# Puritans and Puritanism
# in Europe and America

# Puritans and Puritanism in Europe and America

## A Comprehensive Encyclopedia

### *Editors*

*Francis J. Bremer*
*Tom Webster*

### *Editorial Assistants*

*Susan Ortmann*
*W. Matthew Rice*
*Michael Spurr*

A B C • C L I O

Santa Barbara, California    Denver, Colorado    Oxford, England

Cataloging-in-Publication Data is available from the Library of Congress

# 62330609

09  08  07  06      10  9  8  7  6  5  4  3  2  1

This book is also available on the World Wide Web as an eBook. Visit abc-clio.com for
details.

ABC-CLIO, Inc.
130 Cremona Drive, P.O. Box 1911
Santa Barbara, California 93116-1911

This book is printed on acid-free paper.
Manufactured in the United States of America

Production Team:
Acquisitions Editor          Jim Ciment
Project Assistant            Wendy Roseth
Senior Media Editor          Ellen Rasmussen
Media Manager                Caroline Price
Production Editor            Anna R. Kaltenbach
Editorial Assistant          Alisha Martinez
Production Manager           Don Schmidt
Manufacturing Coordinator    George Smyser

*Tom Webster would like to dedicate this to Ann Milović for so much support, understanding, and willingness to hear about the puritans.*

*Frank Bremer would like to dedicate this to his grandchildren— Adam, Keegan, Kristen, Luca, Lucy, Mac, Molly, Ryan, Taylor, and a player to be named later—who could care less about the puritans at this time, but nevertheless are very precious to him.*

# Contents

# Contributors

## Contributors

Simon Adams
Reader in History
University of Strathclyde
Glasgow
United Kingdom

David J. Appleby
Keele University
Staffordshire
United Kingdom

Margaret Aston
Independent Scholar
United Kingdom

Jeremy D. Bangs
Director
Leiden American Pilgrim
    Museum
Leiden
Netherlands

L. A. Botelho
Professor
Indiana University of
    Pennsylvania
Indiana, PA

Theodore Dwight Bozeman
Professor
University of Iowa
Iowa City, IA

Stephen Brachlow
Professor of Spirituality
Baptist Theological Seminary at
    Richmond
Richmond, VA

Sargent Bush
University of Wisconsin,
    Madison
Madison, WI

Andrew Cambers
Oxford Brookes University
Oxford
United Kingdom

Aaron F. Christensen
Oklahoma State University
Stillwater, OK

John Coffey
Reader in Early Modern History
University of Leicester
Leicester
United Kingdom

Patrick Collinson

David R. Como
Assistant Professor of History
Stanford University
Stanford, CA

James F. Cooper, Jr.
Professor
Oklahoma State University
Stillwater, OK

Will Coster
Department of History
De Montford University
Bedford
United Kingdom

John Craig
Professor, Department of
    History
Simon Fraser University
Burnaby, British Columbia
Canada

Bryan Crockett
Associate Professor, Department
    of English
Loyola College in Maryland
Baltimore, MD

## Contributors

Bruce C. Daniels
Professor of History
Texas Tech University
Lubbock, TX

Michael G. Ditmore
Associate Professor
Pepperdine University
Malibu, CA

David Dymond
University of Cambridge
Cambridge
United Kingdom

Simon Dyton
Cambridge University
Cambridge
United Kingdom

Jackie Eales
Canterbury Christ Church
   University College
Canterbury
United Kingdom

Lori Anne Ferrell
Professor
Claremont Graduate University
Claremont, CA

Amanda Flather

Alan Ford
Professor of Theology
University of Nottingham
Nottingham
United Kingdom

Stephen Foster
Distinguished Research
   Professor of History
   (Emeritus)
Northern Illinois University
DeKalb, IL

Rachelle E. Friedman
Coordinator, History and
   Geography
Lycée Français de New York
New York, NY

Malcolm Gaskill
Fellow and Director of Studies
   in History
Churchill College
Cambridge
United Kingdom

Richard Godbeer
Professor of History
University of Miami
Coral Gables, FL

Mark Goldie
Senior Lecturer in History
University of Cambridge
Cambridge
United Kingdom

Judith S. Graham
Independent Scholar
Newton, MA

Victoria Gregory
King's College, Cambridge
Cambridge
United Kingdom

Polly Ha
Research Fellow
Clare Hall
Cambridge
United Kingdom

Kate Harvey
Cambridge University
Cambridge
United Kingdom

Katherine A. Hermes
Associate Professor of History
Central Connecticut State
   University
New Britain, CT

Ann Hughes
Professor of Early Modern
   History
Keele University
Keele
United Kingdom

Nathan Johnstone
Canterbury Christ Church
   University
Canterbury
United Kingdom

Laura Luder
Dickinson College
Carlisle, PA

Diarmaid MacCulloch
Professor of the History of the
   Church
University of Oxford
United Kingdom

J. Sears McGee
Professor of History
University of California, Santa
   Barbara
Santa Barbara, CA

Michael McGiffert
Editor Emeritus
Omohundro Institute of Early
   American History and Culture
Williamsburg, VA

Jonathan D. Moore
Cambridge
United Kingdom

John Morrill
Professor of British and Irish
  History
Selwyn College, University of
  Cambridge
Cambridge
United Kingdom

David George Mullan
Professor
Cape Breton University
Sydney, Nova Scotia
Canada

Mary Beth Norton
Mary Donlon Alger Professor of
  American History
Cornell University
Ithaca, NY

Catherine Nunn
University of Manchester
Manchester
United Kingdom

Susan M. Ortmann
Graduate Student
University of Delaware
Newark, DE

Elizabeth Reis
Assistant Professor
University of Oregon
Eugene, OR

W. Matthew Rice
Millersville University
Millersville, PA

Sarah Rivett
Assistant Professor
Washington University
St. Louis, MO

Daryl Sasser
Union Theological Seminary
Richmond, VA

Paul S. Seaver
Professor of History Emeritus
Stanford University
Stanford, CA

William Sheils
University of York
York
United Kingdom

Larry A. Skillin
The Ohio State University
Columbus, OH

Stephanie Sleeper
Claremont Graduate University
Claremont, CA

Keith L. Sprunger
Professor of History
Bethel College
North Newton, KS

John Spurr
Professor
University of Swansea
Swansea
United Kingdom

Michael J. Spurr
Millersville University
Millersville, PA

Margo Todd
Walter H. Annenberg Professor
  of History
University of Pennsylvania
Philadelphia, PA

David E. Underdown
Professor Emeritus
Department of History
Yale University
New Haven, CT

Brett Usher

Elliot Vernon
London
United Kingdom

Claire Vivian
Swansea University
Swansea
United Kingdom

Susan Wabuda
Associate Professor of History
Fordham University
Bronx, NY

Dewey D. Wallace, Jr.
Professor of Religion
George Washington University
Washington, DC

James P. Walsh
Professor Emeritus
Central Connecticut State
  University
New Britain, CT

Cassandra Wargo
Dickinson College
Carlisle, PA

Peter Webster
Department of History
University of Sheffield
Sheffield
United Kingdom

Michael P. Winship
E. Merton Coulter Professor of
   History
University of Georgia
Athens, GA

Michelle Wolfe
Postdoctoral Research Fellow
Nottingham Trent University
Nottingham
United Kingdom

Walter W. Woodward
Assistant Professor
University of Connecticut
Hartford, CT

Ralph F. Young
Senior Lecturer, Department of
   History
Temple University
Philadelphia, PA

# Introduction

In its broadest terms, puritanism in the sixteenth and seventeenth centuries was an agenda calling for furthering the perfection of Protestant reform, and it was to be found throughout the British Isles and in the English colonies abroad. Though often studied within the specific context of England or New England, it was a transatlantic movement, and this encyclopedia seeks to make more widely available recent scholarship that emphasizes the broader nature of the subject.

Over the years, claims have been made that credited puritanism with the origins of American democracy, the advancement of the spirit of capitalism, and much else that is cherished in the Western world. Puritans have also been blamed for censoriousness, intolerance, and much that is wrong with the Western world. Both sets of attributions distort the reality, but a proper appreciation of the world of John Winthrop, Oliver Cromwell, and their male and female peers will reveal that the footprints of puritanism are everywhere to be found in the centuries that have elapsed from their day to ours. These footprints are sometimes clearly detectable on the soil of history, and sometimes faint. It is not always clear what direction they are moving in. But the legacy of the puritans has clearly influenced many aspects of the culture of the United States, the British Isles, and some of the Caribbean societies that were part of the seventeenth-century British empire.

Yet historians who can agree on the importance of puritanism cannot agree on what precisely puritanism was. This is partially because for about the first century of the movement it had no institutional form. For the most part, men and women dissatisfied with the Protestant Church of Tudor England refused to leave it, preferring to attempt reform from within and thus joining on occasion with allies who supported them on a particular issue but disagreed with them on others. Where we draw the line between those whose agenda and zeal were sufficient to label them "puritan" and those who do not deserve the name is a question to which different historians will continue to offer different answers. In particular, historians have disagreed over whether Separatists, who clearly shared many of the hopes of other reformers, were puritans or whether their decision to leave the national church requires them to be classified as coming out of the puritan movement but not actually of it. This encyclopedia reflects that ongoing debate since the contributors have not been forced to accept a single definition of puritanism.

The imprecision about how to define puritanism even extends to the way the word is presented. Some scholars, including most of those who focus on American puritanism, capitalize "Puritan" and "Puritanism." Others, primarily students of British religion, use a lowercase $p$. This difference in usage might reflect the fact that the history of seventeenth-century New England does tell a story of a distinct people and ideas that are more clearly definable and thus capable of clearer categorization, while the British story is a less precise one, in which a common orientation, disposition, or temperament manifests itself in different ways at different times and in different circumstances. In editing this encyclopedia we have chosen to allow the individual contributors to decide on whether or not to capitalize the word in their individual essays.

Ironically, in the United States, where the existence of puritanism as a distinct phenomenon has never been in question, scholarship on the subject has been in decline in recent decades. The fascination with the religion of the New England colonists that was central to the work of scholars such as Perry Miller and Edmund S. Morgan has been replaced among most historians with interest in social and cultural aspects of the past. Intellectual history in general, and religious history in particular, are still pursued by researchers in divinity schools and literature departments, but less commonly in history departments. Even those engaged in recent public debates over the role of religion in U.S. life and government neglect the study of the puritan past that is so relevant to these issues.

It is in England, generally recognized as a nation where religion is less vital today than in the United States, that puritan studies have reached new levels of sophistication. Despite—or, perhaps, because of—the challenges of pinpointing exactly who the puritans were and what they believed, a new generation of scholars has embraced the subject. Following in the footsteps of scholars such as Christopher Hill and Patrick Collinson, younger researchers are exploring the relationship of religion in general and puritanism in particular to the shaping of sixteenth- and seventeenth-century England and the neighboring kingdoms of Ireland and Scotland.

This encyclopedia would not have been possible without the assistance of the many scholars on both sides of the Atlantic who still believe in the significance of puritan studies. Many of them have come together over the past decades at conferences on puritanism in England and America hosted in the United States by Thomas More College (1975) and Millersville University of Pennsylvania (1991 and 1999). It is the belief of the editors that those conferences helped shape a network of scholars who have been able to draw upon one another's expert-ise and generosity to help advance their own work and to show the relevance of American and British traditions of puritan scholarship for each other. Certainly, those connections have helped us to enlist the contributors to these volumes.

All this having been said, a true blending of American and British puritan studies would mean looking at all the various topics involved from a transatlantic perspective, but this has not always been possible. Some topics that have captured the enthusiasm of one group of scholars have simply not been investigated on the other side of the Atlantic. Thus, while some essays make insightful comparisons between the ways puritans in different places dealt with a particular issue or implemented a particular idea, others focus largely on topics from a purely American or purely English perspective. It is hoped that the encyclopedia itself, by demonstrating the value of transatlantic comparisons, will encourage more such work, which will perhaps be reflected in a later edition.

It should also be pointed out that the transatlantic approach is not merely something to be found in puritan studies. "Atlantic History" is one of the hot new approaches in historical studies. At the same time, this approach is not as novel as some of its proponents would claim. Indeed, much of puritan studies has always been transatlantic, from the work of the first puritan historians such as William Bradford, John Winthrop, and Cotton Mather, through eighteenth-century authors such as Daniel Neal, down to those who helped set the course for twentieth-century American puritan studies, such as Samuel Eliot Morison and Perry Miller. Through the sixties, seventies, eighties, and nineties, U.S. students of puritan ideas and institutions such as Edmund S. Morgan, David Hall, Stephen Foster, Michael McGiffert, and Michael Winship have placed their work in the broader contexts of not only Anglo-American religion but the Reformation in general. The approach is not new in this community of U.S. scholars, though British historians have been slower to recognize that New England's story may open new insights for them.

*Puritans and Puritanism in Europe and America* consists of a number of different, but related sections.

The collection of **Biographies** attempts to offer brief descriptions of the lives of the men and women who played key roles in the shaping of puritanism in England, New England, Scotland, Ireland, and other places where puritans settled. These are not complete lives, but rather focus on the "puritan" character or contributions of the individual. Included in this section are some who might not normally be thought of as puritans, such as Thomas Cranmer and Edmund Grindal, who helped advance positions that were then embraced by those more clearly puritan. Also included are men such as Matthew Wren and William Laud whose opposition to the movement helped define it or set it off in new directions. Unfortunately, there are relatively few women included in this section, though quite clearly women played an important part in advancing puritanism throughout the Atlantic world and came to be a majority of the formal church members in many New England and English congregations. Their underrepresentation is thus attributable not to their lack of significance but to the lack of surviving evidence that would allow them to speak to us over the centuries.

Given the impact of puritanism on virtually every aspect of life in this period, the section on **Ideas, Events, and Issues** could very well have been twice as long. We have tried to include the obvious topics that will be of interest to scholars and the general public, and we have also attempted to direct interest to areas that are rarely considered. In the process, there are undoubtedly some subjects that have been omitted, and we apologize for that. Readers who do not find a topic in this section are directed to the **Glossary**, where some subjects are explained more briefly.

The selection of **Primary Sources** presented another challenge, since there already exist numerous full volumes of puritan sources, and published puritan writings have become more available through published reprints and electronic access. We attempted a selection that gives some evidence of the puritan spirit as well as examples of advice, agreements, and official positions. We have also tried to include examples of private as well as public writings. Spelling has been modernized in all cases in order to facilitate use by nonspecialists though the hyphenation, capitalization, and punctuation of the original have been to some extent retained, to give the flavor of the period.

A complete bibliography of puritanism would be as long as this entire work. The **Bibliography** presented includes some older but still significant works, while focusing on works published since 1990. For references regarding specific topics, readers should look at the suggestions for **Further Reading** that follow each entry.

*Francis J. Bremer*

# Acknowledgments

This work could not have been possible without the assistance of numerous individuals. First and foremost are the individual contributors, whose entries are evidence of their dedication and scholarship. The members of the Board of Advisors helped shape the content and offered advice when consulted, but are not responsible for the final decisions of the editors on what to include and what to leave out. Dr. Bremer would also like to acknowledge the invaluable assistance of Susan Ortmann, W. Matthew Rice, and Michael Spurr, who aided him in trying to maintain administrative control over the project, and who also contributed essays.

# List of Entries

## Biographies

Abbot, George — Larry Skillin
Abbot, Robert — Francis J. Bremer
Adams, Thomas — Dewey D. Wallace Jr.
Ainsworth, Henry — Francis J. Bremer
Alleine, Joseph — Dewey D. Wallace Jr.
Allen, Thomas — Ralph Young
Alsop, Vincent — John Spurr
Ames, William — Michael McGiffert
Andrewes, Bartimaeus — Patrick Collinson
Angier, John — Catherine Nunn
Annesley, Samuel — Mark Goldie
Archer, Isaac — Michelle Wolfe
Arminius, Jacobus — Francis J. Bremer
Arrowsmith, John — Francis J. Bremer
Ashe, Simeon — Ann Hughes
Aspinwall, William — Francis J. Bremer
Aylmer, John — Brett Usher
Bagshaw, William — Catherine Nunn
Baillie, Robert — John Coffey
Ball, John — Theodore Dwight Bozeman
Ball, Thomas — Theodore Dwight Bozeman
Balmford, Samuel — Francis J. Bremer
Bancroft, Richard — Brett Usher
Barker, Matthew — Francis J. Bremer
Barnardiston Family — Francis J. Bremer
Barrington Family — Francis J. Bremer
Barrow, Henry — Patrick Collinson
Bastwick, John — Francis J. Bremer
Bates, William — Dewey D. Wallace, Jr.
Baxter, Richard — John Spurr
Baynes, Paul — Victoria Gregory
Beadle, John — John Craig
Beaumont, Agnes — Claire Vivian
Bedell, William — Patrick Collinson
Benn, William — Francis J. Bremer
Bernard, Richard — Francis J. Bremer
Bird, Samuel — John Craig
Bird, William — Francis J. Bremer
Blackerby, Richard — Francis J. Bremer
Bolton, Robert — Francis J. Bremer
Bolton, Samuel — Francis J. Bremer
Bownd, Nicholas — John Craig
Bradford, William — Michael G. Ditmore
Bradshaw, William — Stephen Foster
Bradstreet, Anne Dudley — Michael G. Ditmore
Bradstreet, Simon — Susan Ortmann
Brearley, Roger — David Como
Brewster, William — David J. Appleby
Bridge, William — Ralph Young
Brightman, Thomas — Stephanie Sleeper
Brinsley, John — John Spurr
Brocklesby, Edward — Brett Usher
Brooks, Thomas — David J. Appleby
Browne, Robert — Francis J. Bremer
Bruen, John — Francis J. Bremer
Bulkeley, Peter — Michael McGiffert
Bunyan, John — Claire Vivian
Burgess, Anthony — Elliot Vernon
Burgess, Cornelius — Elliot Vernon
Burgess, John — John Craig

**Primary Sources**

# Chronology

1485    Battle of Bosworth: death of Richard III and accession of Henry VII, marking the start of the Tudor dynasty

1494    Poynings' Law lays down that no legislation can be introduced into the Irish Parliament without prior consent of the King

1497    John Cabot, sailing from Bristol, lands in Newfoundland

1502    Treaty of Perpetual Peace between Henry VII and James IV sealed by marriage of James to Henry's elder daughter

1509    Death of Henry VII and accession of Henry VIII

1511    Henry VIII joins the Holy League, papal-led alliance against France

1513    Rise of Thomas Wolsey, who would eventually serve as chief minister in Church (Archbishop of York and Cardinal Legate) and State (Lord Chancellor)

1516    Publication of Sir Thomas More's *Utopia*

1521    Henry publishes *Assertio Septem Sacramentorum* and is given title "Defender of the Faith" by the Pope

1525    First edition of William Tyndale's New Testament in English published

1527    Henry VIII begins negotiations with Rome for an annulment of his marriage to Catherine of Aragon

1529    Wolsey dismissed from all his civil offices; he dies. Thomas More becomes Lord Chancellor

1529    Reformation Parliament meets in first of seven sessions that will extend to 1537

1532    Submission of the Clergy recognizes Henry's superiority over matters ecclesiastical if not matters theological

1532    Sir Thomas More resigns as Lord Chancellor

1532    Death of Archbishop Warham removes obstacle to settlement of Henry's divorce proceedings in England; Thomas Cranmer is appointed Archbishop by the King and approved by the Pope

1532    Anne Boleyn becomes pregnant

1532    Thomas Comwell becomes Henry's chief minister

1533    Cranmer married Henry to Anne Boleyn and subsequently annuls Henry's marriage to Catherine of Aragon; Princess Elizabeth born

1533    Parliament passes the Act in Restraint of Appeals which prevented Catherine appealing to Rome and proclaimed that "this realm of England is an Empire"

1534    Act of Supremacy ends all papal jurisdiction in England by identifying the monarch as head of the church in England

1535    Henry VIII and Thomas Cromwell order the *Valor Ecclesiaticus,* a survey of the wealth of all religious houses

1535    Publication of Miles Coverdale's English translation of the Bible

1535    Execution of Sir Thomas More and Bishop John Fisher for refusing to accept Henry's claim to be supreme Head of the Church

1536    Catherine of Aragon dies; Anne Boleyn executed on charges of treason; Henry marries Jane Seymour

1536    Royal Injunctions order all clergy to instruct youth in the Lord's Prayer; Ten Articles Act brings strong Lutheran influences to bear on religious practice

1536    Dissolution of the smaller monasteries

1536    Pilgrimage of Grace, the greatest of all sixteenth-century rebellions against royal policies; prompted in part by the religious changes of the regime

1537    Prince Edward born; Jane Seymour dies

1537    Thomas Cranmer publishes *The Institution of a Christian Man*

1538    Passage of Act requiring the registration of all baptisms, marriages, and burials in all parishes

1539    Act of Six Articles heralds a theological backlash toward a more Catholic perspective

1539    Dissolution of the Greater Monasteries

1540    Henry marries Anne of Cleves in January and following the annulment of that union in July, marries Catherine Howard

1540    Thomas Cromwell executed

1540    Completion of reforms that produced a new-style corporate Privy Council, combining deliberative and executive functions

1541    Act erecting Ireland into a Kingdom annexed to the Crown of England

1541    Catherine Howard executed for adultery

1542    Lord Deputy St. Leger announces policy of "Surrender and Regrant" in Ireland to bring Gaelic Lords into a feudal relationship with the King

1547    Death of Henry VIII and accession of Edward VI; Edward Seymour, Earl of Hertford, becomes Duke of Somerset and Lord Protector

1547    Dissolution of the Chantries; clerical marriage allowed; the first *Book of Homilies* published

1549    Act of Uniformity imposes first Prayer Book of Edward VI which creates a fully vernacular liturgy

1549    Somerset falls from power following rebellions in South-West and in East Anglia (Ket's Rebellion); power passes to John Dudley, Duke of Northumberland

1552    Second Prayer Book of Edward VI prepared by Cranmer draws on radical Continental Protestant models

1553    Death of Edward VI; Northumberland fails to place Lady Jane Grey on the throne; accession of Mary I

1553    Restoration of the Catholic Mass

1554    Marriage of Mary to Philip II of Spain; reconciliation of England and Rome and restoration of papal jurisdiction

1555    Wyatt's rebellion in Kent; a protest against the Spanish match

1555    Public executions of Protestant "heretics" begin (in all 282 men and women would be burned for heresy during Mary's reign); Cranmer deprived of his offices; over 800 English Protestants (Marian Exiles) go into exile on the Continent, in Protestant centers such as Geneva and Frankfurt

1556    Archbishop Cranmer executed by burning

1558    Marriage of Mary of Scotland to Francis, heir to French throne

1558    Militia Act, the basis of local defense for several centuries

1558    Publication of John Knox's *First Blast of the Trumpet against the Monstrous Regiment of Women*

1558    Death of Mary I and accession of Elizabeth I; France declares Mary of Scotland Queen of England

1559    Acts of Supremacy and Allegiance once more end papal jurisdiction in England and declare Elizabeth to be Supreme Governor of the church; The new Book of Common Prayer represents a step back from the Protestant expression of faith found in the 1552 Prayer Book. Similar provisions approved by the Irish Parliament for the Church of Ireland

1559    Matthew Parker appointed Archbishop of Canterbury

1559    John Knox returns to Scotland from Geneva

1559    Lords of the Congregation rebel against French Catholic domination of Scotland

1560    Elizabeth sends expeditionary force to Scotland and (by the treaty of Edinburgh) forces French to withdraw all troops; Scottish Protestant Lords of the Congregation secure power and the Scottish Parliament abolishes papal jurisdictions and the Mass

1560    Death of Francis II without a child being born to him and Mary

1560    Scots Confession and first Book of Discipline establish structure of a Reformed church

1561    Mary returns to Scotland

1562    Elizabeth nearly dies of smallpox

1563    Convocation approves the Thirty-Nine Articles, the doctrinal creed of the Church of England

1563    First edition of John Foxe's *Actes and Monuments* (or Book of Martyrs)

1566    Archbishop Parker's *Advertisements* require all clergy to wear the surplice

1567    Civil war in Scotland

1568    Mary Queen of Scots escapes to England and is imprisoned (until her execution in 1587)

1569    Northern Rising against Elizabeth I and in favor of Mary Queen of Scots and Catholicism

1570    Pope issues bull of excommunication against Elizabeth calling on her subjects to overthrow her

1570    English Plantation of East Ulster

1570    Thomas Cartwright preaches controversial lectures on the Acts of the Apostles and is removed as Professor of Divinity at Cambridge; he travels to the continent where he will be influenced by the Presbyterian views of Theodore Beza

1571    Ridolfi Plot to depose Elizabeth. Mary implicated but Elizabeth refuses to execute her

1571    Parliament officially approves the Thirty-Nine Articles

1572    An Act of Parliament makes the payment of poor relief mandatory on all householders not themselves in receipt of alms

1572    John Fields and Thomas Wilcox circulate their *Admonition to Parliament* calling for the further reform of the Church

1573    Privy council introduces the "trained bands" or specialist militia alongside the general militia

1573    Brief English invasion of Scotland to secure the position of the Protestant Regent

1576    Publication of William Lambarde's *Perambulation of Kent,* pioneering county history which inspired many others

1576    Edmund Grindal succeeds Matthew Parker as archbishop of Canterbury and relaxes pressures on religious reformers

1577    Archbishop Grindal suspended for opposing the Queen when she orders prophesying to be suppressed

1578    Walter Travers ordained by a synod of Walloon and Dutch ministers to be chaplain to the English Merchant Adventurers in Antwerp

1579    Major rebellion in Munster (the Desmond Rebellion, suppressed 1583)

1579    John Stubbs sentenced to have his hand cut off for criticizing Anglo-French marriage proposals

1580    Jesuit missionaries arrive in England

1580    Thomas Cartwright succeeds Travers as chaplain to the English Merchjant Adventurers in Antwerp

1580    Francis Drake completes a three-year circumnavigation of the globe and is knighted

1581    Parliament approves fines for non-attendance at church by "popish recusants"

1582    Act makes all Catholic clergy found in England liable to execution (more than 100 would be killed by 1603)

| | |
|---|---|
| 1583 | Throckmorton Plot to assassinate Elizabeth |
| 1583 | First royal theater company established |
| 1583 | Edmund Grindal, suspended from his functions as archbishop since 1577, dies and is succeeded by John Whitgift |
| 1583 | Archbishop Whitgift's *Three Articles* aim to identify and prosecute Prebyterian minority in the Church |
| 1584 | Plantation of Munster begun |
| 1584 | The "Black Acts" in Scotland halt the advance of strict Presbyterianism |
| 1585 | First attempt to found a colony in North America (on Roanoke island) |
| 1586 | Privy Council introduces Books of Orders for regulating the work of local JPs, a policy repeated in crisis years until the 1630s |
| 1586 | First engagements involving English troops fighting Spanish troops in the Netherlands |
| 1586 | Babbington Plot uncovered; Mary implicated |
| 1587 | Execution of Mary Queen of Scots |
| 1587 | Walter Travers finishes his *Book of Discipline* as a model for the Presbyterian reforms advocated by some religious reformers. Cope's "Bill and Book," the most concerted Elizabethan attempt to persuade Parliament to reform the Church of England along Presbyterian lines |
| 1588 | Philip II sends the Grand Armada to invade England; it is dispersed by bad weather and the English Navy |

| | |
|---|---|
| 1588 | First of Shakespeare's plays staged (last one first staged in 1613) |
| 1588 | Publication of William Morgan's Welsh translation of the Bible |
| 1588 | Publication of the *Marprelate Tracts* attacking the bishops |
| 1590 | Thomas Cartwright and other Presbyterian leaders arrested for their efforts to change the church |
| 1591 | English troops sent to assist French Protestants in Brittany |
| 1592 | Scottish parliament passes "the Golden Acts" strengthening Presbyterianism |
| 1592 | Cartwright and other leaders released on their promise to desist from further efforts to alter the structure of the church |
| 1593 | Publication of Richard Hooker's *Of the Laws of Ecclesiastical Politie* |
| 1593 | Execution of John Greenwood and Henry Barrow, two leading Protestant separatists |
| 1594 | Nine Years War in Ireland begins |
| 1594 | Walter Travers appointed provost of the new Irish university, Trinity College, in Dublin |
| 1597 | Francis Johnson and a group of English Separatists attempt and fail to establish a colony at the mouth of the St. Lawrence River; Johnson joins the English Separatist congregation in Amsterdam that becomes known as the Ancient Church |
| 1597 | Major codification of the various acts for the relief of poverty into the systematic "Old Poor Law" |

1599    Publication of King James VI's *Basilikon Doron*

1601    Spanish invasion of Ireland (3,500 troops land at Kinsale)

1601    Publication of William Perkins's *Treatise of the Vocations, or Callings of Men*

1603    Death of Elizabeth I and accession of James VI of Scotland to be James I of England and Ireland

1603    James presented with the "Millenary Petition" calling for religious reforms

1603    Surrender of Tyrone ends Nine Years War in Ireland

1604    Hampton Court Conference considers religious reform of the English Church

1604    Richard Bancroft succeeds John Whitgift as archbishop of Canterbury

1604    Treaty of London ends war with Spain

1605    Gunpowder Plot

1605    Publication of Francis Bacon's *Advancement of Learning*

1606    Act of Union of the Kingdoms debated in the Parliaments of England and Scotland but not approved

1606    Probable date of the formation of the Scrooby Separatist congregation under John Smyth and Richard Clifton

1607    Flight of the Irish Earls of Tyrone and Tyrconnel prepares way for English and Scottish plantations in Ulster

1607    Foundation of the Virginia Company

1607    English merchants in Amsterdam gain permission from city authorities to establish an English Reformed Church; John Paget becomes the first pastor of the congregation

1608    First Gaelic Irish translation of the Book of Common Prayer is published; too late to have a significant effect on the efforts to Protestantize Ireland

1608    Scrooby congregation decides to migrate to Amsterdam in the Netherlands; divisions in the Amsterdam Separatist community lead most to move to Leiden the following year with John Robinson as their pastor

1610    James VI and I achieves goal of restoring episcopacy in Scotland

1611    Publication of the Authorized (King James) Version of the Bible

1611    George Abbot succeeds Bancroft as archbishop of Canterbury

1611    Alexander Whitaker, son of the Cambridge puritan leader William Whitaker, arrives in Jamestown as the colony's first minister. He devoted considerable efforts to bringing Christianity to the native population (his most significant achievement in this regard being the conversion of Pocahontas in 1614). He died in 1617

1612    Death of Henry, Prince of Wales, leaving James's younger son, Charles, as heir to the throne

1613    Marriage of James's daughter Elizabeth to the Elector Palatine

1614    The puritan clergyman Lewis Hughes arrives in Bermuda. Three years later he undertakes a religious reformation on the island that included abandoning the Book of Common Prayer

1615 Emergence of George Villers, later Duke of Buckingham (1623), as the new royal favorite

1616 Sir Edward Coke, Lord Chief Justice, is sacked as a judge, the first for more than a century; many more sackings follow later in the century

1617 James makes his only return visit to Scotland after becoming Kind of England

1617 Irish Articles promulgated (they are more unambiguously Calvinist than the English Thirty-Nine Articles of 1563)

1618 Synod of Dort at which British representatives affirm Calvinist teaching and condemn Arminianism

1618 Articles of Perth reform Scottish liturgy, including a demand that those who receive communion do so kneeling

1618 The Bohemian Revolt marks the outbreak of the Thirty Years War; James's son-in-law quickly ejected from his electorate by Spanish troops; James seeks Anglo-Spanish marriage treaty as part of a settlement of the disputes

1620 Members of the Scrooby-Leiden Separatist congregation depart from England in the *Mayflower* and plant the Plimouth colony on Cape Cod; the Pilgrims and the "strangers" who had joined them sign the Mayflower Compact as a voluntary commitment to self-government since they had landed outside the jurisdiction of the Virginia Company, which had granted them a patent

1621 Plymouth's first governor, John Carver, dies and is succeeded by William Bradford, who would hold the office for all but five years until his death in 1657

1623 Prince Charles and the Duke of Buckingham travel to Spain in a vain attempt to win the Infanta's daughter for Charles; they return humiliated and demand war with Spain

1623 Dorchester Company formed to establish fishing bases in New England

1623 Strawberry Bank (later to be Portsmouth, New Hampshire) settled by colonists sent by John Mason

1624 James declares war on Spain and pays Danish mercenaries under Count Mansfeld to recapture the Palatinate; the expedition fails

1625 Death of James VI and I and accession of Charles I

1625 Formation in England of the Feoffees for Impropriations, a group of clergy, merchants and lawyers seeking to purchase church livings and install preaching ministers

1625 Charles marries Henrietta Maria of France, but quickly falls out with France over the honoring of the marriage treaty and over Louis XIII's persecution of Protestants

1625 Charles seeks to cancel all the land grants made by his Stewart predecessors so that he can regrant them on terms more favorable to the Crown and the Church (the Act of Revocation)

1626 Buckingham leads failed expedition against Cadiz

1626   York House Conference upholds Arminian teaching, in effect reversing Dort

1626   Charles I prohibits predestinarian teaching at Cambridge (a similar prophibition applies to Oxford in 1628)

1626   Charles declares war on France

1626   Attempt by the House of Commons to impeach Buckingham; Charles forces to dissolve Parliament

1626   William Bradford and other Plymouth leaders arrange to purchase control of the enterprise from the London merchants who had underwritten the venture

1626   John Robinson dies in the Netherlands

1626   Roger Conant moves the small fishing outpost of the Dorchester Company from Cape Anne to Naumkeag (Salem)

1627   Buckingham leads failed expedition to Île de Rhé (near the besieged Protestant stronghold of La Rochelle)

1628   Parliament passes the Petition of Right, effectively limiting the Crown's right to imprison at will, to billet soldiers on civilians, and to punish those who refused to pay prerogative taxation or make prerogative loans

1628   Buckingham assassinated

1628   William Laud appointed bishop of London

1628   Rev. John White and other members of the Dorchester Company join with London merchants to form the New England Company; the New England Company sends John Endecott to assume control of the settlement at Salem

1628   Plymouth authorities send Miles Standish to break up Thomas Morton's settlement at Merrymount, where Morton is said to provide alcohol and guns to native Americans

1629   Violent scenes mark ending of Charles's third Parliament; seven MPs charged with sedition and imprisoned; Charles embarks on his "Eleven Years Personal Rule"

1629   New England Company reorganizes and receives a royal charter as the Massachusetts Bay Company; John Winthrop and other leaders sign the Cambridge Agreement, signifying their willingness to migrate to New England if they can bring the charter and powers of government with them

1630   Start of the Great Migration to New England as the *Arbella* and her sister ships sail for Massachusetts. Prior to departure Winthrop preaches the lay sermon, "A Model of Christian Charity."

1630   John Winthrop assumes control of Massachusetts Bay from Endecott and moves the center of government from Salem to Boston

1630   Formation of the Providence Island Company to establish a puritan colony off the coast of Nicaragua. Among the principal investors were John Pym, Viscount Saye and Sele, Sir Thomas Barrington, Sir Nathaniel Rich, and other prominent puritans. Their company meetings in the 1630s provided them an opportunity to exchange views and plans about public affairs during the personal rule of Charles I

1631    Freemanship expanded in Massachusetts so that all male church members are eligible for the colony franchise

1631    Clash over church polity in the English Church at Amsterdam between the pastor John Paget and the newly arrived Thomas Hooker

1632    Massachusetts General Court agrees that henceforth the governor will be elected by vote of the freemen and not the colony assistants

1633    William Laud becomes archbishop of Canterbury

1633    Feoffees for Impropriation disbanded by the courts in a case brought by William Laud

1633    Charles I visits Scotland, is crowned, and makes mischief

1633    Thomas Wentworth, later Earl of Strafford, takes up appointment as Lord Deputy in Ireland and begins to introduce his policies of "Thorough"

1633    William Prynne sentenced to lose his ears for libeling the Queen

1633    John Cotton and Thomas Hooker arrive in Massachusetts

1634    Ship Money levied on the coastal regions

1634    John Paget blocks the call of John Davenport to the ministry of the English Church at Amsterdam. The dispute between the two anticipated the divisions between English Presbyterians and Congregationalists in the 1640s

1634    Thomas Wentworth, Lord Deputy in Ireland, forces the Irish Convocation to adopt the English Thirty-Nine Articles and to require ministers to subscribe to them

1634    William and Anne Hutchinson and their family arrive in Boston, having decided to follow John Cotton to the New World

1635    Ship Money extended to inland countries

1635    Disputes between Roger Williams and the Massachusetts magistrates lead to William's banishment

1635    Early settlement of what will become Connecticut. Settlers from Dorchester, Massachusetts, settle the town of Windsor on the Connecticut River; an advance group from Newtown, Massachusetts settles Hartford; John Winthrop Jr., on behalf of a group of English grandees, founds a settlement at Saybrook, at the mouth of the Connecticut River

1636    New canons for the Scottish Church promulgated

1636    Roger Williams, warned off from Plymouth, settles Providence, in what will become Rhode Island

1636    Theophilus Eaton and John Davenport lead a group of mostly London puritans to New England, settling briefly in Boston

1636    Henry Vane is elected governor of Massachusetts

1636    Thomas Shepard's criticism of what he perceives as radical religious views emanating from the Boston, Massachusetts Church, marks the start of the free grace controversy (often misleading called the Antiniomian Controversy) that would divide the colony

1636    The Pequot War begins when John Endecott leads a military expedition against the tribe to punish them for failure to turn over those accused of the murder of English traders

1636    Massachusetts General Court authorized the establishment of a college, which will be named after John Harvard

1637    New Scottish Prayer Book promulgated by proclamation

1637    William Prynne sentenced to lose the stumps of his ears and others their ears for libeling the Bishops

1637    Sermon by the Rev. John Wheelwright inflames the divisions in Massachusetts. Synod at Cambridge defines religious errors presumably espoused by members of the Boston church; John Winthrop elected governor again in preference to Henry Vane. Wheelwright, Anne Hutchinson, and others associated with their views banished from Massachusetts

1637    Massachusetts and Connecticut forces under John Mason attack and destroy the main Pequot village, bringing that war to an end

1637    Davenport and Eaton lead their group in the settlement of New Haven

1638    John Wheelwright moves north and founds the town of Exeter (New Hampshire); William Coddington, William and Anne Hutchinson, and others settle Portsmouth (Rhode Island)

1638    Majority of Scottish political nation subscribe to the National Covenant to withstand religious innovations being advanced by Charles I that would bring the Scottish church into closer alignment with that of England

1638    Judges decide (in the case of *Rex v. Hampden*) in favor of the King's right to enforce the payment of Ship Money

1639    King plans to use English, Irish, and Scottish troops to impose his policies against the Scots. Planned invasion collapses

1639    Towns along the Connecticut River organize themselves under the Fundamental Orders

1639    William Coddington splits with the Hutchinsons and established the town of Newport (Rhode Island)

1639    Robert Keayne, merchant, is admonished by the Boston, Massachusetts church for selling wares at an excessive price

1639    Roger Williams and Ezekiel Holiman establish the first Baptist church in America at Providence

1639    Philip Nye and Thomas Goodwin minister to an independent gathered congregation at Arnhem in the Netherlands

1640    King fails to get support from a Short Parliament to raise troops against the Scots; he attacks Scotland anyway; the Scots defeat him and occupy northeast England; King forced to call the Long Parliament

1641    Constitutional reforms instituted; Strafford executed and other ministers and judges impeached or forced into exile; Triennial Act requiring regular parliaments passed, and prerogative courts and prerogative taxation abolished; Root and Branch Petition demands church reforms

1641    New Haven accepts jurisdiction over neighboring towns and the colony of New Haven adopts a frame of government

1641    Massachusetts General Court adopts the Body of Liberties, a law code

1641    *Bay Psalm Book,* prepared by Richard Mather, Thoams Welde, John Cotton, and John Eliot is published

1641    Massachusetts assumes jurisdiction over Strawberry Bank and Dover settlements in the future New Hampshire

1641    Irish Rebellion against the English Planters leads to widespread massacre of Protestants

1641    The Grand Remonstrance itemized royal misgovernment, remedies achieved, and remedies to be sought

1641    Leading English Presbyterians and Congregationalists agree in the Calamy House Accord to desist from attacking each other's viewpoints while concentrating on reforms of the national Church

1642    King attempts to arrest leading parliamentary critics and fails; King withdraws from London; military and political provocations escalate and the Civil War breaks out; first major battle, the Battle of Edgehill, fails to settle the dispute

1642    Parliament orders the closure of all theaters (ban lasts until 1660)

1642    Three New England puritan clergy arrive in Virginia, invited by Richard Bennett and other settlers of puritan inclination. They will meet discouragement from the colonial government. Many Virginia puritans will move to Maryland in 1648

1643    The English Parliamentarians and the Scottish Covenanters form an alliance formalized in the Solemn League and Covenant; the Scots promise to send 20,000 troops into England and the English promise a federal union of the English and Scottish states and a single system of church government and practice

1643    Parliament calls the Westminster Assembly of Divines to make recommendations for religious reform. New Englanders John Cotton, Thomas Hooker, and John Davenport are invited but decline

1643    The colonies of Massachusetts, New Haven, Connecticut, and Plymouth unite to form the New England Confederation (also United Colonies of New England) for mutual defense

1644    Battle of Marston Moor, the largest of all civil war battles, won by the Parliamentarians and the Scots

1644    Split between advocates of Presbyterianism and Congregationalists in the Westminster Assembly; Congregationalist minority published *An Apologetical Narration* to Parliament requesting toleration within any Presbyterian settlement

1644    Roger Williams's *The Bloody Tenent of Persecution* and John Cotton's *The Keys of the Kingdom of Heaven* are published

1644    Roger Williams, in England, obtains a parliamentary charter for Rhode Island, a colony uniting the settlements at Providence, Newport, and Portsmouth

1644    Publication of John Milton's defence of intellectual liberty, *Areopagitica*

1644 Parliament formally replaces the Book of Common Prayer with the Presbyterian oriented Directory of Worship

1644 Massachusetts General Court formally divides into two separately seated houses, with the Court of Assistants asserting veto rights over lower house (deputies) actions

1644 Parliamentary trial of Archbishop Laud (culminating in his attainder and public execution in Jan. 1645)

1645 New Model Army created and wins Battle of Naseby

1646 King surrenders and First Civil War ends; rise of the Leveller movement calling for more popular government

1646 George Fox begins his ministry; the start of the Quaker movement

1646 Robert Child and others petition the Massachusetts General Court for a broadening of church membership and the franchise, threatening to appeal to Parliament if their demands are not met; petition is rejected, the right of appeal denied, and the leading remonstrants jailed

1646 First session of the Cambridge Assembly in New England, charged with defining church faith and order

1646 John Eliot translates the Bible into the Massachusetts dialect of Algonquian language

1647 Failure of many attempts at peace; Leveller writings – *Heads of Proposals*, *Thve Case of the Army*, *The Agreement of the People* – are published; Army leaders and Levellers debate the fundamentals of governance at Putney church

1647 Nathaniel Ward's *The Simple Cobbler of Agawam* and John Cotton's answer to Roger Williams, *The Bloody Tenent Washed*, are published

1647 William Sayle obtains a parliamentary charter to settle the island of Segatoo in the Bahamas, where he and other puritans who left Bermuda attempted to establish a colony they name Eleutheria. In 1649 they were joined by other puritans exiled from Bermuda by angry royalists following news of the execution of Charles I. In 1650, the church of Boston, Massachusetts raise £800 for the relief of the suffering colonists

1648 King signs an Engagement with dissident Scottish nobles and launches the Second Civil War which his supporters lose

1648 Pride's Purge excludes many of the remaining Presbyterians from Parliament, leaving in control an Independent coalition of Congregationalists, sectarians, and Erastians

1648 Thomas Hooker's *The Survey of the Summe of Church Discipline* is published

1648 Massachusetts adopts a detailed law code, the *Book of Laws and Liberties*

1648 The *Cambridge Platform* is promulgated, defining the New England Way; the platform endorses the Westminster Assembly's Confession of faith and outlines a Congregational form of church order

1648 Richard Bennett and up to six hundred fellow puritans will migrate from Virginia, where they had been subject to increasing government pressure, to the Severn River area of Maryland, where they establish the settlement of Providence

1649 Public trial and public execution of Charles I and abolition of monarchy in England and Ireland; the Scottish Estates proclaim Charles II King of Britain and Ireland

1649 Publication of *Eikon Basilike* begins the cult of Charles I as the martyr-king

1649 The Rump of the Long Parliament acts as interim government of England (until 1653), nominating its own executive Council of State

1649 Organization in England of the Society for the Propagation of the Gospel in New England for the advancement of missionary activities among the Indians

1649 Cromwell leads army of conquest against the Irish Confederates

1650 Cromwell breaks the back of Irish resistance, and returns home to lead invasion of Scotland; he defeats the army of the Covenanters at the battle of Dunbar

1650 Hartford Treaty between New England Confederation and New Netherland Director-General Peter Stuyvesant attempts to settle boundary disputes between the Dutch and English. Stuyvesant's arrest of New Haven colonists bound for the Delaware Bay in the following year leads to a renewal of tensions

1650 Anne Bradstreet's *The Tenth Muse Lately Sprung Up in America* published

1651 Charles II crowned King of Britain and Ireland at Scone; Scots invade England and are defeated at the battle of Worcester; Charles II flees to the Continent

1651 Failed Anglo-Dutch negotiation for a federal union of the two republics

1651 Massachusetts authorities fine and banish three Baptists

1651 John Eliot organizes village for Indian converts at Natick, Massachusetts; this is the first of the "Praying Towns."

1651 English Navigation Ordinances aimed at Dutch carrying trade

1651 Publication of Thomas Hobbes's *Leviathan*

1652 The Act of Settlement threatens to expropriate most Irish landowners and to confine the Catholic population in Connaught between the Shannon and the Atlantic

1652 Spurred by news of the outbreak of war between England and the Netherlands, New Netherland Director General Peter Stuyvesant threatens actions against the Connecticut and New Haven settlements

1653 Cromwell dissolves the Rump Parliament

1653 The Army Council summons a constituent assembly of 144 hand-picked men to prepare a longer-term settlement of the nations of Britain and Ireland (July); referred to as the Nominated or Barebon's Parliament, the Assembly resigns power back into Cromwell's hands (Dec.); he is installed as Lord Protector under *The Instrument of Government*

1654 Harvard president Henry Dunster acknowledges opposition to the practice of infant baptism and resigns

1654 Oliver Cromwell responds to requests for aid from the New Haven colony and commissions Robert Sedgwick and John Leverett (both natives of New England serving in England) to lead an expedition to cooperate with New Englanders in the conquest of New Netherland. When the Anglo-Dutch war ends before the combined force is ready to attack, Sedgwick and Leverett use their force to capture Acadia from the French

1655 Failure of a major Royalist attempt to overthrow Cromwell (Penruddock's Rising); Cromwell appoints the Major Generals

1655 Cromwell dispatches army and naval forces to capture Hispaniola: they fail, but captures Jamaica instead

1656 Cromwell declares war on Spain and makes a treaty with France

1656 Persecution of the Quakers peaks in England with the public torture of James Nayler, convicted by Parliament of "horrid blasphemy"

1656 First Quakers arrive in Massachusetts and are banished

1657 Cromwell declines a parliamentary invitation to become King but accepts a revised paper constitution – *The Humble Petition and Advice*

1657 Ministerial assembly with representatives from Massachusetts and Connecticut recommends what will become known as the Half-Way Covenant, which would allow the baptism of children whose parents were baptized but not full members of the church

1658 Savoy Conference, gathering of Congregationalist clergy in England, adopts *Savoy Declaration of Church and Order*, designed to be the basis for a Congregational national establishment

1658 Death of Cromwell; Richard Cromwell succeeds him as Lord Protector; Richard recalls the Long Parliament and resigns his position

1658 Troubled by reappearance of Quakers, Massachusetts enacts the death penalty for Quakers who return to the colony after banishment

1659 Collapse of the English Republic as political and military leaders struggle with each other for supremacy; the year ends in anarchy

1659 John Eliot's *The Christian Commonwealth*, expressing antimonarchical principles, published in England

1659 William Robinson and Marmaduke Stevenson hanged in Boston under the terms of the 1658 law against Quakers

1660 The General in charge of the Army in Scotland, George Monck, moves south at the head of his troops, occupies London, and calls for free elections; the resulting Parliament (the Convention) recalls Charles II unconditionally upon his issuance of the Declaration from Breda (promising to leave all disputed issues to be settled by Parliament); Restoration of Charles II; Individuals exempted from general pardon for their role in the trial and execution of Charles I (regicides) are tried and executed, including former New Englanders Hugh Peter and Henry Vane. Other regicides seek refuge in New England

1660 Mary Dyer, former "Antinomian" and Quaker, executed in Boston

1661    Savoy conference between Anglicans and Presbyterians fails to produce compromise on forms of worship

1661    Newly elected Parliament seeks a more partisan Cavalier and Anglican settlement

1661    Execution of Quakers in Massachusetts halted by order of Charles II

1661    Massachusetts general Court censures John Eliot for the sentiments expressed in his *Christian Commonwealth*

1662    Act of Uniformity restores Anglican church order and worship "lock, stock, and barrel" and imposes civil disabilities on dissenters; Charles II's attempts to secure liberty for tender consciences by perogative action stymied

1662    Michael Wigglesworth's *Day of Doom* published

1662    Charles II establishes the Royal Society by charter

1662    John Winthrop Jr. obtains a royal charter for the colony of Connecticut that absorbs the New Haven colony into Connecticut

1662    New England Synod of 1662 endorses the Half-Way Covenant and recommends it to the churches of the region, sparking grass-roots debates in many congregations

1663    Rhode Island receives a royal charter

1663    Group of Massachusetts puritans accept an invitation to settle in the Cape Fear area of the Carolinas

1664    First Conventicle Act lays penalties on those attending illegal Protestant services other than those established by law in the Act of Uniformity

1664    Charles II dispatches royal commission to settle boundary disputes and investigate charges against the various New England governments

1665    Great Plague hits London

1665    Five Mile Act bans the clergy who resigned or were ejected in 1662 from living in or even visiting their former parishes

1666    Great Fire of London destroys much of the city

1666    Third Dutch War. English fleet destroyed by the Dutch in the battle of the Medway

1667    Publication of John Milton's *Paradise Lost*

1670    Second Conventicle Act increases penalties on those attending illegal Protestant services other than those established by law in the Act of Uniformity

1672    Charles II issues the Declaration of Indulgence permitting Dissenters to hold licenses to worship outside the Anglican Church

1673    Parliament pressures the Kind to withdraw his promises of religious toleration and passes the First Test Act, imposing new and stringent oaths designed to prevent Catholics from remaining in public office

1675    Wampanoags under Metacom (King Philip) attack Swansea, initiating King Philip's War in New England

1676    Losses from Indian attacks continue to be heavy (estimates of ten percent of the population), but Metacom is killed and the war ends in southern New England.

Fighting continues in northern New England. Christian Indians interned on islands in Boston harbor. Mary Rowlandson taken captive

1676 Fire destroys much of Boston

1676 Edward Randolph arrives in Boston as special agent of the crown to report on enforcement of the Navigation Acts; he exploits divisions in the colony to build a faction favorable to crown intervention in New England affairs

1677 Marriage of James, Duke of York's elder daughter Mary to William of Orange, Stadtholder of the Netherlands

1677 Massachusetts buys out the rights of the Gorges heirs and incorporate what is now Maine into its jurisdiction

1678 Publication of John Bunyan's *Pilgrim's Progress*

1678 Titus Oates's revelations trigger the Popish Plot hysteria that will include efforts to exclude James Stuart (a Catholic) from the succession

1679 Exclusion Crisis peaks and breaks

1679 Reforming Synod in New England adopts the *Savoy Declaration* and urges a thorough reformation of morals and recommitment to the ideals of the founders

1680 New Hampshire separated from Massachusetts and made a royal colony

1681 Charles's opponents overreach themselves; popular concern about the Popish Plot wanes, leading to "the Tory reaction"

1681 Massachusetts General Court grants permission to Boston Baptists to worship in their own meetinghouse

1683 The Rye House Plot, an assassination plot, fails and cost the lives of several republican opponents of the regime, including Algernon Sidney

1684 Complaints against Massachusetts from Edward Randolph and others leads to the abrogration of the Massachusetts charter

1685 Joseph Dudley appointed acting governor of Massachusetts, New Hampshire, and Maine

1685 Death of Charles II and accession of James II; rebellions of the Duke of Monmouth in southwest England and the Earl of Argyll in southwest Scotland were brutally suppressed

1686 James seeks full religious and civil equality for Catholics; Anglicans protest and refuse to cooperate

1686 Royal government creates the Dominion of New England to incorporate the former colonies of Massachusetts (including Maine), New Hampshire, Plymouth, and Rhode Island. The Dominion eliminates the popular basis of government that had existed in most of these colonies. Sir Edmund Andros is appointed Governor General of the Dominion

1687 Connecticut is incorporated into the Dominion of New England (New York and New Jersey will be added in 1688). Andros antagonizes colonists by arbitrary rule, challenges to property titles, promotion of the Church of England, and the levying of taxes. Rev. John Wise is imprisoned for opposition to taxes levied without legislative involvement

1687 James attempts to win over the "Whig" opposition by appointing some to office, and begins a campaign to pack Parliament with supporter of religious liberty. James issues Declaration of Indulgence, attempting to establish toleration by royal prerogative

1687 Publication of Isaac Newton's *Philosophia naturalis principia mathematica*

1688 Seven Bishops tried for claiming the King's Declaration of Indulgence was illegal; they are acquitted of the charge of seditious libel

1688 Increase Mather eludes the Dominion authorities and sails for England to present to James II the colonists grievances against the Dominion

1688 James and his wife have a son after eleven years of marriage, opening up the prospect of a Catholic dynasty

1688 The Glorious Revolution; William of Orange invades England with the support of many Protestants and supporters of parliamentary rights. James flees to France

1689 Convention parliament declares that James's flight is an act of abdication, that the throne is vacant, and invites William and Mary to be joint rulers

1689 The Convention parliament passes the Bill of Rights

1689 Toleration Act grants rights of free religious assembly but no civil equality to Protestant Dissenters

1689 News of the Glorious Revolution leads to uprising in Boston that topples the Dominion of New England. Andros imprisoned

1689 John Locke's influential *Letter Concerning Toleration* published

1689 New England expedition under Sir William Phipps captures the French fortress of Port Royal on the coast of Canada

1690 Connecticut charter restored; Increase Mather lobbies for restoration of Massachusetts charter

1690 King William brings to an end the attempt of James II to regain control of Ireland by his victory at the Battle of the Boyne

1691 William and Mary grant Massachusetts a new charter that restores the popular basis of the General Court but provided for an appointed royal governor. The new charter incorporates the old Plymouth colony into the boundaries of Massachusetts. Increase Mather secures the appointment of Sir William Phipps as the first royal governor

1691 Increase Mather aids in securing a temporary alliance of English Congregationalists and Presbyterians signified by the signing of the Heads of Agreement

1692 Witchcraft episode in Salem Village and surrounding parts of Essex County, Massachusetts

1693 Rhode Island charter restored

1693 Cotton Mather's *Wonders of the Invisible World* published

1699   Publication of the Brattle Street Manifesto marks the appearance of a new liberal faction in New England Puritanism led by William and Thomas Brattle, John Leverett, and Rev. Benjamin Coleman of the Brattle Street Church

1700   Increase Mather forced out of the Harvard presidency

1701   Establishment of Yale College in Connecticut by orthodox clergy

1702   Cotton Mather's *Magnalia Christi Americana* published

# Biographies

# A

## Abbot, George (1562–1633)

Archbishop of Canterbury known for his support of moderate Puritanism and opposition to the rising Arminian faction in church and state. Abbot was born in Guildford, Surrey, in 1562. He first gained fame as a brilliant student at Balliol College, Oxford. Between 1582 and 1597 he earned four degrees, including a Doctor of Divinity, and took holy orders in 1585. Abbot's staunch defense of Calvinist theology at Oxford caught the attention of Thomas Sackville, later Earl of Dorset. Under Sackville's patronage, Abbot took on important administrative posts at Oxford, eventually becoming vice-chancellor of the university in 1603. Abbot's university connections placed him on a committee responsible for translating the Gospels, Acts, and Revelation for the Authorized Version of the scriptures ordered by King James I. This work thrust him into a rapidly rising ecclesiastical career.

Despite having virtually no experience in parochial responsibilities, Abbot was raised to the episcopate at Coventry and Lichfield in 1609 and translated to London in 1610. Completing his meteoric rise, he became archbishop of Canterbury just one year later. As archbishop, Abbot's love of order made him a scourge to nonconformists and recusants alike. His Calvinist theological preference satisfied many Puritans and brought him into conflict with rising Arminian churchmen. The final years of his career were marred by political conflict. Abbot was "retired" to his archiepiscopal residence in Kent after opposing the royal prerogative in

1627. King Charles appointed five bishops, including William Laud, to fulfill the archiepiscopal duties in Abbot's absence. He returned to his duties late in 1628, but Abbot's authority within the church and state never fully recovered before his death in 1633.

*See also:* Bible
*Further Reading*
Nicholas Tyacke, *Anti-Calvinists: The Rise of English Arminianism, c. 1590–1640* (Oxford, 1987); Paul A. Welsby, *George Abbot, the Unwanted Archbishop, 1562–1633* (London, 1962).

*Larry Skillin*

## Abbot, Robert (ca. 1588–ca. 1662)

Church of England clergyman. Abbot received his B.A. from Cambridge, though the details of his education are unknown. It is likely that his first ministry was as an assistant in a Dorset parish. In 1616 he was presented to be vicar of Cranbrook, which living he held until 1643. That parish had a reputation as a strong center of puritanism, and Abbot's fierce opposition to Catholicism would have resonated with his parishioners. As time went on, however, puritan members of the parish became increasingly disenchanted with Abbot's conformity to liturgical practices—such as kneeling at communion—that puritans rejected. In 1641 relations with his parishioners became more strained as he defended episcopacy and took the position that

Parliament had no right to call a national assembly to plan a reform of the church. At that point he moved to Southwick, and then to St. Austin's in London. He was the author of a popular catechism and a volume of directions for the heads of Christian families, and was noted for his opposition to separatism.

*Further Reading*
Patrick Collinson, "Cranbrook and the Fletchers: Popular and Unpopular Religion in the Kentish Weald," pp. 399–428 in Collinson, *Godly People: Essays on English Protestantism and Puritanism* (London, 1983).

*Francis J. Bremer*

### Adams, Thomas (1583–1652)

Eloquent English preacher, sometimes reputed to be a Puritan. Educated first at Trinity and then at Clare College, Cambridge, Adams received the B.A. from the latter in 1602 and the M.A. in 1606. By 1612 he was preaching in Bedfordshire, and in 1614 he became vicar of Wingrave, Buckinghamshire; after 1618 he preached in London (occasionally at Paul's Cross), finally settling at St. Benet's near Paul's Wharf. He was for a while a chaplain to Sir Henry Montague, Lord Chief Justice of England, to whom he dedicated a book in 1618. He was acquainted with Nicholas Tooley, actor and partner in Shakespeare's company, who left ten pounds to Adams with the request that Adams preach the sermon at his funeral. Adams was a Calvinist episcopalian whose Sabbatarianism, commitment to godly preaching, and disaffection toward the Laudian regime (his denunciations of Roman Catholicism seemed inflammatory to Archbishop William Laud) echoed the views of his London Puritan contemporaries, with whom he had little connection. There is no evidence of his support for a Puritan agenda of disciplinary or liturgical change. Apart from a large commentary on 1 Peter, his publications were sermons. A large volume of his collected works appeared in 1629, dedicated to William Herbert, third Earl of Pembroke, who was sympathetic to the "godly." The sermons of Adams are filled with wit, paradox, proverbs, lively images, and illustrations drawn from history and nature. He also used "metaphysical conceits" of the type characteristic of the poetry of John Donne, whom he perhaps knew in the 1620s when both were active at St. Paul's.

*Further Reading*
J. Sears McGee, "On Misidentifying Puritans: The Case of Thomas Adams," *Albion* 30 (1998), 400–418.

*Dewey D. Wallace Jr.*

### Ainsworth, Henry (1571–1622 or 1623)

Separatist leader. Ainsworth was the son of a Norfolk yeoman farmer. He studied at Gonville and Caius College, Cambridge, from 1587 to 1591. Soon thereafter he was attracted to the Separatist movement. It is possible that he spent time in Ireland, whose church many of the godly considered purer than that of England, but around 1593 he joined a group of English Separatists that had settled in Amsterdam. He found employment with a bookseller in that city, and in 1596 he became the teacher in a congregation formed by Francis Johnson.

The Amsterdam congregation was rent by divisions. Ainsworth strove to be a conciliatory force during the first of these disputes, but to little avail. Following this first dispute the Reverend John Robinson and those who had followed him from the area of Scrooby, England, moved on to Leiden to set up their own church. A second schism was led by John Smyth, prompted by his adoption of Arminian views. The third controversy was between Johnson, who believed that the power of excommunication belonged to the church elders, and Ainsworth himself, who maintained that such authority rested in the entire congregation. The dispute led to Ainsworth and his followers withdrawing from Johnson's ministry in December 1610. He ministered to his own followers for twelve years. In addition to his pastoral work, Ainsworth became a noted controversialist, publishing over two dozen works and leaving behind numerous unpublished manuscripts. He became recognized as one of the finest Hebrew scholars of the age, and his works were rooted in his understanding of the scriptures. Most of his books were defenses of the Separatist position, but he also wrote an attack on the Familists; criticized the Anabaptists; published a popular metrical translation of the Psalms (the Ainsworth Psalter) that was widely used by many, including the Pilgrim settlers in Plymouth, Massachusetts; and engaged in attacks on the Church of Rome.

See also: English Puritanism in the Netherlands, Separatists
*Further Reading*
Stephen Brachlow, *The Communion of Saints: Radical Puritan and Separatist Ecclesiology, 1570–1625* (Oxford, 1988); Chaplin Burrage, *Early English Dissenters,* 2 vols. (Cambridge, Eng., 1880); Keith L. Sprunger, *Dutch Puritanism: A History of English and Scottish Churches of the Netherlands in the Sixteenth and Seventeenth Centuries* (Leiden, 1982).

*Francis J. Bremer*

## Alleine, Joseph (1634–1668)

English dissenting minister and spiritual writer. Alleine was born in Devizes, Wiltshire, and entered Lincoln College, Oxford, in 1649, transferring to Corpus Christi in 1651, and receiving the B.A. in 1653. Already notable for fervent piety, he served as chaplain of Corpus from 1653 until 1655, when he accepted a position as assistant to George Newton, vicar of St. Mary Magdalene in Taunton, Somerset. That same year he married Theodosia Alleine, to whom he was not related, and she later wrote his biography. Both he and Newton were ejected from their Taunton parish in 1662 for failure to accept the Act of Uniformity. Alleine remained in Taunton, preaching illegally, until arrested; he was in prison for much of 1663–1664 and again in 1665. His 1664 treatise *A Call to Archippus* urged others to illegal preaching. His posthumous *An Alarme to Unconverted Sinners* (1671), sometimes printed under the title *The Sure Guide to Heaven,* was translated into other languages and frequently reprinted, becoming a classic of Puritan devotion. His *Christian Letters* (1673) contained spiritual exhortations to the congregation from

which he had been separated by imprisonment. Ill when finally released from prison, he went to Bath to restore his health, meanwhile exhorting to piety all whom he met. Calvinist and Presbyterian in outlook, his focus was on the spiritual life. The ardency of his pastoral work and his imprisonment and early death made him a hero and martyr to English Dissenters and New England Puritans.

*Further Reading*
Dewey D. Wallace Jr., ed., *The Spirituality of the Later English Puritans: An Anthology* (1987).

*Dewey D. Wallace Jr.*

## Allen, Thomas (1608–1673)

Influential advocate of New England Congregationalism. Allen was educated at Caius College, Cambridge (B.A. 1628, M.A. 1631). He was assigned to the parish church of St. Edmund's, Norwich, but in 1636 he was silenced by Bishop Matthew Wren for holding Sabbath services in the afternoon, for refusing to read from the Book of Sports, and for not having his congregation kneel for Holy Communion. He removed to Holland for two years before setting sail for New England in 1638. After John Harvard's death, he served as Teacher of the Charlestown Church from 1639 to 1651. During this time Allen married Harvard's widow and was the executor of John Harvard's estate.

In 1652 Allen returned to the mother country and became rector at St. George Tombland in Norwich. In January 1657 he succeeded the first pastor of the Congregational church in Norwich, Timothy Armitage. At this time, though in England, he served on the board of trustees for Harvard, assisting in raising money for the college. He was significant in promoting the "New England Way," with independence (within limits) for each congregation, in England by assisting at the gathering of independent congregations as well as by publishing several of John Cotton's works. In 1655 he published Cotton's *An Exposition Upon the Thirteenth Chapter of the Revelation,* and in 1659 Cotton's *A Treatise of the Covenant of Grace.* The introductions to these works reveal that Allen had close contact with Cotton during the thirteen years he lived in Massachusetts. Cotton's tongue, according to Allen, was "as choise silver," and his writings worth their weight in gold. Allen's most important work, *A Chain of Scripture Chronology* (1659), was published and introduced by William Greenhill, the "evening star" of Stepney. Greenhill wrote that England had greatly benefited from such men as Thomas Allen, whose experience in Massachusetts Bay had enabled him to be influential in the development of Congregationalism and bringing a new dawn to England.

After the Restoration Allen continued to lead Congregational worship services clandestinely in different locations in Norwich.

*See also:* Congregationalism
*Further Reading*
Francis J. Bremer, *Congregational Communion: Clerical Friendship in the Anglo-American Puritan Community, 1610–1692* (Boston, 1994).

*Ralph Young*

## Alsop, Vincent (1630–1703)

Presbyterian minister and controversialist who played a central role in the transformation of Nonconformity into viable, independent denominations. Born at Collingham, Nottinghamshire, where his father, George Alsop, was rector, Vincent Alsop was educated at Uppingham School and entered St. John's College, Cambridge, as a sizar on 13 September 1647. After graduating, Alsop is said to have received orders as a deacon and served as assistant master at Oakham School in Rutland. Benjamin King, minister of Oakham, won Alsop over to Presbyterianism. Alsop married King's daughter, received Presbyterian ordination, and entered the ministry. He served as rector of Wilby, Northamptonshire, from 1658 until his ejection in 1662, but thereafter continued to preach in the area and suffered various penalties, including six months' imprisonment.

Alsop was licensed under the 1672 indulgence as a "Congregationalist" to preach at his own house. In 1675 *Anti-Sozzo*, his witty response to the theology of William Sherlock, established his

reputation as a polemicist. Anthony Wood saw him as the natural heir to Andrew Marvell's crown as the witty defender of Nonconformity. In 1677 Alsop became pastor of the Presbyterian congregation at Tothill Street, Westminster, in succession to Thomas Cawton, and served there until his death. Assisted by John Shower, Alsop maintained the flock through the persecution of the early 1680s, kept up monthly communions, and continued to engage in controversy against the uncharitable impositions of the Church of England in indifferent matters. It became apparent from this polemic that Alsop was effectively wedded to the principle of congregational autonomy. When James II issued his 1687 Declaration of Indulgence, Alsop organized and presented an address of thanks on behalf of the ministers and inhabitants of Westminster and so contributed to the court's propaganda effort. His motives were partly personal, since his son Benjamin had joined Monmouth's rebellion and languished in jail. But they were also more principled. Alsop had recognized that the future of his and other congregations lay in independence rather than reunion with the national church. In this he was typical of the younger generation of Nonconformist leaders.

After the Revolution of 1688–1689 and the Toleration Act, Alsop embraced the opportunity to put Nonconformity on a stronger institutional footing. He took part in the 1694 ordination of Nonconformist clergy in the City of London, the first such occasion since 1662. He encouraged cooperation between the different Nonconformist denominations, becoming a manager of the Common Fund and an enthusiastic supporter of the short-lived "Happy Union," but on the collapse of these ecumenical initiatives he resigned as a Pinners' Hall lecturer and helped to found the Presbyterian Salters' Hall lecture.

*See also:* Declaration of Indulgence, Nonconformity, Pinners' Hall
*Further Reading*
Robert A. Beddard, "Vincent Alsop and the Emancipation of Restoration Dissent," *Journal of Ecclesiastical History* 24 (1973), 161–184.

*John Spurr*

## Ames, William (1576–1633)

Puritan teacher, pastor, and polemicist. Ames was born at Ipswich, Suffolk, into a well-to-do mercantile family that was moderately nonconformist. At Christ's College, Cambridge (B.A. 1598, M.A. and fellow 1601), he came under the influence of William Perkins, evinced exceptional mental powers, and developed a perdurable set of reformist convictions. These he expressed by refusing to wear the prescribed vestments when conducting divine service and by trying to curb students' conventional rowdiness and gambling. The resultant notoriety was heightened by his 1610 Latin translation of William Bradshaw's *English Puritanism*, a work of advocacy for which he supplied a critical introduction.

Forced from the college, barred from pastoral employment (after a brief stint as town lecturer at Colchester, Essex), and threatened with episcopal sanctions, Ames escaped in 1610 to the Netherlands. There for the rest of his life he championed the puritan interest theologically and promoted forms of congregational self-government that would later be adapted for use in England and New England.

At The Hague Ames served as chaplain to the commander of the English troops, Sir Horace Vere, and as preacher to the English residents. Royal pressure engineered by the English ambassador, Sir Dudley Carleton, drove him from these posts by 1619, denied him appointment at the University of Leiden, and pushed him into private life. He spent the next three years in Leiden lecturing to divinity students.

From 1622 to 1632 Ames, now at the peak of his powers, taught theology at the University of Franeker, where he also served as rector after 1626. In his last year of life, he briefly headed an Independent church at Rotterdam. He wished to join the puritan migration to New England but was apparently deterred by considerations of age, health, and purse. Ames married twice and had three children with his second wife, Joane Fletcher, of the literary Fletchers. He died in 1633 from physical trauma brought on by the disastrous flooding of his Rotterdam home.

Ames's thought has Augustinian roots; its dominant tenor is regulative though not legalistic. His social ethic owes a debt to Aquinas and the late medieval schoolmen, his mode of reasoning to Ramus, the formulation of his faith to Calvin and Reformed tradition. He made an aggressive mark in polemical, and a constructive one in practical, divinity. Soon after settling in Holland, he earned intellectual leadership of the contest against Arminianism with four books aimed mainly at the views of Nicholaas Grevinchoven. The last of these, published in 1618 as *Coronis ad Collationem Hagiensem,* helped shape debate at the Synod of Dort, 1618–1619, where he served as doctrinal adviser to the moderator.

Keen to define and defend central commitments of the rising puritan movement, and aiming at an English as well as a Dutch audience, Ames also wrote against Roman Catholicism, as represented by the Jesuit theologian Robert Bellarmine; against Laudian ceremonialism in the English church; and against the radical separatism of Leiden pastor John Robinson, which he had some success in tempering.

Ames's two most important and enduring works are *Medulla S.S. Theologica* (1623; translated as *The Marrow of Sacred Divinity,* 1643), which originated in his Leiden lectures, and *De Conscientia et Eius Iure vel Casibus* (1622; translated as *Conscience with the Power and Cases Thereof,* 1639). Both texts insist that religious profession prove itself in personal discipline and public action. Like Perkins, Ames located the heart of religion in "living to God" and undertook to establish general principles and specific rules for leading a godly life. *Medulla* lays a theological basis for Christian vocation; *De Conscientia* codifies a morality that is both generically Christian and specifically puritan. The most impressive work of its kind by a puritan to date, *Medulla* achieved twelve Latin and three English editions in twenty years and was still current in New England a century later. Ames's other writings include Latin commentaries on the Psalms and the Epistle of St. Peter. Differently constituted sets of his works were produced in English (1643) and in Latin (1658–1661).

Ames's writings gave content, system, and vigor to doctrinal and ethical puritanism. He led in defining the classical federal theology of the 1620s. His scholastic casuistry won critical esteem in puritan circles and beyond. In ecclesiology, his congregational affiliations limited his influence in England but enhanced it in New England, where his views on polity took hold. In New England, too, his ethical teachings remained potent throughout the century.

*See also:* Congregationalism, Conscience, English Puritanism in the Netherlands, Glorification, God, Independency, Predestination, Sin, Soteriology
*Further Reading*
John D. Eusden, *The Marrow of Theology: William Ames, 1576–1633* (Boston, 1968). Douglas Horton, trans., *William Ames by Matthew Nethenus, Hugo Visscher and Karl Reuter* (1965); Keith L. Sprunger, *The Learned Doctor William Ames* (Urbana, 1972).

*Michael McGiffert*

## Andrewes, Bartimaeus (1551–1616)

Founding member of the Dedham Conference. The bulk of his career, however, was spent as town preacher of Great Yarmouth (1585–1616), where his arrival seems to have ratcheted up the movement for godly reformation in that important East Anglian port. Andrewes was born at Bocking, Essex, and matriculated from Jesus College, Cambridge, in 1570, later progressing to a scholarship at St. John's. He took no higher degree than the B.A. (ca. 1577). His early ministry in Essex, at Rochford, Braintree, and Fordham, seems to have enjoyed the patronage of Robert, second Lord Rich, who did more than any other powerful layman to promote the puritan cause in that county. He was ordained priest at Ely in December 1576.

Andrewes was evidently a popular preacher, and in 1583 specimens of his preaching style, whose strengths were said to lie more in exhortation than in doctrine, were published in *Certaine verie worthie, godly and profitable sermons* (republished 1595). They are redolent with the values of intense fellowship among the sermon-gadding, conventicling godly, and imply at many points their partial separation from the rest of mankind.

In 1578 Andrewes became vicar of Great Wenham in Suffolk, thanks, it appears to the wealthy gentleman-clothier William Spring of Lavenham. In 1582 he joined the conference of ministers meeting in and around Dedham, on the Essex-Suffolk border, which on one occasion met in his house. But by 1585 Andrewes was being headhunted by the bailiffs of Yarmouth, who were offering a stipend worth twice what he received at Wenham. So he found that he had "no comfort" in his Suffolk parish and that "his heart was dead in it." The conference held a special meeting, attended by a Yarmouth bailiff, to determine whether it was permissible for him to leave his people for the new post, which was to move from being a "pastor" to the position of "doctor," a demotion in the Presbyterian scheme of things. Most members were against the move, but Andrewes went anyway, demonstrating the impotence of the conference when it came to exercising discipline over its members.

In Yarmouth, Andrewes exhorted a huge congregation of six thousand or more in one of the largest parish churches in England, and from a special new pulpit, ten feet high, which was erected upon his arrival. But after that we hear surprisingly little of him, and all that he published was a catechism with a preface that exhorted the magistrates of Yarmouth to continue in their godly courses, while congratulating them on choosing Robert Dudley, Earl of Leicester, as their steward. Andrewes died a person of moderate substance, with lands and houses in Suffolk and Yarmouth. His son and grandson both received the name Bartimaeus.

*See also:* Dedham Conference
*Further Reading*
Patrick Collinson, *The Elizabethan Puritan Movement* (London, 1967); Patrick Collinson, John Craig, and Brett Usher, eds., *Conferences and Combination Lectures in the Elizabethan Church: Dedham and Bury St. Edmunds, 1582–1590* (Woodbridge, Eng., 2003).

*Patrick Collinson*

## Angier, John (1605–1677)

Puritan clergyman and leading Presbyterian in post-Restoration England. Angier was born in Dedham, Essex, and was baptized on 8 October 1605, the eldest son of John Angier, a clothier. From an early age he intended to enter the ministry. He was educated at the school in Dedham and then at Emmanuel College, Cambridge, where he was awarded B.A. in 1626. He then returned to Dedham, where he came under the influence of John Rogers the puritan lecturer, whose powerful sermons drew audiences in puritan Essex. Subsequently Angier boarded with John Cotton at Boston in Lincolnshire. It was at there that Angier married Cotton's niece by marriage, Ellen Winstanley. He had intended to emigrate to New England with Cotton. However, on a farewell visit to his wife's family in Lancashire in September 1630, he was appointed to Ringley Chapel in Prestwich Parish, where he was twice suspended in September 1631 and again in March 1632. Later in 1632 he was appointed to Denton Chapel in Manchester Parish, where he stayed for the rest of his life. On 28 February 1642 he took the Protestation against the policies of Charles I, and on 13 December 1644 he was empowered to ordain ministers in Lancashire. He became a member of the Manchester Classis that met for the first time on 16 February 1647, on occasion acting as moderator. Also in 1647 he published *An helpe to better hearts, for better times*, which set out a program of godly behavior.

On 3 March 1648 he was one of ninety-two Lancashire ministers who signed the "Harmonious Consent of Ministers" in support of Presbyterian church government. Later in the same year he was also a signatory to the reply of Lancashire ministers to the "Agreement of the People" presented to Parliament by the army.

In common with many Presbyterian ministers, Angier deplored the execution of Charles I and refused the Oath of Engagement (declaration of loyalty to the Commonwealth), although this refusal does not appear to have affected his ministry. In 1651 he was briefly imprisoned in Liverpool with other Manchester Presbyterians when Love's plot to bring Charles Stuart to England as Charles II was discovered. In 1654 he was appointed a minister to assist the commissioners for Lancashire in the ejections of unsuitable ministers. In July 1659 he entered into the accommodation of ministers between Presbyterians and Independents, but this agreement collapsed with Sir George Booth's Cheshire Rising. Although, like many other Lancashire and Cheshire Presbyterians, Angier was apparently aware of the proposed rising, he does not seem to have taken any active part in it. He welcomed the Restoration and on 23 December 1660 signed the Address to Charles II by sixty Lancashire ministers with his friend and colleague Henry Newcome.

Angier did not conform to the restored church, but did not lose his living; he appears, in common with some other Lancashire ministers, to have compromised with authority by permitting the occasional reading of the Book of Common Prayer. Much that is known of his life derives from the biography written by his son-in-law Oliver Heywood, the Nonconformist minister at Northowram in Yorkshire. Angier remained as minister at Denton until his death on 1 September 1677, and he was buried in Denton chapel on 3 September.

*Further Reading*
Oliver Heywood, *The Life of John Angier of Denton,* ed. E. Axon, Chetham Society, new series, vol. 97 (Manchester, Eng., 1937).

*Catherine Nunn*

## Annesley, Samuel (1620–1696)

One of the most prominent Dissenting clergymen of the Restoration era. Born near Warwick, Annesley was educated at Queen's College, Oxford, graduating B.A. in 1639, and was ordained in 1644. He served as chaplain to the Parliamentarian admiral, the Earl of Warwick, and held the rich living of Cliffe in Kent from about 1645. In 1658 he was presented by Richard Cromwell to the vicarage of St. Giles Cripplegate, London, a large parish with a strong puritan tradition. He resigned in 1662, unable to accept the Act of Uniformity, though his puritan uncle, the Earl of Anglesey, pleaded with him to conform. Thereafter, until his death, Annesley was pastor of a substantial congregation at Little St. Helen's in Spitalfields, London. He was several times prosecuted for conventicling. In about 1672 he was described as one of the "Ducklings" who, unlike the more cautious "Dons," was prepared to "take to the water" of complete separation from the Church of England. His congregation included his son-in-law, the publisher John Dunton, and the young Daniel Defoe, later famous as the author of *Robinson Crusoe*. Their connection with him marks a transition from Civil War puritanism to the more secular style of eighteenth-century Dissent. Annesley was a founder manager of the Presbyterian-Congregational Common Fund (1690) and was one of the Salters' Hall lecturers in 1694. In the latter year he officiated at the first public ordination to the Presbyterian ministry since the Restoration. Annesley published a widely read devotional work, the Cripplegate *Morning Exercises* (1661). His wife bore him twenty-four children, of whom three survived him. He was grandfather of Samuel and Charles Wesley, the founders of Methodism.

*See also:* Dissenters, Salters' Hall
*Further Reading*
*Oxford Dictionary of National Biography* (Oxford, 2004).

*Mark Goldie*

### Archer, Isaac (1641–1700)

Clergyman and diarist. The son of the Suffolk Dissenting minister William Archer, Isaac Archer was born in 1641 and died at Mildenhall, Suffolk, 26 April 1700. Attending Trinity College Cambridge from 1657 to 1661, he was ordained priest in 1661. Archer served several Church of England cures in Cambridge and Suffolk, including the curacy of Chippenham, Cambridgeshire, and the vicarage of Mildenhall, Suffolk. As a diarist and minister, Archer's spirituality and ministry reflected the style and experience of evangelical compromise with the Restoration church.

Archer's education at Cambridge and early clerical career were fraught with spiritual ambivalence and filial estrangement. Archer was steeped in an Interregnum Presbyterian style of rigorous self-examination and voluntary religion. However, finding the Book of Common Prayer merely unpalatable, Archer reluctantly conformed, first to retain his place at the university and later to obtain a cure.

Archer's decision to conform sparked a series of bitter conflicts with his father. Outraged at his son's conformity, William Archer pressured his son emotionally and punished him financially, disinheriting him. Despite parental pressure, Isaac Archer picked his own path of partial conformity. He hired curates to read the prayer book while he preached. He maintained ties of affiliation and assistance with local Dissenters and engaged in the personal and domestic piety consonant with the Puritan traditions of his childhood. Archer's diary typifies an introspective style of Restoration evangelical piety. His ministry and relationship with his father poignantly demonstrate the Restoration generation gap between Dissenting fathers and Anglican sons.

*See also:* Dissenters, Nonconformity
*Further Reading*
Matthew Storey, ed., *Two East Anglian Diaries 1641–1729: Isaac Archer and William Coe*, Suffolk Records Society, vol. 36 (Woodbridge, Eng., 1994).

*Michelle Wolfe*

### Arminius, Jacobus (1559–1609)

Theologian whose efforts to reform Calvinist formulations of the doctrine of predestination became extremely divisive. Arminius was born Jacob Harmensen, in the Dutch city of Oudewater, and educated at Utrecht, at the University of Marburg, and then at the University of Leiden. In 1581 he traveled to Geneva to continue his studies there under Theodore Beza and other leading Calvinist theologians. In 1588 Arminius returned to the Netherlands to become minister of the Reformed Church in Amsterdam. In 1603 he left the pastoral ministry to become professor of theology at the University of Leiden.

At the time when Arminius began developing his distinctive theological positions, there were differences within the broader Calvinist community as to precisely how predestination was to be understood. Even in Geneva there was disagreement as to how Calvin's teachings were to be elaborated. As Arminius himself refined his views through the course of these theological debates, he came to believe that God's first decree was to save those who repented and came to believe in Christ as redeemer. God next, according to Arminius, decreed that he would deliver the means necessary for repentance and faith. He also believed that God had foreknowledge of those who would repent and persevere and those who would not. His opponents argued that Arminius reduced God's role to knowing how men would respond as opposed to actually determining who would be saved and who damned.

Following the death of Arminius, some of his followers elaborated on his views in the Remonstrance of 1610. As the controversy continued to rage, a national synod was called to meet in the city of Dort in 1618, with delegates from other Reformed or Calvinist churches invited to attend. The Synod of Dort condemned the teachings of Arminius and set forth its own confession of faith, which affirmed belief in the total depravity of man, unconditional predestination, limited atonement, the irresistibility of God's grace, and the perseverance of the saints. This was far more explicit than anything to be found in Calvin's writings.

Theologians who sought to leave some role for man in responding to God's grace and repenting were quickly branded Arminians, and the term became a shorthand form of abuse that implied movement back toward a Catholic, work-based doctrine of salvation. As with any such label, many of those branded Arminian were not followers of the Dutch theologian.

*See also:* Anti-Calvinism, Arminianism, Predestination, Synod of Dort
*Further Reading*
Carl Bangs, *Arminius: A Study in the Dutch Reformation* (Nashville, 1971); Richard Muller, *God, Creation and Providence in the Thought of Jacobus Arminius* (Grand Rapids, 1991).

*Francis J. Bremer*

## Arrowsmith, John (1602–1659)

Puritan divine. Arrowsmith was born near Newcastle-on-Tyne and studied at St. John's, Cambridge, where he received his B.A. (1620) and M.A. (1623). He became a fellow of St. Catherine's Hall. In 1631 he was installed in the living of St. Nicholas Chapel in King's Lynn, Norfolk.

Arrowsmith was clearly a puritan, though he managed to retain his living through the 1630s. He was one of the members of the Westminster Assembly. In 1644 he was awarded his Doctor of Divinity and made master of his old college, St. John's. In 1647 he was vice-chancellor of Cambridge University. In 1651 he was appointed Regius Professor of Divinity at Cambridge and in 1653 chosen master of Trinity College. Arrowsmith split his attentions between the university and London. Early in the Civil Wars he had obtained the rectory of St. Martin's in Ironmonger Lane. He sided with the Presbyterians in the religious disputes of the 1640s, and in 1645 became a member of the Sixth London Classis. He was a strong opponent of religious toleration and was outspoken in his criticism of the sects and, in particular, those radical religious groups that questioned the need for a university-trained ministry. Three of his sermons preached to Parliament were published, as were three other works. He died before the Restoration brought the puritan regime to an end.

*See also:* Westminster Confession of Faith
*Further Reading*
Samuel Clarke, *The Lives of Sundry Eminent Persons in this Later Age* (1683); John Twigg, *The University of Cambridge and the English Revolution, 1625–1688* (Woodbridge, Eng., 1990).

*Francis J. Bremer*

## Ashe, Simeon (d. 1662)

English puritan clergyman. Ashe was educated at Emanuel College, Cambridge, where he was a protégé of Thomas Hooker, and ordained in 1619. He was probably from Ashby de la Zouch, Leicestershire, and another early mentor was the eminent Puritan minister of the town, Arthur Hildersham. Ashe left a Staffordshire living in the 1630s after opposing Charles I's reissue of the Book of Sports and became chaplain to the radical puritan second Lord Brooke. Ashe was thereby centrally placed within networks of Puritan opposition in the 1630s, a more moderate figure than Lord Brooke, consistently committed to an authoritative national church.

Ashe was involved with John Ball and others in the criticisms of tendencies to separatism sent to Massachusetts ministers in the later 1630s, and from 1640 he became a leader of clerical protests against Laudianism and a crucial figure among Parliamentarian ministers. His militant first sermon to the House of Commons (preached in March 1642) called for the removal of "prelacy" as a prelude to thorough reformation. From the outbreak of war he served as chaplain to the Earl of Manchester's regiment and coauthored a series of newsletters, which included an eyewitness account of the battle of Marston Moor. Following Manchester's eclipse as commander, Ashe concentrated on preaching and Presbyterian mobilization in the city of London, his base for the rest of his life. Throughout the later 1640s Ashe was one of the most determined of the city Presbyterians. He was close to the Scots commissioners resident in London, preached against "toleration," and in favor of commitment to the Solemn League and Covenant, and signed all city declarations against the inadequacies of Parliament's legislation for the church. He was a leader of city protests against the regicide, and although there is no evidence for his own involvement, he was close to the Presbyterian-royalist plotter Christopher Love and, with Edmund Calamy, attended Love on the scaffold. With Calamy and others, Ashe oversaw the posthumous publication of the martyr's works.

For most of his career, Ashe was a lecturer in London, accepting a pastoral charge (of St. Augustine's Watling Street) only in 1655. From October 1651 to January 1655 he acted as assistant to his friend and ally of long standing, Edmund Calamy, at St. Mary Aldermanbury. Despite his lack of a parish living, Ashe was a prominent member of various London classes and of the Provincial Assembly from the mid-1640s until the Restoration. Besides his own publications—mainly of funeral sermons, and other sermons on special occasions—Ashe was an energetic editor of others' works, notably those of Thomas Ball and Christopher Love. Unlike many other Presbyterians, Ashe never came to terms with the Cromwellian regime and welcomed the Restoration of Charles II, but he viewed with alarm the church settlement of 1661–1662. He died just before the enforcement of the Act of Uniformity in August 1662 and was "buried the very evening of Bartholomew Day," when so many Dissenters were ejected from their livings, his funeral sermon preached by Calamy. Despite an apparently unspectacular career, Ashe had clearly prospered, leaving property in the east midlands worth about 5,000 pounds. His fears for the future were seen in the bequest to "forty ministers, my friends in London and elsewhere," with the inscription, "I am not ashamed of the Gospell of Christ."

*Further Reading*
Ann Hughes, *Gangraena and the Struggle for the English Revolution* (Oxford, 2004); Ann Hughes, *Politics, Society and Civil War in Warwickshire, 1620–1660* (Cambridge, Eng., 1987); Anne Laurence, *Parliamentary Army Chaplains, 1642–1651* (London, 1990); Tai Liu, *Puritan London: A Study of Religion and Society in the City Parishes* (Newark, DE; 1986); Elliot C. Vernon, "The Sion College Conclave and London Presbyterianism during the English Revolution," (Ph.D. diss., University of Cambridge, 1999).

*Ann Hughes*

## Aspinwall, William (ca. 1605–1662)

Religious radical in seventeenth-century New England and English Fifth Monarchist. Little is known with certainty of his birth or early life, though his later activities give evidence of his having been well educated. In 1630 Aspinwall and his wife arrived in the Massachusetts Bay Colony. He was the tenth individual admitted to the Boston church, in August 1630, and later in that month was chosen a deacon. A respected merchant, he served the town and colony in a variety of posts: as member of a coroner's jury and a grand jury, as a notary, and as a Boston selectman on two occasions. In 1637 he was chosen one of Boston's deputies to the colony's legislature, called the General Court. Aspinwall was a supporter of Anne Marbury Hutchinson when she was accused of antinomianism. He drafted the petition in support of Hutchinson's brother-in-law and ally Reverend John Wheelwright. As a result he was one of those disarmed and banished from the Bay Colony in 1637. Along with other members of the faction, he migrated to the area of Narragansett Bay and became a signatory of the covenant whereby the town of Portsmouth was organized. Disenchanted with the way things developed there, he may have resettled in the ultraorthodox New Haven colony, and it is clear that within a few years he was seeking a reconciliation with the Massachusetts authorities.

In March 1642 Aspinwall confessed his past errors and was readmitted to the Boston church, and two months later was restored to his political rights in Massachusetts. But his strong biblicism, which had led him in the 1630s to advocate adoption of a Mosaic-style law code formulated by John Cotton, involved him in new disagreements with the colony's magistrates in the early 1650s. The eschatological anticipation that had drawn him to New England and caused him to be excited by the preaching of John Wheelwright during the Hutchinsonian controversy led him back to Cromwellian England in 1653, convinced that the true saints were about to triumph there.

Aspinwall became one of the leaders of the Fifth Monarchist movement. In 1653 he published *A Brief Description of the Fifth Monarchy*, in which he argued for replacing English constitutional principles with laws based solely on scripture. He urged the army to introduce a theocratic regime that would eventually transfer rule to a council of state and administrators composed solely of saints, whose godliness would be attested to by the true churches. By 1655 he had become disillusioned with Cromwell's compromises, but he limited his criticisms to peaceful forms, declining to join any of the plots against the Protectorate. He faded from public view.

*See also:* Fifth Monarchists

*Further Reading*

B. S. Capp, *The Fifth Monarchy Men* (London, 1972); Richard Greaves and Robert Zaller, eds., *Biographical Dictionary of British Radicals in the Seventeenth Century*, vol. 1 (Brighton, Eng., 1982); Philip Gura, *A Glimpse of Sion's Glory: Puritan Radicalism in New England, 1620–1660* (Chapel Hill, 1984); Christopher Hill, *The Experience of Defeat: Milton and Some Contemporaries* (London, 1984); J. F. Maclear, "New England and the Fifth Monarchy," *William and Mary Quarterly* 32: 223–260.

*Francis J. Bremer*

## Aylmer, John (d. 1594)

Bishop of London; earned a reputation as a "hammer of the puritans" during the 1580s. Tutor to Lady Jane Grey and then archdeacon of Stow. Aylmer defended Edward VI's settlement of religion during the first convocation of Mary's reign, thereafter going into exile in 1554. On his return he published *An harborowe for faithfull and trewe subjects* (1559), defending Elizabeth's fitness to rule in the wake of John Knox's *First blast of the trumpet against the monstrous regiment of women*. It contains a famous marginal note, "God is English."

Although he was considered for the episcopal bench in 1559, he remained archdeacon of Lincoln from 1562 until 1577, when Sir Christopher Hatton helped to secure him the bishopric of London. Within days Elizabeth suspended Archbishop Edmund Grindal of Canterbury from his official functions. As dean of the province of Canterbury, Aylmer thereafter exercised a de facto primacy until John Whitgift succeeded Grindal in 1583.

During these years the ecclesiastical commissioners sitting in London, headed by Aylmer, evolved into a full-fledged Court of High Commission, part of whose brief was to discipline nonconformist clergy. It was in this role that Aylmer first emerged as a stern defender of Elizabeth's settlement. After 1583 he vigorously supported Whitgift's drive for ritual conformity by means of clerical subscription to the proposition that the Book of Common Prayer contained nothing contrary to the word of God. Those of his diocesan clergy who would not subscribe, or who subsequently refused the surplice and the "popish" rituals prescribed in the prayer book, found themselves under constant threat of suspension. Although very few were deprived of their livings as a result, Aylmer's efforts played a large part in destroying the conference movement in Essex.

*See also:* Conference Movement, Court of High Commission, Marian Exiles
*Further Reading*
Patrick Collinson, John Craig, and Brett Usher, eds., *Conferences and Combination Lectures in the Elizabethan Church: Dedham and Bury St. Edmunds, 1582–1590* (Woodbridge, Eng., 2003).

*Brett Usher*

# B

## Bagshaw, William (1628–1702)

Born at Litton in Derbyshire on 17 January 1628, the eldest child of William and Jane Bagshaw. He was educated in local schools and became impressed by the ministry of local clergy. He gained the degree of B.A. from Corpus Christi, Cambridge, in 1646, where he was much influenced by the teachings of Drs. Hill, Arrowsmith, and Benjamin Whichcot, all of whom had played some part in the puritan education of this generation of men. At the age of twenty-one he became assistant minister at Attercliffe, Derbyshire, and on New Year's Day 1651 he was ordained by Presbyterian convention by the Classis at Chesterfield.

In early 1652, much against his father's wishes, he became minister at Glossop, Derbyshire, where he stayed until he was ejected in 1662, when he retired to Ford Hall, a family property where he lived until his death. He continued to preach and teach throughout the Derbyshire Peak District, establishing Presbyterian meetings, for which he acquired the title of "Apostle of the Peak." In 1672 he was licensed to preach in various Derbyshire parishes. He was, however, a partial conformist, attending the parish church while preaching elsewhere privately. Following the Act of Toleration, Bagshaw revived meetings in the towns of Derbyshire where he had been licensed in 1672. He was the author of a number of spiritual works.

Bagshaw preached his last sermon on 22 March 1702 on the occasion of the death of William III. He died on 1 April 1702 and was buried in the chancel of the chapel of Chapel-en-le-Frith on 5 April.

*Further Reading*
J. M. Brentnall, *William Bagshaw: The Apostle of the Peak* (London, 1970).

*Catherine Nunn*

## Baillie, Robert (1599–1662)

Scottish divine and Covenanter. Baillie was educated at Glasgow University before becoming minister of Kilwinning in Ayrshire. He was episcopally ordained and was initially in favor of limited episcopacy. However, he opposed the introduction of the Scottish prayer book in 1637 and became a keen supporter of the Covenanter movement. He was a member of the Glasgow Assembly of 1638, which abolished episcopacy, and in 1640 he published *The Canterburians Self-Conviction*, a strong attack on Laudianism and episcopacy that led to his appointment as a Scottish commissioner to London in 1640–1641, where he developed close connections with English Puritans. On his return to Scotland, he was appointed Professor of Divinity at Glasgow in 1642. In 1643, he returned to London as one of the Scottish commissioners to the Westminster Assembly of Divines. He began with great expectations for the prospects of Presbyterianism in England, but was soon frustrated by the delaying tactics of Erastians and Independents in the Assembly and in Parliament. He helped to organize support for a Scottish Presbyterian model in London itself, and he published major works, including *An Historical Vindication of the Government of the Church of Scotland* (1646) and *A Dissuasive from the Errors of the Time* (1645), in which he attacked Independents and sectaries.

Baillie returned to Scotland in 1646 and resumed his duties at Glasgow University. He was appalled by the execution of Charles I, and was sent to Holland in 1649 to persuade Charles II to sign the Covenant. After Cromwell's defeat of the Covenanters at Dunbar, Baillie supported a broad-based alliance with royalists against the English. His stance divided him and his fellow Resolutioners from Samuel Rutherford and other old friends who condemned the alliance. Throughout the 1650s, Baillie was engaged in disputes with these Protesters, although he also encouraged peace negotiations between the two factions. At the Restoration, Baillie refused a bishopric but was appointed principal of Glasgow University. He noted with grim satisfaction the fate of the Independent party in England—"that maleficent crew . . . the two Goodwins, blind Milton, Owen, Sterrie, Lockier." His own Presbyterian party, however, fared little better, and shortly before his death Baillie witnessed the restoration of episcopacy in Scotland and England.

Baillie's *Letters and Journals* (ed. D. Laing, 3 vols., 1841–1842) cover the years 1637–1662 and are a goldmine for the historian of religion in mid-seventeenth-century Britain. As well as being a vital source for the history of the Church of Scotland, they are also full of information and opinion on English puritanism in the 1640s. Baillie was immersed in English ecclesiastical politics during this decade, and his gossipy letters tell us much about the Westminster Assembly and the key figures in Puritan London. By contrast, Baillie's magnum opus, his *Operis Historici et Chronologici* (Amsterdam, 1668), has been almost entirely ignored by scholars.

*See also:* Westminster Assembly
*Further Reading*
McCoy, F. N., *Robert Baillie and the Second Scots Reformation* (Berkeley, 1974).

*John Coffey*

## Ball, John (1585–1640)

Divine, theologian, and controversialist. Entered at Brasenose College, Oxford, around the year 1602, he transferred to St. Mary's Hall and received the B.A. in 1607 or 1608. He was first drawn into the puritan subculture while tutor in the home of Lady Cholmondeley in Cheshire. Through ordination by a sympathetic Irish bishop in 1610, he managed to enter the ministry without subscribing to the doctrine of royal supremacy (that is, acknowledging that the monarch of England was the head of the Church of England) and to the Thirty-nine Articles, a subscription required of all who entered the ministry. He held the curacy at Whitmore in Staffordshire until his death, operating a school and household seminary as well. A regular participant in fasts, conferences, and other projects of the puritan clergy in his county and beyond, he opposed episcopal government and Caroline liturgical trends and was twice imprisoned.

In ecclesiological disputes among the godly in the later 1630s he came to national prominence. His *Trial of the Grounds Tending to Separatism* (1640), *Answer to John Can* (posth., 1642), and *Tryall of the New-Church Way in New-England* (posth., 1644) attacked separatist and semiseparatist ecclesiologies emanating from Old and New England and the Netherlands. A spokesman for moderates who found the Church of England flawed but sound in essentials, he also upheld ministerial primacy against church covenants and other democratizing practices of early Congregationalism. His best-selling *Short Catechisme* (1615 or earlier), his *Treatise of Faith* (1631), and his posthumous *Covenant of Grace* (1645), *Power of Godliness* (1657), and *Treatise of Divine Meditation* (1660) cover much of the ground of Reformed and puritan practical theology.

*See also:* Federal Theology
*Further Reading*
Webster, Tom. *Godly Clergy in Early Stuart England* (Cambridge, Eng., 1997).

*Theodore Dwight Bozeman*

## Ball, Thomas (1590–1659)

Clergyman, apologist, and editor. Born in Aberbury in Shropshire, he matriculated at Queens

College, Cambridge, in 1615 and proceeded to earn his B.A. in 1621. A pupil of John Preston at Queens, he followed him in 1622 to Emmanuel College. There he earned the M.A. and became fellow in 1625. From 1628 to the end of his career he was minister in Northampton.

Drawn into puritan circles at Cambridge, he consulted with an informal conference of like-minded clergy before accepting the call to Northampton, and he helped introduce to Northamptonshire the informal clerical training and devotional exercises devised by Laurence Chaderton at Emmanuel. He shared in a combination lecture and in fast-day rituals, probably conducted a household seminary, criticized Caroline liturgical trends and the Laudian crackdown on nonconformity, and attended the ministerial gathering at Kettering in 1640 that resolved against the "etcetera" oath. In 1631 he subscribed to John Dury's plan for an ecumenical manual of practical divinity, although his own proposed contribution—a theological system in sermonic form—never came to fruition. His *Pastorum Propugnaculum* (1655) defended the trained, ordained ministry against mid-century attacks upon hireling ministers; it revealed moderate Presbyterian convictions. His "Life of Doctor Preston," first published in Samuel Clarke's *General Martyrologie* of 1651, was informed by his intimate knowledge of Preston and the Cambridge scene. With Thomas Goodwin, he edited and published Preston's sermons at the university and before the king.

*See also:* Emmanuel College
*Further Reading*
Webster, Tom. *Godly Clergy in Early Stuart England* (Cambridge, Eng., 1997).

*Theodore Dwight Bozeman*

## Balmford (Bamford), Samuel (d. ca. 1659)

Puritan clergyman and author. Born in London, he studied at Emmanuel College, where he received his B.A. (1616) and M.A. (1619). Balmford's activities over the next few decades are a mystery. He became pastor of St. Alban's Wood Street, London, a parish noted as a center of Presbyterianism.

There he became noted for his pastoral effectiveness. He is primarily known for two posthumous publications. These were *Habakkuk's Prayer applied to the Churches present occasions*, preached on Habakkuk 3:2, and *Christ's Counsel to the Church of Philadelphia*, preached on the text of Revelations 3:11. Both of these were originally preached to the Provincial Assembly of London and they were published in 1659.

*Further Reading*
Tai Liu, *Puritan London: A Study of Religion and Society in the City Parishes* (Newark, DE; 1986).

*Francis J. Bremer*

## Bancroft, Richard (1554–1610)

Archbishop of Canterbury. Bancroft graduated from Christ's College, Cambridge, in 1567, becoming chaplain to Sir Christopher Hatton, Lord Chancellor of England (1587–1591). In February 1589 he preached at Paul's Cross, defending episcopacy as an apostolic institution and criticizing the Church of Scotland. King James VI (later James I of England) demanded, and at Lord Burghley's insistence received, a formal apology. Thereafter Bancroft was partly responsible for unmasking the leading members of the conference movement, whose activities he associated with the pamphleteer "Martin Marprelate" and separatism. In 1593 he published *A survey of the pretended holy discipline* and *Dangerous positions and proceedings*, arguing that not only extremists but also "moderate puritans" within the Elizabethan establishment were potentially subversive and dangerous to the state.

After Hatton's death Bancroft became chaplain to John Whitgift, archbishop of Canterbury, and, after much lobbying on Whitgift's part, was consecrated bishop of London in 1597. His later claim that he had reduced the diocese to a state of conformity is dubious: although many of the radical clergy in Essex and London were disciplined, none was deprived of his living.

Bancroft and Thomas Bilson, bishop of Winchester, took the lead in defending the established church at the Hampton Court Conference, convened by James I in January 1604. Following Whitgift's death in February, Bancroft presided over the first convocation of James's reign. A set of Constitutions and Canons, incorporating Whitgift's Three Articles of 1583, was drawn up and implemented, James demanding that subscription to them should become the yardstick of conformity for all English clergymen.

Translated to Canterbury on 10 December 1604, Bancroft attempted, at James's steady insistence, to impose the Constitutions and Canons throughout the dioceses during his six years as primate. He did not invariably enjoy the cooperation of his suffragan bishops, and historian R. G. Usher's proposition that he single-handedly "reconstructed" the Church of England on Anglican principles was wide of the mark. Essentially an Elizabethan Calvinist with strong disciplinary views, Bancroft appears to have been uninfluenced by emergent Arminian or proto-Laudian theology, and in his will he expressed the wish that the equally Calvinist George Abbot should succeed him as primate.

*See also:* Conference Movement, Exorcism, Hampton Court Conference, Marprelate Tracts, Subscription
*Further Reading*
S. B. Babbage, *Puritanism and Richard Bancroft* (London, 1962); Albert Peel, ed., *Tracts ascribed to Richard Bancroft* (Cambridge, Eng., 1953); R. G. Usher, *The Reconstruction of the English Church*, 2 vols. (New York, 1910).

*Brett Usher*

## Barker, Matthew (1619–1698)

Congregational minister. Barker was born in Northamptonshire in 1619. He studied at Trinity College, Cambridge, receiving his B.A. in 1638 and his M.A. in 1641. He was teaching school in Banbury, Oxfordshire, at the start of the Civil Wars. Moving to London, he ministered for a time to the parish of St. James Garlickhythe, in Garlick Hill.

In a sermon to Parliament in 1648, Barker warned against a Presbyterian settlement and encouraged lay preachers to spread the faith. He preached to Parliament on two other occasions in the 1650s and emerged as a leader of the Congregational movement. Shortly before the Restoration he was named one of the Triers to test the qualifications of ministerial candidates.

Ejected from his living in 1661, he appears to have remained in London, where he was licensed as a Congregational minister in 1672. He labored to unite the various dissenting groups and was one of the original members of the Common Fund and a member of the Happy Union of Dissenting ministers. He died in 1698.

*See also:* Happy Union, Triers and Ejectors
*Further Reading*
Richard Greaves and Robert Zaller, eds., *Biographical Dictionary of British Radicals in the Seventeenth Century*, vol. 1 (Brighton, Eng., 1982).

*Francis J. Bremer*

## Barnardiston Family

One of the leading puritan gentry families in seventeenth-century England. The family's lands were in southwest Suffolk, around Barnston and Kedington. They were early supporters of Protestant reform. Sir Thomas Barnardiston, the head of the family at the time of England's early reformation, spent time in Calvin's Geneva. His son, also Sir Thomas, furthered the reform cause in Suffolk during Elizabeth's reign and married Mary Knightley, whose family was also noted for its support of reformers. His son was Sir Nathaniel Barnardiston (1588–1653).

Sir Nathaniel was a friend and associate of Brampton Gurdon, John Winthrop, Sir Simonds D'Ewes, and other godly gentlemen, as well as being a friend and patron of numerous puritan clergy in East Anglia. He was an opponent of the policies of King Charles I. In 1626 he was imprisoned for refusing the oath as a commissioner appointed by the king to collect what became known as the "forced loan." He was elected to both of the parliaments of 1640 and took a lead in the effort to reform the church. He supported the parliamentary cause in the ensuing Civil Wars, but retired from the Rump Parliament in 1649 at a time when his health was deteriorating. He died in 1653. His wife, Jane, shared his interest in religious reform.

Sir Nathaniel's son and heir Sir Thomas Barnardiston (d. 1659) was elected a member of Parliament, representing Bury St. Edmunds in 1645. He continued to serve during the Protectorate of Oliver Cromwell, but did support the Restoration in 1660. Sir Samuel Barnardiston (1620–1707) was a younger son of Sir Nathaniel. The family had always showed an interest in overseas ventures, and Sir Samuel was chosen deputy governor of the East India Company in 1668. He was elected as a Whig to the parliament of 1672.

*Further Reading*
Richard Greaves and Robert Zaller, eds.,
    *Biographical Dictionary of British Radicals in the Seventeenth Century*, vol. 1 (Brighton, Eng., 1982); *Oxford Dictionary of National Biography* (Oxford, 2004).

*Francis J. Bremer*

## Barrington Family

The Barringtons were patrons of puritan ministers and supporters of Parliament. Sir Francis Barrington (d. 1628) studied at Cambridge University, served as a justice of the peace, and represented the county of Essex in Queen Elizabeth's last parliament. He was knighted in 1603 and became a baronet in 1611. Barrington was one of the most prominent puritan gentry in Essex and took a lead in petitioning Lord Rich in favor of godly clergy who had been suspended from their ministry while numerous scandalous clergy remained in place. He became a close ally of Lord Rich, who supported Barrington's election to the first parliament of King James. There Barrington served on various committees dealing with religious matters. He also lobbied the king on behalf of the puritan cause. His opposition to the loan demanded of Englishmen by King Charles I in 1626 led to his imprisonment in the Marshalsea prison, where John Winthrop requested his son John Winthrop Jr. to visit Barrington and convey his support. Barrington chose

Ezekiel Rogers as his household chaplain and had close contacts with other puritan clergy, including Roger Williams and John Wilson. He lobbied hard to have men sympathetic to the puritan cause elected to the parliament of 1628.

Sir Frances was married to Joan Cromwell, the oldest daughter of Sir Francis Cromwell. She too was zealous in her religious observance and corresponded extensively with clergy on religious matters. That correspondence is an important source for the domestic life and concerns of the puritan gentry.

Sir Thomas Barrington (1589–1644) was the son and heir of Sir Francis and Lady Joan and shared their commitment to the puritan cause. He studied at Gray's Inn, provided legal advice for friends, and then served as a justice of the peace, sheriff for Essex, and then a member of Parliament in 1621, 1624, 1625, 1626, 1628, and both the Short and Long Parliaments of 1640. While not taking a lead in any of the parliaments, he opposed ship money, royal loans, and government-sponsored industrial projects. A moderate puritan, he appears to have shifted to a more radical stance at the time of his father's imprisonment. Sir Thomas corresponded extensively with godly clergy in America and in England and gathered a large collection of biblical commentaries, devotional literature, and printed sermons.

Sir Thomas was an ally of John Pym in the Long Parliament. His close friends included Oliver Cromwell, John Hampden, Sir Thomas Fairfax, Oliver St. John, and Sir William Masham. He helped push through the Grand Remonstrance, supported the abolition of episcopacy, and served as a lay member of the Westminster Assembly. He was also active in keeping Essex loyal to the parliamentary cause. He purged Colchester of royalists, helped to organize troops in the region, and early in the wars commanded a regiment under the Earl of Essex. He died in September 1644.

*Further Reading*
Richard Greaves and Robert Zaller, eds.,
    *Biographical Dictionary of British Radicals in the Seventeenth Century*, vol. 1 (Brighton, Eng., 1982); K. W. Shipps, "Lay Patronage of East

Anglian Puritan Clerics in Pre-Revolutionary England" (Ph.D. diss., Yale University, 1971).

*Francis J. Bremer*

### Barrow, Henry (ca. 1550–1593)

Regarded by denominational historians as a founding father of Congregationalism and as a martyr. He was the leading Separatist of what may be called the second-generational cohort of that movement, following in the footsteps of Robert Browne and Robert Harrison. Barrow was the third son of a Norfolk gentleman who enjoyed cousinly connections with the Bacon family and Lord Burghley, and he had private means. In 1566 he matriculated at Clare Hall, Cambridge, took the B.A. degree in 1569–1570, and, after some undocumented years, entered Gray's Inn in 1576, where he seems to have been intent on enjoying the London scene.

Barrow came to his separatist principles shortly after becoming "a zealous professor," which happened when he heard the stentorian voice of a preacher as he walked past a London church. His separatist conversion came partly from reading Browne's writings in order to confute them, partly through the influence of an obscure early Norfolk Separatist called Thomas Wolsey.

Barrow probably knew John Greenwood in Norfolk, and it was when he came to London to visit Greenwood in the Clink, a prison in Southwark, that he was himself arrested. Barrow had been under observation for some time and was regarded by Archbishop John Whitgift, Richard Bancroft, and their thought police as the man to watch. There followed a series of trials before Whitgift and the Court of High Commission, which lasted from November 1587 into the spring of 1590. In these examinations (for which Barrow himself is our only source) he proved an all too resourceful barrack-room lawyer. Barrow and Greenwood were to spend some years in the Fleet prison, incarcerated under the statute 23 Elizabeth cap. 1 for refusing to attend church, a law that Barrow insisted was never meant for them. On one occasion Barrow had to rebuke the future Bishop Lancelot Andrewes for sug-

gesting that the Fleet, built over an open sewer, was a good place to spend a sabbatical.

Barrow did use his enforced leisure to good effect, producing a stream of writings, including a so-called *Brief discoverie of the false church* (419 closely printed pages), which laid down four reasons for separation, a kind of Separatist quadrilateral. These indicted the established church for (1) false worship, (2) promiscuous membership, (3) false ministry, (4) false and anti Christian government. In the spring of 1593 the bishops sought to include puritan sectaries in new anti-Catholic legislation going through Parliament, a move resisted in the House of Commons. In what looks like spiteful retaliation, Whitgift had Barrow and Greenwood hanged, under the terms of anti-Catholic legislation of 1581. Twice reprieved, once with the nooses actually around their necks, they were finally executed on 6 April 1593. After years in prison, Barrow was still able to leave behind money to support the poor members of the Separatist congregation in London.

*See also:* Congregationalism, Sects, Separatists
*Further Reading*
L. H. Carlson, ed., *Elizabethan Nonconformist Texts*, vols. 3–6, (London, 1962–1970); B. R. White, *The English Separatist Tradition* (Oxford, 1971).

*Patrick Collinson*

### Bastwick, John (1593–1654)

Puritan pamphleteer. Bastwick was born in Writtle, Essex, and studied for a time at Emmanuel College, Cambridge. He studied at the University of Padua and received an M.D. there, after which he returned to Essex and practiced medicine in Colchester, Essex. It is possible that his opposition to Roman Catholicism was exacerbated by his stay in Padua, for he began to write attacks on papistry. His criticisms extended to aspects of the episcopal structure of the Church of England, which led to his being brought up on charges before the Court of High Commission. In 1634 he was excommunicated, expelled from the College of Physicians, fined, and sentenced to prison until he recanted his controversial views.

Prison hardened Bastwick in his opposition to the bishops. He wrote two new tracts against the church, which were published in the Netherlands, one with the assistance of the young John Lilburne. Bastwick was brought before the Star Chamber in 1637, charged with libel against the bishops, sedition, and schismatical writings. He was tried along with William Prynne and Henry Burton. All three were found guilty and sentenced to prison for life. They were also fined, pilloried, and had their ears cut off. Prynne was also branded. Brought for their punishment to the New Palace Yard, the three were defiant and reasserted their views in their addresses to the crowd. They became famous as victims of what was seen as excessive persecution.

The three were set free by Parliament in November 1640. Bastwick was restored to the practice of medicine, and reparations for him were approved, but never fully paid. Bastwick served as a captain in the Leicester trained bands. He also resumed his writing career. Though for a time he expressed sympathy for some of the sectarians, he was himself committed to a Presbyterian reform of the church and wrote a number of tracts against the Independents, and particularly Anabaptists.

*See also:* Crime and Punishment, Star Chamber
*Further Reading*
Richard Greaves and Robert Zaller, eds., *Biographical Dictionary of British Radicals in the Seventeenth Century*, vol. 1 (Brighton, Eng., 1982).

*Francis J. Bremer*

## Bates, William (1625–1699)

English Presbyterian minister. Born in London, the son of a noted physician, he entered Emmanuel College, Cambridge, in 1643, moving to Queen's College, from which he received the B.A. in 1645 and M.A. in 1648. He was vicar of St. Dunstan's in West, London, from at least 1654. Unlike many Puritans, he supported the return of King Charles II in 1660, was named a royal chaplain, and awarded a D.D. from Cambridge in 1661. A member of the Savoy Conference, he was offered the deanery of Lichfield as an incentive to conform, but when he refused compliance with the Act of Uniformity, he was ejected from St. Dunstan's in 1662. He remained in and around London, occasionally preaching. Associated with such moderate Presbyterian Calvinists as John Howe, Richard Baxter, and Thomas Manton (he preached the funeral sermons for the latter two), he joined them in seeking inclusion of Dissenters in the established church. Howe preached the funeral sermon for Bates, praising his avoidance of controversy.

With the accession of William and Mary, Bates delivered addresses before them on the plight of the Dissenters. From 1694 to his death he was pastor to a Presbyterian congregation at Hackney. His published writings encouraged practical religion and decried theological quibbling. *Considerations on the Existence of God and the Immortality of the Soul* (1676) and *The Divinity of the Christian Religion* (1677) were written to show unbelievers that nature and reason as well as scripture declare God's existence and the soul's immortality. Bates represents the emergence of a latitudinarian strain among the dissenting descendants of the earlier Puritans.

*Further Reading*
A. G. Matthews, *Calamy Revised: Being a Revision of Edmund Calamy's Account of the Ministers and others Ejected and Silenced, 1660–2* (Oxford, 1934; reprinted 1988).

*Dewey D. Wallace Jr.*

## Baxter, Richard (1615–1691)

Prominent Presbyterian pastor and author. Baxter did much to shape the political, pastoral, and theological fortunes of seventeenth-century English Puritanism through his powerful personality and writing. Born into a "godly" but impoverished Shropshire family, Baxter received a scanty education; although he did not attend university, he was determined to enter the ministry; in 1638 he was ordained as a deacon, but there is no evidence that he was ever ordained to the full priesthood.

### Early Career
In the early 1640s Baxter served as preacher at Kidderminster in Worcestershire, before joining the

Parliamentarian army as a chaplain in 1645. On returning to Kidderminster, Baxter devoted himself to evangelical preaching and spent two days a week in personal "conference" with his parishioners. By such means he established a voluntary "discipline" in the town, although no more than a third of potential communicants would ever submit to examination before admission to the Lord's Supper. His dismay at the growing influence of the sects led Baxter to form the Worcestershire Association of Ministers for the encouragement of catechizing and "discipline" in 1652. Clergymen in six other counties had followed his lead by the end of 1655, and another seven county associations were eventually established. These cross-denominational associations represented a powerful ecumenical movement within English Protestantism and a backlash against the dangers of spiritual anarchy apparently posed by groups like the Quakers. Baxter also produced a steady stream of devotional, catechetical, and controversial works throughout the 1650s.

## Post-Restoration

Baxter was regarded as one of the national leaders of the moderate Puritans or Presbyterians and was courted by those forging a religious settlement at the restoration of the monarchy in 1660. He became a royal chaplain, declined the offer of a bishopric, prepared position papers for the Presbyterians, and helped to argue their case at the Savoy Conference (1661), where his overeager and tactless initiatives may have hindered his cause. Meanwhile the living of Kidderminster had been successfully reclaimed by its previous minister, and, with the 1662 Act of Uniformity looming, Baxter abandoned his public ministry. In 1661 Baxter married Margaret Charlton (1636–1681), a pious and wealthy woman, and the couple retired first to Acton and then Totteridge, both on the outskirts of London, where Baxter attended the parish church while also preaching privately to his own circle. After Charles II's Declaration of Indulgence (1672), Baxter once again preached publicly in various halls in London. During the 1660s and 1670s he suffered sporadic harassment, but in the early 1680s the authorities increased their pressure on the ageing Puritan leader: in 1683 Oxford University condemned and burnt his book *The Holy Commonwealth* (1659); and in 1685 he was convicted of sedition and imprisoned for nearly two years. He subsequently lived in Finsbury and took advantage of the freedoms established under James II and the 1689 Toleration Act to write and preach until his death on 8 December 1691.

Baxter supplied moral and political leadership to moderate Puritanism. His surviving correspondence is testimony to the respect in which his pastoral, casuistical, and theological skills were held by many Nonconformists and not a few Anglicans. He was a key figure in the abortive attempts to reunite moderate Puritan clergy with the Church of England and recorded much of these secret negotiations in what became his autobiography. Baxter's own attitude toward the Church of England was complex: he leaned toward a "reduced episcopacy" that would not limit the pastoral efforts of the parish clergy; he boasted of the speed with which he and Archbishop James Ussher had agreed on just such a scheme in 1654. But the lordly prelates of the restored Church of England seemed bent on creating and maintaining an authoritarian and rigid church that had no room for men like Baxter. He increasingly suspected that they were "Grotian," his term for those who sought to erect a Gallican, or French-style, Catholicism, and that Charles II and James II were of the same persuasion. At other times, notably under the Cromwells in the 1650s and William III after 1688, Baxter was an enthusiastic exponent of religious reformation by the godly magistrate.

## Influence

For all his combative nature, the elderly Baxter was justified in claiming to have striven for forty-five years in the cause of mutual Protestant understanding and the promotion of basic Christian piety. Convinced that "practical" religion and pastoral work were at the heart of the Protestant ministry, he labored to equip his contemporaries with the necessary tools. Hence his attempt to export the discipline and methods that had worked at Kidder-

*Richard Baxter, Presbyterian pastor and author. (Library of Congress)*

minster and the succession of his best-selling books such as *The Saints Everlasting Rest* (1650), *The Reformed Pastor* (1656), and *The Christian Directory* (1673). Throughout his life Baxter refused to accept any denominational label, preferring to describe himself as "a mere Christian." This did not prevent him from launching ferocious attacks on Baptists, Quakers, Catholics, and some Anglicans, or from associating most closely with the Presbyterians and the ejected ministers. Yet he was out of step with this group in one crucial matter. His first book, *Aphorismes of Justification* (1649), had signaled his unhappiness with the soteriology of Westminster Assembly Calvinism. He feared that both strict Calvinists and radical sectaries were spreading antinomianism, and he devoted both his ministry and his pen to combating this evil. Theologically he can best be described as a Puritan Arminian. Baxter's theology was to be influential among the next generation of Nonconformists, as were his works of practical divinity. His posthu-

mous autobiography *Reliquiae Baxterianae* (1696), edited by Matthew Sylvester, and later rewritten by Edmund Calamy as *An Abridgement of Mr Baxter's History of his Life and Times* (1702), has been a major source for and influence on historians of seventeenth-century English Puritanism.

*See also:* Arminianism, Death and Dying, Declaration of Indulgence, Ejections of Clergy, Pinners' Hall, Predestination, Puritan Best-Sellers
*Further Reading*
Richard Baxter, *The Autobiography of Richard Baxter,* abridged by J. M. Lloyd Thomas, edited by N. H. Keeble (London, 1974); N. H. Keeble and Geoffrey F. Nuttall, eds., *Calendar of the Correspondence of Richard Baxter* (Oxford, 1991); William Lamont, *Puritanism and Historical Controversy* (London, 1996); Geoffrey Nuttall, *Richard Baxter* (Stanford, 1965).

*John Spurr*

## Baynes, Paul (d. 1617)

Nonconformist minister; one of the most influential puritan preachers and casuists of his generation. He was purportedly responsible for many conversions through his sermons and spiritual counsel, and his written works—all of which were published posthumously—reveal both his radicalism and his erudition as a puritan theologian. Notably, he was one of the earliest exponents of a developing congregational, nonseparatist outlook on church government, and his ideas profoundly influenced congregational thinkers of the next generation in both England and New England.

Baynes was born in London but was sent to school in Wethersfield, near Haverhill, probably in the house of the famous godly minister Richard Rogers. He was admitted to Christ's College, Cambridge, in 1591, received his B.A. in 1594, his M.A. in 1597, and was appointed fellow in 1600—a position that he held until 1604. Baynes seemingly led a sinful life as an undergraduate, but relinquished his ungodly ways shortly after his father's death—in fulfillment of his father's dying wish. By 1602, Baynes had risen to eminence when he succeeded the illustrious preacher William Perkins (by whom he was deeply influenced) as lecturer at St. Andrew's, Cambridge.

At St. Andrew's, Baynes's nonconformist practices soon came to the attention of the ecclesiastical authorities. In April 1605, Baynes was in custody for unknown offenses but was eventually released after issuing several pleas to Robert Cecil, Viscount Cranborne. During the episcopal visitation of 1608, he was permanently deprived of his Cambridge lectureship after failing to present a license to preach and refusing to subscribe to the Three Articles.

After his deprivation, Baynes became an itinerant preacher, touring the houses of supportive gentry families, and was famed as a spiritual counselor in cases of conscience. Many individual Christians solicited him for guidance, either in person or by letter. A volume of his correspondence was published in 1620, entitled *Christian Letters*. His *Briefe directions unto a godly life* (1618) was widely read and influential, and many of his sermons were published, including *A caveat for cold Christians* (1618) and *A counterbane against earthly carefulnes* (1618), delivered in Cranbrook, Kent, where Baynes settled for a time. He also compiled several exegetical works, including a commentary on the first and second chapters of Colossians and the first chapter of the Ephesians (1618). This latter work constituted a defense of Calvinism in the face of the threat posed by Arminianism; in it Baynes powerfully defends his Calvinist beliefs.

Baynes's most radical work, *The diocesans tryall*, was published in 1621 under the auspices of the puritan minister and exile William Ames. Responding to the writings of Bishop George Downame, it attacked the *jure divino* (by divine law) defense of episcopacy, that is, the argument that episcopacy was mandated in the New Testament, and offered one of the earliest arguments for a congregational system of church government in a nonseparatist context. His beliefs had an affinity with those of contemporaries William Bradshaw and Henry Jacob. Despite his radical views on church government, Baynes was highly critical of separatism and remained deeply committed to the Church of England.

Baynes was beset by ill health and poverty throughout his life; he eventually died in Cambridge and was buried in St. Andrews on 1 August 1617.

*Further Reading*
Samuel Clarke, *The Lives of Thirty Two English Divines*, 3rd ed. (1677); M. M. Knappen, *Tudor Puritanism* (Chicago, 1939).

*Victoria Gregory*

## Beadle, John (ca. 1596–1667)

Puritan clergyman; best known to history as the author of the *Journal or Diary of a Thankful Christian*, first published in 1656, dedicated to his patrons the Earl and Countess of Warwick, in which Beadle enlarges on the advantages of keeping a detailed diary of spiritual progress. There is some evidence that this work began life as a series of sermons on the Book of Numbers, chapter 33, preached as early as 1644.

Beadle was born at Bramford, Suffolk, about 1596 and was admitted a sizar at Pembroke College, Cambridge, in 1613. He proceeded B.A. in 1617 and M.A. in 1620. He was ordained deacon and priest in 1618 and following his studies in Cambridge spent some time at the household seminary run by Thomas Hooker at Little Baddows in Essex. He came to the attention of Robert Rich, Earl of Warwick, served as his chaplain and, through Rich's patronage, became the rector of Little Leighs in Essex. Beadle with others such as Thomas Shepard, Thomas Weld, and Daniel Rogers, fell foul of Bishop William Laud's visitation in 1630. He was presented for seldom or never reading prayers, failing to wear the surplice, and for baptizing without the surplice or sign of the cross. Beadle appeared before Laud, promised to conform and was dismissed with a canonical admonition.

In 1632, he was preferred to the rectory of Barnstone in Essex. During the Civil War, Beadle was a member of the classis for the county of Essex. A committed Presbyterian, despite the influence of Thomas Hooker, he was ejected in 1662, yet remained in Barnstone until his death in 1667.

*Further Reading*

Tom Webster, *Godly Clergy in Early Stuart England: The Caroline Puritan Movement, c. 1620–1643* (Cambridge, Eng., 1997).

*John Craig*

## Beaumont, Agnes (1652–1720)

Suffolk farmer's daughter who recorded her tribulations as a Nonconformist in a manuscript entitled *The Narrative of the Persecution of Agnes Beaumont.* Initiated into the world of the godly by the preaching and ministerial skills of John Bunyan, she became a devout member of the Bedford church's sister congregation at Gamlinghay in 1672. Her *Narrative,* which remained unpublished until 1760, records the traumatic events leading up to and following her father's sudden death in 1674. Having been rebuked by her father for attending the meetings of Bunyan's congregation, Beaumont was accused of patricide, but she was acquitted after a coroner's inquest. She also fell victim to malicious gossip spread by a former suitor alleging that she was having an affair with Bunyan. During this period she was sustained by her faith. The *Narrative* is a vivid and moving testimony of female piety in a largely patriarchal society that also provides an insight into seventeenth-century filial relationships. Beaumont married twice in later life, first to Thomas Warren (1702), a landowning gentleman who left her part of his estate upon his death (1707), and then in 1708 to Samuel Story who outlived her.

*Further Reading*

Kathleen Lynch "'Her Name Agnes': The Verification of Agnes Beaumont's Narrative Ventures," *English Literary History* 67 (2000), 71–98; John Stachniewski and Anita Pacheco, eds., *Grace Abounding with Other Spiritual Autobiographies* (Oxford, 1998).

*Claire Vivian*

## Bedell, William (1571–1642)

Bishop of Kilmore and Ardagh. Bedell was a paragon of moderate puritan churchmanship, regarded by Bishop Gilbert Burnet as one of the greatest bishops of all time. He came from an Essex farm to enter the newly founded Emmanuel College, Cambridge, as one of the first cohort of students, aged twelve. A lifelong friendship began with Samuel Ward. In 1593 he became a fellow. At some point Bedell acquired the library of William Perkins, all of it later lost in Ireland. In 1601 he became town preacher of Bury St. Edmunds. When new demands for conformity were made in the early years of James I, Bedell decided to conform (but not to subscribe to the Three Articles), much to the disgust of Suffolk's hard-line puritans. In a sermon preached before his bishop, he wished that the name of puritan might be cast into hell, and that everyone might be content to be called Christian. The reconstruction of a puritan continued during a sojourn in Venice, where Bedell served as chaplain to Sir Henry Wotton. He learned Italian, became a friend of Paolo Sarpi, and translated his "History of the Council of Trent" into Latin. Now he knew that Roman Catholics could be Christians too. Bedell returned to Suffolk as rector of Horningsheath, where he remained until his patron, Sir Thomas Jermyn, brought him back into the public eye.

In 1627 he was dispatched to Trinity College, Dublin (a clone of Emmanuel), as its provost, and two years later was preferred to the Irish sees of Kilmore and Ardagh, later resigning Ardagh. Bedell consciously reinvented the image of the model, primitive bishop, holding synods (which made him unpopular with the rest of the Irish hierarchy), walking the streets, growing his own potatoes, and, above all, insisting that those who graduated from Trinity College and his other clergy should communicate in the Irish language. When northern Ireland erupted in rebellion in 1641, Bedell was driven from pillar to post, ousted by the Catholic bishop of the area, whose friendship he had sought without success, and he became part of a train of refugees escorted to the coast by the military. On the way he died, probably of typhus. All that was salvaged was his manuscript Hebrew Bible, acquired in Venice and now in Emmanuel. Bedell was an irenic, we might say, ecumenical, figure. In a famous triangular correspondence with a contemporary of his and Bishop Joseph Hall's who had turned "papist," James Wadsworth, Hall was all bitter polemic, but Bedell wrote as a friend. "You say that you have become a Catholic. Weren't you one before?" Bedell was also a brilliant linguist, who promoted a project to invent a universal language (parodied by Jonathan Swift in *Gulliver's Travels*), although this project was another casualty of the Troubles.

*See also:* Emmanuel College
*Further Reading*
A. Sarah Bendall, Christopher Nugent Lawrence Brooke, Patrick Collinson, *A History of Emmanuel College, Cambridge* (Woodbridge, Eng., 2000); Alan Ford, *The Protestant Reformation in Ireland* (Dublin, 1997); E. S. Shuckburgh, ed., *Two Biographies of William Bedell,* (Cambridge, Eng., 1902).

*Patrick Collinson*

## Benn, William (1600–1681)

Puritan minister. Benn was born in the county of Cumberland, England. He attended Queen's College, Oxford, but did not receive a degree. After serving for a time as a private chaplain, he became a preacher at All Saints Parish in Dorchester. He was an ally of the town's more famous puritan clergyman, John White, and assisted White in some of his programs for social reform.

Following the Royalist seizure of the town in 1643, Benn retreated to London for a time, but he returned to Dorchester in 1646. He served as a member of the Triers for Dorsetshire and also a member of the committee to eject scandalous ministers and schoolteachers. He was ejected from his parish living in 1662 and subsequently imprisoned on a number of occasions for illegal preaching and suspicion of being involved with plots against the Restoration regime. One of his daughters married Nathaniel Mather; another married Theophilus Polwhele.

*See also:* Triers and Ejectors
*Further Reading*
Richard Greaves and Robert Zaller, eds.,
*Biographical Dictionary of British Radicals in the*

*Seventeenth Century,* 3 vols. (Brighton, Eng., 1982).

*Francis J. Bremer*

## Bernard, Richard (1568–1641)

Puritan clergyman and author. Bernard was born in Epworth, Lincolnshire, and retained strong ties to that county, from which most of his patrons came as well. He studied at Christ's College, Cambridge, receiving his B.A. in 1595 and his M.A. in 1598.

Bernard returned for a time to Epworth and was there when he published an edition of Terence in Latin, with an English translation. He was presented to the vicarage of Worksop, Nottinghamshire, in 1601. He appears to have been attracted to the Separatists, affiliating for a time with William Brewster and John Robinson of the Scrooby Separatist congregation. He joined in covenant with men and women from his own and neighboring parishes in which all pledged to aid each other, receive the Lord's Supper together, and avoid listening to "dumb dog" preachers.

In the end, Bernard rejected the separatist stand and published against them, engaging in an exchange with Henry Ainsworth. But despite rejecting separatism, Bernard was a nonconformist and was silenced on at least one occasion by the church authorities. This probably contributed to his move to the parish of Batcombe in Somersetshire. He participated in combination lectures with other godly preachers in the region. Though he appears not to have modified his stance, he was tolerated by the bishop of his new diocese.

He continued to be a prolific writer who demonstrated in his works a great range of interests. He published *A Guide to Grand Jury-men with respect to Witches* (1627), a commentary on the Book of Ruth, and attacks on the Church of Rome and the bishops of the Church of England. He was noted for his use of allegory, particularly in *The Isle of Man* (1627), a work that some believe influenced John Bunyan. One of his more noted works was *The Faithful Shepherd* (1607).

Bernard was a concerned and effective pastor and gathered believers in his home after services to review his sermon and answer questions, and to catechize them. A reformer and nonconformist, he nevertheless was willing to cooperate with reformed bishops. He died in 1641, as the divisions between the king and his puritan subjects were widening.

See also: Witchcraft
Further Reading
Kenneth Fincham, *Prelate as Pastor: The Episcopate of James I* (Oxford, 1990); Tom Webster, *Godly Clergy in Early Stuart England: The Caroline Puritan Movement, c. 1620–1643* (Cambridge, Eng., 1997).

*Francis J. Bremer*

## Bird, Samuel (d. 1603)

Suffolk clergyman and nonconformist. Bird was the son of Samuel Bird of Saffron Walden, Essex. He matriculated pensioner of Queens' College, Cambridge, in 1566, proceeded B.A. in 1570, and commenced M.A. from Corpus Christi College, Cambridge, in 1573. In November 1573 he was elected fellow of Corpus Christi College but vacated his fellowship in 1576; he disappears from the historical record until May 1592 when he became minister of St. Peter's, Ipswich, where he remained until his death in 1603. One Samuel Bird was granted a license to teach grammar throughout the diocese of London on 10 October 1578, and he may have been the schoolmaster of Cockfield, Suffolk, approached in 1585 by the members of the Dedham conference to accept the living of Wenham. His conversion to godliness took place not later than 1580, as his first published work, *A friendlie communication or Dialogue betweene Paule and Demas wherein is disputed how we are to use the pleasures of this life* (1580) attests. The work is notable for its strong attack upon the perils of playing cards and dice and a number of references to his time in Cambridge. Little is known of his ministry at St. Peter's, Ipswich. Bishop Redman's visitation in 1597 uncovered a typical catalogue of nonconformist offenses: failure to wear the surplice, omitting the sign of the cross in baptism, and failing to conduct the annual perambulation around the church bounds, among others. Two volumes of

published lectures (1598) disclose his connections with the godly community in Ipswich.

Further Reading
*Oxford Dictionary of National Biography* (Oxford, 2004).

*John Craig*

## Bird (Byrd), William (d. 1599)

One of the original members of the Dedham Conference. The name was a common one and it is difficult to establish the details of his early life. He may have been the William Bird who graduated from St. John's, Cambridge, in 1556, and he may have been the William Bird whom John Foxe recorded as having been driven out of Dedham during Mary's reign.

Bird became rector of Boxford, Suffolk, in 1563. He had connections with leading reformers in that region of Suffolk. He may have known John Knewstub through connections with St. John's College. Adam Winthrop owned land in neighboring Groton and Edwardstone as well as in Boxford. Winthrop probably was instrumental in bringing his close friend Henry Sandes to Boxford as a lecturer around 1582, perhaps suggesting that Bird was no longer an effective preacher.

Along with Sandes, Bird was one of the original members of the Dedham conference that was organized in 1582. He participated in its meetings and was moderator for some. He died in 1599 and was succeeded by Joseph Bird, who was likely his son. He may also have been related to Samuel Bird, who was a schoolmaster at Cockfield and then minister at St. Peter, Ipswich.

See also: Dedham Conference
Further Reading
Patrick Collinson, John Craig, and Brett Usher, eds., *Conferences and Combination Lectures in the Elizabethan Church: Dedham and Bury St. Edmunds, 1582–1590* (Woodbridge, Eng., 2003).

*Francis J. Bremer*

## Blackerby, Richard (1574–1648)

Puritan clergyman who became noted for his training of aspiring ministers. Blackerby was born at

Worlington, Suffolk, in 1574. He attended grammar school at Bury St. Edmunds and then at the age of fifteen went on to Trinity College, Cambridge, where he received his B.A. and M.A. Blackerby spent nine years at Trinity and achieved a reputation for his mastery of Latin, Greek, and Hebrew. It was likely at Cambridge that he became a supporter of the puritan agenda, and it was certainly there that he became a follower of William Perkins.

Through his puritan connections, Blackerby became chaplain to Sir Thomas Jermyn, one of the noted godly magistrates of Suffolk. He left that post to assume a similar one in the household of Sir Edward Lewkenor, another godly Suffolk gentleman. It is possible that from the start his nonconformity made acquiring a parochial living difficult, and there is no evidence that he ever took holy orders. He did minister to the parish of Feltwell, in Norfolk, for a brief time, but evidently without having been formally instituted or inducted. He did however find occasions to preach, and his effectiveness in the pulpit was attested to by Daniel Rogers and others.

Blackerby's true fame came when he moved to the Essex town of Ashen (Ashdon) and began to receive as boarders young men eager to prepare for the ministry. His was one of the first, if not the first, "puritan seminaries" and certainly the most famous. Later, Richard Greenham, John Cotton, and others followed his example, and such informal institutions were a major factor in the growth of puritanism. In 1629 he moved to Great Wratling, Suffolk, where his son-in-law was rector. Following the opening of the Civil Wars he was called to a congregation at Great Thurlow, where he died in 1648.

*See also:* Household Seminaries
*Further Reading*
Francis J. Bremer, *Congregational Communion: Clerical Friendship in the Anglo-American Puritan Community, 1610–1692* (Boston, 1994); Tom Webster, *Godly Clergy in Early Stuart England: the Caroline Puritan Movement, c. 1620–1643* (Cambridge, Eng., 1997).

*Francis J. Bremer*

## Bolton, Robert (1572–1631)

Puritan clergyman and author. Bolton was born and raised in Lancashire. In 1592 he was admitted to Lincoln College, Oxford, where he demonstrated proficiency in Greek. He transferred to Brasenose College and received his B.A. there in 1596 and his M.A. in 1602. He was appointed lecturer in moral and natural philosophy, and participated in a disputation before King James I when that monarch visited Oxford in 1605. At this stage in his career he demonstrated sympathy for Roman Catholicism and an aversion for puritans. Visiting Cambridge University, he was sharply critical of the famous puritan preacher William Perkins.

Sometime before he received his B.D. in 1609, he was converted to a Reformed view of Protestantism; rejected card playing, dice, and other such pursuits; and decided to enter the ministry. He was inducted to the rectory of Broughton, Northamptonshire, in 1610. There he led his family in a program of pious domestic observance. His personal introspection gave him insight into troubled consciences, which guided his pastoral efforts. He became known as a powerful preacher whom many godly men and women traveled to listen to. His published works were widely read by men and women seeking guidance in their quest for godliness, including John Winthrop.

In addition to preaching often on the theme of the inner life and its spiritual struggles, he also was outspoken in advancing a form of social gospel. He believed in an alliance between godly magistrates and ministers to shape the behavior of the people. He was sharply critical of the arrogance of many of the nation's rulers and the increasing tendency of the upper classes to pursue their own interests to the harm of the common wealth. He was a strong opponent of Catholic interests and a supporter of the Reformed cause in Europe. In advancing these causes, he participated in puritan lectureships and established friendships with prominent clergy such as Arthur Hildersham and John Preston.

*Further Reading*
Tom Webster, *Godly Clergy in Early Stuart England: The Caroline Puritan Movement, c. 1620–1643* (Cambridge, Eng., 1997).

*Francis J. Bremer*

## Bolton, Samuel (1606–1654)

Clergyman and master of Christ's College, Cambridge. Bolton was born in Lancashire, studied at the Manchester School, and entered Christ's College, Cambridge, in 1625. He graduated in 1629 and received his M.A. in 1632. Two years later he became curate at Harrow, Middlesex. In 1638 he was minister of St. Martin Ludgate, in London. He later served as minister at St. Saviour's in Southwark and as a lecturer at St. Anne and St. Agnes in Aldersgate.

In 1642 Bolton was selected as one of the delegates to the Westminster Assembly, called by Parliament to propose a reformation of the English Church. He was highly respected as a preacher, and some of his early publications were collections of fast-day sermons he had preached. He strove for accommodation at a time of widening conflict among various puritan groups.

In 1645 he was chosen master of Christ's College, Cambridge. He served as vice-chancellor of the university from 1650 to 1652. Despite his university responsibilities, he continued to preach in London and Cambridge until his death in 1654.

*Further Reading*
Paul Seaver, *The Puritan Lectureships: The Politics of Religious Dissent, 1560–1662* (Stanford, 1970); John Twigg, *The University of Cambridge and the English Revolution, 1625–1688* (Cambridge, Eng., 1990).

*Francis J. Bremer*

## Bownd, Nicholas (d. 1613)

Puritan clergyman and author of a key work on the Sabbath. The son of Robert Bownd, physician to the Duke of Norfolk, Bownd matriculated sizar from Peterhouse in 1568, and proceeded B.A. in early 1572 and M.A. in 1575. Elected fellow of Peterhouse in 1572, his degrees were incorporated at Oxford in 1577. He was ordained deacon and priest in the diocese of Ely on 2 June 1580, but it is highly doubtful that he ever was rector of Fulbeck, Lincolnshire, as has been claimed. Although he was instituted to the living of Norton, Suffolk, on 3 September 1585, he appears to have been resident in the parish from 1581 as his five children, Hannah, Nathaniel, Abigail, Priscilla, and Susan, were born and baptized in the parish between January 1582 and August 1591. The patron of the living was the godly Suffolk magistrate Robert Ashfield of Stowlangtoft. Following the death of his first wife, Bownd married the widow of John More, the celebrated "apostle of Norwich" who had died in 1592, and he was instrumental in overseeing the printing of a number of More's works. Bownd's mother married as her second husband Richard Greenham, and his sister married John Dod; these links reflect the godly circles of piety and nonconformity in which Bound moved.

Created Doctor of Divinity at Cambridge in 1594, Bownd is best known for *The doctrine of the Sabbath* (1595), which was dedicated to the Earl of Essex with his coat of arms, suggesting that Bownd was one of his chaplains. This work began life as a series of sermons on the Ten Commandments preached in the Bury exercise. Bownd wrote that he had been "solicited to publish my Sermons upon the ten Commandments by certain of my godly brethren auditors of the same" and elsewhere in the work likened the meetings of the godly to "so many firebrands layde together." "Though every man hath some grace of Gods spirit in himself, yet is it greatly increased by conference." Bownd maintained that all Christians were commanded to rest on the seventh day of the week as much as the Jews were on the Mosaic Sabbath, and that the entire day ought to be devoted to acts of worship and godly service. He launched a strong attack on the games and sports that profaned the day, and the work reflected and stimulated the growth of Sabbatarianism among the godly in England. In *The holy exercise of fasting* (1604), Bownd distinguished between public and private fasting, but ruled that private fasts need not be confined to the family of one house, but could include persons "out of divers households gathered together upon their own private motion; yet orderly and in the fear of God." If this suggested a step in the direction of a gathered church, Bownd's dedication of the work to Bishop John Jegon, which assured him "how ready we are, and shall be, to yield obedience to all your lordship's godly proceedings," suggests the opposite. In 1611 he moved to Norwich, where he became rector of the parish of St. Andrews (John More's old parish); he died two years later and was buried in the church on 26 December 1613.

*See also:* Sabbath and Sabbatarianism
*Further Reading*
John Craig, *Reformation, Politics and Polemics: The growth of Protestantism in East Anglian Market Towns* (Aldershot, Eng., 2002).

*John Craig*

## Bradford, William (1590–1657)

Founder, governor, and historian of Plymouth Colony. Born in Austerfield, Yorkshire, Bradford was orphaned by age five. By seventeen he had become a member in Richard Clyfton's Separatist congregation at Scrooby, where he was "adopted" by elder William Brewster and first met John Robinson. Bradford relocated with the Scrooby group to Amsterdam in 1607 and again in 1608 to Leiden, where Bradford in 1611 cashed in his inheritance and became a weaver. In 1613 he married Dorothy May, with whom he had one child. Bradford remained with the smaller group of forty-one Separatists that in 1620 joined with sixty-one "strangers" in boarding the *Mayflower* and eventually landing at what became Plymouth. The enterprise was jointly funded with merchant investors from London. Because the group was supposed to land in Virginia, it had no specific legal or governing status, which led to the agreement to establish a "civil body politic" known as the Mayflower Compact. Dorothy fell overboard and drowned while the *Mayflower* was still at anchor; Bradford remarried Alice Carpenter Southworth in 1623.

In the disastrous first winter, half the group died from malnutrition, including the first governor, John Carver, who was replaced by Bradford; Bradford eventually served as governor for all but five of his thirty-eight years at Plymouth. The first ten years were marked by various ordeals but also saw Bradford display able leadership in various regards: in ironing out peaceable relations with the Wampanoags (which included trade and learning agricultural techniques), in shaping the colony's laws, and in negotiating with the investors (who were often critical of their returns). Of special importance was the agreement reached with the investors in 1627 whereby Bradford and seven others personally assumed the colony's large debts along with certain privileges and rights, although matters were direly complicated by the unscrupulous dealings of Isaac Allerton. Bradford also set himself the task of ferreting out individuals whom he believed posed a threat to the colony, such as John Lyford and Thomas Morton.

In 1630 Bradford began to compose a history, titled simply *Of Plymouth Plantation*. The first book provides a single narrative within the framework of a providential and primitivist interpretation of church history, and culminates with the construction of the first house at Plymouth in December 1620. Bradford worked on the manuscript briefly in 1644, at which time he arranged the second book in the form of annals; he worked on it again from 1646 to 1650, bringing the chronology forward to 1646, at which point it breaks off. Invaluable for its historical worth in various ways, the book is also widely considered a classic of early American literature for its rhetorical polish and Bradford's overall vision. The tone of book 1 is predominantly hopeful and trusting, despite adversity and ordeals, while the tone of book 2 becomes more ironic and even elegiac; the book ends with a list of the original passengers of the *Mayflower*. Bradford wrote a small body of verse, and in his latter years wrote dialogues between the "ancient" and "young" men of the colony and studied Hebrew.

*See also:* Mayflower Compact, Plymouth Colony, Puritan Historians, Pilgrim Thanksgiving (in Primary Sources)
*Further Reading*
Douglas Anderson, *William Bradford's Books: Of Plimoth Plantation and the Printed Word* (Baltimore, 2002).

*Michael G. Ditmore*

## Bradshaw, William (1571–1618)

Preacher and polemicist. He was born in Market Bosworth, Leicestershire, in 1571. Attendance at the grammar school in Ashby-de-la-Zouch, followed by Emmanuel College, Cambridge (B.A., 1593, M.A., 1596), can be said to have determined his subsequent career. At Ashby Bradshaw became acquainted with the Marian exile Anthony Gilby and earned the sponsorship of Arthur Hildersham as well as the protection of the Hastings family. At Emmanuel he came to the favorable notice of its redoubtable master, Laurence Chaderton, who secured for him a position as a tutor to the family of the governor of Guernsey. There he became friends with Thomas Cartwright, as well as with a future bishop, James Montague. When the latter became the first master of Sidney Sussex College, Bradshaw was one of the initial fellows.

Well connected though he was, Bradshaw's uncompromising brand of Puritanism ensured that he would never secure permanent public employment as a minister of the Church of England. Attempts to appoint him to endowed lectureships in Chatham, Kent, and (at a later date) at Christ Church, Newgate, were blocked by episcopal authority, and, until his death in 1618, Bradshaw made do as chaplain to the Redich family of Newhall, Derbyshire.

Bradshaw's claim to historical significance lies in his polemical activities from 1604 through 1608 in the wake of the Puritan discomfiture at the Hampton Court Conference. In a series of works published clandestinely by the London printer William Jones, the militant wing of the Puritan movement sought to disaffiliate itself from the overly moderate representations made at the conference and to rally opinion in its favor in the hopes of bringing on a second conference. Of the seventeen titles assigned to Jones, Bradshaw was responsible for six, and of a further eight printed in the Netherlands in the same cause, three are also his.

Bradshaw's six titles for Jones include his best-known work, *English Puritanisme* (1605). Here he envisions the Church of England as collection of autonomous congregations existing in brotherly communion, responsible only to the civil magistrate should any of them become disorderly. Along with his reiterated rejections of separation from the English church, Bradshaw's views on polity have led to his being enlisted, in company with his fellow workers in the same paper war, William Ames and Henry Jacob, as prophets of the "New England Way." In actual fact, however, Bradshaw drew on strands in the Elizabethan classical movement that favored congregational polity, and he would not have been entirely happy with the constitutions of the New England churches had he somehow lived to see them. Equally, however, the individuals who created and defended the polity of the American Puritans were well aware of Bradshaw's works at a period when they were not easy to acquire, and there are numerous personal links between him and the clergy of the founding generation of the Puritan colonies. If he did not provide the Congregationalists of the 1630s and 1640s with a blueprint for their churches, he can legitimately be claimed as one of their immediate intellectual ancestors.

*See also:* Congregationalism
*Further Reading*
Chaplin Burrage, *Early English Dissenters*, 2 vols. (Cambridge, Eng., 1912); Stephen Foster, *The Long Argument: English Puritanism and the Shaping of New England Culture, 1570–1700* (Chapel Hill, 1991).

*Stephen Foster*

## Bradstreet, Anne Dudley (ca. 1612–1672)

The first individual from the British American colonies to have a volume of poems printed, and a leading poet and writer. Born to Thomas and Dorothy Yorke Dudley, Bradstreet had the advantage of tutoring and the library of the Earl of Lincoln, whom her father served as steward. After childhood sickness, at about age sixteen she married Simon Bradstreet and shortly afterward they, along with her parents, joined the Winthrop fleet in the first wave of the Great Migration to Massachusetts. Her father, one of the original members of the company, frequently served as deputy governor and in other positions; Simon also served in positions of authority throughout his career.

Little is known about Bradstreet before the publication of her book, except that she continued to struggle with illness and also infertility before even-

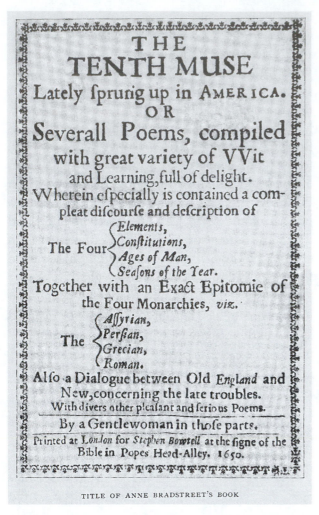

TITLE OF ANNE BRADSTREET'S BOOK

*The title page of American poet Anne Bradstreet's book of poetry,* The Tenth Muse. *(North Wind Picture Archive)*

tually bearing eight children. In 1650, a collection of her poems titled *The Tenth Muse* appeared in London, having been shepherded through the press by brother-in-law minister John Woodbridge. The volume ran to more than 200 pages, comprising commendatory verse by various admirers (including her fellow colonist and author Nathaniel Ward), a group of quaternions (groups of four), a lengthy and unfinished historical account of *The Four Monarchies* in heroic couplets, and a group of elegies and epitaphs for public figures, including the Huguenot epic poet Seigneur du Bartas, Sir Philip Sidney, and Queen Elizabeth. The tone of *The Tenth Muse* is erudite, impersonal, and secular;

a persistent theme is human vanity, but the book has sometimes been characterized as derivative apprentice work. The publication indicates that Bradstreet's poetry was already in some form of circulation, but the reception of the book is not well known; it is possible that Bradstreet in New England felt the lash of rumors about the impropriety of a woman in the masculine role of public poet, but there is no positive evidence. However, she continued to polish poems already published and to produce new ones and other writings throughout the remainder of her life, although the 1666 fire that destroyed her home also consumed her library and manuscripts.

Six years after her death, *Several Poems* (1678) was published by John Foster in Boston; this collection is basically a revision of *The Tenth Muse* expanded with the addition of eighteen poems, many of which are elegies for family members in which her religious views are articulated in verse. Here, Bradstreet achieves a balance between poetic talent and personal concerns; a high point is "Contemplations," widely considered her single greatest achievement.

The third and final phase of her writing is represented in what has come to be called the Andover Notebook (first published in 1867), which contains her spiritual autobiography, various hymn-like poems and prose pieces, and, in her own handwriting, prose "Meditations Divine and Moral" and a poem, "As weary pilgrim." Along with Edward Taylor and Michael Wigglesworth, Bradstreet is now considered one of the three major seventeenth-century American poets.

*Further Reading*
Rosamond Rosenmeier, *Anne Bradstreet Revisited* (Boston, 1991); Ann Stanford, *Anne Bradstreet, The Worldly Puritan* (New York, 1975).

*Michael G. Ditmore*

## Bradstreet, Simon (1603–1697)

Colonial governor. Simon Bradstreet's distinguished career as a colonial statesman is often overlooked due to the recognition afforded his first wife, Puritan poet Anne Bradstreet. The son of a nonconformist minister, Bradstreet was born at Lincolnshire in 1603 and graduated from Emmanuel College. Upon his appointment as assistant to the Massachusetts Bay Company, Bradstreet emigrated to New England. He arrived in the colonies in 1630.

Bradstreet was related to the leadership of Massachusetts Bay Colony through marriage. Anne Bradstreet was the daughter of Governor Thomas Dudley, and Simon's second wife, Anne Gardner, was John Winthrop's niece. Bradstreet served sixty years in public office. Often holding concurrent positions, he remained an assistant of the Bay Company for over forty years, while simultaneously helping to negotiate an agreement with neighboring colonies. His efforts facilitated the founding of the New England Confederation, on which he acted as a Confederation commissioner for thirty-three years.

When Charles II was restored to the English throne, Bradstreet was sent abroad as a liaison and successfully lobbied the king to confirm the Massachusetts charter. However, Charles's demands upon the colony cost Bradstreet support in New England. Despite this, Bradstreet maintained his positive reputation in England and New England. Elected governor of Massachusetts in 1679, he held office until 1686.

When James II revoked the Massachusetts charter and established the Dominion Government, Bradstreet refused any position in the new government because he regarded it as unlawful. Once the colonists revolted against Dominion rule, Bradstreet and others restored order by creating an interim body to govern the colony. When the charter was reinstated, Bradstreet consented to serve as governor until the king's appointee assumed office in 1692.

Through land speculation Bradstreet acquired vast property holdings throughout the colony. Although he had resided in Ipswich, Cambridge, Boston, and Andover, his last years were spent in Salem. He died there in 1697.

*See also:* Anne Dudley Bradstreet
*Further Reading*
*American National Biography* (New York, 1999).

*Susan Ortmann*

## Brearley, Roger (1586–1637)

Minister, and leader of the so-called Grindletonian movement. Born in Lancashire, and apparently raised a puritan, Brearley was ordained as a minister despite the fact that he lacked a university education. While tending to the district attached to the chapel of Grindleton (Yorkshire), Brearley began to broach a series of controversial, perhaps even heretical doctrines, which in the view of his opponents savored of antinomianism and Familism. Tried twice before the York High Commission, Brearley escaped punishment by submitting to the court and promising to conform to the doctrine and discipline of the church. Despite this, his critics persistently charged that Brearley continued to spread his erroneous opinions in the years that followed. Brearley's style of religiosity represented a departure from, and a critique of, prevailing forms of puritan practical divinity; rejecting the strenuous legal regimen of mainstream puritanism, Brearley embraced a form of religiosity that stressed the absolute passivity of the believer in the process of salvation; a species of self-abnegation in which the would-be believer surrendered his or her selfhood prior to salvation; and a profound, indeed mystical, sense of the union between Christ and those who came to be joined to him by faith. Those so joined to God were themselves so transformed that in a certain sense, they could be said to share God's divinity and perfection, claims that explain the consistent charges of Familism lobbed at Brearley and his supporters. This form of piety almost certainly owed something to Continental forms of mysticism, but it also represented a decidedly English, indeed puritan, twist on such ideas. Prior to his death in 1637, Brearley preached successively at Grindleton, Kildwick (Yorkshire), and Burnley (Lancashire); the Grindletonian community that he spawned outlived him, surviving it seems into the 1680s, when his last known follower died.

*See also:* Antinomianism, Family of Love, Sects
*Further Reading*
Theodore Dwight Bozeman, *The Precisianist Strain: Disciplinary Religion and Antinomian Backlash in Puritanism to 1638* (Chapel Hill, 2004); David Como, *Blown by the Spirit: Puritanism and the*

*Emergence of an Antinomian Underground in Pre–Civil War England* (Stanford, 2004).

David Como

*Pilgrim: A Biography of William Brewster* (Falls Church, VA; 1982).

David J. Appleby

## Brewster, William (ca. 1566–1644)

Cofounder and elder of Plymouth Colony. Brewster was born sometime around 1566, possibly in Scrooby, Nottinghamshire. He was educated in Latin and Greek, and studied at Peterhouse College, Cambridge, in 1580, although he appears to have left without graduating. In 1584 he entered the service of the Elizabethan diplomat and politician William Davison, serving until Davison's fall from power in 1587. Brewster returned to Scrooby, acting as the region's postmaster living at Scrooby Manor. Here he began to gather a godly community, which soon attracted the opprobrium of the authorities. An attempted emigration to Holland in 1607 was betrayed, and Brewster was imprisoned. In 1609 the community successfully escaped to Leiden, where Brewster became a teacher and publisher of religious works. He also established a ministry among the English émigrés.

After several brushes with authority, Brewster, returning to England, obtained a land patent in Virginia, largely though the efforts of his friend Sir Edward Sandys. In September 1620 the Brewster family duly sailed for America on the *Mayflower*. In helping to found the colony at New Plymouth, Brewster recommended his ministry and acted as schoolmaster of the colony until 1629. His contemporary William Bradford remembered a sociable and modest man, always ready to offer succor to the needy or oppressed. Brewster died in 1644, leaving behind a huge collection of books, a sword (Massachusetts Historical Society), a chest that had allegedly come with him on the *Mayflower* (Pilgrim Hall Museum, Plymouth, Massachusetts), and a thriving stock of family descendants.

*See also:* English Puritanism in the Netherlands, Plymouth Colony
*Further Reading*
Dorothy Brewster, *William Brewster of the Mayflower* (New York, 1970); Mary B. Sherwood,

## Bridge, William (1600–1670)

One of the celebrated Dissenting Brethren in the Westminster Assembly. He received his B.A. (1623) and his M.A. (1626) from Emmanuel College, Cambridge. After serving in Colchester and Norwich he was silenced for his nonconformity in 1637 by Bishop Matthew Wren, upon which he removed to Holland. There he renounced his Church of England ordination and became first teacher and then pastor of the Rotterdam Church succeeding Hugh Peter in that position after the latter's emigration to Massachusetts Bay. Bridge's colleague at Rotterdam was Jeremiah Burroughes, who was teacher of the church. Throughout the 1630s and 1640s Bridge was in close contact, personally and through correspondence, with many of the other early proponents of Congregationalism: John Cotton, John Wilson, John Davenport, and Thomas Hooker, as well as Thomas Goodwin and Philip Nye who had also gathered a church in Holland at Arnhem. According to Presbyterian critic Thomas Edwards, Bridge and his colleagues in Holland were especially influenced by the Congregationalists of Massachusetts Bay.

In 1642 Bridge responded to Parliament's invitation to nonconformists to return to England. He preached frequently before the Long Parliament and was a principle participant in the Westminster Assembly of Divines (1643–1648). Along with Thomas Goodwin, Jeremiah Burroughes, Philip Nye, and Sydrach Simpson, Bridge was one of the divines who dissented from the presbyterian polity of the majority, and whose plea for a congregational form of polity was published as *An Apologeticall Narration* (1643).

It was also at this time that Bridge returned to Norfolk with the intention of forming a church gathered along congregational lines. Because of the fluid political and military situation during the Civil War, it was decided that it would be more prudent to gather the church in the port town of Yarmouth rather than the inland city of Norwich. In June 1643 Bridge and ten others "entered into Covenant" with one another, promising to acknowledge Jesus Christ "to be our God," to uphold God's ordinances, abstain from sin, and watch "over one another & as need shall be to counsell, Admonish, reprove, comfort, relieve, assist & beare with one another, humbly submitting ourselves to the Government of Christ in his Church." In September, 1643, Bridge was chosen and ordained pastor of this church. The Yarmouth church subsequently went on to become one of the most influential churches in East Anglia during the 1640s and 1650s and was instrumental in advising and assisting at the gathering of congregational churches in Norwich, Couchly, Alby, Wattisfield, Beccles, Woodbridge, and Hapton among others.

Bridge was offered the position of chaplain of the Council of State in 1649, but, reluctant to leave his church, he did not accept. In 1658 he participated in the Savoy Assembly and sat on the committee that wrote the *Declaration of Faith and Order* (Savoy Declaration). After the Restoration, Bridge was ejected in 1662 and went to Clapham and preached at the independent meeting there until his death in 1670.

Along with *An Apologeticall Narration*, Bridge published *Babylons Downfall* (1641), *Reasons of the Dissenting Brethren against certain Propositions concerning presbyterial Government* (1648), *England Saved with a Notwithstanding* (1648), *The Saints Hiding-place* (1647).

*See also: An Apologeticall Narration,* Dissenting Brethren, English Puritanism in the Netherlands
*Further Reading*
Francis J. Bremer, *Congregational Communion: Clerical Friendship in the Anglo-American Puritan Community, 1610–1692* (Boston, 1994); Robert S. Paul, *The Assembly of The Lord* (Edinburgh, 1985).

*Ralph Young*

## Brightman, Thomas (1562–1607)

Minister and millennialist exegete. Thomas Brightman was born at Nottingham in 1562 and attended Queen's College, Cambridge, as a pensioner and taking a B.A., M.A., and B.D. He was a fellow of Queen's College in 1584 and in 1592 was granted the rectory of Hawnes in Bedfordshire. His primary mark on the puritan movement, however, was through the posthumous publication of his major commentary on the Book of Revelation, *Apocalypsis Apocalypseos, or a Revelation of the Revelation* (1609), subsequently reprinted and excerpted throughout the Civil War and Interregnum.

Brightman's millennial exegesis of the prophecies of Revelation linked the Church of England with the Laodicean church condemned there for lukewarmness and tied the reign of the Antichrist to the current age, which had begun with the accession of Elizabeth in 1558. Brightman's literal, historical interpretation of the prophecies of the apocalypse in Revelation demonstrated that the Reformed Churches of Geneva and Scotland would be saved in the coming apocalypse, but the condemned English church would suffer the full wrath of God. Brightman's dire warnings helped to transform puritan disappointment in the progress of reform during the early Stuart period into eschatological visions of the future of the English church and nation, which required extreme vigilance, heightened spiritual duties, and even radical calls for separation and/or transatlantic migration.

*Further Reading*
William Lamont, *Godly Rule: Politics and Religion, 1603–1660* (1969); Avihu Zakai, "Thomas Brightman and the English Apocalyptic Tradition," in Yosef Kaplan, Henry Mechoulan, and Richard H. Popkin, eds., *Menasseh ben Israel and his World,* (1989).

*Stephanie Sleeper*

## Brinsley, John (1600–1665)

Town preacher of Great Yarmouth, Norfolk, and ejected minister. Brinsley was born at Ashby-de-la-Zouch, Leicestershire. His father was a schoolmaster, and his uncle was Joseph Hall, later bishop of Norwich. Brinsley entered Emmanuel College, Cambridge, in 1615, and served as amanuensis to his uncle at the Synod of Dort in 1618. He took his

B.A. in 1619 and his M.A. in 1623 when he was ordained to the priesthood. At some stage he boarded with Arthur Hildersham, the great puritan pastor of Ashby. In 1625 he became schoolmaster at Yarmouth, a notoriously puritan port, and in 1630 the town council appointed him preacher, and the bishop licensed him to preach in the town and diocese. Almost immediately the government sought to silence his preaching, and a tussle over jurisdiction arose between the dean and chapter of Norwich and Yarmouth council. The matter eventually reached High Commission, and Brinsley was deprived of the post. Meanwhile he preached at the Dutch church in Yarmouth until in 1632, when he was forbidden to officiate at all.

Brinsley was protected by Sir John Wentworth of Somerleyton and appointed to livings in Suffolk; he also received the support of Sir Robert Harley. By 1641 Brinsley had resumed his career as preacher at Yarmouth but suffered repeated interruptions and harassment: in 1650 he refused the Oath of Engagement swearing loyalty to the Commonwealth and was ordered to leave the town, only to be allowed back the following year. He was an assistant to the Norfolk Commission of Ejectors in 1654. The high regard in which Brinsley was held is attested by Richard Baxter's suggestion that he was one of the ministers suitable to be a "bishop" in the broad church under consideration in November 1660. In August 1662 Brinsley was ejected from his post, but he continued to reside in Yarmouth until his death in January 1665, when he was buried at St. Nicholas, Yarmouth.

See also: Triers and Ejectors
Further Reading
Tom Webster, *Godly Clergy in Early Stuart England* (Cambridge, Eng., 1997).

*John Spurr*

## Brocklesby, Edward (ca. 1525–1574)

Church of England clergyman and the first put out of his living for refusing to wear the surplice during the Vestiarian Controversy. Brocklesby was born in Lincolnshire. From Eton he went to King's College, Cambridge, in 1542, becoming a fellow and graduating B.A. in 1547. He proceeded M.A. in 1550. In exile in Emden during the reign of the Roman Catholic Mary Tudor, he returned under Elizabeth to become vicar of Hemel Hempstead, Hertfordshire, also ministering in London in the vacant parish of St. Nicholas Olave. Although it was doubtless his activities in London that brought him to the attention of the authorities, it was as vicar of Hemel Hempstead that he was deprived by the ecclesiastical commissioners on 8 May 1565 for refusing to wear the surplice when administering communion. By early 1569 Brocklesby had become rector of Branston, Lincolnshire, and in 1571 was appointed to a prebend (canonry) in Lincoln cathedral. He died in 1574 in possession of both preferments.

See also: Surplice, Vestments
Further Reading
Brett Usher, "Edward Brocklesby, 'the first put out of his living for the surplice,'" in Stephen Taylor, ed., *From Cranmer to Davidson*, Church of England Record Society, vol. 7 (Woodbridge, Eng., 1999), pp. 47–68.

*Brett Usher*

## Brooks, Thomas (1608–1680)

English Nonconformist minister and author. Thomas Brooks was educated at Emmanuel College, Cambridge, matriculating in 1625. During the English Civil Wars he served as a chaplain in the parliamentary navy. At some time in the late 1640s he acquired the position of preacher at St. Thomas Apostle's in London. In March 1648, he was elected rector of St. Margaret's, New Fish Street, London (the Church of England incumbent had been sequestered), and remained in that capacity until the Restoration of 1660. He was also a lecturer at Fish Street Hill, as correspondence with Richard Baxter shows that he had serious disagreements with a fellow lecturer there on the subject of ordination. In 1657, Brooks published the first edition of his most famous work *Apples of Gold*, which was regularly republished until at least 1787.

Brooks was one of almost seven hundred clergy ejected from their livings by the Act for Confirming and Restoring of Ministers (1660). A new rector (although not Brooks's predecessor) was installed in St.

Margaret's in his place. After this first ejection, Brooks preached at St. Nicholas Olave in Bread Street, London. The sermons he delivered there during 1660 were later adapted into a treatise entitled *An Arke for all God's Noahs in a Gloomy Stormy Day,* first published in 1662. On Bartholomew's Day, 24 August 1662, Brooks was ejected from the Church of England, together with almost 1,000 ministers across the nation, for refusing to subscribe to the Act of Uniformity. His valediction appeared in several compilations of Bartholomean farewell sermons (that is, sermons preached on the day of ejection, Bartholomew's Day) published between 1662 and 1664. Despite the attentions of government spies, Brooks continued to preach illegally in London. He risked prosecution and punishment by continuing to publish extensively, adding several new titles to his oeuvre and republishing popular works such as *Apples of Gold* and *Heaven on Earth.* He ignored more natural risks to his life by continuing to work in London during the terrible plague of 1665 and the Great Fire of 1666.

By 1669 Brooks was reported to be lecturing in Hackney, Middlesex. In 1672, following Charles II's Declaration of Indulgence, Thomas Brooks was licensed as a Congregationalist preacher at Lime Street, London. Changed political circumstances led to a renewal of persecution, however, and he was again forbidden to preach in 1676. He died in 1680, but his myriad works of devotion and moral instruction continued to be republished well into the late twentieth century.

*See also:* Nonconformity, Pinners' Hall
*Further Reading*
Alexander B. Grosart, ed., *The Complete Works of Thomas Brooks,* 2 vols. (Edinburgh, 1866–1867); A. G. Matthews, *Calamy Revised: Being a Revision of Edmund Calamy's Account of the Ministers and others Ejected and Silenced, 1660–2* (Oxford, 1934; reprinted 1988).

*David J. Appleby*

## Browne, Robert (1550?–1633)

Separatist. Robert Browne was one of the founders of the Separatist movement that en-couraged the godly to leave the Church of England rather than tolerate its imperfections. His followers were often referred to as "Brownists." He studied at Corpus Christi, Cambridge, and received his B.A. in 1572, following which he was ordained as a minister. He was well connected with some of the nation's leaders, especially Lord Burghley. After a period of teaching and preaching without a license in the Cambridge area, Browne settled in Norwich, where he and Robert Harrison organized a separate congregation. Browne was prosecuted for seditious printing by the bishop of Norwich in 1581 and imprisoned, but later released through the intervention of Burghley.

Following his release, Browne emigrated to Middleburg, Holland, with some of his followers. His major works, *A Book which sheweth the Life and Manners of all true Christians* (1582) and *Treatise of Reformation without Tarrying for Anie* (1582) were both published in the Netherlands and smuggled into England. One of the distinctive features of the Separatists was their unwillingness to associate with puritans who shared many of their views but retained a connection to the national church. Browne himself attacked Thomas Cartwright in print.

Divisions between Browne and Harrison led to Browne being voted out of the separate congregation at Middleburg in 1583. Together with a small number of followers he moved to Edinburgh, Scotland. The authorities there arrested him for his writings and imprisoned him. Released through the intercession of some local authorities, he returned to England in 1584. He was questioned about his works and their distribution by the bishop of London and the archbishop of Canterbury, but he was in ill health and so was allowed to return to his family seat. Recovered, he again ran afoul of the bishops and was excommunicated in 1586.

Following his excommunication, Browne (probably with the aid of Burghley) made his peace with the church authorities and abandoned his advocacy of separatism. He taught school for a few years and then in 1591 was appointed rector of Achurch cum

Thorpe in Northamptonshire. There is no clear evidence that he later reverted to his former beliefs, though some have suggested that he did so. He died in 1633.

See also: Separatists
Further Reading
Stephen Brachlow, *The Communion of Saints: Radical Puritan and Separatist Ecclesiology, 1570–1625* (Oxford, 1988); Chaplin Burrage, *The True Story of Robert Browne* (Oxford, 1906); Albert Peel, *The Brownists in Norwich and Norfolk around 1580* (Cambridge, Eng., 1920); R. B. White, *The English Separatist Tradition from the Marian Martyrs to the Pilgrim Fathers* (Oxford, 1971).

*Francis J. Bremer*

## Bruen, John (1560–1625)

Iconoclast. Bruen was born in the county of Cheshire to a prominent gentry family. He was locally educated and then attended St. Alban Hall in Oxford for two years. Bruen evidently had a strong spiritual experience, from which he emerged as a zealous puritan. Following the death of his father in 1587, he imposed a strong moral regime on his household and estates. This regime included as many as seven sessions of household prayer daily, frequent scripture reading, and the abolition of drinking and traditional sport in the community. The intense piety of the household was matched by a reputation for hospitality.

In 1603 servants of his household destroyed some of the stained glass in the local church. A number of years later, a number of his servants were implicated in further acts of iconoclasm, including the destruction of crosses in parish churchyards. On the later occasion six members of his household were prosecuted in Star Chamber and fined.

See also: Iconoclasm and Iconography
Further Reading
*New Dictionary of National Biography* (Oxford, 2004); R. C. Richardson, *Puritanism in North-West England* (Manchester, Eng., 1972).

*Francis J. Bremer*

## Bulkeley (Bulkley), Peter (1583–1659)

Puritan minister in England and New England. Bulkeley was born to well-to-do parents in Odell, Bedfordshire, attended St. John's College, Cambridge, and in 1610 succeeded his father as rector at Odell and inheritor of a substantial fortune. By his first wife, Jane Allen, who died in 1626, he fathered twelve children. Silenced for nonconformity in 1634 by Bishop William Laud, Bulkeley sold his estate and sailed to New England the following year with his second wife, Grace Chetwode, offspring, and servants.

In Massachusetts in 1636 he helped found the town and church of Concord. As the town's leading citizen and benefactor, he used his wealth to undergird its modest economic life. As the church's "teacher," he ministered for over two decades to the spiritual and moral necessities of his congregation, which survived the loss of numerous members by emigration in 1644 to Connecticut. His son Edward succeeded him as Concord pastor.

Bulkeley served as co-moderator of the 1637 synod that denounced Anne Hutchinson and her errors. His book, *The Gospel-Covenant* (London, 1646; expanded edition, 1651, 1674), comprising sermons of the 1630s, is an important text of Puritan theology. Addressing doctrinal issues in dispute in New England, it takes an orthodox stance that may have helped shape the federal formulas of the Westminster Confession of 1647.

See also: Federal Theology
Further Reading
Michael McGiffert, "The Problem of the Covenant in Puritan Thought," *New England Historical and Genealogical Register* 130 (1976), 107–129.

*Michael McGiffert*

## Bunyan, John (1628–1688)

One of the great figures of seventeenth-century puritanism. He was born at Elstow, Bedfordshire, in 1628, the son of a poor tinker. Bunyan was expected to ply his father's trade and received only a rudimentary education. Yet with a literary output amounting to over sixty works, including the classic

*Pilgrim's Progress,* Bunyan became one of the most prolific religious writers of his age.

There was no history of nonconformity in Bunyan's immediate family; his parents apparently conformed to the Church of England, though neither appears to have had a deeply religious nature. From an early age, however, John was frequently tormented by terrifying dreams and visions of devils and hellfire: events subsequently interpreted as God's chiding in his spiritual autobiography, *Grace Abounding* (1666).

In 1644, two years after the outbreak of the First Civil War and the year of his mother's death, Bunyan was conscripted into the parliamentary army and stationed at Newport Pagnell, Buckinghamshire, until the regiment's demobilization in 1647. Although Bunyan probably did not see any military action during this period, he did encounter the religious radicalism and Puritan preaching that pervaded the ranks of the New Model Army and later governed his life. He married a devout, but poor, Protestant in 1649. As her only dowry, his wife brought with her two pious books: Arthur Dent's *The plaine-mans pathe-way to heaven* (1601) and Lewis Bayly's *Practise of Piety* (1611). These works had a profound effect on the twenty-year-old Bunyan, as they initiated a period of conformity during which he attended church twice daily. Bunyan, however, soon became disillusioned with certain "superstitious" and "idolatrous" elements of Church of England worship, such as the wearing of a surplice, and sought a more pure form of spiritual enlightenment based solely on biblical authority. But his quest for purity proved fraught with complications. Over the next five years he experienced intense spiritual torment and uncertainty, alternating between a state of ecstatic jubilation at the awareness of God's mercy and darkest despair when he felt devoid of God's love. Bunyan emerged from this period a convinced Calvinist with Baptist leanings.

In 1655 Bunyan became a member of the Independent church at Bedford where the Puritan and moderate Baptist John Gifford was pastor. A year later he began to preach publicly to the unconverted and soon came to believe that preaching was

*An English preacher and writer, John Bunyan is best known for* The Pilgrim's Progress, *one of the most widely read books in the English language. (Library of Congress)*

his natural vocation. He also entered into public debate with the newly emerging Quaker movement. His first published tract, *Some Gospel-Truths Opened* (1656), was directed at the "errors" of Quakerism.

The restoration of the monarchy and Church of England changed the position of Puritans like Bunyan. In 1660 he was arrested for holding an illegal conventicle and sentenced to remain in prison until he would agree to conform. His refusal to recant ensured he remained technically a prisoner for the next twelve years, though the terms of his imprisonment were somewhat laxer than we might imagine, as he was permitted to leave jail, travel to London, write, and even preach in his prison cell. Upon his release (1672), he was elected pastor of the Bedford congregation and obtained a license to preach under Charles II's ill-fated Second Declaration of Indulgence. He was summoned to appear before the Archdeacon's Court for failing to attend the services of his local parish church in 1675, but went into hiding rather than obey the summons and was consequently excommunicated. In December of the following year, the authorities caught up with him, and he was imprisoned once again. By the time of his release six months later, Bunyan's fame as a preacher had spread to London, where it was not uncommon for crowds of over a thousand to attend his sermons during the late 1670s. The years 1678–1686 mark Bunyan's major creative period, for it was then that he penned best-selling works such as *The Pilgrim's Progress* (1678) and *The Holy War* (1682). His vivid, plain prose style and frequent use of allegory proved immensely successful and ensured that all his works were widely read. Bunyan died in August 1688 from a chill caught while riding from Reading to London in the rain. He is buried at Bunhill Fields, the Dissenters' burial ground in London.

*See also:* Puritan Best-Sellers
*Further Reading*
Christopher Hill, *A Turbulent Seditious and Factious People: John Bunyan and His Church* (Oxford, 1988); Roger Sharrock, *John Bunyan* (London, 1968); John Stachniewski and Anita Pacheco, eds., *Grace Abounding with Other Spiritual Autobiographies* (Oxford, 1998).

*Claire Vivian*

## Burgess, Anthony (d. 1664)

Prominent Presbyterian clergyman. He was born in Watford, Hertfordshire, and educated at St. John's College, Cambridge, matriculating in 1623 and receiving his B.A. in 1627. He then migrated to Emmanuel College, Cambridge, where he was named a fellow in 1629 and awarded his M.A. in 1630. His college tutors were William Jenkyn and John Wallis.

Burgess was instituted rector at Sutton Coldfield, November 1635, but left in 1642 to become chaplain to the parliamentary garrison at Coventry. In 1644 he was chosen a delegate to the Westminster Assembly and on 25 January 1645 instituted as vicar of St. Lawrence Jewry, London. Burgess preached fast-day sermons to the Lords or Commons on six occasions. Burgess established the Presbyterian discipline at St. Lawrence Jewry in 1645 and was a delegate to the sixth London Classis and the first two London Provincial Assemblies. In 1647 he signed the Testimony of the London Presbyterians against the toleration of heresy.

Burgess returned to Sutton Coldfield in 1649. He was chosen as a clerical assistant to the ecclesiastical commission for Warwickshire and Staffordshire in 1654. He also entered into a long disputation with Richard Baxter over the doctrine of justification, attacking Baxter for his retreat from predestinarian orthodoxy. Despite strong words, Baxter and Burgess remained cordial friends, and Baxter recommended Burgess to Lord Chancellor Hyde as potential bishop in November 1660.

Burgess was ejected in 1662 for nonconformity. He retired to Tamworth in Staffordshire, where he died in October 1664. He was survived by his wife, Sarah, a son, and three daughters: Mary, Abigail, and Ruth. His son, Anthony, followed his father into the church but as a conformist, serving St. Bartholomew-the-Great in London as rector from 1663 until his death in 1709.

*Further Reading*
A. Laurence, *Parliamentary Army Chaplains, 1642–1651,* Royal Historical Society Studies in History, 59 (London, 1990); *Oxford Dictionary of National Biography* (Oxford, 2004); R. S. Paul, *The Assembly of the Lord: Politics and Religion in the Westminster Assembly and the 'Grand Debate'* (Edinburgh, 1985); Elliot C. Vernon, "The Sion College Conclave and London Presbyterianism during the English Revolution," (Ph.D. diss., University of Cambridge, 1999).

*Elliot Vernon*

## Burgess, Cornelius (d. 1665)

Clerical advocate of the reformation of manners and supporter of Presbyterianism. Burgess was born in Somerset. In 1611 he matriculated at Wadham College, Oxford, from which he graduated B.A. on 5 July 1615. In 1616 he migrated to Lincoln College and proceeded M.A. from there on 20 April 1618. Burgess took his D.D. at Oxford in June 1627.

Upon leaving Oxford, Burgess took up the post of household chaplain to Edward Russell, third earl of Bedford. On 21 December 1618 Sir Charles Morison, a client of the Russells, installed Burgess as vicar of Watford, Hertfordshire. In 1620 Burgess was chaplain to Vere's regiment of English volunteers in the Thirty Years' War. Burgess returned to England in about 1621 and was made one of the king's chaplains-in-ordinary. In 1626 he was offered the rectory of St. Magnus in the City of London.

In 1622 Burgess published *A Chaine of Graces* (1622), a work designed to promote the reformation of manners. His other works from the 1620s show Burgess to be a defender of the church (against lay impropriations), of the liturgy, of the divine right of kings, and of tithes.

In the 1630s Burgess began to distance himself from the York House group that was gaining ascendancy in the Church of England. In February 1630 he came into conflict with Bishop Richard Neile for refusing to read prayers before his sermon. He was also reported in 1634 for refusing to read the Book of Sports. In January 1636 Burgess appeared before the church courts for a sermon in which it was alleged that he had attacked the bishops and episcopacy.

By the approach of civil war, Burgess was firmly in the camp of those godly ministers who sought further reformation of the Church of England. On 6 August 1640 he met with John Downham, Edmund Calamy, Arthur Jackson, and John Goodwin to draft a petition against the new church canons. As a client of Bedford, Burgess was charged to meet with his fellow reformers to plan further reformation. Alongside Stephen Marshall, Burgess preached the first fast sermon before the House of Commons on 17 November 1640. He was chosen by the pro-reform ministers on 23 January 1641 to present their petition and remonstrance to the House of Commons. This petition was considered in association with the more radical Root and Branch Petition. Throughout the early 1640s Burgess was associated with the Parliamentarian war party and the Presbyterian clergy. Yet, despite his good standing with the reformers, Burgess often appeared as a moderating and pro-clericalist

voice in the more intense outbursts of 1640s anti-Laudianism. With the convening of the Westminster Assembly in July 1643, Burgess was chosen one of the assessors. Although he initially supported Archbishop Ussher's plan for a reduced episcopacy, he soon threw in his lot in support of a national Presbyterian settlement for the Church of England. Burgess was elected president of Sion College (which had become the London Presbyterian's de facto headquarters) in 1647 and 1648. As a sign of his preeminence among the London ministers, Burgess was the first signatory to the London Presbyterians' *Vindication* against the Army of 1649.

With the coming of the Republic and its general indifference, or even hostility, to Presbyterianism, Burgess faded from the political scene. He appears to have amassed considerable wealth. On 24 April 1654 he was appointed Dr. White's lecturer at St. Paul's. Burgess was then appointed preacher at Wells Cathedral. His purchase of church lands in the wake of the Civil War had made him unpopular with some people, and in 1659 he defended himself by writing *A Case Concerning the Buying of Bishops Lands*. With the coming of the Restoration, he lost all his lands and lived in penury at Watford until his death on 6 June 1665.

*See also:* Primitive Episcopacy, Reformation of Manners

*Further Reading*

*Oxford Dictionary of National Biography* (Oxford, 2004); Elliot C. Vernon, "The Sion College Conclave and London Presbyterianism during the English Revolution," (Ph.D. diss., University of Cambridge, 1999).

*Elliot Vernon*

## Burgess, John (ca. 1561–1635)

Moderate puritan clergyman. Born at Peterborough about 1561, Burgess matriculated at St. John's College, Cambridge, in 1580 and commenced B.A. in 1584 and M.A. in 1587. He was rector of the parish of St. Peter Hungate from about 1587 to 1593. When he was required to wear the surplice, some of his congregation informed him that were he to conform, "they would never profit by his ministry," a view that led to his departure. He held an unknown living in Suffolk before moving to the diocese of Lincoln.

In 1601, Burgess became rector of the third part of the living of Waddesdon in Buckinghamshire and established himself as a leader of the nonconformist clergy in the diocese. When the new canons were being debated in convocation, Burgess was called to preach before the king at Greenwich on 19 June 1604. Burgess took the occasion to issue a plea for moderation concerning the ceremonies of the church and related the story told by Augustus of Pollio's glasses, "which were not worth a man's life or livelihood," applying the tale to the enjoining of ceremonies. James was deeply offended and had Burgess confined in the Fleet. Upon sending a copy of his sermon with a letter of submission to the king and the members of the Privy Council, Burgess was released from prison. On 1 December Burgess led a delegation of thirty ministers from the diocese who presented to James their reasons for refusing to conform. An abridgement of this petition was printed in January 1605.

Burgess's refusal to subscribe to the canons of 1604 resulted in his deprivation on 16 January 1605. He sought to explain his position on ceremonies in a written "Apology," copies of which he sent to Bishop William Chadderton of Lincoln and, thanks to the mediation of Sir Thomas Jermyn of Rushbrooke, Suffolk, to the king. Dr. William Covell was ordered to prepare a response, which was published in 1606 as *A briefe answer unto certain reasons by way of an Apologie delivered to the bishop of Lincolne by Mr J. Burges.* Having failed to win any concessions from the crown, Burgess left England for Leiden, where he studied medicine and in time took the degree of doctor of physic. He also served for a time as chaplain to Sir Horace Vere, governor of the Brill and commander of the English forces in the Low Countries. When Burgess returned to England in about 1612, the king's animus against Burgess pursued him for a time, preventing him from practicing medicine in London. Burgess established himself outside the city in Isleworth, where he built up a successful practice. By June 1616, overtures were being made

to permit Burgess back into the church. He indicated that he was prepared to subscribe to the Three Articles and duly did so, and in 1617, following a brief stint as preacher at Bishopsgate, he became rector of Sutton Coldfield in Warwickshire, where he remained until his death.

In 1620–1621, Burgess served once again under Sir Horace Vere, this time as preacher to the English troops that went to the defense of the Palatinate. In 1631 Burgess published a defense of the lawfulness of ceremonies in which he claimed always to have contended that ceremonies were inexpedient yet lawful. He died on 31 August 1635 and was buried in the chancel of Sutton Coldfield church. His second wife was the eldest daughter of Thomas Wilcox, whose collected expositions he published in a single volume in 1624.

*Further Reading*
Peter Lake, "Moving the Goal Posts? Modified Subscription and the Construction of Conformity in the Early Stuart Church," in Peter Lake and Michael C. Questier, eds., *Conformity and Orthodoxy in the English Church, c. 1560–1660* (Stanford, 2000).

*John Craig*

## Burghall, Edward (1600–1665)

Presbyterian clergyman and author. Burghall was born at Beeston in Cheshire, the son of Hugh and Margaret Burghall. He was baptized at Bunbury, Cheshire, on 9 December 1600. Little is known of his education, but by 1622 he was usher at the school in Bunbury, subsequently becoming the master by 1637.

In 1648 he signed the Cheshire Attestation that endorsed Presbyterian government of the Church of England. By 1651 he was minister at Acton in Cheshire, where he was reported to the Committee for Compounding for refusal to take the engagement and subsequently lost his annual augmentation (supplement to his salary). It was restored to him in June 1654 after he petitioned for arrears. Burghall left a manuscript entitled "Providence Improved," in which he chronicled the events of 1628–1663. It contains an account of his pious reflections on God's punishments for sin and his comments on the uncertain nature of national politics. He was critical of both Catholics and those he branded fanatics, Fifth Monarchists, Anabaptists, and Quakers.

Burghall was ejected in 1662 and retired to Alpraham, Cheshire. He published two sermons: *The perfect way to die in peace* (1659) and *The Great benefit of the Christian education of Children* (1663), which was preached at Acton in Cheshire on 26 May 1662, on the occasion of the founding of a free school there. Burghall died at Alpraham on 8 December 1665 and was buried at Bunbury on 11 December.

*Further Reading*
*Oxford Dictionary of National Biography* (Oxford, 2004).

*Catherine Nunn*

## Burroughes, Jeremiah (1599–1646)

One of the Dissenting Brethren in the Westminster Assembly and a leading proponent of Congregationalism. Burroughes earned his B.A. (1621) and M.A. (1624) at Emmanuel College, Cambridge. It was at Cambridge that he developed lifelong friendships with William Bridge, Sydrach Simpson, Thomas Shepard, and Thomas Welde, as well as his tutor Thomas Hooker. It was also at this time that he began a correspondence with John Cotton. After leaving Cambridge he became parish lecturer at Bury St. Edmunds, Suffolk, where he associated with Edmund Calamy. In 1634 he took the post of rector of Tivetshall, Norfolk. In 1636 he was suspended by Bishop Matthew Wren for refusing to read from the Book of Sports and, for a time, was protected by the puritan Earl of Warwick. The following year he left England for Holland, where he became teacher of the Rotterdam Church where his colleague William Bridge had already been ordained pastor. Not long after their arrival in Holland, both Burroughes and Bridge made a clandestine trip back to Yarmouth in order to bring letters and books to the puritans there. During their stay they lodged with Miles Corbet, the future regicide.

While ministering to their church in Rotterdam both Burroughes and Bridge continued to maintain close connections with New England Congregationalists and seem to have been considerably influenced by their colonial brethren. In fact Presbyterian critic Thomas Edwards acerbically complained that both clergymen had openly proclaimed that they "agree with them of New England, and are of their Church-way."

In 1641 Burroughes returned to England. Though Burroughes was a moderate Congregationalist who did not gather a church, he was appointed morning lecturer at Stepney, Middlesex, by Parliament. Here he became the colleague of William Greenhill, who was evening lecturer. The two men were held in very high esteem by their flock and were dubbed, by Hugh Peter, the "Morning Star" and the "Evening Star" of Stepney. Their expertise and advice was highly regarded, and their lectures and sermons were well attended. Some members of the church even lived as far away as the City and Westminster, yet faithfully attended their sermons.

From 1643 to 1646 Burroughes regularly attended the Westminster Assembly. Richard Baxter, evidently admiring Burroughes's moderate stance, claimed that if all Independents were like Jeremiah Burroughes, episcopalians like James Ussher, and presbyterians like Stephen Marshall, then the ecclesiastical divisions would soon have been healed. Burroughes was a very active participant in the assembly's debates and coauthored with the other four Dissenting Brethren (Thomas Goodwin, William Bridge, Philip Nye, and Sydrach Simpson) *An Apologeticall Narration* (1643), which set forth the minority congregational polity. In his *A Vindication of Mr. Burroughes against Mr. Edwards* (1646, 23), Burroughes, responding to Edwards's accusation that he espoused toleration, claimed that he was never "for a toleration of all things, nay I should be loath to live in England if ever it should be here." He died after a fall from a horse in 1646, before the Westminster Assembly had finished its work.

*See also: An Apologeticall Narration,*
Congregationalism, Dissenting Brethren, English Puritanism in the Netherlands, Independency

*Further Reading*
Francis J. Bremer, *Congregational Communion:
Clerical Friendship in the Anglo-American
Puritan Community, 1610–1692* (Boston, 1994);
Robert Paul, *The Assembly of the Lord*
(Edinburgh, 1985); Tom Webster, *Godly Clergy
in Early Stuart England* (Cambridge, Eng.,
1997).

*Ralph Young*

## Burton, Henry (1578–1648)

Puritan divine and Independent pastor, raised in
the East Riding of Yorkshire in a parish without a
preaching minister. He was educated at St. John's
College, Cambridge, where he fell under the influence of William Perkins and Laurence Chaderton.
He graduated M.A. in 1602 and became a tutor in a
private home before being made clerk of the closet
to Prince Henry. On Henry's death in 1612, Burton
became clerk of the closet to Prince Charles. In
1623, he wrote a book refuting Arminianism and
proving the pope to be Antichrist, but was unable
to get it published. On the accession of Charles, he
expected to remain in his post, but was excluded
from court when he wrote a letter condemning the
popish tendencies of Neile and Laud. He was soon
made rector of St. Matthews, Friday Street, from
where he conducted a vigorous pulpit and press
campaign against popish bishops and popish ceremonies. He was cited before the High Commission
in 1626, imprisoned briefly in the Fleet prison in
1629, and ejected from his parish and imprisoned
in the Fleet in February 1637. Here he was joined
by William Prynne and John Bastwick, and in June
all three were sentenced to stand in the pillory and
have their ears cut off. Their punishment caused a
sensation, and when Burton began his journey
north to Lancaster prison on 28 July, tens of thousands lined the streets to bid him farewell. From
Lancaster, Burton continued to smuggle out writings against the regime, and he was subsequently
moved to Guernsey.

In November 1640, the Long Parliament ordered Burton's release, and alongside Prynne he
was welcomed back to London by a crowd of ten
thousand. However, he had become deeply disillusioned with the Church of England, and in his
*Protestation Protested* (1641), he argued that its
liturgy, discipline, and government were "so many
branches of popery"; reformation would only
begin when the godly re-formed pure "Independent" congregations. Although he was restored to
St. Matthews, Friday Street, as a lecturer, and became rector again in 1642, he proceeded to gather
an Independent congregation within the parish.
His position was close to that of non-separating
Congregationalists like Thomas Goodwin and
Philip Nye, but Burton's more aggressive attacks
on the Church of England meant that he was never
invited to join the Westminster Assembly of Divines. His gathering of a church within a church
also alienated leading parishioners, who had him
removed as rector in 1645. He was closely associated with John Goodwin, who was also ousted from
his parish in 1645, though unlike Goodwin, Burton
remained a traditional Calvinist. His status as a
martyr lent credibility to the Independent cause,
and counterbalanced the Presbyterianism of Bastwick and Prynne. He died and was buried in January 1648.

*See also:* Crime and Punishment, Independency,
Star Chamber, Providences (in Primary Sources)

*Further Reading*
Henry Burton, *A Narration of the Life of Mr
Henry Burton* (1643); R. T. Hughes, "Henry
Burton: The Making of a Puritan
Revolutionary," *Journal of Church and State*, 16
(1974), 421–434.

*John Coffey*

## Byfield, Adoniram (d. 1658–1660)

Clergyman. Byfield was the son of Nicholas Byfield. He matriculated at Emmanuel College, Cambridge, in 1620, and received his B.A. in 1624. In
1629 he obtained curacies at All Hallows, Staining,
Mark Lane, and St. Lawrence Old Jewry in London. He also preached with the later Independent
leader Philip Nye in Hackney. Byfield was criticized in Archbishop William Laud's 1637 visitation
for irregularities in preaching.

Byfield was appointed chaplain to Sir Henry Cholmondeley's Parliamentarian regiment in 1642. He was also appointed, along with Henry Roborough, as a scribe to the Westminster Assembly on 6 July 1643.

In about 1646 Byfield became rector of the parish of Fulham. In around 1652 he moved to Collingbourne Ducis, Wiltshire. Byfield appears to have been a moderate Independent, and he was a signatory to a 1653 petition calling for the propagation of the gospel proposing the licensing of lay preachers. Byfield was appointed as an assistant to the commissioners in Wiltshire for ejecting scandalous ministers, a position he apparently prosecuted with some gusto. He probably died between April 1658 and August 1660.

*See also:* Triers and Ejectors
*Further Reading*
*New Dictionary of National Biography* (Oxford, 2004).

*Elliot Vernon*

## Byfield, Nicholas (1578/9–1622)

Clergyman and author of devotional treatises. He was born in Warwickshire, the son of Richard Byfield, vicar of Stratford upon Avon. Byfield matriculated at Exeter College, Oxford, in 1596 but took no degree. In about 1600 he was appointed lecturer at St. Peter's, Chester, and became curate there in 1608. Byfield was held in high esteem by many of his flock, and in March 1615 his reputation led Sir Horace Vere to present him to the vicarage of the parish of Isleworth in Middlesex.

At Isleworth, Byfield strengthened his reputation as a tireless and fearsome preacher, and he gained the confidence and appreciation of godly gentry such Sir Thomas Hoby. He published at least seventeen works of devotional literature and biblical commentary, both throughout his life and posthumously. His commentaries include an exposition of the Epistle to the Colossians and a commentary on the first Epistle of Peter. Of particular note is his defense of a strict observance of the Sabbath, set out in his controversy with Edward Brerewood.

Despite his fierceness as a preacher and polemicist, Byfield was a moderate puritan who both counseled and practiced conformity to the ceremonies and customs of the Church of England that were not in contradiction to the word of God. Byfield died at Isleworth on 8 September 1622.

*Further Reading*
E. Brerewood, *A learned treatise of the sabaoth* (1630).

*Elliot Vernon*

# C

## Calamy, Edmund (1671–1732)

Historian of Dissent and theorist of toleration. Calamy was the third of a puritan clerical dynasty. His grandfather, Edmund (1600–1666), was prominent in the Civil War era. His father, also Edmund (1634–1685), preached in London from the 1660s and was several times prosecuted for Nonconformity. Both were ejected from the Church of England in 1662. Born in the parish of St. Mary Aldermanbury, London, Edmund Calamy III was educated at puritan academies, at Merchant Taylor's School, and at Utrecht University (1688–1691). In 1691–1692 he studied in the Bodleian Library, Oxford, and began to preach. In 1692 he became assistant pastor to Matthew Sylvester at Blackfriars, London, and lived in the Dissenter enclave at Hoxton Square. In 1694 at Samuel Annesley's meetinghouse in Spitalfields, he was among the first group of men to be publicly ordained to the Presbyterian ministry in London since the Restoration. Calamy was assistant to Daniel Williams at Hand Alley, Bishopsgate (1695–1703), and then succeeded Vincent Alsop as pastor in Westminster. He received doctorates from Scottish universities in 1708. He was a founder trustee of Dr. Williams's Library, today the principal research library for the history of English Dissent. Insofar as the Presbyterians had a leader, that leadership passed from Richard Baxter to Williams to Calamy.

Calamy was one of the most skilful publicists for Dissent in the era after the Revolution of 1688.

His *Defence of Moderate Nonconformity* (1703–1705) was perhaps the most influential work in establishing for eighteenth-century Dissent a commitment to religious toleration of the kind suggested by the philosopher John Locke. Calamy stated that the aged Locke sent him a message commending the work. Even more enduring was Calamy's effort at collecting the lives of the 2,000 puritan ministers ejected at the Restoration (1660–1662), the so-called Bartholomeans (since the day many were ejected was St. Bartholomew's Day, 24 August 1662). The groundwork of this project was the biographical notes that appeared in Baxter's autobiography, *Reliquiae Baxterianae* (1696), which Calamy assisted Sylvester in editing for publication. These notes were expanded in Calamy's *Abridgment of the Reliquiae* (1702), in which the ninth chapter, "A Particular Account of the Ministers, Lecturers, fellows of Colledges, etc., who were Silenced and Ejected by the Act for Uniformity," takes up half the volume. A second edition appeared in 1713, and a *Continuation* in 1727. In turn, the material was reworked in Samuel Palmer's *Non-Conformists' Memorial* (1775) and attained its modern form in A. G. Matthews's essential reference work for Restoration puritanism, *Calamy Revised* (1934; reprinted 1988). Calamy's *An Historical Account of My Own Life*, ed. J. T. Rutt (2 vols., 1824), is a vivid and invaluable record of early Dissent.

*See also:* Dissenters, Popish Plot

*Further Reading*
*Oxford Dictionary of National Biography* (Oxford, 2004).

*Mark Goldie*

## Cameron, John (ca. 1579–1625)

Scottish puritan theologian, whose ideas had a particular impact in France, where he shaped the Protestant theological agenda up to the Revocation of the Edict of Nantes (1685). He was born in Glasgow and attended the city's university, where the curriculum had been reformed by Andrew Melville to include classical and linguistic emphases, and Ramist logic. As a young person he absorbed and held for life the doctrine of the divine right of kings. He graduated M.A. in 1599 and remained to teach Greek for one year. He then went to France, teaching, pastoring, and studying. After studies in Geneva in 1605–1606, he went to Heidelberg, where he presented his thesis in 1608 on the threefold covenant of God with man, making him one of the earliest exponents of an all-encompassing federal theology.

He described three covenants, based respectively on nature (obedience), which was inscribed on every human heart; grace (mercy); and *foedus subserviens*, or *foedus vetus*. This latter was an innovation that addressed the question of justification in terms of the Reformation's emphasis on the dichotomy between the law and the gospel, rescuing *sola gratia* (the doctrine that human beings are saved by grace alone, not by their own fulfilling of the law) from the mire of legalism into which much Calvinist writing had slipped. Cameron returned to Bordeaux as pastor and remained until 1618, when he went to Saumur to fill the post of professor of theology. His hypothetical universalism embodied decrees both universal and particular and made the universal decree of redemption anterior to the particular decree of election. Cameron was rejecting the views of Thodore Beza and other Calvinists who argued that Christ died only for the elect and argued that Christ's sacrifice was hypothetically sufficient for the salvation of all men. But his argument that the will would be able to seek God through moral suasion was perceived by many as close to the heresy of Arminianism. Louis XIII dismissed him in 1621. He taught theology in London for one year and then became principal at Glasgow, promising to impose conformity to liturgical changes demanded by James VI (James I of England). However, he stayed less than one year. King Louis now permitted him to teach at Montauban, where he died as a result of a tumult in 1625, probably at the hands of Protestants hostile toward his royalism.

*See also:* Federal Theology, Grace, Predestination
*Further Reading*
Brian Armstrong, *Calvinism and the Amyraut Heresy: Protestant Scholasticism and Humanism in Seventeenth-Century France* (Madison, 1969).

*David Mullan*

## Carew, Thomas (d. 1616)

Preacher. Carew deserves to be known to history for two reasons: a stormy early career as a radical nonconformist minister in Essex, taking on Bishop John Aylmer of London with the gloves off; and an almost Christian Socialist sermon denouncing the employment practices of the Suffolk clothiers. Perhaps Carew's unusual boldness with both bishops and businessmen reflected his origins, which were close to more famous members of the Carew family and other gentry. Nothing is known of his education, and he was not a graduate. He was ordained by Bishop Edmund Freke, either at Norwich or at Rochester.

In the mid-1580s Carew was a curate at Hatfield Peverel in Essex and a militant nonconformist who was accused by Bishop Aylmer of practicing a "presbytery," and who took an uncompromising line with crypto-Catholics, the so-called church papists. He suffered periods of imprisonment. Carew next turns up in Ipswich, where he was briefly curate of two of the town's parishes in turn, continuing in his defiant nonconformity and incendiary Presbyterian preaching. Then he was on the run again, but the influence of some of the patrons of Puritanism in Essex and Suffolk, including the second Lord Rich and Sir Robert Jermyn, secured

Carew the comfortable living of Bildeston, where he remained rector, now more circumspect in his nonconformity, until his death.

From Bildeston he published two collections of sermons, *Certaine godly and necessarie sermons* (1603) and *Fovre godlie and profitable sermons* (1605). With one exception these were unremarkable in their divinity, borrowing freely from more famous divines such as Richard Greenham and George Gifford. The exception was the sermon published as *A Caveat for Clothiers,* in which Carew took to task the employers of labor in the Suffolk clothing towns, which included Bildeston itself. Deploying a text from the Epistle of James more often taken to apply to landlords, Carew demonstrated with the economic precision of a nineteenth-century blue book that the profits of the clothiers were derived from low wages, so low that only weavers with not too many children and some separate means of livelihood such as a cow or two could hope to survive. Having been told that the rich often left money to the poor in their wills, he suggested that it might be devoutly wished that such rich men would do good by dying quickly, since they did harm as long as they lived.

We do not know how Carew's diatribe was received. He lived on in apparent peace (although the church court records that might have revealed some conflict no longer exist), and when he died in 1616, his main concern was his wife's interest in the tithe corn that was about to be harvested, while he left nothing to the poor.

*Further Reading*
Patrick Collinson, "Christian Socialism in Elizabethan Suffolk," in *Counties and Communities: Essays on East Anglian History,* ed. C. Rawcliffe, R. Virgoe, and R. Wilson (Norwich, Eng., 1996); Albert Peel, ed., *The seconde parte of a register,* 2 vols. (Cambridge, Eng., 1915).

*Patrick Collinson*

## Carter, John (1554–1635)

Clergyman. Carter, born in the county of Kent, was educated at the King's School in Canterbury and then at Clare College, Cambridge. Remaining at the university after receiving his degree, he engaged in theological discussions with Laurence Chaderton, Ezekiel Culverwell, and others.

In 1583 he was appointed vicar of Bramford, a parish in Suffolk under the patronage of the dean and chapter of Christ Church in Canterbury. Carter's puritan stance offended some members of the parish, who complained to the episcopal visitors in 1597 that the clergyman had refused to wear the surplice while officiating at services and had not used the sign of the cross in administering baptism. Though he escaped suspension, the tensions in the parish probably contributed to his decision to leave and assume the rectorship of Belstead, also in Suffolk, in 1617.

Carter was the author of a commentary on the Sermon on the Mount as well as two catechisms. He died in February 1635.

*See also:* Surplice
*Further Reading*
Samuel Clarke, *A Collection of the Lives of Ten Eminent Divines* (1662).

*Francis J. Bremer*

## Cartwright, Thomas (ca. 1535–1603)

Minister, eminent scholar, and foremost leader of Elizabethan Puritanism. Born in Hertfordshire, Cartwright matriculated at Clare Hall as sizar November 1547. In 1550 he became scholar of St. John's while Thomas Lever was master. Although not a Marian exile, Cartwright quitted the university after graduating B.A. in 1554 to clerk for a counselor-at-law and returned to St. John's upon the accession of Elizabeth as fellow of the college in 1560, and of Trinity College in 1562. Having established a reputation for intellectual and rhetorical skill, Cartwright was a natural choice to deliver a philosophical disputation before the queen on 7 August 1564. In 1565 his influence on younger (and more impressionable) minds was seen when the members of his college relinquished their surplices in the evening service after he preached against the surplice.

In 1565 Cartwright was in Ireland serving as domestic chaplain to Adam Loftus, archbishop of

Armagh, who was a fellow of Trinity with Cartwright and commended Cartwright to be his successor. Instead of receiving the appointment, Cartwright returned to Cambridge, receiving his B.D. in May 1567; rising as a star university preacher, in 1569 he became the Lady Margaret Divinity Professor. The new professor of divinity marked the beginning of puritan controversy over ecclesiastical polity in his famous lectures on the first two chapters of Acts. His lectures on the polity of the primitive church threatened the hierarchy and practices of the Church of England, arousing dangerous enthusiasm for presbyterian principles among the students in the university. In December 1570, within a year of his appointment, Cartwright was ejected from his professorship and eventually, in 1572, deprived of his fellowship at Trinity by John Whitgift, then master of the college.

Meanwhile, in 1571, Cartwright had withdrawn with his Presbyterian colleague Walter Travers to Geneva, where Theodore Beza was rector of the university, and the Scottish Presbyterian Andrew Melville was also resident. During the spring of 1572, the puritans in England launched their campaign for further ecclesiastical reform in their *Admonition* to Parliament, spearheaded by John Field and Thomas Wilcox. Though Cartwright was responsible for neither the *Admonition* nor the *Second Admonition,* he had already become a recognized leader of Presbyterianism and was further involved through his response *A replye to an Answere made of M. Doctor Whitgift, against the Admonition to Parliament, A second replie,* and *The rest of the second replie.* Cartwright returned to England from Geneva in April 1572. When the ecclesiastical commissioners of London issued a warrant for his arrest in December 1573, Cartwright retreated to Heidelberg University, where, in addition to *A second replie,* he translated Walter Travers's Presbyterian treatise the *Explicatio* and *A brief discours off the troubles begonne at Franckford.* Following a short period at the University in Basel in 1576, Cartwright moved to the Netherlands, joining the Merchant Adventurers in Middleburg as a factor in 1577, and marrying Alice, sister of John Stubbs, in 1578. Cartwright succeeded

Travers as minister of the Antwerp congregation in July 1580, agitating the queen by further establishing the Presbyterian practices introduced by Travers in Her Majesty's merchant congregation.

While advancing Presbyterianism through his ministry in the Low Countries, Cartwright also championed the cause of the Church of England. He vigorously protested against separatism, expressing his contempt for schism over the puritans' disdain for the surplice in *The rest of the second replie.* However imperfect the Church of England, he argued for its legitimacy against the separatist sect headed by Robert Browne, which had also migrated to Middleburg. When the English Jesuits at Rheims published their translation of the New Testament in 1582, Sir Francis Walsingham and the Earl of Leicester urged Cartwright to compose a refutation, the *Confutation of the Rhemists Translation.* This anti-Catholic undertaking offered Cartwright a generous stipend and the opportunity to prove his loyalty to the queen. Cartwright was also a painstaking preacher and devoted himself to pastoral care. In the Low Countries, he wrote letters to comfort a spiritually distressed Mrs. D. B., while praying with the poor, catechizing, and disciplining his flock when he returned to England. Cartwright also produced nonpolemical works such as *A Treatise of Christian Religion,* which was essentially his own larger catechism. Nonetheless, Bishop John Aylmer committed Cartwright to the Fleet when he returned to England in April 1585, though Cartwright procured release from Burghley shortly after in June and became Master of Leicester's Hospital in Warwick. Whitgift was also apprehensive of the returned exile, refusing to have his *Confutation* published.

Increasing puritan activity in the 1580s was growing intolerable for the most ardent defenders of the church. The seditious Marprelate tracts further agitated the anti-puritans, despite Cartwright and others' strenuous efforts to disassociate themselves from these polemical nonconformist works. The puritans were no longer able to avoid prosecution, for the fact that they were organizing along Presbyterian principles became evident in their Book of Discipline, *A Directory of Church-govern-*

*ment.* In 1591 Cartwright and eight other Presbyterian leaders were arrested and deprived of their ministry for refusing to take the oath before the High Commission and before the Court of Star Chamber. Cartwright and several others suffered from poor health while in prison, and the ministers were released in May 1592. Recovering from ill health, Cartwright served in Guernsey as chaplain at Castle Cornet, while Edmund Snape (who was imprisoned along with Cartwright) was stationed at the Castle of Mont Orgueil in Jersey in 1595. Their aim for reconciliation between the Guernsey and Jersey Presbyteries was realized in 1596 at a Synod for the Channel Islands, and the churches agreed upon a revision of their 1576 Form of Discipline by 1597. While Cartwright continued to minister as chaplain in Guernsey, Edward Lord managed the Hospital in Warwick for Cartwright until the master's return in 1601. Cartwright resumed his ministry at Warwick, preaching until his last days and even dedicating himself the morning of his death on 27 December 1603 in prayer.

*See also:* English Puritanism in the Netherlands; Marprelate Tracts

*Further Reading*

A. F. Scott Pearson, *Thomas Cartwright and Elizabethan Puritanism* (Cambridge, Eng., 1925).

*Polly Ha*

## Caryl, Joseph (1602–1673)

Congregational clergyman. Caryl was born to a gentry family and educated at Merchant Taylor's School before matriculating at Exeter College, Oxford, in 1621. He was ordained in 1627, serving briefly in Battersea before becoming successor to John Preston as preacher at Lincoln's Inn in 1632, a post he held until 1648. It was here he made his reputation, with many of his lectures being published, and he went on to be one of the most frequently call preachers for parliamentary fasts in the 1640s and 1650s.

He was a Congregationalist, associated with the Dissenting Brethren, although he was always inclined to find common ground with the Presbyterians. Indeed, the role of conciliator was one that he frequently took throughout his career. Though he usually voted with the Brethren in the Westminster Assembly, he opposed the publication of their *Apologeticall Narration* as a means to avoid bridges between the parties being burned. Similarly, in late 1643 he signed a tract against the further gathering of churches, hoping that this would minimize ecclesiological conflict during the war. He took on duties to maintain the middle ground. In 1645 he was named a Trier of elders in the fourth London classis and in 1654 as both a Trier and Ejector for clerical candidates. He preached to Parliament immediately after Pride's Purge (when troops of the New Model Army under Colonel Thomas Pride forcibly ejected from Parliament all those who wanted compromise with Charles I) and, with Philip Nye, tried to persuade some of the secluded members of Parliament to return to their seats in early 1649. He tried to defuse the controversy over James Nayler by persuading the Quaker to recant. He also played a prominent role in the Savoy Assembly in 1658, particularly helping to draw up the Declaration of Faith and Order uniting Presbyterians and Congregationalists, an interest he maintained in the restored Long Parliament in 1660. It was natural that he should be one of the ministers chosen to take a letter north to General George Monck in 1659 to ascertain his intentions. His status was such that he was, with Stephen Marshall, one of the chaplains to the commissioners at Holdenby House in 1647 and at Carisbrooke in 1648 (although the king refused to allow him to say grace at meals). He was more welcome as chaplain to the commissioners to Scotland in 1648 and again in 1651. He was also one of the clerics to provide comfort to the family of Oliver Cromwell upon the latter's death.

Caryl accepted the Restoration, and he continued to preach at St. Magnus the Martyr, publishing a denunciation of Venner's Rising in 1661. After his ejection in 1662 he served a congregation in Leadenhall Street, London, surviving allegations of preaching treason in 1663. He was partly supported by John Eliot's salary from the New England Company, partly a reward for his work for the English Society for the Propagation of the Gospel in New England. He received a license to preach after the

Declaration of Indulgence in 1672, a year before his death in 1673.

*Further Reading*
Edmund Calamy, *The nonconformist's memorial . . . originally written by . . . Edmund Calamy*, ed. S. Palmer (London, 1802–3); A. G. Matthews, *Calamy Revised: Being a Revision of Edmund Calamy's Account of the Ministers and others Ejected and Silenced, 1660–2* (Oxford, 1934; reprinted 1988); Tom Webster, *Godly Clergy in Early Stuart England: The Caroline Puritan Movement, c. 1620–1643* (Cambridge, Eng., 1997).

Tom Webster

## Cawdrey, Daniel (1587/8–1664)

Church of England clergyman and Presbyterian minister; born in South Luffinham, Rutland, the son of a deprived puritan minister. He was educated at Sidney Sussex College, Cambridge, then under Alexander Richardson in Barking, Essex, and graduated M.A. from Peterhouse, Cambridge, in 1613. After some years at Little Ilford, Essex, and in London, he was presented to the crown rectory of Great Billing, Northamptonshire, in 1625, going on to be a major activist in the circle of Thomas Ball, centered in Northampton down to the 1640s.

He repeatedly came close to trouble with the authorities. He read the Book of Sports but circulated a manuscript he had coauthored with Herbert Palmer, presenting Sabbatarianism as Jacobean orthodoxy. In 1635 he was described as a leading nonconformist during Archbishop William Laud's archiepiscopal visitation. His churchwardens railed in the communion table at the east end of the chancel, but Cawdrey made this meaningless by placing it tablewise during the communion service, with his *Superstitio Superstes* (1641) making plain his disavowal of the policy. The text was probably circulated in manuscript during the 1630s. In the late 1630s he preached Sunday mornings and afternoons, directly against royal instructions. He refused to contribute to funds for the Bishops' War and explicitly supported the Scottish rebels and rejected the etcetera oath supporting the Laudian canons of 1640.

In the 1640s he was among the most frequent preachers of fast sermons to parliament, taking on a succession of pulpits in London, and active in the London Presbyterian classis from 1644. He was a leading member of the Westminster Assembly, and most of his publications in the 1640s and 1650s contributed to the disputes with the Independents, starting with *Vindiciae Clavium* (1645) against John Cotton. Between 1648 and 1649 he put the emphasis on radicalism from the army, preaching four times to the House of Lords and signing the *London Testimony* (1648) and *Vindication* (1649), all of which linked the person and authority of Charles I and Presbyterianism. He was less active as a controversialist in the 1650s, having returned to Northamptonshire around 1652.

After the Restoration he hoped for a delivery of the broad church promised in the Declaration of Breda and was even recommended to Clarendon for a bishopric. However, he was not only not to become a bishop, he was ejected from Great Billing by the end of 1662. He retired to nearby Wellingborough, where he died two years later.

*Further Reading*
Peter Lake, "The Laudian Style: Order, Uniformity and the Pursuit of the Beauty of Holiness in the 1630s," in K. Fincham, ed., *The Early Stuart Church, 1603–42* (Basingstoke, Eng., 1993); H. I. Longden, *Northamptonshire and Rutland Clergy from 1500*, 6 vols. (Northampton, Eng., 1938–1952); R. S. Paul, *The Assembly of the Lord: Politics and Religion in the Westminster Assembly and the "Grand Debate"* (Edinburgh, 1985); Tom Webster, *Godly Clergy in Early Stuart England: The Caroline Puritan Movement, c. 1620–1643* (Cambridge, Eng., 1997).

Tom Webster

## Chaderton, Laurence (ca. 1536–1640)

One of the very few centenarians of note in preindustrial England; the first master of Emmanuel College, who in his thirty-eight-year tenure saw the college grow to be the largest in Cambridge, and an exemplary puritan divine. Chaderton came from a minor gentry family in Lancashire. He was fond of the sporting life and discovered education and scholarship rather late. At Christ's College Cambridge he was won to the warm evangelical piety of Edward Dering, whereupon his Catholic father cut him off with the proverbial shilling.

Elected to a fellowship in 1568, Chaderton built up a reputation as a theologian and preacher. For half a century he delivered a weekly sermon in St. Clement's Church in Cambridge, and when he gave it up, forty divines testified that they had owed their conversions to his teaching. At Paul's Cross in London in 1579 he uttered an urgent call to national repentance, staking out his puritan credentials. By now Chaderton was married to Cecily Culverwell, a daughter of the wealthy and godly London merchant Nicholas Culverwell, whose other daughter Susan married Chaderton's colleague William Whitaker. This meant forfeiting his fellowship, but Chaderton continued to place recommended students with godly tutors, while relying financially on the generosity of the Culverwell clan.

In 1584 Sir Walter Mildmay founded his new college, Emmanuel, and insisted on Chaderton becoming its master. It was a peculiar foundation, dedicated single-mindedly to the production of godly preaching ministers, its statutes skewed in that direction. It was also poorly endowed (Chaderton as master was paid a miserable fifteen pounds a year), and in consequence became not so much the intended seminary as a fee-paying finishing school for the great, the good, and the godly. Under Chaderton it became notorious for puritan austerity and nonconformity.

Chaderton himself was ideologically and even practically a Presbyterian, his antipathy to episcopal hierarchy most clearly expressed in *A fruitful sermon* on Romans chapter 12 (1584). He was the regular Cambridge correspondent of the London preacher and Presbyterian organizer John Field, and took part in the clandestine conference movement of the 1580s. More publicly, Chaderton, with Whitaker, devoted himself to the defense of Calvinist orthodoxy against its opponents. This was the strategy adopted by the so-called moderate and senior Puritans of Cambridge.

When James I came to the English throne in 1603, he was persuaded to preside over the Hampton Court Conference involving selected bishops and four representative puritan divines, who included Chaderton. Many took this to be a golden opportunity, but the shrewd Chaderton conducted an exercise in damage limitation, saying very little. After the conference, the Canons of 1605 imposed a new test of conformity, with subscription imposed by the energetic Archbishop Richard Bancroft, who was an old friend of Chaderton and his sometime opponent in wrestling matches. Faced with the choice between subscription and deprivation, puritan ministers looked to Chaderton for a lead, while Bancroft warned them to look in any direction but that. There is no evidence that Chaderton ever abandoned his own Presbyterian principles, but with skilful casuistry he urged his correspondents not to forfeit their ministry for the sake of things indifferent. If it was wrong to impose such things on tender consciences, it was almost equally wrong in all circumstances to refuse them. This was to apply a double standard, since in Emmanuel Chaderton was relatively immune from pressures to conform. But it was his tightrope strategy that enabled the preaching ministers who were fanning out from Cambridge in droves to effectively evangelize large areas of England, especially in East Anglia.

In 1622 there was a cunning maneuver by the fellows of Emmanuel, in which Chaderton was probably collusive, to ensure the continuity of the godly tradition in the college. Chaderton resigned the mastership and was replaced by the white hope of late Jacobean Puritanism, John Preston. Thereafter, Chaderton continued to live across the street from the college as he became one of the more venerable institutions of Cambridge. He died on the eve of the English revolution, on 13 November 1640. Chaderton's only daughter, Elizabeth, married the Massachusetts pioneer Isaac Johnson.

*See also:* Emmanuel College
*Further Reading*
A. Sarah Bendall, Christopher Nugent Lawrence Brooke, Patrick Collinson, *A History of Emmanuel College, Cambridge* (Woodbridge, Eng., 2000); A. Hunt, "Laurence Chaderton and the Hampton Court Conference," in S. Wabuda

and C. Litzenberger, eds., *Belief and Practice in
Reformation England* (Aldershot, Eng., 1998);
Peter Lake, *Moderate Puritans and the
Elizabethan Church* (Cambridge, Eng., 1989).

*Patrick Collinson*

### Chapman, Edmund (1538–1602)

Clergyman. Chapman was probably of Suffolk origins. He was educated at Cambridge University, receiving his B.A. from Trinity College in 1599 and
his M.A. in 1562. In 1567 he was appointed university preacher and in 1569 was awarded his B.D. degree. He soon thereafter emerged as a supporter of
Thomas Cartwright. Appointed a prebend in Norwich Cathedral, he was involved with other reformers in the destruction of the cathedral organ. Chapman left Norwich around the time when Edmund
Freke became bishop of the diocese. Whereas
Freke's predecessor, John Parkhurst, was a supporter of church reform, the new bishop was determined to enforce conformity.

A lecturer in Dedham, Essex, in 1582 Chapman
became one of the organizers of the clerical conference that centered on that town. He was suspended from his ministry in 1586, and again in
1588, but he was not prosecuted along with the
other leaders of the conference movement. He
died in Dedham in 1602.

*See also:* Dedham Conference
*Further Reading*
Patrick Collinson, *The Elizabethan Puritan
Movement* (London, 1967); Patrick Collinson,
John Craig, and Brett Usher, eds., *Conferences
and Combination Lecturers in the Elizabethan
Church, 1582–1590* (Woodbridge, Eng., 2003).

*Francis J. Bremer*

### Charnock, Stephen (1628–1680)

Puritan clergyman. The son of a London attorney,
Charnock attended Emmanuel College, Cambridge, receiving his B.A. in 1646 and his M.A. in
1649. After a brief spell as a preacher in Southwark,
he was chosen a fellow of New College, Oxford, in
1650. He became proctor of the college in 1654.

In 1655 he accompanied Henry Cromwell to Ireland as his chaplain. He preached in a number of
Dublin churches and was a member of the committee to approve ministerial candidates and another committee that condemned and recommended the burning of Quaker books. He was an
advisor to the convention that sought to govern Ireland in the unsettled days immediately after the
Restoration. In 1663 he was accused of being involved in a plot against the government, but the evidence was insufficient to convict him.

Shortly thereafter Charnock returned to London. He lost his library in the Great Fire of 1665. In
1675 he was chosen as co-pastor of a Presbyterian
congregation that met at Crosby Hall. A popular
and effective preacher, he avoided denominational
strife and was as comfortable with Congregationalists as with Independents.

*Further Reading*
Richard L. Greaves, *God's Other Children:
Protestant Nonconformists and the Emergence of
Denominational Churches in Ireland, 1660–1700*
(Stanford, 1997); Richard Greaves and Robert
Zaller, eds., *Biographical Dictionary of British
Radicals in the Seventeenth Century*, vol. 1
(Brighton, Eng., 1982); S. J. Seymour, *Puritans in
Ireland* (Oxford, 1921).

*Francis J. Bremer*

### Chauncy, Charles (1592–1672)

Puritan clergyman and president of Harvard College. Chauncy was born in Yardley-Bury, Hertfordshire, in 1592. He studied at Trinity College, Cambridge, receiving his B.A. in 1613 and M.A. in 1617.
He became a fellow of Trinity and college lecturer
in Hebrew and Greek. At this time Chauncy wrote
Latin and Greek verse for various state occasions;
he continued to compose poems for the rest of his
life. To prepare for the ministry, he studied with the
noted puritan cleric Alexander Richardson.

Chauncy served in various parishes from 1624
until 1633. He was a dynamic preacher whose sermons attracted many listeners, including the
prominent puritan peer Lord Saye and Sele, but his
strong puritan views and nonconformity caused

him problems. He resolved to emigrate to New England and arrived in Plymouth, in the colony of the same name, in 1638 and was warmly greeted as one of the most learned members of the clergy to migrate to the colonies. His insistence that baptism required full immersion and that the Lord's Supper only be celebrated in the evening caused controversy that led him to move to the town of Scituate, also in Plymouth, where he found supporters for his views.

Chauncy was chosen president of Harvard College in 1654 and held the position until his death in 1672. He oversaw a traditional curriculum such as he had been familiar with at Cambridge and took responsibility himself for the religious training of the students. Chauncy's stature as a scholar and minister earned respect for Harvard in England as well as New England, but the college struggled financially during his stewardship, in part because of low student enrollments.

While serving as president of Harvard, Chauncy continued to preach and to take stands on the religious controversies of his day. He attacked Socinian doctrines in his *Plain Doctrine of the Justification* (1659). He was a leading opponent of the Half-Way Covenant, which loosened the restrictions on the sacrament of baptism. His *Antisynodalia Scripta Americana* (1662) attacked the changes involved and stirred considerable controversy in the churches, but ultimately he was on the losing side, as most congregations adopted more inclusive membership standards.

*See also:* Half-Way Covenant; Harvard College
*Further Reading*
Cotton Mather, *Magnalia Christi Americana*, 2 vols. (Hartford, 1855); Samuel Eliot Morison, *Harvard College in the Seventeenth Century* (Cambridge, MA; 1936).

*Francis J. Bremer*

## Chauncy (Chauncey), Isaac (1632–1712)

Clergyman and physician. Chauncy was born in 1632 in Ware, Hertfordshire, where his father was vicar. He emigrated to New England with his family while still a child. Entering Harvard College in 1651, he graduated with an M.A. three years later, at which time he returned to England.

Chauncy was presented to a Wiltshire living by Oliver Cromwell in 1656, but ejected under the terms of the Act of Uniformity following the Restoration. He ministered to a private congregation and was cited for absence from services of the Church of England and also for sedition. He received a license as a Presbyterian under the Declaration of Indulgence of 1672. When that was revoked, he settled in London and devoted himself to the practice of medicine.

Despite having accepted a license as a Presbyterian, Chauncy was a proponent of the Congregationalism he had learned in New England, and he continued to write in support of that church polity. In 1687 he returned to the ministry, accepting a call to be pastor of a congregation meeting in Mark Lane, London. He was a member of the Common Fund Board and the Congregational Fund Board. He withdrew from the Happy Union in 1692, in part because of his dissatisfaction with what he viewed as Arminian tendencies among some of his fellow Dissenters. He wrote numerous tracts upholding a strong Calvinist perspective.

In 1699 Isaac Watts joined him as an assistant, and two years later Chauncy resigned as pastor of the Mark Lane congregation. He spent most of his remaining years heading a Dissenting academy in Moorfields. He died in 1712.

*Further Reading*
Francis J. Bremer, *Congregational Communion: Clerical Friendship in the Anglo-American Puritan Community, 1610–1692* (Boston, 1994); Richard Greaves and Robert Zaller, eds., *Biographical Dictionary of British Radicals in the Seventeenth Century*, vol. 1 (Brighton, Eng., 1982); John Langdon Sibley, *Biographical Sketches of Graduates of Harvard University, Volume I, 1648–1658* (Cambridge, MA; 1873).

*Francis J. Bremer*

## Cheever, Ezekiel (1615–1708)

Colonial schoolmaster. Cheever was born in London and educated at Christ's Hospital in that city before entering the University of Cambridge. He was admitted to Emmanuel College, Cambridge, in 1633 but does not appear to have stayed for a degree. He migrated to New England in 1637, settling in the New Haven Colony, where he served as master of the grammar school from 1638 to 1650. He moved to Ipswich, in Massachusetts, where he was schoolmaster from 1650 to 1651. Next he taught at Charleston from 1661 to 1670. His final position was master of the Grammar (Latin) School in Boston from 1670 to 1708. In 1692 he served as secretary to the Court of Oyer and Terminer that tried the accused Salem witches.

Cheever wrote three books. The first two—*Accidence: A Short Introduction to the Latin Tongue* (1645) and *A Short Introduction to the Latin Tongue* (1649) became the primary texts for Latin instruction throughout New England. The last, *Scripture Prophecies Explained* (1685), set forth his belief that the world would be perfected and Christ would come to initiate the millennium before the Last Judgment.

*Further Reading*
James Axtell, *A School upon a Hill* (New Haven, 1974)

*Francis J. Bremer*

## Chidley, Katherine (fl. 1616–1653)

Religious Separatist. Little is known of the wife of Daniel Chidley until the 1620s. At that time she was noted as being active in a Separatist group in Shrewsbury, Shropshire. In 1626 she was presented along with her husband for nonattendance at church and for refusing to be "churched" after childbirth. By the end of the decade the couple had moved to London, where there was a chance of pursuing their faith under less scrutiny.

Chidley was clearly able to read and write and was well versed in the scriptures. In November 1641 she published her first tract, *The Justification of the Independent Churches of Christ,* which was a defense of congregational autonomy, as opposed to the closer ecclesiastical supervision that was part of episcopal and presbyterian forms of church govern-

ment. In the same tract she argued for the autonomy of wives, arguing that the consciences of godly women must not be subject to the authority of ungodly husbands. Two more tracts in 1645 continued her attacks on Presbyterianism, and in particular the Presbyterian clergyman Thomas Edwards. Edwards criticized Chidley and her views in *Gangraena,* in which he claimed that she also had fought with the Congregational clergyman William Greenhill.

By the late 1640s Chidley also had a reputation for political radicalism, being one of the outspoken women associated with the Leveller cause, petitioning Parliament on behalf of the Leveller leader John Lilburne. Her last mark on the record came in 1653 when she was one of the leaders of a group of fellow petitioners who marched on the Nominated (Barebones) Parliament to present their arguments to the members.

*Further Reading*
Ian Gentles, "London Levellers in the English Revolution: The Chidleys and their Circle," *Journal of Ecclesiastical History* 29 (1978), 281–309; *New Dictionary of National Biography* (Oxford, 2004).

*Francis J. Bremer*

## Child, Robert (1613–1654)

Remembered for his 1646 Remonstrance to the Massachusetts General Court. After receiving degrees from Corpus Christi College, Cambridge, Child studied medicine at Leiden and Padua (M.D., 1638). He traveled widely, first arriving in New England in 1641, where he associated with John Winthrop Jr. and invested in an iron works. After losing his investment, he left for England, but he returned in 1645 and in 1646 petitioned, with six other signers, the General Court with a Remonstrance challenging the colony's policies for inconsistent enforcement of English law, demanding the extension of freeman status to all Englishmen in the colony, and seeking to open church membership to all Church of England communicants. The petitioners asserted their right to appeal to Parliament; the General Court rejected any right of appeal. In November, the court charged the petitioners with various offenses and levied fines. Child refused to pay, but "seditious papers" were discovered in his possession when he was about to sail for England and the Remonstrants were once again arrested. Child was assessed an £800 bond but refused to pay and was found guilty of conspiracy. Child finally departed in mid-1647; his treatment was recounted by his brother John in *New-Englands Jonas Cast up at London* (1647), prompting Edward Winslow's *New England's Salamander Discovered* (1647). Child soon abandoned the issue but continued correspondence with the younger Winthrop on scientific and medical issues. In 1651, he composed a "large letter" on English husbandry and left for Ireland, where he worked in agriculture until his death in 1654.

*See also:* Law in Puritan New England, *Laws and Liberties*
*Further Reading*
*American National Biography* (New York, 1999).

*Michael G. Ditmore*

## Clapham, Henoch (fl. 1585–1614)

Preacher and writer. He altered his religious views many times during his life, moving from puritan nonconformist to Separatist, and later to anti-puritan defender of the established church. His life and works illustrate the diversity and instability of the religious climate of early modern England.

After attending Emmanuel College, Cambridge, in the 1580s, Clapham was ordained in the Church of England in 1591, quickly moving from a presbyterian puritan to a separatist position on church government. After a period of imprisonment in 1593, he traveled between Scotland and the Netherlands to develop his understanding of the nature of true church government. By 1596, Clapham was ministering to a Separatist congregation in Amsterdam, where he published several exegetical works, principally *Theological Axioms* in 1597. In 1598, he denounced his former separatist views in *The syn against the Holy Ghoste,* returned to England to preach in London and, like his puritan colleagues, became an outspoken critic of separatism in both his sermons and printed works, most notably *Antidoton* of 1600.

The fluidity of Clapham's beliefs renders him a complex subject to study. He had unstable relationships with both the puritans and the church hierarchy, being imprisoned several times, including in 1603 for his unpopular view that the plague was a moral affliction and not an infectious disease (*Epistle discoursing upon the present pestilence*). Despite moments of ideological unity with puritanism, he was, on occasion, one of its most ardent critics. In 1608, Clapham, now a beneficed minister favored by the archbishop of Canterbury, published two dialogues, *Errour on the Right Hand* and *Errour on the Left Hand,* which condemned divergent religious views from puritanism and separatism through to Catholicism. The central characters, the puritan "Malcontent" and the semi-autobiographical "Flyer," alternate between these positions, but end their spiritual journey favoring "Mediocritie," the representative of the established Church of England.

By 1614, Clapham had been deprived of his living in Kent, after which nothing more about him is known.

*See also:* Providence, Sects
*Further Reading*
*Oxford Dictionary of National Biography* (Oxford, 2004).

*Victoria Gregory*

## Clarke, John (1609–1676)

Baptist preacher, physician, and colonial agent. Clarke was born in Westhorpe, Suffolk. He had some college education and some medical training, possibly at Leiden, and was a puritan by the time of his emigration to Boston, Massachusetts, in November 1637. In the antinomian controversy, he took the side of Anne Hutchinson, and he joined those of her followers who founded Newport, Rhode Island, in mid-1639. There he obtained a large grant of land, practiced medicine, participated in public affairs, and wrote at John Winthrop's request a report upon Hutchinson's "monstrous birth" at Portsmouth, Rhode Island, in

1638. Though never ordained, he became the principal teacher of the church founded at Newport about 1640, mostly by antinomian refugees. The church under his leadership reflected antinomian principles with probable borrowings from English General Baptists. It avoided liturgical formalities, permitted lay preaching, institutionalized free-wheeling discussion of doctrine in meetings distinct from formal worship, avoided a rigid creed, and chose not to ordain a pastor or adopt a covenant. Adopting Baptist principles by 1644, it became the second Baptist church in America, following the one in Providence, which Roger Williams helped found in 1638.

In October 1651 the government of Rhode Island sent him to serve as its agent in London. His aim was annulment of a patent obtained by William Coddington in 1649 that made him governor for life in a colony consisting of the towns of Newport and Portsmouth. Together with Roger Williams, on a similar mission from the mainland towns of Warwick and Providence, Clarke achieved this objective in 1652. Remaining in England, he championed the Baptist cause and in 1652 published his only major work, *Ill Newes From New-England: or, A Narrative of New-Englands Persecution.* Relating the harsh treatment he and two Baptist colleagues received from Massachusetts authorities during a visit to Lynn, Massachusetts, in 1651, it argued for religious freedom both in New and Old England. At mid-decade he joined in the Fifth Monarchist agitations and was jailed and fined. In 1657 he signed a Baptist petition to Cromwell asking him to refuse the crown. When Rhode Island officials learned of the king's restoration in 1660, they began to worry that their charter of 1643/1644 would be challenged and asked Clarke again to act on the colony's behalf. After a long controversy with John Winthrop Jr. over the location of the Connecticut border, at last in 1663 he obtained a new charter. It allowed religious liberty, fixed the colony's boundaries, and established a political structure with substantial powers of self-government. Clarke returned to Newport, resumed preaching at the Baptist church, helped the church weather a Sabbatarian controversy and schism, and served three terms as deputy governor. Retiring from public life in 1672, he died in 1676 and was buried in Newport. He left the bulk of his estate to establish a charitable trust.

*See also:* Rhode Island
*Further Reading*
Sydney V. James, *John Clarke and His Legacies: Religion and Law in Colonial Rhode Island, 1638–1750* (University Park, PA; 1999).

*Theodore Dwight Bozeman*

## Clarke, Samuel (1599–1682)

Biographer. Clarke was a moderate Presbyterian minister. After a long career starting in the 1620s, predominantly as curate of St. Benet Fink, London, and as governor and twice president of Sion's College, he sought accommodation with the post-Restoration regime. He took part in the Savoy Conference, was ejected from his living, and eventually retired to Hammersmith. Here he continued his biographical work, producing expanded new editions and original work such as *The marrow of ecclesiastical historie* (1650, 1654, 1675), *A general martyrologie* (1651, 1660, 1677), *The lives of two and twenty English divines* (1660), *A collection of the lives of ten eminent divines and of some other eminent Christians* (1662), *The lives and deaths of such worthies* (1665), *The lives of thirty-two English divines* (1667, 1677), *The lives of most of those eminent persons* (1675), and *The lives of sundry eminent persons* (1683). He covered a broad spread of history, with *A general martyrologie* providing a potted version of John Foxe's *Actes and Monuments* (1563; popularly known as the Book of Martyrs) brought up to date, but he is most famous for the biographies of clerics and noble professors of the more recent past, frequently adapted from funeral encomia. While his works are a valuable source, his polemical purpose is clear, producing testimonies of puritans of worthy moderation, neither sectarian nor humorless; these are examples by life rather than doctrine. His work fits into a tradition of both Foxeian and classical precedents.

*Further Reading*
Patrick Collinson, "'A Magazine of Religious Patterns': An Erasmian Topic Transposed in English Protestantism," in Collinson, *Godly People: Essays on English Protestantism and Puritanism* (London, 1983); Jacqueline Eales, "Samuel Clarke and the 'Lives' of Godly Women in Seventeenth-Century England," in *Women in the Church on the Eve of the Dissolution*, ed. William J. Sheils and Diana Wood, Studies in Church History, vol. 27 (Oxford, 1990); N. Keeble, *The Literary Culture of Nonconformity in Later Seventeenth-Century England* (Leicester, Eng., 1987).

*Tom Webster*

## Cobbet, Thomas (1608–1685)

New England minister at Lynn (1637–1656) and Ipswich (1656–1685), Massachusetts, and apologist for central Congregationalist doctrines and practices, including infant baptism, church-state relations, and the negative vote. Cobbet's education began at Oxford, but he left in 1625 for training under Dr. William Twisse. Later, he settled as a minister in Lincolnshire until his 1637 emigration to Massachusetts Bay, where he accepted the pulpit in Lynn and ministered with Samuel Whiting until 1656, moving then to Ipswich.

In 1643, he wrote in support of the magistrates' negative vote (veto) in the General Court; the following year (and again in 1666), he delivered the election sermon. Later, he participated in proceedings on the Half-Way Covenant (1657) and also served on various committees: addressing the colony's patent (1661), the founding of the Third Church at Boston (1671), and responding to Gorges-Mason complaints about Massachusetts's jurisdiction (1676). A son taken captive but later released during King Philip's War in 1676 prompted him to write "A Narrative of New England's Deliverances" for Increase Mather. In addition to correspondence and some unpublished manuscripts, Cobbet authored *A Just Vindication of the Covenant and Church-Estate of Children of Church-Members* (1648); *The Civil Magistrates Power in Matters of Religion* (1653), which in-

cludes a rejoinder to John Clarke's *Ill Newes from New England; A Fruitfull and Usefull Discourse Touching The Honour due from Children to Parents, and the duty of Parents towards their Children* (1656); and *A Practical Discourse of Prayer* (1657).

*See also:* Half-Way Covenant
*Further Reading*
Francis J. Bremer and Barbara Bremer, "Thomas Cobbet's *Practical Discourse of Prayer*," *Essex Institute Historical Collections* 112 (1975), 138–150.

*Michael G. Ditmore*

## Coddington, William (ca. 1598/1603–1678)

Founder of Newport, Rhode Island. Born and raised in Lincolnshire, England, Coddington turned to a mercantile career and came to Massachusetts in 1630 as an assistant, later serving as treasurer and also as a deputy. He was settled in Boston by 1633. During the antinomian controversy, Coddington supported John Wheelwright and Anne Hutchinson.

Following Hutchinson's banishment in 1638, Coddington accompanied Hutchinson and others to Portsmouth, Aquidneck (Rhode Island), where he helped establish a scriptural theocracy with himself as judge. After infighting, Coddington and followers withdrew in 1639 to establish Newport on the south end of the island; the two groups combined again by 1640 as a democracy espousing religious toleration and with Coddington elected as governor. He filled this position until 1647, fighting the efforts by Roger Williams to unite Newport and Portsmouth with Providence under a single patent, which Williams succeeded in doing in 1644. Secretly, Coddington negotiated for Aquidneck to join the United Colonies of New England. In 1651, he succeeded in having Williams's patent voided and obtained a patent for Aquidneck, but it was annulled in 1652. In 1656, Coddington submitted to the Williams patent but did not take a major role in government until reorganization under a new royal charter in 1663. Shortly afterward, Coddington shifted to Quakerism. He served as chief magistrate of the colony of Rhode Island in 1674, 1675, and 1678 and wrote one book, *A Demonstration of True Love* (1674), a plea for toleration for Quakers.

*See also:* Rhode Island
*Further Reading*
*American National Biography* (New York, 1999).

*Michael G. Ditmore*

## Cole, Thomas (ca. 1520–1571)

Archdeacon of Essex during the reign of Queen Elizabeth. Little is known for certain of Cole's youth. In 1546 he was headmaster of Maidstone School, and in about 1550 he received his M.A. from Oxford.

In 1551 he was one of a number of "freewillers," as upholders of human free will against the doctrine of predestination were known, from the counties of Kent and Essex who were arrested for their views. He evidently was one of the group who recanted before the authorities. He quickly rehabilitated his reputation with the leaders of the church and in 1553 preached before Archbishop Thomas Cranmer in defense of predestination. Cranmer arranged for the sermon's publication. Shortly thereafter, the Roman Catholic Queen Mary came to the throne, and Cole fled England along with other Marian exiles. He spent most of the next few years in Frankfurt, where he was a supporter of William Wittingham and John Knox, and participated in drawing up the system of discipline for the exile congregation. But he also traveled elsewhere and established a number of contacts with leading Continental Reformers.

Returning to England following the accession of Elizabeth, Cole was presented to the rectory of High Ongar in Essex by Richard, first Lord Rich. Bishop Edmund Grindal appointed Cole as archdeacon of Essex, and he was also appointed Dean of Bocking. He was tireless in his efforts to root out Roman Catholicism. He was one of the godly who called for further reforms, including doing away with the use of vestments. Archbishop Matthew Parker sought to bring him to conformity, but Cole was protected by the influence of Robert Dudley, the Earl of Leicester. The reform cause made significant strides under his administration of the archdeaconry of Essex, as he cooperated with godly lay patrons in the institution of puritan clergy in the parishes of the jurisdiction. He died in 1571.

*Further Reading*
C. H. Garrett, *The Marian Exiles: A Study in the Origins of Elizabethan Puritanism* (Cambridge, Eng., 1938); J. W. Martin, *Religious Radicals in Tudor England* (London, 1989).

*Francis J. Bremer*

## Cole, Thomas (1628–1697)

Puritan Congregational clergyman and head of a Dissenting academy. Cole was born in London and pursued his college education at Christ Church, Oxford, receiving his B.A. in 1649 and his M.A. in 1651. In 1656 he was made principal of St. Mary Hall, Oxford, where he was the tutor of John Locke, among others. In 1659 he became minister at Brampton Bryan, Herefordshire, but he was ejected following the restoration of the monarchy in the following year.

In 1666 Cole opened an academy at Nettlebed, in Oxfordshire. In 1674 he closed the school and moved to London, where he succeeded Philip Nye as minister of the Independent church then meeting at Cutlers' Hall. He was one of the Pinners' Hall lecturers, but did not join the Happy Union between Congregationalists and Presbyterians because of the latter's willingness to seek sacramental union with the Church of England. In 1695 he became one of the managers of the Congregational Fund board. A strong advocate of a high Calvinism, he engaged in many of the disputes that rent the Dissenting religious community of the times.

*Further Reading*
*Oxford Dictionary of National Biography* (Oxford, 2004).

*Francis J. Bremer*

## Collins, John (ca. 1632–1687)

Congregational clergyman. Collins was born in England but migrated to New England with his family when he was still young. He was educated at Harvard College, graduating with his B.A. in 1649 and being awarded his M.A. three years later. He briefly served as a tutor at Harvard, but returned to England in 1653. There he was incorporated M.A. at the University of Cambridge. He was appointed as a preacher in Scotland, which had been reduced to England's control. By 1659 he had become chaplain to General George Monck, who commanded English forces in Scotland.

Following the restoration of the Stuart monarchy, Collins ministered to a Congregationalist church in London. He was one of the original six Pinners' Hall lecturers in 1672 and was a close friend of his fellow New Englander and Harvard graduate Nathaniel Mather. He remained interested in the affairs of Massachusetts and was one of those who recommended Leonard Hoar to be president of Harvard in 1672. He provided the colonists with news of English events and acted as an agent for Massachusetts in accepting and disbursing funds. These efforts were rewarded when the colony awarded him 500 acres of land in 1683. He died in 1687 and was buried in Bunhill Fields, the Dissenter burial ground.

*Further Reading*
Francis J. Bremer, *Congregational Communion: Clerical Friendship in the Anglo-American Puritan Community, 1610–1692* (Boston, 1994).

*Francis J. Bremer*

## Colman, Benjamin (1673–1747)

New England clergyman. Colman was a favorite student of John Leverett at Harvard (class of 1692), and his father and brother were merchants in Boston. Because he was known to be sympathetic to the theological positions of the founders of the new Brattle Street Church in Boston, he was invited by the undertakers to be their pastor. Those who extended the invitation suggested that he be ordained in London. They believed Boston's ecclesiastical order would make it difficult for him to be ordained and installed in their innovative church. They were right, and Colman followed their advice.

The church's short- and long-term success can largely be credited to Colman. His theology was orthodox Calvinist, which allowed him to get along with his peers in New England. When Calvinist doctrine was attacked by either invading or home-grown theologies, Colman stood with the orthodox and thus became a valuable ally. He often spoke on public occasions to the colony, on fast or election days. In addition, his moderate temperament prevented him from getting caught up in pamphlet wars, personal attacks, or pointless dogmatic battles. But, like the church he pastored, he was not exactly normative. He appealed to his congregation's sense of politeness, reasonableness, and civic duty. This made him, in New England Puritan terms, liberal.

*See also:* Brattle Street Church
*Further Reading*
Perry Miller, *The New England Mind: From Colony to Province* (New York, 1953).

*Daryl Sasser*

## Cope, Sir Anthony (1550–1614)

Of Hanwell, Oxfordshire; patron of puritan ministers and promoter of the 1587 bill to revoke the ecclesiastical laws. Cope was influential in godly circles in the nearby town of Banbury, which he represented seven times in parliaments between 1571 and 1601. In 1604 and 1614 he represented Oxfordshire. Cope chose a succession of puritan ministers for the living of Hanwell, whose incumbencies spanned from 1584 until the outbreak of the Civil War. The first was John Dod, who was suspended for nonconformity in 1606–1607. He was replaced by the conformist Robert Harris. In the 1587 session of Parliament, Cope was part of a small puritan pressure group in the Commons, who agitated for a Geneva-style prayer book and Presbyterianism. He introduced what has become known as "Cope's bill and book" in the Commons in February 1587. The text of the bill survives; it stated that the Book of Common Prayer contained "divers imperfections, corruptions and repugnancies." It went on to argue that episcopacy was not agreeable to the word of God.

A separate bill accompanied the proposed new prayer book, which stated that the powers of electing and deposing ministers, admonition, and excommunication rightly belonged to an assembly of ministers and elders rather than to the bishops.

The prayer book recommended by Cope has been identified as a new edition of the *Forme of Common prayers* published by the Dutch printer Richard Schilders. Cope, along with fellow members of Parliament Peter Wentworth, Edward Lewkenor, Ralph Hurlestone, and Robert Bainbridge, were all imprisoned in the Tower of London for holding extra parliamentary meetings to organize their support for these measures. In 1589 the sheriff of Oxfordshire accused Cope and others from Banbury of using the excuse of religion to try to abolish traditional festive pastimes such as maypoles, morris dancing, and Whitsun Ales. As a result, Cope was forced to deny to the Privy Council that he was involved in any suspicious religious meetings. In 1591 the Privy Council ordered that his house be searched for anything that was to be moved in Parliament. His puritan proclivities did not bar Cope from holding local office, and he acted as a justice of the peace for Oxfordshire from about 1582. In the same year, 1582–1583, he was appointed as sheriff of the county and served in that capacity again in 1591–1592 and 1603–1604. In 1589 he was also appointed to supervise the recusants held in Banbury castle, and from 1596 he was a deputy-lieutenant. In 1597 he wrote to Lord Burghley about his concerns about the depopulation bill then being considered by Parliament.

In 1614 Cope spoke in favor of the parliamentary bill against nonresident clergy. In his speech he blamed nonresidency and pluralism on "popery" and argued that "a soul murdering nonresident [is] as dangerous to the soul as a murderer of the body to it." He also complained that there were just as many nonresidents as there had been at the beginning of Elizabeth's reign. He was subsequently appointed to the committee to consider this bill. Robert Harris preached Cope's funeral sermon in 1614 and drew attention to his great respect for learned preachers and his ardent opposition to Roman Catholicism.

*Further Reading*
Patrick Collinson, *The Elizabethan Puritan Movement* (London, 1967); David Dean, *Law-Making and Society in Late Elizabethan England, 1584–1601* (Cambridge, Eng., 1996).

*Patrick Collinson*

## Cotton, John (1584–1652)

Described by his English puritan friend, Thomas Goodwin, as the "Apostle of the Age," Cotton was an intellectual leader of the puritan movement and an influential crafter of congregational church polity.

Cotton left his childhood home in Derby at age thirteen to enter Trinity College, Cambridge, receiving the A.B. (1603) and A.M. (1606) before becoming a fellow of Emmanuel College, where he earned a reputation as an erudite scholar and preacher. He adopted the puritan plain style of preaching in 1609 after hearing Richard Sibbes. His first sermon in this manner converted John Preston. In 1612 he became vicar of St. Botolph's Church in Boston, Lincolnshire. The next year he was granted the B.D. degree and was married to Elizabeth Horrocks. Their home was often full of recent university graduates from Cambridge, Germany, and Holland who sought practical postgraduate training by Cotton.

Soon Cotton was practicing nonconformity, omitting at least some of the ceremonies of the Church of England. He was consequently suspended by Bishop Richard Neile in 1615 and again by Bishop George Montaigne in 1621. From that year, however, the new bishop of Lincoln, John Williams, who respected Cotton's learning, took a lenient approach to his puritan practices. Cotton became known as a judicious consultant on difficult matters of theology and church polity, developing a wide circle of correspondents in the puritan movement.

His ministry was interrupted by an extended affliction with the ague, which took Elizabeth's life in 1631. The next year Cotton married Sarah Hawkred Story, a widow with a ten-year-old daughter. He was ultimately unable to hold out against

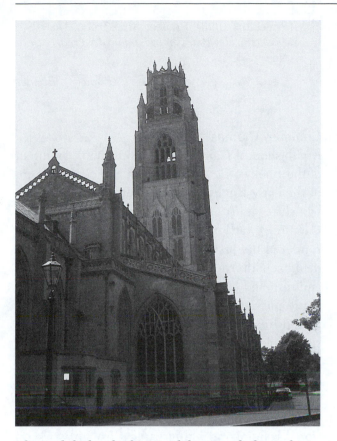

*The English church of St. Botolph's, Lincolnshire, where John Cotton preached and to which Thomas Dudley, Anne Hutchinson, and other future New Englanders came to hear him. (Courtesy Francis J. Bremer)*

church insistence on conformity in the ordinances of worship and went into hiding in 1632, finally notifying Bishop Williams of his resignation in a letter of 7 May 1633. On about 10 July, at the Downs on the Kentish coast, he and Sarah boarded the *Griffin* with other puritan fugitives and sailed for New England. The Cottons' first of six children, Seaborn, arrived during the voyage.

Settling in the new Boston in early September, Cotton was sought by the church there and was soon ordained as teacher, joining the pastor, John Wilson, in a partnership that endured through the final nineteen years of Cotton's life. He was temporarily isolated from most of his New England colleagues during the antinomian controversy (1636–1638). Cotton found himself allied with only John Wheelwright among clerical colleagues, though a large contingent of the Boston laity, led by

Cotton's former Lincolnshire neighbor, Anne Hutchinson, claimed simply to be following Cotton's teachings. The "opinionists," proclaiming a doctrine of "free grace," charged all ministers except Cotton and Wheelwright with preaching a covenant of works and with being themselves unredeemed. Cotton ultimately declared that their views were more extreme than they had professed to him, and he opposed them. He recounted the events of the episode in *The Way of Congregational Churches Cleared* (1648). His own theology of grace is presented in *A Treatise of the Covenant of Grace* (1659). Not long after the controversy ended, he regained his reputation as a judicious and insightful authority on biblical and ecclesiastical matters, consulted by acquaintances on both sides of the Atlantic, as his correspondence shows.

Most of Cotton's published works appeared after his emigration to New England. Books from his English period include *The Way of Life* (1641), *A Brief Exposition of . . . Canticles* (1642), *Christ the Fountain of Life* (1651), *A Brief Exposition . . . of Ecclesiastes* (1654), and *A Practical Commentary . . . upon the First Epistle Generall of John* (1656). His New England writings include the millennialist and anti-Catholic *Powring out of the Seven Vials* (1642) and *An Exposition of the Thirteenth Chapter of the Revelation* (1655). He debated toleration and conscience with the exiled Roger Williams in the "Bloudy Tenent" debate (1644–1652). In the 1640s he staunchly defended the congregational system, whose origin he traced to the martyred saint, Cyprian (ca. 200–258) His catechism for children, *Milk for Babes* (1646), enjoyed popularity in New England households long after his passing, as did the Bay Psalm Book (1640), the first book published in New England, a collaborative translation of the Psalms for which Cotton wrote the preface.

A final illness of more than two months ended on 23 December 1652.

*See also:* Antinomianism, Bay Psalm Book, Cambridge Assembly, Catechisms, Congregationalism, Federal Theology, Fifth Monarchists, Law in Puritan New England, *Moses His Judicials* and Mosaic Law, Toleration, Cotton's

Catechism (in Primary Sources), New Englanders Contemplate England's Wars of Religion (in Primary Sources)

*Further Reading*

Sargent Bush Jr., ed., *The Correspondence of John Cotton* (Chapel Hill, 2001); Everett Emerson, *John Cotton* (Boston, 1990); Lazer Ziff, *The Career of John Cotton: Puritanism and the American Experience* (Princeton, 1962).

*Sargent Bush Jr.*

## Craddock, Matthew (d. 1641)

Merchant, colonizer, member of Parliament. Craddock was the son of a Staffordshire gentleman. He married the daughter of a London merchant and became involved in the wool trade by 1615. Within the next decade he began to expand his business activities into various overseas ventures. He developed interests in the East India Company, the Eastland Company, and the Levant Company. In the late 1630s he served as an officer in the Skinners' Company.

He was also involved in some of England's colonizing activities. Craddock may have been a member of the Dorchester Adventurers, and was certainly a member of the Virginia Company. He was a founder and the first governor of the Massachusetts Bay Company. Craddock supported the move of the company charter and seat of government to New England, though it meant that he lost control over its affairs. He remained a supporter of Massachusetts.

Craddock was an opponent of some of the policies of the Stuart monarchs, particularly the unauthorized collection of tonnage and poundage. As a leading member of one of the guilds, he became active in London politics. He was elected to the Long Parliament and helped to stimulate support for Pym's policies in the city. He was a strong advocate of root-and-branch reform of the church, but he died in May of 1641 before that goal was undertaken.

*See also:* Massachusetts Bay Company
*Further Reading*
Robert Brenner, *Merchants and Revolution: Commercial Change, Political Conflict, and England's Overseas Traders, 1550–1653*

(Princeton, 1993); Frances Rose-Troup, *The Massachusetts Bay Company and Its Predecessors* (New York, 1930).

*Francis J. Bremer*

## Cranmer, Thomas

Archbishop of Canterbury (1489–1556), architect of the Book of Common Prayer, and central figure of the early English Reformation, was of Nottinghamshire gentry stock. Entering Jesus College, Cambridge, at fourteen, in the mid-1510s he surrendered his Jesus fellowship to marry. His wife died in childbirth, and Cranmer was then ordained and resumed his fellowship. He served on a diplomatic mission to Spain in 1527 and in 1529 suggested fresh consultations with European university theology faculties to aid Henry VIII's attempt to rid himself of Catherine of Aragon. He was sent to Italy in 1530, and there the absentee bishop of Worcester, Jerome Ghinucci, made him parson of Bredon (Worcestershire). His break with traditional religion probably came through work on Henry's annulment. During diplomacy in Germany in 1532, he defied clerical celibacy to marry Margarethe, niece of Nuremberg Lutheran leader Andreas Osiander.

Not long after, Henry chose him as archbishop of Canterbury. Consecrated with reluctant papal approval in 1533, he declared Henry's first marriage annulled and facilitated a public royal marriage to Anne Boleyn. When Anne, his religious ally, was executed for adultery, Cranmer granted the king a further annulment (1536). Cranmer and Thomas Cromwell, the king's deputy as head of the English church, collaborated in further reformation, but by Henry's conservative Act of Six Articles (1539), Margarethe was forced to leave England. Having survived Cromwell's fall (1540), Cranmer was the only person at court able to tell Henry of Catherine Howard's adultery (1541). Henry's continuing esteem enabled him to survive efforts by conservatives in 1543 to repeat their destruction of Cromwell. In Edward VI's reign, he was prominent in steering reform, compiling two Books of Common Prayer (1549, 1552), the second being less of a

*Thomas Cranmer, archbishop of Canterbury (1489–1556), and central figure of the early English Reformation. (Library of Congress)*

a heresy trial in 1554, and imprisoned at Oxford with Hugh Latimer and Nicholas Ridley. His morale broken, he signed six recantations, some after he had no doubt been told that he would burn at the stake. He made a last-minute return to Protestantism at his execution, however, publicly repudiating his recantations, and thrusting his right hand, which had signed them, into the flames. Cranmer's firm Erastianism did not appeal to later Puritans, and the Book of Common Prayer, still so notable for his sonorous prose, was too reminiscent of old ceremonial for many; some maintained, probably correctly, that he would have revised it further given opportunity. Nevertheless, his single-minded devotion to Reformation and his frequent quiet ruthlessness toward traditional devotion make him a figure closer to Puritan ideals than his later Anglican admirers would care to admit.

*See also:* Articles of Religion, Book of Common Prayer, Confirmation, Idolatry, Marian Martyrs, Preaching, Vestments
*Further Reading*
Diarmaid MacCulloch, *Thomas Cranmer: A Life* (New Haven, 1996).

*Diarmaid MacCulloch*

compromise than the first. In 1550 he also composed an Ordinal (the order of service by which bishops, priests, and deacons are ordained); he published two books affirming against Bishop Stephen Gardiner that there was no real or corporal presence of Jesus Christ the eucharistic elements of bread and wine. He promoted the Forty-Two Articles (issued 1553, revised 1563 as Thirty-nine Articles, and still the Church of England's doctrinal standard), together with a recasting of English canon law (John Foxe later entitled it the *Reformatio Legum*). John Dudley, Duke of Northumberland, prevented this new version of canon law being enacted; nevertheless Cranmer reluctantly cooperated in Northumberland's and Edward's unsuccessful attempt to make Jane Grey queen succeeding Edward, rather than the Lady Mary, Henry VIII's oldest child.

When Mary nevertheless became queen, Cranmer was convicted at a treason trial in 1553, and at

## Crashaw, William (1572–1626)

B.D., Cambridge, father of the Catholic poet Richard Crashaw, and a well-known puritan preacher at the Inner Temple Church and a minor poet. His published works include sermons, antipapal polemics, dialogues, and a "countrey catechism" called *Milke for Babes*. His 1607 Paul's Cross sermon encompasses several of his concerns. It examines three Babylons: the historical one, the Roman Catholic kingdom of Antichrist, and the "mystical Babylon," the kingdom of sin. The three "little pettie Babylons" that beset the faithful are impropriations of church property, plays, and the abuse of the Sabbath. His overriding concern throughout his career was his animus against the Church of Rome, in which his son took orders long after William Crashaw's death. Such heated anti-Roman polemics as *The Jesuites Gospel* (1610), however, should be balanced against the more tolerant tone of *A Manuall for true Catholikes* (1611). Crashaw's *Manuall* gathers out of "the most misty times of Popery" traditional Catholic prayers, translating them into English for his own readers' edification. Moreover there is some evidence that heat of Crashaw's rhetoric diminished somewhat in his later years. The historian and jurist John Selden, for example, notes that he converted Crashaw from writing antitheatrical polemics.

*Further Reading*
Edward Watkin. "William Crashaw's Influence on His Son," in Watkin, *Poets and Mystics* (London, 1953), pp. 164–187.

Bryan Crockett

## Crisp, Tobias (1600–1643)

Minister. Crisp was born into a wealthy London family. Educated at Eton and Cambridge, Crisp took up livings successively at Newington (Surrey), and Brinkworth (Wiltshire). Although initially inclined to the Arminian ideas that were sweeping the English church in the 1620s and 1630s, Crisp through a now obscure process eventually drifted toward the antinomian form of piety for which he ultimately became famous. Frequently in London during the 1630s, Crisp may have arrived at his unusual ideas through contact with members of the London circle surrounding John Eaton, the famed antinomian heresiarch. In 1642, royalists forced him to flee Brinkworth, and he accordingly returned to London to preach his controversial message of "free grace" openly from the pulpits of the city.

Although he died in 1643, Crisp proved enormously influential. On the one hand, his sermons touched large numbers of people, playing a very significant role in fanning the flames of religious radicalism that were beginning to burn through London during the Civil War. A number of later notorious religious extremists—including the Ranter Lawrence Clarkson, the mystic Jane Lead, and the army radical Henry Pinnell—attested that Crisp had played a formative role in forging their own religious identities. Even more enduringly, Crisp's

sermons, which were first published posthumously by his follower Robert Lancaster in the 1640s and then republished by his son in 1690, continued to exert an influence (and to excite controversy) into the eighteenth century, serving to epitomize the antinomian style of divinity that continued to survive at the margins of the dissenting community.

*See also:* Antinomianism, Pinners' Hall
*Further Reading*
Theodore Dwight Bozeman, *The Precisianist Strain: Disciplinary Religion and Antinomian Backlash in Puritanism to 1638* (Chapel Hill, 2004); David Como, *Blown by the Spirit: Puritanism and the Emergence of an Antinomian Underground in Pre–Civil War England* (Stanford, 2004).

David Como

## Cromwell, Henry (1628–1674)

Army officer and Protectorate administrator. Henry was the fourth son of Oliver Cromwell. He was born in Huntingdon in 1628 and educated at the puritan-favored Felsted School prior to his admission to Emmanuel College, Cambridge, in 1644. Leaving Cambridge before receiving a degree, he studied briefly at Gray's Inn and then joined the army near the end of the first Civil War.

Henry served as a captain of troop under Thomas Harrison. In the summer of 1648 he served under his father in the northern campaign, and then accompanied him to Ireland in 1650 with the rank of colonel. In 1653 he was one of the Irish representatives in the Nominated (Barebones) Parliament. He returned to Ireland to report on the situation there in the following year, and the newly formed Irish Council appointed him to be commander of the army units in Ireland. With the recall of Charles Fleetwood as lord deputy for Ireland, Henry Cromwell became the de facto leader of the country, a position that was finally regularized in 1657 when he was officially appointed lord deputy.

Henry Cromwell's strategy in governing Ireland included an effort to replace military with civilian rule and to reconcile the old Protestant settlers to the new regime. Though he was close to a number of Congregational clergy who had come with him to Ireland, he favored the more conservative Presbyterian elements in the country and sought to exclude Baptists and other sects from influence. His treatment of Catholics was generally harsh, including the internment of priests on western islands.

He remained in Ireland, elevated to the title of lord lieutenant, following his father's death and the institution of his brother Richard as the new Lord Protector. When Richard resigned that post, Henry relinquished his Irish posts and retired to private life. He was allowed to retain his freedom and some of his Irish lands after the Restoration. He died in 1674.

*Further Reading*
R. M. Ramsey, *Henry Cromwell* (London, 1933).

*Francis J. Bremer*

## Cromwell, Oliver (1599–1658)

Soldier and statesman. Cromwell was born as the eldest surviving son of the younger son of a prominent East Anglian landowner, whose wealth was based on monastic spoils handed out by Henry VIII's chief minister, Thomas Cromwell, to his relations. He was a child of the Reformation. Oliver was born and schooled in the small county town of Huntingdon and spent a year at Sidney Sussex College Cambridge, before leaving (1617) because of his father's death. Through his father's sister and through his own wife (Elizabeth Bourchier, daughter of a London fur trader), he had strong links with the godly gentry families of London and East Anglia; and at some point (the most favored date is ca. 1630), he had a conversion experience that made him henceforth a puritan firebrand. There is some evidence that he intended to migrate to Connecticut in 1634, and better evidence that he attended and preached at an underground conventicle in St. Ives (although all eight of his children [born 1624–1638] were baptized in the parish church). By 1636, he could write incautiously of the bishops as "the enemies of God His Truth."

In 1640, probably at the instigation of a godly faction, he was returned to Parliament for the City

of Cambridge and made his reputation for outspokenness whenever religious issues came up. In 1642, he was one of the first to volunteer for military service against the king, and he prevented the gold and silver plate of the Cambridge Colleges being sent to help the royal cause. Between 1642 and 1650 he was prominent both in the military and political arenas. He rapidly rose to command the cavalry of one of the main Parliamentarian armies, that of the Eastern Association (or eight eastern counties), and he became known as "Ironsides" (a soubriquet later transferred to his men). In 1645, when the New Model Army was formed out of the main regional armies, he was (uniquely) exempted from the ordinance that recalled members of Parliament (MPs) to Westminster, and he served both as lieutenant general of the New Model and as an active MP.

By 1648, he had won thirty-eight battles and lost none. He was renowned for recruiting on the basis of radical religious commitment rather than social status and for supporting sectaries as well as supporters of a reformed national church. Indeed he protected the radicals even when they overstepped the mark and plundered their opponents. He was Parliament's most successful and most controversial general. In Parliament he supported a policy of no negotiation before a complete military victory had been secured. In 1647 he supported the army council in deciding to bypass parliamentary attempts to reach a peace settlement by direct negotiation in favor of a settlement that allowed "liberty for tender consciences" for those who did not wish to be part of a national church. When the king refused to negotiate seriously and relaunched civil war, Cromwell persuaded himself that God would have the king destroyed, and he played a key role in putting him on trial and having him executed. He then agreed to lead an army to Ireland to suppress rebellion there, and he did so with great brutality, killing almost all the garrison and several hundred civilians at Drogheda and saying, "It is a just judgement of God upon those barbarous wretches that have imbrued their hands in so much innocent blood." With resistance in Ireland shattered, he returned to lead an invasion of Scotland and again

*A brilliant military commander, Oliver Cromwell was the leader of the English Commonwealth following British Parliament's victory in the English Civil War. Though he was the chief instigator of King Charles I's execution in 1649, he assumed some of the powers of the monarch as Lord Protector. (Library of Congress)*

crushed the armies that upheld the claims of the House of Stuart.

Impatient for the fruits of revolution to be realized (a "reformation of manners," religious liberty for all Protestants who accepted the authority of scripture and the Apostles Creed, greater social justice, and an end to legal corruption and graft), he used military might to dissolve Parliament, establish himself as Lord Protector, and call fresh elections. But the country was too embittered to respond as he wished. Successive parliaments spent more time debating his power than promoting godliness, justice, and peace. He tried to use his generals to bring about moral rearmament programs in the localities; he promoted religious freedom and the Protestant cause abroad; but he made little progress, and he died, exhausted and disillusioned, with his vision unrealized.

His faith was strongly Calvinist, in that he was a firm believer in the doctrine of assurance and was convinced of his own calling to service and salvation. He had a profound belief in God's immanence and providential presence with his people, and his letters and speeches were full of exegetical passages about the workings of providence especially on the battlefield. He read the scriptures constantly and found God's will made manifest in them. "This scripture hath been much stay [*sic*] with me, Isaiah 8 [verses] 8,10,11. Read them, read the whole chapter," he told his friend Oliver St. John in 1648. He saw himself as facing exactly the same challenges as Old Testament heroes and at various points likened himself to Gideon, Moses, and Josiah. But in other ways he was unorthodox. He was violently anticlerical, and among his spiritual advisors only the Congregationalist John Owen could be called orthodox. The others—men like Hugh Peter, Peter Sterry, George Fox—were of a different stamp. He was antiformalist, and (as far as we know) never attended a church service or received Holy Communion after 1642. He believed that God's truth was scattered among the saints in the many Protestant churches. His task was to allow all those with "the root of the matter in them" to evangelize, while permitting those who did not have the root of the matter in them to worship in private but not in public (this limited toleration included even Catholics). So he promoted a loose national church, but made membership optional, and he placed no bar against those outside the church holding public office. In that sense he was far ahead of his time.

He failed in his mission, but his stern, authoritarian moralizing and his vision of a pluralistic religious polity were inspirational for nineteenth-century Dissenters, and the edition of his letters and speeches by Thomas Carlyle was on the best-seller list for almost the whole of Victoria's reign. Today he is commemorated by a Cromwell Association that puts up plaques on the battlefields where he fought and lays a wreath on 3 September (the anniversary not only of his death but of two of his greatest victories) by his statue, which stands on the green next to the Palace of Westminster, home of Parliament.

*See also:* Antichrist, Fifth Monarchists, Independency, Major-Generals, New Model Army, Protectorate, Puritan Revolution, Savoy Assembly, Sects, Triers and Ejectors
*Further Reading*
J. C. Davis, *Oliver Cromwell* (London, 2000); *Oxford Dictionary of National Biography* (Oxford, 2004); R. S. Paul, *The Lord Protector* (Grand Rapids, 1955).

*John Morrill*

## Cromwell, Richard (1626–1712)

Lord Protector of England as successor to his father, Oliver Cromwell. Richard was the third son and heir (after the death of his older brothers) of Oliver Cromwell. His youth kept him from any active involvement in the first Civil War. Though he commanded a regiment in 1647, he did not experience combat. Richard demonstrated little commitment to any political or religious cause and failed to distinguish himself in any of the positions he held, all those positions as a result of his father's prominence. He studied briefly at Lincoln's Inn in 1647. He served quietly in the parliaments of 1654 and 1656. He was appointed chancellor of Oxford in 1657 but had little impact on the university. In that same year he was named to the Council of State.

Exercising his right to name his successor granted him under the Humble Petition and Advice, Oliver Cromwell chose Richard as one of his last actions as Lord Protector. The succession was without incident, but Richard soon demonstrated that he lacked his father's ability to control the many powerful factions that existed in the realm. In particular, he lacked his father's special relationship with the army. He did believe in a civilian settlement, and to advance that called parliamentary elections on the traditional basis, but with the addition of members from Ireland and Scotland. In the months that followed, relations between the Protector, the army, and the parliament quickly broke down. Richard was persuaded to dissolve the parliament, and shortly thereafter withdrew from office, as leading figures decided to recall the Rump Parliament. The result of these events contributed to an unstable situation, which led more and more

of the nation's leaders—most especially General George Monck, commander of the army in Scotland—to conclude that the only viable option for the country was the restoration of the monarchy. Though Richard initially fled to France following the return of Charles II, he was never considered a threat to the Restoration settlement and was allowed to return to England, where he lived out his life in peaceful obscurity.

*See also:* Protectorate
*Further Reading*
E. Hause, *Tumble-down Dick* (New York, 1972); R. W. Ramsey, *Richard Cromwell* (London, 1935).

*Francis J. Bremer*

## Cromwell, Thomas (ca. 1485–1540)

Sixteenth Earl of Essex, spearhead of Henry VIII's Reformation, and the son of a Middlesex tradesman. After colorful if obscure Continental travels, he rose in the service of Cardinal Thomas Wolsey, Henry VIII's chancellor, from the 1510s and transferred to the king after Wolsey's death (1530). Royal councillor in 1531, Master of the Jewels and of the Wards in 1532, king's secretary in 1534, he was the first royal minister to be at home in the House of Commons, using parliamentary legislation to promote annulment of Henry's Aragon marriage through the Act in Restraint of Appeals and subsequent legislation that completed the break with papal jurisdiction. Appointments as vicar-general and vice-gerent in spirituals in 1535 handed him the new royal powers in the Church of England; he was committed to drastic reform, working closely with Archbishop of Canterbury Thomas Cranmer, including in authorizing an English Bible. Evangelical views did not, however, stop him from securing his former ally Anne Boleyn's downfall (1536).

From 1536 he masterminded the dissolution of all monasteries and friaries; he undertook government reforms that, although incomplete and often designed for his political advantage, had long-term importance. His fatal blunder was to be responsible for Henry's Anne of Cleves marriage fiasco (1540). He apparently weathered this storm, even gaining an earldom, but plots by conservative clergy and noblemen secured his arrest and execution. Without Cromwell, Henry's jurisdictional revolution in the church might have been given little chance to make common cause with the Continental Reformation.

*Further Reading*
R. B. Merriman, *Life and Letters of Thomas Cromwell*, 2 vols. (Oxford, 1902).

*Diarmaid MacCulloch*

## Crowley, Robert (ca. 1517–1588)

Early Protestant printer, pamphleteer, and Church of England clergyman. Crowley graduated B.A. from Magdalen College, Oxford, in 1540 and was a fellow until 1542. By late 1546 he was in London, where he produced a stream of verse tracts on social and religious themes. Between 1549 and 1551 he printed several of these himself at premises in Holborn, also publishing other works designed to spread the Protestant message. The most celebrated was William Langland's fourteenth-century satire *The Vision of Piers Plowman*, never before put into print.

Ordained deacon and priest by Nicholas Ridley, bishop of London, in late 1551, Crowley gave up his publishing business. In exile during Mary's reign, he was a signatory to Frankfurt's "new discipline" adopted by members of the exile community in early 1557 but was back in England by early 1559, when his updating of Thomas Lanquet's chronicle, mentioning over 200 Marian martyrs by name, was published as *An epitome of chronicles*.

Thereafter a popular London preacher, Crowley was made archdeacon of Hereford in 1560 and in 1563 was appointed by Bishop Edmund Grindal to the prebend of Mora in St. Paul's Cathedral. He was also associated with John Gough and John Philpot in lectures at St. Antholin's. The three of them emerged, along with Percival Wiburn, as Archbishop Matthew Parker's principal London opponents during the Vestiarian controversy, and they were among the thirty-seven city ministers who, refusing the prescribed vestments in March

1566, were suspended and threatened with deprivation if they did not conform within three months. As a writer, Crowley's most significant contribution to the controversy was *A briefe discourse against the outwarde apparell* (1566), which has been described as "the earliest puritan manifesto."

On 25 June, three months to the day from his suspension, Crowley was duly deprived of the vicarage of St. Giles Cripplegate, to which he had been appointed by the dean and chapter of St. Paul's as recently as autumn 1565. Probably at the same time, he lost his prebend in St. Paul's and his archdeaconry. For the next four months at least, he remained under house arrest with the bishop of Ely; thereafter his movements are unaccounted for until 1569.

During the 1570s Crowley reestablished himself in London, both as a writer and as a clergyman. Although he never returned to the radicalism of earlier days, it must be doubted whether he ever became a conformist in the full sense of the word. He died as vicar of St. Giles Cripplegate, to which he had been readmitted in 1578.

*See also:* Marian Exiles, St. Antholin's, Vestments
*Further Reading*
Patrick Collinson, *The Elizabethan Puritan Movement* (London, 1967); J. W. Martin, *Religious Radicals in Tudor England* (London, 1989); Brett Usher, "Edward Brocklesby: 'The first put out of his living for the surplice'," in Stephen Taylor, ed., *From Cranmer to Davidson*, Church of England Record Society, vol. 7 (Woodbridge, Eng., 1999), pp. 47–68.

*Brett Usher*

## Culmer, Richard (ca. 1597–1662)

Puritan cleric who was famed for his iconoclasm in Canterbury Cathedral in response to the 1643 parliamentary ordinance. He described the incident in his book *Cathedrall Newes from Canterbury* (1644), in which he also attacked episcopacy and argued for presbyterianism. Culmer graduated B.A. in 1618 from Cambridge (Magdalene College) and M.A. in 1621. He was ordained in 1621 and by 1624 had returned to his native Kent, where he acted as curate in parishes near Canterbury. In 1635 he was suspended for three and a half years for his refusal to read the Book of Sports. He canvassed various members of the Long Parliament for patronage and in 1644 was appointed one of the six preachers in Canterbury Cathedral. In 1645 he was intruded into the living of Minster in Thanet, where he refused to use the Book of Common Prayer and was involved in tithe disputes. A man of a contentious nature, Culmer believed that he was opposed by local royalists and sectaries alike. He wrote two tracts in justification of tithes, *The Ministers Hue and Cry* (1651) and *Lawles Tythe-Robbers Discovered* (1655). Culmer was ejected in 1660 at the Restoration. Three anonymous pamphlets attacking Culmer were published in his lifetime. *The Razing of the Record* and *Antidotum Culmerianum* were both printed at the royalist headquarters of Oxford in 1644, and *Culmer's Crown Crackt with his own Looking-Glass* appeared in 1657. They are the source of many erroneous stories about him, which are corrected in a candid account by his son Richard Culmer Jr.—*A parish looking-glasse for persecutors of ministers* (1657).

*Further Reading*

Jacqueline Eales, *Community and Disunity: Kent and the English Civil Wars, 1640–1649* (Faversham, Eng., 2001).

*Jacqueline Eales*

## Culverwell, Ezekiel (ca. 1554–1631)

Church of England clergyman and a leading member of the conference movement. Culverwell was born in London, son of Nicholas Culverwell. He was part of a network of puritan leaders. His eldest sister, Elizabeth, was the mother of William Gouge. Two younger sisters, Cecilia and Susan, married respectively Laurence Chaderton and William Whitaker. His elder brother, Samuel, married a daughter of Thomas Sampson.

Culverwell graduated from Oxford in 1573, proceeding M.A. in 1577. Ordained in about 1585, he became chaplain to Robert, the third Lord Rich, at Little Leighs, Essex, and preacher at nearby Felsted. He joined the conference of ministers led by George Gifford, which met in and around Braintree, in the process becoming a friend of the clergyman Richard Rogers, who frequently mentions him in his diary. It seems likely, therefore, that he stood godfather to Ezekiel Rogers.

Although his nonconformity soon drew the fire of John Aylmer, bishop of London, Culverwell was in 1592 instituted by Aylmer as rector of Great Stambridge, Essex. In 1598 he married, as his second wife, Winifred Barefoot (née Hildersham), possibly the sister of Arthur Hildersham, and was thereafter accepted as a member of the influential Barrington-Hildersham connection. In one of his three extant letters he addressed Lady Joan Barrington as "cousin."

Following the death of Arthur Dent in 1603, he saw Dent's last work, *The Ruine of Rome*, through the press, adding a dedicatory epistle to Lord Rich. In 1605 at Great Stambridge, he solemnized the marriage of Mary Forth to John Winthrop, the future governor of the Massachusetts Bay Colony, who later acknowledged that it was Culverwell's ministry that had converted him to "true religion."

After many citations before the London consistory court following the implementation of the Constitutions and Canons of 1604, Culverwell was deprived of Great Stambridge by the High Commission in 1609 for his continued refusal to observe the ceremonies of the Church of England. Evidently spending the rest of his life in London, he maintained contact with Winthrop and was a friend and correspondent of such leading Calvinist theologians as John Burgess, John Dod, Richard Sibbes, and James Ussher. In his *Treatise of Faith* (1623; 8th ed. 1648), the most important of his handful of published works, he sought to modify the doctrine that Christ died only for the elect. When Alexander Leighton accused him of Arminianism in *A friendly triall of the Treatise of Faith* (Amsterdam, 1624), Culverwell issued a spirited defense—*A briefe answere to certain objections against the Treatise of Faith* (1626)—affirming his adherence to the decrees of the Synod of Dort.

Culverwell was buried in the parish of St. Antholin, London, on 14 April 1631, having made a brief will in July 1630. Among his bequests was one to young Ezekiel Cheever, presumably another godson: £10 and a third of all his Latin books. Culverwell's influence on Gouge, Winthrop (recipient of two his extant letters), Cheever and, perhaps, the family of Richard Rogers earns him an honorable place in the dispersal of the "puritan" tradition of English Calvinism.

*See also:* Conference Movement

*Further Reading*

Patrick Collinson, John Craig, and Brett Usher, eds., *Conferences and Combination Lectures in the Elizabethan Church: Dedham and Bury St. Edmunds, 1582–1590* (Woodbridge, Eng., 2003); David Como, "Puritans, Predestination and the Construction of Orthodoxy in Early Seventeenth-Century England," in Peter Lake and Michael C. Questier, eds., *Conformity and Orthodoxy in the English Church, c. 1560–1660* (Woodbridge, Eng., 2000).

*Brett Usher*

# D

## Danforth, Thomas (ca. 1623–1699)

One of the lay leaders in the settlement of New England. He was born in Framlingham, Suffolk, in 1623 and moved to Massachusetts in 1635 when his family followed the Reverend Thomas Shepard to New England. Thomas was admitted to Shepard's Cambridge, Massachusetts, congregation in 1643 and was admitted to freemanship (the franchise) in the same year. He soon was chosen to various local offices, and in 1657 and 1658 he represented Cambridge in the colony's General Court. Meanwhile, in 1650 he began a long service to Harvard College, as treasurer and later as steward.

In 1659 Danforth was chosen one of the Bay Colony's assistants (a magistrate and member of the upper house of the General Court), and he continued to serve in that role for twenty years. During King Philip's War he became very unpopular in some quarters for his support of the "praying Indians" who had become Christian and were committed to the colony's defense. In 1679 he was chosen deputy governor of Massachusetts and was reelected to that position until the surrender of the charter in 1685. During this period he was a strong defender of the old charter and opposed any concessions to the English government. Following the 1689 uprising against the Dominion of New England, he again assumed the office of deputy governor. Due to the age of Governor Simon Bradstreet, Danforth was effectively the colony's chief executive until the new charter was granted to Massachusetts in 1692.

In religious matters, Danforth was generally a strong defender of the traditional ways of New England Puritanism. He was a fervent enemy of Roman Catholicism and supported harsh measures against Baptists and Quakers. On the other hand, he supported the reform of church membership known as the Half-Way Covenant, seeing the new policy as a means of extending the exercise of church discipline. As a magistrate, he was involved in one of the early examinations of those accused of witchcraft in 1692, but he avoided further involvement and was critical of the subsequent proceedings.

*See also:* King Philip's War
*Further Reading*
*American National Biography* (New York, 1999);
    *Oxford Dictionary of National Biography*
    (Oxford, 2004).

*Francis J. Bremer*

## Darley Family

The Darleys were a Yorkshire family that strongly supported the puritan cause. Sir Richard Darley, aided by his sons Henry and Richard, sheltered the Reverend Thomas Shepard when he was hiding from the authorities prior to his emigration to Massachusetts.

Henry Darley (ca. 1596–ca. 1671) studied at Cambridge University and Gray's Inn. He was a subscriber to various puritan colonial ventures, including the Massachusetts Bay Company, the Saybrook group, and the Providence Island Company, and showed a strong interest in the affairs of New England. He was involved in discussions with the Scottish Covenanters and briefly imprisoned for that in the autumn of 1640. He was a friend and ally of John Pym in the Long Parliament. He remained active in the various parliaments until excluded from the second Protectorate Parliament.

Henry's younger brother Richard was a Merchant Taylor in London in the 1630s. He was recruited to the Long Parliament in 1645 and was generally allied with his brother over the following decade. Following Pride's Purge, when troops of the New Model Army under Colonel Thomas Pride forcibly ejected from Parliament all those who still wanted to negotiate with Charles I, he was in contact with some of the leading advocates of a return to republican forms such as Sir Henry Vane and Henry Neville.

*Further Reading*
Richard Greaves and Robert Zaller, eds.,
   *Biographical Dictionary of British Radicals in the
   Seventeenth Century*, vol. 1 (Brighton, Eng.,
   1982).

*Francis J. Bremer*

## Davenport, John (1597–1670)
Puritan clergyman; a major figure in that reform movement on both sides of the Atlantic.

### England and the Netherlands
Born in Coventry, Warwickshire, he experienced a religious conversion as a young man, after which he matriculated at Merton College, Oxford, in 1613. Two years later he transferred to Magdalen, Oxford, which was known for its puritan sympathies. Davenport left the university before receiving a degree in order to accept a chaplaincy at Hilton Castle, Durham. In 1619 he became curate at St. Lawrence Jewry in the city of London, and in 1624 he was elected vicar of the London parish of St. Stephen's, Coleman Street. Davenport conformed to the liturgical practices of the church, convinced that differences over such matters must be subordinated to the need for a united Calvinist front

*John Davenport, clergyman from Coventry, England, who emigrated to Boston in 1637 and helped found the New Haven Colony in 1638. (Bettmann/Corbis)*

against Catholicism and Arminianism. In 1625 he was awarded both the B.D. and M.A. degrees by Magdalen, Oxford.

The spread of anti-Calvinism in the church, coupled with the rise of a new ceremonialism, drove Davenport toward nonconformity. The failure of England's monarchs to support the Protestant cause on the continent led him to join critics of the government's foreign policy. In 1626 Davenport helped to organize the Feoffees for Impropriations, a corporation that sought to spread puritan influence by purchasing church livings and awarding them to zealous preachers. In that same year he joined with Richard Sibbes, Thomas Taylor, and William Gouge in circulating a letter calling for contributions to aid Protestant refugees from the Thirty Years' War.

In 1633 Davenport joined with Thomas Goodwin, Philip Nye, William Twisse, and other conforming puritans in a meeting at the Ockley, Surrey, home of Henry Whitfield. The meeting had been called to persuade John Cotton and Thomas

Hooker to conform to disputed practices in order to maintain their livings in the church. The outcome, however, was that Davenport himself was persuaded that the demands of the church had become too great and that nonconformity was required of puritan consciences. In consequence, he left England for the Netherlands in December of that year. There he became engaged in a dispute within the Amsterdam church of English exiles. John Paget, whose views were presbyterian, was suspicious of Davenport's congregational principles. Davenport's *Church Government and Church-Covenant Discussed* (1643) and *The Power of the Congregational Churches Asserted and Vindicated* (1672) were written at this time, though printed later. Davenport returned secretly to England in 1636 to prepare to migrate to America.

New England
Accompanied by members of his former congregation of St. Stephen's, Davenport arrived in Boston, Massachusetts, in June 1637. He participated in the Cambridge Synod and the examination of Anne Hutchinson, and advised on the formation of Harvard College. In 1638 he and his followers founded the town and colony of Quinnipiac, later renamed New Haven. The new colony closely reflected Davenport's belief in congregations rigorously restricted to the elect and in civil affairs strongly controlled by the godly.

Following the outbreak of England's Puritan Revolution, Davenport was invited to sit in the Westminster Assembly of Divines, convened in England in 1643 to propose a reform of the national church. He chose to stay in America and offer advice from afar. He was the spokesman for the New England clergy in *An Answer of the Elders of Several Churches in New England* (1643), which sought to explain colonial polity. In other writings he continued to defend Congregationalism from both Presbyterian and sectarian attacks. When the Cromwellian regime collapsed, he was instrumental in providing refuge for the proscribed regicides Edward Whalley and William Goffe. In a series of sermons published as *The Saints Anchor-Hold, in All Storms and Tempests* (1661) he urged the New

Haven faithful to remain committed to their mission despite the Stuart Restoration.

Davenport unsuccessfully opposed the merger of New Haven with the more liberal Connecticut colony in 1662. He was the foremost opponent of the Half-Way Covenant. His career ended in controversy following his acceptance in 1667 of a call to replace the deceased John Wilson as pastor of the First Church of Boston. His claim to have been released for the new post by his New Haven church led to charges of deception. And his strong conservative stand caused a split in his new congregation, triggering a highly charged debate over the autonomy of local congregations, a debate that was further inflamed by his election sermon to the Massachusetts legislature in 1669. He died in March of the following year of a paralytic stroke.

*See also:* English Puritanism in the Netherlands, Feoffees for Impropriations, Half-Way Covenant, New Haven, Predestination
*Further Reading*
Isabel M. Calder, *The Letters of John Davenport* (New Haven, 1938).

*Francis J. Bremer*

## Dent(e), Arthur (ca. 1553–1603)
Church of England clergyman and one of the most popular religious authors of his time. Dent was born at Melton Mowbray, Leicestershire. He graduated B.A. in 1576 from Christ's College, Cambridge. On 17 December 1580 he was instituted rector of South Shoebury, Essex, on the presentation of Robert, the second Lord Rich, grandfather of Robert Rich, the second Earl of Warwick.

The evidence for Dent's involvement in the politico-religious agitation of the 1580s is conflicting, but he was certainly in trouble for refusing the surplice and was involved in discussions about the Book of Discipline (1585–1587). His temperament was, however, essentially irenic, and his ability to edify rural congregations legendary. His *Sermon of Repentance* (1582) was reprinted about thirty-nine times up to 1642. His third published work, *The Plaine-Mans Path-Way to Heaven* (1601)— "wherein every man may clearly see whether he shall be saved or damned"—reached a twenty-fifth edition by 1640. It thus became one of the most frequently reprinted spiritual manuals of its time, and it influenced both John Bunyan, author of the late seventeenth-century classic *Pilgrims Progress*, and Richard Baxter, another influential writer. A forty-first edition appeared as late as 1831. His fourth work, *The Ruine of Rome: or An Exposition upon the whole Revelation,* was with the printer when he died of fever at South Shoebury in January 1603. Ezekiel Culverwell saw it through the press, adding a dedication to Robert, third Lord Rich. It reached a tenth edition by 1656 and found favor with the Evangelical Movement, being reprinted five times between 1798 and 1841. Seven posthumous works appeared during the decade following Dent's death, some perhaps spurious attempts by unscrupulous printers to profit from his popularity.

*See also:* Puritan Best-Sellers
*Further Reading*
Patrick Collinson, John Craig, and Brett Usher, eds., *Conferences and Combination Lectures in the Elizabethan Church: Dedham and Bury St. Edmunds, 1582–1590* (Woodbridge, Eng., 2003); Ian Green, *Print and Protestantism in Early Modern England* (Oxford, 2000).

*Brett Usher*

## Dering, Edward (ca. 1540–1576)

A pattern for the generations of puritan ministers who followed during the period after his early and untimely death. He was a bold preacher who combined the stentorian pulpit style of the Scottish reformer John Knox (they were bracketed together by John Field) with the "affectionate" pastoral skills typical of puritan "practical divinity." Dering came from a family of ancient Kentish gentry, and he was the great-uncle of the prominent Civil War Parliamentarian and antiquarian Sir Edward Dering, who was named for him. He added to this silver spoon in his mouth a golden reputation as a scholar, reckoned to be the best Grecian in England and chosen to make the Greek oration before Queen Elizabeth in Cambridge in 1564. His college was Christ's (B.A. 1560, M.A. 1563, B.D. 1568, fellow,

1560–1570), and he was one of those who turned it into the godliest house in Cambridge (before the founding of Emmanuel). But the imperative of his religious earnestness led him to hide his learning under the bushel of an accessible preaching style and to spit in the face of the prospects held out before him, as chaplain to the duke of Norfolk and well regarded by Archbishop Matthew Parker.

In 1570 he burned his bridges with both Parker and Lord Burghley in letters of stinging rebuke. And he preached a sermon at court before the queen, which should have launched his career but instead made him persona non grata. No Elizabethan sermon was more celebrated (or notorious) or more often reprinted (sixteen editions by 1603). Adopting the role of Nathan in his confrontation with David, Dering held Elizabeth personally responsible for the sorry state of her church. But he continued to have powerful friends in high places, and even Edwin Sandys, as bishop of London, found it impossible to resist the pressure from these friends to protect and even advance Dering. In 1572, the year of the puritan call for religious reform, the *Admonition to the Parliament,* Sandys made him divinity lecturer in St. Paul's, much to the queen's disgust. Dering dissociated himself from some of the principles of the Admonitioners, declared that he was no nonconformist (although he defended the consciences of those who were), and handled the presbyterian issue carefully. The essence of his kind of Puritanism was an ardent zeal for the substance of the gospel and its propagation. In 1572 Dering married Anne Locke, a wealthy widow and former companion and confidante of Knox. She was obliged to share her husband with the many noble and gentle ladies to whom he administered spiritual comfort. They reciprocated with physical ministrations that became more necessary as Dering began to succumb to tuberculosis, from which he died on 26 June 1576, in a set-piece godly deathbed, surrounded by the preachers who recorded his last words.

*Further Reading*
Patrick Collinson, "A Mirror of Elizabethan Puritanism: The Life and Letters of 'Godly Master Dering,'" in Collinson, *Godly People:*

*Essays on English Protestantism and Puritanism* (London, 1983).

*Patrick Collinson*

## D'Ewes, Sir Simonds (1602–1649)

Baronet, antiquarian, scholar, numismatist, lawyer, and country gentleman; best known for his detailed diary of the Long Parliament from 1640 to 1645. An indefatigable collector of books and manuscripts, he planned to write various works he never completed. They included a history of England from the earliest times through the Norman Conquest, an Anglo-Saxon lexicon, a study of Roman coins, and an account of the Pelagian heresy. Despite his social and political conservatism, his fervent opposition to Arminianism shaped his political outlook. His schoolboy letters to his parents contain many indications of his developing puritan religiosity. His New Year's gift to his mother in 1615 consisted of notes taken on sermons he had heard. D'Ewes's *Autobiography,* written in 1637 (but not published until 1845), provides further signs, especially in his account of his time at St. John's College, Cambridge (1618–1620). Required by his lawyer father to leave Cambridge and prepare for a legal career at the Middle Temple, he worked hard at his legal studies, while also exemplifying the unquenchable puritan thirst for "godly" sermons and "godly conference" with like-minded friends.

In London, he heard at least two sermons (and often three) each Sunday. In his own eyes, however, his sermon-gadding and earnest reading of the Bible and the works of numerous Calvinist divines were merely halting first steps on a spiritual search that did not reach its goal until he heard Abraham Gibson preach in Kediton, Suffolk, on 4 July 1625. In a treatise on what he called the "indications" or evidences of salvation composed in 1628, D'Ewes said Gibson's sermon had finally given him a full understanding of the doctrine of predestination, an understanding he then further confirmed by reading *The Life of Faith* by Samuel Ward of Ipswich.

An avid news buff, D'Ewes invariably linked the struggles against the Arminians in England with those of the anti-Habsburg forces in the Thirty Years' War. As sheriff of Suffolk (1639–1640), he dragged his feet on the collection of ship money, which many viewed as an unconstitutional levy in the form it was being requested. Representing Sudbury, Suffolk, in the Long Parliament, D'Ewes spoke out against ship money, the Earl of Strafford, and Laud's Canons of 1640. Although he grew increasingly troubled by what seemed to him the illegal proposals of the men he called the "fiery spirits" and even quarreled with them, his hatred of the Laudians, whom he considered neo-Pelagians, kept him in the Parliamentarian camp. In 1645 he allied himself with the Dissenting Brethren of the Westminster Assembly by publishing a short treatise (*The Primitive Practise for Preserving Truth*), in which he argued against the forcing of "tender consciences" in inessential matters in religion. Ousted from Parliament by Colonel Pride on 6 December 1648, he died about four months later.

*Further Reading*

J. Sears McGee, "Sir Simonds D'Ewes and the 'Poitovin Cholick': Persecution, Toleration, and the Mind of a Puritan Member of the Long Parliament," in *Canadian Journal of History* 38 (2003), 481–491; S. P. Salt, "Sir Simonds D'Ewes and the Levying of Ship Money, 1635–1640," *Historical Journal* 37 (1994), 253–287.

*J. Sears McGee*

## Dickson, David (ca. 1583–1663)

Leading Scottish Presbyterian divine during the early covenanting period. His pious Glaswegian parents first directed him in the same path as his merchant father, but when David proved less than successful, his parents remembered that they had once promised their child to the ministry. Thereupon he was again set to study. He graduated from the University of Glasgow, where he continued as regent before accepting appointment as minister at Irvine, Ayrshire, in 1618. He quickly became an opponent of episcopacy and ceremonies, leading to an appearance before the High Commission on 29 January 1622. He was temporarily deprived and sent to Turriff, but was restored in July 1623, and not troubled thereafter until near the end of episcopacy.

Dickson was famed for his pastoral work and conversions. His services of Holy Communion were attended from far and wide, and his weekday sermons were instrumental in provoking "the famous Stewarton sickness," as his opponents referred to the religious fervor he inspired. In 1638 he went north to attempt to persuade the divines of Aberdeen to subscribe the National Covenant, and late in the same year he preached on the evils of Arminianism to the Glasgow general assembly, which reinstituted Presbyterianism in the Church of Scotland. In the following years he went on to a professorship of divinity at Glasgow, and then in 1650 at Edinburgh, a post of which he was deprived at the Restoration.

Dickson was a federal theologian, and his publications identified him with the puritan notion of the soul physician who treats sin-sick consciences. His *Truth's Victory over Error* was a question-and-answer approach to teaching the Westminster Confession.

*See also:* National Covenant
*Further Reading*
W. K. Tweedie, ed., *Select Biographies*, 2 vols. (Edinburgh, 1845–1857).

*David Mullan*

## Dod, John (1550–1645)

One of the nationally recognized puritan clergymen of his age. Dod was born in Cheshire and educated at the Cheshire School and then Jesus College, Cambridge, receiving his B.A. in 1576 and his M.A. in 1579. He formed a friendship with Thomas Cartwright and joined with fellow Cambridge scholars, including William Fulke and Laurence Chaderton, in discussions of theology and church reform. In 1585 he took up a pastoral ministry at Hanwell, Oxfordshire. He preached twice on the Sabbath and again on Wednesdays, energetically catechized the town's youth, and participated in a combination lecture in nearby Banbury.

As a result of his nonconformity, Dod was suspended from his living in 1604. He retreated to Northamptonshire, where he was sheltered by Sir Erasmus Dryden. There Dod preached at Canons Ashby and neighboring parishes. King James ordered the bishop of Peterborough to investigate Dod's preaching, and in 1614 he was forced into hiding. When King James died in 1625, Archbishop Abbot lifted Dod's suspension. The Knightley family of nearby Fawsley became Dod's patrons. Other puritan gentlemen contributed to his support, including Christopher Sherland, Viscount Saye and Sele, John Pym, and Sir Nathaniel Rich.

Dod remained a resolute nonconformist. He was a target of his local bishop and then of Archbishop William Laud, but his patrons were able to protect him. He was equally well connected with other puritan clergy throughout the country. Among those he considered his friends were John Preston, Richard Sibbes, and Stephen Egerton. In 1632 John Cotton sought and received his blessing when considering emigration to New England. His influence was spread not only through personal connections, but also through his publications, most notably his *A Plaine and Familiar Exposition of the Ten Commandments* (1603).

Dod was close to many members of the parliamentary leadership of the Long Parliament and was harassed by royalist forces when the Civil War broke out. He died at Fawsley on 19 August 1645.

*See also:* Joan Drake
*Further Reading*
Patrick Collinson, *The Religion of Protestants* (Oxford, 1982); William Haller, *The Rise of Puritanism* (New York, 1938); Tom Webster, *Godly Clergy in Early Stuart England: The Caroline Puritan Movement, c. 1620–1643* (Cambridge, Eng., 1997).

*Francis J. Bremer*

## Downame (Downham), George (d. 1634)

Bishop of Derry. He was the son of William, bishop of Chester, and his birth probably took place after his father's consecration in 1561. He became a fellow of Christ College, Cambridge, and professor of logic in 1585. In 1608 he preached a controversial sermon defending the notion "that the episcopall function is of apostolicall and divine institution" he was equally adamant in his antipopery and in his Calvinist theology. This allegiance aided his elevation to the Irish episcopate at Derry in 1616, where his flock included the Scottish settlers who arrived to populate James I's Ulster Plantation. He experienced some difficulty in 1631 when his anti-Arminian St. Paul's Cross sermon, with an additional section on perseverance, was published; Laud sought to suppress it, not only in England but also in Ireland, which was an arbitrary extension of the 1629 articles on publication of controverted themes. He was a moderate disciplinarian toward both Roman Catholics and Presbyterians. His cathedral was completed only in 1633, the gift of the London corporation.

*See also:* International Puritanism, Irish Puritanism
*Further Reading*
*Oxford Dictionary of National Biography* (Oxford, 2004).

*David Mullan*

## Dowsing, William (ca. 1596–1668)

Iconoclast. He was of a yeoman family in Suffolk and moved to Dedham, a puritan parish in the Stour Valley around 1642. He had a remarkable library, and his learning went well beyond his grammar school education, but he would be little known if it were not for fifteen months as commissioner for removing the monuments of idolatry and superstition from all the churches of the eastern association. He acquired this post in December 1643 from the Earl of Manchester, probably through the connections of his lecturer, Matthew Newcomen. During his time as commissioner, he conducted a remarkable inspection and improvement of most of the churches of Cambridgeshire, most of Suffolk, and some of north Essex and south Norfolk, the latter with deputies appointed by himself. Copies of journals contain detailed notes of this systematic "reformation," which included all sixteen Cambridge colleges. He was so overwhelmed by the scale of the idolatry of Kings' College chapel that his work there was not even begun. Elsewhere he worked hard to level chancels, remove "superstitious pictures," take down crosses, and remove inscriptions on tombs that suggested the efficacy of prayers to and for the dead.

As Manchester's star waned and Dowsing became increasingly distressed with the internal squabbles within the Parliamentarian cause and concerned about sectarian liberty, he became less active. In 1646 he seems to have returned to Dedham, still devoted to puritanism but with no public role to take. He maintained his faith, one of many feeling betrayed by the failures of the 1650s but still enough of a puritan to earn fines under the Conventicles Act.

*See also:* Iconoclasm and Iconography
*Further Reading*
Trevor Cooper, ed., *The Journal of William Dowsing: Iconoclasm in East Anglia during the English Civil War*, Ecclesiastical Society (Woodbridge, Eng., 1999); John S. Morrill, "William Dowsing, the Bureaucratic Puritan," in John S. Morrill, Paul Slack, and Daniel Woolf, eds., *Public Duty and Private Conscience in Seventeenth-Century England: Essays Presented to G. E. Aylmer* (Oxford, 1993); John S. Morrill, "William Dowsing and Civil War Iconoclasm," in Trevor Cooper, ed., *The Journal of William Dowsing: Iconoclasm in East Anglia during the English Civil War*, Ecclesiastical Society (Woodbridge, Eng., 1999).

*Tom Webster*

## Drake, Joan (Joanna) (1585–1625)

Sufferer from a well-publicized case of spiritual despair. Joan Tothill Drake was born in Amersham, Buckinghamshire, in 1585, and she died there at her parents' estate in 1625. Under paternal pressure, Joan Tothill with great resistance wed the Surrey esquire Francis Drake in 1603.

A traumatic experience giving birth to her first child prompted her first episode of a prolonged and violent bout of spiritual despair, lasting almost until her death in 1625. As described in Thomas Hooker's 1638 account, *The Poor Doubting Christian Drawn Unto Christ* and in Jasper Hartwell's 1647 version, *Trodden-Down Strength by the God of Strength, Or, Mrs. Drake Revived,* Joan Drake's despair manifested an acutely Calvinist symptomatology. She displayed a nearly unshakable conviction of her own damnation. She alternately attributed this conviction to an absence of any significant signs of regeneration and to her supposed commission of the sin against the Holy Ghost. The knowing and willful rejection of the truth and grace of Christ's divinity (Matthew 12:31–32), known as the sin against the Holy Ghost, was feared by early modern Christians as the ultimate unpardonable sin. Incorporating elements of early modern melancholia and possession cases, her spiritual disorder also included communications from Satan regarding her reprobation, a rejection of church attendance and all forms of household piety, attempts to injure herself by cutting her arms and swallowing pins, and episodes of verbal and physical aggression and blasphemy.

The stature of her family made Joan Drake's case famous among the early Stuart Puritan elite. The attention attracted by her condition and the eagerness of the Drake and Tothill families to provide Mrs. Drake with around-the-clock pastoral care turned her despair into a platform for clerical advancement, a test case for Puritan persuasiveness, and a defense of predestinarian piety. Several distinguished Puritan clergymen wrote and visited; the famous Puritan divines John Dod and Thomas Hooker were successively retained by the Drake family to board with the family and minister to Mrs. Drake. Although eventually successful in moderating her condition, Dod endured abuse and assault with a bedpost from his long-term pastoral client. Stepping in for Dod in 1618, the young Hooker reaped more apparent rewards when he effectively plied Mrs. Drake with Ramist proofs. His work with Mrs. Drake helped to establish his developing reputation. Dod and Hooker's combined efforts calmed her symptoms and reintegrated her into the rituals of church worship and private piety, culminating in a dramatic conversion experience shortly before her death.

Joan Drake's case reflected the gender dynamics of early Stuart pastoral care and the role of despair in Puritan culture. Puritan tropes of a feminized surrender to God had a social context in the Drake case, where salvation was styled as submission to male authority both human and divine. Joan Drake's story was also part of a Puritan discourse about damnation and despair, associated with popular accounts of the sixteenth-century Italian Protestant Francis Spira, who died of despair after recanting his beliefs to the Inquisition. Joan Drake's story shared many of the conventionalized narrative elements of the Spira account. However, whereas the Spira narrative was an account of unrelieved despair and the pastoral failure of a papist priesthood, Joan Drake's narrative was clearly a contrasting tale of conquered despair and the potency of a Puritan ministry.

*See also:* Spiritual Healing
*Further Reading*
Michael MacDonald, "The Fearefull Estate of Francis Spira: Narrative, Identity and Emotion in Early Modern England," *Journal of British Studies* 31 (1992), 32–61; Amanda Porterfield, *Female Piety in Puritan New England: The Emergence of Religious Humanism* (New York, 1992).

*Michelle Wolfe*

## Dudley, Thomas (1576–1653)

Colonial leader. Thomas Dudley was born near Northampton, England. His father evidently died in military service, but friends and family saw to it that he received a grammar school education and was placed in the household of the Earl of Northampton. He volunteered to fight for the Protestant champion Henry of Navarre in France's Wars of Religion but saw no action during his stay in that country.

At some point after his return from France, Dudley became steward to the Earl of Lincoln, whose gratitude and friendship he earned by rigorously managing the earl's affairs so that he was cleared of debt. Dudley himself prospered in this position, and he was able to send two of his sons to Emmanuel College, Cambridge. He met John Preston, the master of Emmanuel, and called upon him for advice on various occasions. When he retired from the earl's service, he settled in Boston, Lincolnshire, where he was a member of the parish of St. Botolph's, whose pastor was John Cotton.

In the late 1620s Dudley became involved in the discussions within the puritan community about emigration to New England, and he was one of a number of Boston area laymen who committed themselves to the enterprise. The Massachusetts Bay Company chose him as deputy governor of the colony, and he accompanied John Winthrop to Massachusetts on the *Arbella* in 1630. He settled in New Towne when that community was intended to be the capital of the colony and felt betrayed when the decision was to locate the capital in Boston instead. He served thirteen one-year terms as deputy governor and was elected governor of Massachusetts in 1634, 1640, 1645, and 1650. He died in 1653. Among his children the one to achieve the most fame was his daughter, Anne Dudley Bradstreet.

Dudley was more precise and rigid than the moderate Winthrop in his approach to the issues facing the colonists, and he often quarreled with his more famous colleague. On more than one occasion other leaders had to mediate disputes between the two men. Dudley was one of the leaders in prosecuting Roger Williams and Anne Hutchinson for their heterodox views. When Hutchinson claimed that she had derived her ideas from John Cotton, Dudley sharply questioned the Boston minister, despite the good relationship they had enjoyed in the old Boston.

*See also:* Anne Dudley Bradstreet, Massachusetts—An Account of the First Year of the Great Migration (in Primary Sources)
*Further Reading*
Robert Charles Anderson, ed., *The Great Migration Begins: Immigrants to New England, 1620–1633*, 3 vols. (Boston, 1995); Francis J. Bremer, *John Winthrop: America's Forgotten Founding Father* (New York, 2004).

*Francis J. Bremer*

## Dugard, Thomas (1608–1683)

Puritan clergyman. Dugard was born in Worcestershire and educated, with his brother William (who became a noted schoolmaster and bookseller), at the Puritan college Sidney Sussex, Cambridge, where their uncle Richard was a tutor. Thomas obtained his M.A. in 1633, and through the patronage of the second Lord Brooke he was appointed as master of Warwick School, following an introduction from Thomas Gataker, a former fellow of Sidney. Dugard was ordained in 1636 but remained as a schoolteacher until appointed to the rich living of Barford, Warwickshire, in 1648. Dugard's diary (covering exactly ten years, from March 1632 to 1642) provides a vivid picture of the sociability of the godly in troubled times.

Dugard's networks comprehended local Puritan ministers and schoolmasters who swapped pulpits, dined together after lectures, edited each other's manuscripts, and debated the dilemmas of conformity, emigration, and attitudes to the Scots. Through Brooke, Dugard was also acquainted with ministers and laymen who were or became prominent national figures in the opposition to Charles I, such as Simeon Ashe, Peter Sterry, John Pym, and Lord Saye and Sele. As rector of Barford in the 1640s and 1650s, Dugard followed a conventionally mainstream Puritan path of opposition to sectarianism and participation in quasi-Presbyterian structures in Warwickshire. Unlike many of his friends, he conformed in 1662, and he died, still rector of Barford, in 1683. Shortly before his death, he had been recognized by the heralds as a gentleman. He published a collection of verse and two tracts as well as contributing prefatory verses to the works of friends such as Ashe and Samuel Clarke.

*Further Reading*
Ann Hughes, "Thomas Dugard and His Circle in the 1630s—a Parliamentary-Puritan Connexion," *Historical Journal* 29 (1986), 771–793.

*Ann Hughes*

## Dunster, Henry (1609–1659)

Puritan clergyman and president of Harvard College. Dunster was born in Bury, Lancashire, and educated at Magdalene College, Cambridge, where he received his B.A. in 1631 and his M.A. in

1634. While there he was influenced by the preaching of William Perkins and Thomas Goodwin. He returned to his native Bury, where he was curate and schoolmaster from 1634 until he migrated to New England in the summer of 1640. Shortly after his arrival in Massachusetts he was elected president of Harvard College. The college had been shaken by the dismissal of Nathaniel Eaton, whose harsh regime had attracted universal disapproval.

Dunster shaped Harvard after the model of the English Cambridge colleges. He introduced the study of Oriental languages. Under his guidance Harvard achieved international respect, while Dunster himself established a wide reputation as a Hebrew scholar. His expertise in that language led to his involvement in the composition of the Bay Psalm Book. Dunster supported efforts to educate Native Americans, and among the college buildings he was responsible for was the Indian College where it was hoped that natives would be educated for the ministry.

Dunster came to believe that there was no scriptural justification for infant baptism. He was forced to resign as college president in October 1654 when he refused to present his son for baptism and would not agree to keep his opposition to infant baptism to himself. After a brief stay in Charlestown, he settled in Scituate, in the Plymouth Colony, where he ministered until his death in 1659.

*See also:* Anabaptists, Harvard College, Plymouth Colony
*Further Reading*
Samuel Eliot Morison, *The Founding of Harvard College* (Cambridge, MA; 1936).

*Francis J. Bremer*

### Duston, Hannah (1657–1737)

New England colonist captured by Native Americans. She was born Hannah Emerson and lived in Haverhill, Massachusetts, on the New England frontier. She married Thomas Duston in 1677, and the couple had thirteen children.

In March 1697 Haverhill was attacked by Native Americans. While Thomas was away from home and able to escape, Hannah's infant child was brutally killed, and she was taken captive and marched north with other colonists who had been captured. During a night when the war party was encamped in the New Hampshire wilderness, Hannah, together with two fellow captives, killed and scalped their captors and escaped back to the puritan settlements. Cotton Mather told her story and compared her to the Old Testament woman Jael, who saved Israel at a time of trial. She was widely applauded by the colonists, who were inspired by her courage in a time when fears of native attacks were widespread.

*See also:* Mary White Rowlandson
*Further Reading*
Carol Berkin, *First Generations: Women in Colonial America* (New York, 1996).

*Francis J. Bremer*

### Dyer, Mary (ca. 1610–1660)

New England dissident and executed Quaker. Mary Dyer emigrated from England to Massachusetts Bay with her husband, William, in 1634 or 1635. They settled in Boston and joined the First Church. Mary was one of the first followers of Anne Hutchinson and followed her into exile in Rhode Island. In 1638, as Anne Hutchinson was excommunicated, it became known that Dyer had given birth to a stillborn, "monster" child. News that she had borne a deformed child quickly spread throughout the colony and beyond. Modern science indicates that the dead child probably suffered from spina bifida along with other abnormalities, but to the Puritans the "monster" was seen as a supernatural sign of God's displeasure with the antinomians.

In 1652 the Dyers returned to England, where Mary became a Quaker. Returning to New England in 1657, Dyer was imprisoned in Boston for being a Quaker, a capital offense, but her husband was able to secure her release. The next year she was expelled from New Haven for preaching her Quaker beliefs. When Dyer returned to Boston to visit two imprisoned Friends (to give Quakers the name they preferred) in 1659, she was again arrested. Dyer was banished and warned never to return.

The Dyers briefly settled in Rhode Island, but Mary again returned to Boston. Imprisoned, Dyer had exhausted the patience and tolerance of the magistrates. She was executed along with two other Quakers on 1 June 1660. A statute of Mary Dyer currently stands outside the State House in Boston.

*See also:* Law in Puritan New England, Mary Dyer's Challenge to the Massachusetts Bay Colony (in Primary Sources)
*Further Reading*
Ruth Talbot Plimpton, *Mary Dyer: Biography of a Rebel Quaker* (Boston, 1994).

*Francis J. Bremer*

## Dyke, Daniel (d. 1614)

With his brother Jeremiah Dyke, a good example of how puritanism gained in respectability as the Jacobean age succeeded the Elizabethan. Their father William Dyke was a true stormy petrel of Elizabethan puritanism, pursued from pillar to post by Bishop John Aylmer of London, although protected by Lady Anne Bacon and, thanks to Lady Anne, her brother-in-law Lord Burghley, her son Anthony, and the Earl of Essex. Daniel was probably the eldest of William's five sons, which would place his birth somewhat before 1584, when Jeremiah was baptized. He matriculated at St. John's College, Cambridge, about 1593, proceeded B.A. in 1596 and M.A. in 1599, from Sidney Sussex College, where he became a fellow in 1606. He took his B.D. at about the same time.

Not much is known of Daniel Dyke outside his religious writings, most of which were published posthumously by Jeremiah. The account in the original *Dictionary of National Biography* is thoroughly confused, mixing up Daniel with his father. Dyke seems to have remained a bachelor, and there is no evidence that he was ever beneficed. It was the patronage of great houses that counted, and supported him: the patronage of Lord and Lady Harington, their son Lord Harington, Dyke's contemporary at Sidney, and a close friend of Prince Henry (oldest son of James I, who died before he could inherit the throne); and his sister Lucy Harington, who as Countess of Bedford was one of the greatest of Jacobean literary patrons. He seems to have served as the Haringtons' chaplain at Combe Abbey near Coventry, where Princess Elizabeth was brought up between 1603 and 1608, and after that at Kew, where the Haringtons had charge of the princess's own household. After Harington and the princess fled from Combe to Coventry on 7 November 1605, in the aftermath of the Gunpowder Plot, Dyke preached before Elizabeth a series of thanksgiving sermons, dealing with that and other recent deliverances in England's providential history, and dedicated to the princess, describing himself as a daily eyewitness of her virtues. Prince Henry, the first Lord Harington, the second Lord Harington, and Daniel Dyke himself all died within a year of each other.

Among Dyke's works, *The mystery of self-deceiving* (dedicated by Jeremiah to the Countess of Bedford, 1615) acquired some fame, went through at least twelve editions, and was much admired by Thomas Fuller. As *La sonde de la conscience*, it achieved a French edition at Geneva, in 1636. According to his brother Jeremiah, Daniel kept a spiritual diary in which he recorded every night the sins of that day, on the Sabbath the sins of the past week, and at the end of the month the "whole transgressions" of that month. The truth is, Jeremiah wrote, the world was not worthy of him.

*Further Reading*
Daniel Dyke, *Certaine comfortable sermons* (1616); *The workes of that late reverend divine D. Dike* (1635); *The second and last part of the workes of D. Dyke* (1633).

*Patrick Collinson*

## Dyke, Jeremiah (1584–1639)

Like his brother Daniel Dyke, one of those divines who placed puritanism in the mainstream of Jacobean life, moving, as it were, across the tracks, religiously and socially, from the radical nonconformity of their father, William Dyke. Jeremiah was baptized at Coggeshall in Essex in 1584, entered Emmanuel College, Cambridge, in 1598, but almost immediately moved to Sidney Sussex, where he took his B.A. in 1602, his M.A. in 1605, and became a fellow, along with brother Daniel.

After a brief incumbency in Cambridgeshire, he became vicar of Epping in 1609 and remained there until his death, thirty years later. The church was in a part of the parish called Epping Upland, two miles from a growing center of population and activity on the road from London into the eastern counties, where there had been a chapel of ease for some centuries. Dyke established a weekday lecture in this chapel that attracted a large auditory, so large that it became necessary to enlarge the building, by public subscription. It is a remarkable fact that Bishop George Montaigne of London, an Arminian and no friend to puritanism, warmly supported the project to extend the chapel to accommodate this sermon-gadding company. On 28 October 1622, Dyke preached at the consecration of the new chapel, dedicating the sermon to his loving and beloved people, and signing off as "your loving Pastor." On 5 April 1628, Dyke preached a fast sermon before the House of Commons, a jeremiad full of warnings of God's judgments, including Halley's Comet, which had appeared in 1618, and the famous "book fish," a portent discovered in Cambridge market in 1626, and of warnings against the departure of "old Truth" in the increase of Arminianism. Dyke was given a silver tankard for his pains. He also preached and published a Paul's Cross sermon (1619). Other works were dedicated to his patroness Lady Katherine Wentworth, Sir Francis Barrington, and the Earl and Countess of Winchelsea. Jeremiah was devoted to his elder brother Daniel and brought all his works to the press after his death, while his son Daniel repeated the compliment by publishing, within a year of his father's death, his *Divers select sermons* (1640). Jeremiah died a man of some substance, dispensing in his will £560 and much valuable household stuff. His son Daniel became Oliver Cromwell's chaplain and died a Baptist in 1688.

*Further Reading*
Jeremiah Dyke, *Two Sermons Preached in 1622 and 1628 by the Rev. Jeremiah Dyke*, ed. B. Winstone (1896); Alexandra Walsham, *Providence in Early Modern England* (Oxford, 1999).

*Patrick Collinson*

## Dyke, William (d. 1608)

Father of Daniel Dyke and one of the more outspoken puritan clergy of the Elizabethan reign. Little is known of William's background and early career. He appears in the historical record as having brushes with the church authorities in Great Yarmouth, Norfolk. In the mid-1580s he was in Coggeshall in Essex. He moved on to the parish of St. Albans, and then to Hemel Hempstead in the diocese of Lincoln. He managed to avoid suspension through the intercession of powerful patrons, including Lady Anne Bacon and her brother-in-law Lord Burghley.

*Further Reading*
*Oxford Dictionary of National Biography* (Oxford, 2004).

*Francis J. Bremer*

# E

## Eaton, John (ca. 1575–ca. 1631)

Minister; one of the first and most prominent preachers of antinomian religious beliefs in early modern England. Born in Kent and educated at Oxford, he was presented to the vicarage of Wickham Market, Suffolk, around 1604. At some point in the next decade, he began to flirt with the heterodox religious beliefs that later made him notorious. Having concluded that mainstream puritan religiosity represented a species of legalism and works-righteousness (that is, righteousness gained by doing good works), Eaton developed his own idiosyncratic version of the theology of grace, which emphasized the gracious, unearned, and passive aspects of justification, and which downplayed, or even denied, the role of the moral law in salvation and the Christian life. Deprived of his benefice in 1619 for his purported antinomianism, Eaton went on to develop a cult following in London and elsewhere, drawing with him disciples who shared his disaffection with mainstream piety and who embraced his version of Christian truth. Together with other like-minded ministers, such as Robert Towne and John Traske, Eaton used pulpit and manuscript to forge a small but vibrant antinomian community, centered in London, which presented a pastoral challenge to the hegemony of dominant puritan ministers. After his death, this community survived and reproduced itself, exploding into the open in the early 1640s, and helping to contribute to the emergence of some of the more extreme forms of sectarianism that flourished in the revolutionary decades.

*See also:* Antinomianism
*Further Reading*
Theodore Dwight Bozeman, *The Precisianist Strain: Disciplinary Religion and Antinomian Backlash in Puritanism to 1638* (Chapel Hill, 2004); David Como, *Blown by the Spirit: Puritanism and the Emergence of an Antinomian Underground in Pre–Civil War England* (Stanford, 2004).

*David Como*

## Eaton, Nathaniel (1609–1674)

Educator and clergyman. Eaton was born in Coventry, Cheshire, England. He matriculated at Trinity, Cambridge, but left before gaining a degree. He then studied briefly under William Ames at the University of Franeker. While in the Netherlands he published a thesis setting out the Sabbatarian views of various theologians. He returned to England after 1634 and became a schoolmaster, teaching briefly in two separate places.

In June 1637 Nathaniel accompanied his brothers Theophilus and Samuel to New England. Eaton was invited to head the new college that was to be named after John Harvard, and took up that position in the fall of 1638. A respected scholar, he got the college off to a good academic start. He gave the school its name and created Harvard Yard. But his regime was a very harsh one. Along with his wife, Elizabeth, he cheated the students by providing them inadequate and poor quality food and drink with the funds allocated to him for that purpose. More seriously, he repeatedly and excessively employed corporal punishment on the students. One year after he assumed this post, the colony's General Court brought him up on charges of maladministration. The court fined him and removed him as head of the college, after which he fled to Virginia. Subsequent examination of the college affairs revealed that Eaton had both embezzled funds and run up unpaid debts in excess of £1,000.

Eaton had little success in Virginia. He next appeared on the Continent, where he received both the Ph.D. and M.D. at the University of Padua in 1647. He then returned to England. His activities over the next decade are unknown, but following the Restoration he conformed to the Church of England and was appointed vicar of Bishop's Castle in Shropshire. In 1665 and again in 1674 he was arrested for debt. On the first occasion he attempted to escape his predicament by perjury and bribery. On the latter occasion he was imprisoned in Southwark, where he died that same year.

See also: Harvard College
*Further Reading*
Samuel Eliot Morison, *The Founding of Harvard College* (Cambridge, MA; 1936).

*Francis J. Bremer*

### Eaton, Samuel (1597–1665)

Puritan Congregationalist clergyman. Eaton was born in the parish of Great Budworth, Cheshire, England in 1597, the son of the vicar of the parish. His education is uncertain, but it is possible that he was a graduate of Magdalene College, Cambridge. He was ordained priest in 1625 and became rector of West Kirby on the Wirral, Cheshire. There and at other places on the Wirral, his puritan practices drew the attention of John Bridgeman, bishop of Chester. He was suspended by the bishop and in about 1634 sailed to Holland, where he joined a group of congregational believers.

Eaton returned to England, as the Dutch climate undermined his health. He found that in his absence he had been fined for nonappearance before the High Commission in York. In 1637, with his brother Theophilus, he sailed for New England, where he was granted land in New Haven. There his congregational views were strengthened. He returned to England in 1640 when he heard that his estate on the Wirral had been destrained for nonpayment of the fine levied by the court at York. By the time he returned, however, the political climate in England was changing, and in a sermon preached at St. John's Church, Chester, in January 1641 he advocated the abolition of episcopacy.

In about 1642 or 1643, Eaton became attached to the regiment of the Parliamentarian Colonel Robert Duckenfield, and by 1647 was chaplain to both Duckenfield's regiment and the garrison at Chester, as well as preacher to the chapel there. It was through Duckenfield's patronage that Eaton, with his fellow Congregationalist preacher, Timothy Taylor, set up the Independent chapel at Duckinfield in Stockport Parish in the east of Cheshire. Eaton resigned his chaplaincy to the Chester garrison and thereafter, with Taylor, drew an enthusiastic congregation that challenged the Presbyterianism in east Cheshire. The Cheshire Presbyterian ministers Henry Newcome and Adam Martindale both recorded the incursions of Eaton's followers into their parishes. Since Eaton had a good reputation as a godly preacher among Presbyterians, Newcome was prepared to hear him preach and to debate church government with him. However, the practice of preaching by lay elders of the church at Duckinfield drew criticism from the Presbyterian clergy.

East Cheshire saw an interplay between the various strands of puritan ideology. Both Independents and Presbyterians viewed with some alarm the rising popularity of the newly emerging Quaker movement, whose influence was beginning to be felt in the northwest of England. In his pamphlet "Quakers Confuted," published in 1654, Eaton entered into a lively and sometimes acrimonious debate with Richard Waller, a Lancashire Quaker, regarding doctrine and church government.

As Eaton held no living, he was not formally ejected, but after the Act of Uniformity of 1662 silenced him, he attended the congregation of John Angier at Denton, Lancashire. He continued to live at Bredbury in Stockport Parish until his death on 9 January 1665. He was buried at Denton on 12 January.

*Further Reading*
R. C. Richardson, *Puritanism in North-West England* (Manchester, Eng., 1992).

*Catherine Nunn*


## Eaton, Theophilus (1590–1658)

One of the wealthiest of the Puritan immigrants to New England; helped found, largely financed, and almost single-handedly ruled the New Haven colony for most of its existence.

Born in Buckinghamshire to a clergyman with high connections in the Elizabethan church, Eaton was sent to London to become a merchant and eventually became an official of the Eastland Company and a royal agent to the Danish court. Eaton was probably brought up with Puritan sympathies, but was willing to tolerate things indifferent, such as kneeling at the Lord's Supper, so long as the church maintained a preaching ministry and a godly communion. In the 1630s, when his spiritual advisor, John Davenport, was forced into exile, and the charter of the Massachusetts Bay Company, of which he was a shareholder, was attacked, Eaton gave up all hope of reformation and organized an emigration to New England.

The group landed in Boston in 1637 and moved on to New Haven, at the mouth of the Quinnipiac River, in 1638. Eaton was instrumental in establishing a political system for the new settlement that restricted the right to vote to regenerate males and a judicial system that eliminated trial by jury. He was then annually elected as first magistrate for the town of New Haven for the rest of his life, and as governor when New Haven became a colony with the addition of new towns.

Eaton ruled with very little opposition. He projected a commanding presence, owned the largest house in town, liberally subsidized the colony's economy, and had a reputation for godliness. But his rule was also responsible. He did not hesitate to employ the gallows when he thought it justified, but the court records show a man more concerned with reclaiming sinners than punishing criminals. When the New Haven church charged his wife with disorderly conduct, slander, and heresy in 1644, he did nothing to spare her the shame of excommunication.

On the evening of his sudden and unexpected death, he repeated his firm determination to remain in New Haven for the rest of his life. His death was a blow from which his colony never fully recovered.

*See also:* New Haven
*Further Reading*
*American National Biography* (New York, 1999); Simeon Baldwin, "Theophilus Eaton: First Governor of the Colony of New Haven," *Papers of the New Haven Colony Historical Society* 7 (1908), 1–33.

*James P. Walsh*


## Edwards, Thomas (1599–1647)

Thomas held rigorously puritan convictions and was a resolute Presbyterian. He branded John Milton a divorcer, and Milton, in return, called him "Shallow Edwards" in his poem, "On the New Forcers of Conscience." But Edwards is remembered by posterity as the author of the most copious denunciation of the Puritan Revolution's radical extremes. He was a polemicist whose tirades and vituperation now earn him significance by providing some of the most detailed accounts of radical puritanism in the period.

Though it is unknown where Edwards was born, he was educated at Queen's College, Cambridge. Having graduated with a B.A. and M.A., he joined Oxford University but continued to live in Cambridge, where he became a university preacher whose severity earned him the title "Young Luther." His unflinching convictions resulted in his imprisonment in February 1627, but he recanted in March 1628 and was released. Edwards soon left Cambridge, however, and received a license to preach at St. Botolph's, Aldgate, in London. His puritanical tendencies soon came to the notice of the authorities, and he was suspended by William

Laud, then the bishop of London. Upon his release he continued his guerrilla preaching against church beautification, the elaboration of church ceremonies, and the emergence of Arminian doctrine and, in July 1640, was prosecuted by the Court of High Commission. Though the outcome is unknown, Edwards himself admits to the "puritan" credentials for which he was prosecuted. In *Gangraena*, he recalls that he "never had a Canonicall coat, never gave a peny to the building of *Pauls*, took not the Canonicall oath, declined Subscription for many years before the Parliament [and] would not give *ne obulum quidem* [not even alms] to the contributions against the *Scots*." This was the career of a puritan preacher who cut his teeth against the Arminian momentum of the English Church during the 1620s and 1630s, after which he became one of the staunchest defenders of Presbyterianism in the 1640s.

When Presbyterian friction with Independency turned into outright conflict in the mid-1640s, Edwards proved to be one of the most ferocious opponents of the "toleration" that Separatist churches desired. In 1641, he published *Reasons Against the Independent Government of Particular Congregations: as also Against the Toleration of Churches to be Erected in this Kingdome* (1641). Though he was not a member of the Westminster Assembly of Divines, he exhorted people to support the Presbyterian cause by frequently preaching in and around London. Edwards cared little that he was rarely paid, because he had married a woman with a substantial fortune. Perhaps as usefully, preaching in so many places allowed him to build a large network of acquaintances and fellow ministers whom he used as informers to furnish him with detailed and lurid accounts of the sectarian menace.

Edwards's next polemical sally, *Antapologia, or A Full Answer to the Apologeticall Narration of Mr. Goodwin, Mr. Nye, Mr. Sympson, Mr. Burroughs, Mr. Bridge, Members of the Assembly of Divines* (1644), consisted of a violent denunciation of the Independent divines identified therein and earned Edwards himself a lectureship at Christ Church, Newgate Street, where he was able to continue building his network of sympathetic associates. He followed this text with an exhaustive account of the sectarian menace that surpassed all previous Presbyterian efforts to describe and denounce religious separatists. The first "part" of this work, *Gangraena: or A Catalogue and Discovery of Many of the Errours, Heresies, Blasphemies and Pernicious Practices of the Sectaries of this Time, Vented and Acted in England in these Last Four Years*, appeared on 26 February 1646, a second "part" appeared on 28 May, and a third on 28 December. During the course of this virulently maledictory odyssey, Edwards relied upon his network of "Ear and Eye-witnesses" to provide accounts of sectarian prayer meetings, sermons, and blasphemous antics, to enumerate 16 kinds of sectary and 266 errors, and to involve himself in bitter feuds with men such as John Lilburne, William Walwyn, John Saltmarsh, and John Goodwin, who considered themselves unjustly denounced in *Gangraena* and whose refutations countered each of *Gangraena*'s successive "parts."

Edwards's final effort against Independency was *The Casting Down of the Last and Strongest Hold of Satan. or, A Treatise Against Toleration and Pretended Liberty of Conscience*, which appeared in 1647. In the same year, however, despite his defenders, such as Josiah Ricraft, Thomas Webbe, Thomas Alle, and John Vicars, Edwards's notoriety prompted him to retire to Holland, from which to continue his polemical battles. Always a small, diminutive man, "a thin and empty bulk" according to his detractors, Edwards quickly succumbed to an ague and died on 27 December 1647. Edwards's puritanism was that of the committed Presbyterian reformer: he defended rather than promoted the "Puritan Revolution" of the 1640s and attempted to counter its radical momentum, which, ultimately, Presbyterianism was unable to halt.

*See also: Antapologia, Gangraena*
*Further Reading*
Thomas Edwards, *Gangraena: or A Catalogue and Discovery of Many of the Errours, Heresies, Blasphemies and Pernicious Practices of the Sectaries of this Time, Vented and Acted in England in these Last Four Years*, facsimile, intro. M. M. Goldsmith and Ivan Roots (Exeter, Eng., 1977); Ann Hughes, *Gangraena and the Struggle*

for the English Revolution (Oxford, 2004); Ann Hughes, "'Popular' Presbyterianism in the 1640s and 1650s: The Cases of Thomas Edwards and Thomas Hall," in Nicholas Tyacke, ed., England's Long Reformation, 1500–1700 (London, 1998), pp. 235–259.

Simon Dyton

## Egerton, Stephen (ca. 1554–1622)

One of the most influential preachers of late Elizabethan London. Egerton succeeded John Field as leader of militant nonconformity in the capital. Fifth son of a London mercer, he graduated B.A. from Peterhouse, Cambridge, in 1576, proceeding M.A. in 1579 and becoming a fellow at the instigation of William Cecil, Lord Burghley. Ordained in 1581, he settled in the London liberty of St. Anne Blackfriars, where in 1585 he married Sara, daughter of Thomas Crooke, preacher of Gray's Inn. By 1586 Egerton was officially described as parish lecturer. He joined the clerical conference organized by John Field, and his reasons for refusing subscription to Archbishop John Whitgift's articles in 1584 are preserved along with Field's in The seconde parte of a register.

Blackfriars was technically exempt from the ordinary jurisdiction of the bishop of London, but Bishop John Aylmer (1577–1594) attempted to bring it under strict episcopal control, in 1589 ordering Egerton to administer communion there or else assist his curate. At the same time, Egerton was, like many leading radicals, employed by the government to examine and refute the leaders of separatism. A record of the conference that he and Thomas Sperin conducted in the Fleet prison with Henry Barrow and John Greenwood on 20 March 1590 survives, along with the exchange of letters that followed. In 1591, pestered with unsolicited messages from Edmund Coppinger, Egerton quickly distanced himself from his fanatical stratagems—an episode that belies the tradition that in 1590 he was imprisoned by John Whitgift, Archbishop of Canterbury, for three years.

In 1598 Bishop Richard Bancroft (1597–1604) again ordered Egerton to observe the ceremonies,

later claiming that he was the only city minister who had not conformed at this time, since Robert Earl of Essex, promising his good behavior, had protected him. In the aftermath of Essex's rebellion in February 1601, Bancroft seized the opportunity to suspend Egerton, claiming that his sermon condemning the uprising was unsatisfactory. When Sir Robert Cecil hinted that a full account of himself might save him from Bancroft's further attentions, Egerton replied with dignity, observing that he had always preached obedience to the civil magistrate. Bancroft reminded Cecil that Egerton had been associated with Field and "acquainted" with Coppinger but agreed to Egerton's restoration if Cecil would "undertake for him."

Under Cecil's protection, Egerton thus remained undisturbed for the rest of Bancroft's episcopate. In March 1603 he and Arthur Hildersham were among the chief organizers of the millenary petition and, with Edward Fleetwood, prepared "instructions" for the delegates to the Hampton Court Conference. In 1604 Egerton, Fleetwood, and Anthony Wotton urged Convocation to consider the revision of the Book of Common Prayer. Following the promulgation of the constitutions and canons of 1604, King James I insisted upon subscription to Whitgift's articles, now incorporated within them, but Egerton still remained undisturbed. According to Sir Thomas Posthumus Hoby, Bancroft passed over Egerton on the grounds that he was not prepared to proceed against lecturers. Yet Bishop Richard Vaughan (1604–1607), apparently on Bancroft's orders as archbishop of Canterbury, seems to have suspended him. Hoby reminded Cecil that Egerton had ministered "twenty-two years without detection" and that since Blackfriars maintained a conforming curate, he himself was not obliged to use the prayer book.

Though Vaughan, sympathetic to moderate puritan aspirations, probably restored Egerton soon afterwards, the experience seems to have induced a self-imposed silence on him for the rest of his life. He perhaps formally relinquished the lectureship in 1607, since Blackfriars was said to lack a preaching minister when in June 1608 Hildersham successfully recommended William Gouge.

In 1620 Egerton received a legacy from his younger sister, Anne Lady Tyndall, whose daughter Margaret had in 1618 married John Winthrop, future governor of Massachusetts. He made his will on 12 April 1622. After some simple bequests, including forty shillings to the poor of Blackfriars, he left everything to his wife Sara as sole executrix, naming William Gouge and Richard Stock among his four overseers. He was buried in Blackfriars on 7 May 1622. In her own will (August 1624) Sara left legacies totalling nearly £600, including £100 to her "loving cousin" Margaret Winthrop, appointing William Gouge sole overseer.

Egerton's translation from the French of Matthew Virel's *A Learned and Excellent Treatise containing all principal Grounds of the Christian Religion* (ca. 1592) reached a fourteenth edition in 1635. *A brief method of catechizing* (1594) achieved a forty-fourth in 1644. He also contributed commendatory prefaces to the works of several godly writers, including Richard Rogers's *Seven Treatises* (1604).

*Further Reading*

Brian Burch, "The Parish of St. Anne's, Blackfriars, London, to 1665," *Guildhall Miscellany*, 3 (1969), pp. 1–54; Leland H. Carlson, *The Writings of John Greenwood, 1587–90* (London, 1962); Albert Peel, ed., *The seconde parte of a register*, 2 vols. (Cambridge, Eng., 1915).

*Brett Usher*

## Eliot, John (1604–1690)

Author, translator, Roxbury minister, and missionary renowned as "Apostle to the Indians." Born in Widford, Hertfordshire, England, and raised in Nazing, Essex, Eliot entered Jesus College, Cambridge, as a pensioner in 1618 and graduated in 1622. He may have applied for ordination in 1625. By the late 1620s Eliot was assisting Thomas Hooker at the latter's school in Little Baddow in Chelmsford, Essex, shortly before Hooker's departure to Holland in response to Laudian pressure.

When the school closed, Eliot migrated to New England, arriving in November 1631 aboard the *Lyon*. Shortly afterward he substituted as pastor in the Boston pulpit during John Wilson's absence. Eliot refused Boston's invitation to a permanent position after Wilson's return, choosing instead to lead the church at Roxbury with Thomas Weld, a position Eliot held until his retirement in 1688. In 1632, he married Anne (or Hanna) Mumford in the first Roxbury wedding; they had six children together. Eliot occasionally found himself in the opposition on political issues, beginning with his questioning of Governor John Winthrop's 1634 treaty with the Pequots, because it had been made without popular consent; after conferring with other ministers (at the behest of the magistrates), Eliot publicly acknowledged his error. Eliot and Weld testified under oath against Anne Hutchinson at her 1637 civil trial, and Eliot also participated in her 1638 Boston church trial. In the late 1630s he contributed, with Weld, Richard Mather, and John Cotton, to the Bay Psalm Book. With Thomas Dudley, Eliot helped establish the Roxbury Latin School in 1645.

Eliot's chief contribution, however, came in the 1640s when, with official support and direction, he turned his attention to evangelizing those Native Americans of eastern Massachusetts speaking the Algonquian language, commencing with two 1646 sermons delivered with a native interpreter at Neponset and at Nonantum. Despite its explicit missionary claims, Massachusetts Bay already lagged behind Roger Williams and Thomas Mayhew when Eliot undertook the task. Eliot set about to master the Algonquian language with the assistance of the native Cockenoe. Eliot's mission effort took three prongs: (1) He began not only to understand the Algonquian language but to translate the Bible and related materials into it; (2) he publicized the missionary effort in the London press as a means to raise funds there; and (3) he focused his effort especially at Nonantum, where there had been a more favorable reception to his sermon than at Neponset.

The works Eliot translated into Algonquian include the Bible (published in 1663 and again in 1685), but also separately, *The Indian Grammar Begun* (1666), *The Indian Primer* (1669), *The Logic Primer* (1672), an abridgement of Lewis Bayly's

*English missionary John Eliot preaches to Native Americans. (Library of Congress)*

*Practise of Piety* (1665), and Thomas Shepard's *Sincere Convert* and *Sound Believer* (1689). The London publications (1643–1671) are collectively known as the "Eliot Tracts" and are variously authored by John Wilson, Shepard, Henry Whitfield, Edward Winslow, and Eliot himself. Of particular interest are *Tears of Repentance* (1653) and *A Further Accompt of the Progresse of Gospele amongst the Indians in New England* (1660), both of which record Praying Indian church relations gathered during attempts to establish a church at Natick (see below). Together with agent Edward Winslow's assistance, the tracts influenced Parliament's 1649 formation of the Society for Propagation of the Gospel in New England (later shortened to the New England Company) to fund and oversee the missionary effort; this was the first Protestant missionary society.

In the late 1640s, Eliot began to plan a separate Praying Indian town, which would be a physically segregated but locally autonomous community, except that Eliot further designed a theocratic government derived from the Old Testament. The General Court provided land not far from Roxbury, and in 1650 it was established as Natick. Eliot described this government in *The Christian Commonwealth* (composed in 1651, but not published until 1659, in London): it involved a hierarchy of rulers divided into "tens, fifties, hundreds, and thousands" (derived from Exodus 18:17–26), reflecting an impulse simultaneously primitivist and millennialist. However, when copies appeared in New England after the Restoration, the concept was roundly rejected: the General Court censured it and ordered all copies destroyed, while Eliot was required to sign a recantation. In 1652, Eliot's attempt at gathering a Praying Indian church at Natick according to proper form failed when the visiting ministers judged that the founding candidates were not mature enough, but a second attempt in

1659 succeeded. Eliot also helped establish the Indian College at Harvard in the 1650s. Eliot continued with his missionary effort, establishing other Praying Indian towns (thirteen others altogether), populated by perhaps as many as 4,000 people, or 25 percent of the New England Native American population. Understandably, Eliot's apostolate, not always popular among New Englanders, was deeply disrupted by King Philip's War. Much suspicion, hostility, and outright violence were visited, often through the General Court, on the Praying Indians before they were ordered into exile on Deer Island, where they stayed for three difficult years. Eliot also reported that virtually all copies of his Algonquian translations of the Bible had been destroyed during the war and that it needed to be reprinted, which was not completed until 1685. According to Ola Elizabeth Winslow, only four of the fourteen Praying Indian towns were rebuilt after the war; certainly, the missionary effort never again reached the same levels in Eliot's lifetime.

*See also:* Indian Bible, King Philip's War, Praying Towns, Society for the Propagation of the Gospel in New England
*Further Reading*
Richard W. Cogley, *John Eliot's Mission to the Indians before King Philip's War* (Cambridge, MA; 1999); Ola Winslow, *John Eliot: Apostle to the Indians* (Boston, 1968).

*Michael G. Ditmore*

### Endecott (Endicott), John (d. 1665)

Governor of Massachusetts; sent by the New England Company to take charge of its settlements near Cape Anne in 1628, concentrated at Salem. There is no reliable record of his life, education, or activities before this time, though his correspondence shows him to have been well read and thoughtful.

Endecott's quick temper and strong religious zeal made his management of the early settlement controversial. He cut down a maypole that the colonist Thomas Morton had erected at a trading post called Merrymount and sent some disaffected colonists back home. Endecott did establish posi-

*John Endecott, who served numerous terms as governor of Massachusetts in the seventeenth century. (Massachusetts Historical Society)*

tive relations with the Pilgrim colonists at Plymouth, drawing on that colony's experience and material support to advance the survival of Salem. He supported the Reverends Samuel Skelton and Francis Higginson in establishing a congregational church at Salem.

With the arrival of the *Arbella* in 1630, Endecott turned over the reins of government to John Winthrop, the recently elected governor of what was now called the Massachusetts Bay Company whose arrival in the Bay signaled the merger of colony and company government. Endecott became an Assistant under the new regime, with the powers of justice of the peace. He again became the center of a storm when he cut the red cross from the English ensign during a muster of the Salem train band in 1634. Winthrop and others agreed with him that the cross was a popish item and quietly eliminated further use of the ensign. But it was feared that Endecott's action might provoke royal action against the colony, and so the

Court of Assistants censured the Salem leader and disabled him from holding office for a year for having shown improper zeal and having acted on his own without consulting his fellow magistrates.

In 1636 he commanded the Bay Colony's expedition to punish the Pequot Indians for the deaths of English settlers in the area that later became Connecticut. His destruction of native villages only accelerated the rift with the natives, which resulted in the Pequot War of 1637 and the almost complete extermination of the tribe.

In 1644 he was elected to a term as governor, distinguishing himself by a new, more conciliatory style. When John Winthrop died in 1649, the colonists again chose Endecott governor, returning him to that post thirteen of the next fifteen years. Bowing to his new responsibilities, he soon moved from Salem to Boston. The "Endecott Era" saw the colony coping with the consequences of England's wars of religion. As governor he was forced to deal in the 1650s with the influx of what the colonists viewed as heresies that had emerged in England during the turmoil of the Interregnum. Baptists were imprisoned, confuted to the satisfaction of the orthodox, and banished or, on occasion, whipped. Endecott sanctioned the execution of three Quakers under the terms of a new laws passed in the 1650s.

The Restoration presented Endecott with another serious challenge to the colony. He worked hard to fend off efforts of the home government to undermine the "New England Way," seeking to preserve the purposes of the colony in defiance of new imperial realities. Under his leadership, Massachusetts appointed agents to represent its cause before the Council for Foreign Relations and developed new ties with English friends in a position to lobby for the colony. John Endecott died in Boston on 15 March 1665.

*Further Reading*
Lawrence Shaw Mayo, *John Endecott* (Boston, 1936).

*Francis J. Bremer*

# F

## Fairclough, Samuel, Jr. (ca. 1625–1691)

College fellow and Congregational clergyman. Born about 1625, presumably in the parish of Barnardiston, Suffolk, Fairclough was the second son of the more famous Samuel Fairclough Senior. He was admitted pensioner at Emmanuel College, Cambridge, in May 1643, commencing B.A. in 1647 and M.A. in 1650. From 1650 to 1656, he was fellow of Caius College, Cambridge. He served as Hebrew lecturer in 1651 and as lecturer in logic in 1658. He relinquished his fellowship with his marriage on 25 October 1655 to Frances Folkes of Kedington and became rector of Houghton Conquest in Bedfordshire. He was ejected from this living in 1662.

In 1672 he was licensed a congregational teacher at Chippenham, Cambridgeshire. He died on 31 December 1691, aged sixty-six, and was buried at Heveningham, Suffolk. Fairclough contributed an "offertory" in verse to the collection of elegies published to commemorate the death in 1653 of his father's patron, Sir Nathaniel Barnardiston. His account of "some remarkable passages of the life and death of Mrs Anne Barnardiston" was published with John Shower's funeral sermon for her in 1682, and he contributed an epistle for the published funeral sermon for his brother-in-law, Richard Shute (1689).

*Further Reading*
*Oxford Dictionary of National Biography* (Oxford, 2004).

*John Craig*

## Fairclough, Samuel, the Elder (1594–1677)

Powerful and popular preacher whose influence spread well beyond his immediate neighborhood of west Suffolk. Fairclough was born on 29 April 1594 at Haverhill, Suffolk, youngest of the four sons of Lawrence Fairclough, vicar of Haverhill. He showed early promise as a scholar and matriculated at Queens' College, Cambridge, in 1608. At Cambridge, Fairclough joined a group of students that met regularly for Bible study, whose numbers included such men as John Davenant, John Preston, and Arthur Hildersham. He proceeded B.A. in 1615 and was ordained priest on 25 February 1616 in the diocese of Norwich.

On the advice of Samuel Ward, famous preacher of Ipswich, Fairclough turned down the offer of a Suffolk living in order to spend time at Richard Blackerby's "seminary" at Ashen, on the Essex-Suffolk border, where he stayed for perhaps three years. It was here that he met Blackerby's eldest daughter, whom he eventually married. In 1619, he accepted the generous offer made by the corporation of King's Lynn to become their lecturer on the handsome terms of a stipend of 100 pounds plus a house. The appointment was not a success. The terms of Fairclough's appointment bred resentment among other ministers in the town, and the success of his ministry angered the town's publicans, as they witnessed their trade decrease. He was presented to the church courts for failing to use the sign of the cross in baptism, and Fairclough decided to leave for a more peaceful living.

Fairclough became lecturer at Clare in west Suffolk, where he came to the attention of Sir Nathaniel Barnardiston, who became his most powerful patron. Fairclough was instituted to the adjoining rectory of Barnardiston on 27 June 1623. When articles were brought against Fairclough for a sermon he had preached and he found himself hauled before the Court of High Commission, Barnardiston went to bat for his favorite preacher and secured the dismissal of these charges. On 10 February 1629, Barnardiston presented Fairclough to the rectory of Kedington, Suffolk, and obtained his institution in a way that completely bypassed the episcopal authorities and the need to subscribe to the Three Articles.

Fairclough was content to settle in Kedington and ministered there for almost thirty-five years, preaching four times a week. His Thursday lectures were clerical fiestas, with as many as twenty fellows and scholars from Cambridge in attendance, as well many ministers from neighboring parishes. The attraction seems to have been a winning combination of scholarship, a dramatic preaching style (he was referred to as Boanerges, "son of thunder," a biblical term often applied to powerful preachers), personality, and practical divinity. Fairclough was not much interested in Presbyterianism and managed to avoid trouble with the ecclesiastical authorities in the 1630s. During the troubled years of the Civil War and the political and ecclesiastical experiments that followed, Fairclough avoided taking sides. Although nominated, he excused himself from attending the Westminster Assembly that commenced work in 1643, and he later declined the mastership of Trinity College, Cambridge. The test of 1662 proved a different matter. Fairclough refused the oath and left Kedington. Barnardiston had died in 1653, and with his old patron and protector gone, Fairclough came out for Nonconformity. His last years were spent peripatetically, as he moved between his children's households. He died at Stowmarket on 14 December 1677, aged eighty-four, and was buried near the vestry door of the church.

*Further Reading*
Samuel Clarke, *Lives of Sundry eminent Persons* (London, 1683); Tom Webster, *Godly Clergy in Early Stuart England* (Cambridge, Eng., 1997).

*John Craig*

## Faldo, John (1633–1691)

Congregational minister; one of the original seven Congregational managers of the Common Fund set up to bring Congregationalists and Presbyterians together. Faldo is said to have been educated at Cambridge, but he did not matriculate. He is said to have preached to "Lilburne's soldiers," but he does not appear to have been a New Model Army chaplain. He was preaching at Chipping Barnet in 1669 and was licensed there (surely in error) as a Presbyterian under the 1672 Indulgence. Between 1673 and 1675 Faldo was engaged in an exchange of pamphlets with William Penn in which he accused the Quakers of blasphemy and quasi popery. In this exchange the influential Presbyterian divine Richard Baxter supported him, but he and Baxter differed over questions of ecclesiology and psalm singing.

In February 1683 Faldo was examined by the lord mayor of London for preaching and fined twenty pounds at the Guildhall Sessions. In 1684 Faldo became minister of the Congregational church at Old Street Square, London, which later relocated to Plaisterers' Hall. In October 1684 Roger Morrice reported that he had been arrested and committed to Newgate. It appears that he was under investigation in connection with the Rye House Plot against Charles II. Richard Lobb claimed in 1686 that Faldo had almost 2,000 in his congregation each Sunday. Faldo embraced the freedom to preach under James II's Indulgence of 1687 and joined in the Congregational address of thanks. After the Toleration Act, Faldo became associated with moves to bring Presbyterians and Congregationalists closer: he helped to manage the Common Fund set up in 1690 and died on the eve of the Happy Union of the two denominations. Faldo also appears to have been a chaplain to the family of Lady Clinton; he published sermons and, posthumously, an abridgement of Jeremy Dyke's *Worthy Communicant* intended for the poor. He was buried in Bunhill Fields, and his funeral sermon was preached by John Quick, who described him as having "an especial hand in the healing of our breaches."

*Further Reading*
Alexander Gordon, *Freedom after Ejection* (Manchester, Eng., 1917).

*John Spurr*

## Fenn, Humphrey (d. 1634)

Nonconformist minister. Fenn's lengthy and influential career provides a good example of the continuities between Elizabethan and early Stuart puritanism. In 1578 he was appointed vicar of Holy Trinity, Coventry, in Warwickshire, where he was associated with Thomas Cartwright and the Presbyterian movement. Fenn was one of the ministers suspended for not subscribing to Archbishop John Whitgift's articles of 1584, he was reinstated with the help of Robert Dudley, Earl of Leicester, who as captain-general chose Fenn to act as one of his chaplains on the 1585 campaign in the Netherlands. In 1588 Fenn was one of the ministers who subscribed to the Presbyterian Book of Discipline, and in 1590 he, Cartwright and others were imprisoned after a Star Chamber case for taking part in the Presbyterian classes held in Warwickshire. While in prison, Fenn counseled Edward Fleetwood, rector of Wigan and prominent among the Lancashire puritan ministers, that ceremonies such as the sign of the cross in baptism were to be refused. The use of the surplice came into the same category, wrote Fenn, but the ministry of those who used the surplice could be accepted. He was released in 1592. In the mid-1620s, he along with the mayor and other citizens of Coventry invited the young Samuel Clarke to lecture in their town. Fenn died on 7 February 1634, and his will contained a sensational and staunchly Presbyterian preamble, which the bishop of Coventry and Lichfield sent to Archbishop William Laud. In the preamble, Fenn endorsed a Geneva-style presbyterian church system and attacked episcopacy as anti-Christian. He argued, however, that separation from the Church of England was unlawful as long as the individual Christian was not forced to approve these corruptions and was able to find a minister capable of administering the sacraments and teaching true doctrine. The preamble was published in 1641, although it was probably circulating in manuscript before that date.

### Further Reading

Humphrey Fenn, *The Last Will and Testament, with the Profession of the Faith of Humfrey Fen,* sometimes Pastor of one of the Churches of Coventry (1641).

*Jacqueline Eales*

## Fenner, Dudley (ca. 1558–1587)

English theologian; born about 1558 and educated at Peterhouse College, Cambridge. He entered in 1575 but left before taking a degree, no doubt because of difficulties arising from his outspoken Puritan opinions. Although trained in theology, he had great difficulty finding a place to serve in the Church of England.

Discouraged at home, Fenner went to the Low Countries once or twice and found work with the English Merchant Adventurers church at Antwerp. This church, pastored by Walter Travers (1578–1580) and Thomas Cartwright (1580–1585), was a Puritan stronghold, and, lacking episcopal supervision, it followed a clear Presbyterian line. In the early 1580s, Fenner joined as co-pastor; Cartwright wrote that they had a joint ministry in the English Church in Antwerp." They shared a distaste for the Anglican liturgy, ordination, and system of bishops, so much so that Fenner, like several other nonconformist English preachers, took ordination (or reordination) at Antwerp from Dutch Reformed pastors, rather than be touched by episcopal hands. The stay in Antwerp confirmed Fenner in his devotion to the Reformed (Presbyterian) way.

In 1582 the merchant church moved to Middelburg, Zeeland, but by that time Fenner had returned to England. In 1583, after some show of nominal conformity, he became assistant to the vicar in the parish church at Cranbrook, Kent. This position did not last long. In 1585 Archbishop John Whitgift demanded strict subscription to three articles of conformity, known as the Three Articles of 1584, which meant subscribing to royal supremacy over the Church of England and the Thirty-nine Articles that laid out the beliefs of the church, as well as to the Book of Common Prayer as containing nothing contrary to the word of God. When Fenner refused to subscribe, Whitgift in June 1585 suspended him. Over the next years, he devoted himself to writing and publishing; and he perhaps returned to the Netherlands to the merchant church. He died in 1587, still a young man in his twenties, and his death was much regretted.

In his short career, he gained great scholarly recognition, even an international following, for his learned theological writings. The author of at least a dozen books, mostly published abroad, he wrote on three topics. First, in company with Travers and Cartwright, he wrote to condemn the episcopal system, which had deprived him and many others, and to support the presbyterian system, which he had experienced at Antwerp. Presbyterianism, he claimed, was the form "prescribed" by Jesus Christ. His *Defence of the Godlie Ministers* (1587) made this case. Second, he wrote systematic theology. His *Sacra Theologia* (1585), with a preface by Cartwright, was one of the first Puritan works of systematic theology and showed English scholarship comparable to the best Reformed theology of the continent. Because it was in Latin, it circulated widely. Thoroughly Reformed in content, it used the covenant concept as the framework, and Fenner laid it out in the dichotomy method of Peter Ramus. His third topic was to promote Ramus's methodology and philosophy, not only for theology, but also for knowledge as a whole. He wrote *The Artes of Logike and Rhetorike* (1584) as a Ramist educational manual. Puritans viewed him as a marvel of learning and courageous church leader.

*See also:* English Puritanism in the Netherlands, Federal Theology, Ramist Logic
*Further Reading*
A. F. Scott Pearson, *Thomas Cartwright and Elizabethan Puritanism, 1535–1603* (Cambridge, Eng., 1925); Keith L. Sprunger, *Dutch Puritanism: A History of English and Scottish Churches of the Netherlands in the Sixteenth and Seventeenth Centuries* (Leiden, 1982).

*Keith L. Sprunger*

## Field, John (ca. 1545–1588)

Officially no more than a minor London clergyman, John Field was the linchpin of the militant wing of Elizabethan puritanism. A Londoner, supported at Oxford by the Clothworkers Company, he probably proceeded B.A. in 1564 and M.A. in 1567, and at his ordination was said to be of Christ Church. He had already attracted the patronage of Ambrose Dudley, Earl of Warwick, and the Dudley brothers continued to protect him.

With the London vestiarian crisis of 1566, in which thirty-seven ministers were suspended for refusing to conform, Field was probably one of the young unbeneficed ministers who took their places, before returning to Oxford. There is evidence to link him with the leading early Nonconformist, Laurence Humphrey, president of Magdalen, and he was an assistant in the great project of the *Actes and monuments* (or Book of Martyrs) of John Foxe, which later provided a model for his own collecting of a "register" of the doings of the puritan ministers. In 1568 he returned to London, preached regularly in the highly irregular parish of Holy Trinity Minories, and became curate in neighboring St. Giles Cripplegate, where all his children were baptized. By 1571 he was living in Grub Street, which was also Foxe's address; another neighbor was the wealthy patron of all godly causes Nicholas Culverwell, with whom Field also collaborated.

In about 1570 Field began with Thomas Wilcox, curate of All Hallows, Honey Lane, to convene clerical meetings, which were the conference movement in embryo. When Field and Wilcox printed *An admonition to the Parliament* in the summer of 1572, Field may already have been suspended from preaching and reduced to schoolmastering, a radicalizing experience of which he complained in letters to one of the fathers of the puritan movement, Anthony Gilby. The *Admonition* presented in a populist and polemical style the anti-hierarchical, presbyterian principles already enunciated in academic lectures at Cambridge by Thomas Cartwright. The authors found themselves in Newgate Prison, where they were visited by some of the original leaders of the radical tendency in the Elizabethan Church, many of whom distanced themselves from the manner as well as the matter of the manifesto. Field claimed sole responsibility for the bitter and brilliant satire that characterized the *Admonition*. Field and Wilcox were in fact puritans of two very different kinds, and later they fell out in a rancorous exchange of letters that the future Archbishop Richard Bancroft gleefully exploited in his anti-puritan writings, when those letters and much of Field's other correspondence fell into his hands.

The influence of the earls of Warwick and Leicester got Field and Wilcox out of prison, after which Field disappeared from view for two years, possibly to the sanctuary of Heidelberg, which also received Cartwright, and where he may have been involved in the publication of further manifestoes. Field's return to London coincided with that relatively peaceful episode in the history of the Elizabethan church during which it was presided over by Archbishop Edmund Grindal, and Field now devoted his pen to the common cause of anti-Catholicism. Leicester secured him a preaching license from Oxford University, and he became lecturer at St. Mary Aldermary, where he preached until again suspended in 1585. But he was still the same Field. He took his great patron severely to task for supporting stage plays, and he exploited a fatal accident at the Paris Garden bear pit to lambaste the new leisure industry.

Although Field had now regained a measure of respectability, he was not very comfortable with it, and the advent in 1583 of Archbishop John Whitgift, with a mission to deal with puritan nonconformity once and for all, was almost a relief. Field now made it his business to work not only against Whitgift but against those moderate puritans who were willing to subscribe to the archbishop's conformist test articles with conditions. He was also active as the national coordinator of quasi-presbyterian conferences that were designed to bolster resistance to Whitgift and to promote a species of presbyterian church order. Field worked closely with the puritan printer Robert Waldegrave and amassed many of the materials that were later exploited in the Marprelate tracts, which Waldegrave printed, documents later published overseas in 1593 as *A parte of a register*. But Field himself was dead before Marprelate ruined the cause for which he had fought. His sons would have been a disappointment. One, Theophilus, became a bishop, and the other, Nathan, an actor and dramatist, who had his apprenticeship in the anti-puritan plays of Ben Jonson.

> See also: *An Admonition to the Parliament,* Book of Discipline, Conference Movement, Martin Marprelate
> *Further Reading*
> Patrick Collinson, *The Elizabethan Puritan Movement* (London, 1967); Patrick Collinson, "John Field and Elizabethan Puritanism," in Collinson, *Godly People: Essays on English Protestantism and Puritanism* (London, 1983); Albert Peel, ed., *The seconde parte of a register,* 2 vols. (Cambridge, Eng., 1915).

*Patrick Collinson*

## Firmin, Giles (1614–1697)

Puritan clergyman in England and New England. He was born in Ipswich, Suffolk. His mother was a kinswoman of John Winthrop. While young he was converted through the preaching of John Rogers of nearby Dedham. He matriculated at Emmanuel College, Cambridge, in 1629, but left the university to engage in the study of medicine.

In 1632 he sailed with his father to New England, settling in Boston and practicing medicine. Firmin returned to England in 1633 but was back in the colony four years later. He was elected a deacon of the First Church in Boston in the closing months of the controversy that divided that church over the teachings of Anne Hutchinson, whose church trial and excommunication he was present for. In 1639 he resettled in Ipswich, Massachusetts.

Firmin returned again to England in 1644. He began his ministerial career in Colchester, Essex (the Elizabethan town called a "City upon a Hill" for its reformed character), and in 1648 he was ordained by a group of Presbyterian clergy that included Daniel Rogers and Stephen Marshall. He became vicar of Shalford, Essex. Firmin believed in the type of regulated and uniform church order such as he had known in New England and became frustrated by the many divergent beliefs and liturgical practices that flourished in England, and especially in East Anglia. He tried to correct this to a degree by promoting the type of voluntary clerical association that had kept New England ministers and churches on the same page. He corresponded with the influential Presbyterian divine Richard Baxter, who shared some of the same views.

When the Act of Uniformity was passed by the Restoration Parliament in 1662, Firmin left the ministry and resumed the practice of medicine. Following King Charles's Declaration of Indulgence of 1672, Firmin was licensed as a Presbyterian clergyman and ministered to a congregation in Ridgewell until his death. In his later years he was drawn into the controversies that developed between Congregationalists and Presbyterians that led to the breakup of the Happy Union. Throughout his English career he expressed his views in print as well as in the pulpit. Among his major works were *A Serious Question Stated* (1651), *Of Schism* (1658), and *Presbyterial Ordination Vindicated* (1660). But his most influential work was *The Real Christian* (1670), in which he dealt with the central puritan issues of conversion and assurance.

*Further Reading*
Francis J. Bremer, *Congregational Communion: Clerical Friendship in the Anglo-American Puritan Community, 1610–1692* (Boston, 1994); T. W. Davids, *Annals of English Nonconformity . . . in Essex* (London, 1863).

*Francis J. Bremer*

## Flavel (Flavell), John (1627–1691)

English Dissenting minister and spiritual writer. He was born at Bromsgrove, Worcestershire, and spent several years at University College, Oxford, before becoming in 1650 the curate and then rector at Diptford, Devon. In 1656 he moved to nearby Dartmouth as lecturer at St. Saviour's, from which he was ejected in 1662 for refusal to conform to the Church of England. Flavel remained at Dartmouth, preaching privately, but had to move his preaching to nearby Slapton after the Five Mile Act of 1665. With the Declaration of Indulgence in 1672, he licensed his house in Dartmouth as a Congregationalist meeting place. First at Dartmouth and then at Slapton, he conducted a small Dissenting academy. In 1682 he moved to London, fleeing persecution in Devon; he was back in Dartmouth

by 1687, where a large meetinghouse was provided for his preaching. He welcomed the Revolution of 1688 for bringing political and religious liberty. Although when at Diptford he had, as a Congregationalist, disputed the Presbyterian views of Allan Geare, in 1691 he presided at a meeting of Devon ministers seeking a union of Presbyterians and Congregationalists. Flavel is best known as the author of works of practical piety such as *Husbandry Spiritualized* (1669) and *Navigation Spiritualized* (1677), both of which went through many editions. These books found moral and spiritual lessons in everyday activities, a type of meditation that contemporaries called "improving the creatures," which was common among Puritans in both Old and New England.

*Further Reading*
A. G. Matthews, *Calamy Revised: Being a Revision of Edmund Calamy's Account of the Ministers and others Ejected and Silenced, 1660–2* (Oxford, 1934; reprinted 1988).

*Dewey D. Wallace Jr.*

## Fleetwood, Charles (d. 1692)

Parliamentary general. As a young law student, Fleetwood took up the cause of Parliament in 1642, and he fought in all three English Civil Wars, campaigning in England, Scotland, and Ireland. At the height of his career, he married Oliver Cromwell's eldest daughter, Bridget, and served as the Protector's Lord Deputy in Ireland, as well as one of his famed major-generals in England.

Fleetwood's cavalry regiment, incorporated into the New Model Army in 1645, was reputed a nest of fanatical preaching Independents. Fleetwood himself often exhorted his men to pray, falling on his knees in front of them. The regiment was prominent in the Army mutinies of 1647. Fleetwood himself, as an elected member of Parliament, served both as a Parliamentary commissioner and as an army representative in the subsequent negotiations.

In 1651, Fleetwood was appointed to succeed the deceased Henry Ireton as commander of forces in Ireland. He was recalled four years later to serve on Cromwell's council. Though he was appointed major-general for the eastern counties, Fleetwood's duties kept him in London, leaving day-to-day administration to his deputies, Hezekiah Haynes, William Packer, and George Fleetwood. With Generals John Lambert and John Desborough, Fleetwood successfully dissuaded Cromwell from accepting the crown. Fleetwood initially supported Richard Cromwell's Protectorate, but later forced him to resign. Appointed commander of the New Model Army, Fleetwood was unable to save the republic, and was politically outmaneuvered by General George Monck. At the Restoration Fleetwood was prohibited from holding public office. He was imprisoned—at one point sharing a cell with George Fox—but eventually released.

*See also:* Major-Generals, Irish Puritanism
*Further Reading*
Christopher Durston, *Cromwell's Major-Generals: Godly Government during the English Revolution* (Manchester, Eng., 2001); Charles H. Firth, and Godfrey Davies, *The Regimental History of Cromwell's Army* (London1940; reprinted 1991); Geoffrey Ridsdill-Smith and Margaret Toynbee, *Leaders of the Civil Wars* (Kineton, Eng., 1977).

*David J. Appleby*

## Forbes, John (ca. 1568–1634)
Scottish Presbyterian divine; the brother of Patrick Forbes, who became bishop of Aberdeen in 1618. He graduated from St. Andrews University in 1583, and in 1593 was ordained to the ministry in the parish of Alford, Aberdeenshire. He was the moderator of the 1605 general assembly at Aberdeen, held in defiance of King James VI's order. In his *Four Sermons* (1635), he made clear his opposition to absolute monarchy, and throughout his career he upheld the autonomy of the church. He was first imprisoned, then sent to London, and finally exiled to the Continent. He described the decay of Reformed polity in the Scottish church from 1584, as well as his own trials in 1605 and 1606, in his *Certaine Records* (published in 1846). In his recorded speeches he appealed to the anti-Catholic Negative Confession of 1581 signed by King James VI in

order to argue that his judges had sworn to uphold Presbyterian polity, thus contributing to the Presbyterian historical appeals that culminated in the National Covenant of 1638. He became a minister of the English congregation of the Merchant Adventurers in Middelburg in 1608 preceded by Travers and Cartwright, and then in Delft from 1621 until 1633, when he was forced out under English pressure. In 1616 he went to London, and King James promised to allow his return, but without effect. In 1619 he was one of those who licensed his nephew, the episcopal theologian John Forbes of Corse. He died of of kidney stone disease in 1634.

*See also:* English Puritanism in the Netherlands
*Further Reading*
Christiaan George Frederik De Jong, *John Forbes (ca. 1568–1634)* (Groningen, 1987).

*David Mullan*

## Fox, George (1624–1690)
Founder of the Society of Friends, popularly known as the Quakers. Fox was born and raised in a puritan household in Leicestershire. His father, Christopher, was a weaver whose neighbors nicknamed him "Righteous Christer." From an early age, Fox displayed a profound religious seriousness, and he left home at nineteen on a spiritual quest. During the years from 1643 to 1647, he wandered around England, arguing with other godly people and identifying most with the Seekers, who were not members of organized churches. Like the godly in general, Fox was hostile to popular festive culture, thirsty for intense experience of the Holy Spirit, and steeped in the scriptures. Unlike more conservative puritans, however, he shared a radical puritan anticlericalism, and he received a revelation that one did not need to be educated at Oxford and Cambridge to preach the gospel.

In the course of his pilgrimage, Fox became convinced that the Inner Light of Christ enlightens every man, a doctrine that fused puritan spiritualism with Arminian universalism. This message galvanized Seekers and other radical puritans exhausted and disillusioned by years of war, unfulfilled

*George Fox, founder of the Society of Friends, better known as the Quakers. (Vincent L. Milner.* Religious Denominations of the World. *Philadelphia: Bradley Garretson, 1872)*

1650s a system of monthly, quarterly, and yearly meetings. He married Margaret Fell in 1669, and together they did much to consolidate Quaker organization in the Restoration period, by establishing the central Meeting for Sufferings in 1675 and maintaining an extensive correspondence with Quaker leaders across Britain, Europe, and America. Fox lived to see the Act of Toleration in 1689, which (surprisingly) included Quakers and allowed them to open their own meetinghouses. Fox's *Journal,* first published in 1694, is one of the classics of English religious literature and presents a vivid account of his own pilgrimage and the birth and growth of the Quaker movement. It perhaps exaggerates Fox's dominance of the movement in its early, rather chaotic, stages, and some historians suggest that figures like James Nayler were equally influential in the early 1650s. But over the first forty years of Quakerism, Fox was the sect's single most important leader.

*Further Reading*

George Fox, *The Journal,* ed. N. Smith (London, 1998); Larry H. Ingle, *First among Friends: George Fox and the Creation of Quakerism* (New York, 1994).

*John Coffey*

hopes of ecclesiastical and political reform, and bitter wrangling among the godly. By the early 1650s, Fox was gathering and organizing a new movement in the north of England, and in 1654 Quaker prophets were sent to other parts of the nation, where they won many converts in London, Bristol, and elsewhere. By 1660, the sect had outstripped the Baptists in its growth and numbered between 40,000 and 60,000. Fox himself was tireless in his travels; he visited Scotland in 1657–1658, Ireland in 1669, North America in 1671–1672, and continental Europe in 1677 and 1684. He was arrested or attacked on numerous occasions and imprisoned eight times for a total of six years. He also published an endless stream of pamphlets.

But like John Wesley in the eighteenth century, Fox was not merely an inspirational preacher and writer; he was also a brilliant organizer who gave structure and coherence to a potentially fissiparous popular movement by developing from the late

### Foxe, John (1516–1587)

Religious reformer and author of *The Actes and Monuments of the English Martyrs* (1563), more commonly known as the Book of Martyrs. He was born in Boston, Lincolnshire, where his father was an affluent merchant. Foxe studied at Brasenose College, Oxford, and received his B.A. in 1537. He became a fellow at Magdalen College and one of the college lecturers in logic. During this period he became committed to the reform cause, earning a reputation as a committed evangelical. But he left the university in 1545 rather than take holy orders.

Over the next few years Foxe found a position as a tutor in the household of the Earl of Surrey and began his career as a translator and author. With the accession of the Roman Catholic Mary Tudor to the throne, he joined other English Protestants in going into exile on the Continent, settling in

Frankfurt. When the exile congregation there divided over the desirability of further reforming the liturgy set forth in the English Book of Common Prayer of 1552, Foxe was on the side of the Scottish Reformer John Knox and William Whittingham favoring further changes. Following Knox's expulsion from the city, Foxe and others moved on to Basel. There he went to work for a printer, which allowed him to become immersed in the world of Continental Protestant scholarship, as well as giving him an opportunity to publish works of his own. While in Basel, he began to show an interest in the history of the church. In the process he became involved in a project of Edmund Grindal, the future archbishop of Canterbury, to gather and publish the stories of Protestant martyrs. Whereas Grindal appears to have desired a focus on those suffering persecution in Mary's England, Foxe showed an interest in earlier English reformers such as the Lollards. When Mary died and most of the exiles returned home, Foxe remained for a time in Basel to complete his book (in Latin) on English martyrs, *Rerum in ecclesia gestarum . . . commentarii* (1559).

Buoyed by widespread praise for the *Rerum,* Foxe returned to England in the fall of 1559 and immersed himself in preparing a larger, English language compendium of the sufferings of England's martyrs. He gathered papers of the Marian sufferers from men and women such as William Winthrop, who had remained underground in England during the persecutions. He also engaged in researching ecclesiastical records, primarily in London and Norwich. Though ordained a priest by his friend Edmund Grindal, now bishop of London, Foxe devoted his main efforts to his research and writing. In 1563 the first edition of the *Actes and Monuments* was published—1,800 pages, which began with an overview of church history from the year 1000, chronicled the corruption of the papacy, and placed the struggles of recent times in a broader context of English church history.

Though he did write other works, Foxe was soon focusing on an expanded version of the *Actes and Monuments,* seeking to utilize the material that was forwarded to him after the publication of the first edition. He also intensified his research in rare books and archives, at the same time reaching out to garner more oral accounts. In the process he also engaged with criticisms of the earlier work, buttressing his arguments where he could and abandoning stories that on further study he found inaccurate. The second edition opened with the apostolic age, included more on struggles on the Continent, and tended to downplay some of the divisions among English Protestants that had been included in the first edition. It was published in two volumes in 1570.

With his reputation even greater following the publication of the new edition, Foxe devoted himself to some other projects that were close to his heart. He edited an edition of Archbishop Thomas Cranmer's work on reforming the code of ecclesiastical law. He prepared an edition of the works of Reformers William Tyndale, John Frith, and Robert Barnes. He also translated some of the great German Reformer Martin Luther's commentaries into English. He engaged in pastoral work at this time as well, most notably in a number of exorcisms in which he was credited with casting out demons. He made efforts to persuade London Anabaptists to recant their heretical views, but was opposed to the burning of two members of the sect at Smithfield in 1575. He continued his attacks on Catholics and urged Jews to convert.

The popularity of the *Actes and Monuments* prompted two further editions, which Foxe worked on, each incorporating some new material and omitting some of the stories from the previous editions. He died in 1587, but his legacy was significant. The *Actes and Monuments* became the unchallenged authority in defining recent history for the English and shaped that history in such a way as to highlight England's importance in God's providential design.

*See also:* Book of Martyrs, Exorcism, Marian Martyrs, Puritan Historians

*Further Reading*

Richard Bauckham, *Tudor Apocalypse* (Appleford, Eng., 1978); Patrick Collinson, "Truth and Legend: The Veracity of John Foxe's Book of Martyrs," in Collinson, *Elizabethan Essays*

(London, 1994), 151–177; William Haller, *Foxe's Book of Martyrs and the Elect Nation* (London, 1963); David Loades, ed., *John Foxe and the English Reformation* (Aldershot, Eng., 1997); David Loades, ed., *John Foxe: An Historical Perspective* (Aldershot, Eng., 1999).

*Francis J. Bremer*

## Fulke, William (ca. 1537–1589)

Theologian and head of a Cambridge college. Born in London, where he received his early education, he entered St. John's College, Cambridge, in 1555. The Roman Catholic reaction of Queen Mary's reign may have led to his decision to enter the Clifford's Inn for the study of law. He was admitted to the Inner Temple in 1560. He returned to St. John's in 1562, at which time he had already published an attack on astrology and a study of meteorology. In both of these he argued for the natural causation of events in the physical world, while also maintaining a belief in divine providence.

Fulke received his M.A. in 1563, after which he became a fellow of St. John's and a college preacher. He was soon identified as one of the more assertive Reformers in the university. He led a puritan faction in the college that rejected the use of prescribed vestments in religious services. This uprising against the established order was suppressed by the end of 1565, but the infighting at St. John's continued. Over the next few years he remained at the center of the religious controversies in Cambridge. He resigned his fellowship and lectured unofficially at the Falcoln Inn in the town. Readmitted to his fellowship, he was promoted to the mastership of the college, which led to sharp attacks that persuaded him to again resign his post. He then left Cambridge to become a chaplain to the Earl of Leicester, who was noted for his patronage of puritan clerics. Leicester appointed him to the living of Great Warley in Essex.

He later moved to a second living in Dennington, Suffolk, appointing a curate to minister to Great Warley.

Protected by Leicester's influence, during the 1570s Fulke emerged as a leading puritan clergyman. He preached often in London churches and was involved with the leaders of the Presbyterian movement within the Church of England. His greatest efforts, however, were reserved for attacks on Roman Catholicism and the defense of the English church against Catholic critics, and these efforts made him more acceptable to the church authorities. He was encouraged by both puritans and the church authorities to undertake the task of answering all Catholic attacks on the English church published since the accession of Queen Elizabeth. Coupled with this task was a series of public disputations that he engaged in with Catholic prisoners, most notably Edmund Campion, the Jesuit, who was eventually executed as a traitor.

In 1578 he was chosen the master of Pembroke College, Cambridge. His record there was mixed. Though he continued to adhere to the views of Calvinism that he believed central to the English church, he did not follow William Perkins and others in their new emphasis on and elaboration of the predestinarian teachings of Calvin. Not only did Pembroke not become a puritan college to the degree that such a label could be attached to Emmanuel, but some of the later critics of English Calvinism such as Lancelot Andrewes and Samuel Harsnett were fellows at Pembroke in the 1580s. Nevertheless, Fulke continued to have strong connections with puritan leaders, who encouraged his ongoing attacks on Rome.

*See also:* Providence
*Further Reading*
*Oxford Dictionary of National Biography* (Oxford, 2004); H. C. Porter, *Reformation and Reaction in Tudor Cambridge* (Cambridge, Eng., 1958).

*Francis J. Bremer*

# G

## Gale, Theophilus (1629–1678)

English Dissenter and learned Calvinist theologian. He was born in Kingsteignton, Devon. In 1647 he entered Magdalen College, Oxford, receiving the B.A. in 1649, and the M.A. in 1652. In 1650 he was made a fellow of the college. He was appointed preacher in Winchester Cathedral in 1657, but at the Restoration in 1660 lost both that position and his fellowship. In 1662 he became a tutor to the sons of Philip Lord Wharton, traveling with them to France, where he became acquainted with Huguenot scholars. By 1666 he was back in London, and thereafter he established an academy for the sons of Dissenters at Newington Green; he also assisted John Rowe in the latter's Congregational church in Holborn, London.

He was the author of writings greatly reputed for their learning by his contemporaries. His monumental *The Court of the Gentiles* (4 vols., 1669–1678), on the basis mostly of philology, maintained that all learning had come down from the ancient Jews, including even the philosophy of Plato, which he reworked and presented as a reformed Platonism, it being his conviction that the Gentiles who borrowed the learning of the Jews had corrupted it. He was a strict Calvinist who insisted strongly on predestination and argued that true moral virtue was impossible without grace. Gale also published works of spiritual edification and was the first English author to write about the French Roman Catholic faction of the Jansenists, whom Gale thought crypto-Calvinists. He bequeathed nearly a thousand books to Harvard College at his death.

*Further Reading*

Norman Fiering, *Moral Philosophy at Seventeenth-Century Harvard* (Chapel Hill, 1981); *Oxford Dictionary of National Biography* (Oxford, 2004).

*Dewey D. Wallace Jr.*

## Gataker, Thomas (1574–1654)

One of the leaders of the puritan movement in the early Stuart church. Born in London, where he received his earliest education, he matriculated at St. John's College, Cambridge, in 1590. He received his B.A. in 1594 and his M.A. three years later. He accepted a fellowship at the newly founded Sidney Sussex College in 1596, but combined his college duties with preaching in the vicinity of Cambridge.

Gataker returned to London in around 1600, tutoring in the household of Sir William Cooke and preaching occasionally at St. Martin-in-the-Fields. In 1601 he was chosen lecturer at Lincoln's Inn, one of the Inns of Court where men trained for the law. In 1611 he resigned that post and accepted the living of Rotherhithe, Surrey. He corresponded with other leading clergy of the day, such as James Usher and Samuel Ward, and was part of the London area's network of godly clergy, lawyers, gentlemen, and merchants. He was respected as a preacher but better known for his publications, in which his religious stand was enhanced by Humanist scholarship.

For the most part Gataker was able to steer clear of clashes with the church hierarchy, though he was briefly imprisoned in 1625 for having provided prefaces for two books condemned as seditious. He was nominated to the Westminster Assembly, where he sided with the Presbyterian majority. He served on various committees, including the one assigned the task of developing a confession of faith. Ill health forced him to withdraw from the activities of the Assembly in 1645, though he retained his pastoral post and wrote a number of tracts against what he deemed the antinomian views of John Saltmarsh. He signed the address against the trial and execution of Charles I. He died in Rotherhithe in 1654.

*Further Reading*
Peter Lake, *The Boxmaker's Revenge: "Orthodoxy," "Heterodoxy," and the Politics of the Parish in Early Stuart London* (Manchester, Eng., 2001); *Oxford Dictionary of National Biography* (Oxford, 2004); Paul Seaver, *The Puritan Lectureships: The Politics of Religious Dissent* (Stanford, 1970).

*Francis J. Bremer*

## Gifford, George (1548–1600)

Church of England clergyman and prolific writer of "sociological" Protestant tracts. Gifford was born in Dry Drayton, Cambridgeshire. Graduating from Christ's College, Cambridge, in 1570, he became an undermaster at Brentwood School, Essex. Although he was still a layman, the archdeacon of Essex allowed him to speak at the "prophesyings" held in Brentwood on the grounds that he was a learned and able teacher.

Ordained by John Aylmer, bishop of London, in 1578, Gifford served a brief curacy at All Saints and St. Peter Maldon, Essex, before his institution as vicar there in August 1582. He was probably the chief organizer at this time of the Braintree conference of ministers. In March 1584 Aylmer suspended him for refusing to subscribe Archbishop John Whitgift's newly imposed Three Articles, and although William Cecil, Lord Burghley, intervened on Gifford's behalf he was deprived by the High Commission in June or July, the only Essex minister to lose his benefice during the subscription crisis.

Compromise was effected, and Gifford remained in Maldon for the rest of his life as town preacher, continuing to lead the Braintree conference. Following a further suspension for refusing the surplice in July 1586, he joined Robert Earl of Leicester in the Low Countries as a chaplain to the English troops. After Sir Philip Sidney was fatally wounded at Zutphen on 22 Sept 1586, Gifford remained with him until he died on 17 October. Gifford wrote *The Manner of Sir Philip Sidney's Death,* perhaps at the request of Lady Rich, the "Stella" of Sidney's sonnets. It remained in manuscript until 1973.

In March 1587, with other members of the Braintree conference, Gifford petitioned Parliament for restoration to his public ministry. He was restored by early 1589, and Aylmer and Whitgift made no further serious attempt to pursue him. He was not examined during the Star Chamber trials of 1590–1591, which followed the exposure of the conference movement and the pursuit of "Martin Marprelate" and the separatist leaders.

One of the most prolific of godly writers, Gifford's works blended practical piety with common sense and the level-headed defense of a moderate, evangelizing Protestant tradition. In 1581 he dedicated to Ambrose Earl of Warwick his most reprinted work, *A Briefe discourse of certaine points of the religion, which is among the common sort of Christians, which may be termed the Countrie Divinitie.* This proved the inspiration for Arthur Dent's even more popular *The plaine-mans pathe-way to heaven* (1601).

A stream of publications followed during the last nineteen years of Gifford's life. In *A dialogue betweene a papist and a protestant* (1582), he coined the phrase "church papist." *A Discourse of the Subtill Practices of Devilles by Witches and Sorcerers* (1587) and *A Dialogue concerning Witches and Witchcraftes* (1593) have appealed to historians for their moderation and to literary critics for their possible influence upon Shakespeare.

What above all carried Gifford through the crisis years of 1589–1591 was his uncompromising denunciation of separatism. From 1588 he conducted a personal campaign against John Greenwood and Henry Barrow, in 1590 publishing *A short treatise against the Donatists of England, whome we call Brownists* and *A Plaine Declaration that our Brownists be full Donatists,* both dedicated to Lord Burghley. *A Short Reply unto the Last Printed Books of Henry Barrow and John Greenwood* appeared in 1591.

Gifford's numerous treatises were complemented by a succession of sermons, over forty in all, published either singly or in bulk. His will (dated 8 May, probated 31 May 1600) appointed his wife, Agnes, as sole executrix and left bequests to six sons and two daughters.

*See also:* Conference Movement, Witchcraft
*Further Reading*
Patrick Collinson, John Craig, and Brett Usher, eds., *Conferences and Combination Lectures in the Elizabethan Church: Dedham and Bury St. Edmunds, 1582–1590* (Woodbridge, Eng., 2003).

*Brett Usher*

## Gillespie, George (1613–1648)

Scottish Presbyterian divine and commissioner to the Westminster Assembly; son of John Gillespie, minister of Kirkcaldy. After his education at St. Andrews University, he refused episcopal ordination, and became domestic chaplain to the Presbyterian Viscount Kenmure, also patron of Samuel Rutherford. On Kenmure's death in 1634, he became chaplain to another radical nobleman, the Earl of Cassilis. In 1637, Gillespie published anonymously his major work, *A Dispute against the English Popish Ceremonies,* which condemned the innovations being introduced into Scottish worship by the Laudians and Charles I. Published in the same year as the Prayer Book controversy in Scotland, the book quickly established Gillespie's reputation in Scotland's resurgent Presbyterian movement.

After the signing of the National Covenant in 1638, Gillespie was ordained minister of Wemyss in Fife, and later in the year he preached before the Glasgow Assembly, which abolished episcopacy.

After a short period as a chaplain to the Covenanter army, he was sent to London in 1640 as one of the Covenanters' clerical commissioners. In 1641, he preached before Charles I in Edinburgh, and in the following year he was made minister of Greyfriars Kirk.

In 1643, Gillespie was appointed as one of the Scottish ministers to the Westminster Assembly, and he remained at the assembly until 1647. He participated fully in the assembly's debates, worked on the committee drafting the Confession of Faith, and preached before the House of Commons in 1644 and the House of Lords in 1645. In the assembly, he crossed swords with Independents like Thomas Goodwin, and Erastians like Thomas Coleman and John Selden. He published a number of works against Erastianism, particularly *Aaron's Rod Blossoming* (1646), one of the major discussions of the relationship between civil and ecclesiastical power in the Scottish Presbyterian tradition. He also wrote extensively against Independents, and his *Wholesome Severity Reconciled with Christian Liberty* (1645) attacked toleration and defended a traditional Reformed doctrine of religious coercion. His posthumously published *A Treatise of Miscellany Questions* (1649) is a fascinating compendium of his opinions on ecclesiology, theology, and politics. In 1645, he presented the Westminster Directory to the Scottish General Assembly, and on his return to Edinburgh in 1647, he presented the Westminster Confession of Faith. He was elected minister of the High Church of Edinburgh, and in 1648 he was appointed Moderator of the General Assembly. He was adamantly opposed to the oath of Engagement that attested loyalty to the Commonwealth, and maintained a radical Presbyterian line until his death.

His manuscript notes on the Westminster Assembly debates were finally edited and published in 1846.

*See also:* Westminster Assembly
*Further Reading*
W. M. Campbell, "George Gillespie," *Records of the Scottish Church History Society* 10 (1949), 107–123.

*John Coffey*

## Gillespie, Patrick (1617–1675)

Scottish Covenanter; younger brother of George Gillespie. Educated at St. Andrews (M.A., 1635), he became minister of Kirkcaldy in 1642 and of Glasgow High Church in 1648. Along with his brother, Samuel Rutherford, and James Guthrie, he belonged to the radical party in the Kirk, and was strongly opposed to compromise with the king. After the regicide in 1649, he insisted that Charles II must not be proclaimed king until he had first subscribed the Covenants (the Scotish National Covenant and the Solemn League and Covenant) and proven his commitment to a Presbyterian settlement.

After the defeat of the Covenanters at Dunbar, Gillespie sided with the Remonstrants, who rejected an alliance with Scottish royalists. He became a key leader of the Remonstrant or Protester party during the 1650s, and was bitterly resented by the moderate Royalist Resolutioners like Robert Baillie. Because they were deeply critical of the Stuarts, the Protesters were initially favored by Cromwell, and in 1653 Gillespie was appointed Principal of Glasgow University. He worked closely with the Cromwellian regime and was regarded as a traitor by many Covenanters. At the Restoration, Gillespie was imprisoned in Stirling Castle. However, in contrast to James Guthrie, who was executed, Gillespie repented of his opposition to the Stuarts and escaped death by asking for the king's mercy. A gifted preacher and theologian, Gillespie wrote extensively on covenant theology, though much of his work remained in manuscript. His posthumous work, *The Ark of the Covenant Opened* (1677), was warmly praised in the preface by John Owen, an old acquaintance of Gillespie from the 1650s.

*Further Reading*
Frances Dow, *Cromwellian Scotland, 1651–60* (Edinburgh, 1979).

*John Coffey*

## Goad, Roger (1538–1610)

College head. Goad was born in Buckinghamshire. He was educated at Eton and then at King's College, Cambridge, where he received his B.A. in 1560 and M.A. in 1563. He was ordained in 1565 and took his B.Th. in 1569 and his D.D. in 1576. While a fellow at King's in 1565, he was critical of the state of religion in the college. In 1570 that became his responsibility when he was elected provost (head) of King's.

Goad was one of those some historians refer to as moderate puritans. He was clearly a dedicated Calvinist in his theology, but he was less critical than others of the church's practices and governance. Thus, he sided with Archbishop John Whitgift as one of the college heads who voted in 1570 to deprive the popular puritan Thomas Cartwright of Cartwright's Lady Margaret professorship. In 1580 he was a member of a panel that examined members of the Family of Love. He joined William Fulke in debating the imprisoned Jesuit Edmund Campion in 1581. He also joined with other moderate puritans in trying to persuade Cartwright to write a refutation of the Catholic Rheims translation of the New Testament. More significantly, in the late 1590s he played a major role within the university in attacking the Arminian views of Peter Baro and William Barrett, a controversy that led to the issuing of the Lambeth Articles asserting the Calvinist position of the church. In 1599 he joined with Laurence Chaderton in confuting the Arminian views of John Overall.

Goad's record as a college head was mixed. He sold off vestments and church ornaments he considered popish in order to build a new library, and he increased the number of preaching fellows at King's. He himself delivered divinity lectures on a frequent basis. But he aroused opposition for his effort to impose a strict dress code and for his efforts as vice-chancellor of the university in 1595 to prohibit football, bear baiting, public swimming, and other popular activities. Some of his critics also charged him with inappropriately using college property for his own benefit.

*Further Reading*
Peter Lake, *Moderate Puritans and the English Church* (Cambridge, Eng., 1983); H. C. Porter, *Reformation and Reaction in Tudor Cambridge* (Cambridge, Eng., 1958).

*Francis J. Bremer*

## Goodwin, John (ca. 1594–1665)

Church of England clergyman, Independent controversialist, and Arminian theologian. Goodwin was born in Norfolk and entered Queen's College, Cambridge, in 1612. He received his B.A. in 1616 and was elected a fellow of the college in 1617. Among his contemporaries at Queen's were senior clergy like John Preston and John Davenant, as well as younger men like Thomas Edwards and Thomas Fuller. In 1625, Goodwin left the college to become vicar of East Rainham in Norfolk. He was also appointed to a lectureship at Yarmouth in 1627, and he became vicar of St. Nicholas, Kings Lynn, in 1629, but was suspended within a year. He also preached at Norwich, Dover, and London, and quickly gained a reputation as a rising star among the godly.

In 1633, Goodwin succeeded John Davenport as vicar of St. Stephen's, Coleman Street, in London, where he soon established himself as one of the city's leading puritan preachers. William Kiffin heard him soon after his arrival in London and was struck by Goodwin's critique of puritan "preparationists," who taught that one must preach the terrors of the law to prepare a sinner's heart for conversion. Goodwin's teaching on justification was also distinctive—he argued that justification involved the sinner being declared righteous on account of Christ's sacrifice, but did not involve "the imputation of Christ's righteousness." This teaching provoked charges of Socinianism from the veteran heresy hunter George Walker in the late 1630s, and it led to a substantial pamphlet debate in 1640–1642, culminating in Goodwin's first major theological work, *A Treatise of Justification* (1642). Goodwin also courted controversy with the church authorities, and he was cited for nonconformity at episcopal visitations in 1635 and 1637. However, he avoided further censure and was able to maintain his living, and in 1639 he warned Thomas Goodwin against fostering separatism from the Church of England. He was well connected with the disaffected godly networks in London and the southeast—besides knowing Thomas Goodwin and Samuel Hartlib, he was also personally acquainted with Lady Clark of Reading, Lady Mary Vere, the Hampden family, and John Pym.

With the recall of the Long Parliament in November 1640, Goodwin and his congregation threw themselves into the movement of protest against Charles I's personal rule. Goodwin published several books of sermons, and in November 1641 he preached and published a fiery sermon entitled *Ireland's Advocate,* which lamented the massacre of Protestants in Ireland and fed fears of a popish plot. In 1642 one of Goodwin's parishioners, Isaac Pennington, was elected lord mayor of London. After the outbreak of Civil War, Goodwin was among the first puritan divines to publish a work of resistance theory, *Anti-Cavalierisme* (1642), which depicted the conflict as a war between Christ and Antichrist. Throughout the Civil War, Goodwin and his followers called for a vigorous prosecution of the war against the king.

At the same time, Goodwin was beginning to establish a gathered church within his parish congregation. By 1644 this had led to conflict with some leading parishioners who feared that the traditional parish organization was being undermined. In 1645, Goodwin was removed from his living and replaced by the Presbyterian William Taylor. In keeping with his Independency, Goodwin joined John Milton, William Walwyn, Henry Robinson, and other pamphleteers in the campaign against Presbyterian uniformity. From 1644 onward, he was engaged in controversy with Presbyterians like Adam Steuart, Thomas Edwards, and William Prynne. Goodwin attacked the Presbyterians as persecutors, and he wrote extensively in defense of a wide-reaching toleration, especially in his tracts *Theomachia* (1644) and *Hagiomastix* (1647). He was frequently accused of heresy, and in 1645 one of his former followers, Samuel Lane, claimed that he was preaching Arminianism. Goodwin set out to refute the accusation, but ended up rethinking the Calvinist doctrine, which he had hitherto accepted. Seeking to vindicate himself from charges of heresy, he published another major theological work, *The Divine Authority of Scripture Asserted* (1647).

In 1647, Goodwin wrote *The Army Harmlesse* to justify the New Model Army's revolt against the Presbyterian-dominated Parliament. He looked to

Cromwell to protect the sects, and participated alongside the Levellers in the Whitehall Debates of December 1648, making the radical tolerationist case against the conservative Independent Philip Nye. Goodwin was also active in supporting the army's political revolution. In early January 1649, his *Right and Might Well Met* defended Pride's Purge, and later in the month he was appointed a chaplain to Charles I in the king's final days. In May, he published a vigorous defense of the regicide, *The Obstructors of Justice*. Soon afterwards, William Taylor was ejected and Goodwin restored as vicar of Coleman Street.

For much of the 1650s, Goodwin was involved in theological and ecclesiastical controversy. In 1651, he published his great defense of Arminianism, *Redemption Redeemed*. The work caused consternation among conservative Calvinists and provoked replies from John Owen, Richard Resbury, and George Kendall. Goodwin also engaged in public disputations with Calvinists like John Simpson and Vavasor Powell, and published a series of books elaborating his new theological perspective, including a commentary on Romans 9 and a short work on the salvation of pagans. However, he was distracted from his promotion of Arminianism by a schism within his own congregation, in which some members (including William Allen and Thomas Lambe) left to become General Baptists. Goodwin published several works defending infant baptism. He also continued his old controversies with the Presbyterians, attacking their calls for censorship. In politics, Goodwin went out of his way to defend the Commonwealth and the Protectorate against their critics, but in 1657, he published a bitter attack on the Cromwellian church settlement, entitled *The Triers or Tormentors Tried and Cast*.

In June 1660, a royal proclamation condemned Goodwin and Milton as defenders of regicide and ordered their arrest. Goodwin went into hiding, and his *Obstructors of Justice* was burned by the hangman. He was eventually given indemnity but excluded from public office. Deprived of his living, he was still able to publish (albeit anonymously) a major catechism entitled *A Door Opening unto the Christian Religion* (1662). He died in 1665. John

Wesley and other Methodists republished his Arminian works in the eighteenth and early nineteenth centuries.

*See also:* Arminianism, *Gangraena*, Independency
Further Reading
John Coffey, *John Goodwin and the Puritan Revolution* (forthcoming); Ellen More, "Congregationalism and the Social Order: John Goodwin's Gathered Church, 1640–1660," *Journal of Ecclesiastical History* 38 (1987).

*John Coffey*

## Goodwin, Thomas (1600–1680)

Puritan minister and theologian; born in Rollesby, Norfolk, raised by religious parents, and enrolled in Christ's College, Cambridge, in 1613. Responding there to the spirited preaching of John Preston and Richard Sibbes, whose sermons he later edited for publication, he made these ministers' mood and manner his own. Engagement with Puritan evangelism probably caused him, in 1619, to transfer to St. Catharine's Hall, where he became a fellow and completed his education. The friendships cemented at Cambridge proved invaluable in the religious and civil struggles that lay ahead.

Goodwin underwent conversion in 1620, but for the next seven years he wrestled painfully with doubts of his salvation. Licensed a preacher of the university in 1625 and chosen lecturer at Trinity Church in 1628 (and promoted to vicar in 1632), he distilled the lessons of his long ordeal into sermons printed in 1636 as *A Child of Light Walking in Darkness*. The book enriched the Puritan study of religious psychopathology and established its author as a rising authority on the theory and practice of evangelical piety.

In or about 1633, Goodwin embraced the principles of voluntaryism, exclusivity, and shared governance that the gathered congregational churches of the Puritan diaspora were putting into practice. No longer able to conform to the state church, he resigned his posts in Cambridge in 1634 and moved to London. There he constructed, and published portions of, a multifaceted program of practical divinity. In 1638, he married Elizabeth Prescot, an alderman's daughter and made his way to Arnhem, Holland, where he joined his friend Philip Nye in turning the city's English church into a model of congregational order. Goodwin returned to London in 1640. His anonymous millennial tract, *A Glimpse of Syons Glory,* came out the next year, followed in 1642 by a sermon series, *Christ Set Forth,* that made his name as a preacher.

During the upheavals of the 1640s, Goodwin and Nye led the Independent faction—known as the Dissenting Brethren—of the Westminster Assembly of Divines in unavailing efforts to moderate the presbyterial reformation of the Church of England. Goodwin also pastored a gathered congregation, St. Dunstan's-in-the-East, preached to Parliament, urged toleration of Baptists and other moderate Dissenters, and aligned himself with Oliver Cromwell. In 1649, Cromwell named him a chaplain to the council of state and, the next year, made him president of Magdalen College, Oxford. There for a decade he preached at St. Mary's, presided over an informal religious fellowship, served on town and county clerical commissions, and extended his scriptural and theological studies. In 1658, Goodwin attended Cromwell's deathbed; in the same year he aided John Owen in drawing up the Congregationalists' Savoy Declaration of faith and order.

Sacked at the Restoration, Goodwin spent his last two decades in London extending his inquiries and heading still another covenanted church. Most of his writings after 1642 remained in manuscript until posthumously brought out in five volumes, 1681–1704. Ranging across revealed and natural theology, the *Works* includes commentaries on Ephesians and Revelation, expositions of election and faith, and meditations on such subjects as creation and the creatures, knowledge of God and Christ, and the work of Christ and the Holy Spirit. It was always Goodwin's fervent desire to set forth Christ crucified for the saving of souls. He meant his doctrinal writings to provide foundations for the edifice of practical divinity to whose building he had devoted his younger years. His teachings on assurance of faith, the seal of the Spirit, and the covenant of grace bear his special stamp.

Goodwin's outlook was ecumenical, his temper irenic, his approach to divine revelation progressive and open-ended, his pedagogy free from scholastic restraint, and his style liberal to the point of prolixity. Notable among his theological ventures is his singularly dramatic elaboration of the covenant of redemption. This revision of federal theology shifted the nexus of grace from covenants made in time between God and elect souls to an originative transaction in eternity between God and Christ for authorizing the plan of salvation to be executed by Christ's willing incarnation and death. Forged in the fires of personal religious experience, Goodwin's presentation of the Trinitarian compact helped settle the concept in the expanding repertory of Reformed belief, where it remains to the present day.

*See also: An Apologeticall Narration,* Congregationalism, Dissenting Brethren, Federal Theology, Independency, Puritan Revolution
*Further Reading*
Robert Paul, ed., *An Apologetical Narration* (Philadelphia, 1963).

*Michael McGiffert*

## Gorton, Samuel (ca. 1592–1677)

Puritan lay radical, author, and founder of Warwick, Rhode Island. Born in Gorton, Lancashire, Gorton received some early education but claimed never to have attended university. He took on the trade of clothier and began to develop radical theological ideas by the 1620s. Gorton migrated to New England in 1636, coincidentally during the antinomian controversy. Despite his sympathy for the radicals, Gorton and a small band of followers (known as Gortoneans, or by the supposed Indian appellation Gortonoges) moved within Plymouth jurisdiction by 1638 but quickly ran afoul of the authorities, the problem stemming from a dispute with his landlord, minister Ralph Smith, and also perhaps from his lay preaching. Gorton relocated by 1639 to Portsmouth with some of the banished radicals, but his prickly behavior got him into trouble with authorities: "Judge" William Coddington had him publicly whipped and banished for Gorton's objection to the theocratic leaning of the government.

Gorton moved to Aquidneck with the Hutchinsons and then by 1641 to Providence, where he purchased land near the Pawtuxet River, but he soon tangled with others (including Roger Williams) over boundaries. Gorton won his case, and the losers appealed to the Massachusetts Bay General Court for protection, which was granted in 1642. Gorton responded with a strongly worded letter of protest (which the General Court calculated as containing twenty-six blasphemous statements). Gorton soon moved on to Shawomet (later Warwick), where he purchased unincorporated land from the Narragansett sachem Miantonomi. Other English settlers in the area, however, led by trader Benedict Arnold, again appealed to the Massachusetts General Court for protection from Gorton and his followers; the Court also produced two minor Narragansett sachems, Sacononoco and Pumham, who had disputed Miantonomi's right to sell the land and had pledged themselves to the colony. Gorton refused to honor a warrant to appear before the court, but soon he and his followers were arrested by a military expedition and brought to Boston to answer charges of heresy and civil disturbance. The group was found guilty, sentenced to irons and labor, and sent into different towns, but their sentences were soon overturned.

After his release, Gorton returned to England to press the issue against Massachusetts before the Earl of Warwick's Commission for Plantations; while there, he was active in radical Puritan circles and began to publish. *Simplicities Defence against Seven-Headed Policy* (1646) recounted his treatment by Massachusetts authorities. *An Incorruptible Key to the CX. Psalme* (1647) pled for toleration by contesting civil magistrates' authority over matters of conscience. In 1648, having obtained letters of safe conduct from the commission, Gorton returned to Warwick to help in establishing the colony without interference. He continued to expound his radical ideas, with *Saltmarsh Returned from the Dead* (1655) and *An Antidote Against the Common Plague of the World* (1657), but was rarely involved in controversy for the remaining two decades of his life. In addition to his published writings, he left a manuscript on the Lord's Prayer

and a 1669 letter of refutation to Nathaniel Morton in response to *New England's Memorial*.

*See also:* Rhode Island
*Further Reading*
Philip Gura, *A Glimpse of Sion's Glory: Puritan Radicalism in New England, 1620–1660* (Middletown, CT; 1984).

*Michael G. Ditmore*

## Gouge, Robert (1630–1705)

Puritan clergyman. Born in Chelmsford Essex, Robert Gouge was sent to Christ's College in 1647. His first position after leaving the university was that of master of a grammar school at Maldon, Essex. During his tenure at the grammar school, Gouge also preached at a local church. He accepted an assignment at St. Helen's in Ipswich in approximately 1652. While in Ipswich, Gouge formed a Congregational church under the patronage of Robert Dunkon. Correspondence written by Samuel Petto, a congregant of Gouge's, refers to the minister as "a very gracious man." The Uniformity Act of 1662 silenced Gouge's preaching, yet he remained in Ipswich for about another decade.

In 1672 Gouge relocated to Coggeshall, Essex, where he was named pastor of a Congregational church. In approximately 1674, Gouge renovated a nearby barn to use as a place of worship. He remained in service in Coggeshall for some thirty years. Gouge published *The Faith of Dying Jacob* in the year 1688. He died in October of 1705.

*Further Reading*
*Oxford Dictionary of National Biography* (Oxford, 2004).

*J. Sears McGee*

## Gouge, Thomas (1605–1681)

Puritan clergyman and ejected minister. Gouge was the eldest son of William Gouge, himself a leading puritan preacher of the early seventeenth century. Thomas attended Eton and then King's College, Cambridge, from which he received his B.A. in 1629 and M.A. in 1633. Though he had been appointed a fellow of King's, he left Cambridge to become curate and lecturer at St. Anne Blackfriars, where his father was rector. He later held livings in Middlesex, at London's St. Sepulchre, and in Surrey.

Gouge sided with the Presbyterian party in the Civil Wars, affirming the Solemn League and Covenant and also joining with fellow Presbyterians in criticizing the execution of Charles I. In 1654 he was appointed an assistant to the London commission for the approbation of ministers. Following his father's death, he completed the elder Gouge's commentary on the Epistle to the Hebrews and saw it into print. He also prepared his own *Christian Directions* (1661), a guide to behavior that urged prayer, Bible reading, and better Sabbath observance, while also warning against activities such as cockfighting, theater, and gambling. He was also outspoken on the need to extend charity to the less fortunate.

Gouge was ejected from his living following the Restoration, but continued to minister to a gathered congregation near St. Sepulchre. He served as treasurer of a fund to aid victims of the Great Fire of London (1665). During the 1660s and 1670s he continued to preach and write about Christian duties. Licensed as a Presbyterian minister in 1672, in that same year he began to travel to Wales to spread the gospel there. He helped to establish charity schools there and raised funds for the publication of a Welsh-language Bible and translations of tracts by puritan authors such as Richard Baxter and Arthur Dent. Gouge was a harsh critic of Catholicism and issued a strong indictment of Catholics, *God's Call to England* (1680), in the aftermath of the Popish Plot.

*Further Reading*
*Oxford Dictionary of National Biography* (Oxford, 2004).

*Francis J. Bremer*

## Gouge, William (1578–1653)

Son of Thomas Gouge the elder. William Gouge was born in Stratford-le-Bow, Middlesex. Gouge spent his childhood in the company of several puritan notables. His mother was the daughter of Nicholas Culverwell and her brothers, Samuel and Ezekiel, were prominent godly clerics. William's uncles through marriage, William Whitaker and Laurence Chaderton, were also noteworthy leaders within the godly community. Gouge attended grammar school at St. Paul's and spent six years at Eton. He then continued his education at King's College at Cambridge receiving his B. A. in 1598 and his M.A. in 1601. Because Gouge took pains to live a spiritual life during these years he gained the reputation of an "arch puritan."

His relatives, believing a clergyman should be wed, evidently pressured Gouge into a marriage to Elizabeth Calton. This triggered a period of depression or spiritual crisis that lasted a few years. He emerged from this dark night of the soul in 1607, when he was actually ordained. In 1608 Arthur Hildersham recommended him to the parishioners of St. Ann Blackfriars, London, where he joined Stephen Egerton in ministering to that parish. He preached twice every Sunday and at a Wednesday morning lecture, drawing such large crowds that by 1617 the church was expanded to provide more room for those who flocked to hear him. Gouge soon achieved a prominent position among the godly preachers of the city. He also earned a reputation as a defender of Calvinist orthodoxy at a time when it was coming under attack from Arminians. His *The Whole Armour of God* (1615) was the first of many publications defending that view. One of his more famous publications was his *Of Domesticall Duties* (1622), in which he set forth advanced views on companionable marriage, including efforts to moderate the notion of wifely submission to their husbands and a strong rejection of the right of husbands to beat their wives, views that were not popular among all of his readers.

Diocesan authorities suspected him of nonconformity, and in fact he administered communion to recipients who were standing as well as kneeling, justifying his practice on the grounds that it was a matter indifferent. Nevertheless, his great popularity shielded him from prosecution, and he avoided being deprived. Gouge had surprisingly warm (if diplomatic) praise for Bishop William

Laud's tolerance of leading London puritans. When Richard Stock died, Gouge relaced him as one of the Feoffees for Impropriations.

In 1643 he was nominated to the Westminster Assembly of Divines. Though ill, he attended the sessions regularly. Gouge emerged as a supporter of Presbyterianism and argued that that system of church government was sanctioned by the will of God. Like many Presbyterians, Gouge was a supporter of the monarchy and was critical of the trial and execution of Charles I. Following the regicide he retired somewhat from the public eye. He died in 1653.

*Further Reading*
*Oxford Dictionary of National Biography* (2004); Paul Seaver, *The Puritan Lectureships: The Politics of Religious Dissent, 1560–1662* (Stanford, 1970).

*J. Sears McGee*

## Gough, John (ca. 1521–1572)

Early Nonconformist leader; son of the London Protestant printer John Gough. According to John Stowe, he was a professional scrivener before ordination by Edmund Grindal, bishop of London, in 1560. On 15 November 1560 he was instituted rector of St. Peter Cornhill, London. He contributed the prologue to an abridgement of Erasmus's *Enchiridion* entitled *A godly boke wherein is contayned certayne fruitfull rules, to bee exercised by all Christes souldiers* (1561), he and was associated with Robert Crowley and John Philpot in lectures at St. Antholin's. Along with Percival Wiburn, Gough, Crowley, and Philpot emerged in 1565–1566 as the principal London opponents of Matthew Parker, archbishop of Canterbury, during the Vestiarian Controversy. In March 1566 they were among the thirty-seven city clergy who, refusing the prescribed vestments, were suspended and threatened with deprivation. Too popular in the city for Parker's liking, Gough and Philpot were in June removed into the custody of Robert Horne, bishop of Winchester, and Crowley into that of Richard Cox, bishop of Ely.

Deprived of St. Peter Cornhill, Gough was released from house arrest in November 1566. Per-

haps spending time as a roving preacher in Essex, he was back in London by February 1569, on 15 January 1570 preaching at the Tower of London before John Feckenham, former abbot of Westminster. When Feckenham circulated a rejoinder in manuscript, Gough countered with *The aunswer of John Gough preacher, to maister Fecknam's obiections against his sermon, lately preached in the Tower* (1570).

In June 1571 Gough again faced examination by Parker, but no more is heard of his activities. His will, dated 27 March 1571, mentions no parish. He describes himself simply as "preacher of the word of God," leaving everything to his wife, Mary. John Gough, "preacher," was buried at St. Bartholomew-by-the-Exchange on 1 February 1572.

*See also:* St. Antholin's
*Further Reading*
Patrick Collinson, *The Elizabethan Puritan Movement* (London, 1967).

*Brett Usher*

## Greenham, Richard (d. 1594)

Pastor and preacher. Greenham was likely born in the early or mid-1540s. He matriculated at Pembroke Hall in 1559 and graduated B.A. in 1564. He received his M.A. in 1567, becoming a fellow of that college. He accepted the living of Dry Drayton, a rural parish of around thirty households located five miles from Cambridge, in the summer of 1570.

In 1573, Greenham was threatened with suspension for refusing to subscribe. Though he signed two letters supporting Thomas Cartwright in 1570, he generally opposed efforts to divide the church. Greenham played a central role in the 1580 anti-Familist campaign. He also attacked Separatists such as Martin Marprelate.

At Dry Dayton, Greenham turned his household into a seminary for young men aspiring to the ministry. His pupils included Arthur Hildersham. Over the years his students took extensive notes on his actions and advice, which were copied and circulated and, along with notes of his sermons, became the core of the five posthumous editions of his *Works*.

In 1591, Greenham moved to London, where he became lecturer at Christ Church, Newgate. He became part of the steady influx of puritans from the provinces in the 1590s that sustained the London nonconformist community, which was under pressure from Bishop Aylmer and Archbishop Whitgift. He remained in London during the virulent outbreak of plague in 1593, preaching a series of well-attended fast sermons. He died late in April 1594 of unknown causes.

*See also:* Household Seminaries
*Further Reading*
Eric Josef Carlson and Kenneth Parker, *Practical Divinity: The Works and Life of Reverend Richard Greenham* (Aldershot, Eng., 1998).

Francis J. Bremer

## Greenhill, William (1598–1671)

Independent minister. Greenhill graduated M.A. from Gonville and Caius College, Cambridge, in 1622. He was a puritan preacher from the start of his career, and after becoming rector of Oakley, Suffolk, in 1629, he became an important figure among the noble professors of East Anglia. He contributed to two combination lectures, in Mendlesham, Suffolk, and at St. George's, Tombland, in Norwich. His radicalism was probably helped by the rule of Matthew Wren as bishop of Norwich, who deprived him in 1636 for refusing to read the Book of Sports. With his close friend Jeremiah Burroughes, he fled to Rotterdam, where they worshipped in the Independent church with William Bridge and Sydrach Simpson. By the end of 1637 Burroughes and Greenhill had returned to East Anglia, smuggling in many seditious books.

By 1641 he was settled in London, and Greenhill and Burroughes were appointed as lecturers to Stepney. He was more peripatetic as a preacher, not least in delivering sermons to fasts both to the House of Commons and the House of Lords through the 1640s. His early stance on church government was as an Independent with a concern to maintain control, joining with moderate Presbyterians and Independents in 1643 to publish *Certaine Considerations* to discourage the further gathering of churches. In the Westminster Assembly he was closely associated with the Dissenting Brethren although he was not a signatory to the *Apologeticall Narration*. He became acclaimed for his exegesis of the Book of Ezekiel, running to five volumes between 1645 and 1662, a learned commentary written with an eye to its contemporary relevance.

Through the 1640s his stance developed: he became a rather more radical Independent, always defending religious toleration but willing to condemn the Levellers. He supported Charles's execution but opposed a government based solely on gathered churches. He recognized the need for further reform in the church, joining with other ministers in 1652 calling for committees to provide oversight, went on to be one of the commissioners proposed by the nominated assembly to perform such work and became one of the Triers and Ejectors for the Middlesex commission in 1657. His willingness to work across the puritan spectrum meant that Richard Baxter recommended him as one suitable for a committee to draw up an account of the common grounds and divisive issues among the godly.

His relations with New England were ambiguous. He was one of a number willing to support missionary work with Native Americans (as he had been willing to support what he saw as Vavasor Powell's similar work with the Welsh). He was seen as a potential source of support for Harvard College in 1671. However, in 1669 he had worked with London Congregationalists writing to the governor of Massachusetts to press for an end to the persecution of Baptists.

In 1659 Greenhill, with other leading Independents, sent delegates to George Monck, trying to find a workable government that did not entail the return of the monarchy. He was, of course, unsuccessful, and in 1660 he was ejected from Stepney. He tried to disassociate himself from Venner's Rising, but he suffered from assumed guilt resulting solely from distrust. His political activities had ended, and he managed to keep ministering to a huge gathered congregation in Stepney for the rest of his life (although he was willing to denounce the hedonism and immorality of the court). During his later years, he was probably best known for his numerous dedicatory epistles to devotional works, a provision he had become noted for in the 1650s. He ended his career as he had begun it, as an active preacher to godly congregations until his death in 1671.

> *See also:* Dissenting Brethren, Savoy Assembly
> *Further Reading*
> Francis J. Bremer, *Congregational Communion: Clerical Friendship in the Anglo-American Puritan Community, 1610–1692* (Boston, 1994); Robert S. Paul, *The Assembly of the Lord: Politics and Religion in the Westminster Assembly and the "Grand Debate"* (Edinburgh, 1985); Tom Webster, *Godly Clergy in Early Stuart England: The Caroline Puritan Movement, c. 1620–1643* (Cambridge, Eng., 1997).

*Tom Webster*

## Greenwood, John (ca. 1560–1593)

Separatist preacher and author. Nothing is known of Greenwood before he matriculated at Corpus Christi College, Cambridge, in 1578. After receiving his B.A. in 1581, he was ordained and accepted the living of Wyam, Lincolnshire, in that same year. In 1585 he chose to leave the national church and was next found attending Separatist conventicles in London in 1587.

Greenwood was arrested, examined, and committed to the Clink prison for his separatism. Henry Barrow, his friend and fellow Separatist, was likewise arrested when visiting Greenwood in prison. The two were tried, fined, and transferred to the Fleet prison in May 1588. There the two men devoted themselves to preparing tracts, letters, and other materials that were smuggled out to be printed and circulated. Greenwood in particular defended separatism against the Essex puritan George Gifford. He saw the Church of England as anti-Christian and took a strong stand against the use of any prepared prayers, including the Lord's Prayer. In March and April 1590, he defended his views in conferences with clerical representatives of the national church, including some puritans. Neither side wavered in their convictions.

Greenwood was released from the Fleet in July 1592 and joined the newly organized Separatist congregation of Francis Johnson as its teacher. But within months he was arrested again, as the government decided to strike hard at the Separatist movement. In March 1593 Greenwood, Barrow, and three other Separatists were convicted of a felony and sentenced to be executed for having written sedition. After two last-minute reprieves, they were hanged at Tyburn on the morning of 6 April. The two men became martyrs to the Separatist cause and came to be regarded as pioneers of Congregationalism.

> *See also:* Sects, Separatists
> *Further Reading*
> Patrick Collinson, "Separation in and out of the Church: The Consistency of Barrow and Greenwood," *Journal of the United Reformed Church History Society* 5 (1992–1997), 239–258; F. Powicke, *Henry Barrow, Separatist (1550?–1622)* (London, 1900).

*Francis J. Bremer*

## Griffith, George (ca. 1618–ca. 1699)

Congregationalist minister. Griffith was born in Montgomeryshire. His family was associated with Sir Robert and Lady Brilliana Harley, and young George entered Magdalen Hall, Oxford, in 1638 as servitor to the Harleys' son Edward. He graduated B.A. in 1642 and in 1645 received his M.A. from Emmanuel College.

Griffith was a powerful preacher and was appointed to a position at the Charterhouse in London in 1648. In 1650 the Haberdasher's Company appointed him lecturer at St. Bartholomew's Exchange. Griffith was soon attracting the attention of some of the nation's religious leaders. Along with John Owen and other ministers, he assisted a committee of the House of Commons in drafting a condemnation of the Socinian Racovian Catechism in 1562. He joined with other Congregational clergy in promoting New England missionary efforts to convert Native Americans. In 1654 he was appointed to the commissions for ejecting scandalous ministers and examining those proposed for the ministry. During that decade he was called upon to preach to Parliament and to assist the government in various other capacities. He played a role in the calling of the Congregationalist Savoy Conference of 1658 and served as the scribe to the gathering. Following the death of Oliver Cromwell, he joined with John Owen and others in agitating for the recall of the Rump Parliament.

Griffith accepted the Restoration of Charles II and denounced a 1661 uprising against the monarch led by Thomas Venner. He ministered to various congregations in London during the following decades. In 1669 he joined in a lectureship at Hackney with other Congregationalists (including Owen and Philip Nye) and a number of Presbyterians. Together with other Dissenters, he rejected King James's request for support at the time of the Glorious Revolution of 1688.

Following that revolution, Griffith joined in the effort to reconcile Congregationalists and Presbyterians. He was one of the managers of the Common Fund established in 1690. During that decade he was also outspoken against a resurgence of antinomianism. He died at some point between making changes to his will in 1698 and the date when the will was proven in 1702.

*See also:* Pinners' Hall, Savoy Assembly
*Further Reading*
Francis J. Bremer, *Congregational Communion: Clerical Friendship in the Anglo-American Puritan Community, 1610–1692* (Boston, 1994).

*Francis J. Bremer*

## Grindal, Edmund (ca. 1519–1583)

Grindal has often been misidentified as a "puritan" archbishop of Canterbury, and no less unfairly censured by High Church historians for weak incompetence. Contemporary assessments were very different, although Grindal's evangelical and pastoral understanding of the nature of the church, and of the episcopal office within it, conflicted with the outlook of Elizabeth I and led to his downfall. It was not Grindal but the downfall of Grindal that contributed to the estrangement of the puritans from the established church.

Grindal was born and raised in a remote region, the west coast of Cumberland. Although the homestead was worth less than a pound a year in rent, the evidence of the house itself, which survives, suggests that the obscurity of his origins has been exaggerated. There were connections that made possible a promising academic and clerical career. At Pembroke Hall in Cambridge he passed through the degrees to that of B.D. (1549) (the doctorate would follow much later) and held a number of senior offices in the university. By the Protestant reign of Edward VI, Grindal, who had been ordained under the old dispensation in 1544, was a marked man: he shone in theological disputations, in which he attracted the attention of William Cecil, and became the most trusted lieutenant of Bishop Nicholas Ridley, whose interests as master of Pembroke he had looked after as its president. He was appointed to prebends in St. Paul's and Westminster Abbey and became one of the king's preachers. Toward the end of the reign, Grindal was nominated for Ridley's see of London, following the intended transfer of Ridley to the north. But then came the Roman Catholic Mary Tudor, and Grindal was one of those who went into exile in Germany, dedicated to a hopeful future by Ridley who, with Grindal's other colleagues, stayed behind to face the music, and the flames. Grindal spent most of the exile in Strasbourg, but also lived in a country parish in order to learn German. Strasbourg was the city of the great Reformer Martin Bucer, at whose feet he had sat in Cambridge, and who was a significant influence.

On Elizabeth's accession, Grindal returned to reclaim the bishopric of London. With other émigré Elizabethan bishops, he was disappointed with the moderate, even incomplete, character of the Elizabethan Religious Settlement and made it his business, with mixed success, to improve on it. His first priority was to ordain and promote to key positions competent, learned, preaching ministers. When some of his favorite clergy refused a peremptory demand to toe the line of conformity, particularly on the issue of the prescribed vestments, Archbishop Matthew Parker, who was not a Marian exile, doubted whether Grindal was the man to handle the vestinarian crisis of 1566. But precisely because of his evangelical aims, Grindal had little patience with nonconformity and was later caustic in his criticism of Thomas Cartwright. Parker, however, and no doubt others, thought that he would be more usefully employed coping with the Catholics of the north than with the godly of London and Essex. Protestantism had had little impact in the north of England, and the Revolt of the Northern Earls in 1569 suggested that there was urgent work to be done, to which Grindal addressed himself, not only dealing severely with remnants of Roman Catholicism but promoting preachers into key positions in market towns, where in the next fifty years they made the Reformation happen.

In 1576 Grindal was the choice of Lord Burghley and other top members of the Elizabethan regime to replace Parker as archbishop of Canterbury, although the queen may have taken some persuading. Parker died a disillusioned conservative, and it was time for a refreshing change. It was not to last long. Within a year the enemies of evangelical Protestantism brought to the queen's attention the preaching conferences, set up in many parts of the country, and called, perhaps unfortunately, prophesyings; these conferences were unauthorized, except by some of the bishops, who in Elizabeth's opinion had exceeded their authority. Ordered, in a face-to-face interview, to suppress the prophesyings and to restrict the number of preachers, a horrified Grindal refused to transmit such an order, conveying his refusal in a letter that challenged the very essence of the royal supremacy, quoting liberally and out of their original context the epistles of St. Ambrose to the Emperor Theodosius. Grindal was suspended and sequestered, and the queen wanted him to be deprived, but this would have sent all the wrong signals to the international community, and her ministers worked hard to keep the archbishop in a state of suspended animation. There were plans for a resignation, but Grindal died in office, on 6 July 1583. Assessments of Grindal by posterity are a litmus test of religious attitudes. High Churchmen called him "false brother" and "perfidious prelate"; John Milton thought him the best of a bad bunch of bishops; Richard Baxter believed that bishops like Grindal could have prevented the Civil War.

*See also:* Prophesyings

*Further Reading*

Patrick Collinson, *Archbishop Grindal, 1519–1583* (London, 1979); Patrick Collinson, *Godly People: Essays on English Protestantism and Puritanism* (London, 1983); William Nicholson, ed., *The Remains of Edmund Grindal* (Cambridge, Eng., 1843).

*Patrick Collinson*

## Hall, Joseph (1574–1656)

Bishop of the Church of England. Hall was born in Ashby-de-la-Zouch, Leicestershire, in 1574 to puritan parents. He entered Emmanuel College, Cambridge, in 1589, where he excelled, becoming a fellow in 1595. His devotional writings brought him to the attention of Henry, Prince of Wales, who made him one of his chaplains in 1608. In 1616 he became dean of Worcester, and in the following year he accompanied King James to Scotland and later defended the Five Articles of Perth (whereby King James had attempted in 1617 to introduce some English practices into the worship of the Scottish church). In 1618 he was one of the English deputies at the Synod of Dort, where his conciliatory line received general applause. Having become bishop of Exeter in 1627, he spent the 1630s maintaining a delicate balance: keeping the approval of the central government while practicing a relatively soft policy with puritans.

In 1640 he produced a tract defending episcopacy by divine right, accepting William Laud's revisions. This tract was followed by a similar anonymous piece, thus entering a vituperative debate with the group of Presbyterian controversialists known as Smectymnuans and the poet and at that time controversialist John Milton during which he maintained the Laudian line. At the same time, having been translated to Norwich, he took a more moderate stance as a member of the Lords' Committee on religion. He, along with other bishops, was imprisoned on the grounds of high treason for a while, and his maintenance was seriously cut. He retired to Higham, near Norwich where he preached, for as long as he was allowed and then wrote devotional treatises until his death in 1656.

*See also:* Smectymnuus, Synod of Dort
*Further Reading*
Kenneth Fincham and Peter Lake, "Popularity, Prelacy and Puritanism in the 1630s: Joseph Hall Explains Himself," *English Historical Review* 111 (1996), 856–881; Joseph Hall, *The Works of the Right Reverend Joseph Hall,* ed. P. Wynter, 10 vols. (Oxford, 1863); Peter Lake, "The Moderate and Ironic Case for Religious War: Joseph Hall's *Via media* in Context," in S. P. Amussen and M. Kishlansky, eds., *Political Culture and Cultural Politics in Early Modern England* (Manchester, Eng., 1995), pp. 55–83; R. A. McCabe, *Joseph Hall: A Study in Satire and Meditation* (Oxford, 1982).

*Tom Webster*

## Hampden, John (1594–1643)

Puritan champion of English liberties and cousin of Oliver Cromwell. Born into a wealthy Buckinghamshire dynasty, Hampden was educated at Magdalen, Oxford. He was first elected a member of Parliament in 1625, and he spent 1627 in prison for refusing to pay a forced loan levied by King Charles I on his leading subjects. Hampden became a household name, however, when he contested the legality of the king's infamous ship money assessment in 1636. Hampden's principle of "no taxation without representation" was cited by Edmund Burke in his *Speech on American Taxation* in 1774 and subsequently by the American colonists themselves. Again elected to Parliament in 1640, Hampden rapidly became one of the leading critics of royal policy and played an important part in the indictment of the king's principal minister, Lord Strafford.

In January 1642 King Charles led a band of armed retainers into Parliament to seize Hampden and four colleagues. However, the "Five Members" and their ally Lord Mandeville were forewarned and escaped arrest. As civil war approached, Hampden helped mobilize Parliament's supporters. He provided a regiment of foot ("Hampden's Greencoats") for the Army of Parliament and led it in combat. On 18 June 1643, Hampden was badly wounded in a clash between royalist and Parliamentarian cavalry at Chalgrove Field, close to his family home. He died six days later, and was buried at Great Hampden. There are several memorials to "the Patriot's" memory in Britain and America, not least towns named in his honor, such as Hampden, Maine.

*Further Reading*
John Adair, *A Life of John Hampden the Patriot, 1594–1643* (London, 1976).

*David J. Appleby*

## Harley Family

Sir Robert Harley (ca. 1579–1656), puritan gentleman and Parliamentarian, was described at his funeral as "the first that brought the gospel into these parts" for his patronage of puritan ministers. Sir Robert graduated B.A. in 1599 from Oxford (Oriel College). Between 1613 and 1615, Sir Robert was at odds with his father over his choice of the moderate puritan, Thomas Pierson, as rector of Brampton Bryan. Harley also cultivated a wide circle of puritan clerics outside the county, including William Gouge, Thomas Gataker, Julines Herring, John Cotton, John Stoughton, and John Workman. Harley believed that his support for nonconformist clergymen led to his loss of court office in the

1630s. Sir Robert's first wife, Ann Barrett, granddaughter of Sir Walter Mildmay, the puritan founder of Emmanuel College, Cambridge, died in 1603, and his second wife, Mary Newport, died in 1622.

In 1623 Sir Robert married Brilliana Conway (ca. 1598–1643), who shared her husband's puritan views. She was the daughter of the secretary of state, Sir Edward Conway of Ragley Hall, Warwickshire, and was born at the English garrison at Brill, Netherlands, hence her unusual Christian name. The survival of approximately 375 of her letters to her husband and to their eldest son, Edward (1624–1700), provides a rich illustration of the Harley family's religious life. Brilliana's letters in the late 1630s to Edward, then at Magdalen College, Oxford, reveal her disapproval of Laudian innovations in ceremonial and church decorations. The debates of the Long Parliament also encouraged her hopes for church reform, and in June 1641 she rejoiced at the progress of the Root And Branch Bill (to be distinguished from the Root and Branch Petition) to abolish episcopacy.

Sir Robert's puritanism strongly colored his actions as a member of Parliament (MP). In the 1620s he took a strongly anti-Catholic and anti-Arminian position. In the Short and Long Parliaments of 1640 he opposed ship money, the Laudian church innovations, and the Scottish war. Lady Harley also took an active pro-Parliamentarian role in the county. In the winter of 1640–1641, she helped to collect information about the parish clergy in Herefordshire for the House of Commons committee for scandalous ministers. In the autumn of 1643, she led the successful defense of Brampton Bryan during a seven-week royalist siege. Her death in October 1643 represented not only a personal blow to Sir Robert, but also the loss of a perceptive observer of the local religious and political scene.

At Westminster, Harley supported the reforming middle group led in the Commons by John Pym, Oliver St. John, and John Hampden. In 1643 he chaired the committee for the destruction of superstitious and idolatrous monuments and later took the Solemn League and Covenant. After

Pym's death, in December 1643, Harley took his place on the committee for the Assembly of Divines. Sir Robert's sympathy for the Scots and his religious Presbyterianism meant that from 1645 he was associated with the political Presbyterian party led by Denzil Holles. Sir Robert's eldest sons, Edward and Robert, served in the Parliamentarian army, and in 1646 Edward was returned to the Long Parliament as MP for Herefordshire. In 1647 Edward was one of the eleven members accused by the army of plotting to restore the king to power, and Sir Robert was anonymously charged with financial and electoral corruption and briefly withdrew from the House. In the autumn of 1648 Sir Robert was appointed to the joint committee that formulated the terms offered by Parliament to the king at Newport. On 6 December 1648, as a result of their support for a settlement with the king, Sir Robert and Edward Harley were excluded from the House of Commons by Pride's Purge. After Charles I's execution, Sir Robert resigned his office as master of the mint, marking the end of his political career. The family was removed from local office until 1654, when Sir Robert and Edward were named to the Herefordshire commission for the ejection of scandalous ministers. This appointment heralded Edward's resumption of local power, although he was once again secluded from the 1656 Parliament.

Sir Robert died in 1656, but his patronage of the puritan clergy was continued after the Restoration by Sir Edward's support for Dissenting ministers, including Richard Baxter. In Charles II's Parliaments, Sir Edward strenuously opposed legislation against the Nonconformists, and in 1688 he and his sons actively supported William and Mary against James II. Sir Edward was the author of two tracts on religious issues, *An Humble Essay Toward the Settlement of Peace and Truth in the Church* (1681), a contribution to the debate about comprehension and indulgence, and *A Scriptural and Rational Account of the Christian Religion* (1695), part of a debate about the reasonableness of the Christian religion, to which the philosopher John Locke and John Toland also contributed at the time.

*Further Reading*
Jacqueline Eales, *Puritans and Roundheads: The Harleys of Brampton Bryan and the Outbreak of the English Civil War* (Cambridge, Eng., 1990).

*Jacqueline Eales*

### Harris, Richard (fl. 1576–1620)

Jacobean minister and theologian of moderate Puritan leanings. Of Shropshire origin, he went up as a pensioner to St. John's College, Cambridge, in 1576 and took his degree in 1579 or 1580. He became a fellow in 1581 and was incorporated at Oxford in 1584. He took his M.A. in 1583, B.D. in 1590, and D.D. in 1595. In 1599 he became rector of Gestingthorpe, Essex. He was involved in collegial meetings with other Puritan clergy. He would appear to have been hired as a lecturer by the Colchester corporation, but was dismissed around 1608. In 1612 he transferred to Bradwell-by-Sea, Essex, in 1612. His will was probated in the Prerogative Court of Canterbury in 1621. His only published work of divinity was an intervention against the Jesuit Martin Becan, who had attempted to exploit differences in the political theology of English theologians. Harris's *Concordia Anglicana de primatu ecclesiae regio; adversus Becanum de dissidio Anglicano* appeared in 1612 and was subsequently translated and published in 1614 as *The English Concord*, containing an addition to deal with Becan's reply to the Latin work.

*Further Reading*
*Oxford Dictionary of National Biography* (Oxford, 2004).

*David Mullan*

### Harrison, Thomas (1606–1660)

Parliamentary military commander and religious radical. The son of a butcher (later mayor) of Newcastle-under-Lyme, Staffordshire, Harrison was sufficiently well educated to take up a career as a clerk to an attorney at the Inns of Court in London. At the outbreak of civil war in England in 1642, Harrison, together with Charles Fleetwood and Edmund Ludlow, enlisted in the Army of Parliament. In 1644, he was appointed major in Fleetwood's cavalry regiment in the Eastern Association Army. The regiment soon became notorious as a nest of Independents and fanatics, and Harrison himself was accused of being an Anabaptist. He was, however, favored by the army's cavalry commander, Oliver Cromwell. Harrison distinguished himself at the battle of Marston Moor in July 1644, as he was chosen to ride to London to report the news to Parliament. He fought at Naseby and then Langport in 1645, where Richard Baxter recalled that he gave thanks for the victory "with a loud voice breaking forth in to the praise of God with fluent expression, as though he had been in a rapture." Soon after the regiment was engaged in Cromwell's storming of Basing House, where Harrison was later accused of killing a royalist officer in cold blood. Elected to Parliament in 1646, and associating with the Fifth Monarchists, he began to argue that the king should be prosecuted for war crimes. In June 1647, Harrison became colonel of his own cavalry regiment. The regiment took part in the army mutinies later that year; but, with the resurgence of civil war in 1648, dutifully joined the defense of northern England against Scottish invasion. In combat at Appleby in August, Harrison, despite being wounded, captured an enemy banner single-handed. One of the Parliamentarian officers reported home that he was a "pious, worthy commander." On his recovery, Harrison and his cavalry were detailed to convey the captive King Charles I to Windsor Castle. Charles feared that Harrison had been sent to murder him, but the king was reassured by the colonel's professional demeanor. In the proceedings that followed, Harrison took a leading part in drawing up the king's sentence and was the seventeenth signature on the death warrant.

Harrison reached the zenith of his career in 1650, acting as commander-in-chief in England, and he fought under Cromwell at Worcester in 1651. Harrison aided Cromwell's seizure of power in 1653, leading troops into Parliament and personally "helping" the Speaker from his chair. Despite this, however, his belief in the millennial rule of the Saints on Earth led him to oppose the formation of Cromwell's Protectorate. By 1655 he was in prison, having been deprived of all military and political office. He was released from close arrest in March 1656, but, incriminated in various Fifth Monarchy plots, he was arrested in April 1657 and again in February 1658. At the restoration of the monarchy in 1660, Harrison refused to follow other regicides in fleeing the country. Throughout his trial and execution in October 1660, he remained adamant that the regicide had been the will of the Lord.

*See also:* Fifth Monarchists

*Further Reading*

Maurice Ashley, *Cromwell's Generals* (London, 1954); Charles H. Firth and Godfrey Davies, *The Regimental History of Cromwell's Army* (Oxford, 1940; reprinted 1991).

*David J. Appleby*

## Harvard, John (1607–1638)

Benefactor for whom Harvard College was named. John Harvard was born into a moderate puritan family in Southwark. He entered Emmanuel College, Cambridge, in 1627 and received his B.A. in 1632 and his M.A. in 1635. He married Ann Sadler in 1636, and the following year he sailed to New England and settled in Charlestown. There is no record of his ordination, but he assisted Zachariah Symmes, the pastor of the Charlestown church, preaching there until his untimely death (of consumption) at the age of thirty-one in 1638. Harvard also served on a committee that worked on a draft of fundamental laws that later served as part of the Massachusetts Body of Liberties. He is most remembered for his bequest of half his estate, valued at 1,700 pounds, and his library of 400 volumes to the new college that had already been founded at New Towne in 1636, before Harvard's arrival in New England. New Towne was renamed Cambridge in May 1638, and the college became Harvard in March 1639.

The books Harvard bequeathed to the college consisted mostly of theological works. In addition there were dictionaries, grammars, and Greek and Latin classics, as well as more recent scientific works.

*Further Reading*
Samuel Eliot Morison, *The Founding of Harvard College* (Cambridge, MA., 1935); Alfred C. Potter, "Catalogue of John Harvard's Library," in *Publications of the Colonial Society of Massachusetts* 21 (1919), 190–230.

*Ralph Young*

## Henderson, Alexander (ca. 1583–1646)

Scottish Presbyterian divine and Covenanter leader; born around 1583 in the parish of Criech, Fifeshire, and educated at St. Andrews University (M.A., 1603). After teaching at the University for some years, he became minister of Leuchars in 1612. At this stage in his career, Henderson enjoyed the patronage of the archbishop of St. Andrews and was aligned with the episcopal party in the Kirk. During the 1610s, however, he switched his allegiance to the Presbyterian faction and opposed the Articles of Perth in 1618. Thereafter, he was closely connected to radical Presbyterian networks, and in 1637 he helped to orchestrate the campaign against the new Scottish Prayer Book. Along with Archibald Johnston of Wariston, he drafted the National Covenant in February 1638 and was elected moderator of the General Assembly in November, masterminding its abolition of episcopacy. In 1639, he became minister of the High Kirk in Edinburgh and wrote manuscript defenses of armed resistance on behalf of the covenant. The King's *Large Declaration* (1639) described him as "the prime and most rigid Covenanter in the Kingdome." In 1640, he was elected rector of Edinburgh University, a position he held until his death.

The success of the Covenanter Revolution was such that in 1640–1641 Henderson was sent as a Scottish Commissioner to London, where he preached to throngs of English puritans. Aware that many English churchmen were reluctant to abolish episcopacy altogether, he published several Presbyterian pamphlets, including *The Unlawfulnesse and Danger of Limited Prelacy* (1641). Later in 1641, Henderson preached before Charles I on his visit to Edinburgh and seems to have developed a good relationship with the king. In 1643, he helped to draft the Solemn League and Covenant and then went to London as a Scottish commissioner to the Westminster Assembly. He participated in drafting the assembly's form of church government, directory of public worship, and catechism. He also preached before the Lords and the Commons, urging them to proceed speedily with reformation of religion. Like the other Scottish commissioners, Henderson was increasingly frustrated by the slow pace of reform in the Westminster Assembly and by the obstructions posed by Independents and Erastians.

In 1645, Henderson participated in negotiations with the king at Uxbridge, and after the royalist defeat, he exchanged a number of papers with Charles about episcopacy in May to July 1646. According to Robert Blair, he and Henderson fell on their knees before the king, pleading with him to accept the peace terms of the Covenanter-Parliamentarian alliance, but to no avail. These fruitless negotiations placed great strain on Henderson's fragile health, and he died on 19 August. He was buried in Greyfriars churchyard, where the National Covenant had been signed in 1638. He was irreplaceable, and in his absence the Kirk became bitterly divided. In his lifetime, he had done more than any other individual since Knox and Melville to shape the Scottish Presbyterian tradition.

*See also:* National Covenant, Solemn League and Covenant

*Further Reading*
John Aiton, *The Life and Times of Alexander Henderson* (Edinburgh, 1836); David Stevenson, *The Scottish Revolution* (Edinburgh, 1973).

*John Coffey*

## Henry, Philip (1631–1696)

Moderate Presbyterian divine and diarist. Philip Henry was an unusual puritan, since he was brought up at Charles I's court and after 1660 lived as a country gentleman at Broad Oak, Flintshire. Henry, the son of a court official, was educated at Westminster School under Richard Busby and at Christ Church, Oxford, from which he graduated B.A. in 1651 and M.A. in 1652. He was a horrified eyewitness to the execution of Charles I.

In the mid-1650s he secured posts as tutor to the sons of John Puleston, Justice of the Common Pleas, at Emral, Flintshire, and preacher at nearby Worthenbury Chapel. In 1657 he received Presbyterian ordination from the Shropshire classis. Henry was a convinced Calvinist, but seems to have favored a modified form of episcopacy, such as that associated with Archbishop James Ussher of Ireland, rather than classical Presbyterianism. In 1658 Worthenbury had become a parish in its own right, and Henry became the incumbent, but this arrangement was reversed in 1660, and he reverted to the role of curate.

Since Henry would not consent to reordination, nor read the services of the Book of Common Prayer, he was discharged in 1661 as incapable of preferment. Although not technically an ejected minister, because he was not an incumbent, Henry henceforth marked St. Bartholomew's Day, 24 August, as the anniversary of his silencing as a preacher. Throughout the 1660s, Henry attended parish churches, but did not take Holy Communion; under the 1672 indulgence, he was licensed to preach at his own house, but did not preach at the same times as the local church services. This arrangement continued until 1681, when he was fined for keeping a conventicle. In the early 1680s he debated ordination with Bishop Lloyd of St. Asaph. He was imprisoned in Chester Castle during the Monmouth Rebellion. After the Toleration Act, Henry once again began to minister to his congregation, now at the same hours as church services, in a building close to his house. Henry published nothing, but left voluminous manuscripts, including a diary, and his son Matthew became a leading Nonconformist clergymen and biblical commentator.

*Further Reading*
Matthew Henry Lee, ed., *Diaries and Letters of Philip Henry* (London, 1882).

*John Spurr*

## Herle, Charles (1598–1659)

Puritan clergyman and author. Herle was born in Cornwall. He studied at Exeter College, Oxford,

receiving his B.A. in 1615 and his M.A. three years later. He briefly served as rector of a parish in Cornwall and then was presented to the living of Winwick, Lancashire.

Herle's first publication, in 1631, was a series of meditations on incidents from scripture that he wrote to demonstrate the devotional richness in English Protestantism. With the outbreak of the Civil Wars he moved to London. In October of 1642 he was invited to preach a fast sermon to the House of Commons and responded with a call for action against sectarian errors, Arminianism, and popery. He became a defender of Parliament's cause, publishing justifications for the war in 1642 and 1643. Herle's publications and sermons gained him greater attention, and he was soon recognized as one of the leading clerical advisors to John Pym and the parliamentary leadership. He was named one of the delegates to the Westminster Assembly charged to reform the church.

As the puritan cause fragmented, Herle was viewed as a Presbyterian, but his stance was moderate, and he argued along with his colleague Stephen Marshall for a middle way. He agreed with the Congregationalists in the Assembly on some points, was a friend of Philip Nye, and licensed the Dissenting Brethren's *An Apologeticall Narration* for publication. Despite sharing common ground on some issues, he rejected the argument for congregational independency, expressing his criticisms in *The Independency on Scriptures of the Independency of Churches* (1643). That tract was answered by the New Englanders Richard Mather and William Thompson, who knew Herle well, in *A Modest and Brotherly Answer to Mr. Herle.*

In the middle of the 1640s, Herle began to spend more of his time in his Lancashire parish. Like many Presbyterians, he seems to have had doubts about the execution of Charles I. There were suspicions that he was in correspondence with royalists in the early 1650s, but he was nevertheless appointed to the Lancashire commission of Triers and Ejectors in 1654. He died in September 1659.

*Further Reading*
Francis J. Bremer, *Congregational Communion: Clerical Friendship in the Anglo-American*

*Puritan Community, 1610–1692* (Boston, 1994); Robert S. Paul, *The Assembly of the Lord: Politics and Religion in the Westminster Assembly* (Edinburgh, 1985).

*Francis J. Bremer*

## Herring, Julines (1582–1644)

Church of England clergyman and minister in the Netherlands. Born in Montgomeryshire, he spent much of his youth in Coventry, where he attended school and demonstrated pronounced religious sympathies. He went on to Sidney Sussex, Cambridge, and received his B.A. in 1604. Returning to Coventry, he was encouraged to study divinity by Humphrey Fenn. Along with his friend John Ball, he sought ordination from a bishop of the Church of Ireland to avoid the required subscription to the Thirty-nine Articles.

Herring's first ministerial position was in the parish of Calke, Derbyshire. His popularity was such that the church could not hold those who came to hear him preach. Among those he influenced at Calke was the young Simeon Ashe. After eight years he was forced from that position and accepted the position of lecturer at St. Almund's in Shrewsbury. There he became a key figure in a network of local puritan clergy that included John Ball, Thomas Pierson, and Robert Nicolls. His refusal to conform to the new church initiatives led to his suspension from the lectureship in the early 1630s. Despite this suspension, he continued to preach at private fasts and other nonpublic occasions. He was outspoken in his criticism of Separatists such as Daniel and Katherine Chidley, and in 1637 was one of thirteen clergymen who wrote to leading New England clergy to express fears that they might be drifting toward separatism.

In 1636 Herring was invited to succeed John Paget as minister of the English Reformed church in Amsterdam. Operating within a Presbyterian system, he expressed his preference for that church order and his opposition to Congregationalism when the Civil Wars broke out in England. He supported the parliamentary cause from afar and welcomed the involvement of the Scots. Herring died in Rotterdam in March 1644 before the outcome of events in England was evident.

*Further Reading*
Francis J. Bremer, *Congregational Communion: Clerical Friendship in the Anglo-American Puritan Community, 1610–1692* (Boston, 1994); Peter Lake, "Puritanism, Arminianism, and a Shropshire Axe-Murder," *Midland History* 15 (1990), 37–64.

*Francis J. Bremer*

## Heywood, Oliver (1630–1702)

Presbyterian minister, evangelist, and autobiographer; pursued his ministry in the Pennines, the hill country of West Yorkshire and Lancashire. Born at Little Lever, near Bolton, Lancashire, Heywood was baptized without the sign of the cross due to the strong puritanism of his parents. In 1647 he entered Trinity College, Cambridge, and there came under the godly influence of Thomas Jollie and Samuel Hammond.

After graduating in 1650, he began preaching in Lancashire and soon secured the post of preacher at Coley Chapel, near the village of Northowram in the parish of Halifax in the West Riding of Yorkshire. On 4 August 1652 he was ordained by the Bury Presbyterian classis. At first he lived with his brother, Nathaniel, who was curate of Illingworth, but in 1655 Heywood married the daughter of the minister John Angier, moved to Coley, instituted monthly celebrations of Holy Communion, and two years later erected Presbyterian "discipline," to much local resentment. Heywood's royalism attracted some suspicion in the later 1650s, especially at the time of Booth's Rising. It was, however, the joint forces of the disgruntled among his congregation and the new vicar of Halifax that succeeded in having him suspended from the ministry in June 1662 and then excommunicated.

Although he occasionally preached by invitation in parish churches in the early 1660s, it was after the Five Mile Act (1665) that Heywood left Coley and began his itinerant evangelism across the northern counties: 1669, for instance, saw him preaching at Bramhome, Dewsbury, Cross Stone,

Sowerby, and Coley. In 1670 he was arrested near Leeds, and his goods were seized to pay his fine under the new Conventicles Act. Under the 1672 indulgence he took out a license as a "Presbyterian teacher," and on June 10 over one hundred of his former parishioners entered into a church covenant with him. At Manchester on 29 October 1672, he participated in the first Presbyterian ordination in the region since the Restoration. After the recall of the licenses, Heywood resumed his peripatetic evangelism: he is said to have traveled 1,400 miles in a single year, preached 105 times in addition to Sundays, and kept 55 fast days and 9 thanksgivings. Convicted of keeping a "riotous assembly" in 1685, Heywood spent almost a year incarcerated in York Castle. He welcomed James II's 1687 Declaration of Indulgence and built a meetinghouse at Northowram, which opened in July 1688, and to which he added a schoolroom in 1693. Heywood was a prime mover in efforts to bring the Happy Union to the north of England. On 2 September 1691 he preached to twenty-four representatives of the Presbyterians and Independents and gained their backing for the "heads of agreement" between the two denominations. Heywood's preaching continued unabated until 1700, when asthma confined him to Northowram, where he died on 4 May 1702. He was buried in Halifax church.

> *See also:* Happy Union
> *Further Reading*
> William J. Sheils, "Oliver Heywood and his Congregation," *Studies in Church History* 23 (1986), 261–277; J. Horsfall Turner, ed., *The Rev. Oliver Heywood B.A., 1630–1702; His Autobiography, Diaries, Anecdote and Event Books*, 4 vols. (Brighouse, Eng., 1881–1885).

> *John Spurr*

### Hibbens, Anne (d. 1656)

Boston excommunicant and executed witch. In England the wife of a man named Moore (and mother of three sons by him), Anne probably emigrated to Boston in the mid-1630s with her husband, William Hibbens. They joined the church in 1639. A prominent merchant, William was elected an Assistant (a justice of the peace and member of the Council of Assistants) in 1643, serving until his death in 1654. He was termed "gentleman" and she "mistress" in the Massachusetts records, thus denoting their high status. Her birth name is unknown, although a misreading of a brief reference has sometimes led to her being erroneously identified as Governor Richard Bellingham's sister.

Anne Hibbens ran afoul of Boston's religious leaders in 1640. Allowed by her husband to supervise some carpentry work in their home, she became convinced that the carpenter had both done a shoddy job and overcharged her. After complaining to her pastor, John Wilson, and the governor, John Winthrop, about having been cheated, she initiated a one-woman crusade against Boston carpenters in general, even importing two carpenters from Salem to support her position. The carpenter she initially targeted, also a church member, contended that she had defamed him. Although church elders repeatedly pressed her to withdraw her charges, she adamantly refused to back down. Even more provocatively, Anne Hibbens insisted that scripture—and a sermon delivered by her other pastor, John Cotton—supported her right to maintain her own opinion, despite her husband's willingness to accept the work as adequate. She thus resisted the standard puritan emphasis on wifely subjection. In early 1641, the Boston church excommunicated her, less for the initial slander than for her disobedience to her husband and her lack of respect for community opinion.

In 1655, following the death of her husband, she was accused of being a witch. Colonial commentators later claimed that William Hibbens had suffered significant financial setbacks prior to his death and that she subsequently became more quarrelsome, angering her neighbors. Whatever lay behind her trial—the records of which do not survive—the jury found her guilty, but her husband's former colleagues, the Assistants, refused to accept the verdict. Accordingly, she was retried before the General Court sitting as a whole. The more numerous deputies outvoted the councilors; she was again convicted and was hanged on 19 June 1656. Anne Hibbens was the third woman executed as a witch in New England and the only high-status woman ever hanged there for witchcraft. (Although in 1692 during the Salem crisis other high-status women were accused, none was executed.)

In two June codicils to her 27 May 1656 will, Anne Hibbens expressed appreciation to her son, Jonathan Moore, who had traveled from England to be with her. She named overseers for an estate of nearly 350 pounds, asking to be buried near her husband.

*Further Reading*
Carol Karlsen, *The Devil in the Shape of a Woman: Witchcraft in Colonial New England* (New York, 1987); Mary Beth Norton, *Founding Mothers and Fathers: Gendered Power and the Forming of American Society* (New York, 1996).

*Mary Beth Norton*

## Higginson, Francis (1587–1630)

Puritan clergyman and New England colonist. Higginson matriculated at St. John's, Cambridge, in 1602 but then moved to Jesus College, where he received his B.A. in 1610 and M.A. in 1613.

Higginson was ordained in 1614 in the diocese of York and began his clerical career as a conformist. Sometime after 1615 he came under the influence of the puritan Arthur Hildersham and gradually shifted toward a nonconformist stance himself. In 1627 he was deprived of his license, and the following year the Court of High Commission began proceedings against him, leading him to offer his services to the Massachusetts Bay Colony.

Higginson settled in Salem, Massachusetts, in 1629 and, together with Samuel Skelton, organized that community's church. Some settlers complained that in their failure to use the Book of Common Prayer and in the forms of governance they introduced, Higginson and Skelton were pursuing a separatist path. Such reports also troubled some English puritans, including John Cotton, who wrote to inquire what was happening in the colony. Higginson contracted a fever and died in August 1630. His influence on the colony remained through publication of a letter he had written to English friends describing the colony and its prospects in very positive terms.

*Further Reading*
Robert Charles Anderson, ed., *The Great Migration Begins: Immigrants to New England, 1620–1633*, vol. 2 (Boston, 1995).

*Francis J. Bremer*

## Higham (Heigham), Sir John (1540–1626)

One of the godly magistrates of Suffolk in the late sixteenth and early seventeenth centuries. He was the son of Sir Clement Higham, who was a judge and speaker of the House of Commons. His mother was Anne Waldegrave, the daughter of another prominent Suffolk family. Sir Clement was a committed Roman Catholic who reached the pinnacle of his influence in the reign of Queen Mary. He resigned from public life with the accession of Elizabeth.

Little is known of John's youth, but it is believed that he studied for a time at Trinity Hall, Cambridge. He entered Lincoln's Inn in 1558 and was called to the bar in 1565. He served as a member of Parliament for Sudbury, Suffolk, in 1563, was named to the Suffolk commission of the peace (making him a justice of the peace) in 1573, and knighted in 1578.

Whereas his father was a stalwart Catholic, Sir John became known as one of the principal magistrates, along with Sir Robert Jermyn, who were responsible for transforming the Stour Valley region of East Anglia into what some have called a "godly kingdom." He also cooperated with evangelical clergy in trying to advance religious reform in the region. In the 1580s his support for the godly faction in Bury St. Edmunds led to a clash with Bishop Edmund Freke and the temporary removal of Higham and Jermyn from the commission. He was selected the member of Parliament for Ipswich in 1584 and was returned to represent the county in the parliaments of 1586 and 1604. There he continued his efforts for reform. In the parliament of 1586 he spoke in favor of the speedy execution of Mary Stuart, Queen of Scots. His death in 1626 was a major blow for those who sought to preserve the strength of puritanism in Suffolk.

*Further Reading*

Francis J. Bremer, *John Winthrop: America's Forgotten Founding Father* (New York, 2003); Diarmaid MacCulloch, *Suffolk and the Tudors: Politics and Religion in an English County, 1500–1600* (Oxford, 1986); *Oxford Dictionary of National Biography* (Oxford, 2004).

Francis J. Bremer

## Hildersham, Arthur (1563–1632)

Puritan minister; undoubtedly a key figure within the puritan movement in late Elizabethan and Jacobean England. Frequently in trouble with the ecclesiastical authorities, he played a vital role in internal communications within the godly community and was renowned not only for his ministry but also for his activism in promoting reform in the church.

Hildersham was born in Stetchworth, Cambridgeshire, into an illustrious Catholic family with royal connections. Destined for the Catholic priesthood, Hildersham was sent to school in Saffron Walden, Essex, where he was converted to Protestantism by the headmaster. He matriculated at Christ's College, Cambridge, in 1576, but was removed by his father in 1578 in the hope that Arthur would continue his studies in Rome. Arthur refused and was consequently disinherited, yet he secured the patronage of a distant cousin, the puritan Earl of Huntingdon, Henry Hastings, and returned to Cambridge, where he graduated B.A. in 1581 and M.A. in 1584. Although his election to a fellowship in 1583 was vetoed by the master of the college, he was appointed Reader in Divinity at Trinity Hall, Cambridge, through the help of Hastings.

At Cambridge, Hildersham came to believe profoundly that further reform of the established church was required. As a result of his campaigning to achieve this, together with his nonconformist practices, a turbulent relationship with the ecclesiastical authorities formed. In 1587, Hildersham was appointed lecturer at Ashby-de-la-Zouch, Leicestershire, and minister in 1593. Although he spent the most part of his long ministry there, he was admonished and silenced numerous times for his nonconformity.

Many of the sermons he preached at Ashby were published, notably his *CLII lectures upon Psalme LI* (1635) and *CVIII Lectures upon the fourth of John* (1632). Hildersham also compiled several works of godly instruction, including *The doctrine of communicating worthily in the Lord's Supper* (1619), in which Hildersham encouraged the godly to receive Holy Communion regularly, and *The doctrine of fasting and praier* (1633), in which he promoted days of fasting and humiliation in order to facilitate closer communion with God through prayer.

In addition to his ministerial duties, Hildersham was a key link in the godly communications network, often organizing employment for fellow ministers such as William Bradshaw. He played a central role in drafting and promoting a series of carefully coordinated godly petitions presented to King James I shortly after his accession, including the millenary petition of 1603. Although he narrowly missed out on representing the puritan cause at the Hampton Court Conference, he was one of twenty-seven more radical puritan activists who lobbied the official delegates. In 1604, Hildersham, and another thirty or so Nonconformist ministers from the diocese of Lincoln, personally presented a petition to the king at Hinchingbrooke, arguing for less severity in the enforcement of conformity. The petition was secretly printed in 1605, possibly with the help of Hildersham, in *An abridgement of that booke*. The petitioning campaign ultimately backfired, and the king, enraged by the petitions, consequently ordered the enforcement of full conformity in the ministry.

After the virtual failure of the reinvigorated puritan reform campaign, Hildersham fell victim to the new drive for conformity and was himself deprived in April 1605 by Bishop William Chaderton for ceremonial nonconformity. Yet Hildersham remained a prominent member of godly lectures and meetings held at Ashby and the surrounding areas. In 1606, he ingratiated himself with the bishop of the diocese of Coventry and Lichfield, when he defended the established church against a group of

Separatists at a conference held in the house of Lady Isabel Bowes. He was restored to the lectureship at Ashby in 1609, but was silenced again in 1611, after the heretic Edward Wightman scurrilously claimed to have derived his views from Hildersham's teachings. Hildersham was in fact a fierce opponent of separatism and publicly opposed the semiseparatist church established by Henry Jacob in Southwark in 1616.

In trouble again, Hildersham was imprisoned in London in 1615 for refusing to take the "ex officio" oath. Having been released on bail, Hildersham went into hiding, failed to appear when summoned by the Court of High Commission, and was excommunicated, fined 2,000 pounds, and sentenced to prison. He was branded "the prime ring-leader of all the schismatical persons in that countrey," and "well worthy of severe punishment." He was then invited to the exiled church in Leiden, but chose to remain in England, taking refuge in the London homes of sympathetic gentry families. In 1625 he eventually regained his preaching license and returned to Ashby, but he was deprived again in 1630 for refusing to wear the surplice. He was reinstated in late 1631, but died in March 1632.

*Further Reading*
Thomas Cogswell, *Home Divisions: Aristocracy, the State and Provincial Conflict* (Manchester, Eng., 1998); Peter Lake, *Moderate Puritans and the Elizabethan Church* (Cambridge, Eng., 1982).

*Victoria Gregory*

## Hill, Thomas (d. 1653)

Puritan clergyman and college head. The first clear evidence of Hill is his matriculation at Emmanuel, Cambridge, in 1618. He graduated in 1623, became a fellow of the college, and received his M.A. in 1626. Three years later he was ordained. He was one of the young men who studied with John Cotton at Boston, Lincolnshire, as he prepared for his B.D. While at Emmanuel, he preached regularly at the Cambridge parish of St. Andrew the Great.

In 1633 he was presented to the living of Titchmarsh, Northamptonshire, by the Earl of Manchester. While serving that parish, he also came into contact with other leading puritan families, including those of Lord Brooke and the Earl of Warwick. These connections probably were behind Hill's appointment to a House of Lord's committee on religious reform in 1641. Over the next few years he was named a member of the Westminster Assembly, became a regular preacher at Westminster Abbey, and preached to Parliament. In 1645 he was initially named to be the master of Emmanuel College, but was soon moved to the more prestigious post of master of Trinity, Cambridge. Despite his college responsibilities, he preached every Sunday at St. Michael's Church and also preached often in the parish of All Saints. A number of his sermons were published. Hill died in December 1653.

*Further Reading*
Victor Morgan, *A History of the University of Cambridge, Volume II, 1546–1750* (Cambridge, Eng., 2004); *Oxford Dictionary of National Biography* (Oxford, 2004).

*Francis J. Bremer*

## Hoar, Leonard (1630–1675)

Clergyman, president of Harvard College. Following Hoar's father's death in 1638, his mother Hoar migrated with her children to New England, settling in Braintree, Massachusetts. Hoar attended Harvard College, receiving his A.B. in 1650 and his M.A. three years later.

Like many Harvard graduates of this period, Leonard journeyed to England to pursue a career in the ministry of the reforming English church. In 1656 he was presented by Oliver Cromwell to the post of rector at Wanstead, Essex, which he held until he was ejected following the Restoration. In the following years he pursued interests in botany and medicine, formed friendships with Robert Boyle and other members of the Royal Society, and received the degree of Doctor of Physic from Cambridge University in 1671.

In 1672 Hoar returned to New England. He was chosen to succeed Charles Chauncy as president of Harvard College, but his tenure was not very successful. He was in part the victim of disaffection sowed by unsuccessful candidates for the post. The fellows and students turned against Hoar, and a number of them left the college. Hoar's position soon became untenable, and he resigned the post in March 1675. Yet his vision for the college had been a forward-looking one. He sought to introduce experimental science into the curriculum and provided equipment to do so. He secured a new charter that gave more power to the college fellows and less to the overseers. He died in Boston on 28 November 1675.

*Further Reading*
Samuel Eliot Morison, *Harvard College in the Seventeenth Century* (Cambridge, MA, 1935); John Langdon Sibley, *Biographical Sketches of Graduates of Harvard University,* vol. 1 (Cambridge, MA, 1873).

*Francis J. Bremer*

## Hobart, Peter (1604–1679)

Presbyterian minister at Hingham, Massachusetts. A controversial and divisive minister of the first church at Hingham, Massachusetts, Hobart was born on 13 October 1604 in the English village of Hingham. He studied at Cambridge, where he received a bachelor's degree in 1625 and a master's in 1629. Six years later, Hobart immigrated to New England and helped found the Massachusetts town of Hingham. When the church was gathered in 1635, Hobart became its first pastor.

In a colony founded on Congregational polity, Hobart's attempts to control church affairs without the consent of the members proved divisive within his own congregation and troubled clergymen throughout New England. A council was eventually convened that condemned his practices. Hobart's reputation as a troublesome maverick was further strengthened in the "Hingham mutiny" of 1645, in which he and several followers rebelled against an unpopular court-appointed militia officer. In so doing, the men of Hingham accused Governor Winthrop of exceeding his powers and initiated impeachment-like proceedings against him. Winthrop was ultimately acquitted of all accusations. In later years Hobart continued to attempt to increase his power by limiting lay participation in church admissions, dismissals, and discipline. The battles

that took place because of this persistent Presbyterian stance plagued his ministry until his death on 20 January 1679.

*Further Reading*
Perry Miller, *Orthodoxy in Massachusetts* (Cambridge, MA, 1939).

*Aaron Christensen*

## Hoby, Sir Edward (1560–1617)

Controversialist. Born at Bisham, Berkshire, in 1560 and educated at Eton and Trinity College, Oxford (B.A. and M.A. in 1576), Hoby traveled in Europe between 1576 and 1578, before returning to study at the Middle Temple. The nephew of William Cecil, Lord Burghley, Hoby became prominent at court and was knighted following his marriage to Margaret Carey in 1582. He gained lucrative royal licenses for the trade of iron and wool and represented Queenborough, Berkshire, Kent, and Rochester in Parliament. Prominent in Elizabeth's foreign policy, Hoby helped to secure James I's accession and became a Gentleman of the Privy Chamber. He died in 1617.

In his *Letter to Mr T. H.* (1609), Hoby attacked Theophilus Higgons, formerly minister of St. Dunstan's Fleet Street and Censor of Christ Church, Oxford, for converting to Rome. He demonstrated that Higgons was a doctrinal puritan who tore down Oxford's maypoles but had converted to escape creditors, gain preferment, and desert his troublesome wife. Hoby attacked the Jesuit John Floyd, who had converted Higgons. *A Counter-Snarle For Ishmael Rabshacheh* (1613) and *A Curry-combe for a Coxe-combe. Or Purgatories Knell* (1615), ridiculed Floyd's "vision" of Elizabeth I's ghost and his proof of purgatory using the apocryphal Book of Maccabees. In *A Curry-combe*, a lively dialogue against purgatory, Hoby argued that souls went either to heaven or hell, that the early church knew no purgatory, and that differences among Catholic authors proved it a satanic fiction.

*Further Reading*
Bruce Gordon and Peter Marshall, eds., *The Place of the Dead* (Cambridge, Eng., 2000).

*Andrew Cambers*

## Holdsworth, Richard (1590–1649)

Holdsworth can only be called a Puritan if it is acknowledged that a Puritanism eschewing nonconformity, but "orthodox" in its Calvinism and rejection of Catholicism, was the dominant tendency in the Jacobean Church. Born in Newcastle-upon-Tyne, the son of the vicar, Holdsworth was admitted to St. John's College Cambridge in 1607, where he became a fellow in 1613. His patron Sir Henry Hobart presented him to a benefice in Yorkshire, which he soon exchanged for the London rectory of St-Peter-le-Poer. In 1629 he became Professor of Divinity at Gresham College, and later president of the London clergy guild of Sion College.

He was the doyen of the London preachers of his day. He was also an outstanding pedagogue, whose "Directions for Students in the University" explain why he was so much loved by his pupils. Disappointed of the mastership of his own college in 1633, Holdsworth was elected the fourth master of Emmanuel in 1637 and proved to be the best head that house ever had. As the storm clouds of revolution and civil war gathered, Holdsworth suffered the fate of all moderates caught up between polarizing extremes. Originally in good odor with Parliament, he was one of those propounding a scheme of so-called reduced episcopacy, and he was offered one of the bishoprics (Bristol) intended to promote a settlement between the parties (and was the only one to refuse). But if one had to choose sides, Holdsworth could only be a royalist, and soon his actions in contributing to Charles I's fighting fund and preaching a sermon before the king, which the university printed, made him "delinquent" in the eyes of Parliament. When the university elected him Lady Margaret Professor in succession to Samuel Ward, this was regarded as a provocation, and he was imprisoned in the Tower. Cambridge never saw him again, and he died, still under a cloud, on 22 August 1649. His enormous library of more than 10,000 books eventually found its way to the University Library, where to this day it forms the core of the collection of early printed theological and religious books.

*Further Reading*
A. Sarah Bendall, Christopher Nugent Lawrence Brooke, Patrick Collinson, *A History of*

*Emmanuel College, Cambridge* (Woodbridge, Eng., 1999); John Twigg, *The University of Cambridge and the English Revolution, 1625–1688* (Cambridge, Eng., 1990).

*Patrick Collinson*

## Hooke, William (1601–1678)

Puritan clergyman in New England and England. Hooke was born in Hampshire and educated at Trinity, Oxford. He received his B.A. in 1620 and his M.A. in 1623. After his ordination he served as vicar in Axmouth, Devon. His preaching and nonconformity forced him from the pulpit, and he migrated to New England in 1637. He first served as pastor to the Taunton congregation in the Plymouth Colony. In 1644 he joined his friend John Davenport in the New Haven ministry.

Hooke was related to Oliver Cromwell through his wife, Jane Whalley Hooke. It was likely Cromwell who assisted him in the English publication of two fast sermons, *New England's Tears for Old England's Fears* (1641) and *New England's Sense of Old England and Ireland's Sorrowes* (1645). In 1656 he returned to England. Cromwell named him to be one of his household chaplains and appointed him to be master of the Savoy Hospital. He became one of the leaders of the Congregational clergy in London and was a member of the Savoy Assembly that prepared the Savoy Declaration of Faith and Order.

Hooke continued to preach in London after he was ejected from his post following the Restoration. He continued to correspond with friends in New England such as John Davenport and his kinsmen, the regicides Edward Whalley and William Goffe. He died in 1678 and was buried in Bunhill Fields, the Dissenter burial ground.

*See also:* Savoy Assembly, New Englanders Contemplate England's Wars of Religion (in Primary Sources)
*Further Reading*
Francis J. Bremer, *Congregational Communion: Clerical Friendship in the Anglo-American Puritan Community, 1610–1690* (Boston, 1994).

*Francis J. Bremer*

## Hooker, Richard (1554–1600)

Church of England clergyman and theologian. Though his ideas were not widely known or debated in his lifetime, his *Laws of Ecclesiastical Polity* set the Church of England on a course that increasingly diverged from Continental Protestantism. Hooker studied at Corpus Christi College, Oxford, and received his B.A. in 1574 and M.A. in 1577, then becoming a fellow of the college. A sermon he preached at Paul's Cross, London, in 1584 led to Bishop John Aylmer and Archbishop Edwin Sandys recommending his appointment as master of the Temple a year later. His teachings on the nature of faith were attacked by Walter Travers, the lecturer at the Temple, as outside orthodox Calvinist views.

*The Laws of Ecclesiastical Polity* developed out of his debates with Travers and became one of the first major works of English theology and philosophy to be written in English. The first part of that work appeared in 1593, and the final parts were not published before Hooker's early death in 1600. At the heart of the work was an expansion of the areas of *adiaphora*, "things indifferent," that is, matters not expressly regulated by scripture, which could therefore legitimately be decided by earthly magistrates. This expansion was based on the idea that the interpretation of God's will relied heavily on past experience and on human reason as well as on scripture itself. While not departing significantly from the essentials of Reformed theology, Hooker's positions directly challenged some of the other positions of the puritan movement. He was perhaps the first to argue that the Elizabethan settlement was not merely a compromise of the time but the ideal form for the Church of England. He criticized overemphasis on preaching and placed greater emphasis on the sacraments and on liturgical prayer and ceremonies, in many ways anticipating the views that would later be expressed by bishops such as William Laud.

*See also:* Adiaphora
*Further Reading*
Patrick Collinson, "Hooker and the Elizabethan Establishment," in A. S. McGrade, ed., *Richard Hooker and the Construction of Christian Community* (Tempe, AZ, 1997); Peter Lake, *Anglicans and Puritans? Presbyterianism and English Conformist Thought from Whitgift to Hooker* (London, 1988); Diarmaid MacCulloch, *Reformation: Europe's House Divided, 1490–1700* (London, 2003); B. D. Spinks, *Two Faces of Elizabethan Anglican Theology: Sacraments and Salvation in the Thought of William Perkins and Richard Hooker* (Lanham, MD, 1999).

*Francis J. Bremer*

## Hooker, Thomas (1586–1647)

Preacher, theologian, and a prime mover in the creation of the colony of Connecticut; born in Leicestershire. His birth year is usually given as 1586, and his birthplace as Marefield, although it is more likely to have been Birstall. Little is really certain about his early life before his matriculation at Cambridge in 1604.

### English Career

At Cambridge a B.A. in 1608 was followed by an M.A. in 1611, after which Hooker served for a further seven years as a lecturer and catechist at Emanuel College. His conversion experience took place at some point in his Cambridge career and apparently entailed an unusually intense and painful sense of conviction that he was a sinner.

In 1618 Hooker became rector of St. George's in Esher, Surrey, coming into immediate contact with the famous spiritual valetudinarian Joan Drake. Mrs. Drake's travails required the efforts of a succession of divines, of whom Hooker was the most successful in bringing her from despair to a sense of conversion. Upon Mrs. Drake's death in 1625, Hooker took up the position of lecturer at Chelmsford in Essex and at some point also began keeping a grammar school at nearby Little Baddow, employing John Eliot as his usher. The power of Hooker's pulpit oratory made him something of a celebrity in Essex, and in addition, he was the center of a combination of private seminary and ministerial "exercises" that looked back to the Elizabethan "prophesyings" and forward to the clerical associations of Puritan New England. Younger ministers in attendance on the master were said to

*Thomas Hooker and his followers immigrate to Connecticut to start their own colony in 1636. (Library of Congress)*

"trade upon his stock" in their own sermons. Hooker also formed a covenanted religious society that anticipated in many particulars the full-blown Congregationalism of the "New England Way," only without the officers and the sacraments.

Hooker's own difficult conversion, as well as his years with Mrs. Drake, seem to have determined his lifelong engagement with the anatomy and psychology of the would-be believer's path to salvation. Whether imprecatory or consoling, Hooker was always concerned with the states the committed but as yet unconverted believer ordinarily must pass through as preparation for saving grace, the fragmented and extended nature of the later stages of the order of salvation, and the degree to which pu-

tative saints could claim assurance of their salvation. His sermons on these subjects from the later 1620s, when published, proved his most popular works: the three most reprinted titles (*The Poore Doubting Christian, The Soule's Humiliation,* and *The Soule's Preparation*) collectively ran to seventeen editions in the ten years 1631 to 1640, amounting to upwards of 30,000 copies.

In 1628 Hooker is to be found in association with Nathaniel Ward in a complicated intrigue over the mastership of Emanuel, indicating that by that date he was already a well-entrenched figure among the ministers claiming the protection and patronage of Robert Rich, second earl of Warwick. Indeed, among Warwick's protégés Hooker in this period is matched for topical and political commentary in his sermons only by the inveterately partisan Hugh Peter. These activities, along with his prominence in Essex, attracted the attention of the London diocesan authorities, culminating in a summons in 1630 to appear before the Court of the High Commission.

## Netherlands

Hooker promptly went in to hiding, and the next year, 1631, he escaped to the Netherlands. His sermon *The Danger of Desertion,* preached on the occasion of his exile, contains the famous metaphor of God shipping away his Noahs and his Lots to New England. Hooker's stay in the Netherlands was to no purpose, other than to bring him in contact with William Ames. He was unable to take up any permanent position at English churches in Amsterdam and Delft because of suspicions about his allegedly Separatist leanings, and he in his turn dismissed Dutch religion as cold and formalist. In spring 1633 he returned to England briefly in order to prepare for migration to America.

## New England

Hooker arrived in Boston, Massachusetts (in the company of John Cotton and Samuel Stone), in September 1633 and immediately joined a company of Essex migrants at Newtown (now Cambridge). Before the year was out they had formed a covenanted church, which called Hooker and Stone to be their co-ministers. By 1635, however, the Newtown people were complaining of being "stinted" for land, while Hooker himself was tiring of the Bay Colony's penchant for divisive controversies. Repeated attempts to get the Massachusetts General Court to sanction a removal to a location beyond the colony's patent failed, whereupon a portion of the Newtown company removed in 1635 to what is now Hartford, Connecticut. They were followed in 1636 by the remainder of Newtown, as well as Hooker himself, and by colonists from Dorchester and Watertown, who founded the Connecticut towns of Windsor and Wethersfield. Relations with the authorities in the Bay Colony remained strained into the early 1640s.

Hooker played a prominent role in New England ecclesiastical affairs for the rest of his life. He returned to the Bay to serve as the co-moderator (with Peter Bulkeley) of the 1637 synod that condemned Anne Hutchinson and her followers for antinomianism and again, in the company of John Haynes, in 1639 to confer over a potential confederation of the New England colonies. In 1643 he presided (this time in conjunction with Cotton) over another synod in the Bay, which politely but explicitly distinguished the New England Way from Presbyterian alternatives and declared that the churches of the mother country would never be right until refounded on the basis of individual covenants.

At home in Connecticut, Hooker in 1638 cheered on the session of the colony's General Court that wrote the colony's *Fundamental Orders* with an election sermon that was unusual in its emphasis on the right of the electorate "to set the bounds and limitations of the power and place" of those whom they elected. He also continued his exploration of the process of conversion through the sermons published posthumously as *The Application of Redemption* (1656–1657) and *A Comment upon Christ's Last Prayer* (1656).

When an invitation to Cotton, John Davenport, and Hooker to attend the Westminster Assembly arrived in 1642, all three declined, but characteristically it was Hooker who commented tartly that he did not intend "to go 3,000 miles to agree with three men." In 1645, however, at the behest of the clergy generally, he prepared the longest of the various apologias for New England's church polity, *A survey of the Summe of Church-Discipline* (not published until 1648 and then in truncated form). In manuscript the *Survey* may have had some influence on the synods of 1646 and 1647 that wrote the Cambridge Platform, the classic statement of New England Congregationalism, but its author was too ill to attend either meeting.

Hooker died in Hartford on 7 July 1647. Upon receipt of the news, John Winthrop wrote in his *History*, "He shall need no other prayse, the fruit of his labors in both Englandes shall preserve an honorable and happye remembrance of him for ever."

## Assessment

Hooker's historical reputation has suffered to an unusual degree from one form or another of tendentious misinterpretation. Part of the problem lies in his bibliography: no definite canon was established until 1975, while his most popular printed works appeared without any editorial control. Over and above this problem, however, his significance has been muddled by the frequent use of anachronistic or exaggerated antinomies. Changes in sensibility have wrought their havoc as well, so that even his much admired prose style—economical, remorselessly logical, and punctuated by flashes of rhetorical brilliance—is sometimes today damned as closed, cajoling, and coercive. Hooker was a forceful and talented individual of some significance in England and of great importance in New England. He deserves to be judged by friend and critic alike in his own context and for his own sake.

*See also:* Joan Drake, Connecticut, English Puritanism in the Netherlands, Spiritual Healing
*Further Reading*
Sargent Bush Jr., *Writings of Thomas Hooker: Spiritual Adventures in Two Worlds* (Cambridge, MA, 1980); Frank Shuffleton, *Thomas Hooker, 1586–1647* (Princeton, 1977).

*Stephen Foster*

## Hooper, John (ca. 1500–1555)

Bishop of Gloucester. From Somerset and a former Cistercian monk, he fled England in 1540 because of his evangelical views; experience of Zürich (1547–1549) further radicalized him. Lord Protector Edward Seymour Duke of Somerset appointed him chaplain on his return, and he was active in debating with unitarian radicals. In 1550–1551 he refused to accept the bishopric of Gloucester if he must swear to the Royal Supremacy using an oath mentioning the saints, or wear certain traditional vestments at his consecration. He eventually backed down on the latter point, having found no prominent supporters other than the London Stranger Church Superintendent Jan Laski, which showed the limits on institutional change in Edward VI's church. He proved a model Protestant bishop, assiduous in his diocesan court (his diocese was reunited with Worcester in 1552), but he earned hostility from local conservatives for refusing to administer confirmation and for ostentatiously possessing both a family and a long beard. He was an obvious target for the Roman Catholic Mary I, although he had rallied to her rather than Jane Grey. His death at the stake in Gloucester was unusually agonizing. He became an example for Puritans of how the English episcopate might develop, although his outspoken advocacy of divorce in cases of marital breakdown, and his reservations about the growing ascendancy of predestinarian theology, were not in line with future mainstream Puritan thought.

*See also:* Vestments
*Further Reading*
E. W. Hunt, *The Life and Times of John Hooper (c. 1500–1555), Bishop of Gloucester* (Lewiston, 1992).

*Diarmaid MacCulloch*

## Hopkins, Edward (1602–1657)

London merchant who supported the Puritan cause on both sides of the Atlantic. He helped organize the New Haven Colony, served Connecticut for many years, and ended his life back in England as a Commonwealth official. Born in Hertfordshire to obscure parents, he was patronized by a rich relative, who set up Hopkins as an overseas trader. Hopkins prospered, and for the rest of his life was a very wealthy man.

Known for devotions so intense that he went into a trancelike state, Hopkins became associated with Puritans like John Davenport and Theophilus Eaton, whose stepdaughter Hopkins married in 1630. Like them, Hopkins hoped that the Church of England could be reformed from within, until those hopes were crushed by the rise of William Laud. In 1637, he joined Eaton and Davenport in planning the emigration that resulted in the founding of New Haven, an act that signified separation from the national church.

Although Hopkins was a frequent visitor to New Haven, he made his primary residence in Hartford and gave most of his service to the Connecticut colony. Nearly every year from 1640 to 1652, he was annually elected governor or deputy governor, and he was constantly busy in the colony's economic development, its Indian affairs, and its relations with the Dutch in New Netherland. He was also important in organizing the New England Confederation, an alliance of the Puritan colonies.

Hopkins returned to England in 1652. He had some regrets about his original emigration, his wife's mental health was deteriorating, and he wanted to serve the regime of Oliver Cromwell. Upon arrival in London, he was appointed as a naval commissioner, a post he held until his death five years later. He was elected to the House of Commons in 1656, where he served on committees concerned with trade and the war against Spain.

*Further Reading*
*American National Biography* (New York, 1999); Thomas Davis, *Chronicles of the Hopkins Grammar School* (New Haven, 1938).

*James P. Walsh*

## Hopkins, Matthew (ca. 1620–1647)

Self-styled "Witchfinder General," chiefly responsible for the interrogation of about 250 East Anglian people as witches, of whom over a hundred were hanged. Hopkins was probably born in the Suffolk parish of Great Wenham in the 1620s, where his father, James, was rector and an active participant in local puritan society. Hopkins senior corresponded with John Winthrop in New England and willed that his son Thomas should emigrate. Matthew was the youngest of six children to survive infancy. Little is known about his early life, but tradition has it that he was articled as a lawyer in a shipping office in Ipswich.

By 1644, Hopkins was living in the Essex port of Manningtree, where he claimed to have detected a coven of witches, who would have killed him but for his godly election. In March 1645, Hopkins joined forces with another zealous gentleman, John Stearne, with whom he questioned witchcraft suspects from Manningtree and surrounding villages. Hopkins and Stearne crossed the Stour estuary into the puritan heartland of Suffolk, where they continued to exploit local anxieties about the devil, as well as the godly backlash against quasi-Catholic episcopal policies of the 1630s. The witchfinders used illegal methods of torture to extract confessions from prisoners, who included the unpopular (and possibly Laudian) vicar of Brandeston. Sometimes working independently, they moved into Norfolk, Huntingdonshire, Northamptonshire, Bedfordshire, Cambridgeshire, and the Isle of Ely—a route that, in part, resembled that taken by the puritan iconoclast William Dowsing.

In the winter of 1646, criticisms of Hopkins's campaign made by a Huntingdonshire vicar were voiced again at the Norfolk assizes. By this time, it is probable that Hopkins was already weak with the consumption from which he died in the summer of 1647. John Stearne went home to compose a defensive memoir, then retreated into historical obscurity.

*See also:* Witchcraft
*Further Reading*
Malcolm Gaskill, ed., *The Matthew Hopkins Trials*, vol. 3 of James Sharpe and Richard M. Golden, eds., *Writings on English Witchcraft, 1560–1736* (London, 2003); Malcolm Gaskill, *Witchfinders: A Seventeenth-Century* Tragedy (London, 2005); Jim Sharpe, "The Devil in East Anglia: the Matthew Hopkins Trials Reconsidered," in Jonathan Barry, Marianne Hester, and Gareth Roberts, eds., *Witchcraft in Early Modern Europe: Studies in Culture and Belief* (Cambridge, Eng., 1996), pp. 237–254.

*Malcolm Gaskill*

## Howe, John (1630–1705)

Presbyterian clergyman and advocate for puritan union. Howe was born in Leicestershire in 1630 but moved with his family to Ireland after his father was suspended from the ministry for praying publicly that Prince Charles (eventually Charles II) might not be raised in popery. The family fled Ireland following the uprising of 1641. Howe entered Christ College, Cambridge, in 1647, where he befriended Henry Field, Ralph Cudworth, and others, but then moved to Brasenose College, Oxford, in 1648, receiving his B.A. there two years later. In that same year he was chosen to be chaplain at Magdalen, Oxford, where the Congregationalist Thomas Goodwin was college president.

Howe received his ordination from the Presbyterian Charles Herle in 1652, and in 1654 he accepted the perpetual curacy of Great Torrington in Devon. There he began his lifelong efforts to bring together Congregationalist and Presbyterian clergy. A local member of Parliament brought him to the attention of Oliver Cromwell, who named Howe to be a domestic chaplain. As a member of the Protector's household, he would have been in contact with Thomas Goodwin and other Congregationalist leaders such as John Owen and William Hooke. In 1658 he attended the Congregationalists' Savoy Conference as an observer. Following the death of Oliver Cromwell, Howe continued to serve the new Lord Protector, Oliver's son Richard. At that point his friend Nathaniel Mather introduced him to Mather's brother, Increase, whom Howe appointed to take his place temporarily in Great Torrington. However, following Richard Cromwell's stepping down from the Lord Protectorship, Howe returned to his parish.

Howe refused to conform to the Restoration church and was ejected from his living in 1662. Over the next years he remained in the southwest, mostly preaching in private homes and writing various works of theology. In 1670 he moved to Ireland, where he was allowed to preach in Antrim with the approval of the local bishop and archbishop. In 1675 he returned to England and accepted the co-pastorate of the Presbyterian congregation that met at Habersdashers' Hall. He became one of the leading Dissenting clergyman in the city, still working to unite the various puritan denominations, while yet hoping for acceptable terms that would allow comprehension within the national church.

Faced with renewed government action against Dissenters in the early 1680s, Howe was persuaded to accompany Philip, fourth Baron Wharton, to the continent. He remained in Holland until 1687, when James II issued his first declaration of indulgence. Recognized as one of the leaders of the Dissenters, he was chosen in 1689 to deliver a speech of welcome to King William and Queen Mary on behalf of Presbyterians and Congregationalists. He joined with Matthew Mead, his old friend Increase Mather (in England again seeking a restoration of the Massachusetts charter), and others in seeking to unite the Dissenters, combining with them in drafting the "heads of agreement" that led to the Happy Union of London Presbyterian and Independent (Congregational) ministers. He was chosen one of the directors of the Common Fund for the support of needy ministers and ministerial students. He also participated in a combination lectureship at Pinners' Hall that involved both groups. The union soon dissolved over charges that published sermons of Tobias Crisp that Howe and others had verified as genuine actually contained antinomian views. Efforts by Howe and others to save the union failed. Together with other Presbyterians, Howe withdrew from the Common Fund and the Pinners' Hall lectureship and established their own lectureship at Salters' Hall. He continued to be seen as one of the elder statesmen of the Dissenting community until his death in 1705.

*See also:* Conventicles Acts, Pinners' Hall
*Further Reading*
Francis J. Bremer, *Congregational Communion: Clerical Friendship in the Anglo-American Puritan Community, 1610–1692* (Boston, 1994); Edmund Calamy, *Memoirs of the Life of the Late Reverend John Howe* (London, 1724); Alexander Gordon, *Freedom after Ejection* (Manchester, Eng., 1917).

*Francis J. Bremer*

## Howie, Robert (ca. 1565–? [between 1641 and 1647])

Theologian. Howie was born in Aberdeen of a merchant burgess, and graduated M.A. from King's College, Cambridge, in 1584. He may have made his first contact with Ramism during that time. After graduation he, along with his friend John Johnston, went to the Continent. Howie found his way to the university in the German state of Herborn, where he remained until 1588. The new faculty there included Caspar Olevianus, a founder of federal theology, and Howie defended a thesis on the subject while at Herborn. In 1588 he matriculated at the University of Basel, and in 1591 published his only important work of theology, *De Reconciliatione Hominis cum Deo*. That same year he and Johnston returned to Scotland. Before the end of the year he was appointed a minister of Aberdeen. He was then a convinced Presbyterian, but by mid-1597 he had begun to move toward episcopacy. As minister of Dundee from March 1598 he maintained his support for the king's program of episcopacy. In 1607 James VI nominated him to take Andrew Melville's place as principal of St. Mary's College, St. Andrews.

In the following years he was active in the defense of episcopacy, but by the middle of the 1620s his attachment to episcopacy had grown colder, so that in November 1638 he signed the National Covenant and continued as principal. In 1641 Samuel Rutherford brought to light Howie's embezzlement of college funds. He kept his salary, but was deposed from his academic post. He died in obscurity, date unknown.

*Further Reading*
James K. Cameron, ed., *Letters of John Johnston, c. 1565–1611, and Robert Howie, c. 1565–c. 1645* (Edinburgh, 1963).

*David Mullan*

## Hubbard, William (ca. 1621–1704)

Minister at Ipswich, Massachusetts, and historian. His family migrated to New England in 1635 and settled at Ipswich. Hubbard graduated with the first class at Harvard in 1642 but did not become a minister until age thirty-five (1656) at Ipswich, where he teamed with Thomas Cobbet. In 1671 Hubbard joined in castigating Boston First Church's underhanded manner of obtaining John Davenport and then protested the General Court's harsh censure of the ministry in the matter. At the magistrates' request, Hubbard delivered the 1676 election sermon, *The Happiness of a People in the Wisdome of their Rulers Directing*. In 1677 Hubbard's *A Narrative of the Troubles with the Indians in New-England* was published, treating especially King Philip's War. By 1680 Hubbard had begun an extensive history of New England, largely indebted to Governor Winthrop's manuscript journal as well as to works by Edward Johnson and Nathaniel Morton. In 1682, the General Court voted to pay Hubbard the sum of £50 for the work, and in 1683 agreed to advance half the sum if he submitted a fair copy for the press, which he did. But it remained unpublished until 1815, when it appeared as *A General History of New England from the Discovery to MDCLXXX*. Also in 1682, Hubbard delivered both a fast-day sermon and a funeral sermon for Major-General George Denison (published 1684 as *The Benefit of a Well-Ordered Conversation*). Finally, in 1701 he cowrote with John Higginson *A Testimony, to the Order of the Gospel, in the Churches of New-England*.

See also: Puritan Historians
Further Reading
American National Biography (New York, 1999).

*Michael G. Ditmore*

## Hughes, George (1603–1667)

Presbyterian clergyman. Hughes shone as a young scholar at Corpus Christi College, Oxford, where he graduated B.A. in 1619; he then transferred to Pembroke College as one of its first fellows, graduating M.A. in 1625. He was later incorporated in Cambridge, receiving his B.D. in 1633. About 1628 he became lecturer at All Hallows, Bread Street, London, with his maintenance paid by the Feoffees for Impropriations. After he was suspended in 1636, John Dod helped gain him a chaplaincy to Lord Brooke. He became vicar of Tavistock, Devon, and chaplain to the Earl of Bedford in 1638. After the war forced him to take flight, he became vicar of St. Andrew's, Plymouth. Thereafter he was the predominant Presbyterian minister in the county. In 1648 he wrote and gained seventy-two clerical signatures to *The Joint Testimonie* calling for adherence to the Solemn League and Covenant and for greater religious discipline. In the 1650s he was central to the establishment of a quasi-Presbyterian association in Devon bringing ministers from a broad denominational background together.

He was cast out of Plymouth, apparently by visiting commissioners, a week before St. Bartholomew's Day in 1662, the day of mass ejections of the clergy who refused to conform. He is claimed as the first minister of the Treville Street Presbyterian church in Plymouth. In 1665 he was accused of holding conventicles and imprisoned in nearby St. Nicholas Island for nine months. His friends gathered bail, and he was released on condition that he live at least twenty miles from Plymouth. He accordingly retired to nearby Kingsbridge, where he died two years later.

*Further Reading*
S. K. Roberts, *Recovery and Restoration in an English County: Devon Local Administration, 1646–1670* (Exeter, Eng., 1985); M. Stoyle, *From Deliverance to Destruction: Rebellion and Civil War in an English City* (Exeter, 1996).

*Tom Webster*

## Hughes, Lewis (ca. 1570–ca. 1646)

Puritan clergyman in Bermuda. Hughes was rector of St. Helen, Bishopsgate, in London at the start of the seventeenth century. There he was involved in supporting the servant Mary Glover, of his parish, in accusing Elizabeth Jackson of being a witch. Hughes pushed for and achieved a trial in which Jackson was found guilty. Following the trial, Hughes and four clerical colleagues performed an exorcism on Glover, a prohibited practice that led to his deprivation.

In 1614 Hughes accepted an offer from the Virginia Company to serve as a minister in the new colony of the Somers Isles, or Bermuda. There Hughes demonstrated his puritan leanings by dispensing with the Book of Common Prayer in services and having the congregation elect four elders to govern the church. His views contributed to clashes he had with the first two governors of the colony during his tenure, but he became a close friend of Governor Nathaniel Butler, who introduced the Genevan liturgy of the Channel Islands into Bermuda.

When Hughes traveled to England in 1620 to organize support for the colony, he was attacked for his nonconformity, but was nevertheless allowed to return to the colony. There he became one of four councilors who took over control of the colony's administration following Butler's departure. Following a change in the colony's English leadership, Hughes was removed from his ministry and returned to England. He published various works defending himself, his beliefs, and his actions, but remained generally obscure.

*Further Reading*
*Oxford Dictionary of National Biography* (Oxford, 2004).

Francis J. Bremer

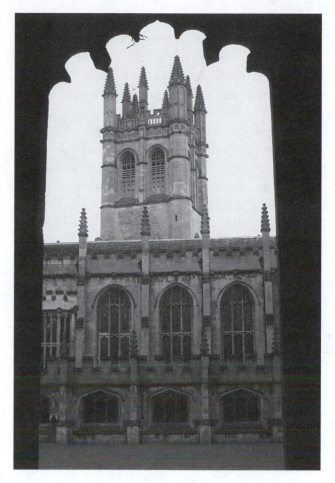

*Some of the buildings of Magdalen College, Oxford University, where Laurence Humphrey was head of the college and where John Davenport and other Puritans studied. (Courtesy Francis J. Bremer)*

## Humphrey, Laurence (ca. 1525–1589)

College head and puritan leader. Humphrey was born in Buckinghamshire and received his university education at Magdalen, Oxford, where he received his B.A. in 1549 and his M.A. in 1552. After receiving his B.A., he was chosen a perpetual fellow of the college. He was one of the fellows who strongly supported the reformation of the English church begun by Henry VIII and carried on by Edward VI.

Humphrey spent the Marian regime in exile, first in Zürich and then for a time in Basel. He worked as a translator for local printers, along with John Foxe and John Bale. In 1558 he moved to Geneva, where he joined the English congregation there. While in exile he began publishing religious works

of his own calling for further reform of English Protestantism through the purging of those popish remnants that had remained at the close of Edward's reign. Following the accession of Elizabeth to the throne, he returned to England and to his fellowship in Oxford.

Humphrey's rise at Oxford was rapid. He was named Regius Professor of Theology and then, in 1561, was elected president of Magdalen. Even at that time he was emerging as one of the sharpest critics of the use of liturgical vestments. Efforts by Archbishop Matthew Parker and others to get him to conform to the prescribed practices failed, and Humphrey might well have lost his position at Magdalen, had it not been for support from Robert

Dudley, the Earl of Leicester, from the Duke of Norfolk, and from John Foxe. Though these friends were able to deflect any efforts to remove him from the college, his continued stance in the Vestiarian Controversy clearly cost him further preferment in the church, possibly even a bishopric.

Under Humphrey's leadership, Magdalen became a nursery for the production of reformed, that is, puritan, clergy during the 1570s and 1580s. Humphrey also labored to purge Roman Catholic fellows and practices from other Oxford colleges, particularly during his term as vice-chancellor of the university from 1571 to 1576. The last decades of Humphrey's life were troubled by divisions within his college. Some of the new generation of reformers that he had nurtured came to see him as insufficiently zealous. In addition, disputes over the interpretation of college statutes pitted him against some of his own fellows, many of whom began to accuse him of high-handed and arbitrary governance. Despite these internal quarrels, his broader reputation continued to grow as he devoted himself to new published attacks on Roman Catholicism.

*See also:* Vestments
*Further Reading*
Patrick Collinson, *The Elizabethan Puritan Movement* (London, 1967); C. M. Dent, *Protestant Reformers in Elizabethan Oxford* (Oxford, 1983).

*Francis J. Bremer*

### Hutchinson, Anne Marbury (1591–1643)
Religious dissident and founder of Rhode Island. The daughter of a one-time silenced Church of England minister, Francis Marbury, and Bridget Dryden Marbury, Hutchinson was born in Alford, Lincolnshire; in 1612, she married prosperous Alford merchant William Hutchinson and bore fifteen children between 1613 and 1636.

In 1634, the Hutchinson family and related members, including brother-in-law John Wheelwright, joined the Great Migration to Massachusetts, apparently at the behest of Anne, who had felt unsettled by the removal a year earlier of minister John Cotton in response to Laudian persecution. The Hutchin-

sons settled in Boston and, despite doubts about her religious persuasion, soon became involved members of both church and state, with William serving as Boston deputy and as appraiser to particular courts. The Hutchinsons, like others in England and New England of the Puritan variety, soon began to keep conventicles in their house, which reportedly attracted sizable crowds (sixty to eighty people); rumor had it that Hutchinson herself engaged in some form of teaching or scriptural explication, perhaps to a mixed-gender audience, both of which would have been daring. Hutchinson also may have been a midwife; at least she assisted midwives at various births. Meanwhile, by late 1636 it became apparent that a divisive split was developing in the Boston church, especially around the issue of Wheelwright's proposed position as minister there.

The opposition revealed that there were more sensitive and broad-ranging theological and ecclesiological issues involved, including the exact nature of salvation and, therefore, the foundations for church membership. Hutchinson, developing concepts from Cotton, had moved toward a position that denied the practice of scrutinizing sanctification to infer justification. Hutchinson's influence in the conflict may be surmised from the fact that when the area ministers conferred with Cotton in October 1636, she also was summoned; what she said then was later used as evidence against her. The 1637 synod, called to quell the controversy, specifically prohibited conventicles, probably targeting the Hutchinsons; however, the Hutchinson conventicles continued.

In November, the General Court, once again under the control of John Winthrop and Thomas Dudley, took decisive action against the various dissidents, including Hutchinson. Called before the court, Hutchinson was charged with traducing the ministers and with defying the order against conventicles. After two days of stymied interrogation, Hutchinson uttered a confession of sorts, in which she explained her position and the basis for it, saying that God had empowered her to judge ministers. She further admitted to experiencing "immediate revelation," meaning that particular Bible passages had a prognostic power for her. Finally,

*Anne Hutchinson was one of the members of the Boston, Massachusetts, congregation who advanced views of grace and salvation that were attacked by the orthodox majority as "antinomian." She was one of a number banished for her challenge and settled in what became Rhode Island. (Library of Congress)*

she uttered a divine curse against the court (and its posterity) for their proceedings against her. After further deliberation, and after two ministers delivered their testimony under oath, the court banished her but, as it was already winter, ordered her to be held under house arrest in the Roxbury home of minister Thomas Weld. During the winter, she was visited by other ministers several times, who discovered that she held other equally alarming theological opinions, for which she was formally tried by the Boston church in March 1638. She was formally admonished at the end of the first week, but, despite an apparent change of heart, was excommunicated the following week.

Hutchinson and family and various supporters (including Boston magistrates William Aspinwall and William Coddington) then departed for the island of Aquidneck, where, with the help of Roger Williams, they purchased land from the Narragansetts and soon established Portsmouth, although further division ensued. In September 1638 Hutchinson was delivered of a "monstrous birth" (medical historians have diagnosed it as a hydatidiform mole, an abnormal mass formed in the uterus; news of this was interpreted by some as the judgment of Providence on antinomians, as Mary Dyer's "monstrous birth" had been, and widely dispersed in New England and in old England by Winthrop and Cotton. Following the death of her husband, William, in 1642, and fearing encroachment of Massachusetts Bay into their territory, Hutchinson and the remaining family members moved on to Dutch territory on Long Island, where, in the following year, all but one daughter were killed in an Indian massacre. The account of the colony's dealings with Hutchinson and the other radicals was publicized in *A Short Story*, published in 1644; Presbyterian heresiographers in the 1640s and 1650s quickly seized on the Hutchinson episode to embarrass John Cotton and to rouse alarm about the dangers of religious toleration. In the nineteenth and twentieth centuries, however, Hutchinson's reputation changed, and she became widely revered as a martyr both for religious toleration and for women's rights.

*See also:* Antinomianism, Crime and Punishment, Family Piety, Law in Puritan New England, Rhode Island, Anne Hutchinson's Statement (in Primary Sources)
*Further Reading*
Michael Winship, *Making Heretics: Militant Protestantism and Free Grace in Massachusetts, 1636–1641* (Princeton, 2002).

*Michael G. Ditmore*

## Hutchinson, Lucy (1620–1681)

Biographer. She was born Lucy Apsley, in the Tower of London, where her father was lieutenant of the Tower. She received a better education than common for women of this period, learning to read and write not only in English but in Latin. Her mother encouraged her in a puritan orientation, and from an early age she was an eager gadder to sermons. Following the death of her father, her life was unsettled, with movement between one branch of the family to another. This ended when she married the Northamptonshire gentleman John Hutchinson in 1638.

John enlisted in the Parliamentarian army shortly after the outbreak of the first Civil War, and in 1643 he was appointed governor of Nottingham and Nottingham Castle. He was one of those who signed the death warrant for Charles I in 1649. Following the wars the couple retired to their Owthorpe estate in Nottinghamshire. During this time Lucy began the translation of some of the poetic works of the Latin poet Lucretius.

At the restoration of the monarchy in 1660, John Hutchinson was in danger of being exempted from the pardon granted by Charles II to some of those he deemed responsible for the execution of his father. Family influence saved him from danger on this occasion, but in 1663 he was arrested on charges of being involved in a planned uprising against the monarchy. He was imprisoned and died in jail.

Lucy continued her interests in poetry but also devoted herself to vindicating her husband, writing "The Life of John Hutchinson of Owthorpe in the County of Nottinghamshire," a work that when eventually published offered important insight into the period. She attended sermons preached by John Owen and devoted herself to writing defenses of orthodoxy against heresy and atheism.

*Further Reading*
Lucy Hutchinson, *Memoirs of the Life of Colonel Hutchinson,* edited by J. Sutherland (Oxford, 1973); *Oxford Dictionary of National Biography* (Oxford, 2004).

*Francis J. Bremer*

# J

## Jackson, Arthur (ca. 1593–1666)

Presbyterian divine and ejected minister. Jackson was born at Little Waldingfield, Suffolk. He was orphaned young, and his uncle supported him at Trinity College, Cambridge, where he took a B.A. in 1614 and M.A. in 1617. He left Cambridge in 1619 when he married, and he was ordained in 1620 at London, where he was first lecturer and then from 1625 rector of St. Michael's, Wood Street. Jackson rapidly emerged as a leading London Presbyterian. He was a member of the first London classis and on the Committee of London's Provincial Assembly; he was appointed to ordain ministers in 1644, and he became president of Sion College in 1646. In 1649 he became rector of St. Faith's near St. Paul's and seems to have withdrawn from vestry business at St. Michael's (although he did not formally resign that parish until 1655).

As a royalist, Jackson protested against the trial of Charles I and refused to testify against the Presbyterian plotter Christopher Love, for which he was fined 500 pounds and imprisoned for several months in the Fleet. In 1660 Jackson presented Charles II with a Bible as he passed through St. Paul's Churchyard, and in 1661 he was a commissioner for the Presbyterians at the Savoy Conference. He was ejected from St. Faith's in 1662, and according to informers, he then lived in Whitefriars, an extraparochial jurisdiction near the Temple, where he preached to conventicles, before retiring in about 1665 to Hadley and then Edmonton in Middlesex. Here he died in August 1666, but he was buried in the ruins of St. Michael's, Wood Street. Jackson published a series of annotations on the Bible.

*Further Reading*
*Oxford Dictionary of National Biography* (Oxford, 2004).

*John Spurr*

## Jacob, Henry (1563–1624)

Preacher and writer of books on Puritan ecclesiology. Jacob was born at Cheriton, Kent, in 1563. He entered St. Mary Hall, Oxford, in 1581 and earned the B.A. and M.A. (1586). He stayed on at Oxford as precentor at Corpus Christi College, but by 1590 he had left the university. His sympathies were with the Puritans, and although he was ordained, there is no evidence that he ever served as pastor of the Church of England. After Oxford, his activities and means of livelihood for several years are vague, although he published some books and his name appeared on petitions. On two occasions, in 1603 and 1605, he landed in jail for Puritan "insolence."

Without prospects in England, he went to the Netherlands. He probably slipped back and forth several times. By 1610 he was in Leiden, where he and William Ames and Robert Parker, fellow exiles, entered into discussions with John Robinson, the Separatist leader. The chief topics were separatism (Robinson) versus nonseparatism (Jacob, Ames, and Parker) and the nature of the church. Which side influenced the other? A major interpretative question is whether these meetings molded Jacob's thinking about independency of congregations or whether he had these ideas previously, without Separatist influence. Jacob began to speak out about an ideal church dedicated to pure membership but not in complete secession from the Church of England. In1616 he returned to London, and put his theories into action, forming a congregation at Southwark. The Jacob church was a group of believers gathered for voluntary worship and functioning independently from the established church. Jacob did not fully renounce the Church of England, although he kept a good distance from it. The "Jacobites" believed that every congregation should be gathered on the basis of a covenant and that each such congregation should be independent and self-governing. In 1622 he immigrated to Virginia, where his activities are unknown, and he died there in 1624.

Jacob's radical views on church government caused quite a stir in Puritan circles. Until then, most Puritan nonconformists were either Separatists or non-Separatists working to bring in a reformed church. Jacob, like William Ames, Robert Parker, and William Bradshaw, wanted a middle position of independently functioning congregations without declaring formal separation from the Church of England. The Jacobites left open the possibility of occasional fellowship with other church groups. Separatists saw it as too little, only a "Samaritan" or mixed church; traditional Puritans saw it as going too far.

Recent church historians use labels like "semi-Separatist" if they stress Jacob's connection to separatism or "non-separating Congregationalism" if they emphasize a tie to mainstream Puritanism. Jacob's teachings eventually were absorbed into the Congregationalist movement. Jacob wrote many books, all published in Holland, which gave his ecclesiological views. See especially his *Reasons Taken Out of Gods Word* (1604), *Divine Beginning of Christs True Church* (1610), and *Declaration and Plainer Opening* (1612).

*See also:* Congregationalism, Independency

*Further Reading*
Stephen Brachlow, *The Communion of Saints: Radical Puritan and Separatist Ecclesiology, 1570–1625* (Oxford, 1988); Murray Tolmie, *The Triumph of the Saints: The Separate Churches of London, 1616–1649* (Cambridge, Eng., 1977).

*Keith L. Sprunger*

## Janeway, James (1636–1674)

English Dissenter and spiritual writer. Janeway was born in Lilly, Hertfordshire, where his father was a curate. He matriculated at Christ Church, Oxford, in 1656 and received the B.A. in1659. He left Oxford at the Restoration and lived for a while at Windsor. He preached in London in 1665, the plague year, during which many of the conforming clergy left the city. Later he preached to a Dissenting congregation in Rotherhithe, Surrey. He was licensed as a Presbyterian following the Declaration of Indulgence in 1672. On at least two occasions he narrowly escaped arrest for illegal preaching.

Janeway is best known as a spiritual writer whose works focused on holy dying and heavenly mindedness. *Heaven Upon Earth* (1667), calling attention to the recent plague and fire in London, warned of the importance of befriending God before it was too late. *Death Unstung* (1669), a funeral sermon, described the joys of heaven but cautioned believers against assuming their deaths would be easy. *A Token for Children* (1672) told stories of the holy deaths of pious children and was still being reprinted in the nineteenth century. *Invisibles, Realities, Demonstrated in the Holy Life and Triumphant Death of John Janeway* (1673) narrated the spiritual ecstasies and words of wisdom that accompanied the untimely death of his younger brother. *Mr. James Janeway's Legacy to His Friends: Containing Twenty-Seven Famous Instances of God's Providences in and about Sea-Dangers and Deliverances* was published posthumously in 1683.

*Further Reading*
Dewey D. Wallace Jr., ed., *The Spirituality of the Later English Puritans: An Anthology* (Macon, GA, 1987).

*Dewey D. Wallace Jr.*

## Jeake, Samuel (1623–1690)

Nonconformist preacher and lawyer. Jeake was born in Rye and raised in what appears to have been a godly household. The religious influence may have come from his mother, who was the daughter of a Sussex clergyman, John Pierson. Entries in his letter book from the 1640s reveal his support of the parliamentary cause. In 1651 Jeake became town clerk of Rye. After the passage of the Protectorate's Marriage Act, he also served as registrar for births, deaths, and marriages. During this decade he also preached on occasion to a gathered congregation, though he is not known to have had any formal training for the ministry.

Following the Restoration, Jeake lost his posts in the town, but he continued to offer legal advice and services. He also became the minister to the town's Nonconformist congregation, which for a time at least met in his home. Jeake also wrote extensively on civic and religious matters. He maintained a correspondence with John Allin, the puritan vicar of Rye from 1653 to 1662, who had moved to London. Jeake took a strong public position during the Exclusion Crisis, leading to renewed persecution of him and his flock. He fled to London and only returned to Rye a few years before his death. During his life he accumulated a personal library of about 2,100 tracts, books, and pamphlets, which included works of theology, politics, literature, and science.

*Further Reading*
Anthony Fletcher, *A County Community in Peace and War: Sussex, 1600–1660* (London, 1975); *Oxford Dictionary of National Biography* (Oxford, 2004).

*Francis J. Bremer*

## Jermyn, Sir Robert (1539–1614)

Puritan magistrate and lay patron. Robert was the son and eventually heir of Sir Ambrose Jermyn of Rushbrooke Hall in Suffolk. He was admitted to the Middle Temple in 1561 and may have previously studied at Corpus Christi College, Cambridge.

In 1577 Sir Ambrose died, and Sir Robert was named to the Suffolk Commission of the Peace (thus becoming a justice of the peace). Along with allies such as Sir John Heigham and Sir Edmund Lewkenor, Jermyn contributed to the development of a strong godly culture in the region. In achieving this goal, the magistrates were closely allied to the area's puritan clergy, contributing to Queen Elizabeth's remark that her county of Suffolk was so well governed because "the magistrates and ministers go together." Among the more important clergy in this alliance was Jermyn's friend John Knewstub, who later dedicated one of his books to Jermyn and the other "gentlemen in Suffolk whom the true worshipping God hath made right worshipful."

In 1583 Jermyn, along with Heigham, was removed from the commission for their support of the godly faction in Bury St. Edmunds against Bishop Edmund Freke. Though he was not restored to the commission until 1593, Jermyn continued to serve the cause of reform. He was chosen to represent Suffolk in the parliaments of 1584 and 1586. He served as deputy lieutenant of the county. In 1585 he accompanied the Earl of Leicester's expedition to the Netherlands, though he had to return in less than a year for reasons of health. Following his return to the commission he served as *custos rotulorum,* in essence the chair of the justices. He was also important as a patron of puritan clergy. Adam Winthrop, who knew him well, called him "a pious man and a lover of true religion."

*Further Reading*
Patrick Collinson, *The Elizabethan Puritan Movement* (London, 1967); John Craig, *Reformation, Politics and Polemics: The Growth of Protestantism in East Anglian Market Towns, 1500–1610* (Aldershot, Eng., 2001); Diarmaid MacCulloch, *Suffolk and the Tudors: Politics and Religion in an English Country, 1500–1600* (Oxford, 1986).

*Francis J. Bremer*

## Jessey (Jacie), Henry (1601–1663)

Puritan nonconformist; during the 1640s and 1650s, Baptist-leaning minister of the famed semi-Separatist congregation that had been founded by Henry Jacob and ministered to by John Lathrop in London. Jessey was born 3 September 1601 in

West Rounton, North Riding, Yorkshire, the son of the rector of Rounton. He entered Cambridge in 1618, taking his B.A. from St. John's in 1623 and M.A. in 1626. He was ordained in 1627 and served as vicar of Aughton, East Riding, Yorkshire, until 1634, when he was deprived for nonperformance of ceremonies and for removing a crucifix from the church. In 1637 he took charge of a gathered congregation in Southwark, London, that had been organized by Henry Jacob. That Southwark congregation practiced adult baptism, and by 1644 Jessey rejected infant baptism himself. The congregation went through several divisions throughout the 1640s and 1650s and was the origin of many Separatist London churches as well as the Particular Baptists. Jessey's own fortunes rose during the Interregnum period during which he was one of nine men whose approval was required to sanction the publication of any new translation of the Bible, he conducted a biweekly lecture series at All Hallows the Great in London, and he became associated with Fifth Monarchy men Christopher Feake and Thomas Venner after 1653.

In the 1650s, Jessey's lifelong interest in Hebrew and Rabbinical literature and sympathy for Jews led him to set up a charity for impoverished Jews in Jerusalem. Jessey had adopted Sabbatarianism, or the observance of the Jewish Sabbath, during the late 1640s. He also facilitated the mission of Rabbi Menasseh ben Israel to England to discuss Jewish readmission and influenced Cromwell's decision to allow Jews to resettle in England. Jessey's belief in millennialism and the role of the Jews in the coming apocalypse informed his support of their readmission to England. His millennialist views also appeared in the annual publication of his *Scripture Kalendar* (or *Scripture Almanack*), which detailed his moderate Fifth Monarchist position in the interpretation of the five earthly monarchies of the Book of Daniel.

Jessey was removed from his position at Southwark at the Restoration and spent his remaining years alternating periods of imprisonment with assisting members of his congregation in the Netherlands and England. He died 4 September 1663, and his broadsheet elegy, "A pillar erected to the memory of that holy, humble, and faithful servant of Iesus Christ, Mr. Henry Jesse," was published shortly after his death. Jessey never married.

*Further Reading*

Barbara Ritter Dailey, "The Visitation of Sarah Wight: Holy Carnival and the Revolution of the Saints in Civil War London," *Church History* 55 (1986), 438–455; David Katz, *Philo-Semitism and the Readmission of the Jews to England, 1603–1655* (1982); B. R. White, "Henry Jessey: A Pastor in Politics," *Baptist Quarterly* 25 (1973), 98–110.

*Stephanie Sleeper*

## Johnson, Edward (1598–1672)

One of the staunchest defenders of the Massachusetts Bay Colony. Johnson played several roles, but is best remembered as the author of the history, *The Wonder-Working Providence of Sion's Savior in New England*. This work, in contrast to those written by William Bradford and John Winthrop, was not intended as an official record of a colony's founding. Rather, Johnson wanted his history to be a record of the battle between the forces of good and evil in New England. He came to New England in 1630, probably aboard the *Arbella*, as an Indian trader. Little in his background suggested that Johnson would become the fervent puritan that he did. He had grown up in a reformist atmosphere in Canterbury, but his early training was preparation to become a joiner. After returning to England for a brief period, Johnson settled in Massachusetts for good in 1636, experiencing religious conversion during the antinomian controversy. Soon after, he achieved prominence in a number of local positions: he helped to found the town of Woburn, Massachusetts, and served as clerk, selectman, militia captain, and deputy to the General Court.

*The Wonder-Working Providence* combined both fact and vision. The history, first published in 1654, attempted to provide a year-by-year account of the history of Massachusetts. Johnson often confused the course of events and reported some of them incorrectly. More important is the way in which Johnson expressed his sense that the Puritans were soldiers of Christ engaged in actual battle against Satan's forces who wished to destroy the new Jerusalem. As such, the work is better considered allegory than history. At the same time as describing New England as a millennial battlefield, *The Wonder-Working Providence* suggests that Johnson had developed a sense of pride in his new home and that its history was worth recording. Johnson offers another voice to help with comprehending the first-generation puritan experience, one freed from the constraints that limited Governors Bradford and Winthrop.

*See also:* Puritan Historians
*Further Reading*
Stephen Arch. "The Edifying History of Edward Johnson's *Wonder-Working Providence*," *Early American Literature* 28 (1993), 42–59.

*Rachelle E. Friedman*

## Johnson, Isaac (1601–1630)

One of the early settlers of Massachusetts. Johnson was a man of great potential who died before it could be realized. He was the step-grandson of Laurence Chaderton, the master of Emmanuel College, Cambridge, where Isaac matriculated in 1614. The young man received his B.A. in 1618 and his M.A. in 1621, following which he was ordained into the ministry. Rather than seeking a clerical position, he entered Gray's Inn to study law. In 1623 he married Lady Arbella Clinton, the daughter of the third Earl of Lincoln. Two years later he received a large inheritance from his paternal grandfather.

Johnson showed an interest in migration as early as 1627, and he played a role in the meeting of some of the leaders of the Massachusetts Bay Company at Sempringham, the seat of his father-in-law. He became an assistant of the Bay Company and a large investor in its operations. His decision to migrate was an important one, his prominence being recognized by the rechristening of the fleet's flagship the *Arbella* in honor of Johnson's wife. Settling in Massachusetts, both the Johnsons died in 1630, during their first year in the colony. They had no children.

*Further Reading*
Robert Charles Anderson, ed., *The Great Migration Begins: Immigrants to New England, 1620–1633*, vol. 2 (Boston, 1995).

*Francis J. Bremer*

## Jollie, Thomas (1629–1703)

English Dissenting minister. Jollie was born near Manchester and entered Trinity College, Cambridge, in 1646, apparently leaving without a degree. In 1649 he was called as curate to the chapel district of Altham, Lancashire, where he gathered a covenanted congregation. He went to London in 1658 to participate in the Savoy meeting of Congregational Churches that produced the Savoy Confession of Faith. After the Restoration the churchwardens of Altham complained that he neither used the Book of Common Prayer nor provided the sacraments for all in the parish; the Act of Uniformity forced him from his position at Altham in August 1662. He was arrested five times for illegal preaching, and twice imprisoned. In 1667 he moved to Wymondhouses, Lancashire, where he preached, often at night to avoid arrest. He licensed meeting places there under the 1672 Act of Indulgence. After the Toleration Act, he preached to a congregation at Wymondhouses, where he died. In 1659, 1675, and 1693 he participated in conferences seeking the union of Presbyterians and Congregationalists.

Interested in New England, he corresponded with ministers there, including Increase Mather, seeking their opinions on ordination and on the question of to whom the sacraments should be administered. He was dubious about the New England practice of the half-way covenant. His *Note Book* is an example of a Puritan diary and evinces his ardent piety (he spent one whole day each month in prayer and meditation) and recognition of special providences in the deaths of persecutors. His only publications, *The Surey Demoniac* (1697, with John Carrington as coauthor) and *A Vindication of the Surey Demoniac as No Imposter* (1698), defended an exorcism in which Jolly had participated. The Church of England conformist Zachary

Taylor attacked him for fraud and fanaticism in regard to this exorcism.

*Further Reading*
H. Fishwick, *The Note Book of the Rev. Thomas Jolly*, Chetham Soc., new series 33 (Manchester, Eng., 1894).

*Dewey D. Wallace Jr.*

## Jones, Samuel (1628–1697)

Welsh Nonconformist clergyman and founder of a Dissenting academy. He received his B.A. from Jesus College, Oxford, in 1652, having previously spent time at All Souls and Merton Colleges. He was admitted a fellow of Jesus and received his M.A. in 1654. At some point he became a dedicated puritan, and in 1657 he was admitted to the vicarage of Llangynwyd in Glamorgan. He was forced to give up his living following the Restoration's Act of Uniformity, but continued to preach in private homes. While he may have been imprisoned for a brief time, his own status and that of his lay patrons kept him from severe persecution. He established the first Dissenting academy in Wales at Brynllywarch. In addition to his work there in training future ministers, he also taught the children of gentry families.

*Further Reading*
*Oxford Dictionary of National Biography* (Oxford, 2004).

*Francis J. Bremer*

## Josselin, Ralph (1617–1683)

Essex clergymen whose diary reveals the world of the godly in rich detail. Josselin was born on 26 January 1617 at Roxwell in Essex, the son of John Josselin, a failing farmer. Ralph was educated at Bishop's Stortford and at Jesus College, Cambridge. Despite disruptions caused by money problems, Josselin gained his B.A. in 1637 and his M.A. in 1640. He decided upon a clerical career and was ordained in February 1640. On 28 October he married Jane Constable of Olney and in March 1641 was instituted as vicar of Earls Colne in Essex. The parish had a puritan reputation thanks to the Harlakenden family, the patrons of the living and lords of the manor, and to the influence of a previous vicar, Thomas Shepard, who had emigrated to New England. Josselin, who had a godly upbringing and was a convinced Calvinist, disliked the ceremonial and other policies of Archbishop Laud. At his own ordination Josselin had refused to bow to the altar, and taking advantage of the Long Parliament's religious reforms of 1641 and 1642, he removed suspect imagery from his church; he joined in appeals to Parliament to further the work of godly reformation.

As the 1640s progressed, Josselin backed attempts to create a godly England and a strong national church: he took the Solemn League and Covenant, signed an Essex petition in support of a national church settlement proposed by the Westminster Assembly, and was ready to serve within a Presbyterian church structure. Locally, he denounced popular recreations and festivities, including dancing on the village green, and demanded regular church attendance. He sought to limit participation in Holy Communion to those parishioners who were worthy of the sacrament. When this proved impossible, Josselin suspended the celebration of the sacrament in his parish for almost a decade. At the same time, however, he gathered a group of godly parishioners for private prayer meetings. This group, which he referred to in his diary as "the society," was probably the nucleus of those who received the sacrament when he restored it in 1651. Josselin detested the sects and was particularly alarmed by the emergence of the Quakers. Politically, he was a moderate Parliamentarian, wary of the Levellers and other radicals, concerned by the regicide (the execution of Charles I), but consoled by a strong sense of divine providence directing public affairs. In the late 1640s and 1650s, he was a convinced millenarian.

Surprisingly Josselin retained his living at the Restoration. His conformity to the liturgy of the Church of England was partial and grudging, yet despite several encounters with the church courts for offenses such as not wearing the surplice Josselin managed to escape prosecution and died in possession of his living. Josselin's importance lies in the intimate self-portrait of his diary. Covering his whole adult life, the diary is most detailed between 1644 and 1664 when Josselin was making almost daily entries. It reveals not only his inner life, including his anxieties, dreams, and spiritual state, but also the minutiae of his domestic life and his community. It provides a picture of his economic position and his farming, the weather, the price of goods, and the state of crops and livestock. He records his own and his family's health, relations with his wife, children, and neighbors, foreign and national affairs, and, above all, his own dealings with God.

*Further Reading*
Alan Macfarlane, ed., *The Diary of Ralph Josselin 1616–1683* (London, 1976); Alan Macfarlane, *The Family Life of Ralph Josselin: An Essay in Historical Anthropology* (Cambridge, Eng., 1970).

*John Spurr*

# K

## Keayne, Robert (1595–1656)

Colonial merchant. Born in Berkshire County, England, in 1595, Robert Keayne was the son of a butcher named John Keayne. At age ten Robert took up residence in the Cornhill, London, home of John Heyfield. Apprenticed to Heyfield, a merchant tailor, Keayne became familiar with the Cornhill district, which served as a center for trade and commerce. Robert remained a resident of Cornhill until 1635, when he relocated his family to New England.

Keayne prospered during his years in England. At age twenty he finished his training and gained admittance to The Free Merchant Tailor's Company of London. This guild, founded and chartered in 1503, represented the business interests of merchants in the cloth trade and tailors. The guild regulated cloth merchants' economic activities and recruited apprentices such as Keayne. Two years after his admittance to the Merchant Tailor's Company, Robert married Anne Mansfield. The marriage, a fortuitous event, tied Robert to a well-established family. Anne's brother, Reverend John Wilson, became one of the most influential puritan clerics to eventually settle in New England.

By 1623 Londoners recognized Robert Keayne as a "gentleman," and his acceptance as a member of the honorable artillery company of London underscored Keayne's achievement. Though he and his wife, Anne, suffered the loss of three of their four children in infancy, overall Keayne led a rela-

tively contented life in London. While he lived in London, Keayne, one of the puritan, or godly, Christians, took every opportunity to gad about to hear a variety of sermons. His comprehensive sermon notes provide excellent information about which godly ministers engaged in preaching during 1627–1628. As a member of the godly flock, Keayne's first recorded interest in the puritans' New England colony comes from a reference to his membership within the group of "adventurers behind the Plymouth Colony."

Keayne emigrated with his family to New England in 1635. Whether he left England for financial or religious reasons is unknown. Most likely a mix of both drove him to board the ship *Defense*. Keayne traveled in good company to the New World. He and his family enjoyed the company of the Reverend John Wilson, and Reverend Thomas Shepard traveled onboard ship. Once in Boston, Keayne gained a reputation for sharp business dealings. Despite his appointment to a Boston committee handling land allotments, his election as a selectman, his election as a representative to the General Court, and his service in a variety of other colonial offices, Keayne never overcame his reputation for economic misconduct.

On several occasions he was called before the colonial court to answer for alleged business transgressions. He was accused of overcharging for goods, of stealing two hundred pounds that had been entrusted to him for delivery to persons in New England, and of drunkenness. Perhaps the most well-known case against Robert Keayne involved Goody Sherman, a New England matron, who insisted Keayne stole her sow.

Robert Keayne died in 1656. Whether saint or sinner, Keayne's Last Will and Testament, which covered some 158 pages, explained his side of his public trials. This famous document tells readers much about philanthropy in New England. Moreover, Keayne's sermon notes provide a wealth of information about godly religious beliefs in England and New England.

*See also:* Works and Salvation (in Primary Sources)
*Further Reading*
Bernard Bailyn, "The Apologia of Robert Keayne," *William and Mary Quarterly* 7 (October 1950).

*Susan Ortmann*

## Kiffin, William (1616–1701)

Particular Baptist minister; born in London of poor stock. In the 1630s he attended conventicles and in 1638 rejected arguments for a state church, joining what was to become Devonshire Square Baptist Church. Here he delivered his first sermons, becoming a Particular Baptist in 1642 and being central to the first Confession of Faith in 1644. Throughout the 1640s and 1650s he was an eminent spokesman for the movement, taking on his role as critical to the establishment of the fledgling movement, in and beyond London, not least in dissuading Baptists from joining with Fifth Monarchists. By the end of the 1650s he was on good terms with Oliver Cromwell and sat as member for Middlesex in his last parliament. In February 1660 he was arrested by order of General George Monck, the first of many such experiences through the rest of his life.

After the Restoration he played an important part, intervening on behalf of other Baptists in trouble with the authorities. He also contributed to many debates that served to maintain the unity of the Particular Baptists, most notably writing against the more ecumenical stance of John Bunyan, author of the classic allegory of the Christian journey, *Pilgrim's Progress.* In 1681 Kiffin's *A Sober Discourse of Right to Church-Communion,* advocating

the closed membership of Particular Baptist congregations, was probably the most important contribution to this controversy. Upon the 1672 declaration of indulgence, he acquired a license to preach, and he remained active even after the declaration was withdrawn a year later.

After the Act of Toleration of 1689, Kiffin was a major figure in convening the first national assembly of Particular Baptists where the second Confession of Faith was adopted. During the less persecutory regime of William and Mary, Kiffin continued his ministry at Devonshire Square, and did so all through his final years, albeit with some assistance. His contribution to the development of the movement into a visible denomination was considerable, not least for the help he gave in maintaining a sense of unity in both theological and practical terms in times of persecution.

*Further Reading*
W. Orme, *Remarkable Passages in the Life of William Kiffin* (London, 1823); Murray Tolmie, *The Triumph of the Saints: The Separate Churches of London, 1616–1649* (Cambridge, Eng., 1977); B. R. White, *The English Baptists of the Seventeenth Century,* rev. ed. (Didcot, Eng., 1996).

*Tom Webster*

## Knewstub, John (1544–1624)

Minister, and a leader of the Elizabethan puritan movement in Suffolk. Knewstub was born in Kirkby Stephen in Westmoreland in 1544. He graduated from St. John's College, Cambridge, in 1564, and three years later he was admitted to the fellowship of that college. He soon emerged as a member of the puritan faction in the university, joining others in petitioning against the wearing of clerical vestments. Among his university friends were John Still, Henry Sandes, and Adam Winthrop. His first publication, in 1577, was a series of *Lectures . . . upon the Twentieth Chapter of Exodus,* which he had delivered while he was at Cambridge, setting forth the developing covenant theology.

Knewstub first gained national attention when he preached the 1576 Good Friday sermon at Paul's Cross in London. His subject was the Family of Love, and opposition to the Familist sect preoccupied him over the next five years. In 1581 he helped to prepare and promote a bill against the Family of Love that was introduced into the parliament that met in the early months of 1581.

Meanwhile, in 1579 he was presented to the living of Cockfield, Suffolk. In 1582 he hosted a gathering of Suffolk clergy, which organized a clerical conference similar to and connected to that in Dedham. He was well connected with prominent puritans at the royal court, and in 1585–1586 Knewstub served as a chaplain to the Earl of Leicester on the latter's expedition to the Netherlands.

Back in Suffolk, Knewstub emerged as the leader of the combination lecture that functioned at Bury St. Edmunds. In the latter part of Elizabeth's reign he was one of the dominant figures in the puritan movement in the Stour Valley borderland between Suffolk and Essex. He traveled throughout the region, preaching and visiting clerical colleagues such as Richard Rogers, Ezekiel Culverwell, and Stephen Egerton, as well as lay supporters of the movement such as the Winthrops. His advice was sought on the appointment of clergy to various posts. He was consulted by the townsmen of Bury St. Edmund in the choice of town preachers. In 1592 he joined with Lawrence Chaderton, Roger Goad, and John Still, among others, in recommending John Ward of Haverhill to be town preacher of Ipswich. Though he was often cited in visitations for omitting to wear the surplice and for refusal to sign with the cross in baptism, no actions were taken against him. In addition to his opposition to these church rituals, he was noted for his advocacy of fasts and strict Sabbath observance.

In 1603 Knewstub was chosen as one of the puritan spokesmen at the Hampton Court Conference. When the sought-for reforms were denied, he pleaded with the king for tolerance of those in Suffolk who desired to avoid use of the surplice and signing with the cross in baptism, but his plea was rejected. Correspondence between his friends William Bedell and Samuel Ward indicates that at this time Knewstub was concerned with the possible consequences of continuing nonconformity and was seeking a curate who would conduct services while wearing a surplice. This stratagem failed, and in 1606 he was presented to the church courts for not using the sign of the cross in baptism and for not wearing the surplice. Again in 1611 he was cited for not wearing the surplice. Yet both times he escaped deprivation.

Knewstub continued to play a prominent role in efforts to foster the piety of the godly in the Stour Valley, and he preached strongly on the need to exercise Christian love to all members of the community. In 1605 he preached the funeral sermon for Robert Welche of Little Waldingfield and joined with fellow clergyman in carrying the coffin to the graveyard. He joined with Richard Rogers of Wethersfield, Essex, in acting as spiritual physician to an Essex youth. In 1613 September he joined with John Winthrop Groton, Henry Sandes the lecturer of Boxford, and others in a covenanted spiritual association pledged to remember each other in their prayers every Friday and to meet annually to renew their communion. In 1618 he preached the funeral sermon for Richard Rogers.

Knewstub died at Cockfield and was buried on 31 May 1624. He had preached what might be called a social gospel, urging his listeners to exercise charity toward their neighbors, and contemporary testimony indicates that he practiced what he preached. Richard Rogers in his diary referred to his friend Knewstub as "in prayer unwearied," and a man of "rare humility, joined with great knowledge and wisdom" who was noted for "his bearing of wrongs" and "bountiful liberality with mercifulness."

*See also:* Conference Movement

*Further Reading*

John Craig, "'The Cambridge Boies,'" in Susan Wabuda and Caroline Litzenberger, eds., *Belief and Practice in Reformation England* (Aldershot, Eng., 1998); Christopher Marsh, *The Family of Love in English Society, 1550–1630* (Cambridge, Eng., 1994); Irvonwy Morgan, *The Godly Preachers of the Elizabethan Church* (London, 1965).

*Francis J. Bremer*

## Knightley, Sir Richard (ca. 1610–1661)

Staunch supporter of John Pym in the Long Parliament in opposition to the policies of Charles I. Knightley was the son of Richard Knightley of Staffordshire, who was in turn heir to his cousin, Richard Knightley of Fawsley, Northamptonshire. He was educated at Lincoln College, Oxford, and Gray's Inn, and was part of his Fawsley cousin's Puritan connection, which included John Hampden, whose daughter he married in 1637. When his cousin died in 1639, his father inherited Fawsley, and Sir Richard was elected by Northampton in both the Short and Long Parliament, where he sat from 1640 until his seclusion in 1648. Although he was not a major landowner until his father's death in 1650, he pledged money for Parliament's defense in 1642, supported Pym in the debate on the Grand Remonstrance and served as a teller for the majority when it came to a vote. In 1643 he presented the grievances of his shire, supported the Solemn League and Covenant, and, when Pym died in December, served as a pallbearer. Knightley was active in late 1647 on the Commons committee setting conditions for negotiations with the king, but a year later he opposed the trial of the king, and so he was excluded in Pride's Purge and briefly imprisoned. In 1651 he was licensed to go abroad but returned to serve in Richard Cromwell's Parliament. In February 1660 he was elected to the Council of State and was rewarded at the Restoration with a Knighthood of the Bath.

*Further Reading*
David Underdown, *Pride's Purge* (Oxford, 1971).

*Paul Seaver*

## Knowles, John (ca. 1606–1685)

Puritan clergyman and Massachusetts colonist. Knowles was born in Lincolnshire and educated at Magdalene College, Cambridge, from 1620 to 1627. He moved in puritan circles, sharing a room with Richard Vines and befriending Matthew Newcomen. In 1623 he became a fellow at St. Catherine's College, where Richard Sibbes was master, and in 1627 he was ordained. In 1635 he was elected by the aldermen of Colchester, Essex, as lecturer, the latest in a long line of godly ministers. Here he was close to John Rogers, being present at his deathbed and delivering his funeral sermon in 1636. He backed Newcomen as Rogers's successor at Dedham. In 1637 he pushed William Dugard as Colchester's schoolmaster ahead of a candidate favored by Archbishop William Laud. He was noted by Laud as avoiding Holy Communion, presumably to avoid having to kneel and was summoned for preaching at a burial service without the surplice. To evade disciplinary measures, he resigned his lectureship and, in 1639, sailed for New England.

He was accepted as co-pastor with George Philips at Watertown, Massachusetts, and sat on the Board of Overseers at Harvard College. In 1642 he responded to a Virginian request for an evangelical mission but returned to Watertown a year later when the governor of Virginia imposed liturgical conformity there. After Philips's death in 1644, he served alone and was joined by John Sherman in 1647. He was sympathetic to godly rule in England, being a signatory to a letter congratulating Oliver Cromwell on his campaign in Ireland. In 1651 he returned to England, becoming lecturer at Bristol cathedral, then going on to serve as Congregational minister at other churches in the city. He was present at the Savoy Assembly in 1658, an attempt to reconcile Presbyterians and Congregationalists. However, he never forgot his colonial connections; in 1659 he became one of a board of English trustees aiming to raise funds for Harvard College.

After the Restoration he became lecturer at All Hallows the Great in London, only to be deprived in 1662. Thereafter he continued to preach, mostly at Little Eastchamp, London, and was one of many Nonconformist ministers who stayed on during the plague of 1665. He raised the suspicions of the authorities when he took part in a project raising money for suffering Polish Protestants in the 1660s. When the Declaration of Indulgence was promoted in 1672, he served a Presbyterian church in the parish of St. Catherine-in-the-Tower. In the same year he declined an offer of the presidency of Harvard College, choosing to continue his English ministry until his death in 1685.

*Further Reading*

Francis J. Bremer, *Congregational Communion: Clerical Friendship in the Anglo-American puritan community, 1610–1692* (Boston, 1994); A. G. Matthews, *Calamy Revised: Being a Revision of Edmund Calamy's Account of the Ministers and others Ejected and Silenced, 1660–2* (Oxford, 1934; reprinted 1988); Tom Webster, *Godly Clergy in Early Stuart England: The Caroline Puritan Movement, c. 1620–1643* (Cambridge, Eng., 1997).

*Tom Webster*

## Knox, John (ca. 1513–1572)

Known as the greatest of the Scottish Protestant reformers.

### Early Life

Knox was born in Haddington, East Lothian, of burghal stock. He studied for a time at St. Andrews University, and he probably acquired legal training under the supervision of the noted jurist John Weddell; in 1540 Knox acted as a notary. At some point he was admitted to minor orders. In 1544 he was tutor of the sons of local lairds. Influenced by the martyr George Wishart (d. 1546), Knox became a Protestant, and in 1547 he joined the assassins of Archbishop Beaton, whom they held responsible for Wishart's burning, under siege in St. Andrew's Castle. He was subsequently called to serve as preacher in the town. When the castle fell to the French in July, he was sent to the galleys for nineteen months. Thereafter he went to England and gained some prominence as a preacher in the north. He was appointed a chaplain to Edward VI in 1551 and helped complete the second Book of Common Prayer, contributing the Black Rubric, an explanation that kneeling while receiving Holy Communion implied no adoration or idolatry of the elements of bread and wine. In October 1552 Northumberland recommended him for elevation to the see of Rochester, though in days to come the two fell out. Knox was dissatisfied with some of the ceremonies of the English church, though he was not utterly opposed to some form of episcopal office. In June 1553 he was sent as preacher to Buck-

*John Knox was the predominant figure in the Scottish Protestant Reformation of the sixteenth century. (Library of Congress)*

inghamshire, but several months after the Roman Catholic Mary Tudor's accession to the throne of England he took refuge on the Continent.

### Geneva and Scotland

In 1554 Knox went from Geneva to Frankfurt, where he was pastor of the English congregation until liturgical conflict—he and William Whittingham were opposed to set lay responses in the liturgy—led to his return to Geneva in March 1555. There, he and Christopher Goodman became ministers of the English congregation, until later in 1555 Knox went to Scotland, where he preached freely. In July 1556 he returned to Geneva, where he had again accepted a call. In May 1557 he was called back to Scotland, but when he arrived at Dieppe in October he received a letter to the contrary. Sharp exchanges followed, with the result that Knox did not return, but some of his supporters signed what is called the first band, a Protestant covenant, on 3 December 1557. He returned to Geneva and published six works during 1558, including the *Book of Common Order,* an English version of the Genevan service book, which reflected his rejection of set forms of worship.

Knox made his return to Edinburgh on 2 May 1559; he was denied passage through England because of his infamous *First Blast of the Trumpet against the Monstrous Regiment of Women.* An attack on the rule of the female Queen Mary, it was not taken well by her successor Queen Elizabeth. In July he accepted the call to become minister of Edinburgh, and he was instrumental in the preparation of the Scots Confession and the first Book of Discipline (1560), which supplied a structure for the Reformed church. The discipline, as the proposal was referred to, included a permanent eldership, and also, ambiguously, superintendents, quasi-episcopal figures. However, he was never able to gain for the Protestant church all the financial resources of the Catholic Church, and thus his vision could not be implemented in its entirety. In 1561 Mary Stewart returned from France following the death of her husband King Francis II, and Knox attacked her and her Roman Catholic allegiance with the zeal of an ancient prophet decrying the worship of Baal. He preached the sermon at the coronation of James VI in 1567, thus siding against the queen in the civil war, having adopted the opinion that Christians were bound to wage war against ungodly rulers. The king's party was led by the re-

gent, James Stewart, Earl of Moray, who was assassinated in 1570, whereupon Knox's influence declined. He died of apoplexy in Edinburgh on 24 November 1572.

Knox's name is so strongly identified with the Scottish Reformation in great part because he alone wrote its history (*History of the Reformation of Religion within the Realm of Scotland,* first complete edition 1644). He bequeathed a legacy of unremitting opposition to anything redolent of popery; an ecclesiastical structure that helped, unwittingly or otherwise, to lay the foundations for presbyterian polity; the unfettered use of the pulpit to interpret the Bible to contemporary hearers, and not just in *spiritualia.* His concern for discipline and pastoral care likewise foreshadowed the advent of puritanism in Scotland and in England; and it was he who imported the notion of covenanting into Scotland from Edwardian England.

*See also:* Book of Discipline
*Further Reading*
Roger A. Mason, ed., *John Knox and the British Reformations* (Aldershot, Eng., 1998); Jasper Ridley, *John Knox* (Oxford, 1968).

*David Mullan*

# L

## Lathrop, John (1584–1653)

New England clergyman. Lathrop was born in the East Riding of Yorkshire. He matriculated at Christ Church College, Oxford, but soon moved to Cambridge, where he received his B.A. at Queen's College in 1606 and his M.A. in 1609. He was ordained in 1607 and in 1609 became perpetual curate of the parish of Egerton, in Kent.

In 1624 Lathrop resigned his curacy. He had evidently been won over to a semi-Separatist position, and he moved to London, where in the following year he was chosen pastor of Henry Jacob's independent congregation. The decision by one of the congregants to have a child baptized in the national church led to heated debates in the congregation and the call by some to formally and completely separate from the Church of England. Lathrop resisted those demands and also defended his semi-Separatism in debates over independency with John Davenport of St. Stephen's Coleman Street.

In 1632 one of Bishop William Laud's pursuivants arrested Lathrop and some of his followers for conducting an unlawful conventicle. Imprisoned for two years, he was released on bond in 1634, around which time he decided to emigrate. Arriving first in Boston, he settled in Scituate, a town in the Plymouth Colony, where he organized a new church and was chosen its pastor. Disputes over land led to his relocating in Barnstable in the same colony in 1639. He ministered to the congregation there until his death in 1653.

*Further Reading*
*American National Biography* (New York, 1999).

*Francis J. Bremer*

## Laud, William (1573–1645)

Archbishop of Canterbury and one of the principal opponents of puritan reform. William Laud was born in the town of Reading, the son of a prosperous clothier. He was educated at the town grammar school and then went on to matriculate at St. John's College, Oxford, in 1589. St. John's had been founded during the reign of Queen Mary and still retained a strong Catholic influence. He received his B.A. in 1594, his M.A. in 1598, and his B.D. in 1604. He was elected a senior fellow of the college in 1601. While still at Oxford, he took a number of positions that led the future archbishop of Canterbury George Abbot and others to raise questions about his orthodoxy, and the charge that he was a papist began during these years, though there was never any actual basis for the accusation.

Laud's advancement in the church began in 1608 when Richard Neile, later archbishop of York, named William as his chaplain. Three years later he was made a royal chaplain, and by 1612 he was regularly preaching at the king's court. In 1611 he succeeded to the presidency of St. John's College. Abbot tried unsuccessfully to prevent his election and in 1615 criticized a sermon Laud preached as smacking of popery. In fact, by this time Laud was attacking Presbyterians as being as bad as papists.

*William Laud's efforts to return the "beauty of holiness" to the church contributed to charges of "Arminianism" and his support of the royal authority led him to seek to purge Puritans from the church. (Corbis)*

The dispute eventually reached the king who, with Neile defending his protégé, decided in Laud's favor.

In 1621 Laud was elevated to bishop of St. David's. He rarely visited the diocese, staying instead at Richard Neile's London residence of Durham House where he could be close to the court. In the 1620s Durham House became the center of a group of young clergy who sought to reintroduce what they saw as the "beauty of holiness," and whose views included some that were opposed to orthodox Calvinism and—to some at least—smacked of Arminian heresy. Laud's advancement was aided by his close friendship to King James's favorite the Duke of Buckingham.

The new king, Charles I, was initially closer to Lancelot Andrewes, whom Laud admired, than to Laud himself. Following Andrewes death, however, it was Laud who became the close ally of the king. In 1627 he became bishop of London, a diocese that included not only the city but the entire county of Essex, both puritan hotbeds. At the same time Laud was also playing an important role in advising the king on matters of government. He quickly emerged as the principal opponent of the puritans in the church and of the critics of the king's policies in the state. He worked to convict of treason the author of a tract opposing the so-called forced loan whereby Charles I attempted to raise funds without parliamentary approval. As head of the Privy Council's Commission for Regulating Plantations, he prosecuted an attack on the charter of the Massachusetts Bay Colony, and he tried to suppress further puritan emigration to New England. His efforts to rebuild the power and wealth of the church set him at odds with many lay interests. He successfully attacked the Feoffees for Impropriations, a corporation that sought to spread puritan influence by purchasing church livings and awarding them to zealous preachers. He emphasized conformity to the prescribed forms of church worship and was relentless in seeking the deprivation of nonconformists. He favored moving altars back to their position in the east end of the church and railing them in with altar rails. Most serious, perhaps, was his support of clear opponents of traditional Calvinism such as John Cosin and Richard Montagu.

In 1633 he was elevated to the post of archbishop of Canterbury and renewed the practice of metropolitan visitations to reinforce the drive for conformity. He reinvigorated the Court of High Commission. Clashes with puritan clergy such as Thomas Shepard became evidence of his determination. He played an important role in the prosecution of the lawyer and pamphleteer William Prynne in the Court of Star Chamber. He advised and assisted Charles I in seeking to bring the churches in Ireland and Scotland into closer conformity with the Church of England. The revisions of the Scottish canons and prayer book that ensued helped to precipitate the uprising in that northern kingdom.

The Long Parliament ordered Laud imprisoned. In 1644 he was tried for subverting the religion of the realm and for contributing to the subversion of England's laws. He was convicted by ordinance and executed in 1645.

*See also:* Altar Policy, Anti-Calvinism, Antipopery, Arminianism, Book of Sports, Conscience, Court of

High Commission, Feoffees for Impropriations, Smectymnuus, Vestments, Visitation

*Further Reading*

Charles Carlton, *Archbishop William Laud* (London, 1987); Julian Davies, *The Caroline Captivity of the Church: Charles I and the Remoulding of Anglicanism* (Oxford, 1992); Anthony Milton, *Catholic and Reformed: The Roman and Protestant Churches in English Protestant Thought, 1600–1640* (Cambridge, Eng., 1995); Nicholas Tyacke, *Anti-Calvinists: The Rise of English Arminianism, c. 1590–1640* (Oxford, 1987).

*Francis J. Bremer*

## Lechford, Thomas (d. ca. 1642)

Lawyer in colonial Massachusetts. Little is known about the birth and youth of Thomas Lechford. He clearly was trained for the law and was a member of Clement's Inn (an inn of chancery that trained students in certain legal tasks), though not admitted to the bar. A few facts known about his early history indicate that he aligned himself with the puritan critics of the church. He was a solicitor for the lawyer and subversive pamphleteer William Prynne and claimed that he was imprisoned for his role in Prynne's defense. He also attended the sermons of Hugh Peter at St. Sepulchre, London, prior to that clergyman leaving England for Rotterdam.

In 1638 Lechford migrated to Massachusetts, arriving shortly after the culmination of the controversy that centered on Anne Hutchinson. In this highly charged atmosphere, some of Lechford's own religious views came under scrutiny, particularly his acceptance of episcopacy. Doubts about his orthodoxy led to his being denied church membership and thus the right to be a freeman.

In June 1639 Lechford recommended to the colony's General Court a series of practices for better regulating proceedings at law. These included appointing an official recorder of proceedings and a court secretary to write verdicts and prepare writs. Lechford was likely disappointed when he was not awarded an official position, but he supported himself by preparing legal documents such as conveyances and wills. In the summer of 1639, he represented a couple in a property suit and was disciplined by the General Court for trying to influence the jurors.

The longer he stayed in the colony, the more he became critical of New England religious practices. His dissatisfaction was increased by the failure of his career to take off. Though he was not the only colonist with legal experience in England—John Winthrop, for instance, had been an attorney of the Court of Wards and Livery—the colonial leadership did not encourage the activities of attorneys and indeed later prohibited anyone from charging fees for representing defendants in court.

Lechford returned to England in 1641. The following year he published *Plain Dealing, or, Newes from New England*. In this tract Lechford expressed his preference for an episcopal establishment and criticisms of colonial practices, but his evenhanded description of New England practices makes the work a valuable resource for historians.

*See also:* Worship in Massachusetts (in Primary Sources)

*Further Reading*

Thomas Lechford, *Note-Book Kept by Thomas Lechford* (Cambridge, MA, 1885).

*Francis J. Bremer*

## Lee, Samuel (1625–1691)

Congregationalist minister in England and New England. He was born in London and educated there at St. Paul's School, then entered Magdalen Hall, Oxford, in 1647, and in 1648 Wadham College, Oxford, receiving the M.A. that year. In 1649 he became a fellow of Wadham; led by its Warden, John Wilkins, Wadham was becoming a center of the new science. In 1655, responding to the wishes of Oliver Cromwell, he became rector of St. Botolph's, Bishopsgate, London, a post that he resigned in 1659, the year in which his *Orbis Miraculum*, an illustrated treatise on the biblical temple of Solomon, was published. After the restoration of Charles II in 1660, Lee preached in and around London to Dissenting meetings; in 1677 he became joint pastor with Theophilus Gale of the Congregationalist meeting in

Holborn, London. In 1679 he became pastor to a Congregationalist meeting in Newington Green, a London suburb, where he stayed until 1686, when he sailed for New England. There he became the pastor of the newly founded Congregational church in Bristol, Rhode Island. Attempting to return to England after the Glorious Revolution of 1688, he was captured by French pirates and taken to France, where he died. In his later years he published many works of edification bearing such titles as *The Triumph of Mercy* and *The Joy of Faith*. He was highly reputed both for his classical learning and his knowledge of natural science. He was a friend of Charles Morton, another Wadham student and enthusiast for the new science, and brought many scientific books with him to New England, which were left there.

*Further Reading*
*Oxford Dictionary of National Biography* (Oxford, 2004).

*Dewey D. Wallace Jr.*

## Leicester, Robert Dudley, Earl of (1532/3–1588)

The Earl of Leicester owes his reputation as "captain-general of the puritans" primarily to a Roman Catholic polemic of the 1580s, in which he was accused of exploiting puritan hostility to Mary, Queen of Scots, in order to manipulate the succession. His personal tastes, patronage of the stage, and complicated love life were difficult to reconcile with puritan moralizing and made him an easy target for charges of hypocrisy. But his extensive religious patronage was more than political opportunism. Although he apparently conformed to the Roman Catholic Church under Mary Tudor, his 1582 will expresses clear predestinarian views, and from the beginning of Elizabeth's reign he was prominent in the advancement of the preaching clergy.

No less consistent was his opposition to deprivations (to depriving ministers of their benefices) for what he regarded as trivial acts of nonconformity, an opposition that can be detected as early as the Vestiarian Controversy of 1564–1566. As the example of Thomas Cartwright shows, Leicester's political influence made him a very effective protector on the personal level. His tolerance of dissent was genuine—he was prepared to accept considerable personal criticism from the godly—but it was also a consequence of his relatively unsophisticated grasp of ecclesiastical politics. He was prepared to challenge the bishops openly (even Archbishop John Whitgift), while denying sincerely any intention of subverting the episcopal order. His death in 1588 has been considered a turning point in puritan politics, for no future statesman displayed a similar sympathy for godly causes.

*See also:* English Puritanism in the Netherlands
*Further Reading*
Simon Adams, *Leicester and the Court* (Manchester, Eng., 2002).

*Simon Adams*

## Leigh, William (1550–1639)

Clergyman. Leigh was born in Lancashire and educated at Brasenose College, Oxford, where he received his B.A. in 1573 and his M.A. in 1578. He then returned to Lancashire to take up the ministry. That region was noted for strong remnants of Roman Catholicism, and the area authorities had established five centers where yearly synods were to be conducted to propagate the gospel. Leigh was moderator of the synod in Preston and was also appointed a justice of the peace.

Following a brief return to Oxford, where he was vice-principal of Brasenose, he returned to the north. He was a forceful preacher and a man of puritan piety who was critical of the shortcomings of the church in the region. In 1612 he was involved, both as a justice of the peace and as a minister, in the prosecution of the twelve accused Lancashire witches. As a justice he took the statement of the afflicted fourteen-year-old girl, and he later preached the sermon when the ten convicted witches were hung.

*Further Reading*
*Oxford Dictionary of National Biography* (Oxford, 2004).

*Francis J. Bremer*

## Leighton, Alexander (ca. 1570–1649)

Scottish critic of the Stuart Church of England. Leighton was educated at the University of St. Andrews, receiving his M.A. in 1587. During the early seventeenth century he was a lecturer in the area of Newcastle upon Tyne, but in 1617 he migrated to the Netherlands and enrolled as a medical student at the University of Leiden. While pursuing his studies there, he made contacts with some of the publishers of English Separatist works.

Leighton settled in London in 1619. Denied a license as a physician because he had received holy orders, he practiced medicine anyway. He also participated in illegal religious conventicles and joined Henry Jacob's congregation. In the mid-1620s he began to publish his religious views, including criticism of episcopacy, a call for England to provide military support for the Protestant cause on the continent, and an attack on stage plays. Briefly imprisoned, Leighton soon resumed his calls for reform. He organized a petition to be presented to the parliament called in 1628 and then traveled to the Netherlands, where he published *An Appeale to the Parliament, or, Sions Plea Against the Prelacy* (1628) in which, among other things, he claimed that the assassination of the king's favorite, the Duke of Buckingham, was a sign from God.

Shortly after his return to England in 1630, Leighton was arrested and brought to trial for sedition before the Star Chamber. Degraded from holy orders, he was whipped, pilloried, and had his left ear cut off and his face branded with the letters "S.S.," indicating a sower of sedition. He was then incarcerated in the Fleet prison. He remained in prison until freed by parliamentary order in 1641. The following years he was rewarded for his sufferings with an appointment as keeper of Lambeth Palace, which had been turned into a military prison. He visited Scotland over the next years. He was likely the author of a tract published in 1648 warning Londoners of the power of the army. He died in 1649.

*See also:* English Puritanism in the Netherlands
*Further Reading*
Stephen Foster, *Notes from the Caroline
    Underground: Alexander Leighton, the Puritan
    Triumvirate, and the Laudian Reaction to
    Nonconformity* (Hampden, CT, 1978).

*Francis J. Bremer*

## Lever, Thomas (1521–1577)

Marian exile and evangelical religious reformer. Lever received his B.A. from St. John's College, Cambridge, in 1542, became a fellow of the college in 1543, and was awarded his M.A. in 1545. At Cambridge he formed a friendship with the Humanist Roger Ascham and became one of the leaders of the evangelical reform movement in the university. In 1550 he preached at St. Paul's in London and also before King Edward VI. In these sermons he called for reform of the church and of education. But he also embraced the social gospel that was being advanced by some of the leading evangelicals, criticizing the rich for exploiting the poor. In 1551 the king appointed him master of St. John's.

Following the death of King Edward in 1553, Lever supported the claim of Lady Jane Grey to the throne. When that cause failed and the Catholic Mary Tudor became queen, Lever resigned his position at St. John's and joined others who sought refuge on the continent. He visited Zürich, where he formed a friendship with the Reformer Heinrich Bullinger, but settled first in Geneva. Visiting Frankfurt, he became engaged in dispute with his fellow exile John Knox over the proper prayer book to be used by the English exile congregations. He then moved on, settling in Arau.

Following the death of Queen Mary and the accession of Elizabeth, Lever returned to England. He was soon out of favor with the queen, probably for questioning her plan to assume the title of supreme head of the church; she settled for that of supreme governor. He was appointed archdeacon of Coventry in 1559, but his radical stances probably denied him greater preferment. Though he agreed to the Thirty-nine Articles, he was opposed to the wearing of the surplice and sought to intercede for those who were persecuted for taking that stance. He was very outspoken in trying to raise the standards for the ministry, and he took the radical position of arguing that local congregations should have a say in the selection of their ministers. He encouraged clerical prophesyings in his archdeaconry as a means of improving the preparation of clergy. Lever died in 1577.

See also: Lectures and Lectureships, Prophesyings
*Further Reading*
*Oxford Dictionary of National Biography* (Oxford, 2004).

Francis J. Bremer

## Leverett, John (1616–1679)

Soldier in the parliamentary army and governor of the colony of Massachusetts. Leverett was born in Boston, Lincolnshire. His family were members of St. Botolph's Parish in that town and in 1633 followed their pastor, John Cotton, to the new Boston in Massachusetts. John began his career as a merchant. He joined the Boston Artillery Company in 1639 and was included in a Massachusetts commission to deal with the Narragansett Indians in 1642.

In 1644 Leverett returned to England and received a commission as a captain in the regiment of Thomas Rainsborowe. Returning to New England after four years of service, he began to play a larger role in the political affairs of the colony. He was elected a selectman of the town of Boston in 1651 and was also chosen to represent the town in the General Court, the colony's legislature. He was placed on delegations to warn the French against encroachments on the northern frontiers of Massachusetts (now the state of Maine) and to settle disputes over New England's western frontier with the Dutch in New Netherland. With the outbreak of the First Anglo-Dutch War, Leverett and his father-in-law, Robert Sedgwick, journeyed to England to seek English support against the Dutch colony. Oliver Cromwell sent them back to New England with four ships, 200 troops, and authorization to raise colonial militia for an attack on New Netherlands. The war came to a conclusion before the expedition could sail, and it was redirected north, where Sedgwick seized some French outposts.

Leverett intended to remain in New England after this success, but he was sent to England by the Massachusetts authorities to serve as the colony's agent to the Protectorate government. His reports helped to shape the colonial understanding of and support of Oliver Cromwell. He returned to America in 1662, following the Restoration.

Over the next decade Leverett served in a variety of governmental positions and also served as major-general of Massachusetts. In 1674 he was elected the colony's governor, a position he held until his death in 1679. He was thus governor during King Philip's War, the devastating conflict with the Native American tribes that had been organized by the Wampanoag leader Metacom (King Philip to the English). He promoted an offensive strategy against the tribes, which gradually achieved victory and effectively destroyed the native societies of southern New England. As governor he approved the sale of Native American captives into slavery in the West Indies.

*Further Reading*
*American National Biography* (New York, 1999); Francis J. Bremer, *Congregational Communion: Clerical Friendship in the Anglo-American Puritan Community, 1610–1692* (Boston, 1994); Douglas Leach, *Flintlock and Tomahawk: New England in King Philip's War* (New York, 1958).

Francis J. Bremer

## Lobb, Stephen (ca. 1647–1699)

A prominent and disputatious Congregationalist clergyman of the Restoration era. He was the son of Richard Lobb, member of Parliament, of Liskeard, Cornwall. His education is unknown. In 1672 he was licensed to preach at his father's house. In 1680 he coauthored with John Humfrey defenses of Dissent against Edward Stillingfleet's *Mischief of Separation*. In 1681 he settled in London as pastor of a congregation in Swallow Street, moving to Fetter Lane in 1685. Implicated in the Rye House Plot, he was arrested in August 1683. His *True Dissenter* (1685) encouraged the term "Dissenter," which he took to represent "thorough nonconformity," that is, complete separation from the Church of England. He thought that the practice of occasional conformity was wrong. When in 1687 James II issued his Declaration of Indulgence (a prerogative edict suspending the penal laws), Lobb was among the minority of Dissenters who published an address of thanks. He thereupon became a favorite at court and an active agent in James's campaign to lure Dissenters into a coalition with Catholics in support of repeal of the Test and Corporation Acts and the penal laws. In this stance he had a few colleagues, notably the Quaker William Penn and the Presbyterian Vincent Alsop. It brought him deep unpopularity and the nickname "the Jacobite Independent." From 1692 to 1699 he was at the heart of the theological quarrel between Calvinists and Arminians that rent the Dissenters. He published a series of attacks on Daniel Williams and the deceased Richard Baxter, implying that their abandonment of Calvinism led them into Socinianism. In 1694 his side in the dispute took over the Pinners' Hall lectureship, the other side taking Salters' Hall. Of Lobb's three clergyman sons, two conformed to the Church of England.

*See also:* Pinners' Hall
*Further Reading*
*Oxford Dictionary of National Biography* (Oxford, 2004).

*Mark Goldie*

### Locke, Anne Vaughan (b. ca. 1530)

Outspoken advocate of religious reform during the reign of Queen Elizabeth. She was well educated and fluent in languages. She may have learned her Reformed beliefs from her stepmother, who had previously been the wife of Henry Brinklow. In 1552 she began a friendship with John Knox, who lodged with the Lockes at that time.

Anne and her husband, the merchant Henry Locke, remained in London after the accession of Queen Mary. In 1656 she began a correspondence with Knox, who persuaded her to join the exile community in Geneva. There she devoted some of her time to translating into English Calvin's sermons on the song of Hezekiah. Returning to England after the accession of Queen Elizabeth, she continued to correspond with Knox (who was soon in Scotland) and to solicit support for the Scottish Reformation from London merchants. She seems to have adopted Knox's criticisms of the pace of reform in England and may have been one of the women whose support of those opposing the requirement that clergymen wear special vestments in performing religious ceremonies was commented on by Bishop Edmund Grindal.

Following the death of her husband in 1571, Anne married the popular Reformed preacher Edward Dering. Dering praised her for her support during the crackdown on puritans in London. Following his death in 1575, Anne wed for the last time, marrying Richard Prowse, who was three times mayor of Exeter. In 1590 she again published a translation, this time a work offering comfort to the Protestants in the Netherlands. No record of her death has been found. Her correspondence with Knox offers valuable insight into the views of an educated woman who was committed to the reform of the church.

*Further Reading*
Patrick Collinson, "John Knox, the Church of England and the Women of England," in R. A. Mason, ed., *John Knox and the British Reformations* (Aldershot, Eng., 1998); Patrick Collinson, "The Role of Women in the English Reformation Illustrated by the Life and Friendships of Anne Locke," in Collinson, *Godly People: Essays on English Protestantism and Puritanism* (London, 1983).

*Francis J. Bremer*

# M

## Manton, Thomas (1620–1677)

English Nonconformist minister and author. The son of a Devon minister, Thomas Manton was baptized in March 1620 at Lydeard St. Lawrence, Somerset. He attended Wadham College, Oxford, gaining considerable academic recognition over the succeeding years, finally becoming a Doctor of Divinity in 1660. Manton was ordained into the Church of England as a deacon at Exeter at the age of twenty and served as lecturer at Colyton, Devon. In July 1645, he was appointed rector of Stoke Newington and soon began to acquire a reputation as a preacher and author.

Manton's support for Parliament in the English Civil War was tempered by a suspicion of the aims of the Independents. In 1649 he was a signatory to the *Vindication,* a Presbyterian document opposing the execution of King Charles I. The execution of the minister Christopher Love by the parliamentary authorities in 1651 caused further tension between Presbyterians and the new republic. Manton's funeral sermon for Love was published several times, as *The Naturall Man's Case Stated* (1652). In 1652 Manton succeeded Obadiah Sedgwick as rector of St. Paul's, Covent Garden. Despite his disapproval of radical elements within the government, Manton sat on several official commissions and appears to have found favor with Cromwell, being appointed lecturer at Westminster Abbey in 1655.

Alarmed at the political turmoil that followed Cromwell's death in 1658, Manton began to contemplate the return of the monarchy. In February 1660 he traveled to Holland with Edmund Calamy, Edward Reynolds and William Spurstowe to negotiate with the exiled Charles II. After the Restoration, Manton took part in attempts to arrive at a comprehensive religious settlement, attending the Savoy Conference of 1661. At the same time, however, he was attacked in the Cavalier press for his part in the republication of *Smectymnuus* (a provocative critique of episcopal government first published in 1641). Finding himself unable in conscience to comply with the Act of Uniformity, Manton was one of many hundreds of Puritan ministers ejected from the Church of England on St. Bartholomew's Day, 24 August 1662. His farewell sermon was published in concert with several other leading Nonconformists, further enraging Cavalier-Anglican detractors. However, Manton issued a letter utterly disavowing the sermon published in his name, a letter that was gleefully published by his principal critic, Roger L'Estrange, in an attempt to coerce other ministers to issue similar retractions. Manton continued to preach privately to leading Puritan gentry, such as Lord Wharton, but was constantly harried by the authorities. He was reported in 1669 for not receiving Holy Communion and in 1670 was arrested under the provisions of the Five Mile Act and committed to the Gatehouse prison in London for six months.

Following Charles II's Declaration of Indulgence in 1672, Manton was licensed as a Presbyterian preacher at his house in Covent Garden. But when times again turned against the Noncon-formists, he experienced further persecution, with at least one of his meetings being forcibly broken up by soldiers in 1675. He died on 18 October 1677 and was buried at Stoke Newington.

*See also:* Ejections of Clergy, Pinners' Hall
*Further Reading*
A. G. Matthews, *Calamy Revised: Being a Revision of Edmund Calamy's Account of the Ministers and others Ejected and Silenced, 1660–2* (Oxford, 1934; reprinted 1988); Rev. Thomas Smith, general ed., *The Complete Works of Thomas Manton, D.D., With A Memoir of the Author by the Rev. William Harris, D.D., and an essay by the Rev. J. C. Ryle,* 22 vol. (London, 1870–1875).

David J. Appleby

## Marshall, Stephen (ca. 1594–1655)

Prominent Presbyterian minister and preacher to Parliament. Marshall was born in Godmanchester, Huntingdonshire, to a poor family. He matriculated at Emmanuel College, Cambridge, as a pensioner in 1615, graduating B.A. (1618), M.A. (1622), and B.D. (1629). In 1618 he became chaplain to the Barnardiston family in Clare Priory, Suffolk, possibly acting as lecturer at Clare and attending Richard Blackerby's household seminary at nearby Ashen, Essex. In 1619 he succeeded Richard Rogers as lecturer at Wethersfield, Essex, and was very successful. In 1625 he was instituted as vicar in neighboring Finchingfield, and here he established his reputation. He was renowned as a painful (diligent) preacher, delivering moving sermons with more passion than rhetorical decoration, and met with pastoral success in counseling his patron, Sir William Kempe, and restoring him to society.

In the following years his stature grew. He remodeled the parish vestry and worked at advancing the reformation of manners through local activity and enlisting the help of the provincial magistracy. He was also a regular visitor to many pulpits across Essex. Furthermore, he became an important spiritual and practical advisor to other godly ministers and to the noble professors of the Reformed religion in Essex, particularly the Rich and Barrington families. His prominence grew as he kept his benefice through the 1630s while many colleagues were deprived or exiled, placing his evangelical vocation above his distaste for the pressures exerted against his nonconformity.

At the start of the 1640s he emerged as one of the major clerical reformers in parliamentarian politics. He was nominated as one of the preachers at parliamentarian fasts in 1640 and onward, many of which were printed. Marshall joined with Cornelius Burges, Matthew Newcomen, Edmund Calamy, and others to advance the godly cause, being crucial in the ministers' "petition" and "remonstrance" delivered to the Commons in January 1641. From this circle also emerged the pamphlets of "Smectymnuus," critical contributions to the ecclesiological debate of the early 1640s. In them his movement from supporter of a reformed "primitive" episcopacy to a proponent of moderate Presbyterianism can be traced. Marshall was also central to the Root and Branch Bill (which resulted from the Root and Branch Petition) to abolish episcopacy and also to the efforts to paper over the emerging ecclesiological cracks within the godly cause. Once war broke out, he left London for a while to act as chaplain, preaching to the Earl of Essex's troops and persuading the forces at the crucial battle of Edgehill that God was on their side.

In mid-1643 he traveled to Edinburgh as one of the Westminster Assembly's commissioners, promoting the Solemn League and Covenant and returning to deliver John Pym's funeral sermon at the end of the year. For the next three years his work was dominated by the Westminster Assembly. He operated as a pragmatic Presbyterian, holding the Erastians at bay and constantly seeking accommodation with the Independents. He drafted the section of the directory on preaching, but his moderation made him seem untrustworthy to the more conservative Scottish Presbyterians. By 1646 he spoke for the assembly against the extreme Erastianism of Parliament but, remaining a pragmatist, went on to play a prominent role in the Hinkford classis in Essex.

He spent the end of the decade in his favored role as broker. He accompanied the commissioners sent to negotiate with the king at Newcastle in January 1647 along with Joseph Caryl, with whom he went on to act as an unpopular chaplain to the king at Holmby House. In early 1648 he returned to Scotland to help repair the alliance and played an active role in the ecclesiological debates in the Isle of Wight. He preached to the Commons two days after Pride's Purge and seems to have been uneasy about the execution of Charles I.

He was never so central a figure after 1649, although he still played a part. He preached to the Barebones Parliament and acted as a commissioner to draw up the "fundamentals of religion" as part of the loose-limbed ecumenism of the 1650s. In 1654 he was appointed as one of the "Triers," those given the task of assessing candidates for the ministry. He took his final ministerial post, becoming town lecturer of Ipswich, Suffolk, in 1651. However, he was beginning to suffer from gout, and in 1655 he started to suffer from consumption. He died on 19 November 1655 and was buried in the south aisle of Westminster Abbey with great solemnity. Following the Restoration, in September 1661 his remains were taken up and cast into a pit at the back door of the prebendary's lodgings in the churchyard of St. Margaret's, Westminster.

*See also:* Smectymnuus
*Further Reading*
Tom Webster, *Stephen Marshall and Finchingfield* (Chelmsford, Eng., 1994).

*Tom Webster*

## Martindale, Adam (1621–1686)

Presbyterian clergyman; born in Prescot, Lancashire, England, in September 1621. Unusually for one intending to become a Presbyterian minister, he had no university education, and was a product of an impressive program of self-education. In 1641 he became a civilian clerk to the Parliamentarian army at Liverpool. There he entered into religious debate with radical officers. In 1646, he was invited to preach at Gorton near Manchester, where he observed the debate between Presbyterians and Independents taking place in the town. In July 1649 he was ordained by Presbyterian convention by the eighth London Classis and accepted an invitation to minister to the congregation at Rostherne, Cheshire.

His appointment to Rostherne was not universally welcomed. Martindale was an outspoken, if sincere, character, and his criticism of the ungodly was resented. He strongly resisted the growing popularity of the Quaker movement and deplored Independent lay preaching in his parish.

At the Restoration, Martindale retained his living, although he was imprisoned for countenancing conventicles. Following the Act of Uniformity in 1662, he was ejected by the bishop of Chester. He turned to school teaching, and for a time he taught mathematics at Manchester Grammar School. In about 1670 he was appointed chaplain to Lord Delamere, and in 1672 he was licensed to preach in Rostherne. Between ejection and his death, Martindale traveled widely, visiting friends and sympathizers among Dissenters. He died in September 1686 and was buried at Rostherne on 21 September.

*Further Reading*
Martindale, Adam, *Life of Adam Martindale written by himself*, ed. Richard Parkinson, R. Chetham Society, old series, vol. 4 (Manchester, Eng., 1845); *Oxford Dictionary of National Biography* (Oxford, 2004).

*Catherine Nunn*

## Marvell, Andrew (1621–1678)

English poet, Parliamentarian, and supporter of Puritans. He was born in Winestead-in-Holderness, Yorkshire, where his father was rector. In 1624 the family moved to Hull, where Marvell attended the Hull Grammar School. He entered Trinity College, Cambridge, in 1633, receiving the B.A. in 1639. He left for the continent in 1641 or 1642, remaining there for about four years. Back in England, he was tutor to the daughter of Thomas, Lord Fairfax, and then to a ward of Oliver Cromwell. He praised Cromwell in several poems. In 1657 he was named Latin Secretary and assistant to John Milton. In 1659 he was elected to Parliament for Hull and served in succeeding parliaments until his death. He published defenses of the

Dissenters John Howe and John Owen, the latter in *The Rehearsal Transpros'd* (in two parts, 1672–1673), a satiric response to the anti-Puritan writer Samuel Parker, whom Marvell condemned for intolerance and for abandoning the Calvinist grace-centered theology of the earlier Church of England. In 1677 he published anonymously *An Account of the Growth of Popery and Arbitrary Government in England,* defending political and religious liberty. In a parliamentary speech of that same year he warned against the growth of the power of the bishops. He was alarmed by the possibility that the Duke of York would succeed to the throne and undo the Protestant Reformation in England. His poems, most of which were published posthumously, express conventional themes of love and nature expressed in distinctive and witty ways, but also reveal his religious convictions, as in "Bermudas," a celebration of God's providence, and "The Coronet," which employs imagery of the suffering Christ.

*Further Reading*
John M. Wallace, *Destiny His Choice: The Loyalism of Andrew Marvell* (Cambridge, Eng., 1968).

Dewey D. Wallace Jr.

*Cotton Mather, son of Increase, was one of the leading clergymen of late-seventeenth- and early-eighteenth-century New England and an author of histories and medical works, as well as religious treatises.* (The Illustrated Book of All Religions. *Chicago: Star Publishing Company, n.d.*)

## Mather, Cotton (1663–1728)

American Congregational minister, historian, dabbler in science, and author of more than four hundred publications. Mather was born into an illustrious ministerial dynasty. His father was Increase Mather, and Richard Mather and John Cotton were his grandfathers. His fraught relationship with his father, whom he was rarely able to please, perhaps accounts for his childhood stutter. Mather entered Harvard College at twelve. He was ordained in 1685 and joined his father at the North Church in Boston. He remained in that post for the rest of his life as the most prominent and controversial minister in Massachusetts. Although Mather never traveled far from Boston, he was an ambitious man, and he projected himself successfully on a transatlantic stage. Most of his important books were published in England, and he had a voluminous correspondence with prominent Europeans; he received an honorary doctorate from the University of Glasgow in 1710, and he was elected a fellow of England's most prestigious scientific organization, the Royal Society, in 1713.

Mather lived in a period of great social and cultural changes, changes that he did not always handle skillfully. In 1692, he wrote an apology for the Salem witchcraft trials, the last significant witchhunt in either England or British North America. Mather's book, *The Wonders of the Invisible World,* came out as the Massachusetts government was shutting the trials down. His unfortunate timing insured that his predominant posthumous reputation would be as a superstitious bigot with blood on his hands. Other inept political interventions over his life left him with a wide range of powerful enemies.

But more often Mather attempted to bend with changes and adapt them for his overriding evangelical purposes. In what might be called his earliest scientific writing, *Memorable Providences, Relating to Witchcrafts And Possessions* (1689), he described possessed children in Boston. In doing so, Mather deliberately followed English writers like Joseph Glanville who were fighting a rearguard battle to prove the existence of the demonic (and thus confute atheism) by new canons of scientific demonstration. In 1715, he finished a far more fashionable manuscript that was published in London six years later, *The Christian Philosopher.* This was a venture in the new physico-theology, a popular genre that demonstrated the existence of a wise and benevolent creator through the latest scientific discoveries. In 1721, in response to a local smallpox epidemic, Mather encouraged experimentation with vaccination, for which he got a bomb thrown through his window.

Mather severely felt the loss of the Massachusetts Charter in 1691 and with that loss, the end of puritan self-rule. One of his ways of coping was his decision in 1693 to compile a massive ecclesiastical history of New England, the *Magnalia Christi Americana* (London, 1702)—"Whether *New England* may *Live* any where else or no, it must *Live* in our *History!*" The *Magnalia* is a hodgepodge consisting of biographies of important leaders and accounts of church affairs, the demonic, and Indian wars. Mather presented as harmonious a version of New England's past as he could allow himself while still acknowledging the region's many conflicts. The *Magnalia* remains an invaluable source for historians and Mather's most important literary production.

In Mather's time, elite religion placed an increasing emphasis on lack of dogmatism and toleration. Neither of these had been puritan virtues. Mather's most notable response came in the 1710s. Always a firm believer in the imminent approach of the millennium, in that decade Mather began seeking a unity between evangelical Christians of diverse creeds in preparation for Christ's return. That unity was to come not through doctrinal agreement, but through what he called "vital piety." His ecumenical impulses even caused him to reach out to Anglicans and Quakers.

Other important works by Mather include *Manuductio ad Ministerium*, a manual for prospective ministers, and *Ratio Disciplinae Fratrum Nov-Anglorum* (1726), an invaluable survey of Congregational church practices. *Bonifacius, or Essays to do Good* (1710) was written to encourage the performance of good works. It influenced Benjamin Franklin and was popular among nineteenth-century evangelicals.

Mather was not able to get all of his important work published. A medical treatise, "The Angel of Bethesda," did not appear in print until 1972. From 1693 to the end of his life, Mather labored on his "Biblia Americana," an enormous and useful compendium of scripture commentaries from a wide variety of authors. It remains in manuscript, in seven large folio volumes.

Mather was vain, painfully self-conscious, insecure, quick to meddle but hypersensitive to criticism, and possessed of prodigious amounts of energy. Married three times, he had fifteen children, thirteen of whom died before him.

*See also:* Brattle Street Church, *Magnalia Christi Americana*, Old Age, Puritan Historians, Sermon Notes, Witchcraft
*Further Reading*
Richard F. Lovelace, *The American Pietism of Cotton Mather: Origins of American Evangelicalism* (Grand Rapids, MI, 1979); Kenneth Silverman, *The Life and Times of Cotton Mather* (New York, 1984); Michael P. Winship, *Seers of God: Puritan Providentialism in the Restoration and Early Enlightenment* (Baltimore, 1966).

*Michael P. Winship*

## Mather, Increase (1639–1723)

Prolific author, minister at Boston's Old North (Second) church (1664–1723), Harvard College president, and colonial agent. The son of Dorchester minister Richard Mather and Katherine Holt Mather, Increase received his B.A. from Harvard in 1656 and, while residing in Ireland and England, an M.A. from Trinity College, Dublin, in 1658. While in England he made numerous connections with religious and political leaders that were to be useful to him and to New England.

*Increase Mather, one of the foremost colonial clergymen of the second half of the seventeenth century. (Massachusetts Historical Society)*

After the Restoration he returned to New England and in 1662 married Maria Cotton; among their ten children was Cotton Mather, who later served as minister with Increase. At the 1662 synod, Mather, along with Harvard president Charles Chauncy and New Haven minister John Davenport, vigorously opposed the loosening of baptismal privilege and church membership now known as the Half-Way Covenant. Mather pressed his case even after losing at the synod and later at the General Court. In 1664 Mather accepted an invitation to become teacher to Boston's Second Church, a position he held until his death. Mather turned toward chiliasm and increasingly defended the values of the founding generation of Massachusetts against what he saw as a declension. In 1670, following the death of his father, he published *The Life and Death of that Reverend Man of God Mr. Richard Mather.*

In the 1670s, Mather adopted a prophet's mantle, warning the "Rising Generation" against innova-

tions and deviations by invoking jeremiad rhetoric against social and spiritual failings and advocating a return to *First Principles of New-England* (the title of a 1675 book). A high-point was his 1674 double sermon *The Day of Trouble Is Near,* which, employing covenantal rhetoric, called for particular social and ecclesiastical reforms, pointed toward chiliasm, and vaguely prophesied a coming war. When King Philip's War actually broke out in the summer of 1675, Mather felt vindicated and interpreted the war as divine punishment to call back and correct God's people; he thereby influenced the General Court legislation against "Provoking Evils." Toward the end of the war, Mather began a narrative that largely interpreted it in biblical terms; published in 1676, the book competed with a slightly different interpretation shortly after offered by William Hubbard. Mather continued to promulgate his views. In a 1677 election sermon, *The Danger of Apostasy,* Mather specifically held magistrates responsible for declension. He began urging churches to engage in "covenant renewal." Mather's efforts led to the Reforming Synod of 1679, summarized in *The Necessity of Reformation* (1679).

In the 1680s, Mather's interests turned toward science and natural phenomena, especially concerning astronomy and comets, as evidenced in *Heaven's Alarm to the World* (1681), and he organized the Boston Philosophical Society. He engaged in a project of collecting, organizing, and editing a large array of providential tales, published in *An Essay for the Recording of Illustrious Providences* (1684), which was bolstered by his own *The Doctrine of Divine Providence* (1684).

In the latter half of the 1680s, Mather was consumed with political matters. In response both to Gov. Andros's imposition of Anglican order and to James II's Act of Indulgence, Mather was dispatched to England, where he stayed four years to lobby on behalf of the colony's interests. There he witnessed the Glorious Revolution; then, along with Sir Henry Ashurst, Elisha Cooke, and Thomas Oakes, he continued to lobby, especially concerning the rebellion against Andros. Mather was instrumental in negotiating a new charter for Massachusetts in 1691, which fundamentally changed the government, especially by relinquishing election of the colony's governor to royal appointment. Although Mather had done his best under trying circumstances, the new charter made him unpopular in New England.

In 1692, Mather's public opposition to the admissibility of spectral evidence led to the dismissal of the Salem witch trials. A strong Harvard supporter, Mather in 1685 had served as president pro tempore of Harvard, instituting several curricular and disciplinary changes; in 1692, he drafted a new charter for Harvard, with himself as president, although the Privy Council voided the charter four years later, prompting Mather to draft a new charter under which, because of Cambridge residency requirements, he would eventually resign the presidency. But this charter, too, was rejected in 1699; under the new proposal, Mather spent 1700–1701 in residency at Cambridge before being replaced with Samuel Willard. In the meantime, however, he labored to prevent what he viewed as growing liberalism at Harvard and elsewhere, futilely opposing the establishment of the Brattle Street Church and what he saw as presbyterial relaxation of membership standards by Solomon Stoddard at Northampton. Throughout his remaining years, Mather continued to preach, publish, and agitate against the growing innovations and latitudinarianism he saw challenging the Puritan order of New England.

*See also:* Providence, Reforming Synod of 1679
*Further Reading*
Michael Hall, *Increase Mather: The Last American Puritan* (Middletown, CT, 1988); Kenneth B. Murdock, *Increase Mather* (Cambridge, MA, 1925).

*Michael G. Ditmore*

### Mather, Nathaniel (1630–1697)

Congregational minister. Nathaniel Mather was the second son of Richard Mather and brother of Samuel and Increase Mather. He was born in Much Woolton, Lancashire, and traveled with his family to Massachusetts in 1635. There he attended Harvard College, graduating with an M.A. in 1647.

Mather returned to England to seek a pulpit from which he could aid in the cause of reformation. In 1656 Oliver Cromwell presented him to be vicar of Barnstable in Devonshire. There he formed a friendship with John Howe and became a member of the Devonshire Association. It is likely that he was one of the delegates at the Congregationalist Savoy Assembly in 1658. Ejected from his benefice in 1662, Nathaniel left England with the aid of Matthew Mead and became pastor of an English congregation in Rotterdam. When his brother Samuel died in 1671, Nathaniel accepted the call to replace him as pastor of the New Row Congregational church in Dublin. He published some of Samuel's works and led a drive to raise funds in Dublin for the relief of New Englanders suffering from King Philip's War. In the aftermath of the Rye House Plot, persecution of Dissenters in Dublin was stepped up, and Nathaniel left Ireland to accept the pastorate of the Lime Street Church in London, succeeding another former New Englander, John Collins, who had died in 1687.

Nathaniel provided his brother Increase and other colonists information on English and Irish religious and political developments and followed events in New England closely. He assisted Increase when the latter came to England to secure New England rights that had been undermined by the revocation of the Massachusetts charter. Nathaniel also joined with John Howe, George Griffith, and other Dissenting clergymen in encouraging William of Orange to seize the throne from James II in the Glorious Revolution.

Nathaniel initially worked for the unity of Nonconformists and supported the Heads of Agreement between Congregationalists and Presbyterians that his brother Increase had helped to organize. He was one of the original managers of the Common Fund in the early 1690s. Nathaniel remained suspicious of Presbyterians, however. He attacked Daniel Williams in 1693 for preaching Arminian views, a dispute that led to the breakup of the union and the withdrawal of the Presbyterian clergy from the jointly sponsored Pinners' Hall lectureship. Mather was one of the clergy then named to the vacant positions at Pinners' Hall. He died in London in 1697 and was buried in Bunhill Fields.

*See also:* Pinners' Hall
*Further Reading*
Francis J. Bremer, *Congregational Communion: Clerical Friendship in the Anglo-American Puritan Community, 1610–1692* (Boston, 1994); Richard L. Greaves, *God's Other Children: Protestant Nonconformists and the Emergence of Denominational Churches in Ireland, 1660–1700* (Stanford, 1997); John Langdon Sibley, *Biographical Sketches of Graduates of Harvard University, Volume I, 1648–1658* (Cambridge, MA, 1873).

*Francis J. Bremer*

## Mather, Richard (1596–1669)

New England "founder," Congregational apologist, and Dorchester, Massachusetts, pastor. Father of the famous Increase Mather and grandfather of the celebrated Cotton Mather, Richard Mather was himself one of the leading figures in the history of early New England. Born in 1596 and educated at Oxford, Mather arrived in Massachusetts Bay in 1635 and began his ministry in First Church of Dorchester the following year. He served his church for thirty-three years. As an apologist for the Congregational system of church polity; Mather's importance was second only to that of John Cotton. Mather penned several tracts that sought to explain and justify church practices in Massachusetts Bay, the most important of which was arguably *Church-Government and Church-Covenant Discussed* (London, 1643). Mather's role was also central in the construction of the Cambridge Platform of 1648, which New England Congregationalists regarded as their official "constitution" of church government.

As much as any one man, Richard Mather may be also considered as the father of the so-called Half-Way Covenant, which, in response to declining church membership rates, eased admission requirements by allowing the children of baptized but unregenerate members to be baptized. A synod of lay and clerical delegates recommended implementation of this "innovation" in 1662. Though the

*Richard Mather, one of the leading New England clergymen of the first generation and the principal promoter of the Half-Way Covenant. (Circer, Hayward, ed.,* Dictionary of American Portraits, *1967)*

Half-Way Covenant granted churchgoers only limited membership privileges, Mather and his allies soon found themselves facing a storm of vocal opposition from a minority among the colony's laity and a small number of ministers, who insisted that the Half-Way Covenant represented a sinful departure from previous church practices. Clerical opponents included Mather's own son Increase, and the dispute over the implementation of the measure was the most significant to face Massachusetts Congregationalists prior to the Great Awakening. Attempting to mediate a dispute over the Half-Way Covenant at the First Church of Boston in 1669, the aged Mather was physically locked out of the church by opponents. He shortly thereafter fell ill and died days later. In response to a deathbed plea, Mather's shocked and grief-stricken son Increase abruptly reversed his position on the Half-Way

Covenant to become one of the colony's strongest advocates of the measure, which most churches increasingly began to implement by the 1680s and 1690s.

See also: Bay Psalm Book, Cambridge Assembly, Half-Way Covenant
*Further Reading*
B. R. Burg, *Richard Mather of Dorchester* (Lexington, KY; 1976).

*James F. Cooper*

## Mather, Samuel (1626–1671)

Congregational minister. Mather was the son of Richard Mather and Katherine Holt. He was born at Much Woolton, Lancashire, in 1626 and emigrated with his parents and three brothers to New England in 1635. Mather studied at Harvard College, graduating M.A. in 1643 and becoming the first graduate named a fellow. Refusing a call to the ministry of Boston's Second Church, he returned to England instead. His New England connections with leading English Congregationalists secured for him a position as chaplain to Thomas Andrewes, the lord mayor of London who had earlier been a member of Thomas Goodwin's Arnhem congregation. In 1650 he became a chaplain at Magdalen, Oxford, where Thomas Goodwin was president. He accompanied his friend Sidrach Simpson to Scotland. During the next two years he preached occasionally at Leith.

In 1654 Philip Nye recommended him as a preacher to the Council of State in Ireland. Two years later he was called to the ministry of the church of St. Nicholas in Dublin, where his colleague was Samuel Winter. Mather was also a lecturer at Christ Church, a fellow of Trinity College, Dublin, and one of the leading puritan clergy in the country, with a close relationship to Henry Cromwell during the latter's administration of Irish affairs. He served as one of the commission to approve ministers in County Cork.

Following the accession of Charles II, Mather preached a sequence of two controversial sermons in September of 1660, urging Charles to assume the role of a reforming Hezekiah and identifying various church practices as needing reform. He warned that if such reforms were not instituted and, worse, "If you super-adde the sin of Persecution to the sin of Superstition, you will be quickly ripe for final Ruine," as "the Lord himself will fight against you." The authorities prohibited Mather from further preaching. He sent his sermon notes to New England, where they were published in 1670 through the efforts of his brother Increase.

Deprived of his living, he returned to Lancashire, where he had been born, and ministered to a parish there until ejected in 1662. He then returned to Dublin, preaching regularly to a congregation on New Row in that city. He urged cooperation between Congregationalist, Baptist, and Presbyterian Dissenters, particularly in *Irenicum: or an Essay for Union,* which was published posthumously in 1680. But his irenic interests were limited to orthodox Calvinists. He was critical of the Fifth Monarchist Jeremiah Marsden and preached *A Defence of the Protestant Christian Religion Against Popery* (1672). Another of his interests was typology, and his sermons on *The Figures or Types of the Old Testament* were published by his brother Nathaniel in 1683.

Mather died in October 1671. Samuel was soon succeeded by his brother Nathaniel as pastor of the New Row congregation.

*Further Reading*
Francis J. Bremer, *Congregational Communion: Clerical Friendship in the Anglo-American Puritan Community, 1610–1692* (Boston, 1994); Richard L. Greaves, *God's Other Children: Protestant Nonconformists and the Emergence of Denominational Churches in Ireland, 1660–1700* (Stanford, 1997); A. G. Matthews, *Calamy Revised: Being a Revision of Edmund Calamy's Account of the Ministers and others Ejected and Silenced, 1660–2* (Oxford, 1934; reprinted 1988); John Langdon Sibley, *Biographical Sketches of Graduates of Harvard University, Volume I, 1648–1658* (Cambridge, MA, 1873).

*Francis J. Bremer*

## Mayhew, Thomas, Jr. (1621–1657)

Puritan missionary in New England. Mayhew was born in England. His father, Thomas Mayhew, was a merchant and an associate of Matthew Craddock, the first governor of the Massachusetts Bay Colony. The elder Mayhew became engaged in New England when he agreed to manage some of Craddock's properties in Massachusetts. He prospered in New England and in 1641 became proprietor of Martha's Vineyard, Nantucket, and other islands off the coast through a grant from Sir Ferdinando Gorges, who claimed property rights to the entire region.

The younger Mayhew had accompanied his father to New England in 1631 and was educated in the town schools of Medford and Watertown. He was tutored in the classics as a means of preparing for a ministerial career, but he never proceeded to university. He moved to Martha's Vineyard with his father in 1641 and there became interested in the welfare of the Native Americans on the island. He learned their language and was soon preaching to them. By 1651 he had converted close to two hundred. Visitors who were impressed with his work, as well as with the missionary efforts of John Eliot on the mainland, solicited support for his efforts. He involved native converts as pastor, teacher, and elders of the congregation he formed. He died while journeying to England in 1657 to seek further support for his efforts.

*See also:* Praying Towns, Society for the Propagation of the Gospel in New England
*Further Reading*
Henry Whitfield, *A Farther Discovery of the Present State of the Indians of New England* (New York, 1865 reprint of 1651 publication).

*Francis J. Bremer*

## Mead, Matthew (1629–1699)

Congregational pastor, "ejected minister," and Whig radical. Mead was born at Leighton Buzzard, Bedfordshire, in 1629 or 1630 and educated at Eton; he became a scholar of King's College, Cambridge, in 1648 and a fellow in 1649, but resigned in 1651, possibly to avoid the Oath of Engagement declaring loyalty to the Commonwealth. He later told Richard Baxter that he had left without a degree and in need of further guidance about philosophy and divinity.

In 1653–1654 Mead energetically pursued the rectory of Great Hill, Buckinghamshire. He gained presentation to the living by the Great Seal (the decision of the government), disputed the rights of the patron, and was even temporarily installed with the help of troops, but ultimately lost his case. Subsequently Mead became morning lecturer at St. Dunstan's, Stepney, and on 28 December 1656 he was admitted as a member of the Congregational church led by William Greenhill, vicar of Stepney. Several promotions and preferments came Mead's way in the 1650s, including service as assistant to the Buckinghamshire and Middlesex Commissioners, preacher to the Council of State, and lecturer at St. Bride's, Fleet Street, London. In January 1658 he was admitted as curate of the chapel of St. Paul's at Shadwell in the parish of Stepney.

At the Restoration Mead lost most if not all of his positions: he appears to have held on to his lectureship at St. Sepulchre's, Holborn, until at least October 1661. But he was under suspicion for preaching sedition. In 1663 he crossed to the Netherlands. He may have been in London during the Great Plague of 1665; he had certainly returned from exile by 1669, when he accepted a post as assistant to William Greenhill pastor of the Stepney Congregational church. After Greenhill's death in 1671, Mead succeeded him as pastor. He was ordained by John Owen, Joseph Caryl, and others on 14 December 1671. In September 1674 a purpose-built meetinghouse was opened at Stepney. The four pine pillars supporting the roof had been presented to Mead by the States of Holland; the building contained a secret attic for the congregation's use in times of persecution. Mead and his congregation were harassed: he was repeatedly arrested and fined; and his meetinghouse was attacked and its furniture destroyed by the authorities.

Detained in the aftermath of the Rye House Plot, he was released, only to be ordered by the Middlesex Sessions to conform to the public worship of the Church of England. In 1683 he succeeded John Owen as one of the Pinners' Hall lecturers. Mead moved in radical Whig circles: he had links to Scottish dissidents and was a friend of

Robert Ferguson. In 1685 he was deputed to stir up the citizens of London on behalf of the Monmouth Rising, but his halfheartedness was criticized. He once again left for the Netherlands—in 1686 at Utrecht he preached "with a foaming mouth . . . that Babylon might be destroyed in England and her brats dashed against the walls"—but he returned to take advantage of the 1687 Indulgence. That November he preached at Grocers' Hall before the mayor. After the Revolution, the Stepney meetinghouse was extended with galleries, and the congregation settled the adjacent house and garden on Mead. Mead joined in the creation of the Happy Union of Presbyterians and Congregationalists, preaching on "two sticks made one" (Ezekiel 37:19) at Stepney on 6 April 1691. He sought to appear moderate when the Union foundered, but he remained in the Pinners' Hall Lecture and was one of the founders of the Congregational Fund Board in December 1695. He died in October 1699 and was buried at Stepney. John Howe preached his funeral sermon. Mead's own publications were almost all sermons.

*See also:* Happy Union, Pinners' Hall, Salters' Hall
*Further Reading*
Richard L. Greaves, *Secrets of the Kingdom: British Radicals from the Popish Plot to the Revolution of 1688–9* (Stanford, 1992).

*John Spurr*

## Mildmay, Lady Grace (born Sharington) (1552–1620)

Author of devotional manuscripts and an accomplished healer. Lady Grace Sharington Mildmay was born in 1552, the middle daughter of a Wiltshire gentry family. Grace Sharington wed the young Northamptonshire courtier and gentleman Anthony Mildmay in 1567. Predeceased by her husband, Lady Mildmay died at Apethorpe, Northamptonshire, in 1620.

During her husband's frequent absences on diplomatic missions, Lady Mildmay constructed a "spiritualized household" regime of piety and medical charity typical of many godly gentlewomen of the period. Lady Mildmay's memoir and papers described a domestic routine of devotional reading and closet prayer, medical good works, and strict avoidance of frivolous and ungodly society. Her written meditations, composed for her daughter and grandson, reflected a doctrinally flexible and firmly Protestant personal piety, which prized godly sociability and the textual world of the Geneva Bible and condemned religious innovation and the potential corruption of popery, but conceptually alternated between notions of a predestined election and a forgiving and freely offered grace.

Both her memoir and meditations exhibited a conventional understanding of Elizabethan and early Stuart womanhood. Feminine submission and self-control were both gendered and Christian virtues. Piety provided Lady Mildmay with an ideological encouragement to feminine obedience. It also offered her a means to cope with the challenges of a difficult husband and occasional marital problems, as she very conventionally styled her submission to Sir Mildmay's temper and insensitivities as an act of Christian discipline and acceptance of God's will.

Lady Mildmay's life and writings demonstrate the ambiguities confronted by historians of women, religion, and Puritanism in the Elizabethan and early Stuart period. She exemplifies how the shared Humanist ideals of godly domesticity, the politically circumscribed roles of many women, and the different practical approaches and needs brought to Protestant piety by women have rendered older delineations of "Calvinist," "Arminian," "Conformist," and "Puritan" tricky to apply. A consummate domestic Protestant, Lady Mildmay synthesized elements of voluntary religion, sacramental piety, and antipopery, forming a practical piety and Protestant identity that fit her feminine context as a relatively retiring matron in the upper ranks of the Elizabethan and early Stuart gentry.

*Further Reading*
Patricia Crawford, *Women and Religion in England, 1500–1720* (London, 1993); Linda Pollock, *With Faith and Physic: The Life of a Tudor Gentlewoman, Lady Grace Mildmay, 1552–1620* (London, 1995).

*Michelle Wolfe*

## Mildmay, Sir Walter (before 1523–1589)

Chancellor of the Exchequer under Elizabeth I and founder of Emmanuel College, he was part of the core of the Elizabethan regime, a very Protestant core. His career had begun in the later years of Henry VIII in the Court of Augmentations, which dealt with the property and personnel of the dissolved monasteries. Second in command to two lord treasurers, it was Mildmay who ran the Elizabethan Exchequer. He had been born across the road from the fish market in Chelmsford, but ended his days as proprietor of a large estate in Northamptonshire. Although no one at the time would have called him a puritan, we may well do so. His own archive contains papers relating to the trials and tribulations of puritan ministers. However, Mildmay was a loyal servant of his mistress, and thus had to act as the prosecutor of Archbishop Edmund Grindal, and of William Davison, his colleague who was scapegoated for his part in the execution of Mary Queen of Scots. But he was not an unprincipled servant, and he boldly opposed the marriage of Elizabeth to the French Duke of Anjou.

Mildmay had spent two years at Christ's College, Cambridge, and he must have welcomed its Elizabethan transmogrification into the college of Edward Dering and Laurence Chaderton. He endowed the college with property that provided for the stipend of a preacher, a Greek lecturer, and six scholarships, and he gave the library a collection of Greek and Latin texts. But the masters of Christ's were not always godly enough for Mildmay's taste, which must be why he decided to leave as his memorial a new college, entirely devoted to the production of godly, learned, preaching ministers to serve the church at large. (The idea that his intention was to subvert the established church by laying the cuckoo's egg of Presbyterianism in its nest was a later, High Church invention.) This was not a piece of personal vanity on Mildmay's part, since he called the college not after his own name but "Emmanuel."

If Mildmay was the personification of careful housekeeping in his public, Exchequer, role, he was stingy and penny-pinching in his own affairs,

and kept his son and daughter-in-law (who, as Lady Grace Mildmay, was the earliest English woman diarist) on short commons. Consequently he roped in numerous other benefactors to help endow his college, and, though he is often credited with the purchase (for £550) of the site of Emmanuel, it was in truth the wealthy London merchant Richard Culverwell, Chaderton's uncle by marriage, who put up the money. The endowment was not sufficient to fulfill all of the founder's dreams for the college, and Chaderton, who was an essential part of the strategy, received a very inadequate stipend. Mildmay died worth nearly £7,000 in cash and plate, besides his estate.

*See also:* Emmanuel College
*Further Reading*
A. Sarah Bendall, Christopher Nugent Lawrence Brooke, Patrick Collinson, *A History of Emmanuel College, Cambridge* (Woodbridge, Eng., 1999); Stanford E. Lehmberg, *Sir Walter Mildmay and Tudor Government* (Austin, TX, 1964).

*Patrick Collinson*

## Milton, John (1608–1674)

Pamphleteer, political apologist, and poet-prophet, who stood at the center of the "Puritan Revolution." His prominence as a "puritan" during this period must therefore acknowledge not only his political significance and theological opinions, but his poetic and literary achievements, which cannot be divorced from his puritan credentials and for which he is chiefly remembered.

Milton's childhood rector in London was the puritan Richard Stock. At St. Paul's School, Milton's tutor was for a while Thomas Young, who later became one of the Presbyterian Smectymnuans, controversial pamphleteers whom Milton defended in print. Due to the church establishment's efforts to restore order to the Church of England in "puritan" Cambridge, however, Milton turned against the idea of a clerical career during his time at Christ's College, which he had entered in 1625. In 1632, he graduated from Cambridge with a B.A. and M.A. cum laude (having therefore subscribed twice to

*John Milton, British poet. (Hulton-Deutsch Collection/Corbis)*

the graduates' Oath of Conformity) and retreated to Horton, in Buckinghamshire, to pursue his own course of further study. Though he voiced dissatisfaction with the English clergy in his elegy "Lycidas" in 1637, he was not yet a committed puritan.

In 1638, Milton embarked upon the grand tour of the Continent. In Geneva, he met the Arminian Hugo Grotius; in Rome, he met numerous Italian (and Catholic) Humanists. While in Italy, he was shocked to learn about the Bishops' Wars, which had erupted in England and Scotland. He cut his journey short, returning to London because he thought it wrong to continue his travels while his fellow Englishmen fought for "liberty" at home. Though it might be thought odd for a man with puritan inclinations to spend time in Rome, it is in fact possible that his experiences in Europe galvanized and moulded his theological and political convictions, identified by Milton himself at this point with "liberty."

Back in England, Milton engaged in heated debates about the nature of the Church of England and remarked that the men and women who had sought to extend the Elizabethan Settlement in the past, to free the English Church from her Catholic origins, were "strait . . . branded with the Name of Puritans." Despite such "scandalous misnaming," Milton's own puritan credentials can be appreciated by examining the program of political and religious reform in his prose works. In his five antiepiscopal tracts, Milton revealed his Presbyterian convictions, while vociferously attacking bishops, ecclesiastical ceremonies, and church courts. His unhappy marriage to Mary Powell in July 1642 prompted him to question the church's prohibition of divorce on the grounds of incompatibility, most notably in *The Doctrine and Discipline of Divorce* (August 1643). The label "puritan" lacked sufficient impact to truly deride what became Milton's notorious view of marriage; instead, his opponents branded him a Divorcer. In response to this widespread paper persecution, Milton set about arguing for the liberty of the press in *Areopagitica* (November 1643).

In 1645, Milton's *Poems* were published, which established his poetic rather than his puritanical credentials. Indeed, other men whose poetical works were published at about the same time were Royalists such as John Cleveland, Edmund Waller, Robert Herrick, and Abraham Cowley. Milton soon went on to write his Sonnet XII, which attacked the more radical puritans who used his divorce tracts to justify the promiscuity for which he was blamed; afterwards, he turned on his old Presbyterian allies as "the New Forcers of Conscience," suggesting that presbyters were little better than the bishops against whom they had both initially campaigned. Puritanism was a broad movement in which, and even against which, Milton can be seen to develop.

In 1649, Milton was commissioned by Parliament to defend regicide in *The Tenure of Kings and Magistrates* (February 1649) and refute Charles I's *Eikon Basilike* in *Eikonoklastes* (October 1649). He later wrote a series of *Latin Defences,* which vindicated the Commonwealth and himself on the European stage. In March 1649, he was appointed Latin Secretary to the Council of State and worked as the government censor. True to his convictions set out in *Areopagitica*, he allowed the publication of a Socinian manifesto, the Racovian Catechism, which was nevertheless subsequently burned. It is likely that during this period that Milton began rationalizing his own beliefs in *De Doctrina Christiana*, which was only discovered in 1825. This work reiterates Milton's free-thinking, scripturally obsessed approach to right religion: his opposition to state interference in religious affairs and individual conscience, as well as to infant baptism, a paid clergy, the indissolubility of marriage, the doctrine of the immortality of the soul (as well as arguing for its common materiality with the body), the unity of the Trinity, creation ex nihilo (from nothing), and the Calvinist insistence upon the inability of human beings to secure their own salvation. If puritanism and Independency did indeed disintegrate into a great number of separating congregations and conventicles during the 1640s and 1650s, Milton's sect was a very small one: himself.

At the Restoration, Milton did not flee Old England, though his hypothetical New England exploits are described in Peter Ackroyd's fictional *Milton in America*. Instead, he boldly defended the Commonwealth until he was captured, arrested, and fined. The poet and dramatist William Davenant and the member of Parliament and closet poet Andrew Marvell interceded on his behalf, and he was released. Milton set to work preparing *Paradise Lost* for publication and it appeared in 1667; *Paradise Regained* and *Samson Agonistes* were published together in 1671. These poems dramatize Milton's unorthodox and increasingly introverted religious and political convictions. The baroque glory and Latinate complexity of *Paradise Lost* in particular, however, does not adhere to the plain style characteristic of much puritan expression.

Milton spent the remainder of his days preparing historical, geographical, and scholarly works, which he had already written, for the press. He died of gout on 9 November 1674 and was buried in St. Giles Cripplegate. He is considered to be posterity's most vocal defender of the Commonwealth. His fanatical piety, scriptural convictions, and commitment to Protestant England are indeed essentially puritan, but his theological opinions (Anti-Trinitarianism, Arminianism), his consistent acquiescence in traditional Anglican practices (his children were all baptized; he was buried according to the rites of the English Church), and his Humanist learning and delight in poetry and music suggest that the label "puritan" is as inadequate now to describe John Milton as it was in the seventeenth century.

*See also:* Antichrist, Anti-Trinitarianism, Arminianism, Puritan Revolution, Sin

*Further Reading*

Arthur F. Barker, *Milton and the Puritan Dilemma* (Toronto, 1942); Nathaniel H. Henry, *The True Wayfaring Christian: Studies in Milton's Puritanism* (New York, 1987); Christopher Hill, *Milton and the English Revolution* (London, 1979); A. L. Rowse, *Milton the Puritan: Portrait of a Mind* (London, 1977).

*Simon Dyton*

## Mitchell, Jonathan (1624–1668)

New England clergyman. Mitchell was born in England, in Halifax, Yorkshire, in 1624. His parents were puritans who migrated to Massachusetts in 1635. His witnessing the sudden death of a family servant contributed to his personal conversion and to his determination to enter the ministry.

Mitchell entered Harvard College in 1645 and graduated with an M.A. in 1647. Three years later he was elected a fellow, and he soon became college tutor. In 1650 he also succeeded Thomas Shepard as pastor of the Cambridge congregation following Shepard's death. According to Cotton Mather's account, Mitchell was a powerful preacher. In a colony election-day sermon he delivered in 1667, he coined the phrase "errand into the wilderness" to refer to New England's mission from God.

In 1662 Mitchell was appointed, along with Daniel Gookin, to be one of the colony's first licensers for the press. He was one of the advocates of modifying baptismal requirements in the Synod of 1662 and afterwards became one of the leading proponents of the "Half-Way Covenant," as proposed by the synod.

*Further Reading*
*American National Biography* (New York, 1999);
    John Sibley, *Biographical Sketches of Graduates
    of Harvard,* vol. 4 (Cambridge, MA, 1873).

*Francis J. Bremer*


## More, John (ca. 1542–1592)

An English clergyman known as "the apostle of Norwich." More was born in Westmorland and studied at Christ's College, Cambridge, receiving his B.A. in 1563 and shortly thereafter being elected a fellow of the college. He was strongly influenced by the Reformer Thomas Cartwright and was one of the signatories of a petition commending Cartwright in 1570. Two years later, Bishop John Parkhurst appointed him to the living of Aldborough, Norfolk.

In 1573 More became one of the two preachers at St. Andrew's Church in Norwich, Norfolk, where he remained until his death. He was a popular preacher who was credited with bringing many to a heightened awareness of their relationship to God. More often preached three times on a Sunday. But he was a nonconformist and was summoned before Bishop Parkhurst for refusing to wear the surplice; the bishop tried to persuade him to conform and defended More in correspondence with Archbishop Matthew Parker. In 1576 More joined with other Norwich clergy in petitioning against the imposition of disputed ceremonies and was suspended from the ministry by Bishop Edmund Freke, the new bishop of the Diocese of Norwich. He signed a submission, which was probably sufficient to have his suspension lifted, but he found himself in trouble again when Archbishop John Whitgift required subscription to his Three Articles in 1584. Together with around sixty other clergy of Norfolk, More submitted to the archbishop reasons for refusing to subscribe.

His reputation as the apostle of Norwich was based on his preaching and character. An effective preacher himself, More was an advocate for more and better preaching in the church. He used his stature in the puritan movement to advise lay patrons of church livings and to assist fellow ministers. He published nothing in his lifetime, but a number of his treatises and sermons appeared after his death in 1592, brought to print by Nicholas Bownd, who was his successor at St. Andrews and his literary executor.

*See also:* Surplice
*Further Reading*
Patrick Collinson, *The Elizabethan Puritan
    Movement* (London, 1967); Patrick Collinson, *The
    Religion of Protestants* (Oxford, 1982); *Oxford
    Dictionary of National Biography* (Oxford, 2004).

*Francis J. Bremer*


## Morrice, Roger (ca. 1628–1702)

Puritan minister, political diarist, and historian. Morrice was the son of a yeoman farmer in the parish of Leek in the north Staffordshire moorlands. He matriculated at Magdalen Hall, Oxford, in 1651, then migrated to Catharine Hall, Cambridge, in 1654. He graduated B.A. in 1656 and M.A. in 1659. He was vicar of Duffield, Derbyshire, from 1658 until 1662, when he was ejected under the Act of Uniformity. For some part of the next three decades he was chaplain in London to Denzil, Lord Holles, and to the eminent lawyer Sir John Maynard. Both were Parliamentarian veterans of strong puritan persuasion, who had sought since the 1620s to limit the powers of the Crown. Morrice became well-off, presumably by the largesse of his patrons, and he spent generously on the education of young men for the Dissenting ministry.

Morrice occasionally surfaces in contemporary sources as a chronicler and collector of manuscripts. He helped Edmund Calamy list the ejected of 1662, and he supplied manuscripts to the Anglican historian John Strype. Under the will of Richard Baxter, Morrice was responsible, with Matthew Sylvester, for distributing Baxter's library. (Among recipients of books was the future deist firebrand John Toland.) Morrice followed Baxter's "middle way," both in the theological retreat from Calvinist orthodoxy and in pursuit of the ecclesiastical ideal of accommodation with Anglicanism through "comprehension."

Morrice's importance is twofold. He left a journal of his own times and a large manuscript collection on puritan history, housed in Dr. Williams's Library, London. The first is indispensable to historians of later Stuart England, the second to those of Elizabethan puritanism. The Entring Book is an immensely detailed account, about a million words long, of public affairs from 1677 until 1691. Morrice must have become, in effect, a full-time journalist, perhaps supplying newsletters to a group of Presbyterian-Whig politicians. This circle included the Holleses, Maynards, Hampdens, Harleys, Foleys, Hobarts, Howes, Pagets, and Swinfens. In the Entring Book Morrice emerges as self-effacing, astonishingly well-informed, diplomatic, and an astute barometer of public opinion. The diary is a valuable source for high politics, religious history, state trials, the flow of news and information, and much else, such as public festivals and entertainments, dueling, and the theater. Morrice was especially concerned with the fate of Dissent, when persecuted, when wooed by James II, and when grudgingly tolerated in 1689, and, more broadly, with the fate of English Protestantism in the face of the Counter-Reformation. He acted as go-between in Anglican-Dissenter negotiations, particularly on the eve of the Revolution of 1688, helping to seal a Protestant coalition against the Catholic monarch James II.

Morrice hoped to write the history of puritanism. He drafted an outline in the 1690s, but his hope was not fulfilled, and the job was done by Daniel Neal in the *History of the Puritans* (1732). The principal aim of his surviving drafts was to demonstrate that the values that came to be labeled puritan had been at the heart of English Protestantism since the Reformation. The spirit of "true religion" had only latterly, toward the end of Elizabeth's reign and after, been subverted by the "hierarchists." He approved of several early bishops, such as the Marian martyr John Hooper and the Jacobean archbishop George Abbot; but despised Archbishops Richard Bancroft and William Laud. Morrice's materials today serve the study of the earliest Presbyterians, particularly John Field, whose campaigns for a purer preaching ministry are recorded in his Register, Morrice's luck-

iest manuscript find. Field was often in trouble for nonconformity, yet spurned the excesses of the sectaries. Morrice continued this tradition. In the Entring Book he deplored the opposing zealots, the "hierarchists" and "fanatics," whilst applauding the "sober churchmen" and "old Puritans." Morrice was a last voice of old puritanism, yearning for a reunited and reformed national godly church, before permanent denominational separation became unavoidable after 1689.

Morrice's elaborate will reveals his friendships. His pallbearers were senior Presbyterian ministers, including Vincent Alsop, John Howe, Daniel Williams, Edmund Calamy, and Matthew Sylvester. He was also close to latitudinarian clergy of the established church, Bishops Edward Fowler, Richard Kidder, and John Moore. He appointed as his principal executor the puritan-Whig member of Parliament Edward Harley.

*Further Reading*
Roger Morrice, *The Entring Book,* 5 vols., ed. Mark Goldie et al. (forthcoming).

*Mark Goldie*

## Morton, Charles (1627–1698)

Educator and minister in Old and New England. He was born in Cornwall, where his father was a rector, and educated first at Queen's College, Cambridge, before changing to Oxford, where he finished his education at Wadham College, a center of new scientific study under its warden, John Wilkins. He was awarded the B.A. in 1649 and the M.A. in 1652. In 1653 he became vicar of Takeley in Essex, then moved to Cornwall, where he became rector of Blisland from 1655 until his ejection at the restoration of Charles II in 1660. He preached privately at St. Ives, Cornwall, until moving to London in 1666. In 1672 he was licensed to preach as a Presbyterian under the terms of the Declaration of Indulgence.

By 1675 he was conducting an academy at Newington Green, on the outskirts of London, for the instruction of young men of Dissenting families to whom the universities were closed. In addition to classical and theological studies, Morton instructed his pupils in natural science, the school being equipped with a laboratory. Morton's manuscript "Compendium Physicae" summarized scientific learning for his pupils; never published, it was used at Harvard College as late as 1728.

Suspected of disloyalty to the monarchy, he was forced by harassment to abandon his school in 1685 and move to New England in 1686, where he had some expectation of being offered the presidency of Harvard. But with the royal governor Edmund Andros recently arrived in Massachusetts, it proved impolitic to name Morton to the presidency of Harvard, though he was named to its corporation and occasionally lectured there. Instead he became the pastor of the First Church of Charlestown, Massachusetts, where he continued until his death. His insistence that he be merely installed as Charlestown pastor rather than reordained and his advocacy of ministerial associations introduced Presbyterian views to New England Congregationalists. In 1687 he publicly criticized the revocation of the Massachusetts charter, for which he was tried for sedition, but acquitted by the jury. His only significant publication was *The Spirit of Man,* a treatise on the relationship of personal temperament to morality and divine grace. An enthusiast for the new science and a transmitter of it to New England, he felt that it revealed the power and wisdom of God in creation. Theologically he was a moderate Calvinist, whose preaching emphasized practical morality.

*Further Reading*
Samuel Eliot Morison, "Charles Morton," *Publications of the Colonial Society of Massachusetts,* vol. 33 (1940), pp. vii–xxix.

*Dewey D. Wallace Jr.*

## Mosse, Miles (1558–1615)

Clergyman who promoted reform in Elizabethan Suffolk. Mosse was born in Chevington in 1558, son of Miles Mosse, a yeoman, and studied at the grammar school in Bury St. Edmunds. He became pensioner of Gonville and Caius College, Cambridge, in 1575, where he proceeded B.A. in 1579 and M.A. in 1582. He was ordained priest in 1583 and was licensed to preach in 1584. In 1585 he was appointed vicar of St. Stephens, Norwich, and the following year moved from Norwich to Bury St. Edmunds, where he served as preacher of the parish of St. James. He was on close terms with the godly ministers of west Suffolk, an association presided over by John Knewstub and including such men as Nicholas Bownd, Walter Allen, and Reginald Whitfield, with important ties to Laurence Chaderton in Cambridge. While in Bury, Mosse proceeded to the Cambridge degrees of B.D. in 1589 and D.D. in 1595. In 1597, he accepted the rectory of Combes, one of the wealthier livings in the archdeaconry of Sudbury, to which he was instituted on 27 May and where he remained until his death in 1615. Author of several works, he quarreled famously with his conformist neighbor Thomas Rogers, who in 1589 launched a calculated attack on Laurence Chaderton's anonymously published sermon on church government. For his pains, Rogers found himself excluded from the exercise, which he blamed on Mosse, taking his published revenge with *Miles Christianus* (1590), ostensibly a clash over the merits of reading versus preaching. Perhaps Mosse's most lasting achievement was the erection in 1595 of the parish library of St. James in Bury St. Edmunds, to which he persuaded the neighboring clergy, gentlemen, and townsmen to donate books; by 1599 the collection numbered more than 200 volumes.

*Further Reading*
John Craig, *Reformation, Politics and Polemics: The growth of Protestantism in East Anglian Market Towns* (Aldershot, Eng., 2002).

*John Craig*

# N

## Negus, William (ca. 1559–1616)

Church of England clergyman and member of the conference movement in East Anglia. Negus graduated B.A. from Trinity College, Cambridge, in 1578 and became assistant town preacher in Ipswich, Suffolk, with whose authorities he made a covenant in early 1584. By June of that year he had joined the Dedham conference of ministers.

Differences between Negus and Robert Norton, Chief Preacher of Ipswich, resulted in factional strife in the town, and by October 1584 Negus had been suspended by the bishop of Norwich, Edmund Freke. Although his Dedham colleagues urged him to remain in Ipswich if reasonable terms could be negotiated, Negus accepted an offer by Robert, third Lord Rich, of the rectory of Leigh, Essex. He was instituted there by John Aylmer, bishop of London, on 31 March 1585.

In July 1586 Aylmer suspended him for refusing to wear the surplice. Negus's own account of the interview survives, along with a petition from his parishioners not to desert them for "such a trifle." Despite his steady opposition to the ceremonies of the Book of Common Prayer, he continued at Leigh into the reign of James. On 20 March 1609, however, he was deprived by the High Commission, along with three other Essex clergy, including Ezekiel Culverwell.

He was buried at Leigh on 8 January 1616. His library and manuscripts were bequeathed to his youngest son, Jonathan, later vicar of Prittlewell, Essex, who published his father's only known work, *Man's Active Obedience, or the Power of Godliness* (1619).

*See also:* Surplice
*Further Reading*
Patrick Collinson, John Craig, and Brett Usher, eds., *Conferences and Combination Lectures in the Elizabethan Church: Dedham and Bury St. Edmunds, 1582–1590* (Woodbridge, Eng., 2003).

*Brett Usher*

## Newcome, Henry (1627–1695)

Presbyterian clergyman in the north of England. Henry Newcome was born in Caldecot, Huntingdonshire, in September 1627. He was educated at Oxford, where he was awarded B.A. in 1647 and M.A. In 1651, he became schoolmaster at Congleton, Cheshire. There he came to the attention of John Ley, Presbyterian member of the Westminster Assembly, who encouraged Newcome's enthusiasm for puritanism. In 1648, Newcome was ordained by Presbyterian convention at Sandbach, Cheshire, and in 1649 appointed minister to Gawsworth Parish, where he cultivated friendships with men with a strong preference for Presbyterianism.

In 1657, Newcome was appointed minister at the church in Manchester, Lancashire. There he became an active member of the Presbyterian classis. Following the Restoration, he continued to preach in Manchester and surrounding towns. The Act of Uniformity of 1662 was for Newcome a test of conscience that prevented him from jeopardizing his hopes of immortal life in favor of worldly preferment. Despite a petition from the people of Manchester, he failed to be appointed fellow at the restored collegiate church.

From 1662 until his death, Newcome found himself considered a Dissenter by conformists. This distinction distressed him, as he never ceased to hope for puritan reformation of the Church of England. Despite conformist legislation, he continued to minister to sympathizers, and in 1672 he was licensed to preach in Manchester under the Declaration of Indulgence. After 1689, he was licensed preacher to the Presbyterian congregation in Manchester. Newcome died in September 1695.

*Further Reading*
Henry Newcome, *Diary, 1661–1663,* ed. T.
Heywood, Chetham Society, old series, vol. 18
(Manchester, Eng., 1846).

*Catherine Nunn*

## Newcomen, Matthew (ca. 1610–1669)

Presbyterian minister. Newcomen was born around 1610 in Colchester, Essex. He matriculated at St. John's College, Cambridge, in 1626, graduating B.A. (1629) and M.A. (1633). He spent some time studying with John Rogers, the lecturer of Dedham whom he succeeded upon the latter's death in 1636. It was here that he won his fame as a pastor and preacher, preaching along the Stour Valley, with particular acclaim being recorded for an appearance at Stowmarket, Suffolk, where his friend Thomas Young was vicar. He kept his post through the 1630s, benefiting from Dedham's distance from London and Bishop William Juxon's relatively underachieving regime.

From 1640 on he spent more time in London, not least as a contributor to the weekly meetings at Edmund Calamy's house, where the clerical contribution to the cause was marshaled. He contributed to the ecclesiological debate of 1641 as one of the "Smectymnuans." Their treatises were more antiepiscopacy than pro-Presbyterian, and part of their reticence is explained by an agreement of November 1641, adopted by Newcomen and others, to minimize ecclesiological infighting among the godly.

Newcomen preached fast sermons to parliament on several occasions, trying to foster unity among the godly against the common enemy. The same ethos shaped his actions in the Westminster Assembly, where he was a convinced Presbyterian with an eye to accommodation with the Independents. His willingness to compromise remained into 1645, but it never extended to the antinomians and was also ultimately frustrated by the Erastians in Parliament and the intransigence of the Independents. In 1646 he was central in drawing up an assertion of the *ius divinum* of church censures and helped to draft a petition in response to Parliament's ordinance effectively uniting church and state. More positively, he was one of the main authors of the Westminster Assembly's catechism.

His attention returned to Essex as he became marginalized in the later 1640s, and he was crucial in drawing up and distributing the *Essex Testimony* (1648) and the *Essex Watchmen's Watchword* (1649). These promoted the Solemn League and Covenant and the Directory for Worship, the Confession of Faith, and the Humble Advise for Church Government, products of the Westminster Assembly. Regretting the developments of the late 1640s, he concentrated on his ministry through the 1650s, taking a place on the Commission for Scandalous Ministers for Essex in 1654 but focusing on Dedham. In 1655 he succeeded his friend Stephen Marshall as town lecturer for Ipswich, Suffolk.

In 1661 he joined the Savoy House Conference and worked for a broad church. He was created Doctor of Divinity in 1661 but declined to become a royal chaplain and could not subscribe to the Book of Common Prayer. He accepted a call to become pastor at the English Church in Leiden in 1662. He became a Dutch citizen in 1666 to avoid being called home during hostilities and seemed settled in the Netherlands, where he died during the plague of 1669.

*See also:* Smectymnuus
*Further Reading*
*Oxford Dictionary of National Biography* (Oxford, 2004).

*Tom Webster*

## Norton, John (1606–1663)

Leading preacher and controversialist, as well as the author of America's first biography. Born in Bishop's Stortford, Hertfordshire, he matriculated at Peterhouse, Cambridge (A.B. 1624 and A.M. 1627). He taught school at Bishop's Stortford, also serving as curate of the local church. While in Stortford, he was converted by the puritan preaching of Epping's Jeremiah Dyke. He then served as chaplain to Sir William Masham of High Laver, Essex, but by the early 1630s his objection to the ceremonies of the Church of England turned his thoughts to emigration. Successive embarkations in 1634 and 1635 were threatened by storms at sea—described in Thomas Shepard's *Autobiography*—but he finally arrived at Plymouth in October, 1635, preaching there throughout that winter. He then moved to Ipswich, where he was called as teacher in February 1638, serving alongside Nathaniel Rogers.

In 1645 Norton's colleagues, knowing his mastery of Latin and his considerable forensic skill, assigned him the task of answering a series of questions about congregational polity from the Dutch minister, William Apollonius. Norton skillfully defended the "New England Way" in *Responsio ad Totam Quaestionum . . .* (1648). He played an important role in the Cambridge Synod of 1646 and in the debates that resulted in the Cambridge Platform of 1648, the basic statement of church discipline for all New England Congregationalists.

Norton was again asked to reply to a controversial tract when Springfield's founder, Thomas Pynchon, published *The Meritorious Price of Our Redemption* (1650), which the magistrates considered heretical and duly burned on the Boston Common. Norton's *A Discussion of the Great Point in Divinity, the Sufferings of Christ* (1653) explained the importance of Christ's suffering to Protestant belief in the individual soul's access to grace and redemption. His most famous work, however, was *The Orthodox Evangelist* (1654), a description of the soteriology of conversion.

As John Cotton was dying in December 1652, he named Norton as his ideal successor. Despite Ipswich's protracted attempts to retain him, Norton was finally installed as Boston's teacher on 23 July 1656. Norton meanwhile wrote *Abel being Dead, Yet Speaketh* (1658), a life of Cotton, a model for many later hagiographical biographies about the first-generation leaders.

Though his preaching and particularly what Cotton Mather called his "gift of prayer" contributed to his sustained popularity, Norton's enjoyment of universal respect was compromised, first by his leadership in the suppression of Quakers in New England, which he defended in *The Heart of N-England Rent* (1659), and by his 1662 service as joint emissary with Simon Bradstreet to King Charles II's court in England. Though they deflected a threat to the colony's charter, their conciliatory acceptance of religious toleration met with vehement opposition from New England traditionalists, who charged Norton with disloyalty to the colony's basic tenets. His death in an apoplectic attack occurred soon thereafter in his Boston home.

*Further Reading*

Edward J. Gallagher, Introduction to John Norton, *Abel Being Dead Yet Speaketh (1658), A Biography of John Cotton* (facsimile, Delmas, NY, 1978); Cotton Mather, "Nortonus Honoratus, The Life of Mr. John Norton," in *Magnalia Christi Americana* (London, 1702).

*Sargent Bush Jr.*

## Noyes, James (1608–1656)

Presbyterian sympathizer and colleague of Thomas Parker at Newbury, Massachusetts. Born in Wiltshire, England, on 22 October 1608, Reverend James Noyes studied at Oxford, but quit early to join his cousin Thomas Parker in teaching school at Newbury, England. In March 1634, they immigrated to New England and one year later helped found the town of Newbury, Massachusetts.

As ministers, Noyes and Parker became notorious in the Massachusetts Bay Colony for their Presbyterian views on church government. Both advocated measures that would ease membership requirements, and both sought to enhance their authority as church governors at the expense of lay participation. Their attempts to diminish lay rights were widely resisted by members of the congregation. The feuds that ensued between the developing factions hampered the entire ministry of Noyes and Parker and were the source of great alarm to many neighboring churches. A ministerial council convened in 1643 to condemn their practices, and in the 1670s even the General Court was forced to step in to help resolve the disputes and to contain the Presbyterian sentiments that divided Newbury. The attempts to bring peace to the town ultimately succeeded only after the tenures of Noyes and Parker came to an end.

Before his death on 22 October 1656, James Noyes wrote three major works: *A Catechism for Children* (1641); *Moses and Aaron* (1661); and *The Temple Measured* (1647), which outlined many of his Presbyterian perspectives.

*Further Reading*
Joshua Coffin, *A Sketch of the History of Newbury, Newburyport, and West Newbury* (Boston, 1845); James F. Cooper, *Tenacious of their Liberties: The Congregationalists in Colonial Massachusetts* (New York, 1999).

*Aaron Christensen*

## Nye, Philip (1595–1672)
One of the leaders of seventeenth-century English Congregationalism.

### Early Career
Philip Nye was born and raised in the English county of Sussex and matriculated at Brasenose College, Oxford, in 1616. He soon transferred to Magdalen Hall and received his B.A. in 1619 and M.A. in 1622. He began to preach as early as 1620, but his first ecclesiastical living was when he was named curate of All Hallows Staining in 1627. In 1630 he was lecturer at St. Michael's Cornhill in London.

From the start of his career Nye was well connected with the leaders of the puritan clerical movement. Along with Thomas Goodwin and John Davenport, he was one of the participants in a clerical conference at the Ockley home of Henry Whitfield in 1632 that was called to persuade John Cotton to conform to the practices of the church in order to remain in his Boston (England) living. In the end, it was Cotton who persuaded Nye and some of the others that conformity to the new demands of the bishops could no longer be justified. His own orthodoxy now suspected by the authorities, Nye may have considered following John Davenport to the Netherlands in 1633, but in the end he stayed for the time in London. Between 1636 and 1639 he joined with Thomas Goodwin in publishing six works of Richard Sibbes.

Nye had already demonstrated support for various puritan colonizing ventures. He was one of the early members of the Massachusetts Bay Company and continued to support that venture through the 1630s and later. He also had links to the Providence Island Company. In 1632 he became one of the individuals who initiated plans to establish a colony, to be governed by John Winthrop Jr., at Saybrook, in what became southern Connecticut.

In the end, Nye migrated not to the New World, but to the Netherlands, where around 1639 he joined Thomas Goodwin and John Archer in ministering to a congregation of English exiles at Arnhem. Goodwin and Nye had maintained contact with friends such as John Cotton and John Davenport who had settled in America, and the Arnhem congregation followed the practices of the Congregational churches in New England, including limiting full membership to those deemed to be godly.

### Nye and the Puritan Revolution
With the calling of the Long Parliament and that body's commitment to reform the Church of England, Nye, along with other exiles, returned to England. He spent a brief time in Hull, where he laid the groundwork for the organization of a small congregation on the New England and Arnhem pattern. In April 1642 the Earl of Manchester appointed him to a living in Huntingdonshire, and in the same month he was named as one of the delegates to the Westminster Assembly of Divines.

Well connected with leaders of the parliamentary party, in 1643 Nye and Stephen Marshall were named to accompany the parliamentary commission that met with a Scottish delegation to draft the

Solemn League and Covenant. He is generally credited with the phrasing of the commitment to reform England according to the practices of "the best reformed churches in Christendom," which was capable of a broader interpretation than the Scots realized. He presented the draft agreement to Parliament in September 1643 and preached to that body on the occasion.

In the Westminster Assembly Nye joined with his friend Thomas Goodwin and others in arguing the case for adoption of the "New England Way" in preference to the Presbyterian plan advocated by Robert Baillie and the other Scottish delegates to the Assembly. Having agreed to an accord (Calamy House Accord) with the leading proponents of Presbyterianism that neither side would publicly attack the other, Nye and Goodwin sought to advance the Congregational cause by facilitating the publication of tracts written by John Cotton and other New Englanders. They were especially challenged to distinguish their proposals from the anarchy of separatism, which Presbyterians claimed was the ultimate outcome of a Congregational approach to polity.

The rise of radical sects led many to turn toward the greater ecclesiastical control promised by Presbyterianism, and it became apparent that the Westminster Assembly would recommend a Presbyterian settlement. Fearing that Parliament would accept such a recommendation, Nye and his fellow Dissenting Brethren issued *An Apologeticall Narration* (1643), in which they sought the right to maintain their own churches, independent of any such national church. In fighting to prevent an effective Presbyterian national church, Nye and his fellow Congregationalists were forced into an alliance of convenience with others who sought to remain independent, some of whom espoused beliefs and practices that Nye found abhorrent. At the same time, he accepted much of the other work of the Assembly, including the Westminster Confession of Faith, and he wrote the preface to the Assembly's *Directory of Public Worship.*

Even after Parliament adopted a Presbyterian settlement, Nye remained an important figure in the nation's debates. He preached before Parliament on a number of occasions, as well as preaching a Sunday sermon and delivering a weekly lecture at St. Margaret's in Westminster. He remained close to Stephen Marshall and other moderate Presbyterians. He served on a committee charged with sending ministers into the north of England in 1646. He participated in the army debates at Whitehall in 1648, siding with Henry Ireton in accepting the authority of the civil magistrates in matters of religion, in particular their duty to act against false faiths.

During the 1650s Nye helped to shape a new religious establishment. He joined with John Owen and others in proposing a religious settlement that would tolerate all who accepted the "fundamentals" of true Christianity. He was close to Oliver Cromwell, who named him one of the "Triers" to test candidates for the ministry. In 1658 he was one of the members of the Congregationalists' Savoy Conference and helped draft its Declaration of Faith and Order, which derived largely from the New England Cambridge Platform and represented the New England Way that Nye had long ago adopted. He continued to seek to reconcile moderate Presbyterians to a Cromwellian Church that would have reunited the major groups of the original puritan movement.

## Last Years

Following the restoration of the monarchy in 1660, Nye was initially excluded from the clemency granted by Charles II on account of his prominent role in the events of the preceding decades. That decision was reversed, however, and his life was spared on his agreement to never hold civil or ecclesiastical office. He continued to believe in the right of the civil magistrate to order religion and believed that God had a purpose in the changing fortunes of the godly. He worked on a history of the puritan movement that was likely destroyed by the great London fire of 1666. Returning to London after the devastation, he was a lecturer in the Hackney combination lectureship. In 1672 he was licensed to preach to a Congregational church, but died later that year.

*See also: An Apologeticall Narration,*
Congregationalism, Dissenting Brethren,
Independency, Pinners' Hall, Savoy Assembly,
Toleration
*Further Reading*
 Francis J. Bremer, *Congregational Communion:*
   *Clerical Friendship in the Anglo-American*
   *Puritan Community, 1610–1692* (Boston, 1994);
Keith L. Sprunger, *Dutch Puritanism: A History*
*of English and Scottish Churches of the*
*Netherlands in the Sixteenth and Seventeenth*
*Centuries* (Leiden, 1982); Murray Tolmie, *The*
*Triumph of the Saints: The Separate Churches of*
*London, 1616–1649* (Cambridge, Eng., 1977).

*Francis J. Bremer*

# O

## Oakes, Urian (ca. 1631–1681)

Clergyman and Harvard president. Born in England, in 1640 he accompanied his family to Massachusetts, where they settled in Cambridge. Urian's father, Edward Oakes, served as town selectman, as representative to the colony's General Court, and as a militia commander during King Philip's War.

Urian studied at Harvard and graduated in 1649. He returned to England in 1654, serving first as a private chaplain and then as a parish minister in Hampshire. He was ejected following the restoration of the monarchy in 1660. He taught grammar school for a time and ministered to a Nonconformist congregation. In 1671 he traveled back to New England, where he had been invited to succeed Jonathan Mitchell as pastor of the Cambridge church. He preached a series of jeremiads, warning the colonists about their failure to live up to the standards of their fathers. He also became involved in the governance of Harvard, first as a member of the Board of Overseers and then as an elected member of the Harvard corporation.

When the unpopular Leonard Hoar resigned the presidency of the college in 1675, the corporation invited Oakes to take the position. He did so on an acting basis only, because he did not wish to give up his ministry. In 1680 he finally accepted the presidency, though with the stipulation that he could continue to minister to the Cambridge church. He died of a fever a year later.

*See also:* Reforming Synod of 1679

*Further Reading*
Samuel Eliot Morison, *Harvard College in the Seventeenth Century* (Cambridge, MA, 1936).

*Francis J. Bremer*

## Owen, John (1616–1683)

English Calvinist theologian and Congregationalist leader. He was born at Stadham, Oxfordshire, where his father was vicar, and according to the son, a "non-conformist." Educated at Queen's College, Oxford (B.A. 1632, M.A. 1635), Owen left in 1637 to serve as chaplain successively in two gentry families before moving to London in 1642. In London he attended the sermons of leading preachers and experienced an assurance of grace. The publication of *A Display of Arminianism* in 1643 brought him to the attention of Parliament, which appointed him to the rectory of Fordham, Essex. In 1646 the House of Lords made him vicar of Coggeshall, Essex, and after reading John Cotton's *The Keyes of the Kingdom of Heaven*, he adopted Congregationalist views on church government and gathered a church within his parish. In 1647 he again attacked Arminianism in *The Death of Death in the Death of Christ*. Owen was first invited to preach before Parliament in 1646, when he called for the toleration of gathered churches. He also preached before Parliament on 31 January 1649, the day after the execution of King Charles I, declaring that the overthrow of a monarch who commanded unrighteousness was justified. In that and

*John Owen, English Calvinist theologian. (Library of Congress)*

other sermons he expressed hopes for a coming millennial kingdom.

Owen advanced quickly in the government of Oliver Cromwell. He went with Cromwell to Ireland in 1649 and was involved in the management of Trinity College, Dublin. Back in England in 1650, he was appointed preacher to the council of state. That same year he accompanied Cromwell to Scotland. In 1651 he was appointed Dean of Christ Church, Oxford, and ordered to preach at St. Mary's church on alternate Sundays; from 1652 to 1657 he was vice-chancellor of Oxford University. In 1653 the Doctorate of Divinity was conferred upon him by the university. As Cromwell's deputy he promoted university reform. As adviser to Cromwell he helped design the system of Triers and Ejectors for the reform of the clergy and served on committees dealing with such matters as clergy for Ireland, translation of the Bible, the determination of fundamental doctrines, and the readmission of Jews to England.

Opposed to the restoration of the monarchy, he was deprived of his deanery in 1660, and upon the arrival of Charles II, he was in danger for complicity in the execution of Charles I; but with influential friends and an international reputation as a theologian protecting him, he retired to Stadham, where he preached to a small circle. After 1663 he lived mostly in London, apart from brief stays at Stadham. His meetings were often spied on by informers, and in 1683, after the discovery of the Rye House Plot, of which he apparently knew beforehand, he was arrested but freed because of insufficient evidence for prosecution.

Owen remained a leader and spokesman for the Congregationalist Puritans in England until his death. In 1658 he was a leader in the meeting that produced the Savoy Confession of Faith, a revision of the Westminster Confession of Faith that reflected Congregational polity and some of his distinctive theological emphases; it also represented his determination to wed the Congregationalists (or Independents as they were often called) to strict Calvinism. After the Restoration Owen declined invitations to both the Netherlands and New England and preached in London to a congregation that included former Cromwellian leaders. On several occasions he conferred with the king as a representative of the Dissenters.

In his writings after 1660 Owen upheld toleration for Protestant Dissenters against royalist detractors and wrote extensively in defense of Calvinist orthodoxy against Quakers, Roman Catholics, Arminians, and Socinians. At one time or another in his career he defended in print each of the five major points of the Synod of Dort. Among his most important writings after the Restoration were several treatises on the Holy Spirit and a massive commentary on the Epistle to the Hebrews. As a theologian, Owen exemplified the high Calvinist emphasis on the divine decrees and utilized the scholastic method that characterized much seventeenth-century Reformed orthodoxy. In treatises on the spiritual life he promoted a piety stressing the supernatural power of renovating grace, which he thought had been eroded by a graceless moralism that he associated with Arminians and Socinians. He is widely regarded as the most important English Calvinist theologian of the later seventeenth century.

*See also:* Arminianism, Christology, Comprehension, Grace, Independency, Pinners' Hall, Sin

*Further Reading*
Peter Toon, *God's Statesman: The Life and Work of John Owen* (Grand Rapids, MI, 1973); Carl R. Trueman, *The Claims of Truth: John Owen's Trinitarian Theology* (Carlisle, PA, 1998).

*Dewey D. Wallace Jr.*

# P

## Paget, John (d. 1638)

English pastor at Amsterdam and writer of books defending the presbyterian system. He was from the Paget family of Leicestershire, but the exact date and place of his birth are unknown. At Trinity College, Cambridge, he gained the B.A. in 1595 and the M.A. in 1598. He served as rector of Nantwich, but in 1604, because of puritan nonconformity, the bishop ejected him. In 1605 he went into exile in the Netherlands, serving first as a military chaplain and then as pastor of the English Reformed at Amsterdam (1607–1637).

In the Netherlands he supported the Dutch Reformed Church and took session in the Dutch classis. In his church, he favored Calvinistic theology and the Reformed (presbyterian) church government. The English Reformed Church served the English refugee population of Amsterdam, but Paget had much competition. The city had many English churches, some for Separatists (led by Henry Ainsworth and Francis Johnson) and Anabaptists (led by John Smyth). Another emerging party, influenced by the ideas of William Ames and Henry Jacob, was non-separating but "congregational" in approach. He was against all of these.

Paget wrote several books. Most important were *Arrow against the Separation* (1618), against Brownism, and *Defence of Church-Government, Exercised in Presbyteriall, Classical, & Synodall Assemblies* (posthumous, 1641), which supported traditional Reformed polity against Congregationalist Puritanism. By his writing and preaching, Paget was a vehement defender of English Presbyterianism against rival forms of Puritanism.

*See also:* English Puritanism in the Netherlands
*Further Reading*
Keith L. Sprunger, *Dutch Puritanism: A History of English and Scottish Churches of the Netherlands in the Sixteenth and Seventeenth Centuries* (Leiden, 1982).

*Keith L. Sprunger*

## Pagit (Paget), Eusebius (ca. 1551–1617)

One of the most uncompromisingly radical of Elizabethan puritan ministers. A native of Northamptonshire, he entered Christ Church Oxford as a chorister at the age of twelve. He suffered some kind of injury (it is not altogether clear whether to his arm or his leg) while taking part in a religious procession and habitually signed himself "lame Eusebius Paget." He was subsequently at Christ's College, Cambridge, where he graduated B.A. in 1567. Archbishop John Whitgift claimed that he was unlearned, although this seems to have been a prejudicial judgment, given that Pagit published a number of works, including a translation of John Calvin's *Harmonie upon the three evangelists* (1584).

Pagit was rector of the town of Old from 1569, and of Lamport, from 1572, both Northamptonshire livings. He was soon showing his radical colors. In a sermon preached in 1572 at Greenwich (he seems to have had naval connections, and he owned a house at Deptford), he compared the Elizabethan bishops to abbots and cardinals. Nonconformity led to the loss of both livings, but Pagit remained in Northamptonshire as a kind of "ranging apostle," preaching in the prophesyings, and especially in the exercise at Southam, Warwickshire, which brought the institution into disrepute in 1576. He was also ministering in the household of his uncle and patron, John Isham. A catechism, ascribed to "Robert Openshaw" but in fact by Pagit, by the 1630s reached almost thirty editions, all containing Pagit's account of how his catechizing had worked with everyone in the family, down to milkmaids and kitchen boys.

In 1581 the patronage of the Earl of Bedford and the influence with Sir Richard Grenville of Sir Francis Hastings, brother of the Earl of Huntingdon, secured Pagit the rectory of Kilkhampton in north Cornwall, and he also preached in nearby Barnstaple. Pagit was joined at Kilkhampton by one of the Scottish Presbyterian ministers in temporary exile, David Black, who started up a school for the sons of the gentry that the two called the Reformed college. With their students, Pagit and Black turned this part of the world upside down, invading the parishes of conformable ministers and libeling them in a manner that anticipated the Marprelate tracts, with which the name of Pagit was immediately associated. After the whole affair had been exposed in the Court of High Commission, Pagit was again deprived (1585).

Little is known of his movements for the next few years, although he probably resorted to schoolmastering. In 1591 he wrote of men who were loath that he should have enough leisure to swallow his own spittle. In 1604 he obtained the rectory of St. Anne and St. Agnes, Aldersgate Street, London, which he held until his death, thirteen years later. His son Ephrain Pagit, author of the famous *Heresiography* (1645), turned away from his father's puritanism.

*Further Reading*
Patrick Collinson, *The Elizabethan Puritan Movement* (London, 1967); William J. Sheils, *The Puritans in the Diocese of Peterborough,*

Northamptonshire Record Society, vol. 30 (Northampton, Eng., 1979).

*Patrick Collinson*

## Palmer, Herbert (1601–1646)

Puritan clergyman and member of the Westminster Assembly of Divines. Palmer was born at Wingham, Kent, England, in 1601 and baptized on 29 March. He had a godly upbringing, much influenced by his mother, which inspired him from an early age to enter the ministry. In about 1615 he entered St. John's College, Cambridge, and was awarded B.A. in 1619, M.A. in 1622, and later in 1632, B.D. He subsequently became fellow of Queen's College, Cambridge, and was ordained in 1624. In 1626 he was appointed lecturer at St. Alphage's, Canterbury. Samuel Clarke, whose record of Palmer's life is the source of what is known of him, presents a picture of a godly man, much opposed to the growing enthusiasm for ritual that was evident in the English church. His proficiency in French gave him the opportunity to preach to the French community in Canterbury.

Palmer had detractors among both Separatists and ritualists. Clarke says little of Separatist objections to Palmer, but makes much of ritualist opposition. Three years after Palmer's appointment, he found his lectureship opposed by the dean of Canterbury Cathedral; however, popular demand and assurances as to his orthodoxy secured his appointment.

In 1632 Palmer was appointed university preacher, and in February of the same year was presented to the living of Ashwell in Hertfordshire by William Laud (then Bishop of London). In his defense at his trial in the House of Lords in 1644, Laud cited this appointment in his favor. Palmer was by this time known to be of Presbyterian persuasion. He was diligent in preaching, catechizing the young, and paying attention to the moral development of all members of society. The major targets of puritan reform—drunkenness, swearing, and general laxity of social behavior—were of concern to him. These concerns ran parallel to ideals of Sabbatarianism and the proper regulation of the godly household.

With the political shifts in England in the 1640s, Palmer found his beliefs coming into focus. In 1643 he was appointed one of the first members of the newly commissioned Westminster Assembly of Divines, whose brief was to oversee the puritan reformation of the Church of England. He was appointed assessor to assist the prolocutor in cases of absence and, as an acknowledged conscientious member of the assembly, was known for his championship of Presbyterianism. His increased duties at Westminster led him to appoint a deputy at Ashwell; he thereafter spent most of his time in Westminster, where, loath to surrender ministerial duty, he preached in local parishes.

In April 1644, Palmer was appointed president of Queen's College, Cambridge. There he undertook the reformation of the college, being eager to appoint fellows of puritan tendency and good education. Palmer died in August or September 1646, having been active in the debates of the Westminster Assembly until at least April of the previous year. His collaboration with Daniel Cawdrey on *Sabbatum Redivivum* and his work on a catechism acceptable to the Westminster Assembly perhaps show his influence on the politics of church government in the early 1640s. Herbert Palmer was buried in New Church, Westminster.

*Further Reading*
Samuel Clarke, *Lives of Sundry Eminent Persons* (1683).

*Catherine Nunn*

## Parker, Robert (ca. 1654–1614)

Clergyman. Parker first enters the historical record when he entered Magdalen College, Oxford, in 1575. He received his B.A. in 1582 and his M.A. in 1587. He was a fellow of the college from 1585 to 1593, and during that time he began to show signs of rejecting some of the policies of the church. He refused to wear required vestments and avoided subscribing to the canons of the church. Despite this nonconformity, he was able to obtain positions in the church through the efforts of his patron, Henry Herbert, the second Earl of Pembroke.

Parker's *Scholasticall discourse against symbolizing with Antichrist in ceremonies* was published in the Netherlands in 1607 and clearly marked him as a puritan reformer. Suspended from the ministry, he took up residence in the Netherlands, settling in Leiden, where he had contact with John Robinson's Separatist congregation. Parker rejected separatism, however, and in 1611 moved to Amsterdam, where he joined John Paget's English Reformed congregation and was soon elected an elder of the church. The congregation welcomed his preaching and sought to call him as co-pastor. But Parker rejected Paget's Presbyterian views, believing (like the Congregationalists) that synods were for advice only. In 1613 Parker moved on again, serving as a chaplain to English troops on the continent. He died in 1614.

Parker's second work, *De descensu domini nostri Jesu Christi ad inferos* (1611), dealt with theological arguments concerning Christ's descent into hell. Two other works were published after his death. *Exposition of the Pouring out of the Fourth Vial* (1650) focused on the Book of Revelation. *De Politeia Ecclesiastica Christi* (1616) dealt with church polity. While accepting the value of synods with limited authority, he asserted the importance of congregational government.

Parker's son, Thomas, became an important figure in New England Puritanism.

*Further Reading*
A. C. Carter, *The English Reformed Church in Amsterdam in the Seventeenth Century* (Amsterdam, 1964); Keith L. Sprunger, *Dutch Puritanism: A History of English and Scottish Churches of the Netherlands in the Sixteenth and Seventeenth Centuries* (Leiden, 1982).

*Francis J. Bremer*

## Parker, Thomas (1595–1677)

Presbyterian minister at Newbury, Massachusetts. The Reverend Thomas Parker, who presided over the first church in Newbury, Massachusetts, from its gathering in 1635 to his death on 24 April 1677, was born into an affluent and highly educated family in Wiltshire, England, on 8 June 1595. Upon his graduation from the University of Leiden in 1614, Parker returned from Holland to teach school and preach in Newbury, England, until his immigration to New England twenty years later. With his cousin and longtime colleague James Noyes, Parker led a party of families to the banks of the Ouascacunquen River, later named Parker River in his honor, where they settled the town of Newbury, Massachusetts.

As ministers, Parker and Noyes quickly gained the attention of their congregation and the entire coastal region as they instituted a Presbyterian form of church government in a society founded on Congregational ideals and practices. In particular, the Newbury clergymen attempted to ease membership requirements and to expand their ministerial authority beyond the bounds of standard Congregational orthodoxy. Their practices alarmed both local church members and most clergymen of Massachusetts Bay. A power struggle that emerged between Parker supporters and the growing anti-Presbyterian faction in Newbury troubled Parker throughout his ministry. During a more than thirty-year conflict in Newbury, numerous outside councils and conventions were called upon to mediate between the feuding parties. In 1643, a convention of elders met at Newbury and determined that "formal" exercise of church power did belong to the church officers and that well-behaved Christians were at least acceptable as candidates for membership, but that lay consent was necessary in decisions pertaining to church government. The vague results of the convention, however, did little to slow the growth of the contentious spirit in the small town.

By 1665, John Woodbridge, a Presbyterian sympathizer, had replaced the deceased James Noyes as Parker's assistant. Reenergized, Parker once again began to push openly for more authority, demanding that his approval be required in all church matters and that lay participation be limited to silent consent. In 1669, the anticlerical faction decided to suspend Parker from his duties as minister at Newbury. When neighboring elders failed to resolve the dispute, the General Court, ultimately siding with the dissenters, ordered Woodbridge to step down and suggested that Parker allow the laity a voice in church matters by the raising of hands, reaffirming standard Congregational practices. Although this council and others like it provided temporary relief, Parker's Presbyterian policies caused continual contention in Newbury and were a source of much concern among Congregationalists throughout New England.

Thomas Parker set forth his Presbyterian views on church government in a 1644 publication entitled *A Letter on Church Government*. His other works include *The Prophesies of Daniel Expounded* (1649) and two Latin titles: *Methodus Gratiae Divinae* (1657) and *Theses de Traductione Peccatoris ad Vitam* (1664).

*See also:* James Noyes

*Further Reading*

Joshua Coffin, *A Sketch of the History of Newbury, Newburyport, and West Newbury* (Boston, 1845); James F. Cooper, *Tenacious of Their Liberties: The Congregationalists in Colonial Massachusetts* (New York, 1999).

*Aaron Christensen*

## Parris, Samuel (1653–1720)

Danvers pastor during Salem witchcraft controversy. Born in London in 1653, Samuel Parris entered Harvard College but never graduated. He left Harvard in 1673 for an inherited Barbados plantation. After this venture—and several other commercial endeavors—proved unsuccessful, the failed merchant assumed the pastorate of the church of strife-ridden Salem Village (modern Danvers, Massachusetts) in 1689. The infamous Salem witchcraft controversy began in Parris's own home in 1692, with the strange "afflictions" of his niece and his daughter. Parris, among many others, strongly believed that the girls had been bewitched by members of the local community. Numerous other "victims" raised similar charges; hysteria developed and spread to neighboring towns; and eventually hundreds stood accused of witchcraft. Nineteen people were convicted and hanged by Massachusetts authorities; another was "pressed" to death.

Parris's role in the witchcraft tragedy has been debated for centuries. In the aftermath of the affair, contemporaries condemned him utterly; later historians described him as a pitiless man of blind zeal and even a madman. More recent historians dismiss suggestions that Parris "caused" the calamity, but point out that he contributed to the atmosphere of hysteria by overemphasizing the possibility that pious church members might secretly be witches and by publicizing the afflictions through group fasts and prayer sessions rather than isolating the "victims" from the community, a strategy that had succeeded in stemming the spread of hysteria in previous witchcraft cases. Parris's sermons suggest that, well in advance of the crisis, he helped to create a climate conducive to hysteria, warning repeatedly that Satan's minions were coming to destroy the godly.

Shortly after the controversy ended, most church and civil authorities deeply regretted the affair and acknowledged numerous errors in judgment. Parris stubbornly refused to admit any wrongdoing, prompting angry churchgoers in his congregation to demand his ouster from office. He belatedly apologized to his congregation for his actions during the controversy, but, at the urging of a ministerial council, he resigned from his office in 1696. Parris died in obscurity in 1720.

*See also:* Salem Witchcraft, Witchcraft
*Further Reading*
James F. Cooper Jr. and Kenneth P. Minkema, eds., *The Sermon Notebook of Samuel Parris* (Boston, 1993); Larry Gragg, *A Quest for Security* (New York, 1990).

*James F. Cooper*

## Parsons (Persons), Robert (1546–1610)

Best remembered as a missionary Jesuit priest, an English expatriate who worked to reconvert his native land to the Roman Catholic faith. In the end his efforts were unsuccessful, but he did exert considerable influence on English Protestants as well as Catholics.

Parsons entered Balliol College, Oxford, in 1563 and took B.A. and M.A. degrees in 1568 and 1572.

In 1574 he was forced to resign his fellowship at Balliol, probably due to his increasingly apparent Catholic sympathies. He went to Louvain, spent time with the Jesuit William Good, and entered the Society of Jesus at Rome. Ordained in 1578, he was appointed two years later to accompany Edmund Campion and others on a secret mission to England, a mission Parsons himself may have conceived. Scholars dispute whether the mission was primarily pastoral, undertaken to offer support and devotional instruction to English Catholics, or political, designed to orchestrate a Catholic takeover. The latter view has gained ground in recent years, but it should be remembered that pastoral and political ends are not mutually exclusive: Parsons very likely went to England for both reasons. While there he preached, wrote religious books and pamphlets, and set up a secret printing press.

When Campion was arrested in 1581, Parsons escaped to Rouen. Thereafter he worked from abroad, establishing five seminaries for training English priests in Spain and France and engaging in polemical exchanges with English Protestants. Perhaps his best-known exchange is with Thomas Morton on the legitimacy of equivocation, the Jesuit practice of offering only a partial answer under interrogation, completing the answer mentally rather than vocally.

In addition to polemics, Parsons wrote the widely influential *Christian Directorie* (1582, rev. 1585), a devotional treatise the puritan Edmund Bunny expurgated of its explicitly Catholic elements and republished. Together, the two versions comprise perhaps the most popular devotional handbook of Elizabethan England.

*Further Reading*
Ronald Corthell, "Robert Persons and the Writer's Mission," in Arthur F. Marotti, ed., *Catholicism and Anti-Catholicism in Early Modern English Texts* (1999).

*Bryan Crockett*

## Penry, John (1563–1593)

Religious radical. Penry was a native of Wales who entered Peterhouse, Cambridge, in 1580. He received his B.A. four years later. After taking a year off, he returned to Cambridge in 1585 but then migrated to Oxford, receiving the M.A. from St. Alban Hall in 1586. Convinced that the English church was insufficiently reformed, he refused to be ordained.

Penry devoted himself to trying to advance the cause of the gospel in his native Wales. He published a treatise calling for greater attention to preaching there and persuaded a Welsh member of Parliament to bring it before that body. Archbishop John Whitgift denied that Parliament had the right to meddle in religious matters and arranged for Penry to be prosecuted before the High Commission for treason and heresy. A month in prison did not deter Penry, who proceeded to use the printer Robert Waldegrave to publish further calls for reform. Penry soon joined with Waldegrave in running the secret press and was thus involved in some degree with the printing of the Marprelate tracts in 1588. Shortly thereafter he relocated in Scotland, where James VI proclaimed him an outlaw in 1590.

Though he had been a supporter of Presbyterianism prior to his sojourn in Scotland, his experiences there disillusioned him with that polity. Returning to England in 1592, he continued to be involved in publications advocating reform of the English church. In London he joined the Separatist congregation of Henry Barrow and John Greenwood, then under the ministry of Francis Johnson. Penry was arrested in 1593. He was tried shortly after the execution of Barrow and Greenwood, and he was convicted and met the same fate in May of 1593.

*See also:* Martin Marprelate, Separatists
*Further Reading*
 Chaplin Burrage, *The Early English Dissenters in the Light of Recent Research,* 2 vols. (Cambridge, Eng., 1912); Patrick Collinson, *The Elizabethan Puritan Movement* (London, 1967); D. J. McGinn, *John Penry and the Marprelate Controversy* (New Brunswick, NJ, 1966).

*Francis J. Bremer*

## Perkins, William (1588–1602)

Theologian. William Perkins was born and raised in the English county of Warwickshire. He studied at

*William Perkins, English Puritan theologian. (Archive Photos/Getty Images)*

Christ's College, Cambridge, where he received his B.A. in 1581 and his M.A. in 1584. His family appears to have been relatively affluent, and various accounts support each other in categorizing Perkins as leading an idle and dissolute life as an undergraduate. But following his receipt of the B.A., he had a conversion experience that changed his personal life and led him to the study of theology. He became a fellow of Christ's in 1584 and held that position until he resigned it a decade later.

Perkins soon became one of the luminaries of Cambridge. In his early ministry he preached to prisoners in the local jail. He was appointed lecturer at St. Andrew's Church, and his sermons attracted large numbers of both students and townsfolk. He is best described as a moderate puritan. His closest friendships were with Laurence Chaderton, Richard Greenham, and other puritans, but he was did not concern himself much with issues of liturgy or church governance. His primary focus was doctrine, and he was a powerful advocate of Calvinism and an opponent of Roman Catholicism. In the latter case he did on occasion take positions against practices such as kneeling to receive the Eucharist. And he did support the puritan Presbyterian clergy who were brought up on charges in 1590–1591.

Perkins made his greatest mark as a theologian, and his works were highly regarded in England, on the Continent, and later in New England. His approach to theology was influenced by the approach of Peter Ramus, who sought to understand things by dividing them. Some of the diagrams in Perkins's works reveal that Ramist approach. In terms of the content of his theology, Perkins was influenced by some of the followers of Calvin, such as Theodore Beza. His most significant contributions to the debates of his time were on the subjects of predestination and moral theology.

Perkins attempted to go beyond Calvin in teasing out the nature of predestination. In his *De Praedestinationis Modo et Ordine* (1598) and *God's Free Grace and Man's Free Will* (1602), Perkins taught that God had by immutable decree chosen some men to be saved and condemned others to damnation even before creation. In keeping with this belief, he advanced a doctrine of limited atonement, arguing that Christ only died for the benefit of those who were of the elect. These works brought a sharp attack from the Dutch theologian Jacobus Arminius and others.

Though he believed that the elect were chosen from before creation and that nothing could alter God's decree, Perkins also devoted himself to examining the question of how the elect could gain assurance of their salvation. He believed that sanctification could bring assurance. Indeed, he argued that sanctification was "an infallible sign of salvation." He devoted himself to exploring cases of conscience, seeking to establish the nature of sanctified behavior. He set forth individual measures to look for, such as fervency at prayer, heartfelt repentance for sin, and engaged attendance at sermons. But he also stressed the importance of the social dimension of Christian behavior, pointing to the need for charity in one's treatment of others. Through works such as *A Discourse of Conscience* (1596) and the posthumous *The Whole Treatise of the Cases of Conscience* (1606), Perkins established a reputation as a master in dealing with cases of conscience.

Perkins's goal in stressing sanctification as a means of gaining assurance was to relieve the elect of the anxiety that came with trying to determine if one had saving faith. But the task of judging whether one's behavior was truly sanctified could be equally difficult. Perkins himself acknowledged that the evidence of sanctification was "often feeble and weak." Other writers sought to spell out in ever more detail the path of righteousness, with the result that many came to doubt that they could ever achieve the precise path of behavior being described as signaling their justification.

*See also:* Conscience, Glorification, Grace, International Puritanism, Justification, Plain Style, Predestination, Soteriology, Synod of Dort, Witchcraft

*Further Reading*

Theodore Dwight Bozeman, *The Precisianist Strain: Disciplinary Religion and Antinomian Backlash in Puritanism to 1638* (Chapel Hill, 2004); Ian Breward, ed., *The Works of William Perkins* (Abingdon, Eng., 1970); David R. Como, *Blown by the Spirit: Puritanism and the Emergence of an Antinomian Underground in Pre–Civil War England* (Stanford, 2004); L. Wright, "William Perkins: Elizabethan Apostle for Practical Divinity," *Huntington Library Quarterly* 3 (1939–1940), 171–196.

*Francis J. Bremer*

## Peter, Hugh (1599–1660)

Puritan clergyman in England and New England who was executed as a regicide. Born in Cornwall, Hugh Peter was educated at Trinity College, Cambridge, where he earned his B.A. in 1617–1618. It was in Cambridge that he began his association with Richard Sibbes, John Preston, John Cotton, and Thomas Hooker. After receiving his M.A. in 1622, he preached at St. Sepulchre's, London, where he was very successful in "converting sinners."

*Hugh Peter, English Puritan clergyman. (Archive Photos/Getty Images)*

## Netherlands

In 1628 Peter became a member of the Massachusetts Bay Company, and after being silenced by Laud in 1629, he migrated to Holland. In 1632 he reorganized the English church in Rotterdam along Congregational lines after corresponding with John Cotton in New England. In fact, according to Presbyterian critic Robert Baillie, the first Congregational church in Holland "was that of Rotterdam, which Mr. Peters did draw from its ancient Presbyteriall constitution, to that new frame which it seemeth he also learned by Mr. Cottons Letters from New England." Peter's position in Rotterdam was pivotal, for he was a link connecting the prehistory of Congregationalism with its future history. William Ames, one of the progenitors of "non-separating Congregationalism," became (a few months before his death in 1633) Hugh Peter's co-pastor at Rotterdam.

During the five years he was pastor of the Rotterdam church, Peter had a significant impact on the other English puritans in exile, most notably the future Dissenting Brethren who, in dissenting from the Westminster Assembly, later published *An Apologeticall Narration* (London, 1643). Two of them—Thomas Goodwin and Philip Nye—were influenced by Peter's church when they gathered a congregation in Arnhem. The other three carried on in Rotterdam after Peter left for New England. William Bridge succeeded Peter as pastor, and Jeremiah Burroughes became teacher, while Sydrach Simpson was a member.

## New England

In 1635 Hugh Peter sailed to New England, where he became an influential member of the community at Salem. Peter became pastor of the church there and worked briefly with Roger Williams, who was teacher. It was Peter who excommunicated Williams and was one of Anne Hutchinson's chief accusers at her trial in 1636. In 1637 he was appointed overseer of the college and began lobbying for Salem as the home for the proposed college. However, the site for the college, shortly thereafter named Harvard, was established in Newtown. Peter was also very active in supporting the economy of Salem by helping to promote the nascent shipbuilding, salt, and glass industries.

## England's Civil Wars

In 1641 Hugh Peter and Thomas Weld were sent to England on a mission to raise funds for Harvard College and for the conversion of the Indians, to secure tax concessions for ships involved in the New England trade, "and to advance the 'glorious reformation' of church and state which the Bay Colony understood had at last begun in England." Hugh Peter considered the last objective to be the most important aspect of the mission, and subsequently events conspired to keep him in England working for this goal.

In England Hugh Peter traveled with the army as chaplain under General Thomas Fairfax, where his chief role was to exhort the troops prior to each battle. He also served as Oliver Cromwell's secretary and preached frequently before Parliament. This position was not only important enough to cause him repeatedly to postpone his return to

New England, but also gave him a platform from which to spread his views throughout England. Presbyterian polemicist Thomas Edwards, profoundly troubled over the growing respectability of the Independent cause, expressed his distress about Peter's efforts to proselytize in England. As the army's chaplain, Edwards wrote, Peter was able to spread Independency throughout England, for now he was "an Ubiquitary here and there, in this Countrey, and that Countrey, in the Army and at London: when ever the Independents or some other Sectaries are about any great designe or businesse, he must be sent for." As he accompanied Cromwell around the country, Peter was, according to Edwards, "carefull to propagate his Church-way at home as well as abroad, and that in all haste, and at once to over-spread the Kingdome with it."

To his adversaries, Hugh Peter had rapidly achieved notoriety as a far-too-effective promoter of Congregationalism. Both Anglicans and Presbyterians regarded him as a malicious seducer of innocent persons to Independency. Edwards bitterly observed that many men in England had adopted erroneous Congregational principles through contact with Peter. "Would they in New-England," Edwards lamented, "endure one or more Presbyterians to live among them, and to go up and down their Countrey, and in chief Towns and places to preach against, cry down their Churches and Church Government, and to extoll and cry up a contrary way, as Mr. Peters and others do here?" Although the histrionic Edwards was exaggerating when he called Peter "the Vicar Generall and metropolitaine of the Independents both in New and Old Englande," there is no question that Hugh Peter was a prime mover behind the spread of Congregationalism.

Peter was responsible for the publication of one of the most important treatises on the "New England Way." In 1637, hoping to discredit New England Congregationalism, a group of English Presbyterians published *A Letter of Many Ministers in Old England, requesting The judgment of their Reverend Brethren in New England concerning Nine Positions.* In 1642, after the Presbyterian challenge had been expanded to thirty-two ques-

tions, Richard Mather, with the approval of other New England clergymen, sent a reply to England. This work found its way into Hugh Peter's hands. He added an introduction and published it in June 1643 as *Church-Government and Church-Covenant Discussed, In an Answer of the Elders of the severall Churches in New-England to Two and thirty Questions, sent over to them by divers Ministers in England, to declare their judgements therein.* The publication was timed to coincide with the opening of the Westminster Assembly, thereby making accessible a concise compendium of the New England Way to the divines who would be debating which form of polity ought to be adopted.

In introducing Mather's tract, Hugh Peter began by beseeching Presbyterians to be open-minded and not allow their preconceived notions about the validity of the New England Way to obscure the truth: "The onely way I know to reach Gods mind in Worship will bee to love the truth for its owne sake." He then pressed the case for the adoption of Congregationalism. Since episcopacy in England had been successfully rooted out, he declared, there were only two options left to be considered for the structure of churches—Independency and Presbyterianism. Actually it was inaccurate to call Congregationalism "Independency," Peter argued, for "we know not any Churches Reformed, more looking at sister Churches for helpe then ours doe, only we" have neither discovered in Scripture nor "from any friend or enemy, that we should be under Canon, or power of any other Church." In matters of polity, then, there is no power authorized by God higher than that of the individual congregation.

In 1651 Hugh Peter published his own book *Good Work for a Good Magistrate,* in which he proposed certain political reforms in England based on those already prevalent in Holland and New England. He believed that good men rather than good laws should be the guiding forces in society, and, for him, the authentic philosopher-king was the visible saint who would seek "to advance true Religion." For this reason he was concerned with the role of higher education and of a trained, educated clergy. "Godlie and tractable" men, regardless of class or social position, should be supported by scholarships and educated for the ministry. Once they were qualified, they would be elected to ministerial office in gathered congregations "according to that waie of New-England, set forth by Hooker and Cotton."

During his seven years in New England, Hugh Peter was vigorously intolerant of opinions that appeared to be a threat to the existence of the Bible Commonwealth—most notably antinomianism, encountered in the controversy that swirled around Anne Hutchinson. However, in *A Word for the Armie* (London, 1647) he wrote that in order for Independents to succeed in establishing the rule of the saints, a policy of toleration would have to be adopted so that the aid of other Dissenters could be enlisted in overthrowing the king. Only through a policy of toleration could the Reformation be brought to fruition. Thus, Hugh Peter diverged from his colonial brethren by expediently accepting a broader toleration—a concept that he now entreated Massachusetts Bay to adopt as well. "Ah sweet New England!" he wrote John Winthrop, "& yet sweeter if divisions bee not among you, if you will give any incouragement to those that are godly & shall differ etc. I pray doe what you can herin, & know that your example in all kinds swayse here."

It was Hugh Peter who delivered a sermon before Parliament in December 1648 during the trial of Charles I in which he urged Parliament to condemn the king to the executioner's block. During the Interregnum his prominence continued to ascend. In 1649 he accompanied Cromwell to Ireland and in 1650 spent two months in Wales where he helped gather Independent congregations. In 1651 Parliament put him on the commission to revise the laws. It was reported he was one of the most vocal and active members, even though his training was in theology not law. By the Restoration, Royalists considered him one of the most influential and dangerous Puritans in the country, and he was exempted from the Act of Indemnity. Although denying his guilt as a regicide, he was tried, condemned, and, on 16 October 1660, executed according to the procedure reserved for traitors—he was hung, drawn, and quartered.

*See also:* Congregationalism

*Further Reading*
Francis J. Bremer, *Congregational Communion: Clerical Friendship in the Anglo-American Puritan Community, 1610–1692* (Boston, 1994); Geoffrey F. Nuttall, *Visible Saints: The Congregational Way, 1640–1660* (Oxford, 1957); Raymond P. Stearns, *The Strenuous Puritan: Hugh Peter 1598–1660* (Urbana, 1954); Raymond P. Stearns, "The Weld-Peter Mission to England," *Publications of the Colonial Society of Massachusetts* 32 (1937), 188–246.

*Ralph Young*

## Petto, Samuel (ca. 1624–1711)

Congregationalist clergyman. Petto was admitted sizar at St. Catharine's College, Cambridge, 15 June 1644 and received his B.A. in 1647. He was appointed as rector of South Elmham St. Cross, Suffolk in 1648. Petto was also appointed rector of the neighboring parish of Homersfield in January 1657 and was appointed an assistant to the Suffolk commission of Triers and Ejectors that examined clerical credentials in October 1657.

Petto was of the Independent persuasion in religion and entered into debates with the Presbyterians Matthew Pool and John Collinges concerning the validity of lay preaching in 1658–1659 and in the 1680s and 1690s regarding the justification of infant baptism.

Petto was ejected in 1660 and in 1669 moved to Wortwell, Norfolk, where he preached around the Yarmouth region. With the coming of the Declaration of Indulgence, he was licensed as a Congregationalist at his house at Wortwell and at the house of John Westgate at Redenhall on 8 May 1672. In the mid-1670s, Petto gathered a congregation in the town of Sudbury, Suffolk, and appears to have received the favor of the town's mayor John Catesby, who apparently let him live in the vicarage house of All Saints, Sudbury.

In 1693 Petto published *A faithful narrative of the wonderful and extraordinary fits, which Mr Thomas Spatchett, minister of Dunwich and Cockley, was under by witchcraft*, relating to the bewitching of Spatchett. He also entered into the debate on optics in the Philosophical Transactions of the Royal Society in 1699. Petto died in Sudbury in 1711 and was buried in the churchyard of All Saints, Sudbury, on 21 September 1711.

*Further Reading*
*Oxford Dictionary of National Biography* (Oxford, 2004).

*Elliot Vernon*

## Phillips, George (ca. 1593–1644)

Puritan minister and colonist. He studied at Caius College, Cambridge, receiving his B.A. in 1613–1614 and his M.A. in 1617. He served as vicar at Boxsted, Essex, and was actively associated with other puritan clergy in the region; his views on church government were endorsed by his friend John Rogers. Phillips and his family joined the Great Migration to New England in 1630, sailing with his East Anglian neighbor Governor John Winthrop. Phillips settled in Watertown, Massachusetts, where a church covenant was signed in July 1630 and Phillips was selected to be the pastor of the church.

Phillips was a strong advocate of congregational polity and labored to establish the autonomy of local churches, yet rejected calls for separation from the Church of England. He is believed to have been the author of *The Humble Request of his Majesties Loyall Subjects, the Governor and Company Late Gone for New England* (1630), which stressed that the colonists were not severing their connections with the national church. He served as one of the committee charged by the Massachusetts General Court, the colony's legislature, to compile the laws issued in 1641 as the *Body of Libertyes.* In 1642 he was appointed to the Board of Overseers of Harvard College. He died at Watertown on 1 July 1644.

Phillips wrote on a number of the religious disputes of the times. He composed a defense of the sacraments against Baptist views. In 1643, however, Thomas Lamb published *A Confutation of Infants Baptisme,* and following Phillips's death friends arranged for his earlier work to be published as a refutation of Lamb. Phillips's *A Reply to a Confuta-* *tion of Some Grounds for Infant Baptisme* (1645) was welcomed by English Congregationalists and others disturbed by the spread of Baptist views. While maintaining that the outward forms of ceremonies and sacraments were less important than the spiritual truth that underlay them and denying that baptism was a guarantee of saving grace, Phillips defended the importance of infant baptism for the growth of the church.

*Further Reading*
Henry Foote Wilder, "George Phillips, First Minister of Watertown," *Proceedings of the Massachusetts Historical Society* 63 (1930), 193–227; Timothy L. Wood, "'A Church Still By Her First Covenant': George Philips and a Puritan View of Roman Catholicism," *New England Quarterly* 72 (1999), 28–41.

*Francis J. Bremer*

## Phillips, John

One of a number of obscure clerical figures who put their energies into composing both religious tracts and journalistic pamphlets, ballads, and funeral verses. He was probably born in London, son of Robert Phillip, a clothworker. Phillips referred to himself on occasion in print as a "student in divinity" and "preacher of the Word of God" and was a student at Queen's College, Cambridge, but appears to have left the university without taking a degree. Phillips was an active and prolific writer from the mid-1560s until the early 1590s. His works were primarily directed to a popular audience, as in his examination of Essex witches published in 1566 or his treatment, published in 1581 by Robert Waldegrave, of the child prophet, William Withers, whose emergence from a coma resulted in a series of alarming predictions about the fate of sinful England. His religious tracts included anti-Catholic polemic, prayers, and warnings to repentance. He was also active as a writer of printed epitaphs and verse memorials, commemorating Margaret Douglas, Countess of Lennox (1578), Sir Philip Sidney (1587), and Sir Christopher Hatton (1591). Several of his works are no longer extant, and it is not known when or where he died. His activities may be usefully compared to those of fellow writers and clerics such as John Andrewes, Arthur Gurney, and William Averell. He is not to be confused with John Phillips of Emmanuel College, Cambridge, who was vicar of Faversham in Kent from 1606 until his death in 1640.

*Further Reading*
W. W. Greg, "John Philip—Notes for a Bibliography," *Library*, 3rd series, 1 (1910), 302–328, 396–423; Alexandra Walsham, *Providence in Early Modern England* (Oxford, 1999).

*John Craig*

## Philpot, John (1516–1555)

Clergyman and Protestant martyr. Philpot was born into a prominent Hampshire family and entered Winchester College at the age of ten. There he showed a great facility for the study of Hebrew. In 1533 he was admitted to New College, Oxford. There he would have associated with some of the country's earliest advocates of Protestantism. His own leaning toward the new faith may have been strengthened by a tour of Italy he undertook prior to 1541.

A zealous Protestant by 1548, Philpot preached in his native Hampshire despite the opposition of Bishop Stephen Gardiner. In 1551 Gardiner was removed from his see and replaced by John Ponet, who quickly appointed Philpot to be archdeacon of Winchester. Following the accession of Mary Tudor to the throne in 1553, Philpot resisted the queen's efforts to return England to the church of Rome. He preached against Catholic doctrines at the convocation for the archdiocese of Canterbury. Within a year he was deprived of his post, excommunicated, and imprisoned. He wrote a series of pastoral letters from prison that were later published by John Foxe in his *Actes and Monuments of the English Martyrs* (1563), popularly known as the Book of Martyrs.

Philpott was tried and convicted of heresy in December 1555 and burned at the stake on 18 December. Some of his papers were preserved by William Winthrop and later given to Foxe.

*Further Reading*
*Oxford Dictionary of National Biography* (Oxford, 2004).

*Francis J. Bremer*

## Phips, Sir William (1651–1697)

Governor of Massachusetts during the Salem Witchcraft Trials. Born into a poor family in Woolwich, Maine, on 2 February 1651, Sir William Phips rose to prominence as a treasure-hunter in the Caribbean. King James II, who received a substantial portion of the bounty recovered from a sunken Spanish ship, knighted William in June 1667. After distinguishing himself over the next two decades as a protector of the English colonies against the French in a few sea skirmishes, Phips was appointed governor of Massachusetts in 1691.

Due to his humble background and lack of theological training, Phips was ill prepared for the ecclesiastical nightmare that marred his short tenure as governor. Returning from England in the spring of 1692, Phips found the small village of Salem engaged in the famous witchcraft hysteria. With over 100 accused witches already awaiting trial, the new governor appointed a special tribunal to try the accused. While Phips was away on a military campaign, his appointed tribunal, which permitted "spectral" evidence in the trials, condemned 19 accused witches, while another was crushed to death. Upon his return in October, Phips immediately dissolved the special court he had created and forbade the use of spectral evidence in future cases. As the public became more cynical about the continued trials over the next few months, Phips, in an attempt to restore order, ultimately discharged all remaining suspects. He died in England on 19 November 1697, having served a short and unpopular term as governor of Massachusetts.

*See also:* Law in Puritan New England, Salem Witchcraft
*Further Reading*
Emerson W. Baker and John G. Reid, *The New England Knight: Sir William Phips* (Toronto, 1998).

*Mary Beth Norton*

## Pierson, Thomas (ca. 1570–1633)

As rector of Brampton Bryan, Herefordshire, from 1612 until his death, Pierson was responsible for introducing moderate puritanism into this region of the Welsh marches. Pierson was a native of Cheshire and graduated B.A. in 1594 from the puritan enclave of Emmanuel College, Cambridge, proceeding M.A. in 1597. He was ordained in 1599 and acted as lecturer in two Cheshire parishes, where he was active in the famous case of the possession of Thomas Harrison, a local Northwich boy. Pierson returned to Cambridge in 1603 as editor of the works of the influential William Perkins. At Brampton Bryan Pierson was reported to the diocesan authorities for adapting the Book of Common Prayer and declining the use of the surplice and the sign of the cross in baptism. He was treated leniently, partly because he was no Separatist and partly because of the power of his patron, Sir Robert Harley. Pierson also set up several combination lectures for the local clergy in order to counter the lack of preaching in the marches. His stepson, Christopher Harvey, prepared two of Pierson's works for the press after his death—*The Cure of Hurtfull Cares and Feares* (1636) and *Excellent Encouragements against Afflictions* (1647). Both books are anti-Catholic and anti-Arminian in tone and demonstrate Pierson's predestinarian beliefs. In his will, Pierson left 441 theological books to be used as circulating library by local puritan clerics. Some of the books survive today in the parish library of More, Shropshire.

*Further Reading*
Jacqueline Eales, "Thomas Pierson and the Transmission of the Moderate Puritan Tradition," *Midland History* 22 (1995), 75–102.

*Jacqueline Eales*

## Pigge, Oliver (fl. ca. 1550–1591)

Puritan preacher in Elizabethan England. The evidence for Pigge's life consists of a few scraps of information, leaving much shrouded in obscurity. He may have come from a family of that name that lived in and around Colchester. He matriculated pensioner from St. John's College, Cambridge, in 1565 and graduated B.A. in 1570. He was ordained deacon in 1571 and instituted rector of Abberton, near Colchester, on the presentation of Mrs. Katherine Audley. Resigning Abberton not later than 2 December 1578, Pigge moved to the Suffolk living of Rougham, close to Bury St. Edmunds, whose rector, William Tey, was a founding member of the Dedham conference. Here Pigge's nonconformity roused the enmity of Sir Robert Drury, patron of the living, and Pigge soon found himself suspended by Edmund Freke, bishop of Norwich, and having to appeal to the Privy Council for assistance.

Pigge was an important member of the classical or conference movement at this time, corresponding with John Field, the organizing secretary in London and disclosing details of the meetings of more than sixty ministers from neighboring counties at Cockfield, Suffolk, John Knewstub's living, to discuss how far the Book of Common Prayer might be tolerated. His preaching won him favor with the godly Suffolk gentlemen, Sir Robert Jermyn and Sir John Higham, to whom he dedicated *A comfortable treatise upon the latter part of the fourth chapter of the first epistle of saint Peter*, published in 1582. In spite of their protection, he was imprisoned at Bury St. Edmunds in July 1583 when the Crown dealt severely with the perceived threat of separatism in the area. Perhaps as early as 1585, Pigge left Suffolk for Hertfordshire, serving in 1587 as one of the Hertfordshire delegates, together with William Dyke, to a synod held in Cambridge. He may have been preaching in the town of Dorchester in April 1589 with a view to being engaged as the town's preacher, but if so he proved unsuccessful. Little is known of the last years of this red-bearded minister, apart from the fact that he was supported by Lady Bridget Russell, second wife of Francis Russell, second Earl of Bedford, who may have preferred him to a lectureship in Watford.

*Further Reading*
*Oxford Dictionary of National Biography* (Oxford, 2004).

*John Craig*

## Polwhele, Theophilus (d. 1689)

Congregationalist clergyman. Polwhele was born in Cornwall but was living in the county of Somerset when he was admitted to Emmanuel College, Cambridge, in 1644. His tutor there was the future archbishop of Canterbury William Sancroft. Polwhele received his B.A. in 1648 and was appointed to a Dorset parish. He married the daughter of William Benn, which united him with that prominent Dorchester clergyman.

In the early 1650s he moved to Carlisle, and in 1654 he was named a member of the committee for ejecting scandalous ministers for the counties of Cumberland, Durham, Northumberland, and Westmorland. He continued to move, and in 1660 he was in Devon when he signed an address to Charles II from the Congregational clergy of that county. He was ejected in 1660, but continued to preach illegally, running afoul of the authorities on a number of occasions. Following the Declaration of Indulgence of 1687 he was appointed the first minister of a Congregational meetinghouse in Tiverton.

*Further Reading*
*Oxford Dictionary of National Biography* (Oxford, 2004).

*Francis J. Bremer*

## Powell, Vavasor (1617–1668)

Welsh clergyman and Dissenter. Powell was born near Knighton, in the county of Radnorshire, in 1617. He was influenced by the preaching of Walter Craddock, and by 1640 he had gathered a following by his own preaching. Two years later he had moved to London, where he preached at St. Anne and St. Agnes. Sometime between 1643 and 1646 he became vicar of Dartford, Kent.

In 1650 Powell was named as an approver of the Act for the Propagation of the Gospel in Wales. He was empowered to remove and replace any clergy considered to be unfit for their ministries. During this period his Calvinist orthodoxy came to include support for the Fifth Monarchists, and he became known for his enthusiastic preaching style. In 1652

complaints were lodged with the authorities charging that Powell traded in church lands and spoke against the government. He was arrested when he criticized the Protectorate and identified Oliver Cromwell as the "vile person" named in the Book of Daniel.

Despite his concerns about the Protectorate, he joined in fighting a royalist insurrection in 1655 and was arrested following the restoration of the monarchy in 1660 for refusing to submit to the oath of supremacy and allegiance. In prison he wrote *The Bird in the Cage Chirping*, an apologia for his actions in propagating the gospel in Wales. Released in 1667, he preached the coming of the Fifth Monarchy in London in March of 1668. Arrested again, he died in prison in October 1668.

*See also:* Fifth Monarchists
*Further Reading*
*Oxford Dictionary of National Biography* (Oxford, 2004).

*Michael Spurr*

## Preston, John (1587–1628)

In his prime perhaps the most influential and esteemed leader of the godly in both church and state. Intimately involved in the politics of the Jacobean court, Preston simultaneously exerted a profound influence on the development of a distinctly puritan approach to popular piety.

### Life and Career

Born to a farming family at Upper Heyford, Northamptonshire, in 1587, Preston matriculated at King's College, Cambridge, in 1604, thanks to the support of a rich uncle. In 1606 he moved to Queens' College, and he was elected a fellow there in 1609, proceeding M.A. in 1611.

Although a lay prebendary of Lincoln Cathedral, Preston was more interested in medicine and astrology than in theology at this time. However, some time around 1611 or 1612, Preston experienced a spiritual awakening through a sermon by John Cotton. Preston immediately turned to the study of divinity and was ordained priest in the Diocese of Peterborough in June 1614.

In March 1615 Preston was chosen to engage in a public philosophical disputation before King James. Preston excelled, and was offered a place at court but declined. He received the B.D. in 1620 and soon became dean and catechist at Queens'. In 1621, thanks to his close relationship with George Villiers, the Marquess of Buckingham, Preston finally accepted a place in court as chaplain-in-ordinary to Prince Charles. In May 1622 Preston was elected preacher to the Honourable Society of Lincoln's Inn. In October 1622 Preston became master of Emmanuel College. In July 1623 Arthur Chichester, with Sir Edward Conway and Buckingham, obtained a D.D. for Preston, through a personal mandate of the king. In 1624 Preston took up an additional post in Cambridge of Trinity lecturer.

By now Preston had reached the peak of his career, and for a while Buckingham continued to seek preferment for Preston. However, Buckingham was quietly undergoing a change of allegiance in an anti-Calvinist direction. In February 1626 at the York House Conference, Buckingham's new agenda became clear to Preston, and a wedge was driven between them. As a result, Preston's influence at court began to wane.

Soon Preston's health also began to decline. By May 1628 he was seriously ill, probably with tuberculosis. On his deathbed he was visited by Sir Richard Knightley, John Dod, Laurence Chaderton, and Lord Saye and Sele. Then on 20 July, Preston died. He was buried on 28 July in Fawsley parish church, and Dod preached the funeral sermon.

## Publications, Theology, and the Issue of Conformity

Preston's vast printed legacy of over 100 editions in the three decades following his death comprises mainly sermonic as opposed to systematic material. These sermons indicate that Preston was definitely the "hotter sort of Protestant" and a strict Sabbatarian. Although his plain-style preaching was on occasions militantly antipapist and anti-Arminian, and his court sermons frequently addressed the contemporary political scene, Preston's works are almost entirely consumed with matters of spiritual experience and practical piety. Many attributed their spiritual awakening to Preston's searching preaching, including some eminent Puritans such as Thomas Shepard. Preston was an exemplary "experimental predestinarian" and also embraced the system of English Hypothetical Universalism.

Although John Hacket, later bishop of Coventry and Lichfield, slighted Preston as one with a puritanical instinct to purge the church of the remnants of corrupt religion, there appears to be no direct surviving evidence for this, nor any evidence of Preston's attitude to vestments, the signing of the cross in baptism, or episcopacy. Outwardly, Preston was a moderate, or fully conforming, Puritan.

But he was not complacent about the ecclesiastical status quo, and inwardly Preston was a reformer. In 1620, Preston clashed with the ecclesiastical authorities over his failure to use the Book of Common Prayer at a lecture in St. Botolph's church, Cambridge. A recantation and written apology saved him his place at the university, but it appears that Preston still covertly worked to support the reformation of the English church along Puritan lines. He was a keen friend and supporter of those renowned for a more defiant stance toward their mother church, and, as master of Emmanuel, he fostered the growth of Puritanism within the established church, while himself, like the eminent politician that he was, strategically avoiding fruitless direct conflict with the authorities.

*See also:* Emmanuel College, Federal Theology
*Further Reading*
Thomas Ball, *The Life of the Renowned Doctor Preston* (Oxford, 1885); Jonathan Moore, *Hypothetical Universalism: John Preston and the Softening of Reformed Theology* (Grand Rapids, MI, forthcoming); Irvonwy Morgan, *Prince Charles's Puritan Chaplain* (London, 1957).

*Jonathan Moore*

## Pricke, Robert (d. 1608)

One of those ministers of Suffolk whom Robert Reyce in his "Breviary of Suffolk" (1618) identified among the great "commodities" of the county. He was virtually the private chaplain of an exemplary puritan gentleman, Sir Edward Lewkenor, since Lewkenor's parish of Denham had few inhabitants and the church was (and is) tiny. Pricke, like many inhabitants of central Suffolk (where he seems to have originated; he probably never went to the university) had an alias, Oldmayne, the name that his son Timothy preferred to use. His principal patron was not so much Lewkenor as Lewkenor's mother-in-law, Martha Higham, aunt of Sir Robert Jermyn, who lived at Denham, ensured that Pricke was the first curate in two centuries to enjoy the full value of the living, and when she died left forty pounds to build the parsonage house, which still exists.

Lewkenor, although not a big man locally, was a very active parliamentarian, and his papers include the letter that Pricke wrote to him at the time of the 1584 parliament, spurring him on to his best endeavors for the cause of the church. In 1605, Lewkenor and his wife died on successive days from smallpox, deaths that profoundly moved the academic community in Cambridge, and Pricke preached the funeral sermon. He published *The doctrine of superioritie, and of subjection* (1609), the politics of which may suggest that the association of Puritanism with rebellious resistance was merely contingent and not a necessary one. Pricke was succeeded as curate of Denham by his son Timothy (Oldmayne), whose entire life was spent in this small village.

*Further Reading*
Patrick Collinson, "Magistracy and Ministry: A
    Suffolk Miniature," in Collinson, *Godly People:
    Essays on English Protestantism and Puritanism*
    (London, 1983).

*Patrick Collinson*

## Prynne, William (1600–1669)

Pamphleteer and lawyer; born near Bath, graduating M.A. from Oriel College, Oxford, in 1621, admitted a student at Lincoln's Inn in the same year, and called to the bar in 1628. He is best known as an astonishingly prodigious writer, who produced more than two hundred pamphlets, most of them controversial. In the 1630s he was tried twice for sedition in the Star Chamber. The first time was for

*William Prynne, English puritan pamphleteer. (Archive Photos/Getty Images)*

his work against plays, *Histrio-Mastix: The Player's Scourge,* which might have been insensitive but was not, as charged, an attack on the Crown. He was sentenced to have his ears cut off, fined 5,000 pounds, and sentenced to life imprisonment. In 1637 he was tried again, having been able to write and publish *Old Antithesis to the New Arminianism* and *Newes from Ipswich* while in prison. The first was a theological attack on Laudianism, the second an account of Bishop Matthew Wren's visitation in East Anglia. Once again he was found guilty of sedition and sentenced to have his ears fully cropped this time, and the initials "S.L." burnt into his cheeks. The initials stood for "seditious libeler," but puritans declared they stood for "stigma of Laud." This sentence turned him into a major puritan martyr, along with Henry Burton and John Bastwick, suffering for similar offenses.

In 1640 he believed in an Elizabethan episcopalian replacement for Laudian bishops, seeing

Joseph Hall and John Williams as successors to Whitgift. He became a more root-and-branch reformer by 1641 but never a complete Presbyterian, always looking for an Erastian solution, with a confidence in an uncorrupted royal absolutism. His account of William Laud's crimes and trial, *Canterburies Doome* (1646), was intended to show the archbishop's Romanist subversion of the Crown. However, by the time he became a member of Parliament (MP) in 1649 he was turning his attention to an alternative source of Jesuit subversion, initially to the Levellers and then presenting Pride's Purge and Charles I's trial and execution as a popish plot.

Prynne spent the start of the 1650s imprisoned without trial and was an opponent of the Commonwealth and Protectorate throughout the decade. At the Restoration he served as an MP for Bath in both the Convention and Cavalier Parliaments. Although many royalists still saw him as the seditious writer of the 1630s, Charles II and Clarendon were willing to give him credit for his work as a royalist in the 1650s. Charles appointed him as keeper of records in the Tower of London, a perfect post for such a devoted antiquarian. His last years were spent producing a succession of tomes arguing the case for a conservative constitutionalism. He continued his puritanism of spirit and lifestyle, publishing a few tracts against duels, taverns, and the drinking of healths, works decidedly out of kilter with the more libertarian royal court but always accompanied by expressions of loyalty. Anthony Wood depicted him almost as a Jacobean relic. It should be noted, however, that he never lost his distrust of papists, seeing the Quakers as masked papists and blaming Jesuits, naturally, for the Great Fire of London (1665). This conviction was still part of Prynne when he died in 1669.

*See also:* Star Chamber, Theater and Opposition
*Further Reading*
E. W. Kirby, *William Prynne: A Study in Puritanism* (Cambridge, MA, 1931); W. Lamont, *Marginal Prynne* (London, 1963); J. G. A Pocock, *The Ancient Constitution and the Feudal Law* (Cambridge, Eng., 1957).

*Tom Webster*

## Pym, John (1584–1643)

Parliamentary leader who has been seen as the greatest strategist of the Long Parliament's war effort in the early stages of the English Civil War. He was born into an old Somerset family on the fringes of the county elite, but his father died when he was a few months old, and he was brought up in the home of his step-father Anthony Rous, a godly magistrate (sheriff of Cornwall in two very significant years—1588, the year of the Spanish Armada, and 1603, the year James I succeeded Queen Elizabeth—and executor of the will of Sir Francis Drake). He studied at Broadgates Hall, Oxford, and the Middle Temple and settled down to a life as a small landowner with minor local offices—notably as a receiver of Crown lands in Hampshire, Wiltshire, and Gloucestershire. He was elected to all the parliaments of the 1620s as well as the Short and Long Parliaments, always for rotten boroughs on the patronage of "godly" peers. From 1620 on he was a widower who lived in other men's houses, and he was a tireless advocate of their public causes.

He became a "man of business" for the godly Earls of Pembroke, Bedford, and Warwick, helping them with estate management and more particularly with their colonial ventures in New England and in the Caribbean. He wrote copious reports for his patrons. From the outset, Pym's career is marked by exceptional self-belief, by exceptional anti-Catholic paranoia, and by what Stephen Marshall, in his funeral sermon, referred to as his "unweariableness." In 1621 and 1624, he was one of the outspoken advocates of war with Spain. In 1625 he spearheaded a series of bills against papists, saying "If they gain but a connivancy, they will press for a toleration; then strive for an equality, and lastly aspire to such a superiority as may work the extermination both of us and our religion." In 1626, he was prominent in the attempt to impeach the king's chief minister, the Duke of Buckingham, for mismanaging the war with Spain and promoting false religion (Arminianism), and he dominated the Committee on Religion, delivering fourteen reports from the committee to the House of Commons. In 1628, he led the attack on the Arminians Richard Montagu and Roger Manwaring, accusing the latter of "conspiring with the Jesuits and the Church of Rome to disturb the Government"—pure paranoia. By the dissolution in 1629 and the beginning of the Personal Rule, as the period is called during which the king ruled without Parliament, he was a leader of opposition (though not the central leader) to Charles I's style of government. In the 1630s he was heavily involved in the Providence Island colonization scheme; he became a patentee of the Saybrook colony (and may have seriously consideration emigration). His religious position is best illustrated by the pew erected in his home parish on the site of the old high altar, as a good position from which to hear sermons every Sunday morning and afternoon.

When Charles I was forced to recall Parliament in 1640, Pym took a key role. Working closely with his allies in the Lords, he made the major speeches setting the agendas of the Short and Long Parliaments, saying, "The root of the grievances I think to be an intended union between Rome and ourselves." For two years he worked for reformation in church and state. He sought a reconciliation for a while, but his ineradicable belief in the popish plot brought him to see the necessity of confrontation. His hand is to be seen in the timing of initiatives, in the development of a strong propaganda drive—allowing many of his own speeches to be published and hiring outstanding polemicists (like Henry Parker) to write what it would have been dangerous for him to write under his own name. He does not seem to have had a theological objection to episcopacy, but he was persuaded that there would be no safety from popery so long as the office of bishop remained in the royal gift and that the Presbyterian option was the prudent way forward. He had no time for separatists and wanted strong, effective, "pure" Protestant forms of worship and discipline. He was willing to work with religious radicals to build an effective war effort, as so many wavered or looked for compromise. Once war broke out, he was tireless in building the administrative machinery of war—new taxes, conscription, the Solemn League and Covenant—even as his body succumbed to bowel cancer, from which he died on 8 December 1643. Both Houses of Parliament suspended business to attend his funeral in Westminster Abbey, after which he was interred in Henry VII's chapel—from which his corpse was evicted and thrown into a ditch at the Restoration.

*Further Reading*
J. H. Hexter, *The Reign of King Pym, 1640–1643* (Cambridge, MA, 1940); Conrad Russell, "The Parliamentary Career of John Pym 1621–1629," in P. Clarke, A. Smith, and N. Tyacke, editors, *The English Commonwealth, 1549–1642* (New York, 1979).

*John Morrill*

## Pynchon, William (ca. 1590–1662)

Entrepreneur, founder of Springfield, Massachusetts, and controversial author. Born in Springfield, England (near Chelmsford, Essex, where he likely knew Thomas Hooker and John White), to a prosperous family, Pynchon came into his inheritance at age twenty-one and became one of the original patentees of the Massachusetts Bay charter and a signatory of the Cambridge Agreement.

Pynchon arrived in Massachusetts in 1630 with Winthrop's fleet, settling first at Dorchester and then at Roxbury by 1631. In 1632 Pynchon paid £25 for beaver-fur trading privileges, an early indication of his economic activity. He served as colony treasurer (1632–1634) and was reelected annually as an assistant until 1637, shortly thereafter relocating to Agawam (renamed Springfield in 1641) on the Connecticut River, a promising location for trade; he served again as assistant from 1642 to 1651, when he returned to England. Pynchon was centrally involved in establishing the new town government, which under his leadership came under the jurisdiction of Massachusetts Bay. In 1638, there was controversy concerning Pynchon's handling of corn purchases from Indian trade during a grain shortage, but, though accused and fined by Connecticut authorities for price gouging and trying to monopolize trade, Pynchon seems to have been ultimately exonerated.

Pynchon was involved in two early witchcraft cases: in 1648, he served on the General Court that

*William Pynchon, one of the original patent holders for the Massachusetts Bay Company. (Library of Congress)*

sentenced Margaret Jones to be executed for witchcraft (the first such execution in Massachusetts Bay); then in 1649–1651, he was involved in the cases against Mary and Hugh Parsons of Springfield. But Pynchon became especially notorious for the first of his theological publications, *The Meritorious Price of Our Redemption,* first published in London in 1650. Drawing on the ideas of Anthony Wotton, Robert Smith, and Hugh Broughton, Pyn-

chon defended the belief that Christ had only made atonement for the sins of the elect, against Arminian and Lutheran versions, but, as Michael P. Winship has shown, he departed from more orthodox Puritanism on covenant theology. When copies first arrived in New England in October of that year, it roused such furor and indignation that the General Court condemned it for "many errors & heresies generally condemned by al orthodox writers" and ordered it to be publicly burned, its author to appear before the court, and Ipswich minister John Norton to prepare a response. Pynchon made his first appearance in May 1651; after conferring with leading ministers, Pynchon shortly made a statement that he had "not spoken . . . as [he] should have done."

After further threats and delays, Pynchon departed for England before a May 1652 court deadline and never returned, settling at Wraysbury. But he continued to promulgate his views in print: *The Jewes Synagogue* (1652); *A Farther Discussion of that Great Point in Divinity, the Sufferings of Christ* (1655), and a second time with the misleading title *The Meritorious Price of Our Redemption,* a refutation of Norton's response; *A Treatise of the Sabbath* (1654); and *The Covenant of Nature with Adam Described* (1662).

*Further Reading*
American National Biography (New York, 1999); Michael Winship, "Contesting Control of Orthodoxy Among the Godly: William Pynchon Reexamined," *William and Mary Quarterly,* 54 (1997), 795–822.

*Michael G. Ditmore*

# Q

## Quick, John (1636–1706)

Presbyterian minister. Quick was born in Plymouth, Devon, England, and baptized there on 19 June 1636. He was educated at Exeter College, Oxford, awarded B.A. in 1657, and ordained by Presbyterian convention on 2 February 1659. In 1658 he was appointed minister at Churchstow with Kingsbridge, Devonshire, and subsequently perpetual curate of Brixton, Plympton. At the Restoration he kept a low profile and after a while recommenced his ministry, which he continued until December 1663. His activities drew the attention of Seth Ward, the restored bishop of Exeter. Quick was arrested while preaching and imprisoned, not only for Dissent, but also for refusal to cease preaching. In the winter of 1664, he was bound over in the sum of forty pounds by Devon Assizes and imprisoned for three months. In 1672 he was licensed to preach in Plymouth, but after the withdrawal of his license was once more imprisoned, with other Dissenting preachers, at Plymouth.

Upon his release Quick moved to London and ministered to a congregation in Covent Garden. In 1680 he was appointed pastor to the English church at Middleburg in Holland. His appointment was short lived, and he returned to London in 1681, where he became interested in the welfare of French Protestant refugees. Quick was prosecuted on a number of occasions for preaching, but following the Toleration Act in 1689, he became minister to a Presbyterian congregation in Bartholomew Close, Smithfield, London. John Quick died in 1706 and was buried at Bunhill in London on 7 May 1706.

*Further Reading*
*Oxford Dictionary of National Biography* (Oxford, 2004).

*Catherine Nunn*

# R

## Ranew, Nathaniel (d. 1678)

Congregational puritan clergyman. Ranew, who may have been born in Essex, was admitted sizar at Emmanuel College, Cambridge, in 1617 and proceeded B.A. in 1621 and M.A. in 1624. His degree was incorporated at Oxford in July 1627. His first living was the parish of St. Andrew Hubbard, Little Eastcheap in London, where he remained until he became rector of West Hanningfield in 1645. He did not remain long in West Hanningfield, as he was instituted by parliamentary order in 1647 to the vicarage of Felsted, Essex. Like his Cambridge contemporary John Beadle, Ranew came to the attention of Robert Rich, second earl of Warwick, who lived at Leigh Priory and who supported Ranew with an annual stipend of twenty pounds.

Ranew took an active part in the ecclesiastical changes of the late 1640s and 1650s as a member of the East Hinckford classis and one of those who subscribed to the "Testimony of Essex Ministers in the Province of Essex" issued in 1648. With the passage of the Act of Uniformity in 1662, Ranew was ejected from Felsted. In a curious move, he was instituted to the vicarage of Coggeshall in March 1661, but there is no evidence that he ever took possession of this living. He moved to Billericay, Essex, was licensed as a Congregational preacher in 1672, and was buried there on 17 March 1678. The only work known to have been published by Ranew was his tract on Christian meditation dedicated to Mary, Countess of Warwick, entitled *Solitude improved by Divine Meditation* (London, 1670).

*Further Reading*
*Oxford Dictionary of National Biography* (Oxford, 2004).

*John Craig*

## Rich, Mary, Countess of Warwick (1625–1678)

Diarist and patron of Puritan ministers. Mary showed her determined nature at a young age when she refused to consent to an arranged marriage and chose instead to marry Charles Rich, younger son of Robert Rich, second Earl of Warwick. Mary's father, the Earl of Cork, was eventually persuaded to agree to the marriage, which took place in 1641. Mary moved to the Earl of Warwick's country estate at Leighs Priory near Felsted in Essex, where she was welcomed into an extended family.

Warwick and his relatives were arguably the leading Puritan family in England, and Mary, already of a godly disposition, was soon influenced by their piety. For the remainder of her life, she spent part of each day in the garden at Leighs in prayer and meditation. On the deaths in quick succession of the Earl of Warwick and his eldest son, the earldom passed to Mary's husband, Charles, in 1659. The new countess's eagerness for "edifying discourse" and godly sermons made Leighs Priory a favorite resort for Puritan ministers. After the ejection of hundreds of Puritans from the Church of England in August 1662, the Countess of Warwick provided support and succor for several Nonconformist ministers from Essex and London. As patrons of many livings across southern England, however, the Earl of Warwick and his wife did not break all ties with the state church, and in her later years the countess counted at least two bishops among her friends. She survived her husband by five years.

*Further Reading*
Charlotte Fell Smith, *Mary Rich, Countess of Warwick (1625–1678): Her Family and Friends* (London, 1901).

*David J. Appleby*

### Rich, Sir Nathaniel (1585–1636)

Parliamentary puritan and colonizer. Rich was born in Essex and was probably the eldest son of a London alderman and sheriff. He was the cousin and ally of Richard Rich, the second Earl of Warwick.

Nathaniel Rich was admitted to Gray's Inn, one of the Inns of Court, in 1610. He was knighted in 1617. As early as 1615 he had become involved in colonizing ventures as a member of the Bermuda Company. He was also a supporter of the Virginia Company, and he was a member of the faction that challenged Sir Edwin Sandys's leadership of that venture. When Virginia became a royal colony in 1624, he became a member of the commission advising the king on the colony. Shortly thereafter, however, he emerged as a strong parliamentary critic of Charles I and his advisor the Duke of Buckingham. He became an ally of John Pym, and along with Pym took a lead in pushing for the Petition of Right and complaining about the spread of Arminian influences in the Church of England. Following the dissolution of parliament in 1629, he redevoted himself to colonizing efforts, this time with a focus on puritan efforts. He helped in the negotiations that led to the grant of the Massachusetts Bay Company charter and was one of the organizers of the Providence Island Company. He died in 1636.

*Further Reading*
Richard Greaves and Robert Zaller, eds., *Biographical Dictionary of British Radicals in the Seventeenth Century*, 3 vols. (Brighton, Eng., 1982).

*Francis J. Bremer*

### Rich, Sir Robert, Second Earl of Warwick (1587–1658)

English politician, admiral, and colonial entrepreneur. Educated at Emmanuel College, Cambridge, Robert Rich was later noted by friends and enemies for his charisma, geniality, and godliness. He was created a Knight of the Bath in 1603, and the influence of his family ensured his election as member of Parliament for Maldon, Essex, in 1610 and 1614. In 1619 he succeeded his father as Earl of Warwick. An astute and energetic businessman, with an Elizabethan taste for licensed piracy, Warwick was prominent in the development of English plantations in the Bermudas. Together with his brother, the Earl of Holland, Warwick joined Lord Saye and Sele, Lord Brooke, and John Hampden to found the Providence Company. As head of this and several other entrepreneurial companies, Warwick went on to develop colonies such as Massachusetts (1628) and Connecticut (1635).

Lord Warwick emerged as a leader of the Puritan opposition to Charles I. Now fabulously rich, he was so powerful and popular in his native county that he was known as the King of Essex. He refused to pay the king's forced loans and ship money tax, and, as the patron of many parish livings, stoutly resisted Archbishop William Laud's ecclesiastical policies. As a punishment for such defiance, Charles I stripped him of the Lord Lieutenancy of Essex. By 1641, however, with the king attempting to placate his critics with offices and favors, Warwick was appointed a Privy Counsellor, and, among other honors, reinstated as lord lieutenant. More significantly, he also succeeded the sickly Earl of Northumberland as Admiral of the Fleet.

At the outbreak of civil war in England in 1642, Warwick's charisma and popularity among his

*Robert Rich, second Earl of Warwick and Lord High
Admiral. (Hulton Archive/Getty Images)*

sailors helped ensure that the bulk of the navy declared for Parliament. Warwick, confirmed as
Parliament's Lord High Admiral, proved an active
and highly competent wartime leader. When the
nobility and members of Parliament were required to relinquish their commands in 1645 by
virtue of the Self-Denying Ordinance, Warwick
was keenly missed. He used his enforced sabbatical to ensure the incorporation of Providence
Plantations (today's Rhode Island). In 1648, when
many ships' companies mutinied and defected to
the royalist side, Parliament charged Warwick
with raising another fleet. This makeshift navy
proved so effective that the royalists, despite
their reinforcements, were chased from the seas.
During this second civil war, Warwick's magnificent stately home at Leighs Priory, near Chelmsford, Essex, was raided by royalist forces and
plundered.

In the revolution following Parliament's victory,
Warwick disapproved of the abolition of the monar-

chy and the House of Lords. Nevertheless, he supported Cromwell's seizure of power and remained
loyal to the Protectorate. In November 1657, Warwick's grandson and namesake, Robert, married
Cromwell's youngest daughter, Frances. Sadly, this
was the pinnacle of the family's power: young
Robert Rich died within months, followed quickly
by the Earl of Warwick himself, on 19 April 1658.
Warwick was buried at Felsted in Essex, with his
funeral sermon preached by Edmund Calamy. The
city of Warwick, Rhode Island, was named after
him by Samuel Gorton.

*Further Reading*
William Addison, *Essex Worthies* (London, 1973).

*David J. Appleby*

### Robinson, John (ca. 1575–1 March 1625)

The Pilgrims' Leiden pastor and continuing inspiration. He wrote several theological works, the
most important being A *Justification of Separation*
(1610), reissued in 1639 during renewed discussions on church order. Robinson attended Corpus
Christi College, Cambridge, 1592–1603 (B.A., ordained and made fellow, 1597; M.A., 1599; dean,
1600). He became assistant minister of St. Andrew's, Norwich, in 1603. Dismissed for nonconformity around 1606, he lived in Norwich through
early 1607, preaching occasionally elsewhere without license. As he was revisiting Cambridge, sermons by Laurence Chaderton (on Matthew 18:17)
and Paul Baynes (on Ephesians 5:7–11) influenced
Robinson toward separating from the Church of
England. In the summer of 1608, Robinson fled to
Amsterdam with the Scrooby Separatists led by
Richard Clifton and those of Gainsborough led by
John Smyth. When Smyth and his followers became Anabaptists, hoped-for congregational unity
disintegrated. Robinson became the pastor of over
100 people who moved to Leiden (1609), preaching to them three times a week.

Registered in the University of Leiden (1615),
Robinson became friends with Johannes Polyan-
der and Festus Hommius, who invited him to debate predestination against Simon Episcopius.

Robinson was on friendly terms with the ministers of Leiden's English Reformed Church, Robert Durie (father of John Durie, the ecumenical pioneer) and Hugh Goodyear. Robinson's ideas on separation and election were clarified in responses to attacks by Joseph Hall and Richard Bernard. Robinson agreed with William Perkins's views on predestination (published 1598). Discussion of Perkins had revived in the Netherlands with the posthumous appearance in 1612 of Jacobus Arminius's long rejoinder to Perkins's pamphlet, and the publication of a Dutch translation of Perkins in 1617. Besides debating, Robinson contributed to this fray by republishing Perkins's *Catechism Concerning Church Government*, with additions of his own, in 1623, followed the next year by a response to an Arminian pamphlet by John Murton that elicited from Robinson a defense of the doctrines promulgated by the Synod of Dort. Robinson's ideas shifted from a rigid separatism to allowing the hearing of godly puritans such as William Ames, Robert Parker, and Henry Jacob, who visited him in Leiden, as did William Aspinwall. Robinson's congregation asserted its agreement with the Calvinist doctrines in the *Harmony of Confessions* (1586).

Robinson's farewell sermon to the Pilgrims leaving for America, 1620, included the common sentiment of those who believed in the possibility of further reform that their faith should remain open to ongoing divinely inspired insight, and not petrify as Robinsonianism. This has been seized on to credit him with a liberal attitude more characteristic of later times. Though such claims may be exaggerated, Robinson's cautious openness evidently influenced the Plymouth colonists, who did not participate in witchcraft hysteria nor execute Quakers or other dissidents, and who attempted to treat Indians fairly before the courts. This perceptible attitude of toleration may be partly ascribed to Robinson's discussions in 1617 with the Mennonite Pieter Twisck, author of a compilation of statements in favor of religious toleration, *Religions Vryheyt* (Hoorn, 1609).

*See also:* English Puritanism in the Netherlands, Plymouth Colony

*Further Reading*
Walter H. Burgess, *John Robinson* (London, 1920); Timothy George, *John Robinson and the English Separatist Tradition* (Macon, GA, 1982).

*Jeremy Bangs*

## Rogers, Daniel (1573–1652)

Puritan preacher. Rogers came from a noteworthy clerical family in East Anglia. His father was Richard Rogers, which meant that he was related to Ezekiel Rogers, Nathaniel Ward, Samuel Ward of Ipswich, and John Rogers. Two of his sons also went on to become puritan ministers. He was educated at Christ's College, Cambridge, where he became close friends with Paul Baynes and William Ames before becoming lecturer at Wethersfield, Essex, in 1625. He stayed there until his death in 1652. He established a reputation as one of the most popular preachers in the county, a major figure in the clerical network and a spiritual aide to noble professors such as the Barrington and Rich families. He was untroubled for his nonconformity until William Laud's second visitation in 1631. Anticipating discipline, he submitted a petition signed by moderate puritan ministers. His license to preach was suspended in September upon his refusal to sign the Three Articles. He attended a demonstration against Laudian policies at the end of the month.

For the rest of the decade he worked to keep the pulpit at Wethersfield active, bringing in ministers from across the region, and maintained his ministry as far as was possible. He organized and contributed to religious exercises at home and elsewhere and produced printed devotional works. He was prominent in his support for Robert Rich, Earl of Warwick, in 1640. He resumed his parochial duties through the 1640s and was part of an appeal in 1649 to limit toleration to those who signed the Solemn League and Covenant and the first of the signatories to *The Essex Watchmen's Watchword* (1649), protesting against the Leveller manifesto, the Agreement of the People.

*Further Reading*
T. W. Davids, *Annals of Evangelical Nonconformity in Essex* (London, 1863); Giles Firmin, *The real*

*Christian or, A treatise of effectual calling* (1670); H. F. Waters, *Genealogical Gleaning in England* (1901); Tom Webster, *Godly Clergy in Early Stuart England: The Caroline Puritan Movement, c. 1620–1643* (Cambridge, Eng., 1997); Tom Webster and Kenneth Shipps, eds., *The Diary of Samuel Rogers, 1634–1638*, Church of England Record Society, vol. 11 (Woodbridge, Eng., 2004).

*Tom Webster*

## Rogers, Ezekiel (1588–1660)

Congregational minister and New England colonist. Rogers was born at Wethersfield, Essex, the son of Richard Rogers, the lecturer there, and the younger brother of Daniel Rogers. He was a gifted minister but prone to altercations with patron and parishioners. He graduated M.A. from Christ's College, Cambridge, in 1608 and his nonconformist resolutions encouraged him to take a place as chaplain to the Barrington family of Hatfield Broad Oak from 1610. Possible disagreement led to his talent being placed in their wealthy but distant living of Rowley in Yorkshire in 1621. He thrived there until the new regime of Richard Neile brought more exacting standards of conformity; in fact, his ministry was so valued that Neile worked hard to persuade him to compromise. In 1636 he was suspended and fell into an argument with his patrons about their intentions to replace him; this argument was not resolved before his departure for New England in 1638. He established a settlement, also called Rowley, in Massachusetts and became a major figure in the colony. He preached the election sermon in 1643, touching nerves with the suggestion that no one should be governor twice, and he similarly offended some of his auditors when he preached at the 1647 synod. He responded to demands for his preaching by establishing a fortnightly lecture at other towns, securing an assistant at Rowley, the root of some division, as he was said to have neglected his flock. Highly valued as a minister, he saw out his last years at Rowley.

*Further Reading*
T. Gage, *The History of Rowley* (Boston, 1840); R. C. Marchant, *The Puritans and the Church Courts in the Diocese of York, 1560–1642*

(London, 1960); Cotton Mather, *Magnalia Christi Americana* (London, 1704); H. F. Waters, *Genealogical Gleanings in England* (Boston, 1901).

*Tom Webster*

## Rogers, John (ca. 1570–1636)

Church of England clergyman, of a godly family, and part of a puritan clerical stock within Essex and Suffolk. His uncle was Richard Rogers, the famous lecturer of Wethersfield, and it was Richard who provided for his nephew's troubled education at Emmanuel College, Cambridge. He was related by blood or marriage to Daniel and Ezekiel Rogers, and Nathaniel and Samuel Ward, and he was the father of Nathaniel Rogers. For most of his career John Rogers was lecturer of Dedham at the extreme northeast corner of Essex and the diocese of London. The distance from authority provided relative freedom from episcopal discipline, and once he settled in this strongly puritan parish in 1605, he was to stay until his death in 1636.

He was most acclaimed as a passionate preacher, wining applause from Thomas Goodwin and being described by Thomas Hooker as "The prince of all the preachers in England." The demands of judging faith and living a faithful life are very much the focal point of his two main works, *The Doctrine of Faith* and *A Treatise of Love*. A substantial exposition of the First Epistle of Peter was published posthumously in 1650. His ministry in Dedham allowed him to concentrate on his preaching priorities and to establish a godly parish. It also provided an environment where he seems to have established a household seminary. He made Dedham famous as a center for auditors gadding to sermons. Indeed his last trouble with the authorities was brought on by Bishop Matthew Wren wanting to hire horses in Ipswich while he was traveling on visitation, only to be told that they had all been taken by townsfolk to ride over the border to hear Rogers preach.

His attitude to conformity was complicated. Giles Firmin recalled that "tho' he did conform, I never saw him wear a surplice, nor heard him use but a few Prayers; and those, I think, he said *memoriter*, he did not read them: but this he would do in his Preaching, draw his fingers around his throat, and say, Let them take me and hang me up, so they will but remove these stumbling Blocks out of the Church." For most of his career, his place in Dedham allowed him to neglect ceremonies with relatively little trouble. However, his priorities placed nonconformity well below preaching in terms of importance. He condemned those who lost permission to preach for refusing to conform. When he came to the attention of Bishop William Laud, particularly in 1631, he was suspended and came to the difficult decision to subscribe to the Three Articles. When Bishop Wren was annoyed with the unavailability of horses in 1636, the bishop was apparently determined to silence him, and Archbishop Laud ordered Rogers to suspend the lecture as a health caution during the plague. When he was not allowed to renew his preaching when the sickness had abated, he realized that it was effectively suppressed and, according to the puritan sources that carry this anecdote, "this strooke him to the harte." He died on 18 October 1636. The manner of his death placed him in the martyrology of the 1630s and served as an example of the underhand and anti-Christian ways of the Laudian hierarchy.

*See also:* Directions for Godly Living (in Primary Sources)
*Further Reading*
T. W. Davids, *Annals of Evangelical Nonconformity in Essex* (London, 1863); Cotton Mather, *Magnalia Christi Americana* (1704); H. F. Waters, *Genealogical Gleanings in England* (Boston, 1901); Tom Webster, *Godly Clergy in Early Stuart England: The Caroline Puritan Movement, c. 1620–1643* (Cambridge, Eng., 1997).

*Tom Webster*

## Rogers, Nathaniel (1598–1655)

Congregational minister. Rogers was born in Haverhill, Suffolk, the second son of John Rogers, the lecturer of Dedham, Essex. After graduating M.A. from Emmanuel College, Cambridge, in 1621 he had a spell as chaplain, possibly with the Crane family in Coggeshall, Essex, whose daughter he married. In 1627 he became curate to John Barkham, a friend of William Laud, at Bocking, Essex. Initially the relationship was good, as Rogers eschewed issues of nonconformity, winning a reputation as a fine preacher. However, in 1631 Thomas Hooker convinced him of the necessity of nonconformity, and after he delivered a sermon without a surplice, Barkham suggested that it was wise for him to move on.

Rogers became rector in Assington, Suffolk, where his patron was Brampton Gurdon, which took him into John Winthrop's circles. The company of clergymen such as Henry Jessey contributed to his radicalization. In 1636 Rogers emigrated, aware of the likely disciplinary attentions of Bishop Matthew Wren. He arrived in New England in the midst of the antinomian controversy and contributed a calming voice to the synod of 1637 that was applauded. In 1638 he joined John Norton as pastor at Ipswich, Massachusetts, successor to Nathaniel Ward. He remained there for the rest of his life, winning admiration for his divinity, although his exacting standards limited his publications to a letter to a member of Parliament calling for thorough social and ecclesiastical reformation.

*Further Reading*
Cotton Mather, *Magnalia Christi Americana* (London, 1704); Nathaniel Rogers, *A letter discovering the cause of Gods continuing wrath against the nation, notwithstanding the present endeavours of reformation* (1644); H. F. Waters, *Genealogical gleanings in England* (Boston, 1901); Tom Webster, *Godly Clergy in Early Stuart England: The Caroline Puritan Movement, c. 1620–1643* (Cambridge, Eng., 1997).

*Tom Webster*

## Rogers, Richard (1551–1618)

Puritan divine and author. Rogers was born in Moulsham, a parish of Chelmsford, Essex, and baptized there on 29 June 1551. He matriculated as a sizar at Christ's College, Cambridge, in 1566 and graduated A.B. in 1571, in which year he was ordained deacon and priest. He later migrated to Caius College and received his M.A. in 1574.

Within a year of his ordination, Rogers was serving as curate of Radminster, Essex. There he mobilized prosperous godly men to assist him in governing the parish. In 1577 Rogers accepted a lectureship at Wethersfield, Essex, where he was to achieve his greatest fame, but where his parish evangelizing appears to have been less successful than at Radminster. In 1583 he and twenty-six fellow ministers in Essex were suspended after petitioning against Archbishop John Whitgift's Three Articles, but he was restored to his ministry after eight months through the intervention of an influential puritan layman. Though he ran into trouble with the ecclesiastical authorities for his nonconformity in 1598 and 1603, on those occasions as well he emerged unscathed, due to the intercession of aristocratic friends.

In the 1580s he joined the effort of puritan clergy to form associations to better assist each other in spreading reform. He signed the "Book of Discipline" and was one of the members of the Braintree conference, where he formed a friendship with Ezekiel Culverwell, then vicar of Felsted, with whom he would often meet to discuss matters such as "our Christian estate, . . . God's mercy in our calling to the fellowship of the gospel, . . . the true testimonies of faith, and . . . the great comfort which by continuing herein doth come unto God's people." While it is clear that Wethersfield became an occasional gathering place for like-minded clergy, we know less about the Braintree association than we do of the more famous conference at Dedham.

Rogers prepared a set of daily devotions for godly life at the request of his fellow conference members and later expanded that into his most significant work, *Seven Treatises containing such directions as is gathered out of the Holie Scriptures,* which was published in 1603 and again two years later with a dedication to King James I. This was the most important work of puritan practical divinity produced by his generation of clergymen and retained readers into the twenty-first century. *Seven Treatises* is a detailed discussion of conversion and the godly life. Beginning with faith and justification, it proceeds to an account of sanctification as the fruit of salvation and then dwells on the means by which the godly life is to be obtained and a detailed discussion of the daily direction by which one could preserve and produce the fruits of faith and sanctification.

The clergyman's own concern with living the godly life is manifest in his diary, where he recorded not only details of his personal devotions but also his contacts with other saints on occasions of conviviality and at times of fasts. His preaching attracted the godly from throughout the region of the Stour River valley. John Wilson was attracted to a pastoral post in Sudbury so that he could hear and be near Rogers, whose *Seven Treatises* Wilson had read as a Cambridge undergraduate. Many of Rogers's sermons addressed the social dislocations caused by the economic crisis associated with the decline of the cloth industry in East Anglia. He preached a form of social gospel, encouraging the rich to treat the poor with Christian charity. Despite his fame among his peers, Rogers was not comfortable with all aspects of his pastoral ministry. He was frustrated with the lack of Christian piety of members of his congregation and impatient with catechizing the youth who studied in the town school that was located in his home.

Rogers married twice. Among the children of his first marriage were two sons, Daniel and Ezekiel, both of whom followed their father into the ministry. Daniel eventually followed Stephen Marshall in the Wethersfield lectureship that his father had held and became a noted puritan minister during the Interregnum. Ezekiel migrated to New England, where he served in the ministry in Massachusetts. Following the death of his first wife, Richard married Susan Ward, the widow of the Reverend John Ward of Haverhill, Suffolk, who brought a number of children to the marriage. Three of Rogers's stepchildren also entered the ministry. Samuel Ward became the noted puritan lecturer in Ipswich, Suffolk. John Ward became a noted puritan preacher. Nathaniel Ward was rector of Stondon Massey, Essex, before emigrating in 1634 and becoming one of the leaders of the Massachusetts Bay Colony. In addition to supervising the education of his sons and stepsons, Rogers also assisted his nephew John Rogers, later lecturer of Dedham, in attaining a Cambridge degree.

Rogers died at Wethersfield on 21 April 1618. John Knewstub preached his funeral sermon and the noted Stephen Marshall followed him in the Wethersfield lectureship.

*Further Reading*
Patrick Collinson, *The Elizabethan Puritan Movement* (London, 1967); T. W. Davids, *Annals of Ecclesiastical Nonconformity in the County of Essex* (London, 1863); M. M. Knappen, *Two Elizabethan Puritan Diaries* (Chicago, 1933); Irvonwy Morgan, *The Godly Preachers of the Elizabethan Church* (London, 1965).

*Francis J. Bremer*

## Rogers, Samuel (ca. 1613–ca. 1643)

Puritan clergyman and diarist. Samuel Rogers was not a minister of any importance in the sense of making a great impact on the world, as his active ministry was short and he had too little time to make a reputation as a noteworthy clergyman. He probably died early in 1643 at the age of thirty. He did, however, leave a diary that covers the years from 1634 to 1638 and gives insight into the life of a minor player living through a period of considerable change. He was the son of Daniel Rogers. He studied at Emmanuel College, Cambridge, from 1629 until August 1635, when he became chaplain to Lady Margaret Denny in Bishop's Stortford, Hertfordshire. In December 1637 he took a similar post with Lady Mary Vere in Hackney on the edge of London. His journal gives regular "reviews" of preachers and laity in his accounts of services and spiritual exercises. From Stortford he developed a close relationship with William Sedgwick and his contacts broadened in London. Vere's favorite minister was John Goodwin, and there were visits from luminaries like John Dod. Rogers's diary provided a space for expression of his anger and confusion caused by Laudian sympathizers and particularly by Bishop Matthew Wren. These feelings, and his frustration with those he regarded as reprobate, make comprehensible his virtual dependence on gadding to sermons, fasts, and household exercises with like-minded people. Ac-

cess is also gained to the puritan perspective on the impact of Laudianism on East Anglia and London.

*See also:* Espousal Imagery
*Further Reading*
Tom Webster and Kenneth Shipps, eds., *The Diary of Samuel Rogers, 1634–1638*, Church of England Record Society, vol. 11 (Woodbridge, Eng., 2004).

*Tom Webster*

## Rollock, Robert (ca. 1555–1599)

Scottish Reformed theologian and first principal of Edinburgh University. Rollock was born near Stirling and educated at St. Andrews University under the leading Presbyterian, Andrew Melville. After graduation Rollock became a regent at the university, before moving in 1583 to the new Edinburgh college, established by James VI. He became principal in 1585, was appointed professor of theology in 1587, and remained at the college until his death in 1599. Under his direction, Edinburgh University adopted a curriculum that combined Aristotelianism with Ramism. It became a major center for the training of Reformed preachers, whom Rollock introduced to the Heidelberg Catechism and the writings of leading Continental Reformers John Calvin and Theodore Beza. He was a charismatic teacher, famed for his piety, and he left a deep impression on pupils like Robert Boyd and John Welch. He was moderator of the General Assembly in 1597, but alienated Presbyterians by accepting the ecclesiastical policies of James VI. Rollock was Scotland's leading Reformed theologian in the late sixteenth century and a pioneer of Scottish covenant theology. He gained a considerable reputation as a biblical commentator, and his commentaries on the Pauline epistles were highly praised by Theodore Beza. From 1590 onward, his various works were published by presses in Edinburgh, Geneva, Heidelberg, and Herborn.

*See also:* International Puritanism
*Further Reading*
*Select Works of Robert Rollock*, ed. W. M. Gunn, 2 vols. (Edinburgh, 1826).

*John Coffey*

## Rous, Sir Anthony (1605–1677)

Parliamentary army officer and government official. Rous began his public career as a captain of foot in the parliamentary army in 1644, but was promoted to the rank of colonel in the following year. A Cornishman, he was also a member of that country's governing committee. In 1653 he was named to the Council of State. He served the Protectorate in a variety of capacities, including excise commissioner, admiralty commissioner, a member of the Cornish committee of Ejectors, and the Ejectors' assistant to Major General John Desborough. He was a strong supporter of Oliver Cromwell and was elected to the Protectorate Parliament of 1656.

Following the death of Cromwell, he signed the Truro petition demanding a free parliament. In 1660 the Rump appointed him to be governor of Pendennis Castle, but he was soon removed by General George Monck. Rous was elected to represent Helston, Cornwall, in the Restoration parliament, but his election was ruled void because of suspicions that he was a Presbyterian.

*Further Reading*
*Oxford Dictionary of National Biography* (Oxford, 2004).

*Michael Spurr*

## Rous, Francis (1579–1659)

Lay puritan who had one of the longest political careers on record in Stuart England. Throughout it, he fought for the Calvinist cause and against Arminianism and Roman Catholicism. Born in Cornwall and the son of a close friend of Sir Francis Drake, Rous studied at Broadgates Hall in Oxford (B.A., 1597), Leiden University, and the Middle Temple in London. A deep religious experience led him to leave his legal studies to study theology. First elected to Parliament in 1626, he served in every parliamentary session from then until his death in 1659. On 26 January 1629, his speech in the House of Commons against the rising Arminian faction characterized it as a Trojan horse that would open Protestant England up to defeat by the pa-

*Francis Rous, English Puritan Member of Parliament. (Archive Photos/Getty Images)*

pacy and its Spanish ally. He believed that the result would be the overthrow of political liberty and religious truth as he understood those terms, a conviction very similar to the one that animated Rous's stepbrother and close ally, John Pym.

In the Long Parliament, Rous helped lead the drive against the Laudians. His fellow members of Parliament appointed him provost of Eton College in 1643 and made him one of the lay members of the Westminster Assembly, doubtless in recognition of the knowledge of religious issues that he had displayed in a stream of published works that had begun with his *Meditations of Instruction* in 1616. His *Testis Veritatis* (1626) defended double predestination against the accused supposed Arminian Richard Montagu, and his *Catholick Charity* (1641) defended Protestants against the charge of uncharitableness made by a Catholic polemicist, Sir Toby Mathew. Mathew's short work appeared in 1630, and Rous wrote his long rejoinder soon after, but was prevented from publishing it during the

1630s by the Laudian authorities. During those years, however, the manuscript circulated in puritan circles and was read by Pym and others. In 1645 he coauthored an anonymously published treatise (*The Ancient Bounds*) in favor of tolerating "tender consciences" in the church settlement then being negotiated. Although remarks in Robert Baillie's letters have led scholars to put Rous among the Presbyterians, the argument in this treatise, with its advocacy of the toleration sought by those called the Dissenting Brethren in the Westminster Assembly, shows that he leaned toward Independency instead.

In 1649, an anonymously published tract appeared that argued that the Rump regime was de facto England's government and should be obeyed so long as its commands were lawful. Rous's authorship of this piece, *The Lawfulnes of obeying the Present Government,* soon became known. Rous sat on Cromwell's council of state and accepted appointment as one of Cromwell's Triers. He also served as speaker of the Barebones Parliament and must have been complicit in the plot to end it and return power to Cromwell. Rous's close association with the Lord Protector further supports the notion that he was sympathetic to Independency.

See also: Westminster Assembly
Further Reading
J. Sears McGee. "Francis Rous and 'scabby or itchy children': The Problem of Toleration in 1645," *Huntington Library Quarterly* 67 (2004), 401–422.

*J. Sears McGee*

### Rous, John (1584–1644)
Puritan preacher. Rous studied at Emmanuel College, Cambridge, receiving his B.A. in 1603 and his M.A. in 1607. He was ordained in 1607 and began his ministry in Norfolk. In 1623 he was presented to the living of Santon Downham in Suffolk. Following the death of his father in 1631 he moved to the nearby parish of Brandon, remaining there until his death in 1644.

In 1625 he began to keep a diary in which he recorded items of everyday life, clerical concerns,

his travels, and news of the day, as well as copying into it verses and contemporary writings. It is an important source that offers insight into puritan life and concerns.

Further Reading
Oxford Dictionary of National Biography (Oxford, 2004).

*Michael Spurr*

### Rowlandson, Mary White (ca. 1638–1710)
Author of a narrative describing her captivity at the hands of Native Americans. Mary White was likely born in England shortly before her parents migrated to New England in 1639. The family settled in Lancaster, Massachusetts, and prospered. Around 1656 she married Joseph Rowlandson, who became the minister of Lancaster.

Lancaster was still a frontier community at the time when King Philip's War broke out in 1675. Natives attacked the town in February 1676, and Mary Rowlandson and all three of her children were captured along with other settlers. She was eventually ransomed in May of that year. Two of her children were also released, but her six-year-old daughter died in captivity from wounds suffered in the attack.

Rowlandson's fame arises from *The Sovereignty and Goodness of God*, her account of her captivity, which was published in 1682. It tells of a journey of over a hundred and fifty miles from Lancaster into the northern New England wilderness, the physical and emotional challenges she experienced, and her trust in her God. It was one of the few publications by a seventeenth-century New England woman.

See also: King Philip's War
Further Reading
Michael Robert Breitwieser, *American Puritanism and the Defense of Mourning: Religion, Grief and Ethnology in Mary Rowlandson's Captivity Narrative* (Madison, 1990).

*Francis J. Bremer*

### Rutherford, Samuel (ca. 1600–1661)
Scottish Presbyterian minister, theologian, and political theorist. Rutherford was born around 1600

near Crailing in southeast Scotland. A key early influence was the minister of Crailing, David Calderwood, a Presbyterian polemicist who was deprived of his charge in 1617 for protesting against royal ecclesiastical policies. Rutherford entered Edinburgh University in 1617 and graduated in 1621. During this time, he associated with radical Presbyterians who led protests against the Five Articles of Perth and organized illegal conventicles. In 1623 he was appointed regent of humanity at the university, but was removed from his post in 1626 due to the premarital pregnancy of his future wife, Eupham Hamilton.

In 1627 he became the minister of Anwoth in Galloway. It was here that he gained a reputation as a tireless pastor and activist. He established a network of connections with the gentry of southwest Scotland and orchestrated a Presbyterian campaign against royal ecclesiastical policy. His activities came to the attention of the authorities, and in 1636 he was deprived of his charge and placed under house arrest in the episcopalian stronghold of Aberdeen. Frustrated at his confinement, Rutherford released a torrent of letters to godly women, nobles, lairds, burgesses, and ministers all over Scotland in 1636 and 1637, many of which were copied and circulated among devout Presbyterians. Following the signing of the National Covenant in February 1638, Rutherford became a leading figure among the Covenanter clergy. In October 1639, he was appointed professor of divinity at New College, St. Andrews, a post he held until 1660.

Between November 1643 and November 1647, Rutherford was in London as one of the Scottish commissioners to the Westminster Assembly. In these four years he participated in the assembly's debates over church government and published a number of major works, including *Lex, Rex: or the Law and the Prince* (1644), an erudite and sometimes bitter defense of armed resistance to Charles I. He also published major works against Independency and Erastianism, *The Due Right of Presbyteries* (1644) and *The Divine Right of Church Government and Excommunication* (1646). His calls for the suppression of dissent earned him a place in Milton's sonnet "On the New Forcers of Conscience under the Long Parliament." In *A Free Disputation against Pretended Liberty of Conscience* (1649), Rutherford condemned radical Puritan tolerationists and reasserted the traditional Protestant doctrine of religious coercion.

By the time he prepared to return to Scotland in November 1647, Rutherford was aware that the assembly's achievements were jeopardized by the rising strength of the Independent party backed by the army. A month after his return to Scotland, the moderate Covenanters signed an Engagement with Charles I. Rutherford campaigned vigorously against this alliance. The defeat of the Engagers' army at Preston in August 1648 allowed the radical Presbyterians to establish a militant "kirk party" regime, but also prepared the way for the Independents' revolution in England. After the execution of Charles I in January 1649, the Covenanters proclaimed Charles II king of Great Britain and Ireland.

When Charles visited Scotland in July 1650, he was subjected to a lengthy speech from Rutherford expounding the duty of kings. The Covenanter defeat at Dunbar in September 1650 came as a shattering blow and split the movement into two factions. The moderate Resolutioners wished to forge a new alliance with the Engagers, but Rutherford supported the hard-line Remonstrants, or Protestors, who insisted on further purging of church and state. Throughout the 1650s, the Remonstrant-Resolutioner dispute bitterly divided the Church of Scotland, and Rutherford became alienated from many former friends. He continued to preach and to publish major theological works.

In September 1660, following the restoration of Charles II, copies of *Lex, Rex* were publicly burned, and Rutherford was deprived of his position in the university and his charge in the church, and confined to his own house. He was cited to appear before Parliament on a charge of treason, and his friends feared that he might well face execution. Early in 1661, however, Rutherford fell seriously ill. On 8 March, he issued a last will and testament, and near the end of the month, he died.

Rutherford's posthumous reputation rested on his *Letters*, which were first published in the

Netherlands in 1664 and quickly became a classic of evangelical Protestant piety. They were lavishly praised by Richard Baxter and C. H. Spurgeon and have been republished no fewer than eighty times in various English editions, and at least fifteen times in Dutch.

*Further Reading*
Andrew Bonar, ed., *Letters of Samuel Rutherford* (Edinburgh, 1984); John Coffey, *Politics, Religion and the British Revolutions: The Mind of Samuel Rutherford* (Cambridge, Eng., 1997).

*John Coffey*

# S

## St. John, Oliver (1598–1673)

Lawyer and politician, the grandson of a peer, and the son of a prominent Bedfordshire gentlemen. He was educated at Queens College, Cambridge (where he formed a lifelong friendship with Oliver Cromwell), and at Lincoln's Inn. A sound legal career was transformed by his role as attorney for John Hampden in the latter's challenge to Charles I's "arbitrary" collection of ship money (1637–1638).

Returned to Parliament for the Earl of Bedford's "pocket borough" of Totnes in 1640, he was an outspoken critic of the king's fiscal policies, and a leading figure in the impeachment of the Earl of Strafford. He was made solicitor general in Charles's attempt in May 1641 to reach an accommodation with his critics, and that muted his voice for a while, but there was never any doubt that he would stick with his close colleagues in the godly grouping in both houses of Parliament. He was one of those who had been a conformist puritan to 1640, yearning for the church to be cleansed of the dregs of popery, but he became persuaded that the episcopal office was too discredited to survive. He drafted the bill for the outright abolition of bishops read on 27 May 1641. In general, his religious views were, and remain, cloudy. He was Erastian, godly, and predestinarian, and he came to accept the case for a loose national church with a measure of ease for tender Protestant conscience. But his mind was a lawyer's mind with a dash of pragmatism. He supported the Anglo-Scots alliance, but cooled to the Covenant. He was prominent in the trial and execution of Archbishop William Laud and later prominent in negotiating the Union of England and Scotland and in failing to negotiate a Union of England and the Netherlands. He was made Lord Chief Justice of Common Pleas in 1648 and was willing to serve as a judge during the Commonwealth and Protectorate; but he took no part in the trial of the king, and he resisted attempts by Cromwell to make him a prominent supporter of his regimes by, for example, serving in his new House of Lords. He was pardoned at the Restoration but barred from public office, and he spent his final years building and enjoying a magnificent Dutch-style house near Peterborough.

*Further Reading*
William Palmer, *The Political Career of Oliver St. John* (Newark, DE, 1993).

*John Morrill*

## Saltonstall, Sir Richard (ca. 1586–1661)

American colonist and supporter of the Massachusetts Bay Colony. Saltonstall, the son of a prominent family of clothiers, used his wealth to support the settlement of the Massachusetts Bay Colony. He was knighted on 23 November 1618 and served as justice for the West Riding, 1625–1626. Saltonstall joined the Massachusetts Bay Colony on 4 March 1629 and was elected assistant in 1629 and 1630. Among the services provided by Saltonstall

*Richard Saltonstall, one of the early leaders of the Massachusetts Bay Company. (Massachusetts Historical Society)*

were financial assistance to the company and his fellow colonists, including a 500 pound loan; also, he arranged for provisions to be sent ahead of the settlers. Saltonstall arrived in the colony in 1630 and personally led the settlement of Watertown. Despite a substantial land grant—588 acres—in the new settlement, Saltonstall returned to England in April 1631, where he maintained ties with the colony. He sent a letter to Boston's clergy in 1651, chastising them for the persecution of minority sects, particularly the Baptists. His subsequent colonial ventures in Connecticut failed, resulting in heavy financial losses. Saltonstall opposed royal interests during the civil wars and was awarded the position of commissioner of the high court in 1650. Wanted for sedition following the Restoration, Saltonstall managed to avoid arrest until his death in 1661.

*See also:* Cambridge Agreement
*Further Reading*
Robert Charles Anderson, ed., *The Great Migration Begins: Immigrants to New England 1620–1633,* vol. 3 (Boston, 1995); *Oxford Dictionary of National Biography* (Oxford, 2004).

W. Matthew Rice

### Saltonstall, Richard (1610–1686)

Colonial magistrate. Saltonstall first journeyed to Massachusetts in 1630, where his family helped found Watertown, but went back to England in 1631 to study law. Having returned to the colony in 1635, Saltonstall helped found Ipswich and served as its magistrate. He also played a role in the government of Massachusetts, serving as assistant 1637–1649, 1664, and 1680–1682. In addition to keeping magistrate's court at Ipswich and Newbury, and on the Piscataqua River, Saltonstall was the alternate commissioner of the New England Confederacy in 1644 and substitute agent of the colony in 1660. He was also a member of the military. During the 1640s Saltonstall, along with several other Ipswich men, agitated against Governor John Winthrop. Saltonstall opposed the Life Council, which would have given magistrates life terms in the General Court, as well as Winthrop's potential involvement in Acadia. Saltonstall supported those colonists who decried the stipulation of church membership for voting and holding office; he also protested slavery. Saltonstall returned to England in 1649 and lent his support to Oliver Cromwell, serving as commissioner of the High Court of Justice, 1650. The remainder of Saltonstall's life was divided between Massachusetts and England. During one of his last visits to the colony, he donated 450 pounds to Harvard College. Saltonstall died in Lancaster, England, 1686.

*Further Reading*
*American National Biography* (New York, 1999); Robert Charles Anderson, ed., *The Great Migration Begins: Immigrants to New England, 1620–1633,* vol. 3 (Boston, 1995).

W. Matthew Rice

## Sampson, Thomas (ca. 1517–1589)

Minister and advocate for reform. Little is known for certain about Sampson before his receipt of a B.A. from Cambridge University in 1542. In 1547 he was admitted to the Inns of Court for the study of law. The following year he was licensed to preach, and in 1550 he was ordained, along with his friend John Bradford. His strong belief in the need for more reform of the church was signaled by his refusal at the time of his ordination to wear the prescribed clerical vestments. He received the support of Bishop Nicholas Ridley and was appointed to the rectory of All Hallows, Bread Street, in London.

In 1554, following the accession of Queen Mary, Sampson fled to the continent in the company of Edmund Grindal and Richard Cox. During his exile he traveled from place to place, rather than settling with any one congregation. On his return to England following the succession of Elizabeth, he was considered for a bishopric, but he was too skeptical about the newly emerging settlement to accept such responsibility. He did, in 1561, accept the position of dean of Christ Church, Oxford. Lord Robert Dudley, soon to be Earl of Leicester, helped to secure his appointment. At Christ Church, Sampson oversaw the destruction of images and other remnants of Catholicism in the college and received permission to preach in his doctoral garb rather than the prescribed surplice. Along with his colleague Laurence Humphrey, the president of Magdalen College, he helped to spread puritan views within the university.

By the mid-1560s the refusal of Sampson and Humphrey to wear ecclesiastical vestments became a cause of growing contention between the two men and Archbishop Matthew Parker. In 1565 Sampson was deprived of his living. After a brief incarceration, he was permitted to preach in London (not officiating in the sacraments) without wearing the surplice. He continued to criticize the inadequate reform of the national church, eventually alienating many of his former friends and supporters.

*Further Reading*
Patrick Collinson, *The Elizabethan Puritan Movement* (London, 1967); C. M. Dent, *Protestant Reformers in Elizabethan Oxford* (Oxford, 1983).

*Francis J. Bremer*

## Sanderson, Robert (1587–1663)

Famous casuist and preacher who was, like George Abbot, James Ussher, and others, an episcopalian who remained Calvinist in his soteriology throughout his long career. Urged to modify his position on predestination by various Arminians, Sanderson not only refused but continued to condemn their views in his writings. A Yorkshireman, he earned his academic degrees at Lincoln College, Oxford (B.A., 1605; M.A., 1607; B.D., 1617; D.D., 1636). From 1619 to 1660, he was rector of Boothby Pagnell, Lincolnshire, but he preached frequently at Charles I's court. Although willing to take the etcetera oath in 1640, he urged the king to refrain from pressing it, and he worked on a House of Lords committee in 1643 to forge a religious settlement. Keen to sustain a united Protestant front against Roman Catholicism, he would yield neither to the Arminians on one side nor to those who sought to abolish both episcopacy and the Anglican liturgy on the other. The latter stance was engendered partly by his differences with John Cotton in nearby Boston. In his parish, Sanderson transposed the language of prayer book ceremonies in order to sustain the Anglican liturgy in spirit while altering its wording enough to avoid sequestration. Consecrated bishop of Lincoln in October 1660, he also contributed to important revisions of the Book of Common Prayer of the restored Church of England.

*Further Reading*
Peter Lake, "Serving God and the Times: The Calvinist Conformity of Robert Sanderson," *Journal of British Studies* 27 (1988), 81–116.

*J. Sears McGee*

## Sandes, Henry (1549–1626)

Member of the conference movement in the Stour Valley in the 1580s. Sandes was likely born in Lancashire and studied at St. John's College, Cambridge. At Cambridge he met and formed friendships with John Knewstub, John Still, and Adam Winthrop, among others, and it was there that his commitment to the reform of the English church was probably formalized. In 1578 he was instituted vicar of Preston, Suffolk, presented to the living by Robert Reyce, a kinsman of the Winthrops.

A few years later Winthrop was probably also involved in Sandes's move to Boxford. The Winthrop manor of Groton was in the neighboring Suffolk town of Groton, but Adam Winthrop held property in Boxford and other towns in the region. Sandes was preacher at Boxford for at least forty years and also preached at Groton church. He was also a member of a market-day combination lecture at Boxford that was supported by the Winthrops and other local puritans. Much of his energy was devoted to making this part of the Stour valley a godly community. He was involved in the creation of a Free Grammar School in Boxford and one of its first governors, along with Knewstub, Winthrop, and other prominent clerical and lay leaders in the region. Sandes would also have been involved in the drafting of a social covenant for Boxford in 1596.

Sandes was one of the clergy who responded to John Knewstub's call to gather at Cockfield in May 1582 to discuss how the godly were to spread their message while also responding to new pressures for conformity. The outcome was the creation of a number of separate but linked local clerical conferences. Sandes was an active member of the Dedham conference and appears to have also met regularly with the ongoing conference centered at Cockfield. The minutes of the Dedham conference reveal him to have been a strict Sabbatarian. He promoted the development of better church discipline, but appears to have been willing to cooperate with sympathetic bishops in the creation of a reformed church. The correspondence of John Winthrop shows that Sandes played an important role in the religious life of the Winthrops and had a strong influence on Adam Winthrop's son John, the future governor of Massachusetts.

*Further Reading*
Francis J. Bremer, *John Winthrop: America's Forgotten Founding Father* (Oxford, 2003); Francis J. Bremer, "The Heritage of John Winthrop: Religion along the Stour Valley, 1548–1630," *New England Quarterly* 70 (1997), 515–547; Patrick Collinson, John Craig, and Brett Usher, eds., *Conferences and Combination Lectures in the Elizabethan Church, 1582–1590* (Woodbridge, Eng., 2003).

*Francis J. Bremer*

## Savage, Thomas (1607–1682)

Supporter of Anne Hutchinson during the free grace (antinomian) controversy in New England. He arrived in Boston in April 1635 and was admitted to the church the following month. In 1637, he married William and Anne Hutchinson's daughter Faith and simultaneously helped form Boston's Artillery Company. He was one of six Massachusetts Bay Company members disarmed for supporting Hutchinson, and upon her exile, Savage followed her to Rhode Island. He soon returned, however, and was rapidly reconciled with the Boston authorities. Thereafter, until his 1682 death, Savage was a pillar of the colony. He became Speaker of the Deputies to the General Court in 1659 and a colony assistant from 1680 until his death. He rose to the rank of major in the Artillery Company and helped command Massachusetts forces during King Philip's War. Savage's testimony against the radical minister Richard Wayte in 1640 and his later opposition to Quakers suggests he never fully endorsed the church's radical extremes. In the 1660s, Savage promoted adoption of the Half-Way Covenant and helped found Boston's third church (Old South) in 1669. His early support for Hutchinson may have combined familial loyalty with acute indignation at the Boston leadership's lack of tolerance. The former exile was eulogized by Reverend Samuel Willard in *The Righteous Man's Death: A Presage of evil approaching*, Boston, 1684.

*Further Reading*
Louise Breen, *Transgressing the Bounds: Subversive Enterprises among the Puritan Elite in Massachusetts, 1630–1692* (New York, 2001);

Michael Winship, *Making Heretics: Militant Protestantism and Free Grace in Massachusetts, 1636–1641* (Princeton, 2000).

*Walt Woodward*

## Scottow, Joshua (1618–1698)

Merchant, commentator on New England's history, and controversial frontier magistrate. Resident in Boston by 1634, Joshua Scottow became a prominent merchant who challenged Massachusetts leaders on numerous occasions. In 1669, he left the First Church to protest the selection of a pastor hostile to the Half-Way Covenant and, along with other dissidents, founded the Third Church.

Scottow began purchasing land in Maine in 1660 but did not move to the northern frontier until after 1670. During King Philip's War he commanded the fort at Black Point (Scarborough), his actions and nonactions earning him a reputation for selfishness and cowardice among other frontier dwellers. Although his good name was in tatters locally, he retained the confidence of Massachusetts officials, who named him commander of Fort Loyal in Falmouth (now Portland) during King William's War. On 20 May 1690, after a five-day siege, he surrendered the fort to a combined force of French and Indians. Most of the surviving defenders were slaughtered on the spot, but he and a few others were carried into Canadian captivity, whence he was ransomed the following October by Sir William Phips.

Thereafter he returned to Boston, where he published two tracts, *Old Mens Tears for their own Declensions . . .* (1691) and *A Narrative of the Planting of the Massachusetts Colony anno 1628 . . .* (1694), both of which lamented the course of events in the colony.

*Further Reading*
Mary Beth Norton, *In the Devil's Snare: The Salem Witchcraft Crisis of 1692* (New York, 2002).

*Mary Beth Norton*

## Sedgwick, Obadiah (1600–1658)

Puritan clergyman and preacher to Parliament. Sedgwick was born in the country of Wiltshire. He initially studied at Queen's College, Oxford, but migrated to Magdalen Hall, receiving his B.A. in 1620 and M.A. in 1623. Following his ordination he served as chaplain to Horace, Lord Vere of Tuilbury, who commanded English forces in the Netherlands. While there he corresponded with John Davenport, whom he may have known through Oxford connections.

In 1630, Sedgwick became curate and lecturer of St. Mildred, Bread Street, London. He was a popular preacher and a puritan, and in 1637 he was censured and suspended from his living. The following year he preached to the London Artillery Company, a group that his friend Davenport had also preached to. Sedgwick was befriended by the Earl of Warwick, who presented him to the living of Coggeshall, Essex.

Following the opening of the Long Parliament, Sedgwick returned to London. He preached the first fast-day sermon before Parliament in 1642, and, serving briefly as a chaplain to the regiment of Denzil Holles, he was present at the battle of Edgehill. In 1643 he was named one of the licensers of religious books. He was a member of the Westminster Assembly of Divines. Though a strong supporter of the Scottish alliance and inclined to Presbyterian forms of church organization, he was not rigid in these views. He continued to preach to Parliament and to publish his own works through the 1640s and remained an important force into the 1650s.

*Further Reading*
Richard Greaves and Robert Zaller, eds., *Biographical Dictionary of British Radicals in the Seventeenth Century*, 3 vols. (Brighton, Eng., 1984); John F. Wilson, *Pulpit in Parliament: Puritanism during the English Civil Wars* (Princeton, 1969).

*Francis J. Bremer*

## Sedgwick, Robert (1613–1656)

Military commander and merchant. Sedgwick emigrated to Boston in 1635; he moved to Charlestown in 1637. Sedgwick played a leading role in the economy of Massachusetts. Originally he was an importer and fish dealer, but his later investments were aimed at developing Boston's shipping and industrial potential. He funded the building of ships and wharves, as well as other projects. Sedgwick was elected to the Massachusetts legislature in 1636, 1638–1644, 1648, and 1649. He was also involved in military matters, serving as captain of the Charlestown militia in 1636, commander of the colony's artillery company in 1641, 1645, and 1648, commander of Castle Isle in 1645, and major-general of the colony in 1652.

Sedgwick used his military experience to press England's interests against its colonial rivals. He took part in a failed plot against the Dutch in 1644. In 1653, during the first Anglo-Dutch War, he appealed to Cromwell for permission to campaign against the Dutch; Cromwell gave Sedgwick his blessing and supplied him with several ships and 200 soldiers to aid in the enterprise. The force reached Boston in 1654 but, before action could be taken against the Dutch, it was discovered that hostilities had ended. Sedgwick turned his attention to Acadia, using his troops to capture French forts at Port Royal, St. John, and Pentagoet. In 1655, Cromwell placed Sedgwick in command of twelve ships and several hundred soldiers and sent him to the Caribbean. Sedgwick was instrumental in helping to establish a permanent English colony in Jamaica, where he died in 1656.

*Further Reading*
*Oxford Dictionary of National Biography* (Oxford, 2004).

W. Matthew Rice

## Sewall, Samuel (1652–1730)

New England Puritan, judge, councilor, and merchant. Sewall was born 28 March 1652 at Bishop Stoke, Hampshire, England. "Out of dislike to the English Hierarchy," his grandparents had emigrated to Newbury, Massachusetts, in the 1630s, and his parents, Henry Sewall and Jane Dummer Sewall, were married there in 1646. But the harsh New England climate caused Jane's parents to return to England the following winter, and the

*Samuel Sewall, Massachusetts merchant and magistrate of the late seventeenth century. He served as one of the judges in the Salem witchcraft trials and wrote the first colonial book attacking the practice of enslaving Africans. (Library of Congress)*

young couple accompanied them. Henry made what was to be a visit to New England in 1659 to secure his late father's estate, but the Restoration in England made it prudent for him to remain in the colonies and send for his family, who arrived in 1661.

Reverend Thomas Parker of Newbury prepared Samuel Sewall to enter Harvard College in 1667. He graduated B.A. in 1671 and M.A. in 1674 and was later an overseer. In 1676, he married Hannah, the only living child of John Hull, the wealthy merchant, silversmith, mint master, and treasurer of the Massachusetts Bay Colony, and a founder of the Third (South) Church. Now Sewall put aside any plans for the ministry and began to learn "the manner of the Merchants." He became a member of the South Church in 1677, just before the birth of the first of his fourteen children, of whom only six lived to maturity.

Sewall became a freeman in 1678, and the following year joined the Ancient and Honorable Artillery Company. He managed the Boston printing press from 1681 to 1684. At his father-in-law's death in 1683, Sewall took over his merchant business and property interests and assumed many of his civic and political roles. At the end of 1683, Sewall became a (nonresident) deputy to the General Court from Westfield and was elected to Hull's place as captain of the South Company of Militia, though he resigned the command in 1686 because of an order to put the cross in the colors. Each year from 1684 to 1686, Sewall was elected to the seat Hull left vacant on the Court of Assistants.

In November 1688, Sewell traveled to England to attend to family property interests and matters related to the abrogation of the Massachusetts Bay charter in 1684 and the establishment of the royal government in 1686. Thus he was absent from New England during the revolt against Governor Edmund Andros in the spring of 1689. When Sewall returned, he resumed his place on the Court of Assistants. He was named to the Governor's Council under the new Province Charter of 1691 and re-elected annually until his retirement in 1725. In May of 1692, Sewall was appointed commissioner of oyer and terminer for the Salem witchcraft proceedings. In December of that year, despite the disfavor into which the witchcraft court had fallen, Sewall was made a justice of the Superior Court of Judicature, becoming chief justice in 1718, a position he retained until his resignation in 1728. Alone among the witchcraft judges, Sewall publicly recanted, standing in the South Church on a 14 January 1697 fast day, while Reverend Samuel Willard read on his behalf a bill in which he assumed the "Blame and Shame" for his part in the trials. Sewall was judge of probate for Suffolk County from 1715 to 1728 and held numerous municipal offices.

From 1699 until his death Sewall was a commissioner (and much of the time secretary and treasurer) of the Company for the Propagation of the Gospel in New England. His published writings include an antislavery tract, *The Selling of Joseph, A Memorial* (1700), and other religious works and poetry.

The diary Sewall kept from December 1673 to October 1729 is a rich source of religious, political, and especially social history, and his most enduring legacy. Sewall reveals himself to have been an affectionate and engaged father. He tells of his son Samuel's difficulties as a student and apprentice, and of his troubled marriage to Rebeckah, daughter of Governor Joseph Dudley; of daughter Elizabeth's religious fears; of daughter Hannah's life as an invalid; of son Joseph's rise to the ministry of the South Church; of daughter Mary's death in childbed; and of daughter Judith's marriage to William Cooper, minister of the Brattle Street Church. Though Sewall was deeply religious and constant to Puritan ways (he abhorred periwigs and Christmas-keeping), his diary entries extend well beyond the spiritual, providing a remarkable record of his everyday interactions with notable and ordinary New Englanders. He rode the arduous court circuit until he was seventy-six; watched with the sick and bore the dead to their graves; took into his home several children, including an Indian boy whom he prepared for Harvard; and enjoyed setting the tune for the psalms at the meetinghouse.

Hannah died in 1717. Sewall remarried first Abigail (Melyen) Woodmansey Tilley and second Mary (Shrimpton) Gibbs. He died 1 January 1730 and was buried in Boston's Granary burying ground.

*See also:* Domestic Relations, Law in Puritan New England, Salem Witchcraft, Society for the Propagation of the Gospel in New England
*Further Reading*
Judith S. Graham, *Puritan Family Life: The Diary of Samuel Sewall* (Boston, 2000); David D. Hall, "The Mental World of Samuel Sewall," *Worlds of Wonder, Days of Judgment: Popular Religious Belief in Early New England* (New York, 1989); *Oxford Dictionary of National Biography* (Oxford, 2004); T. B. Strandness, *Samuel Sewall: A Puritan Portrait* (East Lansing, MI, 1967).

*Judith S. Graham*

## Shepard, Thomas (1605–1649)

Puritan minister in England and New England. Son of a Towcester, Northamptonshire, grocer and his wife, Shepard received his early education from teachers who embraced the emerging Puritan program of personal and social godliness, attended Emmanuel College, Cambridge, where he took the B.A. and M.A. degrees, and in 1627 became a minister of the Church of England. In 1624, he committed himself to Christ and the Puritan cause. His autobiographical memoir charts a conversion that largely conformed to Puritan expectations, although perhaps more fraught than many. From its traumas he drew the basic model for his subsequent preaching on judgment and redemption.

Shepard's early ministry was disrupted by episcopal crackdowns on nonconformists and dissidents. Shepard preached three years at Earles Colne, Essex, till silenced by Bishop William Laud; served as chaplain in a pious gentry household in Yorkshire, where he married his first wife, Margaret Touteville; preached for a while in the vicinity of Newcastle; went into hiding; and finally, his English options having run out, sought refuge in the Puritan outpost in New England. After a narrow escape from shipwreck on a first attempt, followed by more months under cover, he sailed for the Massachusetts Bay Colony with Margaret (died 1636) and son Thomas, landing at Boston in October 1635 and settling in Newtown (soon to be renamed Cambridge).

Shepard's preaching bears marks of his bruising conversion, his evangelical Calvinist mind-set, the public strife of his times, and his own stormy experience, along with his direct observations of the generic sinfulness of humanity, above all his own. His English sermons published as *The Sincere Convert* (1641) harp on "the small number of true believers and the great difficulty of saving conversion." His American series in *The Parable of the Ten Virgins* (1660) presents perhaps the most searing analysis of religious hypocrisy in Puritan literature. His private journal—the largest of its kind from his era—reveals the many agonies and few epiphanies of his never-ending yearning for proofs of divine compassion and approval.

Shepard adhered to the minority party of Puritans who espoused so-called congregational principles of church order. The 1636 ceremony that created the Newtown church and installed him as its minister proved exemplary for the "New England Way," as towns spread across eastern Massachusetts and beyond. By deed and word Shepard became one of the Way's strong definers and defenders.

The model's makers envisioned holy communions with active, intimate rapport of pastor and people. They hoped to ensure purity of membership by obliging each candidate for admission to present a persuasive relation of individual experience of saving grace. This requirement became a primary, and problematic, earmark of the new church order. The extensive notes Shepard took on confessions given in his meetinghouse document with unmatched clarity the stress-filled lives of Puritan laypeople who aspired to be, and be acknowledged as, "visible saints." Their cases were often unclear, but Shepard, who was familiar with the ambiguities of spiritual data and ever alert to deceit, but eager to discern sincerity of heart, typically awarded the benefit of the doubt.

He extended no such judgment of charity to Anne Hutchinson and other Dissenters in the antinomian, or free-grace, controversy that racked Massachusetts from 1636 to 1638. Convinced that failure to crush Hutchinson and her errors amounted to treason against God, Shepard became her harshest accuser; his charges sparked the struggle and kept it burning to the bitter end. Also in service to the godly community, he counseled students in training for ministry at Harvard College, which he helped establish; championed the government's military smashing of hostile Indians and supported John Eliot's missionary work; helped provide the theological rationale for the *Cambridge Platform of Church Discipline* (1648); produced influential texts such as *The Sound Believer* (1645) and *Theses Sabbaticae* (1649); and with wives Joanna Hooker and Margaret Boradel raised three of four surviving sons to be New England ministers after him.

*See also:* Conversion Process, Sabbath and Sabbatarianism
*Further Reading*
Michael McGiffert, ed. *God's Plot: Puritan Spirituality in Thomas Shepard's Cambridge,* 2nd

ed. (Amherst, 1994); Thomas Werge, *Thomas Shepard* (Boston, 1987).

*Michael McGiffert*

## Sherfield, Henry (1572–1634)

Lawyer and iconoclast. Sherfield was baptized at Winterbourne Falls, near Salisbury. He is believed to have been educated in small country schools, and there is no evidence that he ever matriculated at Oxford or Cambridge. Despite this, he did study at Lincoln's Inn and was called to the bar in 1606. By that time he was clearly committed to the cause of puritan reform.

As his career developed, Sherfield earned a reputation for being extremely ambitious and even "violent" toward his enemies. He was appointed an attorney of the Court of Wards and Liveries and used that position to enhance his local influence in Salisbury, Southampton, and Winchester. He was chosen to represent Southampton in the parliaments of 1614 and 1621 and was chosen recorder of Southampton in 1618. In 1623 he was also elected recorder of Salisbury, and he represented that town in the parliaments of 1624 and 1629. In Parliament he became recognized as a strong opponent of papists, and he advocated laws that would require Protestant education of Catholic youth.

Sherfield also brought his reforming zeal to bear in his parish of St. Edmunds, Salisbury. In October 1630 he destroyed one of the stained glass windows in the church that Bishop John Davenant had ordered to be protected. He was brought before the Star Chamber for his offense, fined a substantial amount, and ordered to make a public submission to the bishop. His enemies raised questions about his financial accounts in 1633, which threatened to further embarrass him. He died, however, in the following year.

*See also:* Iconoclasm and Iconography
*Further Reading*
*Oxford Dictionary of National Biography* (Oxford, 2004).

*Michael Spurr*

## Sherman, John (1613–1685)

New England magistrate and then clergyman. Sherman first attended St. Catherine's, Cambridge (without taking a degree) and then Trinity College, where he earned his A.B. in 1629 and his A.M. in 1633. One of his teachers at Cambridge was the passionate preacher John Rogers, whom he consulted before making the decision to remove to New England aboard the *Elizabeth* in 1635. First he settled in Watertown, Massachusetts, then removed to Wethersfield, Connecticut, and from there to Milford. He was elected magistrate to the New Haven General Court in 1640. In 1647 he returned to Watertown where he succeeded George Phillips as minister of the church. From 1647 to 1685 he was one of the overseers of Harvard College. He held the significant position of moderator of the Reforming Synod in Cambridge in 1679. Sherman gained renown as an amateur astronomer as well as a compiler of almanacs. His epitaph proclaims him "a man distinguished for his piety, character and truth; a profound theologian; as a preacher a veritable Chrysostom; unsurpassed in his knowledge of the liberal arts, particularly mathematics." One of his descendents, Roger Sherman, was a signer of the Declaration of Independence and was also instrumental at the Constitutional Convention in working with Benjamin Franklin to achieve the "Great Compromise."

*Further Reading*
Samuel Eliot Morison, *The Founding of Harvard College* (Cambridge, MA, 1935).

*Ralph Young*

## Sibbes, Richard (1577–1635)

One of the most influential puritan divines of the seventeenth century. Born in Tostock, Suffolk, Richard Sibbes, the firstborn son of a wheelwright, challenged his father's career aspirations for him and entered St. John's College, Cambridge. After receiving his B.A. and M.A. degrees, in 1608 Sibbes was appointed one of the college fellows. Upon earning his B.D. he also accepted a lectureship at Holy Trinity in Cambridge. Due, however, to

Sibbes's puritan leanings, he was deprived of both positions in 1615. Yet Sibbes had already earned the respect of his peers as a preacher, and he enjoyed the benefit of important friends. Therefore in 1617, with the help of Sir Henry Yelverton, he was chosen to fill an influential preaching spot at Gray's Inn, London, the largest of the four great Inns of Court.

At one point in his life Richard Sibbes held three prominent appointments simultaneously. Not only did he preach at Gray's Inn, but Sibbes was also elected to serve as Master of St. Catherine's Hall, Cambridge, and in 1633 he returned to Holy Trinity at the behest of King Charles, who appointed him "to its perpetual curacy." Despite his personal humility, Richard gained the reputation of celebrated preacher and pastor. Moreover, his connection with important persons in England helped neutralize the level of criticism directed toward him. He was an active member of the Feoffees for Impropriation and one of those who solicited aid for Protestant refugees from the Thirty Years' War.

During his lifetime, Sibbes allowed the publication of only three of his works. Two of the texts are collections of sermons titled, *The Saint's Safety in Evil Times* and *The Bruised Reed and Smoking Flax*. The third publication was a treatise called *The Soul's Conflict with Itself and Victory over Itself by Faith*. Sibbes's work on clarifying how the Holy Spirit functions in a Christian's everyday life proved especially significant. According to Sibbes, godly persons "entertained the Spirit" within their souls. His theology of the Holy Spirit explained the "indwelling" or living presence of the Spirit in the soul, how the soul is "sealed" by the Spirit, how the Holy Spirit grieves within us when we fail in our duty to God, and how the Spirit works to give comfort to the battered soul. Sibbes instructed his listeners that the Spirit must be accepted as an integral part in every facet of Christian life. His views influenced John Cotton, among others. They represented what has been called the mystical strain in puritanism.

Richard Sibbes had a considerable impact on the nature and content of puritan thought and preaching in both England and the New England colonies. He labored tirelessly to make biblical theology accessible and relevant to the godly layperson. Though he never married, throughout his distinguished career Sibbes continued to extend his network of friendships with other godly ministers, teachers, and laypersons. In 1635 he died at Gray's Inn.

*See also:* Feoffees for Impropriations, Human Nature, Soteriology
*Further Reading*
Mark Dever, *Richard Sibbes: Puritanism and Calvinism in Late Elizabethan and Early Stuart England* (Macon, GA, 2000).

*Susan Ortmann*

## Simpson, John (1615–1662)

Fifth Monarchist preacher. Simpson was a native Londoner who studied at Exeter College, Oxford, receiving his B.A. in 1635 and his M.A. in 1638. He emerged in 1642 as one of the leading antinomian preachers in London, clashing with conservative clergy and arguing that Christ was even to be found in common animals such as hogs and dogs. Though sometimes labeled a Baptist, he placed no reliance on any outward forms. In 1643 Parliament ordered him suspended from his London lectureship and banned him from preaching, but he ignored their orders.

As the Civil Wars progressed, Simpson's radical views became more acceptable, but he again became a center of controversy when he preached to Parliament in 1651 and used the occasion to attack the professional clergy and university education. By then he was a close associate of Major-General Thomas Harrison, and he served as a major under Harrison in the campaign against the Scots invasion of 1651 aiming to restore Charles II to the throne.

Simpson believed in the imminence of the millennium, and on December 1651 he joined with Christopher Feake in calling a London meeting that has been seen as the beginning of the Fifth Monarchist movement. Simpson was a strong critic of Oliver Cromwell and the Protectorate regime. Imprisoned for a time and then banned from preaching in London, he violated the order and, called before Cromwell, denounced the Protector to his face. Dismissed with a caution, he nevertheless continued his opposition for a time. He was ejected from his church livings at the Restoration. He defended the regicides in a public sermon in October 1660, then was arrested, but released after swearing the oaths of allegiance and supremacy. He died not long after his release.

See also: Antinomianism
Further Reading
Richard Greaves, *Saints and Rebels* (Macon, GA, 1985); Richard Greaves and Robert Zaller, eds., *Biographical Dictionary of British Radicals in the Seventeenth Century*, 3 vols. (Brighton, Eng., 1984).

*Francis J. Bremer*

## Simpson, Sidrach (ca. 1600–1655)

One of the five Dissenting Brethren (along with Thomas Goodwin, Philip Nye, Jeremiah Burroughes, and William Bridge) responsible for writing the *Apologeticall Narration,* which sparked the debate over church polity that divided the Westminster Assembly in the early 1640s. A popular preacher in London, Simpson fell afoul of William Laud and was convened before the archbishop in 1635. Soon thereafter, chafing at the bands of episcopal discipline, Simpson emigrated to Holland in 1638. He joined an independent church in Rotterdam but soon fell out with its teacher, William Bridge. Simpson then started a new church in Rotterdam. The persistent rivalry between Bridge and Simpson led eventually to their both exiting Holland, much (it would appear) to the relief of the authorities there.

Simpson was back in London by 1641, where his heretofore dangerous positions were now approved of in a world turned upside down, and where he was reunited, at least politically, with Bridge. In 1643 Simpson preached a fiery sermon before Parliament on 26 July, warning them against moderation in matters of the spirit: "If you would have a thorough Reformation . . . first, take heed of Policy . . . Policy doth with Religion as Ammon did with Tamar, when it has its will of it, it thrusts it out-of-doors." He was also made a member of the Westminster Assembly in 1643, the year that saw the publication of the *Apologeticall Narration.*

The *Narration* eschewed the Presbyterian government urged by the Scots but also disdained the charge of separatism, with which the narrators claimed to have been "falsely charged." It may thus be read more as a statement advocating toleration of "tender consciences" than as an apologia for Independency, although the narrators' advocacy of a polity they preferred to label "congregational" certainly left them open to the label. By 1645 Simpson and his fellow Dissenting Brethren had formed a subcommittee of the assembly charged with producing their own statement on church polity. Their model provided for forms of church discipline, order, ordination, and excommunication, which allied them in many ways with mainstream Presbyterians in the assembly. In matters of church government, however, their emphasis on the authority of the individual congregation allied them with the sectarians and their voluntary meetings.

Simpson had been admitted to Emmanuel College, Cambridge, in 1616; his degree status is uncertain. In 1650, he was appointed master of Pembroke Hall, Cambridge, and obtained livings in London: first at St. Mary Abchurch, where he set up a congregational polity, and, later, at St. Bartholomew, Exchange, in 1653. He was briefly imprisoned for preaching against the Lord Protector. He died in 1655, and was buried in the last of the several churches he served, St. Bartholomew's. Besides his wife, Simpson left at his death an impressive estate, a son who went on to become a zealous high churchman of some renown in the Restoration, two printed fast sermons, and several other polemical and religious tracts, some of which he wrote with his fellow dissenting apologists in the 1640s. Works under his sole authorship include the following: *The Anatomist Anatomiz'd* (1644), *The Judgment of the Reformed Churches* (1647), *A Plain and Necessary Confutation of Antichristian Errors* (1654). Several other of his works were published posthumously.

See also: *An Apologeticall Narration,* Congregationalism, Dissenting Brethren, English Puritanism in the Netherlands, Independency

*Further Reading*
John Spurr, *English Puritanism, 1603–1689* (Basingstoke, Eng., 1998).

*Lori Anne Ferrell*

## Skelton, Samuel (1593–1634)

New England clergyman. Skelton was born in Lincolnshire, England, in 1593 and received his B.A. (1611) and M.A. (1615) from Clare Hall, Cambridge. Following his ordination he was named rector of Sempringham, and probably also served as a chaplain to the Earl of Lincoln. He was one of the first ministers sent to New England by the Massachusetts Bay Company in 1629. Together with Francis Higginson, he helped organize the Salem church in July 1629, and he was chosen pastor of that congregation. Some of the settlers, particularly John and Samuel Browne, complained about Skelton's preaching and the practices of the Salem congregation, but the minister was supported by his colleague and by the local governor, John Endecott. As Massachusetts grew, in 1633 Skelton expressed some concern about the possibility that clerical conferences as they were evolving might threaten congregational autonomy. He died in August 1634.

*Further Reading*
Francis J. Bremer, *Shaping New Englands: Puritan Clergymen in Seventeenth Century England and New England* (Boston, 1994).

*Francis J. Bremer*

## Smyth, John (d. 1612)

Separatist leader. Smyth was the minister of a Separatist congregation at Gainsborough, England, that, together with the Scrooby congregation led by Richard Clifton and John Robinson, fled in 1608 to Amsterdam, where Smyth rebaptized himself and some followers, constituting what they considered the only pure congregation on earth. Smyth had studied under Francis Johnson at Christ's College, Cambridge (1586–1598; M.A., 1593; fellow, ordained 1594), before his appointment as city preacher in Lincoln (1600). Dismissed for offending upright citizens in 1602, he moved to Gainsborough and preached without a license (1604, 1606). Following his arrival in Amsterdam, Smyth engaged in acrimonious written debates with Clifton; Smyth pronounced all defenders of infant baptism heretical. Union with Smyth thus out of the question, Robinson led the Scrooby group to Leiden (1609). Smyth then decided that through their practice of adult baptism Amsterdam's Waterlander Mennonites were a true church. "A Short Confession" (1610) epitomized Smyth's mature, non-Puritan theology and included Mennonite views on free will, the Incarnation, and the magistracy (which was forbidden to true believers). Smyth and most of his followers signed it and were eventually accepted as Mennonites, first as an allied congregation, then as joiners whose adult baptism was valid. Some of Smyth's congregation, however, refused this particular "further light" and accused their former friends of apostasy. Led by Thomas Helwys, they returned to England and founded a congregation seen as the origin of the General Baptist movement.

*See also:* English Puritanism in the Netherlands

*Further Reading*
W. H. Whitley, editor, *The Works of John Smyth*, 2 vols. (Cambridge, Eng., 1915).

*Jeremy Bangs*

## Snape, Edmund (1576–1608)

One of the members of the Northamptonshire classis and a friend to such godly luminaries as Thomas Cartwright and Henry Travers, Snape is the subject of several vitriolic asides (most of these marginal) in Richard Bancroft's *Dangerous Positions* (1593). In Bancroft's anti-puritan and anti-Scottish work, Snape is identified as a minister who "most friendly entertained" presbyterial discipline, who "charg[ed] the present government with persecution" in a 1590 letter to his father, and who carried on a seditious correspondence with Travers in London.

Snape took deacon's orders in 1575 but refused to serve the Church of England unless a congregation directly called him. Fortuitously, the church of St. Peters, Northamptonshire, did call him in the year of his diaconal ordination. In 1576, Snape traveled with Thomas Cartwright to the Channel Islands to assist Huguenot ministers in devising a form of church discipline. After sojourns in Jersey and Exeter, Snape went to Oxford, where he received the B.A. from St. Edmund Hall in 1581, and the M.A. from Merton three years later. Snape then returned to the parish of St. Peters, where he remained until his death.

*Further Reading*
Richard Bancroft, *Daungerous positions and proceedings, published and practiced within this iland of Brytaine* (1593).

*Lori Anne Ferrell*

## Some, Robert (1542–1609)

Chaplain to the Earl of Leicester and participant in the Martin Marprelate controversy. Whether he "became respectable with age and increasing responsibility," as one biographer claims, or whether (as seems more likely) his moderate ecclesiological positions simply balanced out his more unyielding theological opinions, Some's career as a controversialist typifies the complex, seemingly paradoxical doctrinal and ecclesiological milieu of late sixteenth-century conforming Calvinism, or "moderate Puritanism."

Some's theological opinions, advertised extensively in his polemical treatises and sermons, were resolutely cast from the mold set by Calvin. He aligned himself with the Cambridge party opposing Peter Baro's espousal of the doctrine that the elect to reprobation are damned as much for their sins as in response to eternal decree. Some also publicly opposed the doctrines espoused by John Overall, who was a protégé of Baro's and an anti-Calvinist in the mode of Lancelot Andrewes.

But Some's stringent Calvinism must be weighed in the balance with his fierce advocacy of ecclesiastical conformity in the Marprelate affair, in which his first contribution, *A Godly Treatise containing and deciding certain questions moved of late in London and other places, touching the ministry, sacraments, and church* (1588), defended such positions as "The godly are not polluted which receive the Sacrament at the hands of an unpreaching minister" and "A Godly Prince may and ought to compel his Subjects (if any refuse) to the external service of God." *A Godly Treatise* so provoked John Penry that Penry chose to answer it in a stinging tract entitled *M. Some laid open in his coulers* (also 1588), which denounced Some as the "snappishest gentleman who ever penned a distempered discourse." Not one to let snappish controversy rest once it had been aroused, Some answered Penry's tract later that same year.

Some matriculated at St. John's College, Cambridge, where he took the B.A. (1561–1562), M.A. (1565), B.D. (1572), and D.D. (1580). His academic career compassed the range of opportunities offered by the colleges of Cambridge: he served Queen's College as bursar and vice president in the late 1560s and early 1570s, and he was made master of Peterhouse in 1589. He was vice-chancellor of the university in 1590, 1599, and 1608. He was also rector of the church in Girton (a town near Cambridge). Some wrote several treatises in addition to his anti-Marprelate tracts of 1588, among them works on the sacraments and the Lord's Prayer, and against the Anabaptists Barrow and Greenwood. His membership in the more evangelical wing of the Elizabethan church is attested to by the nineteenth-century reprinting of his treatise on the church (bound with James Pilkington's *Exposition on Nehemiah* in 1585) by the Parker Society.

*Further Reading*
Patrick Collinson, *The Elizabethan Puritan Movement* (London, 1967).

*Lori Anne Ferrell*

## Sparrowhawke, Edward (d. 1678)

A minor minister whose unwillingness to play his cards close to his chest brought him briefly into the spotlight. He seems to have come from the Stour valley and was educated at Emmanuel College, Cambridge. It appears that he returned to his roots, holding a curacy in the Suffolk part of the Stour valley after he graduated M.A. in 1625. He was suspended from this post and then appears as curate and lecturer at St. Mary Woolchurch, London, in the early 1630s. In 1635 he was disciplined for preaching against bowing at the name of Jesus. He withdrew to Coggeshall, Essex, where he had family. In 1637 he was reported to have been holding conventicles. In March of that year he responded to visitation sermons promoting the altar policy in very strong terms, delivering a jeremiad that enumerated the judgments upon the land: bad harvests, the plague, recession, and high taxation. All these were caused, he claimed, by "our Altars and such superstitious adoration, bowing at names and such new idolatrous mixtures of religion, and the treading down of Gods people," comparing Charles I to Manasseh, the king of Judah who erected altars to strange gods and consorted with witches and wizards. His whereabouts are unknown until 1643, when he was given the rectory of Black Notley, Essex, a post he held until his ejection after the Restoration. He moved to the north of the county, near Colchester and stayed at Boreham until his death in 1678.

*Further Reading*
T. W. Davids, *Annals of Evangelical Nonconformity in Essex* (London, 1863); Tom Webster, *Godly Clergy in Early Stuart England: The Caroline Puritan Movement, c. 1620–1643* (Cambridge, Eng., 1997).

*Tom Webster*

## Spurstowe, William (ca. 1605–1666)

Presbyterian minister. Spurstowe was born in London and educated at Emmanuel College, Cambridge, receiving his B.A. in 1623, M.A. in 1630, and D.D. in 1649. He was connected to John Hampden and was chaplain to Hampden's regiment in the early stages of the English Civil War. He joined with Stephen Marshall, Edmund Calamy, and others as one of the authors of the Smectymnuus tracts and a member of the Westminster Assembly of Divines.

Spurstowe was a leader of English Presbyterians. He was one of those who negotiated with Charles I in 1648, and he strongly opposed the trial and execution of the king. Following the Restoration, he became one of the chaplains in ordinary to Charles II and labored to bring about an inclusion of Presbyterians in the restored national church. When this effort failed, he resigned his church living and went into retirement.

*See also:* Smectymnuus
*Further Reading*
G. R. Abernathy, *The English Presbyterians and the Stuart Restoration, 1648–1663* (Philadelphia, 1965); Tai Liu, *Discord in London: The Puritan Divines and the Puritan Revolution, 1640–1660* (Newark, DE, 1973).

*Francis J. Bremer*

## Sternhold, Thomas (d. 1549)

Instigator of the collection of versified psalms later to become the Sternhold and Hopkins "Old Version." His early life is unclear. Evidence survives connecting him both with Hampshire and with Awre in Gloucestershire. It is thought he attended Christ Church, Oxford, but did not take a degree. Sometime in or before 1538 he joined the household of Henry VIII, as one of the grooms of the robes. It is probable that he represented Plymouth in the parliament that met in January 1545. In parallel to the work of the French court poet Clement Marot, who published a similar collection in 1540, Sternhold rendered some forty of the psalms into the simple "common meter" ballad form. The first edition of the collection, containing some nineteen psalms, was the *Certayne Psalmes*, printed in Cambridge, which can roughly be dated as from after 1547 by its dedication to Edward VI. A second edition of 1549 contained eighteen more, and the full forty appeared in 1562. Sternhold died on 23 August 1549.

The motivation for Sternhold to embark on this project is unclear. It is certain that such "holy songs" were in vogue at the court under the influence of Catherine Parr, who herself wrote devotional literature. However, the suggestion that Sternhold was driven by a desire to see all secular songs replaced by the psalms is one that cannot be substantiated, deriving only from a preface to an edition appearing after his death. To class Sternhold as a "puritan" before the term existed would therefore be a mistake. The holy songs were to be delighted in, alongside other, secular, music.

See also: Psalms
Further Reading
Rivkah Zim, *English Metrical Psalms: Poetry as Praise and Prayer, 1535–1601* (Cambridge, Eng., 1987).

Peter Webster

## Sterry, Peter (1613–1672)

English Puritan mystic. Sterry was born in Southwark and entered Emmanuel College, Cambridge, in 1630, receiving the B.A. in 1634 and the M.A. in 1637, having become a fellow in 1636. In 1639 he became a chaplain to Robert Greville, Lord Brooke, later a general in the parliamentary army. In 1643 Sterry was named to the Westminster Assembly, where he was associated with those Independents known as the Dissenting Brethren. By 1645 he was preaching sermons with millennial themes to the House of Commons. In 1649 he was named a chaplain to the Council of State, and later he was a chaplain to Oliver Cromwell, whom he strongly supported and whom he advised and served in matters of religious policy. After Cromwell's death, he became chaplain to Philip Sidney, Viscount Lisle. Sterry was suspected of disloyalty to the restored monarchy, but found safety at the West Sheen estate of Viscount Lisle, in Richmond, south of London, where there gathered a devout circle dubbed by Sterry the "lovely society."

Apart from sermons, Sterry's writings were published posthumously. Notable was his *Discourse of the Freedom of the Will* (1675). Sterry advocated religious toleration and was a Platonist with strong ties to the Cambridge Platonists, especially Benjamin Whichcote. He was also a mystic who was familiar with the writings of the early seventeenth-century German mystic Jakob Böhme (in English, Jacob Boehme), reveled in the beauty of nature, and employed erotic imagery drawn from the biblical Song of Solomon to describe the soul's union with God. Unpublished manuscripts by Sterry confirm his universalist conviction that God's predestinating love would bring all persons to salvation. His theological and spiritual writings, which are characterized by literary grace and poetic invention, are suffused with a Calvinist emphasis upon divine grace.

See also: Espousal Imagery, Grace
Further Reading
Vivian de Sola Pinto, *Peter Sterry: Platonist and Puritan* (Cambridge, Eng., 1934).

Dewey D. Wallace Jr.

## Still, John (ca. 1544–1608)

Bishop. Little is known of Still prior to his matriculation at Christ's College, Cambridge, at the start of the Elizabethan reign in 1559. He received his B.A. in 1562, his M.A. in 1565, and his B.D. in 1570. Early on he earned a reputation as a powerful preacher. He attracted the attention of Matthew Parker, the archbishop of Canterbury, who presented Still to a number of church positions, including rector of Hadleigh (1571), dean of Bocking (1572), and archdeacon of Sudbury (1577). He also advanced at Cambridge. In 1570 he was appointed to succeed Thomas Cartwright as Lady Margaret Professor of Divinity. In 1574 he was elected master of St. John's College, and in 1577 he moved to the mastership of Trinity College.

He was sympathetic to those who sought further reform of the church and had argued that leniency be extended to Thomas Cartwright when that divine was challenged for his Presbyterian views. Still made a number of friends at Cambridge who later became leading figures in East Anglian Puritanism, among them John Knewstub, Henry Sandes, and the layman Adam Winthrop. In fact, he became very close to the Winthrops. Adam Winthrop married Still's sister Alice. Though she died soon thereafter, the two men remained close. Still arranged for Winthrop to hold offices at St. John's and Trinity college. Winthrop's brother William stood surety for the first fruits paid by Still's brother George. And John Still likely stood as godfather to Adam Winthrop's son John, the future governor of Massachusetts.

As archdeacon of Sudbury, Still supported the efforts of lay and clerical puritans to create a godly kingdom along the Stour River, while nevertheless opposing those nonconformists who separated from the church. In 1593 he was chosen to be Bishop of Bath and Wells. There too he sought to curb nonconformity, while protecting godly clergy who were largely conformable from being deprived of their livings. He died in 1608.

*Further Reading*
Francis J. Bremer, *John Winthrop: America's Forgotten Founding Father* (New York, 2003); Patrick Collinson, *The Elizabethan Puritan Movement* (London, 1967); P. M. Hembry, *The Bishops of Bath and Wells, 1540–1640* (London, 1967).

*Francis J. Bremer*

## Stock, Richard (1569–1626)

Noted London preacher. Stock was born in York and educated at St. John's, Cambridge, where he studied under the master of the college, William Whitaker, and received his B.A. in 1590 and his M.A. in 1594. He was incorporated M.A. at Oxford in 1595 and elected fellow at Sidney Sussex, Cambridge, in 1596, but did not serve, becoming chaplain to Sir Anthony Cope of Hanbury, Oxfordshire, to Lady Lane of Burton-on-the-water, Gloucestershire, and rector of Standlake, Oxfordshire. He was in London lecturing at St. Augustine's by 1603, when he preached a Paul's Cross sermon against local taxes that burdened the "meaner sort." He was briefly curate at St. Mildred's Bread Street, and in 1604 he became curate and lecturer at Allhallows Bread Street, where he succeeded the rector, Thomas Edmunds, in 1611, and where he remained as rector and lecturer until his death in 1626.

Stock was remembered in several merchants' wills, along with the prominent puritan ministers William Gouge, Stephen Egerton, and Ezekiel Culverwell. He saw Whitaker's *An answere to the Ten reasons of Edmund Campian* through the press in 1606; his Paul's Cross sermon against the papists was published in 1609; *The doctrine and use of repentance* in 1610; a funeral sermon, *The churches lamentation for the losse of the godly* in 1614, and *A learned and very usefull commentary upon the whole prophesie of Malachy* in 1641. The Anglican Thomas Fuller claimed that Stock's preaching was approved by all that were judicious and religious.

*See also:* Feoffees for Impropriations
*Further Reading*
Paul Seaver, *The Puritan Lectureships* (Stanford, 1970).

*Paul Seaver*

## Stoddard, Solomon (1643–1729)

Controversial Northampton, Massachusetts, revivalist; grandfather and mentor of Jonathan Edwards. The Reverend Solomon Stoddard, whose ministry in the frontier village of Northampton, Massachusetts, endured fifty-six years, was one of the most dominant and controversial figures in the late Puritan movement. Born on 4 October 1643 and dying on 11 February 1729, Stoddard's career spanned a time of crucial significance in the history of New England Puritanism. As an undergraduate at Harvard, Stoddard was influenced by the debates that resulted in the adoption of the Half-Way Covenant in 1662, the year of his graduation. While working on a master's degree over the next three years, he studied the theology of many Presbyterian divines. Once hired as pastor in Northampton in 1672, Stoddard wasted no time implementing his Presbyterian views.

Stoddard first made his views public in 1687, in *The Safety of Appearing,* and clarified his views further in his *Doctrine of Instituted Churches* of 1700. In the latter work, Stoddard justified the Half-Way Covenant and went beyond its precepts, arguing that baptism should be even more freely offered and that all churchgoers should enjoy the benefits of the sacraments, including the Lord's Supper. The Northampton clergyman rationalized that since the human eye could not ultimately discern a saint from a sinner, "visible" sainthood was a human device not founded in scripture. Therefore, full church membership should be extended to all desiring applicants, and church covenants should no longer be utilized. He also believed that all members were entitled to the Lord's Supper as a possible part of God's elite, arguing the ordinance was not a seal of sainthood, but simply a springboard to eventual conversion, or a "converting ordinance."

Within five years of his ordination as pastor at Northampton, the young minister thus admitted all but openly scandalous Christians to full church membership and participation in all sacraments. These practices threatened to shake the foundations of the "New England Way," as it ignored the previous requirement of a regenerative experience and a direct ancestral bloodline to a covenanted member. Additionally, by allowing this new breed of church member to fully partake of the Lord's Supper, Stoddard challenged the colony's founders, who considered participation in the sacred ordinance to be a seal of one's sainthood. This unique doctrine earned him an enormous amount of support in the upper Connecticut River Valley, but put him at odds with most of the Congregational clergymen of Massachusetts Bay. Increase and Cotton Mather began a pamphlet- and book-writing campaign against him, accusing the inland minister of innovations against the founders of the colony. The public feud between the Mathers and Stoddard only seemed to add to his reputation as a powerful and outspoken critic of the "New England Way." He became so influential and prominent in the valley and on the coast, that friends and foes alike dubbed him "Pope Stoddard."

Stoddard was also distinguished as an early revivalist. His emotional sermons depicting the punishments of hell enabled him to bring people into the church in great numbers. During his ministry, in fact, he was able to invoke at least five distinct "harvests," in which numerous people converted in a short amount of time. Stoddard's 1714 work, *A Guide to Christ,* even offered suggestions to other ministers on how they could lead a person to conversion through emotional preaching. This book became widely read and influential throughout New England during the religious revivals of the Great Awakening.

In addition to his significance as an innovator and revivalist, Stoddard was also well known as the grandfather of the famed Great Awakening preacher, Jonathan Edwards. As a mentor and predecessor of Edwards in Northampton, Stoddard left his grandson a pulpit that was to become enormously significant during the Great Awakening. Although Edwards ultimately sided with the Mathers in terms of church admittance requirements and the sacraments, the style of evangelical preaching and revivalism for which he was known emulated his grandfather.

*See also:* Reforming Synod of 1679
*Further Reading*
Paul Lucas, *Valley of Discord: Church and Society along the Connecticut River* (Hanover, NH, 1976); Perry Miller, *The New England Mind: From Colony to Province* (New York, 1954); Patricia J. Tracy, *Jonathan Edwards, Pastor: Religion and Society in Eighteenth-Century Northampton* (New York, 1979).

*Aaron Christensen*

## Stone, Samuel (1603–1663)

"Teacher" from 1635 to 1663 of the first Puritan church established in Hartford, Connecticut; ably defended the development of a "congregational way"; famously described the ideal Congregational church as "a speaking aristocracy in the face of a silent democracy." Stone, born in Hertford, probably joined the Puritan movement after entering Emmanuel College, Cambridge, in 1620, and in 1630 was appointed to a Puritan lectureship at Towcester in Northamptonshire. In 1633, he was invited to accompany Thomas Hooker, who was about to lead a migration to New England. In 1635, he preceded Hooker to Connecticut, and named Hartford, Connecticut, after his birthplace in England.

Stone left many of his sermons in manuscript form, but his most important work, *A Congregational Church is a Catholike Visible Church . . . ,* was published in London in 1652. In reply to attacks by English Presbyterians that a system of independent churches was philosophically illogical, Stone argued that the universal, catholic church was a "genus," a sort of essence, or "quiddity," of which individual churches, like the one in Hartford, were a "species." Christ, he concluded, had founded a congregational system, and not a "catho-like, integral, political church," the sort of system that Presbyterians wanted Parliament to establish. His performance earned him the title of "Doctor Irrefragabilis" from Cotton Mather.

Stone believed that all residents within a parish, if not morally scandalous, were obliged to attend the Lord's Supper, and to have their children baptized. Church members were therefore a "democracy," but because they were not necessarily regenerate, they were obliged to quietly acquiesce in the rule of the godly men who held office in the church, the "aristocracy." Stone knew his definition did not describe reality. In 1653, he and his congregation fell into a long, bitter dispute that finally ripped the church asunder. By then, if not before, Stone must have realized that democracies are never silent.

*Further Reading*
*American National Biography* (New York, 1999); Paul Lucas, *Valley of Discord: Church and Society along the Connecticut River, 1636–1725* (Hanover, NH, 1976).

*James P. Walsh*

*William Stoughton presided over the Salem witchcraft trials. (Library of Congress)*

## Stoughton, William (1630–1701)

Chief judge of the Salem witchcraft trials in 1692–1693. Born in Rotherhithe, Surrey, Stoughton came to Dorchester, Massachusetts, with his parents in 1632. As a member of the Harvard College class of 1650, he trained for the ministry, thereafter going to England to preach and to study at Oxford (where he received an M.A.). In 1662 he returned to Massachusetts, where he speculated in land and assumed various public responsibilities. First appointed a county judge in 1674, he performed judicial duties periodically thereafter and occasionally represented Massachusetts as an envoy, both in other colonies and in England.

Following the abrogation of the original Massachusetts charter in 1684, Stoughton served first in the interim government of his friend Joseph Dudley and, after November 1686, as a councilor in the Dominion of New England under Sir Edmund Andros. Although he urged Andros to surrender peacefully on 18 April 1689, during the Massachusetts phase of the Glorious Revolution, Stoughton did not actively participate in the Dominion's overthrow. After an office-holding hiatus, he was appointed lieutenant governor under the charter of 1691.

The new governor, Sir William Phips, arriving in May 1692 to find more than thirty people in jail awaiting trial for witchcraft, immediately established a nine-member Court of Oyer and Terminer with William Stoughton as chief judge. Although no formal records survive from the trials and thus details of the proceedings are largely lost, contemporary critics observed that Stoughton pursued the accused witches with particular zeal. It was he, for example, who directed the jury that initially acquitted Rebecca Nurse to reconsider its verdict (subsequently altered to "guilty").

Respected for both his judicial experience and his theological training, Stoughton seems to have dominated events in the Salem courtroom. He adamantly insisted that God would never permit the devil (ultimately under divine control) to create an afflicting specter in the shape of an innocent person. Accordingly, the testimony of victims that they had been assaulted by certain people in spectral form became a major determinant of guilt—at least until critics began to argue in late summer that Stoughton's reasoning was flawed and that Satan, the quintessential liar and trickster, could deceive humans' perceptions. In late October the critical clamor over spectral evidence grew so loud that Governor Phips dissolved the court. When in January 1693 trials resumed in regular courts and without reliance on spectral evidence, Stoughton continued as chief judge, although he angrily abandoned that post briefly upon learning that Phips had reprieved the remaining people who had been convicted but not yet executed.

When Phips was recalled to England in 1694, Stoughton as lieutenant governor assumed the leadership of the colony, a role in which he continued until his death in 1701 with only a brief respite in 1699–1700. William Stoughton never married.

*See also:* Salem Witchcraft
*Further Reading*
Peter Hoffer, *The Salem Witchcraft Trials* (Lawrence, KS, 1997); Mary Beth Norton, *In the Devil's Snare: The Salem Witchcraft Crisis of 1692* (New York, 2002).

*Mary Beth Norton*

## Strong, William (d. 1654)

Congregationalist minister. Strong was probably from Dorset, though we know little of his youth. He graduated with his B.A. in 1631 from St. Catharine's College, Cambridge, and was elected a fellow in February 1631. He took his M.A. in 1634. In July 1634 he was suspended as a fellow and stripped of his degrees for denying episcopacy.

Strong was appointed as rector of Moor Crichel, Dorset, in 1640, but with the coming of civil war in 1643 he fled to London. There he was appointed lecturer at St. Dunstan-in-the-West, Fleet Street in 1644. Strong replaced the Presbyterian Andrew

Perne as minister of the parish on 14 October 1647. Strong was one of the favored ministers of the successive Parliamentarian regimes. In 1645 he was appointed as a preacher at the morning exercises at Westminster Abbey and in 1646 replaced Edward Peale as a member of the Westminster Assembly.

In the debate between Presbyterians and Independents on the issue of church government, Strong was initially a moderate or parochial Independent. In August 1648 he was appointed a trier of ministers for the Presbyterian twelfth London classis and joined in instituting the Presbyterian eldership at St. Dunstan's. However, by late 1650 Strong was in controversy with his parish concerning the imposition of Congregationalist principles on the parish and left to gather a congregation at Westminster Abbey.

Highly regarded by Oliver Cromwell throughout the Commonwealth period, he was appointed in 1654 as one of the Cromwellian Triers to test candidates for the ministry; he was probably active in this role when he died in June 1654. Although he was afforded the honor of burial in Westminster Abbey by the Cromwellian regime, his remains were exhumed in 1661 and thrown into a pit in the churchyard of St. Margaret's, Westminster.

*Further Reading*
*Oxford Dictionary of National Biography* (Oxford, 2004).

*Elliot Vernon*

## Stubbs, John (ca. 1541–1590)

Religious writer. Stubbs was a native of Norfolk and graduate of Trinity College, Cambridge (B.A. 1561), but his formative experiences were at Lincoln's Inn, which he entered in 1562. There he associated with a group of zealous Protestant reformers who were dissatisfied with the reforms of the Elizabethan church. He was admitted to the bar in 1572. During the 1570s he may have been involved in published criticisms of the inadequacies of the church.

In 1579 Stubbs published *The Discovery of a Gaping Gulf*, which was a criticism of a proposed marriage between Queen Elizabeth and the Duke of Anjou. He objected because the duke was a Catholic and such a union would be in violation of God's will and law. Implicitly he was calling into question the queen's dedication to Protestantism. Elizabeth was furious at this unsolicited advice and initially wished to have Stubbs and some of the men who had distributed his tract hung. After an initial felony prosecution had failed, Stubbs was retried for sedition in the court of Queen's Bench. He was convicted and sentenced to have his right hand cut off and to be imprisoned. He remained in the Tower of London until 1581.

Stubbs insisted during his punishment on his loyalty to the queen. Indeed, after his right hand was cut off, he is supposed to have taken off his hat with his left hand and cried out "God save the Queen." In 1589 he was elected member of Parliament for Great Yarmouth, in Norfolk. He drew up a petition against the use of the ex officio oath (which forced individuals to incriminate themselves) against puritan ministers and continued to urge further reform of the church. He accompanied an English force to France in 1590, where he died.

*Further Reading*
Patrick Collinson, *The Elizabethan Puritan Movement* (London, 1967); Wallace MacCaffrey, *Queen Elizabeth and the Making of Policy, 1572–1588* (Princeton, 1981).

*Francis J. Bremer*

# T

## Taylor, Edward (ca. 1642–1729)

Westfield minister and among the foremost of American poets before 1800. Born in Sketchley, Leicestershire, England, of yeoman farmer background, Taylor's refusal to subscribe to the 1662 Act of Uniformity eventually led to his migration to New England in 1668, where he matriculated at Harvard as an upperclassman. After graduation, in 1671 he accepted an invitation to pastor at Westfield, a frontier community, although he did not formally gather the church until 1679. Taylor married Elizabeth Fitch in 1674; three of their eight children survived infancy. About 1692 he married Ruthy Wyllis, with whom he had six children. His fifty years of ministry at Westfield was marked by three conflicts: (1) in the 1680s and 1690s, a disagreement with neighboring minister Solomon Stoddard over membership and communion; (2) in 1713–1715, a disciplinary issue in his congregation, in the course of which he withheld communion; and (3) his dissatisfaction with the location of a new meetinghouse erected in 1721–1722.

With the exception of a funeral elegy for a Westfield deacon and verses printed by Cotton Mather, none of Taylor's voluminous writings were printed until the 1930s; they include a gospel harmony (as works were called that showed how the various Gospels were in harmony with each other), sermons collected in *Christographia* and *Upon the Types of the Old Testament;* a *Treatise Concerning the Lord's Supper;* and a large number of poems. Chiefly he is remembered for a manuscript titled *Poetical Works,* which includes a verse drama *Gods Determinations,* a group of *Occasional Meditations,* and especially the *Preparatory Meditations,* composed over a forty-three-year period. Taylor's verse is chiefly in the metaphysical vein, given to elaborate yet homely imagistic conceits and rough metrics, but within an orthodox Calvinistic view.

*Further Reading*
*American National Biography* (New York, 1999).

*Michael G. Ditmore*

## Taylor, Thomas (1576–1632)

Puritan clergyman. Taylor was born in 1576 at Richmond, Yorkshire, and made an impression as a rising star at Christ's College, Cambridge. He became a fellow and the Wentworth Hebrew lecturer from 1599 to 1604. He also became an important part of the spiritual brotherhood within the university, becoming close friends with John Preston, John Cotton, and Richard Sibbes. He clashed with the authorities after a sermon in 1608 that denounced Archbishop Richard Bancroft's treatment of puritans. (This reputation may have delayed the award of his doctorate, which he did not receive until 1628, incorporated at Oxford in 1630.) Threatened with degradation, he moved to Watford, possibly as vicar, and by 1612 to Reading, close to his brother. There he established a very productive household seminary. He produced an extraordinary wealth of devotional works, showing himself very much the disciple of his mentor at Cambridge, William Perkins. In 1625 he was elected curate and lecturer at St. Mary's Aldermanbury, London, and was representative of the mainstream clerical puritanism of the early Stuarts. He flourished in London and was renowned as a preacher and as spiritual advisor to the godly. He was loosely connected with the Feoffees for Impropriations and, later, with John Dury's ecumenical project. There was a reprimand earned for his part in an effort to raise support for the Protestants in the Palatinate; otherwise his ministry continued undisturbed until he retired in 1630 and moved to Isleworth away from the London air. Here he died in late 1632.

*Further Reading*
"The Life of Dr Taylor," in *The Works of Dr Thom. Taylor* (1653); "The true relation of Doctor Thomas Taylor," in *The Works of Thomas Taylor* (1659); Samuel Clarke, *The lives of thirty two English divines in A general martyrologie* (1677); Paul Seaver, *The Puritan Lectureships: The Politics of Religious Dissent, 1560–1662* (Stanford, 1970); Tom Webster, *Godly Clergy in Early Stuart England: The Caroline Puritan Movement, c. 1620–1643* (Cambridge, Eng., 1997).

*Tom Webster*

### Throckmorton, Job (1545–1601)

One of the most outspoken of Elizabethan puritan members of Parliament, which became apparent when three of his speeches delivered in the 1586 parliament were discovered in the 1950s. He was the eldest son of the large family of Clement Throckmorton of Haseley, Warwickshire. After spending time in Oxford (B.A. 1566), he inherited an estate burdened with debt. He was not active in local politics. So when he sought a parliamentary seat in 1586, intent on the speeches he was to make about Mary Queen of Scots, religion (in support of the "Bill and Book" that sought to introduce Presbyterianism), and foreign policy (expressing an undiplomatic outrage), he campaigned as a carpetbagger in Warwick. Two years later came the Marprelate tracts. Throckmorton

was in this literary conspiracy up to his neck, and in addition to circumstantial evidence, comparison of the tracts with Throckmorton's speeches and with the only printed pamphlet he acknowledged has convinced modern scholars that if the libels had a single author, that author was Throckmorton. He said that he was not Martin and didn't know Martin. But since "Martin" did not exist, that was true. Eventually Throckmorton seems to have reverted to obscure privacy, dying suddenly, intestate, in February 1601. Pay no attention to the original *Dictionary of National Biography*, which unfortunately confuses him with another Throckmorton, a religious melancholic who ended a lifetime of religious doubt undergoing treatment from John Dod.

*See also:* Marprelate Tracts, Martin Marprelate
*Further Reading*
L. H. Carlson, *Martin Marprelate, Gentleman* (San Marino, CA, 1981); J. E. Neale, *Elizabeth I and Her Parliaments, 1584–1601* (London, 1957); J. E. Neale, *The Elizabethan House of Commons* (London, 1949).

*Patrick Collinson*

### Tombes, John (1602–1676)

Baptist minister. Tombes was a student at Magdalen Hall, Oxford, where he received his B.A. in 1621, his M.A. in 1624, and his B.D. in 1631. At Oxford he was noted as an extraordinary linguist. In 1623, while catechist at Magdalen, he began to doubt the scriptural basis for infant baptism, though he did not resolve the matter to his own satisfaction for some time.

Tombes became a preacher at Leominster, Herefordshire, in 1630 and became noted for his opposition to ceremonies and general puritan stance. His support for Parliament in 1642 forced him to abandon Leominster. After a brief stay in Bristol, he relocated in London. There he finally came to a public rejection of infant baptism. His friend Stephen Marshall arranged for him to be appointed a preacher at the Inns of Court, where he would not be called upon to perform baptisms. He continued to write and speak out against the practice, engaging in a debate with Richard Baxter, and agreeing to a statement of his views being dispatched to New England by his friend Henry Jessey. His close connections with orthodox Calvinists who were Presbyterians and Congregationalists led to his being appointed during the Protectorate as one of the national triers for the approbation of candidates for the ministry.

Tombes returned to Leominster in the 1650s, but lost his living at the Restoration due to his opposition to infant baptism. During the following decades, he continued to advocate his Baptist views, but also wrote attacks on separatism and Socinianism, and defended Calvinist doctrinal positions.

*Further Reading*
Richard Greaves and Robert Zaller, eds., *Biographical Dictionary of British Radicals in the Seventeenth Century*, 3 vols. (Brighton, Eng., 1984).

*Francis J. Bremer*

## Tomkys, John (d. 1592)

Protestant preacher, who was to the town of Shrewsbury, in a small way, what John Calvin was to Geneva. He was not the first Protestant preacher in the town, but his arrival in 1582 ratcheted up the reformation of manners, imposed under a code of seventy-nine articles, as though they were Ecclesiastical Ordinances. When Tomkys died ten years later, his passing was, says a local chronicler, lamented by all "perfect protestants," by which we may understand Puritans. Tomkys came to Shrewsbury from his native Staffordshire. Little is known of his education except that it was funded by Sir Richard Pipe, a lord mayor of London of Staffordshire origin. He published translations from French and Latin of works by the Zürich reformer Heinrich Bullinger. Tomkys was a client of the Earl of Leicester and preached before the earl on the occasion of a notable civic visit to Shrewsbury. The most notorious episode in Tomkys's by no means peaceful apostolate in Shrewsbury occurred when he led an attack on a kind of maypole set up annually by the Company of Shearmen, a bone of contention in this town dominated by the politics of cloth and the competing interests of the various parts of the industry. He was subjected to the indignity of a charivari (in America, a shivaree), and three years later, after his time, further trouble over the "Shearman's Tree" led to a murder.

*Further Reading*
Patrick Collinson, "The Shearman's Tree and the Preacher," in *The Reformation in English Towns, 1500–1640,* ed. Patrick Collinson and John Craig (Basinstoke, Eng., 1998); A. B. Somerset, ed., *Records of Early English Drama: Shropshire* (London, 1994).

*Patrick Collinson*

## Tompson, William (1598–1666)

New England clergyman. Tompson was born in Lancashire and educated at Brasenose College, Oxford, where he received his B.A. in 1622. He was a friend of Lancashire puritans Richard Mather and Charles Herle. He emigrated to Massachusetts in 1637. He preached initially in what was to become Maine and then settled as the minister of Braintree, Massachusetts. In 1642 he traveled to Virginia, responding to a plea from puritans in that colony that their New England friends help them by dispatching clergymen. The royal governor of that colony soon cracked down on the puritan efforts, and Tompson returned to Massachusetts. According to Cotton Mather, depression kept Tompson from exercising his ministry for a time. He published two books, both in collaboration with his friend Richard Mather. The first was *A Modest and Brotherly Answer to Mr. Charles Herle* (1644), in which they defended the colonial system of Congregationalism against Herle's Presbyterian objections. The other was a call for cooperation between the two religious groups, published in 1650 as *An Heart-Melting Exhortation with a Cordial Consolation.*

*Further Reading*
Francis J. Bremer, *Shaping New Englands: Puritan Clergyman in Seventeenth-Century England and New England* (Boston, 1994).

*Francis J. Bremer*

## Trapnel, Anna (fl. 1642–1660)

Puritan prophet generally associated with the millennial Fifth Monarchist movement. At the age of fourteen she began to repeat sermons informally, claiming that the Holy Spirit was the source of her voice. This was the typical style of most midcentury Puritans in such matters. In January 1654, however, she also began to receive visions and revelations. The form of these was based on scriptural examples of prophetic visions. In one she saw the throne of God, surrounded by his angels singing, "Holy, Holy, Holy." This vision is similar to the one described in Isaiah 6:3. Trapnel attracted many preachers to hear her utterances, including John Simpson and Henry Jessey.

The content of the visions was unusual for the strength of the political message, as shown in her *Strange and Wonderful Newes from White-Hall* (1654) and *Anna Trapnel's Report and Plea* (1654). They also emphasized the humility and repentance exemplified by the New Testament, rather than the more popular Old Testament emphasis on judgment and retribution. Overall, Trapnel's image is contrary to the traditional image of the Old Testament prophet: utterer of censorious lamentations, which foretold woe and destruction. As a female prophet, she followed in the tradition of the handmaid of God, established by the female saints and mystics of the medieval Church. However, the most important aspect of her style of prophecy was its emphasis on silence, making her work possibly a precursor to Quaker speech forms.

*See also:* Antinomianism, Fifth Monarchists, Conversion Narratives (in Primary Sources)
*Further Reading*
Phyllis Mack, *Visionary Women: Ecstatic Prophecy in Seventeenth-Century England* (Berkeley, 1992).

*Kate Harvey*

## Travers, Walter (ca. 1548–1635)

Intellectual leader of Elizabethan puritanism. Travers matriculated at Christ's College, Cambridge, in 1560. He was the eldest of five children (four sons and one daughter) in the family of a godly goldsmith of Brydelsmith Gate, Nottingham. At Cambridge, Travers migrated to Trinity College, where he demonstrated both his academic promise and his puritan persuasions. In 1569, he was elected senior fellow at Trinity, where Thomas Cartwright was also a fellow. Under growing hostility toward puritans arising from new controversy over church polity and with John Whitgift's appointment as vice-chancellor, Travers departed from the university to Geneva in 1571 with his brother Robert Travers, also fellow of Trinity, and with Thomas Cartwright. Theodore Beza was rector of the Geneva Academy at the time and welcomed the English exiles along with the Scottish Presbyterian Andrew Melville. While in Geneva, Travers devised England's first systematic treatise on Presbyterian church government, *Ecclesiasticae Disciplinae et Anglicanae Ecclesiae ab illa Aberrationis plena e verbo Dei & dilucida explicatio*. Travers printed the *Explicatio* anonymously in 1574, and in the same year Thomas Cartwright's translation with his preface appeared in England as *A full and plaine declaration of Ecclesiasticall Discipline owt off the word off God, and off the declininge off the churche off England from the same*. Travers maintained correspondence with Geneva after his return to England in 1575. Although his letters have not been found among Beza's correspondence, one of Beza's letters to Travers in 1582 is still extant.

Travers's Continental career extended to the Low Countries. On 8 May 1578 he became the first minister for the English merchants in Antwerp and was ordained according to the Presbyterian model advocated in his *Explicatio*. Cartwright continued to cultivate Presbyterianism in the merchant congregation following Travers's ministry in 1580, securing the congregation's favoring of Presbyterianism into the seventeenth century. Meanwhile Lord Burghley received Travers as his household chaplain and as tutor to young Robert Cecil, later Earl of Salisbury. Burghley further employed Travers as reader of the Temple Church in London through Bishop John Aylmer's recommendation. When Richard Alvey, master of the Temple Church, requested Travers as his successor in 1584, Travers's ordination in Antwerp came into question, and Travers was unwilling to be reordained, defending the legitimacy of his ministry. Instead Travers became lecturer, while Richard Hooker was appointed the master. No more than a year later, the two learned divines engaged in a famous controversy, which climaxed in their pulpit battle over the basis on which Roman Catholic forefathers were saved, resulting in Travers's suspension and the silencing of his ministry. While the question of church government did not arise in their public debate, it had been a chief reason for Hooker's preferment over Travers as master of the Temple. Following Travers's ejection from office, he appealed to the Privy Council for restoration to the ministry. Although Travers was not restored, Hooker answered his supplication and, provoked by Travers's appeals concerning church polity, embarked on his foundational treatise for the Church of England, *Of the Laws of Ecclesiastical Polity.*

Travers was meanwhile active as moderator for meetings of the London classis, even hosting Presbyterian synods at his house in the late 1580s. In 1584, he appeared as puritan spokesman with Thomas Sparke at the Lambeth conference. The conference was called in protest to Archbishop John Whitgift's Three Articles and the suspension of ministers who failed to subscribe. At the same time that Travers participated in clandestine Presbyterian activity and appeared publicly to defend the puritans, he wrote on behalf of England against a Continental epistle in favor of Catholics in England in 1583. The epistle appeared as a preface to an English translation of Fr. Robert Person's *De persecutione Anglicana Epistola* by an unknown author with the initials G. T. Travers, who is also known for an additional anti-Catholic treatise on behalf of England, entitled *Vindiciae Ecclesiae Anglicanae,* which appeared in 1630.

Travers is most often noted for his primary role in writing the Book of Discipline, entitled *A Directory of Church-government.* While Travers's *Explicatio* was a sophisticated argument for the principles of Presbyterianism, the Book of Discipline provided instructions for the implementation of Presbyterian government. In the Star Chamber trial of 1591, the Book of Discipline became the court's primary evidence against Thomas Cartwright and other main leaders of the Presbyterian movement. Travers, however, managed to escape prosecution in the trial. He departed from London on 22 July 1592 to the Netherlands, returning to the English Merchant church, which had since relocated to Middleburg. In 1594, Travers secured a position as Provost of Trinity College, Dublin, through the favor of Lord Burghley. Travers succeeded Adam Loftus as second provost of Trinity, yet he is known to be the first provost concerned with the workings of the college. He was also mentor to James Ussher at Trinity and continued his correspondence with Ussher, later archbishop of Armagh, after his return to London in 1598, where Travers remained until his death in January 1635. Travers's later years have for the most part remained unknown, though his commonplace book, dating into the late 1620s, reveals his collection of revenue from lease of Wickford Hall in Essex. Just as Travers established an international network through his time spent in Geneva and in the Low Countries, he continued during his later years to study the works of Continental Reformers such as Heinrich Bullinger, in addition to contemporary authorities such as Pierre Du Moulin the Elder and Johann Heinrich Alsted. Travers's library, which he bequeathed to Sion College, further demonstrates his extensive reading of Continental theologians.

*See also:* English Puritanism in the Netherlands, Irish Puritanism

*Further Reading*

Polly Ha, "English Presbyterianism, 1590–1640" (forthcoming Ph.D. diss., University of Cambridge); S. J. Knox, *Walter Travers: Paragon of Elizabethan Puritanism* (London, 1962); A. F. Scott Pearson, *Thomas Cartwright and Elizabethan Puritanism* (Cambridge, Eng., 1925).

*Polly Ha*

## Tuckney, Anthony (1599–1670)

Tuckney would have been surprised, before the Civil War, to hear himself described as a Puritan, since he would have been content to categorize himself (if at all) as a defender of the "good old doctrine" of the Church of England, Calvinism. We can, perhaps, with the benefit of hindsight, call him an establishment Puritan, taking account of the fact that in the 1630s he preached sermons on official occasions, including a visitation sermon before the visitor for Archbishop William Laud. But why a Puritan at all? Tuckney was a prominent scion of Emmanuel College, a fellow of the college from 1619. He served as chaplain to the fourth Earl of Lincoln, whose sister married his contemporary Isaac Johnson, with her husband embarked on the first fleet for Massachusets, and soon died there. He maintained a lifelong friendship with his school friend and chamber fellow at Emmanuel, Samuel Whiting, minister at Lynn in Massachusetts from 1636 to 1679, and he was keenly interested in things American. Tuckney had been sent off to Boston, Lincolnshire (his native county), to experience what John Preston called the "seasoning vessel" of the household of John Cotton, who was his cousin, and when Cotton left Boston for another Boston, Tuckney succeeded him as vicar and preacher of Boston, where he was instrumental in founding a parish library, which still exists.

The events of the 1640s drew Tuckney closer to the center of things, and in 1643 he became a member of the Westminster Assembly of Divines, where he took a leading role in the construction of both the Catechism and the Shorter Catechism. By now we may call him a Presbyterian. In 1645 Richard Holdsworth was removed from the mastership of Emmanuel, and after the brief interlude of the headship of Tuckney's close friend Thomas Hill, presently transferred to Trinity, Tuckney became the sixth master of the college. When the Westminster Assembly completed its deliberations, Tuckney moved back to Cambridge, after delicate negotiations with Holdsworth. In 1653 he became master of St. John's. In both colleges he earned a reputation as a strict disciplinarian. By this time, the Calvinist Tuckney was something of a theological dinosaur, his old-fashioned views dramatized in what became a famous correspondence with the Cambridge Platonist Benjamin Whichcote, once his pupil at Emmanuel but now provost of King's.

Whichcote was accused of departing from the spiritual, plain, powerful tradition for which Cambridge had been famous.

With the Restoration of 1660, Tuckney's world collapsed. He resigned both Boston and St. John's. He withdrew to London, but later moved to the Midlands. The Great Fire of 1666 destroyed his considerable library. He returned to London and died in 1670. His four wives included the widow of Thomas Hill and (his fourth) the widow of his fellow Assembly man, William Spurstowe.

*See also:* Emmanuel College, Westminster Catechisms, Westminster Confession of Faith
*Further Reading*
A. Sarah Bendall, Christopher Nugent, Lawrence Brooke, and Patrick Collinson, *A History of Emmanuel College, Cambridge* (Woodbridge, Eng., 1999); S. Salter, ed., *Moral and Religious Aphorisms*, (London, 1753).

*Patrick Collinson*

## Twisse, William (1578–1646)

Theologian born near Newbury, Gloucester. He showed early signs of intelligence and shone at New College, Oxford, with George Abbot as a tutor, becoming a fellow and graduating D.D. in 1614. His early work was to assist in the translation of Bradwardine's *De causa Dei contra Pelagium*, and this work won the approval of James VI (of Scotland) and I (of England), who placed him as chaplain to his daughter Elizabeth in Heidelberg, although the appointment was short lived. In 1620 he took the living at Newbury. He held this post until the town fell to the royalists in the early 1640s.

His reputation was mainly based on his scholarship and, though he could be fairly acerbic in his writings, this was a rather bookish, detached learning. His standing was such that Charles I was willing to allow him to ignore the Book of Sports and to defy the the policy of moving the altar back to the east end of the church and railing it off. As a controversialist theologian, he won acclaim for his critique of Thomas Jackson's Neoplatonic work on the creed. Twisse denounced this work as worse than Arminianism. Indeed his next work, of greater impact, was a defense of William Perkins's predestinarianism against the assault of the Dutch theologian Jacobus Arminius. He was also willing to provide an early criticism of John Goodwin's stand on free will and to caution Thomas Goodwin and John Cotton for what he saw as their flattering of human capacities in justification. These works brought him attention across Europe.

In 1641 he was a natural member of Bishop John Williams's committee reviewing Laudianism. In 1643 he was a delegate to the Westminster Assembly and was chosen as its prolocutor. However, his work in London saw him move beyond his finest years, and by 1645 poor health made him resign from an active role in the assembly. In March 1645 he collapsed in the pulpit, took to his bed and died a year later. He was given a state funeral in Westminster Abbey attended by members of Parliament. In 1661, however, a royal proclamation had him disinterred and cast into a pit in the churchyard of St. Margaret's, Westminster.

*Further Reading*
Samuel Clarke, *The lives of sundry eminent persons in this later age* (1683); S. Hutton, "Thomas Jackson, Oxford Platonist, and William Twisse, Aristotelian," *Journal of the History of Ideas* 39 (1978), 635–652.

*Tom Webster*

# U

## Udall, John (ca. 1560–1592)

Preacher and author. Though his family lineage is often disputed, it is probable that John Udall was related to a family from Wickham in Hampshire. Educated as a cleric at Cambridge, as an undergraduate Udall developed a close association with the Welsh radical John Penry. During this time he also adopted puritan leanings.

While serving as curate at Kingston upon Thames, Udall gained a reputation as an eloquent preacher. The volumes of sermons he produced for publication identified him with godly ideals. The first, *Amendment of Life,* was published in 1584. *Obedience to the Gospell* and *Peter's Fall* soon followed. In 1586 he was called before the Court of High Commission at Lambeth for having undermined England's established church. However, the patronage of influential friends enabled him to retain his position in the ministry. Rather than being a discouragement, this experience served to strengthen his commitment to the views of the godly.

Udall retained his association with John Penry, and in 1588 became connected, along with Penry and others, to the publication of a series of anticlerical pamphlets that were printed under the pseudonym Martin Marprelate. During this enterprise Udall continued to preach openly about the need for reform in the Church of England. Due to his candid criticisms of the church, Udall was again called before the Court of High Commission in 1588. This time he was deprived of his living. After a few months Udall was invited to resume his clerical duties in the town of Newcastle-upon-Tyne. He accepted. While Udall was engaged in serving his new congregation, many of the Marprelate tracts were being released. Every effort was being made to identify the authors of the pamphlets. In 1590 Udall was arrested on the suspicion that he had authored the Marprelate tracts, which had been deemed seditious by Archbishop John Whitgift and other members of the Court of High Commission. Though sentenced to death, eventually Udall received a pardon from Archbishop Whitgift. However, he died shortly thereafter. His Hebrew grammar and dictionary, *Key to the Holy Tongue,* was published in 1593, following his death.

*Further Reading*
*Oxford Dictionary of National Biography* (Oxford, 2004).

*Susan Ortmann*

## Ussher, Henry (ca. 1550–1613)

Archbishop of the Protestant Church of Ireland. Ussher was born in Dublin, Ireland, and sent to Magdalene College, Cambridge, for his university education. There he associated with a number of the leaders of the English puritan movement. Following his B.A. (1570), he continued his studies at Paris and then Oxford, where he received his M.A. from University College in 1572. He returned to Dublin as treasurer of Christ Church in 1573, was made archdeacon of Dublin in 1580, and archbishop of Armagh and primate of Ireland in 1595. Throughout his Irish career he campaigned for the creation of an Irish university, and in 1592 he was rewarded for his efforts when Trinity College, Dublin, was chartered.

*Further Reading*
Colm Lennon, *The Lords of Dublin in the Age of the Reformation* (Dublin, 1989).

*Francis J. Bremer*

### Ussher, James (1581–1656)

Church of Ireland bishop and scholar. Ussher was born into a well-established and prosperous Dublin family on 4 January 1581. In 1594 he entered the newly founded Protestant university, Trinity College, Dublin, where he was educated under the tutelage of two English Presbyterian exiles, Walter Travers and Henry Alvey. He stayed on at Trinity to become a fellow and professor of Theological Controversies, a post that he held till 1617. In 1601 he was ordained, and in 1605 became chancellor of St. Patrick's Cathedral. In 1621 he was appointed to the see of Meath; two years later he was made a Privy Counsellor; and in 1625 King James promoted him to the archdiocese of Armagh.

Ussher had two parallel careers, one as a scholar, and the other as ecclesiastical administrator and politician. His first published work in 1613 was *Gravissimae quaestionis, de Christianarum ecclesiarum . . . continua successione et statu, historica explicatio,* a Foxean attempt to trace the descent of the Protestants from the early church through an often bizarre collection of mediaeval heretics. He also wrote and lectured on controversial and antipapal theology, publishing in 1624 a lengthy treatise, *An answer to a challenge made by a Jesuit in Ireland.* In addition he made major contributions to patristic studies and to the history of the early church in Britain and Ireland, the former through his edition of the true Ignatian letters, and the latter through his monumental 1639 book, *Britannicarum ecclesiarum antiquitates.* But perhaps his most influential work, at least within Ireland, was

*James Ussher, archbishop of Armagh and theologian who fixed the date of Creation precisely at 4004 B.C.E. (Bettmann/Corbis)*

his *A discourse of the religion anciently professed by the Irish and British* (published under this title in 1631), which set out to show how the early Irish church of Patrick and his followers was, to all intents and purposes, Protestant, and that the reformed Church of Ireland was therefore its rightful heir, thus providing the origin myth for the Church of Ireland right down to the twentieth century. Ussher traveled regularly to England during the 1610s and 1620s, making close contacts with prominent English academics, such as William Camden, John Selden, and John Cotton, and moving easily in Calvinist and puritan circles.

Politically and theologically Ussher was fiercely anti-Catholic, but, at the same time, deeply deferential to royal authority, which he saw as divinely ordained. These instincts clashed in 1626–1627, when King Charles sought to negotiate the graces (privileges) that would have involved the concession of toleration to Catholics, leading Ussher and his fellow Protestant bishops to speak out publicly against the proposal, which was dropped. In the period after the arrival of Lord Deputy Wentworth in Ireland, however, Ussher's influence over church policy declined. In the 1634 convocation, he fought to preserve the independence of the Irish church, opposing the imposition of the Thirty-nine Articles and the English Canons of 1604 on the Church of Ireland. His defeat was followed by his retreat from political matters, as he focused upon his archiepiscopal see and his studies. He didn't reenter the world of political affairs until he left for England in 1640, where he remained permanently after the 1641 rising in Ireland and was sucked into the politics of the Long Parliament. He played a subsidiary role in the events leading up to the Civil War, engaging in polemic with Milton over episcopacy, advising parliament and the king, proposing a compromise between episcopacy and presbyterianism, and ministering to the Earl of Strafford before his execution. Though his opposition to popery and his Calvinism led Parliament to court him, even to the extent of nominating him to serve in the Westminster Assembly, Ussher refused such blandishments and made it clear that his primary loyalty lay with the king, whom he followed to Oxford. After Charles's defeat, Ussher returned to London, where he concentrated upon his studies, and largely kept to himself. He retained, however, his saintly and scholarly reputation among both Anglicans and puritans: Richard Baxter sought his support for his schemes of reconciliation, and when Ussher died on 21 March 1656, Oliver Cromwell ordered that the state should pay for his funeral in Westminster Abbey.

*See also:* International Puritanism, Irish Articles,

Irish Puritanism, Primitive Episcopacy, Westminster Assembly, Westminster Confession of Faith

*Further Reading*

Alan Ford, "James Ussher and the Godly Prince in Early Seventeenth-Century Ireland," in Hiram Morgan, ed., *Political Ideology in Ireland, 1541–1641* (1999), pp. 203–228; R. B. Knox, *James Ussher, Archbishop of Armagh* (Cardiff, 1967).

*Alan Ford*

# V

## Vane, Sir Henry (1613–1662)

Radical politician and lay theologian. Vane, son of a Privy Counsellor to Charles I, had a religious conversion in his mid-teens that left him assured of his salvation and inclined him toward nonconformity. In 1635, he went to Massachusetts and took up residence in Boston. The colonists, dazzled by his high status and the force of his personality, elected him governor in May 1636. Vane was already demonstrating a prodigious appetite for theological speculation, and he aligned himself with the most heterodox elements in the rapidly emerging religious dispute that nineteenth-century historians misleadingly dubbed the Antinominian Controversy.

Vane was voted out of office the next May, after vigorous electioneering against him by Massachusetts's lay and ministerial leaders, and he returned to England in August. Charles I appointed him secretary of the navy in 1639, and he took a seat in Parliament in 1640. When the Civil War broke out in 1642, Vane switched sides and emerged as a political and ecclesiastical radical, pressing for war with the king and the abolition of episcopacy. Energized by millenarian hopes, he was a vigorous promoter of religious liberty and a protector of sects. Vane became a major player in both domestic and foreign affairs for the duration of the Long and Rump Parliaments. Next to Cromwell himself, Vane may have been most responsible for the eventual dominance of the radical Independent faction over Parliament. Vane broke with Cromwell when Cromwell dissolved the Rump Parliament in 1653,

and he retired from active politics until Cromwell's death in 1658. During his retirement, Vane published his major religious treatise, *A Retired Mans Meditations* (1655), along with various commentaries on the contemporary political scene, and as a religious teacher acquired a circle of admiring "Vanists." Cromwell had him imprisoned for five months in 1656. Vane returned as a major radical political figure when the Rump was reinstated upon Cromwell's death, and he threw in his lot with the army in the last desperate attempt, opposed by

*Henry Vane, governor of the Massachusetts Bay Colony from 1636 to 1637. (Library of Congress)*

many moderate puritans, to block the return of Charles II in 1660. Charles promised indemnity to all except those who were involved in the execution of his father. Vane should have been covered by the indemnity, but he was deemed too dangerous to leave free and became the single exception. After two years in prison, Vane was put on trial for treason. At his trial, he proved militantly unapologetic about his past and about the necessity for kings to be subordinate to Parliament. His failure to be submissive ensured his death, as he knew it would. Vane was beheaded on Tower Hill on 14 June 1662.

*See also:* Independency
*Further Reading*
Violet A. Rowe, *Sir Henry Vane the Younger: A Study in Political and Administrative History* (London, 1970); Michael P. Winship, *Making Heretics: Militant Protestantism and Free Grace in Massachusetts, 1636–1641* (Princeton, 2002).

*Michael P. Winship*

## Vere, Lady Mary (1580–1670)

Patron and friend of puritan ministers. Born Mary Tracy, she was first married to William Hoby and then in 1607 to Sir Horace Vere, who was the commander of English forces in the Netherlands in the 1620s and 1630s. A woman of noted piety, she befriended numerous puritan clergy, including William Ames, John Preston, John Dod, William Spurstowe, and Obadiah Sedgwick; Sedgwick served as a chaplain to her husband in the Netherlands. Her own chaplain was Samuel Rogers, the son Daniel and grandson of Richard Rogers. Her relationship with the puritan clergyman John Davenport is particularly well documented. She assisted Davenport in gaining the living of St. Stephen's, Colman Street, London, in the early 1620s, and she is said to have cared for the Davenports' son when the clergyman and his wife first migrated to New England in the 1630s. Her support of New England was evident when she supported the efforts of Josiah Glover in establishing the first printing press in the colonies.

In the 1650s, Lady Vere personally held eight advowsons in the country of Essex and used them to place puritan ministers in those parish livings. Her

five daughters all married prominent supporters of the puritan cause, including Anne, who married Thomas Fairfax, the Parliamentarian general.

*See also:* English Puritanism in the Netherlands
*Further Reading*
Richard Greaves and Robert Zaller, eds., *Biographical Dictionary of British Radicals in the Seventeenth Century*, 3 vols. (Brighton, Eng., 1984).

*Francis J. Bremer*

## Vicars, John (1579 or 1580–1652)

Author; a lay proponent of Presbyterianism. Vicars was born an orphan at Christ's Hospital, London. He matriculated at Queen's College, Oxford, but did not take any degree. Following his time at Oxford, Vicars returned to Christ's Hospital as usher and later schoolmaster. He translated Virgil's *Aeneid* in 1632 and also wrote a number of volumes of verse focusing on godly themes current at the time.

Vicars was a lifelong friend of John Bastwick and William Prynne and delivered Bastwick's *Letany* to John Lilburne for printing in the publishing conspiracy that led to the pillorying of Henry Burton, Bastwick, and Prynne in 1638.

During the Civil War, Vicars was a Parliamentarian in politics and a Presbyterian in religion. His main works are accounts of the battles of the Parliamentarian armies. He was also involved in controversies with sectaries and the Levellers. Vicars played an important role in the movement to institute Presbyterianism in London during the Civil War. He was a signatory to the London citizens' petition of 18 November 1645 calling for the institution of Presbyterianism in the parishes. From 1646 he served as one of the ruling elders at the Presbyterian stronghold of Christ Church, Newgate Street, with the minister William Jenkyn and lecturer Thomas Edwards. Vicars was also a delegate to the Fifth London Classis and the London Provincial Assembly.

Vicars was married to Jane and had a son, John, and two daughters, Frances and Hester. He died at Christ's Hospital on 12 April 1652.

*Further Reading*
Elliot C. Vernon, "The Sion College Conclave and London Presbyterianism during the English

Revolution" (Ph.D. diss., University of Cambridge, 1999).

*Elliot Vernon*

## Vincent, Nathaniel (1638–1697)

Nonconformist preacher. Vincent was educated at Corpus Christi College, Oxford, receiving his B.A. in 1656 and his M.A. the following year. He began his preaching career in 1658 in Pulborough, Sussex. The following year he was ordained and presented to the rectory of Langley Marish, Buckinghamshire, where he remained until he was ejected in 1662 as a consequence of the Restoration. He then became chaplain to the family of Sir Henry Blount, a position he held for three years.

Vincent's reputation grew as a result of sermons he preached in London following the Great Fire of 1666. Over the next few years he preached illegally in various locations in London and the surrounding countryside, with his sermons interrupted on a number of occasions by the arrival of troops. He was captured in the summer of 1670 and sent to the Marshalsea prison in Southwark, across the Thames from London. He was visited often by his followers, which caused his removal to the Gatehouse in Westminster. There he composed his *A Convert from the Storm.*

Vincent was eventually released and resumed his preaching in 1671. In 1672 he was licensed as a Presbyterian teacher and continued both to preach and publish. *The Morning Exercise Against Popery* (1675) included works by other Nonconformists as well as his own. He also published *The Little Child's Catechism* (1679) and several funeral sermons. In 1683 he was brought before the quarter sessions at Dorking, Surrey, on charges of conducting a conventicler, but he was released on a writ of error. He was arrested again in 1686 and charged with involvement in Monmouth's Rebellion, but he was again set free.

In 1692 his own congregation fractured, with sixty members joining the rival Southwark congregation of Richard Fincher. In that same year he declined an invitation to serve as one of the managers of the Common Fund of Presbyterians and Con-gregationalists. He died in 1697 and was remembered for his compassion for the sick and poor and his "great zeal against bold intruders into the work of the ministry."

*Further Reading*
*Oxford Dictionary of National Biography* (Oxford, 2004).

*Michael Spurr*

## Vincent, Thomas (1634–1678)

English dissenting minister. Born at Hertford, he was the elder brother of Nathaniel Vincent, also a Nonconformist preacher. He entered Christ Church, Oxford, in 1648, receiving the B.A. in 1652 and the M.A. in 1654. He left Oxford to become a chaplain to Robert Sidney, Earl of Leicester, and in 1657 became rector of St. Mary Magdalene, Milk Street, London, from which he was ejected in 1662 for refusal to submit to the Act of Uniformity. After ejection he assisted Thomas Doolittle in the latter's Dissenting academy at Bunhill Fields, London. During the plague year of 1665, he preached courageously in London parish churches abandoned by their frightened conformist incumbents. In 1669 he was preaching in a large room in Bishopsgate Street, London, and in May 1670 he was fined for illegal preaching. He was licensed as a Presbyterian under the terms of the 1672 Declaration of Indulgence. He was the author of *An Explicatory Catechism* (1673), of an attack upon William Penn and the Quakers (*The Foundation of God Standeth Sure*, 1668), and of published sermons. He was best known for works that struck the note of judgment, such as *Christ's Certain and Sudden Appearance* (1667) and *God's Terrible Voice in the City* (1667), which drew moral and spiritual lessons from the plague and fire of London. A collection of his "holy and profitable sayings" was published posthumously (1680). Vincent was an important Puritan spiritual writer of the Restoration era.

*Further Reading*
A. G. Matthews, *Calamy Revised: Being a Revision of Edmund Calamy's Account of the Ministers and others Ejected and Silenced, 1660–2* (Oxford, 1934; reprinted 1988).

*Dewey D. Wallace Jr.*

# W

## Waban (ca. 1600–ca. 1684)

Native American convert to Christianity. Waban was a leader of a native community west of Boston at the time of the settlement of that colony in 1630. His observations of the new arrivals decided him to throw in his lot with the English, and when John Eliot arrived in his village to preach in 1646, Waban offered his wigwam for the clergyman's use and embraced the Christian message. He also provided for his eldest son to be raised in an English family to learn their language and customs.

When Eliot received the land to found Natick as the first of the colony's "Praying Towns," Waban was one of those who joined the new community. By 1655 he had emerged as the native leader of Natick, and because of that town's importance he exerted a strong role over the expanding network of Christian native communities. His warnings about the Wampanoag threat were unheeded, and, together with many other native converts, he experienced internment on an island in Boston harbor during King Philip's War because their loyalty was not fully trusted. Following the conflict, Waban returned to Natick, remaining there until his death, though with a much diminished influence.

*See also:* Praying Towns
*Further Reading*
H. von Lonkhuyzen, "A Reappraisal of the Praying Indians: Acculturation, Conversion, and Identity at Natick, Massachusetts, 1646–1730," *New England Quarterly* 63 (1990), 396–428; Daniel Mandell, "'Standing By His Father': Thomas Waban of Natick, 1630–1722," in R. Grumet, ed., *Northeastern Indian Lives, 1630–1816* (Amherst, MA, 1996).

*Francis J. Bremer*

## Waldegrave, Robert (ca. 1554–1604)

Printer of religious tracts. Robert Waldegrave, the son of Richard Waldegrave of Blockley, Worcestershire, was born near the Welsh border around the year 1554. Following his father's death, Robert was apprenticed in 1568 to a stationer named William Griffith. The first publication attributed to Waldegrave was a book of prayers entitled *The Castle for the Soule* (1578). This book connects Robert to English clerics preaching godly doctrines. By 1584 Waldegrave had printed a set of sermons by John Udall, an active godly minister.

The relationship between Udall and Waldegrave continued, and it is most likely through this association that Waldegrave developed ties to John Penry. From this association, Waldegrave was linked to the Martin Marprelate controversy begun in 1588. Perhaps this connection best identifies him with Puritanism. Though there is dispute over the authorship of the tracts, Waldegrave is recognized as the printer of the tracts. Waldegrave's press was seized once he was identified as the printer of the pamphlets. Though he continued his work in secret for a time, Waldegrave left the Marprelate Press in 1589 and moved his family to Scotland the following year.

Through his relationships with Udall and Penry, Waldegrave had established ties to Presbyterian clerics. While in Scotland, he earned a living by printing their publications. Waldegrave also was engaged as a printer by James VI of Scotland and was later appointed the King's Printer. Thus he enjoyed royal protection during his tenure in Scotland. Waldegrave was accused of treason in 1597, thus severing his relationship with King James. Having successfully refuted the charge, Waldegrave returned to England. At the time James ascended to the English throne, Waldegrave regained his license to publish from the Stationers Company of London. His death in 1604 occurred shortly thereafter.

*See also:* Martin Marprelate
*Further Reading*
*Oxford Dictionary of National Biography* (Oxford, 2004).

*Susan Ortmann*

## Wallington, Nehemiah (1598–1658)

London puritan artisan, prolific diarist, and writer. Wallington was born in the parish of St. Leonard's, Eastcheap, the tenth of twelve children and the fourth son of John Wallington Sr., citizen and turner (d. 1638), and his wife, Elizabeth (d. 1603), and followed his father and elder brother into the turner's trade. He was in many respects the quintessential puritan, introspective, bookish, sermon-going, scrupulous in business, and constantly struggling for an even-tempered acceptance of life and of himself, which he believed should accompany assurance of election. He followed the fortunes of Protestantism during the Thirty Years' War and Parliament during the Civil War. Although he served conscientiously as a lay elder in the Fourth London Classis from 1646, his Presbyterianism was based on his desire for parish discipline, and his only quarrel with the Protectorate was that it did not bring the godly reformation he had long prayed for. Wallington was never apprenticed but was admitted to the Turners' Company by patrimony in 1620. Within a year he married Grace Rampaigne, sister of two brothers. One of her brothers was a godly minister, whose letters of comfort Nehemiah preserved and whose widow, Sarah, and her two children, lived with the Wallingtons from 1635 until Sarah's death in 1654. The other brother was a planter in Ireland killed during the rebellion in 1641, whose son Charles was taken in by the Wallingtons and served as Nehemiah's apprentice until his freedom in 1655. Nehemiah's freedom as a turner and marriage followed two years of mental breakdown during which, doubting his salvation, he made a number of suicide attempts, which were compromised and complicated by his desire to protect his father and the puritan community from the disgrace of such an ungodly act. It was then that he first began to write, initially a record of his sins and God's mercies, part diary, part commonplace book, which he continued intermittently into the 1630s. Work and family responsibilities—he was helped by his father and older brother, by the friendship and counsel of Henry Roborough, the curate and lecturer at St. Leonard's, by the steady common sense and strength of Grace, and perhaps by the discipline of writing itself—prevented any further breakdown, but the death of their first child, a daughter, in 1625, led to a fresh crisis, during which Wallington confessed that he forgot all his promises and covenants with God and was inconsolable until reminded by Grace that their daughter had gone to a better home in heaven. Their three sons all died, and only their daughter Sarah, born in 1627, survived to adulthood and to marry in 1647 a young godly turner, John Houghton.

Unlike his father and older brother, both of whom were liverymen in the Turners' Company, Wallington never left the yeomanry. Although he apparently worked steadily at his craft, he had no head for business and struggled all his life to find some balance between the demands of his calling as a turner and the more compelling demands of his calling as a Christian. He regularly rose very early in the morning to write before private prayer in his closet and public prayers with his household. He admitted to buying too many books and had a library of more than 200 works, beginning with William Gouge's *Of Domestical Duties,* purchased soon after his marriage. In 1638 Wallington was indicted, along with Henry Burton, John Bastwick, and William Prynne in their famous Star Chamber case for seditious libel, and, although confessing that he had had a copy of Prynne's *News from Ipswich,* he was soon dismissed. In 1654 when he catalogued his own writings, he listed fifty notebooks, ranging from his diary to memorials of God's judgments against Sabbath breakers, commonplaces from scripture and various puritan guides to the godly life, sermon notes, a volume of collected letters, several volumes detailing the mercies he had received, and several volumes of political news collected during the 1640s. Aside from a book called "The Mighty Works of the Lord, which is a Prop to Faith," which he gave to his wife, and a book on patience, which he left to his half-sister Patience, he bequeathed all his notebooks to his son-in-law. He had little else to leave and apparently made no will.

*See also:* Family Piety
*Further Reading*
Paul S. Seaver, *Wallington's World: A Puritan
    Artisan in Seventeenth-Century London*
    (Stanford, 1985).

*Paul Seaver*

*Sir Francis Walsingham, sixteenth-century English diplomat and statesman who was highly influential during Queen Elizabeth's reign. (Bettmann/Corbis)*

## Walsingham, Sir Francis (ca. 1530–1590)

Member of Parliament and diplomat. Walsingham was resident in France on the day of the St. Bartholomew's Day massacre (24 August 1572), during which unsettled and dangerous time he offered protection to the English resident in Paris (whose cohort included Sir Philip Sidney).

As secretary of state for Elizabeth I, Walsingham is of interest to students of Puritanism for his consistently zealous Protestant views, which shaped his approach to foreign policy and his advice to a queen who in the main preferred the more moderate views of Lord Burghley. He served as ambassador to France (where he attempted to persuade the government to tolerate the Huguenots) in the early 1570s, and to Scotland (where he was sent to gauge the relationship of James VI to the Roman Catholic supporters of the king's mother) in the early 1580s. Walsingham excelled at the art of espionage: he is credited with unraveling several Catholic intrigues against Elizabeth, including the Ridolfi Plot of 1569 and the Babington conspiracy of 1585. He persuaded the queen to sign the death warrant for Mary Queen of Scots, and he received the first intelligence reports of an armada sailing for England from Spain in the waning months of 1587.

*Further Reading*
Read Conyers, *Mr. Secretary Walsingham and the
    Policy of Queen Elizabeth* (Oxford, 1925).

*Lori Anne Ferrell*

## Ward, John (d. 1598)

Puritan preacher. Though he was famous in his day and the father of two more famous preachers, little survives to put flesh on the bare bones of the life of John Ward, preacher of Haverhill and Bury St. Edmunds in Suffolk. There is no evidence that John Ward ever studied either at Cambridge or Oxford.

It seems most probable that the monumental inscription erected for him in the church in Haverhill is accurate in stating that he preached the Gospel "at Haverhill and Bury [St. Edmunds]" for thirty-four years. Ward died in 1598, and this would date his arrival in Haverhill to 1564. Thus he cannot be the student of the same name identified as Ward in Charles Cooper and Thompson Cooper's *Athenae Cantabrigiensis.* Ward's appointment as one of the town preachers in Bury St. Edmunds was short-lived. Appointed in 1597, he served only a year before his death. Almost nothing is known of his long ministry in Haverhill, although it is entirely probable that he was suspended from his ministry in Haverhill by John Aylmer, bishop of London in 1584. William Whitaker, eminent divine and master of St. John's College, openly admired Ward's exegetical ability: "Give me John Ward for a text" was his oft-repeated comment. His sons, Samuel, Nathaniel, and John, were all born in Haverhill and all went on to study at Cambridge, Samuel and Nathaniel becoming eminent preachers in their own right. Ward's widow married Richard Rogers of Wethersfield in Essex.

*Further Reading*
John Craig, *Reformation, Politics and Polemics: The growth of Protestantism in East Anglian Market towns, 1500–1610* (Aldershot, Eng., 2002).

*John Craig*

## Ward, Samuel (1572–1643)

Master of Sidney Sussex College, Cambridge; an archetypal moderate puritan. As a student in Christ's College (B.A. 1593, M.A. 1596), he was a devoted follower of William Perkins (who helped him with his college debts) and Laurence Chaderton. His diary and sermon notebook attest to his fervent evangelicalism, his commitment to biblical studies, and especially his intensely introspective piety: he listed in painful detail his most trivial sins, both of commission and attitude, bemoaning his sleepiness during college sermons, the "sluggishness" of his spiritual affections, his penchant for overindulging in plums swiped from the college trees. Ward also used his diary to express anxieties about "sins of the land" and the state of the Church of England, afflicted increasingly by clergy "too pontifical and papistical" and by creeping Arminianism. His puritan pedigree beyond question, he was elected fellow of Emmanuel College in 1596 (B.D. 1603), and in 1610 (the year of his D.D.) master of the newest puritan foundation, Sidney Sussex.

There are good grounds, however, to attach "moderate" to Ward's puritanism. He supported episcopacy, maintaining lifelong friendships with Calvinist bishops like James Ussher, William Bedell, and John Davenant. And however devoted he was to training a preaching ministry, he was a pluralist. The king rewarded his work on translation of the Authorized Version of the Bible (1604–1611—he was assigned the Apocrypha) with a prebend in Wells, a royal chaplaincy, the archdeaconry of Taunton, a canon's stall in York, and rectories in Hertfordshire and Norfolk. He did preach sermons on occasion, his language redolent with emotion, fervently exhorting his auditors to repentance. He also called for stricter ecclesiastical discipline. But he visited Taunton rarely, relying on surrogates and curates to serve his judicial and pastoral functions. To be sure, a speech impediment may have disinclined him to preach regularly, and he did appoint puritans to act for him in his archdeaconry court; however, his multiplication of offices may render his puritanism at least problematic.

As master of Sidney and in 1620–1621 vice-chancellor of the university, Ward had to balance the demands of administration and scholarship. He introduced geographic and scientific studies to his students, fretted over the college accounts, and played host to visiting scholars, including in 1627 Lord Brooke's radically republican history lecturer, Isaac Dorislaus (though Ward's own inclination seems to have favored monarchy). The preponderance of both his scholarship and his actions as a member of the vice-chancellor's court, however, was devoted to maintaining Calvinist orthodoxy and simplicity of worship in the face of rising Arminianism and ceremonialism. An outspoken Calvinist, he was one of the five British delegates sent by James in 1618 to the Synod of Dort. There he was associated with another delegate, John Davenant, as a supporter of hypothetical universalism; however, his argument that Christ's death created only the possibility of salvation for all, remaining merely potential for the reprobate, gave no real ground to Arminianism. In 1623 he became Lady Margaret Professor of Divinity, from which position he continued his vigorous defense of strict predestinarianism, most evident in his 1625 university sermon, published as *Gratia discriminans* the following year. His posthumously printed *Opera nonnulla* (1658) displays consistent and thoroughgoing Calvinism. Sidney's chapel, unconsecrated, maintained a table rather than an altar. Small wonder that the college under his direction attracted puritan students, including Oliver Cromwell, Thomas Edwards, and the sons of Samuel Ward of Ipswich, John Rogers, and Thomas Gataker.

After Charles's accession in 1625, Ward found his theological position increasingly under fire in the university, as newly imposed Arminian heads of colleges came to outnumber their more conservative brethren on the vice-chancellor's court. The court began to exonerate accused anti-Calvinists (and on occasion even Catholics) who would have been prosecuted and deprived by its antecedents. In 1629 Ward was himself censured by vice-chancellor Matthew Wren for purchasing a copy of William Prynne's *Anti-Arminianisme,* and a few years later he reported to Ussher that he had been reprimanded for defending puritans in consistory.

At the outbreak of war in 1642, Ward declined financial aid to both sides, but neither his neutrality nor the invitation he received to join the Westminster Assembly could prevent his imprisonment in St. John's College by Parliamentarian troops occupying Cambridge in 1643. There he contracted his fatal illness, a moderate puritan scholar sacrificed to the radicalism of his more headstrong brethren.

*Further Reading*

Margo Todd, "'An Act of Discretion': Evangelical Conformity and the Puritan Dons," *Albion* 18 (1986), 581–599; Margo Todd, "Puritan Self-Fashioning," *Journal of British Studies* 31 (1992), 236–264.

*Margo Todd*

## Ward, Samuel (of Ipswich) (1577–1640)

An enormously popular preacher, who exercised a profound influence upon the town of Ipswich for more than thirty years. Born in 1577, Ward came from preaching stock, being the son of John Ward, preacher of Haverhill, Suffolk. He was admitted a scholar of St. John's College, Cambridge, on 6 November 1594 on the nomination of Lord Burghley. He proceeded B.A. in 1597, became a fellow of Sidney Sussex College in 1599, and commenced M.A. in 1600. At about this time, he succeeded his father as lecturer at Haverhill, and it was during this time that he forged links with the Fairclough family. His tenure at Haverhill was not to last long. On 1 November 1603, he accepted the office of town preacher offered him by the corporation of Ipswich on the handsome terms of a salary of a hundred marks and rented accommodation. The following year he married Deborah Bolton, a widow of Isleham, Cambridgeshire, and resigned his fellowship at Sidney Sussex College. His standing among the burgesses of Ipswich was reflected in the increases made to his salary—an increase to 90 pounds in 1611 was followed by another increase to 100 pounds in 1617.

These were years of constant preaching from the pulpit of St. Mary-le-Tower, and it was about this time that Ward organized the famous town library of Ipswich. Yet there was another side to this popular preacher with the plain style. In 1621 Ward, a talented caricaturist, produced a picture showing the king of Spain conversing with the pope and the devil and compared this plotting to the planning of the ill-fated Armada of 1588 and the Gunpowder Plot of 1605. When Count Gondomar, the Spanish ambassador in London, complained of the insult to his sovereign, Ward was examined by the Privy Council and briefly imprisoned before he was permitted to return to Ipswich. This marked the first of two clashes with the ecclesiastical authorities on account of his puritan practices. In 1622, Ward was called before Samuel Harsnet, bishop of Norwich, on charges of nonconformity. Ward appealed to the king, who referred the matter to the examination of Lord Keeper Williams, who negotiated successfully with Harsnet on Ward's behalf. He may have been briefly inhibited from preaching in August 1623, but the details of this episode are unclear.

A sterner test came in 1635 when Ward fell foul of Archbishop William Laud. In November 1635, Ward was charged with a number of offenses, including preaching against the Book of Sports and against bowing at the name of Jesus. He was alleged to have said that the Church of England was ready to ring the changes and that religion and the gospel "stood on tiptoes ready to be gone." Ward was suspended from his ministry and imprisoned. On his release, Ward moved to Rotterdam, where he eventually ministered with William Bridge. His exile was short lived, as he returned to Ipswich by April 1638, although whether or not he enjoyed the freedom of his ministry is not clear. He died in March 1640 and was buried on 8 March 1640 in the church of St. Mary-le-Tower. As a mark of deep gratitude and respect, the town of Ipswich continued paying Ward's annual stipend of 100 pounds to his widow and eldest son for as long as they lived. Ward, with the sometime editorial assistance of Thomas Gataker, Ambrose Wood, and his younger brother Nathaniel, published a number of immensely popular sermons between 1615 and 1624. A collection of his eminently quotable sermons and treatises appeared in 1627 and again in 1636.

*See also:* Gunpowder Plot

*Further Reading*

Frank Grace, "'Schismaticall and factious humours': Opposition in Ipswich to Laudian Church Government in the 1630s," in David Chadd, ed., *Dissent in East Anglia,* vol. 3 (Norwich, Eng., 1998), pp. 97–120; Samuel Ward, *Sermons and Treatises* (1627); Tom Webster, *Godly Clergy in Early Stuart England: The Caroline Puritan Movement, c. 1620–1643* (Cambridge, Eng., 1997).

*John Craig*

## Watson, Thomas (d. 1686)

English Puritan minister. From Yorkshire, he entered Emmanuel College, Cambridge, in 1635, and was awarded the B.A. in 1639 and the M.A. in 1642. By late 1647 he was preaching in London at St. Stephen, Walbrook. On 7 December 1648, the day after Pride's Purge, Watson preached a fast-day sermon before the Rump Parliament implying criticism of the purge and decrying the spread of heresy. He was not voted the usual thanks for his sermon nor asked to print it. In 1649 he was one of fifty-two London ministers who signed "A Testimony to the Truth of Jesus Christ," which called for Presbyterian government in the English Church in order to restrain the growth of heresy. That same year he signed *A Vindication of the Ministers of the Gospel,* in which some Puritan clergy denied complicity in the execution of Charles I. In 1651 he was imprisoned for several months for involvement in the plotting of the minister Christopher Love, who was executed in 1651 for corresponding with the future Charles II and the former queen, Henrietta Maria.

After the Restoration, Watson was ejected (1662) as rector of St. Stephen, Walbrook. A sermon of that year (*A Word of Comfort for the Church of God*) steeled the godly to face persecution. An informer reported him for illegal preaching in 1664 and 1665. In 1666 he took the Oxford oath not to attempt change in the government of church or state. In 1669 he was reportedly preaching in a large meetinghouse in London; in 1672 (under the terms of the Declaration of Indulgence) he was licensed to preach as a Presbyterian, but in 1683 and 1685 he was prosecuted for illegal preaching. His health failing, he retired to Essex, where he died. His *Ark of Divine Contentment* passed through fifteen editions between 1653 and 1682. *The Holy Eucharist* emphasized that sacrament as a means of grace, and his posthumous *A Body of Practical Divinity* (1692) consisted of 176 sermons explaining the Shorter Catechism of the Westminster Assembly. His writings disclose moderate Calvinism, a focus on the spiritual life, and considerable classical, Hebraic, and patristic learning.

*Further Reading*

A. G. Matthews, *Calamy Revised: Being a Revision of Edmund Calamy's Account of the Ministers and others Ejected and Silenced, 1660–2* (Oxford, 1934; reprinted 1988).

*Dewey D. Wallace Jr.*

## Weld (Welde), Thomas (1595–1661)

Puritan clergyman and colonial agent. Weld was baptized in Sudbury, Suffolk, in 1595, matriculated at Trinity College, Cambridge, in 1611 and was ordained in 1618. After a spell at Haverhill, Suffolk, from 1619, he became vicar of Terling, Essex, in 1624, and he became an important figure in the circles of spiritual exercises in the county. He was prominent in the fasts and conferences established by Thomas Hooker and attended by ministers like John Rogers and Stephen Marshall. In concert with the parish elite he advanced a program of reformation of manners and established a household seminary, one of whose pupils was Thomas Shepard. In late 1630 Bishop William Laud summoned him and required him to sign the Three Articles. After several months of equivocation, he refused and was thus excommunicated. At the end of 1631, with a number of other ministers, he remonstrated with Laud after a visitation sermon and was called before High Commission for entering the church while excommunicated. After considering Scotland and Ireland, he emigrated to Amsterdam and then Massachusetts in 1632.

Having been appointed first pastor of Roxbury, where he served with John Eliot, Weld became a member of the first synod of New England and played an important role in the antinomian controversy. Roxbury's proximity to Boston meant there were many dissidents, and Weld worked hard to restore orthodoxy. In 1638 he became an overseer of Harvard College, and later that year he began working with Eliot and Richard Mather on a translation of the psalms, published in 1640 as *The Whole Booke of Psalmes*. This text, usually known as the Bay Psalm Book, was the first book printed in the English colonies in North America.

In 1641, at the request of the General Court, he accompanied Hugh Peter to England to raise funds for Massachusetts. Despite initial success, his increasing preoccupation with English affairs and failure to prevent Roger Williams's plan to acquire a patent to all Narragansett territory led to his dismissal in 1645. He and Peter accompanied Alexander, Lord Forbes, on his 1642 expedition to Ireland, and he was involved in a plot to save Archbishop Laud from the death penalty by having him tried in New England. His publication of John Winthrop's account of the antinomian troubles, with his own assessment added, won the castigations of English Congregationalists, as it emphasized the intolerance of the New England Way. His reputation was improved, to a degree, by two works, one, *An Answer to W. R.* (1644) being an answer to William Rathband's attack on Congregationalism, the second *A Brief Narrative of the Practices of the Churches in New England* (1645).

After a short spell at Wanlip, Leicestershire, he became rector of St. Mary's, Gateshead, Durham, in 1650. He became embroiled in a harsh pamphlet war with Quakers. He remained there until 1657 when he retired, which was probably a judicious move, as his intolerance seems to have alienated his congregation. He seems to have moved to London, signing a declaration disowning Venner's Rising in 1661, shortly before his death.

*See also:* Bay Psalm Book

*Further Reading*

R. Howell, "Thomas Weld of Gateshead: The Return of a New England Puritan," *Archaeologia Aeliana*, 4th series, 48 (1970); R. P. Stearns, "The Weld-Peters Mission to England," *Publications of the Colonial Society of Massachusetts* 32 (1937); Tom Webster, *Godly Clergy in Early Stuart England: The Caroline Puritan Movement, c. 1620–1643* (Cambridge, Eng., 1997); Keith Wrightson and David Levine, *Poverty and Piety in an English Village: Terling, 1525–1700*, 2nd ed. (Oxford, 1995).

*Tom Webster*

## Wemyss (also Weemes), John (ca. 1579–1636)

A minister in the Church of Scotland from Lathocker in Fife and a scholar who was an important student of Judaism. Wemyss was born about the year 1579. He received his M.A. from St. Andrews in 1600. He preached in Hutton, Berwickshire, until his transfer to Dunse in 1613. Archbishop Spottiswood of St. Andrews chose Wemyss to attend the 1618 preliminary assembly at Perth designated to compile articles of practice in accord with the Church of England. At Perth he served as a ministers' representative.

The assembly's Articles of Perth were highly contentious. Wemyss refused to perform the ritual as prescribed by the articles. The High Commission charged him in 1620 with contempt and insubordination, dismissing him with a reprimand and remonstrance from the archbishop. Afterwards, Wemyss withdrew from religious politics and devoted himself to Judaist, or philo-Semitic, theology.

Wemyss was one of the earliest scholars who saw Judaism as an important component of the Puritan movement. His major works include *The Christian Synagogue*, published in 1623; *Portraiture of the Image of God in Man* in 1627; *The Lawes of Moses, Ceremoniall, Morall, and Judiciall*, in 1633; and finally *A Treatise of the Foure Degenerate Sonnes, viz., the Atheist, the Magician, the Idolater, and the Jew*, in 1636. These works argue for learning from the Jews, at the same time they warn of the Jews' threat to Christianity and propose measures to curb Jewish influence once they are allowed into a Christian country.

In seventeenth-century Scotland and England, Wemyss's primary importance lay in the development of toleration of the Jews in a Christian country, an idea that he did not live to see come to fruition but for whose fruition he laid the groundwork. His works can be found in the library inventories of many New England colonists and almost certainly influenced John Cotton's proposed law code, *Moses His Judicialls,* presented to Massachusetts Bay Colony in 1636, as well as Roger Williams's opinion that Jews should be welcomed to New England. John Eliot became an "apostle to the Indians" in part because of Judaist literature. Wemyss died in 1636. In 1655 Cromwell accepted the reentry of the Jews into England.

*Further Reading*
Oxford Dictionary of National Biography (Oxford, 2004).

*Katherine Hermes*

## Whalley, Edward (d. ca. 1674–1675)

Officer in Parliamentarian Army and one of Cromwell's major-generals. A cousin of Oliver Cromwell, Edward Whalley left his trade as a woollen draper to fight for Parliament in the English Civil Wars. He rose to become one of the Lord Protector's major-generals, responsible for the imposition of godly rule across a large section of England.

Whalley fought in all three Civil Wars, initially as an officer in Cromwell's own double-regiment of horse, and then as colonel of his own regiment in the New Model Army. Whalley's Puritanism was generally moderate; a member of Thomas Goodwin's congregation during the 1650s, he was claimed at various times both by Presbyterians and Independents. His regiment, however, soon became a notorious hive of political and religious sectarianism, to the discomfort of its regimental chaplain, the moderate Presbyterian Richard Baxter.

Whalley sat as one of King Charles's judges in January 1649, and he signed the king's death warrant. He actively supported Cromwell's assumption of power in 1653. In 1655, when Cromwell experimented with direct military dictatorship, Whalley was appointed to govern the East Midlands. Although he dutifully proceeded against delinquents, alehouses, and scandalous ministers, Whalley proved a notably tolerant major-general. Unlike his colleagues, he permitted horseracing and took a keen interest in administering effective justice throughout the region.

On the Lord Protector's death in 1658, Whalley declared for Richard Cromwell, but his regiment refused to follow him. As a regicide, Whalley expected little mercy after the restoration of the monarchy. He fled to New England with his son-in-law, William Goffe, and is believed to have died in Hadley, Massachusetts, around 1675.

*See also:* Major-Generals
*Further Reading*
Christopher Durston, *Cromwell's Major-Generals: Godly Government during the English Revolution* (Manchester, Eng., 2001); Charles H. Firth and Godfrey Davies, *The Regimental History of Cromwell's Army* (Oxford, 1940; reprinted 1991).

*David J. Appleby*

## Wharton, Philip (1613–1696)

Puritan leader in the parliamentary opposition to Charles I. Wharton succeeded his grandfather as fourth Lord Wharton in 1625 and in the following year began his studies at Exeter College, Oxford. He was a puritan with strong convictions and a spokesman for the reform party in the House of Lords in the Short and Long Parliaments. With the outbreak of the Civil Wars, he became an officer in the army of the Earl of Essex and participated in the battle of Edgehill.

His strong religious views led to his appointment as one of the lay members of the Westminster Assembly. Though he initially followed the Scottish proposals, he came to advocate a greater liberty for conscience. Though he was opposed to the trial and execution of Charles I and subsequently withdrew from active politics, he remained on good terms with Oliver Cromwell. Following the restoration of the monarchy in 1660, Wharton again became active in the nation's affairs. He supported puritan members of Parliament who fought in the Cavalier Parliament for relief for their cause. Following the passage of the Clarendon Code, he used his influence to protect Dissenters and promote their cause. On the accession of James II in 1685, he left England, taking up residence in the Netherlands. He supported William of Orange's invasion of England in 1688, and following the Glorious Revolution he became one of the new monarch's privy councilors.

*Further Reading*
Richard Greaves and Robert Zaller, eds., *Biographical Dictionary of British Radicals in the Seventeenth Century*, 3 vols.(Brighton, Eng., 1982).

*Francis J. Bremer*

## Whately, William (1583–1639)

Noted puritan preacher. Whately was born into a prominent puritan family in Banbury, Oxfordshire. He graduated B.A. from Cambridge (Christ's College) in 1601 and proceeded M.A. at Oxford (St. Edmund's Hall) in 1604. In 1605 he was appointed curate and lecturer at Banbury and vicar in 1610. Whately's eloquent and learned preaching made Banbury synonymous with puritanism, and in 1614 the great dramatist Ben Jonson satirized the Banbury godly as hypocrites in *Bartholomew Fair.* Whately was presented to the church authorities in 1607, inter alia for preaching against ceremonies and adapting the Book of Common Prayer to his own use. Whately's sermons demonstrate his belief in predestination and his view that preaching was the chief guide to godliness. His works on salvation, including *The redemption of time* (1606) and *The new-birth: or, A treatise of regeneration* (1618), were highly popular, although he was careful to avoid theological controversy in his publications. He also wrote two conduct books, *A bride-bush* (1617) and *A care-cloth* (1624), although he repudiated the first edition of *A bride-bush* as published without his permission. The expanded 1619 edition can therefore be regarded as definitive. In it he argued that it was lawful for a man to beat his wife in certain circumstances, a view opposed by the majority of churchmen. Whately also argued that an innocent spouse should be allowed to divorce and remarry in cases of adultery or desertion, an opinion that the High Commission forced him to recant in 1621. Whately's death was widely mourned by the godly, and his links with other puritan clergy were marked by the gift of his ring to the aged John Dod, vicar of Fawsley.

*See also:* Marriage
*Further Reading*
Jacqueline Eales, "Gender Construction in Early Modern England and the Conduct Books of William Whately," in R. N. Swanson, ed., *Gender and Christian Religion*, Studies in Church History, vol. 34 (Woodbridge, Eng., 1998), pp. 163–174.

*Jacqueline Eales*

## Wheelwright, John (ca. 1592–1679)

Contentious puritan minister whose involvement in the antinomian controversy dogged him throughout his life. Born into a landowning family of Saleby, Lincolnshire, Wheelwright attended Sidney Sussex College, Cambridge, where he first knew Oliver Cromwell. Wheelwright received the A.B. degree in 1615 and the M.A. in 1619. Two years later he married Marie Storre, whose father was vicar of Bilsby, Lincolnshire. He succeeded to that post on the death of his father-in-law in 1623. After Marie died, Wheelwright married Mary Hutchinson, sister-in-law of Anne Marbury Hutchinson, in 1630.

Wheelwright lost his position at Bilsby in 1632 when convicted of simony. The Wheelwrights emigrated in mid-1636. His nomination for a clerical position at Boston was opposed by Governor John Winthrop, so he settled instead at nearby Mt. Wollaston. In 1636 the antinomian, or free grace, controversy erupted in the Massachusetts Bay Colony. Wheelwright delivered a fast-day sermon on 19 January 1637, bluntly comparing the colony's clergy with the likes of Herod and Pilate and suggesting that violence against authority was sometimes a necessary consequence of strong belief. This inflammatory sermon led to the charges of sedition and contempt of authority, of which he was convicted later that year. After several months' delay in sentencing, while the court futilely hoped he would moderate his position, he was disfranchised and expelled from the colony.

Though invited to join other exiled "opinionists" in Aquidneck (later Rhode Island), he chose instead to go north to Piscataqua, where in 1638 he and some faithful followers established the town of Exeter. He served as minister there until 1643, when the area was annexed by the Massachusetts Bay Colony. He then moved to Wells on the coast of southern Maine. Finally, in 1644 he successfully appealed to the Massachusetts Bay General Court and to Governor Winthrop to have his banishment repealed. This enabled him in 1647 to move to Hampton, then a part of Massachusetts. In 1654 he gave an election sermon in Boston, but the next year he took his large family back to England where Cromwell was Lord Protector. Little is known of his residence in England, though one document shows his residence as "Belleau," which was the Lincolnshire seat of Henry Vane, a strong ally of the defeated faction in New England while serving as the youthful governor in 1636–1637.

In London, he published *A Brief, and Plain Apology* (1658) in which he claimed—as he always had—his orthodoxy. This, not *Mercurius Americanus* (1645), which is often incorrectly ascribed to him, was his last defense. After the monarchy's restoration and the subsequent beheading of Vane in 1662, Wheelwright returned to Massachusetts. At age seventy, he became the minister at Salisbury, where he served until his death at eighty-seven.

*See also:* Anne Marbury Hutchinson, Antinomianism
*Further Reading*
Charles H. Bell, *Memoir of the Reverend John Wheelwright,* Publications of the Prince Society, vol. 9 (1876), pp. 1–78; Michael P. Winship, *Making Heretics: Militant Protestantism and Free Grace in Massachusetts, 1636–1641* (Princeton, 2002).

*Sargent Bush Jr.*

## Whitaker, Alexander (1585–1617)

Puritan clergyman in the Virginia colony. Alexander Whitaker was the son of the puritan theologian and college head William Whitaker. Through his mother, Susan Culverwell Whitaker, he was related to other puritan figures such as Laurence Chaderton, William Gouge, and Arthur Dent. His father died when he was young.

Alexander attended Eton and entered Trinity College, Cambridge in 1602. He would have known Adam Winthrop, the auditor of the college, who had been a friend and admirer of William Whitaker, and also John Winthrop, Adam's son and a student at Trinity. In 1609, following his graduation and receipt of his M.A., he was ordained a clergyman. Two years later he journeyed to the Virginia colony as minister to the settlement of Henrico, on the James River. Given his complaints about the reluctance of English clergy who opposed the wearing of the surplice to come to America, where such conformity was not enforced, it is likely that puritan scruples about the use of vestments was at least part of his reason for emigration. He was interested in the Native Americans, whom he hoped to convert, and wrote about their religion in some of his letters home. His most famous success was the conversion and baptism of Pocahontas. He died of drowning when crossing a creek in the colony in 1617.

*Further Reading*
Karen Kupperman, *Indians and English: Facing Off in Early America* (Ithaca, NY, 2000); H. C. Porter, "Alexander Whitaker: Cambridge Apostle to Virginia," *William and Mary Quarterly* 14 (1957), 317–343.

*Francis J. Bremer*

## Whitaker, William (1548–1595)

Master of St. John's College, Cambridge, and a leading university divine in the late sixteenth century, primarily due to his indefatigable writing against popery. Whitaker's religious positions reflect the theological and ecclesiological views of Elizabethan moderate Puritanism. He was a supporter and promoter of the royal supremacy, episcopacy, and conformity in matters *adiaphoric.* But Whitaker was also a staunch Calvinist who assisted in the writing of the Lambeth Articles of 1595.

Whitaker's reputation for "Puritanism" may stem from his clash with the Anti-Puritan (but reliably Calvinist) Archbishop John Whitgift in the William Barrett affair of 1595. Whitaker also moved in the social circuit of the Elizabethan godly elite, first marrying the sister-in-law of Lawrence Chaderton, and then, after her death, taking as his second wife the widow of Dudley Fenner.

A fellow of Trinity College, Cambridge, Whitaker was educated at expense of his uncle, Alexander Nowell, dean of St. Paul's. He was appointed canon of Norwich cathedral in 1578. In 1580, he was appointed Regius Professor of Divinity, the same year he was appointed chancellor of St. Paul's. In 1582, Lord Burghley and Archbishop John Whitgift appointed Whitaker to the mastership of St. John's College, Cambridge.

As befitted his fierce Calvinist partisanship, Whitaker wrote theological works arguing against both German Lutheranism and Roman Catholicism. His great work, *De Auctoritate Scripturae*, dedicated to Whitgift, was published in 1594. A posthumous edition of many of Whitaker's works was published in 1610 in Geneva.

*Further Reading*
Peter Lake, *Moderate Puritans and the Elizabethan Church* (Cambridge, Eng., 1982).

*Lori Anne Ferrell*

## White, John (1575–1648)

Minister and colonial promoter. John White, minister at Dorchester (Dorset), was born at Stanton St. John near Oxford in 1575. He was educated at Winchester and New College, Oxford (M.A., 1601), and was a fellow of the college until he became rector of Holy Trinity, Dorchester, in 1606.

White's strict Calvinism was at first unpopular in Dorchester. But after a disastrous fire in 1613, he became famed for his preaching. Dorchester should be rebuilt as a Reformed community, he taught, where idleness and sin would be eradicated by attacking their roots: poverty, ignorance, and disease. Helped by a now puritan corporation, White promoted the expansion of poor relief; a hospital where children were taught godliness and obedience; an elementary school; and improved care for the sick and elderly. The program was financed partly by a municipal brewery, partly by the charitableness of the townspeople, who gave freely both for Dorchester's own needs and those of distressed people elsewhere. Dorchester's contributions to towns visited by plague or fire far exceeded those from other places of comparable size. White's reforms led to improved church attendance and a dramatic fall in illegitimate births, though a less marked decline in disorderly behavior.

Before 1642, White was a conforming minister of the Church of England. The innovations in the direction of increased ceremonialism associated with Archbishop William Laud made him uncomfortable, but in a 1633 assize sermon he still preached obedience to authority. A year later, however, he narrowly avoided suspension for refusing to read the Book of Sports, and soon afterwards was in trouble with the High Commission over the Feoffees for Impropriations. But the diocesan authorities treated him mildly, and he was never punished for his churchwardens' failure to rail in the communion table.

White's other major preoccupation was transatlantic settlement. He was involved in the formation of the Dorchester Company (later absorbed by the Massachusetts Bay Company) and its transformation from a predominantly fishing enterprise into one promoting immigration to New England. In 1630 he oversaw the departure of a group from Dorchester and the surrounding area who established the town of Dorchester, Massachusetts. White frequently offered John Winthrop advice and encouragement; at one time he considered going to Massachusetts himself.

The Civil War pushed White into more extreme positions. In 1640 he still thought that episcopacy could be reformed; by 1642 this was no longer realistic. He became an active member of the Westminster Assembly, in which he supported the Presbyterians against the Independents; after the fall of Dorchester to the Royalists in 1643, Parliament appointed him minister at Lambeth. He returned to Dorchester in 1646, in failing health but still opposing toleration of the radical sects: in March 1647 he held a public fast at St. Peter's church to denounce their heresies and blasphemies. He died on 21 July 1648.

*See also:* Poor Relief
*Further Reading*
Frances Rose-Troup, *John White: The Patriarch of Dorchester* (New York, 1930); David Underdown, *Fire from Heaven: Life in an English Town in the Seventeenth Century* (London, 1993).

*David Underdown*

## Whitfield (also Whitefield and Whitfeld), Henry (ca. 1591–1657)

Congregational clergyman and supporter of missionary activities among the Native Americans. Whitfield studied at New College, Oxford, in 1610, but evidently did not stay for a decree, leaving Oxford to pursue legal training at the Inns of Court. He was ordained and inducted as rector of St. Margaret's, Ockley, Surrey, in 1618 and ministered there until 1638.

Whitfield resigned his living, sold his estate, and migrated to New England in 1639, taking a number of parish families with him at his own expense. His was the first ship to sail directly from England to the new colony of New Haven. While crossing the Atlantic, Whitfield and a group of his fellow emigrants drew up a covenant that became the foundation of the town they named Guilford, on land they purchased from the local Native Americans. Whitfield served as pastor there for eleven years without pay.

In 1650, discouraged by the New England wilderness and encouraged by letters from English friends, Whitfield left Guilford and returned to England, where he resumed his ministry at a parish in Winchester, where he died in September 1657. He retained an interest in New England affairs, and particularly in the mission to the Indians. Whitfield knew of John Eliot and his missionary efforts and had also been impressed with the missionary work of Thomas Mayhew Jr. In England he became a member of the Society for the Propagation of the Gospel in New England and in 1651 published *The Light Appearing More and More towards the Perfect Day*, which related in great detail the work of Mayhew and Eliot. He was later involved in the publication of *Strength out of Weakness* (1652) and further reports in 1555.

*Further Reading*
*American National Biography* (New York, 1999).

*Francis J. Bremer*

## Whitgift, John (ca. 1532–1604)

Archbishop of Canterbury. Whitgift was born in Lincolnshire and graduated B.A. from Pembroke Hall, Cambridge, in 1554. He remained in Cambridge for the next twenty-three years, holding a variety of university posts. Despite his flirtation with nonconformity during the Vestiarian Controversy of 1564–1566, in 1567 he was appointed both as Regius Professor of Divinity and master of Trinity College. In 1571 he was promoted dean of Lincoln, conscientiously dividing his time between his duties there and in Cambridge.

When in 1570 Thomas Cartwright, his successor as Lady Margaret Professor of Divinity, comprehensively attacked the provisions of the Elizabethan settlement in a series of lectures, Whitgift emerged as his most implacable opponent. As vice-chancellor of the university, he sanctioned Cartwright's removal from his professorship. When *An Admonition to the Parliament* (1572), by John Field and Thomas Wilcox, was immediately followed by *A Second Admonition,* perhaps by Cartwright, Whitgift was chosen to counter this burgeoning Presbyterian threat in print. *An answere to a certen Libel intituled, An admonition to the Parliament* also appeared before the end of 1572. Cartwright hit back with *A Replye to an answere* (1573). Whitgift countered with *The Defense of the Aunswere* in 1574. Although Cartwright published *The second replie . . . agaynst Maister Doctor Whitgiftes second answer* (1575), Whitgift never returned to the subject in print, perhaps in part because Edmund Grindal's elevation as archbishop of Canterbury in 1576 marked a temporary cessation of hostilities.

In April 1577 Whitgift was consecrated bishop of Worcester, succeeding Grindal as primate in September 1583. Supported by John Aylmer, bishop of London, and other like-minded bishops, he immediately initiated a campaign for clerical conformity by means of subscription to a series of articles (popularly known as the Three Articles, to distinguish them from the official Thirty-nine Articles). The sticking point for many clergy was that the Three Articles included the proposition that the English prayer book contained nothing contrary to the word of God. Months of strife ensued, and by September 1584 Whitgift was forced by the Privy Council to modify his strategy. Henceforth the Three Articles were used only selectively as a cat-and-mouse tactic against the activities of the most prominent radicals.

Whitgift was a learned, energetic Calvinist of considerable administrative ability, but this divisive opening gambit in some respects crippled his twenty-year primacy—not least because many of those appointed to the episcopal bench during those years were far from sharing his authoritarian views. Although he enjoyed the unwavering support of Elizabeth, he did not invariably see eye to eye with William Cecil, Lord Burghley, or his son Sir Robert Cecil, and during the 1590s he seems to have had some difficulty in securing the promotion of his protégés—Richard Bancroft, his chaplain and successor as archbishop of Canterbury included. Whitgift died in February 1604, one month after speaking on the opening day of the Hampton Court Conference.

*See also: An Admonition to the Parliament,* Anti-Calvinism, Articles of Religion, Dedham Conference, Lambeth Articles, Subscription
*Further Reading*
Patrick Collinson, *The Elizabethan Puritan Movement* (London, 1967); Peter Milward, *Religious Controversies of the Elizabethan Age* (London, 1977); Brett Usher, *William Cecil and Episcopacy* (Aldershot, Eng., 2003).

*Brett Usher*

## Whiting, Samuel (1597–1679)

Served as pastor at Lynn, Massachusetts, for more than forty years after successive prosecutions for nonconformity in his English parishes, Lynn Regis and Skirbeck. A native of Boston, Lincolnshire, he was educated at Emmanuel College, Cambridge, receiving his A.B. (1616) and A.M. (1620). A brief undated autobiographical letter to John Cotton tells of his soul-searchings there.

With his second wife, Elizabeth St. John, and two children, he emigrated in April of 1636, settling in Saugus, renamed Lynn after Whiting's former residence. Not prolific as a published writer, he was known for his moderation, cheerfulness, and devout spirituality. He was a proficient Hebraist and Latinist, evidence of which is his 1649 oration at Harvard College, "Oratio, Quam Comitijs Cantabrigiensibus Americanis Peroravit." He became an overseer of Harvard in 1654. His best-known work is his brief biography of Cotton, *Concerning the Life of the Famous Mr. Cotton,* written soon after Cotton's death but unpublished until Thomas Hutchinson's 1769 collection of colonial writings. The Cotton biographies by John Norton and Cotton Mather depended heavily on Whiting's account, which dwells mainly on Cotton's English years. He was a staunch defender of the church's authority when challenged by civil authority. Two volumes attest to his preaching style and content: *A Discourse of the Last Judgement* (1664), which condenses many sermons to notes, and his work on inward devotion and prayer, *Abraham's Humble Intercession for Sodom* (1666).

*Further Reading*
William Whiting, *Memoir of Rev. Samuel Whiting, D.D* (Boston, 1872).

*Sargent Bush Jr.*

## Wigglesworth, Michael (1631–1705)

Longtime minister and physician at Malden, Massachusetts, and the most popular poet in colonial America. His long narrative poem in ballad meter, *The Day of Doom* (1662), was America's first best-seller.

Religious persecution drove his parents from their native Yorkshire to New Haven in 1638. Schooled by Ezekiel Cheever, Michael entered Harvard College in 1647, studying medicine until his conversion in 1650 or 1651 redirected him to the ministry. He earned the A.B. and A.M. degrees and was appointed tutor and fellow of the college. During this period (1652–1654), he wrote and delivered two orations on the topic of eloquence.

In 1654 Wigglesworth was invited to preach at Malden. As his diary for this period shows, he suffered from spiritual and psychological doubts as well as sexual anxiety and health problems that delayed his full commitment to the ministry at Malden. He married Mary Rowley, on 18 May 1655 and five months later settled in Malden. He was ordained as teacher of the Malden congregation in the spring of 1657, though already suffering from the ill health that compromised his ministry for the next thirty years. Mary's death in December 1659 apparently deepened his tendency to depression. Unable to serve his congregation adequately, and beset with sharp criticism and reduced salary, he turned to poetry as a means of teaching. Motivated by the demise of the Puritan regime in England, Charles II's restoration, perception of New England's spiritual decline, and recent disputes over the Half-Way Covenant, he composed his dramatization of the Day of Judgment, *The Day of Doom* (1662), which sold all 1,800 copies in the first year. Doggedly descriptive, the poem's power rests in its narrative force, its rhythmic regularity, and its unmistakably didactic purpose. Four more American editions appeared before his death, and it remained a staple of New England religious life for generations.

In 1662, when a drought suggested God's displeasure to him, he also wrote a jeremiad attacking New England's spiritual failings, *Gods Controversy with New England*, which remained unpublished until the nineteenth century. His poetic talent was further demonstrated eight years later when he published *Meat Out of the Eater*, a poem reflecting more interest in figurative language and the paradoxes at the heart of Christian belief than his earlier works.

After twenty years of widowhood, to great scandal, Wigglesworth in 1679 married his housekeeper, Martha Mudge, a woman twenty-five years his junior. They had six children, and Wigglesworth almost miraculously regained his physical and mental health, returning to full activity and wide reputation as a godly and effective minister. After Martha's 1690 death, Wigglesworth married Sybil Avery Sparhawk in 1691, who bore his eighth child and second son. In 1705, Cotton Mather preached his funeral sermon, "A Faithful Man."

*See also:* Puritan Best-Sellers
*Further Reading*
Ronald A. Bosco, ed., *The Poems of Michael Wigglesworth* (Lanham, MD, 1989); Richard Crowder, *No Featherbed to Heaven: A Biography of Michael Wigglesworth, 1631–1705* (East Lansing, MI, 1962).

*Sargent Bush Jr.*

## Wilcox, Thomas (ca. 1549–1608)

Wilcox may be defined as a puritan, not only on his track record as Nonconformist and "practical" divine, but because in a publication of 1581 he accepted the designation, while regretting its invention by the Roman Catholic Nicholas Sanders. Wilcox was at Oxford in the mid-1560s but left without a degree, becoming curate of the London parish of All Hallows Honey Lane. In June 1572, he joined forces with John Field in publishing the Presbyterian manifesto, *An admonition to the Parliament,* which was deemed seditious, earning its authors more than a year in the Fleet prison. Wilcox played second fiddle to Field, composing "a breife confession of Faythe" under his direction. Later the two fell out, in a correspondence exploited by the anti-puritan Richard Bancroft.

It is not clear whether the cause of the split was a moral or ideological error on Wilcox's part. Was this why Wilcox in many of his prefaces went beyond normal convention in describing himself as a grievous sinner? Bishop John Aylmer of London was in favor of exporting Wilcox and his kind to the Catholic north. Wilcox did go north, but only as far as Hertfordshire, where he became a curate in Hemel Hempstead Parish and cultivated the patronage of Lady Anne Bacon, spending time in the Bacon household at Gorhambury. It was probably Wilcox who put together, and at Gorhambury, the puritan archive amassed by Field and known to history as *A parte of a register* (published overseas in 1593) and the manuscript "Seconde Parte of a Register." Wilcox developed into one of the most sought-after puritan casuists of his time. Some of his letters of spiritual comfort were published, but others survived (until the late seventeenth century) only in manuscript form, the recipients reading like a Who's Who of the great and good of Elizabethan England, including the Countess of Sussex, Sir Francis and Lady Walsingham, and Robert Beale. But his particular patrons were the Harlakenden family of Kent, from whom he and his wife, Annah, received an annuity of £13.6s.8d, plus £6.13s.4d for their son Elijah.

If all the many books signed "T. W." were his, he published twenty-five, dedicated to a variety of great patrons, who included the third Earl of Bedford and his countess, the very literary Lucy. In 1604, Wilcox presented Prince Henry with a trans-

lation of the influential Huguenot Philippe de Mornay's *Traité de la verité de la religion chrétienne . . .* (1581), *A woorke concerning the trewnesse of the christian religion,* which had been begun by Sir Philip Sidney and continued by Arthur Golding. In this he declared his unswerving loyalty to Henry's royal father. There is evidence that Wilcox had acted as an intermediary between the English puritan interest and James before his accession. In 1624, long after his death, Wilcox received the ultimate accolade of a collected edition of his *Works,* something that never happened to John Field.

*See also: An Admonition to the Parliament,* Book of Discipline
*Further Reading*
Patrick Collinson, *The Elizabethan Puritan Movement* (London, 1967); A. Peel, ed., *The seconde parte of a register,* 2 vols. (Cambridge, Eng., 1915).

*Patrick Collinson*

## Willard, Samuel (1640–1707)

New England Puritan minister and vice president of Harvard College. Willard was born 31 January 1640 in Concord, Massachusetts, the son of Simon Willard, who, along with Reverend Peter Bulkeley, was among those who first settled the town in 1635. Bulkeley probably prepared Samuel for Harvard, where he graduated B.A. in 1659, and M.A. at some later time, but not in the customary course of three years. In 1664, Willard was ordained minister of the newly gathered church in the frontier town of Groton, and he married Abigail, daughter of Reverend John Sherman of Watertown. But in March 1676, during King Philip's War, Groton was devastated by an Indian attack, and the surviving residents temporarily abandoned the town.

Willard and his family settled in Boston, where he regularly assisted the ailing Reverend Thomas Thacher at the Third (South) Church, a congregation formed in 1669 by members of the First Church who favored the acceptance of the Half-Way Covenant. Willard was admitted to membership in the South Church in February 1678, installed as teacher shortly after, and with Reverend

Thacher's death in October, became sole minister to the congregation. Abigail had died in 1676, after the birth of their sixth child. In 1679 Willard married Eunice, the daughter of magistrate Edward Tyng, and she bore him fourteen more children.

When Sir Edmond Andros arrived as governor in 1686, two years after the abrogation of the Massachusetts Bay charter, he demanded for Church of England believers the use of the Congregational meetinghouses. Willard and his fellow church leaders resisted, but as Easter approached in 1687, Andros ordered the South Church sexton to ring the bell and open the church for Anglican worship. Willard's congregation was required to submit to the intrusion until the Andros regime was overthrown in the revolution of 1689, an event in which the minister took a prominent role.

Though a guardian of Puritan orthodoxy, Willard evidently reconciled himself to the changes wrought by the Massachusetts charter of 1691, which provided for a Crown-appointed governor, a franchise based on property and not Congregational church membership, and toleration of religious dissent. In 1700, Willard encouraged the Boston ministers to extend recognition to the progressive orthodoxy of Reverend Benjamin Colman's new Brattle Street Church, and he secured the South Church's approval of another liberal, Reverend Ebenezer Pemberton, as his colleague minister.

Willard's was a voice of moderation during the Salem witchcraft hysteria of 1692. Two decades earlier, as minister in Groton, he had overseen with notable prudence the healing of a young servant, Elizabeth Knapp, who was believed to be possessed. He again came forward to urge the Salem court to adhere to high standards of evidence in the proceedings and to exercise caution in giving credence to accusations.

In 1701 Willard assumed the leadership of Harvard after Reverend Increase Mather was forced from the presidency, largely because of Mather's reluctance meet the requirement that he leave his Second (North) Church congregation and reside at the college. Named vice president, Willard was permitted to remain in his pulpit, spending only one or two nights a week in Cambridge, and still exercise full authority over the college. The author of numerous theological writings and treatises, Willard's principal work is *A Compleat Body of Divinity* (1726). He died 12 September 1707.

*See also:* Harvard College

*Further Reading*

Ernest Benson Lowrie, *The Shape of the Puritan Mind: The Thought of Samuel Willard* (New Haven, 1974); Seymour Van Dyken, *Samuel Willard, 1640–1707: Preacher of Orthodoxy in an Era of Change* (Grand Rapids, MI, 1972).

*Judith Graham*

## Williams, Roger (ca. 1603–1683)

The founder of Rhode Island Colony and an advocate of religious liberty.

### Life

Williams was born in London early in the reign of James I. His family was of modest means, and it was by the patronage, probably indirect, of the famed lawyer Sir Edmund Coke, that he was able to attend Pembroke College, Cambridge. He graduated B.A. in 1627 and, rather than involve himself in the corruptions of the Church of England, took a post as chaplain in the Masham household in Sussex. But with Bishop William Laud becoming more aggressive, Williams and his young bride, Mary Bernard, sailed for Boston, Massachusetts, arriving in February 1631. He was quickly offered the town's pulpit on an interim basis, but refused on account of the lack of Separatist rigor among the people. Thus he turned to the more radical folk of Salem, but the colonial magistrates blocked his settlement there. So he went off to Plymouth, where he assisted the minister for two years. Even there, however, his opinions were somewhat startling, and in 1633 he returned to Salem where he assumed office and began agitating again.

The year 1635 brought the crisis to a head, as the magistracy sought to have Williams returned to England. For a time, John Cotton, minister in Boston, tried both to protect and to persuade Williams, but in the fall he was sentenced to banishment, the grounds including his advanced separatism and his view that the king of England had no power to grant Indian land to English settlers. The execution of the decree was deferred due to Williams's ill health, and in January 1636 he fled to Providence rather than be seized and shipped back to England. He took part in founding a Baptist church there in 1638, but soon left to become a Seeker. In later years he worked to secure a colonial charter for his haven of religious freedom, spending the years 1643–1644 and 1651–1654 in England. *The Bloudy Tenent of Persecution* (1644) was published in England; it was his first major work on liberty of conscience. In 1672 he engaged in a public disputation with Quakers.

Work

At some point, probably even before crossing the Atlantic, Williams had become an advanced Separatist and had also absorbed a method of biblical interpretation that was to lead him beyond the mainstream of Puritan thought. That hermeneutics, typology, was by no means new in the seventeenth century. In fact, it is an ancient Hebraic form of exegesis whereby previous events are linked to the present; in Christian hands it was an important method of linking the two testaments of the Bible. The "type" is the original event; the "antitype" is a later event that builds upon the former but advances its meaning; the former is a shadow, the latter a clarification and fulfillment. One example consists of the great high priest Melchizedek and Jesus Christ, as described in Hebrews.

No Reformed theologian could do without typology, but among the early English General Baptists, typology was allowed freer play than among most contemporary exegetes. What Williams drew from these men, including the Separatist John Smyth, was a more radical and consistent application of typology whereby the Old Testament, most significantly Israel and its monarchy, was spiritualized; so that Israel became, not a model for contemporary "Christian" societies under a godly magistrate, but an earthly type of a radically separatist church of the faithful and of Christ the heavenly king, who ruled over a kingdom not of this world. Thus did

Williams subvert the very foundation of the aspirations of some Englishmen to create new elect nations in covenant with God. He showed the self-understanding of the Massachusetts Bay Colony, which saw itself as a city on a hill, to be threadbare and lacking any authentically biblical basis.

Williams combined this form of exegesis with the Reformed doctrine of predestination. He argued that if God knows his own, the elect, how then can these people be lost? If their salvation is secure, arguments that alternative, indeed heretical, teachings could lead people to ruin in the next world appear futile. So the magistrate can have no function in the maintenance of pure religion—in theory, and also in practice in Rhode Island colony. The civil authority tends only to the protection of persons and property. This blending of an advanced typological exegetical method and an insistence upon the doctrine of predestination marks the high point of Williams's innovations in Christian thought and paved the way to John Locke's *Letter concerning Toleration* (1685).

*See also:* John Winthrop, Indian Bible, International Puritanism, Plymouth Colony, Rhode Island, Seekers, Toleration

*Further Reading*
Edwin S. Gaustad, *Liberty of Conscience: Roger Williams in America* (Grand Rapids, MI, 1991); W. Clark Gilpin, *The Millenarian Piety of Roger Williams* (Chicago, 1979); Ola Elizabeth Winslow, *Master Roger Williams* (New York, 1957).

*David Mullan*

## Wilson, John (ca. 1591–1667)

Puritan clergyman in England and New England. John Wilson's father was a chaplain to Archbishop Edmund Grindal, and the youth was raised in comfortable circumstances. He attended Eton and in 1605 entered King's College, Cambridge. There he was influenced by the puritan preachers of the university and by his reading of Richard Rogers's *Seven Treatises* (1604). He traveled to Dedham to hear Rogers preach. Wilson's rooms at Cambridge became a meeting place for similarly minded men such as William Ames. When he received his B.A.

in 1610, his puritan sympathies were evident enough for him to be denied a fellowship in his college, which was generally not sympathetic to the reform movement. He studied for a year at the Inns of Court in London, there making the acquaintance of William Gouge. Wilson returned to Cambridge, taking up residence at the puritan stronghold of Emanuel College and received his M.A. in 1613. It is likely that while at Emmanuel he formed friendships with John Cotton and Thomas Hooker.

Wilson preached for a time in godly families until 1618, when he accepted the post of lecturer in Sudbury, Suffolk. Just as he had traveled from Cambridge to hear Richard Rogers, university students such as Thomas Goodwin, William Bridge, and Jeremiah Burroughes now journeyed to Sudbury to hear him. While at Sudbury he also met the nearby puritan gentleman John Winthrop and likely supported the unsuccessful attempt to get Winthrop elected as one of Sudbury's members of Parliament in 1626.

Wilson became one of the early members of the Massachusetts Bay Company and accompanied John Winthrop to the colony in 1630. There he was chosen the pastor of the First Church in Boston. He traveled back to England in 1631, 1634, and 1635 to settle affairs there and to persuade his wife to join him in New England. In 1633 John Cotton joined him in the Boston pulpit. The relationship between the two men was strained by the controversy over free grace that centered on Anne Hutchinson. The so-called antinomian controversy divided that church and plunged the colony into turmoil, with Cotton being identified by the enthusiasts as their inspiration and Wilson attacked by them for teaching a covenant of works. In the end, the two men worked to heal the divisions and resumed a productive relationship in guiding the church.

Wilson served as chaplain to the forces sent by Massachusetts against the Pequot Tribe in the Pequot War of 1637, but he was one of the early advocates of converting the Indians. On one occasion he took the orphaned son of one of the local sagamores into his home to protect and educate.

Wilson outlived many of his contemporaries and faced challenges that they never confronted. In the 1650s he was a fierce opponent of Quaker missionaries who traveled to New England. Faced with declining church memberships in the 1650s and 1660s, he became a supporter of the Half-Way Covenant, which modified membership in such a way as to extend baptism to more youth.

*Further Reading*
*American National Biography* (New York, 1999).

*Francis J. Bremer*

## Winslow, Edward (1595–1655)

Founder of Plymouth, colonial agent, and author. By 1617 Winslow had joined the English Separatist congregation at Leiden, worked as a printer with William Brewster, and married Elizabeth Barker. He migrated with the Leiden group to New England in 1620; his wife died the following year, and his remarriage two months later was the first in Plymouth Colony. Winslow was instrumental in forging the settlers' treaty with the Wampanoags and later in a land purchase from that tribe's leader, Massasoit. He contributed to *A Relation or Journal* (1622) and wrote *Good Newes from New-England* (1624). Winslow often traveled to England on colony matters; in 1627 he helped arrange a new deal with merchant investors in which he and a small group of other settlers assumed the colony's debts. He served at Plymouth as an assistant and on three occasions as governor and helped draft the Plymouth law code. During the 1640s he helped organize the New England Confederation. In 1646, he went to England and defended the colonies against accusations made by Samuel Gorton (in *Hypocrisie Unmasked,* 1646) and Robert Child (in *New-Englands Salamander Discovered,* 1647). In 1648, he published *The Glorious Progress of the Gospel Amongst the Indians in New England.* In 1654, Oliver Cromwell appointed Winslow to head an Anglo-Dutch committee to assess claims against the Dutch for destroying English ships in neutral Dutch ports. In 1655 Winslow participated in the campaign against Santo Domingo and Jamaica, during which he died of tropical fever and was buried at sea.

*See also:* Society for the Propagation of the Gospel in New England, Thanksgiving, Pilgrim Thanksgiving (in Primary Sources)
*Further Reading*
*American National Biography* (New York, 1999).

*Michael G. Ditmore*

### Winter, Samuel (1603–1666)

Puritan clergyman and college head. Winter was born in Temple Balsall, Warwickshire, and educated at the King Henry VIII School in Coventry. He then studied at Emmanuel College, Cambridge, where he came under the influence of John Preston. Through Preston's influence he then went to Boston, Lincolnshire, where he prepared for the ministry in the household seminary run by John Cotton. He began his ministry in Nottinghamshire and was a lecturer at York.

By the time the Civil Wars began, Winter was not only a puritan but an advocate of Congregationalist polity. In 1650 he settled in Dublin, Ireland, as a chaplain to the parliamentary commissioners charged with governing that country. In 1651 he began to act as Provost of Trinity College, Dublin, a post that was confirmed in 1562. He worked hard to revitalize the college by collecting back rents, and he sought to make it an important force for the spread of Protestant influence, developing schemes to make new preachers proficient in the Irish tongue. He formed a friendship with Increase Mather, who studied for his M.A. at Trinity after immigrating from New England, and that relationship continued strong for the rest of his life. Winter was also committed to opposing the spread of Baptist views in Ireland. Following the collapse of the puritan regime he lost his post at Trinity. He died in 1666.

*Further Reading*
T. C. Barnard, *Cromwellian Ireland* (London, 1975).

*Francis J. Bremer*

### Winthrop, Adam (1548–1623)

Puritan layman and lawyer. Adam was a younger son of Adam Winthrop, master of the Clothworkers

*The tomb of Adam Winthrop, father of Massachusetts governor John Winthrop, by the chancel door of the parish church of Groton, England. (Courtesy Francis J. Bremer)*

Company. Though born in London, he moved as a young man to Groton Suffolk when his father retreated there to avoid the religious scrutiny of the Marian regime. He was sent to school in Ipswich, Suffolk, where he studied under John Dawes, who was himself a Marian exile and translator of Protestant works, including Calvin's *Institutes*. While studying under Dawes, Adam came to the attention of Roger Kelke, the town preacher of Ipswich, who was also the master of Magdalene College, Cambridge. In 1567 Adam matriculated at Magdalene.

Cambridge in the late 1560s had a strong puritan presence, and Adam Winthrop, his own religious views likely shaped by his godly older brother William, gravitated to the reformers. Among those he formed friendships with were John Knewstub and Henry Sandes. He also became friends with John Still, whose sister he married. Rather than complete a college degree, in 1574 Adam enrolled at the Inner Temple, one of the Inns of Court in Westminster where lawyers were trained. Ten years later he was admitted to the bar through the sponsorship of the Earl of Leicester, a patron of puritan clergy. It is likely that either John Still or John Knewstub had brought him to the earl's attention.

Adam returned to Groton, where he served for a number of years as steward of Groton Manor, which had been inherited by his older brother John. John Still secured for him the position of receiver of rents for St. John's College and then the post of auditor of Trinity College. Adam also managed some of Still's affairs in the town of Hadleigh, and performed legal services for other godly gentlemen. Gradually he obtained small amounts of land for himself in Groton and the neighboring towns of Boxford and Edwardstone. He followed the cause of religious reform and helped to bring Henry Sandes to Boxford as lecturer. From his diary and other writings we know that Winthrop followed the cause of godly reform on his visits to London and Cambridge. In Suffolk, the Winthrop home was frequently visited by clergymen such as Knewstub. He was the type of godly layman whose energies on behalf of reform helped to establish puritanism in the Stour River valley during the late sixteenth century.

Following the death of his first wife, Adam had married Anne Browne. She gave birth to the couple's only son, John Winthrop, in 1588. Adam was close to his son as young John grew up. At some time around 1612 he joined with his son in buying Groton Manor in young John's name from Adam's brother John, who had settled in the Munster Plantation in Ireland. This purchase enabled young John Winthrop to become a respectable landowner, facilitating a career that would lead to membership on the Suffolk Commission of the Peace and ultimately to his being governor of the Massachusetts Bay Colony.

See also: John Winthrop, William Winthrop
*Further Reading*
Francis J. Bremer, *John Winthrop: America's Forgotten Founding Father* (New York, 2003); Martin Wood, "Adam Winthrop of Groton,

Suffolk, 1548–1623" (M.A. thesis, University of Essex, 1998).

*Francis J. Bremer*

## Winthrop, John (1588–1649)

A member of the Suffolk, England, Commission of the Peace and the governor of the Massachusetts Bay Colony. He led the Great Migration to New England in 1630 and was the principle architect of the region's political culture.

### Family Background and Early Life

Winthrop was born on 12 January 1588 in Edwardstone, Suffolk, the son of Adam Winthrop and Anne Browne, but baptized in Groton. His uncle William had been a member of the underground congregation in London during the reign of Queen Mary and subsequently a supporter of reform in the reign of Elizabeth, associating with leaders like John Foxe, John Field, and others. John's father, Adam, the youngest, studied at Magdalene College, Cambridge, where he formed a friendship with John Still, John Knewstub, Henry Sandes, and others who were later active in pursuing the further reform of the English church.

The Winthrop household was deeply religious, and those who were already key figures in the effort to reform the Church of England were guests at the Winthrop home during John's youth. John was tutored by John Chaplin and probably attended the grammar school at Bury St. Edmund's. 1601 he matriculated at Trinity College, Cambridge. Two years later, however, he gave up his university studies to marry Mary Forth, the daughter of John Forth of Great Stambridge, Essex, who was bailiff for the Rich family lands in Rochford Hundred. The couple spent much of the next decade in Great Stambridge, where John was influenced by the preaching of Ezekiel Culverwell, and where he first recorded in his diary intense experiences of union with God, which were to periodically refresh his faith and which he described in terms of conjugal union with Christ.

In 1613 John purchased the family home of Groton Manor from his uncle John, and settled there as the lord of the manor. Two years later he was named to the Suffolk Commission of the Peace, making him one of the Suffolk justices of the peace. Following the death of Mary Forth Winthrop from complications of childbirth in June 1615, John married Thomasine Clopton of Groton. One year later she died. He vividly described her lingering death in his spiritual diary. John married for a third time in 1618, taking as his wife Margaret Tyndal of Great Maplestead, Essex.

### New England Pioneer

The Stour River valley region in which Winthrop was born and raised had a reputation as an area where religious reform and social equity were achieved through the cooperation of a zealous magistracy and a preaching ministry. But by the 1610s darkness seemed to be closing in on that godly kingdom due to new governmental and religious policies. Having considered emigration to Ireland, Winthrop joined the Massachusetts Bay Company, and in August 1629 he joined with a group of the investors who met at Cambridge and reached an agreement committing themselves to migrate to the colony and bring the charter with them. In October of that year, his fellow investors chose him governor of the company.

In April of 1630 he sailed on the *Arbella,* one of four ships carrying a total of almost 700 passengers to New England. Before leaving he signed his name to "The Humble Request," which asserted the emigrants' continuing affiliation with the Church of England, and preached a lay sermon, "A Model of Christian Charity," in which he expressed the goals of the new plantation. Setting forth an organic view of society in which "in all times some must be rich some poor, some high and eminent in power and dignity; others mean and in subjection," he nevertheless stressed that, regardless of each individual's status, all were equally important as members of the same body. Asserting the themes of the social gospel that he had often heard preached in the Stour valley by clergymen such as Knewstub and Thomas Carew, he reminded his fellow colonists that they should commit themselves to "be knit together in this work as one man" to "entertain each other in brotherly Affection" and "mourn together, labor, and suffer together, allways having before our eyes our . . . Community as members of the same body." In the same sermon he spelled out his conviction that in embarking on their venture the colonists entered into a covenant with God and that they were under an obligation to form an exemplary society that would serve as an inspiration for men everywhere. "We must Consider that we shall be as a City upon a Hill," he said, "the eyes of all people are upon us."

### Shaping a New Society

Winthrop served as governor of the colony for twelve one-year terms (1629–1634, 1637–1640, 1642–1644, and 1646–1649). In every other year he served as deputy governor or one of the assistants, the board of magistrates that evolved into an upper house of the legislature. Though he was not unchallenged, there is no questioning the fact that he was the key figure in shaping the colony and its institutions in its formative decades. He took the lead in extending freemanship (the franchise) beyond the original stockholders who had migrated. His efforts to shape the governing institutions of Massachusetts were heavily influenced by his experience as a member of the Suffolk Commission of the Peace.

As an individual magistrate, Winthrop was noted for the leniency of his decisions, despite the opposition of some colonists, notably Thomas Dudley, who sought a more rigorous regime. A man of his times, Winthrop disdained and opposed innovations that would lead to what he dismissed as "mere Democracy," the "meanest and worst of all forms of Government." However, his instincts for moderation and compromise led him to accept and shape a greater popular participation in government over time. Under his watch the colony expanded steadily and towns were granted large powers of self-government, confirmed in legislation of 1636. Relations between church and state were close, but each was independent. The magistrates sought and generally accepted the advice of the clergy, who formed the bulk of the colony's university elite, but they reserved and on occasion exercised their right to reject that advice. Churches relied on the nurturing support of the civil government and acknowledged the right of the state to appoint days of fast and thanksgiving and to enforce the first table of the Commandments, but bristled at any suggested state interference in the affairs of the congregations. Winthrop also presided over the foundation work for the colony's education system. Laws were passed requiring the heads of household to see to the education of their children and servants and requiring towns to support teachers from public funds. In 1636 Harvard College was founded to ensure the colony a future supply of lay and clerical leaders.

## Challenges to the New England Way

It was during Winthrop's life in Massachusetts that the colony was confronted with the challenges of Roger Williams and Anne Marbury Hutchinson. Roger Williams defended Native American claims to the land against the king's grant of it in the charter, rejected the government's enforcement of the first four commandments, and urged all the colony's churches to repudiate their ties to the Church of England. When Williams first expressed controversial views, Winthrop was able to heal the opening division, but Winthrop was not in office as governor when, in 1635, the colony's General Court in October 1635 ordered Williams to be sent back to England. Winthrop, who admired and liked the young clergyman, warned Williams, allowing him to escape the colony's jurisdiction and settle in the territory that later became Rhode Island.

Winthrop was far more troubled by the controversy in the Boston church and in the colony that resulted from the radical religious views expressed by Anne Hutchinson and her supporters. The dispute was not over toleration of different views, which neither side believed in, but over which view of grace and salvation all would be expected to subscribe to. Winthrop's election to the governorship in 1637 signified the triumph of the orthodox party. A synod of representatives of the region's churches condemned the errors circulating, and the General Court sentenced ringleaders of the dissidents, including Hutchinson and her brother-in-law Rev-

erend John Wheelwright, to banishment on grounds of sedition. In contrast to his relationship with Williams, Winthrop had no sympathy for Anne Hutchinson and expressed strong condemnation of her and her opinions in his *Short Story of the . . . Antinomians* (1644), which was later published in England by Thomas Welde. In dealing with these and other dissidents, Winthrop kept himself focused on the need to maintain the unity of Massachusetts, though he was willing to tolerate forms of diversity that did not threaten the objectives of the colony.

During the English Civil Wars, Winthrop and the Massachusetts government supported the Parliamentarian cause. Fasts were held and prayers offered for the success of the Parliamentarian army. Reference to the king was dropped from the colony's oath of allegiance in May 1643, and two years later the General Court issued an order forbidding any support for the royalist cause. Despite the urging of some, Winthrop decided not to return to England to share in the building of a godly commonwealth, but his son Stephen returned, served in the army, and later in Cromwell's government, and John Winthrop Jr. often traveled back and forth between the colonies and the mother country. While welcoming assistance from Parliament, Winthrop resisted any action that would have recognized the colony's subjection to that body. When he died, the outcome of the Civil Wars was still in doubt.

## Legacy

Winthrop's service to the colony was not limited to what he accomplished in office. He expended his own wealth to assist those in need. He had built and launched a bark called the *Blessing of the Bay,* which helped in the exploration of the region and the establishment of trade. Having as a youth considered a career in the ministry, he delivered sermons as a lay preacher both in Boston and other communities. As he negotiated the colony's course in its dealings with Crown, tribes, and Catholics, Winthrop recorded the day-to-day affairs of the colony in a journal, which grew to three large manuscript volumes. Published long after his death as *A*

*John Winthrop, first governor of Massachussets. (Massachusetts Historical Society)*

*History of New England*, the work is a remarkable historical document. It combines extended treatments of the major events that shaped the colony with providential tales and information on weather, the progress of crops, and other items of everyday life. It has been the most important source for writing the history of early Massachusetts from William Hubbard and Cotton Mather in the colonial era to the present day. His extensive correspondence and other manuscripts were handed down through various members of the Winthrop family until gathered and catalogued by Robert Charles Winthrop in the late nineteenth century. He arranged for them to be deposited in the Massachusetts Historical Society, where they form the single largest extant collection of family papers from the first century of American history.

Historians have been generous in their assessments of the governor. Winthrop's religious faith was grounded on his intense personal experience of God's love and manifested itself in a social gospel. While insisting on unity, he did not demand ab-

solute uniformity in belief and practice, accepting a creative conversation on how the religious and secular goals of the society could best be accomplished. His charity was not always evident—most notably in his dealings with Anne Hutchinson—but he was more understanding than many of his contemporaries of the need to adapt principles to the realities of the New World. This willingness to negotiate the shaping of new institutions enabled his colony to avoid the crises of authority that disrupted the stability of other early colonies.

*See also:* Cambridge Agreement, Law in Puritan New England, Massachusetts Bay Colony, Massachusetts Bay Company, "Model of Christian Charity," Providence, Puritan Historians, Conversion Narratives (in Primary Sources), Covenants— Covenants of Private Christians (in Primary Sources), Death and Dying (in Primary Sources), Directions for Godly Living (in Primary Sources), Social Order (in Primary Sources)
*Further Reading*
Francis J. Bremer, *John Winthrop: America's Forgotten Founding Father* (New York, 2003); Richard S. Dunn, *Puritans and Yankees: The Winthrop Dynasty of New England, 1630–1676* (Princeton, 1962); Edmund S. Morgan, *The Puritan Dilemma: The Story of John Winthrop,* 2nd edition (New York, 1999).

*Francis J. Bremer*

## Winthrop, John, Jr. (1606–1676)

Puritan governor, physician, and alchemist. His scientific beliefs led him to adopt tolerant religious principles that influenced his emigration from Massachusetts, as well as his amicable relations with religious outcasts, mild treatment of Quakers, leniency toward witchcraft suspects, and efforts to mediate disputes within Connecticut's Puritan congregations.

The son of Massachusetts Bay Colony's first governor was born 12 February 1606 at Groton, England. In 1622 he entered Trinity, Dublin, and later studied law at London's Inner Temple. Science proved more interesting, however, especially alchemy, the early form of chemistry that linked practical experiment to spiritual and utopian ideals. With a friend, Winthrop sought to produce the

Alkahest, an alchemical panacea, and the philosopher's stone, which was supposed to be able to purify lead into gold.

Winthrop brought his spiritual and scientific aspirations to America in 1631. Through improvements in mining, metallurgy, medicine, and agriculture, he hoped New England might become a model of economic development and spiritual regeneration. He searched for mineral deposits and established a salt works and an advanced ironworks. He developed unique alchemical medicines that made him New England's most sought-after physician.

Neoplatonic scientific beliefs positing that humans had only imperfect understanding of the operations of nature influenced Winthrop's religious views. Since no person had perfect knowledge of divine intent, tolerance of religious diversity seemed desirable. By pooling imperfect knowledge—in religion and science—men could collectively improve human spiritual and temporal conditions. Leading English Puritans shared such tolerant views, but they met stiff resistance in Massachusetts.

One of the staunchest defenders of New England "orthodoxy"—which allowed only limited dissent—was Winthrop's father. While the elder Winthrop led the prosecution of Anne Marbury Hutchinson, the younger Winthrop (who as assistant might have joined the prosecution) avoided her trial altogether. In the case of Robert Child, arrested for petitioning to worship in New England as he had in Old, the son again absented himself from a prosecution his father led.

Dissatisfaction with Bay conservatism probably influenced Winthrop's immigration to Connecticut in 1636. Winthrop sought to establish at New London an alchemical research center to pursue divinely granted scientific breakthroughs. He befriended many whose beliefs had made them outcasts in Massachusetts: Samuel Gorton, Roger Williams, and the Quaker William Coddington. When Connecticut's puritan churches became wracked by conflicts over the Half-Way Covenant, Winthrop attempted to mediate these disputes by promoting religious tolerance. His support for freedom of conscience helped him acquire Connecticut's royal charter from Charles II in 1662, the same year he helped found the Royal Society. Winthrop also changed Connecticut's record as New England's fiercest prosecutor of witchcraft. As governor (1657, 1659–1676), Winthrop was chief magistrate in witchcraft trials. He used this authority to overturn convictions, stage-manage trials, and otherwise ensure that witches would be spared execution. In 1669, he helped establish a legal definition of witchcraft that ended executions in Connecticut permanently. Winthrop died in Boston in April 1676, while urging moderate treatment of native combatants in King Philip's War.

*See also:* Connecticut, Pequot War
*Further Reading*
Robert C. Black III, *The Younger John Winthrop* (New York, 1966); Richard S. Dunn, *Puritans and Yankees: The Winthrop Dynasty of New England, 1630–1676* (Princeton, 1962).

*Walt Woodward*

## Winthrop, Margaret Tyndal (ca. 1591–1647)

Third wife of John Winthrop, governor of Massachusetts. Margaret was born into a gentry family in Great Maplestead, in the English county of Essex. Her father was a master of the Court of Chancery. Her mother, Anne Egerton, was related to a number of prominent puritan clergy, including Stephen Egerton. Margaret was taught to read and write, and her piety and interest in religious literature were encouraged.

In 1618 she married the widower John Winthrop, whose first two wives had died. Her family had some reservations about the match, due to Winthrop's unsure title to his Groton estate and a concern that he was not distinguished enough for her. But the objections were overcome through the intercession of the ministers Stephen Egerton and Ezekiel Culverwell, as well as that of Winthrop's Mildmay kin. Furthermore, the two had clearly formed a close attachment spiritually as well as romantically.

Margaret was mother to Winthrop's four young children from his first marriage as well as bearing

*The parish church in Groton, Suffolk, England, where the Winthrops worshipped, and Groton Hall, one of their residences. (Courtesy Francis J. Bremer)*

five of her own. During the first twelve years of their marriage John was often absent, and Margaret, with the assistance of her father-in-law, Adam, managed the family estate. Their frequent separation provided the opportunity for frequent correspondence, which has provided us with an extraordinary collection of love letters between a puritan couple of this time period. A new form of separation occurred when John immigrated to New England in 1630 and Margaret remained behind for a year to wrap up the family's affairs. Prior to departing, the two agreed to set aside five to six o'clock every Monday and Friday to think of one another and enter into spiritual communion with each other till the time they were reunited.

Once in Massachusetts Margaret continued to provide support for her husband during the trials of the early colony, though they no longer had many occasions for the correspondence that is so reveal-

ing for the earlier period. Nevertheless there is ample evidence that she was a trusted advisor to her husband as well as a wife. Her judgment and kindness made her much appreciated by the local citizens as well. She died in May 1647 of a respiratory disease.

*See also:* John Winthrop
*Further Reading*
Francis J. Bremer, *John Winthrop: America's Forgotten Founding Father* (New York, 2003); Alice Morse Earle, *Margaret Winthrop* (New York, 1895).

*Francis J. Bremer*

### Winthrop, William (1529–1582)

Merchant and promoter of godly reform. William Winthrop was the eldest son of Adam Winthrop, master of the Clothworkers, and he followed his father into that company. It is possible that his mother, Alice Hunne Winthrop, was the daughter of William Hunne, who was seen as an early Protestant martyr as a result of his death while opposing Roman Catholic practices.

The Winthrops were members of the London parish of St. Peter's Cornhill Street, where William's religious views were likely shaped by the strong reformer and rector, John Pulleyne. When the Roman Catholic Queen Mary came to the throne in 1553, Adam Winthrop, William's father, retreated to the family's lands in Suffolk to avoid close inspection of his religious views. William moved into the neighboring parish of St. Michael's Cornhill and joined one of the underground congregations in the city. It is likely that some of the secret Protestant worship meetings were held on one of the Winthrop ships on the Thames. William also had contacts with imprisoned Protestants, offering financial support to them and preserving some of their papers, which he later handed on to John Foxe, who recorded the sufferings of that time in his *Actes and Monuments of the English Martyrs* (1563), popularly known as the Book of Martyrs.

With the accession of Queen Elizabeth in 1558, Winthrop was able to act openly on behalf of reform. He was a friend of Foxe and of the reformer

John Field. As a churchwarden of St. Michael's, he helped to advance reform in that parish, where the church organ was sold to buy copies of Foxe's *Actes and Monuments* and John Calvin's *Institutes of the Christian Religion* (1536). He was involved with the stranger churches (Protestant congregations of foreign nationals living in London); he assisted the Spanish congregation in finding a place to worship, raised funds for the French church, and was elected an elder of the Italian church.

Winthrop recommended a number of fellow members of the Marian underground to church authorities. He also used his wealth to promote the placement of godly preachers in parishes in London and in Suffolk. On numerous occasions he stood surety for the fees that clergy had to pay when they were inducted into a living. It is possible that he was too generous in supporting reform, or perhaps he made bad business decisions. At any rate, in 1577 he had to sell his home to provide apprenticeships for his sons. The following year he was himself placed on the charity of the parish and lived the remaining years of his life in one of the residences for the poor in the churchyard of St. Michael's. He was remembered by his brother, Adam Winthrop, as "A good man, without harm, and a lover of piety."

*See also:* Adam Winthrop, Marian Underground
*Further Reading*
Francis J. Bremer, "William Winthrop and Religious Reform in London 1529–1582," *London Journal* 24 (1999), 1–17.

*Francis J. Bremer*

## Wise, John (b. 1652)

Pastor of Ipswich Second (or "Chebacco Parish") Church in Massachusetts, author, Congregational defender. Born in Roxbury, Massachusetts, in 1652, John Wise graduated from Harvard College in 1673. After preaching in Branford, Connecticut, for four years, he was ordained pastor of the Second Church of Ipswich in 1683. In 1687, during the imposition of the short-lived Dominion of New England, Wise was arrested and jailed for publicly urging citizens to resist taxation without represen-

tation. He gained further renown for his chaplainship during the siege of Quebec, as well as for his support of victims who were unjustly accused during the Salem witchcraft hysteria.

By the turn of the century, Wise found himself at odds with many ministers in Massachusetts over issues of church government. Clergymen were increasingly coming to believe that Congregationalism was too "democratic," in granting members significant decision-making powers within local churches. These concerns reached a culmination in 1701 when Cotton Mather produced a number of formal "Proposals" to reform government within local Congregational churches, mainly by modifying and reducing lay initiatives in church affairs. In response to these proposals, and to the more autocratic sentiments among the clergy in general, Wise wrote two lengthy (and often satirical) pamphlets to defend existing Congregational practices: The *Churches Quarrel Espoused* (1710) and *A Vindication of the Government of the New England Churches* (1717). In the former, Wise cautioned readers that clerical efforts at "reform" in fact threatened to destroy lay liberties and the Cambridge Platform, Massachusetts's "constitution" of church government. He further blamed rising church disorder on clerical authoritarianism rather than excessive lay liberties in church affairs.

Wise's essay was significant insofar as it justified Congregational practices not merely on scripture grounds, as had been the case with previous Congregational apologists, but on the basis of constitutionalism and free consent as well. In *A Vindication*, Wise extended his thinking in emphasizing connections between Congregational principles and principles drawn from reason, natural rights, and English constitutional government. Wise also launched into a lengthy and more general defense of the principles and practices of democracy, which helped earn for him a reputation among later scholars as one of America's first democrats. *The Churches Quarrel* and *A Vindication* were reprinted and enjoyed some popularity in 1772, resonating with political spirits that arose during the Revolutionary crisis.

In his efforts to defend traditional Congregational practices, Wise enjoyed the support of a significant, if undetermined, number of allies in the clerical community. Unsurprisingly, many ordinary churchgoers delighted in the witty and often sarcastic barbs that Wise hurled at those ministers who sought to enhance their own church power at the expense of the laity. A divided clergy found it impossible to convince ordinary churchgoers to adopt significant changes in church government. Owing in no small measure to the opposition that Wise ignited, Mather's Proposals were ignored by nearly all churches in Massachusetts.

*Further Reading*
George Allen Cook, *John Wise: Early American Democrat* (New York, 1952); Perry Miller, *The New England Mind: From Colony to Province* (New York, 1953).

*James F. Cooper*

## Wood, Thomas (ca. 1520–ca. 1577)

Thanks to the letter book compiled by his son Ambrose, Thomas Wood is possibly the best-known puritan layman of Elizabeth's reign. A soldier at Boulogne and in Scotland in the reign of Edward VI, during the reign of the Roman Catholic Mary Tudor he was one of the four founders of the exile community at Frankfurt-am-Main in June 1554. He followed John Knox to Geneva in 1555 and was elected an elder of the English congregation in December 1557. After returning to England, he served as clerk of the council of the garrison of Newhaven (Le Havre) in 1562–1563. He was still a servant of the Crown in 1568, but in 1570 retired to Groby in Leicestershire. Wood knew Sir William Cecil and the Earls of Leicester and Warwick well, and he had no hesitation about warning them directly of godly discontent with the course of ecclesiastical policy, especially the suppression of the exercises, or prophesyings, at St. Antholin's (London) in 1566 and Southam (Warwickshire) in early 1576. Over the latter, Wood famously elicited a long personal defense from Leicester. In exile Wood had apparently accepted Knox's criticisms of the Edwardian prayer book, and in the 1570s he expressed

strong hostility to the episcopate. It is not entirely clear, though, whether he returned from Geneva a convinced Presbyterian, or whether his disenchantment with the established church was a reaction to the bishops' campaign for uniformity.

*Further Reading*
*Oxford Dictionary of National Biography* (Oxford, 2004).

*Simon Adams*

## Woodbridge, Benjamin (1622–1684)

Presbyterian clergyman. He was son of John Woodbridge (1582–1637), rector of Stanton Fitzwarren, Wiltshire, and Sarah (1593–1663), daughter of Robert Parker, the author of *De politeia ecclesiastica Christi* (1616).

Benjamin matriculated at Magdalen Hall, Oxford, 9 November 1638, but he left the university when he immigrated to New England in 1639 to join his brother John. Woodbridge resumed his studies at Harvard College, graduating B.A. in 1642. He then returned to England, taking his M.A. at Magdalen Hall on 16 November 1648. During the Civil Wars, Woodbridge was a Presbyterian, and on 18 May 1648 he succeeded William Twisse as rector of Newbury, Berkshire. He was appointed one of the clerical assistants for Berkshire to the Cromwellian Triers in 1654.

Woodbridge was a polemicist for Calvinist orthodoxy, publishing *Church-members set in joynt* against lay preaching in 1648 (under the pseudonym Filodexter Transilvanus). Between 1652 and 1654, Woodbridge entered into a pamphlet dispute with William Eyre, attacking Eyre's antinomianism and defending the orthodox doctrine of justification by faith.

At the Restoration, Woodbridge was made one of Charles II's chaplains-in-ordinary and in 1661 was chosen as one of the puritan commissioners at the Savoy Conference. Woodbridge refused the canonry of Windsor in 1662 and did not subscribe to the Act of Uniformity, instead facing ejection from his living on 24 August (St. Bartholomew's Day) 1662. But Woodbridge wavered in his noncomformity. He agreed to be ordained by the bishop of Salisbury at Oxford in October 1665, yet remained a Nonconformist and was licensed as a Presbyterian under the Declaration of Indulgence of 1672. He died at Newbury on 1 November 1684 and was buried on 4 November.

*Further Reading*
*Oxford Dictionary of National Biography* (Oxford, 2004).

*Eliot Vernon*

## Wotton, Anthony (1561?–1626)

Minister and religious controversialist. A rising star in Elizabethan Cambridge, Wotton earned the attention of the Earl of Essex, who named the young divine to a chaplaincy in 1594; a year later, however, he lost out the Regius professorship in divinity to John Overall, at which point Wotton left Cambridge for a brief stint as professor of Gresham College. Wotton's career was not without controversy; apparently a firm Nonconformist, he appears to have largely removed himself from the hierarchical structure of the church, choosing after 1600 to earn his living by lecturing at the East London parish of Allhallows Barking. He was suspected of complicity in Essex's rising; was implicated in the movement for further godly reform early in James's reign; was engaged in protracted and often bitter printed disputes with Roman Catholics throughout the early seventeenth century; lived long enough to attack the alleged Arminianism of Richard Montagu in print; and perhaps most famously, Wotton suggested revisions to the standard reformed doctrine of justification, revisions that were assaulted as Socinian innovations by the young puritan divine George Walker. Walker's charges led to a protracted feud, involving many of London's most famous godly ministers, and although in the end Wotton was largely exonerated of the charges, his reputation suffered within European protestant circles. Nevertheless, Wotton's subtle revisions to the doctrine of justification proved intriguing to some later English theologians. In different ways, his thought influenced a number of antinomian theorists, as well as the allegedly heretical New England lay theologian William Pynchon, and, most spectacularly, the famous independent minister John Goodwin, who recycled and refined Wotton's ideas, bringing them to a broader audience, including the young Richard Baxter.

*Further Reading*
Theodore Dwight Bozeman, *The Precisianist Strain: Disciplinary Religion & Antinomian Backlash in Puritanism to 1638* (Chapel Hill, 2004); David Como, *Blown by the Spirit: Puritanism and the Emergence of an Antinomian Underground in Pre-Civil War England* (Stanford, 2004).

*David Como*

## Wren, Matthew (1585–1667)

Church of England bishop. Matthew Wren studied at Pembroke College, Cambridge (B.A., 1605; M.A., 1608), and began his career in the church upon his ordination in 1611. He became a household chaplain to Lancelot Andrewes, then Bishop of Ely. By 1621 he had become one of the chaplains to King James I.

In 1625 Wren was made master of Peterhouse College, Cambridge, and began to attract adverse attention from puritans for his liturgical preferences. He supervised the building of a new college chapel, which included a railed-in altar, decorated roof, and elaborate furnishings—all in keeping with the views of those churchmen who advocated a return to the "beauty of holiness." He also supported the controversial theological opinions of Richard Montagu, defending Montagu against the attacks of Samuel Ward, the university's Lady Margaret Professor of Divinity.

Wren accompanied King Charles I on the monarch's 1633 visit to Scotland and may have contributed to drafting the subsequent demands for the reordering of the rites of the Church of Scotland. In 1634 he was elected bishop of Hereford. In 1635 he was elected bishop of Norwich, in the heart of puritan East Anglia. Here, working to serve the goals of the king and of Archbishop William Laud, he set out to impose obedience to the new policies for ordering church services and to force puritans to conform. He was credited with being responsible for driving many puritan clergy into exile in the Netherlands or New England.

In 1638 Wren was elected bishop of Ely. There he continued his policy of enforcing conformity. Wren had become one of the most detested opponents of puritan reformers, and, shortly after the assembling of the Long Parliament, he was brought up on charges and in December 1641 was sent to the Tower of London, where he remained in confinement for eighteen years. He was restored to his bishopric with the return of the monarchy and participated in the crafting of the Restoration religious settlement.

*Further Reading*
*Oxford Dictionary of National Biography* (Oxford, 2004).

*Francis J. Bremer*

### Wright, Robert (ca. 1550–1624)

Puritan clergyman. Wright was born in the county of Essex. He matriculated at Christ's College, Cambridge, in 1565, and he completed his B.A. in 1569 and his M.A. in 1572. He left the university two years later to follow Thomas Cartwright abroad. He furthered his studies at the University of Heidelberg until 1576, when the collapse of the Calvinist regime there led him to return to England.

After preaching at various aristocratic households, in 1579 he had settled at Rochford Hall in Essex, one of the homes of Robert, the second Lord Rich. He formed the household into the equivalent of a Congregational church. His preaching and catechizing stirred up the opposition of some regional clergy, who reported his activities to the authorities. Following the death of Lord Rich, Wright traveled to Antwerp, where he was ordained by clergy there. An attempt to regularize his position at Rochford Hall by securing him a preaching license from Bishop John Aylmer led to a clash in which Richard Rich, uncle of the third Lord Rich, assaulted the bishop. A trial before the High Commission led to the brief imprisonment of Rich and Wright.

Following his release (on agreeing to the appropriateness of English ordination and the Book of Common Prayer) Wright settled in Friering, Essex, and claimed to have received a preaching license from Archbishop Edmund Grindal. He was likely one of the founders of the ministerial conference centered on Braintree, George Gifford being one of his fellow members. Bishop Aylmer suspended him from his living in 1584, but he soon relocated as town preacher in Ipswich. He continued active in the Braintree conference and in 1585 represented that conference along with Gifford in a national gathering of puritan clergy in London.

Implicated in the Marprelate controversy, Wright moved on once again, leaving Ipswich and succeeding William Fulke as rector of nearby Dennington, where he remained for the rest of his life.

*Further Reading*
Patrick Collinson, *The Elizabethan Puritan Movement* (London, 1967); *Oxford Dictionary of National Biography* (Oxford, 2004).

*Francis J. Bremer*

# Y

## Yates, John (ca. 1590–1660)

Congregationalist minister with an appetite for controversy. Yates was educated at Emmanuel College, Cambridge (M.A. 1611 and B.D. 1618), and at the household seminary of Alexander Richardson at Barking, Essex; colleagues included Thomas Hooker and William Ames. He went on to be lecturer at St. Andrew's, Norwich, and, from the mid-1620s to 1658, rector of Stiffkey, Norfolk, a presentation of Sir Nathaniel Bacon. He is best known for his work against Arminianism; his first work of 1615 was a defense of the influential puritan theologian William Perkins against the Dutch theologian Jacobus Arminius. After disciplinary trouble with Bishop Samuel Harsnet, he collaborated in an attack on his theology in the parliament of 1624. In 1625 he was, with Nathaniel Ward, cosignatory to a petition to be presented to the House of Commons by John Pym as an assault on Richard Montagu, then chaplain to James I. He went on to appear before a committee assessing Montagu's heterodoxy and was called before King James, who castigated him. He wrote *Ibis ad Caesarum* (1626), a reply to Montagu's *Appello Caesarum* (1625), claiming that Montagu had misrepresented the Church of England. He is less visible after this. He was one of four "proto-trustees" in Norwich, assisting the Feoffees for Impropriations in London in their work of supplying pulpits with godly ministers. His ecclesiology is more probable than definite. In a work of 1622 there are hints of favoring primitive episcopacy, but he later assisted in producing editions of the works of Jeremiah Burroughes and William Bridge, both more famous Congregationalists. In his last year he signed a denunciation of Venner's Rising of 1660.

### Further Reading

K. L. Sprunger, "John Yates of Norfolk: The Radical Puritan Preacher as Ramist Philosopher," *Journal of the History of Ideas* 37 (1976), 697–706; Nicholas Tyacke, *Anti-Calvinists: The Rise of English Arminianism, c. 1590–1640* (Oxford, 1987); Tom Webster, *Godly Clergy in Early Stuart England: The Caroline Puritan Movement, c. 1620–1643* (Cambridge, Eng., 1997).

*Tom Webster*